DATA ABSTRACTION

THE OBJECT-ORIENTED APPROACH USING C++

McGRAW-HILL SERIES IN COMPUTER SCIENCE

Fundamentals of Computing and Programming
Computer Organization and Architecture
Systems and Languages
Theoretical Foundations
Software Engineering and Databases
Artificial Intelligence
Networks, Parallel and Distributed Computing
Graphics and Visualization
The MIT Electrical Engineering and Computer Science Series

FUNDAMENTALS OF COMPUTING AND PROGRAMMING

***Abelson and Sussman:** *Structure and Interpretation of Computer Programs*
 Bergin: *Data Abstraction: The Object-Oriented Approach Using C + +*
 Kernighan and Plauger: *The Elements of Programming Style*
***Springer and Friedman:** *Scheme and the Art of Programming*
 Tremblay and Bunt: *Introduction to Computer Science: An Algorithmic Approach*
 Tucker, Bradley, Cupper, and Garnick: *Fundamentals of Computing I: Logic, Problem Solving, Programs, and Computers*
 Tucker, Bradley, Cupper, and Epstein: *Fundametals of Computing II: Abstraction, Data Structures, and Large Software Systems*

*Co-published by The MIT Press and McGraw-Hill, Inc.

DATA ABSTRACTION

THE OBJECT-ORIENTED APPROACH USING C++

Joseph Bergin
Pace University

McGraw-Hill, Inc.

New York   St. Louis   San Francisco   Auckland
Bogotá   Caracas   Lisbon   London   Madrid
Mexico City   Milan   Montreal   New Delhi
San Juan   Singapore   Sydney
Tokyo   Toronto

DATA ABSTRACTION
THE OBJECT-ORIENTED APPROACH USING C++

This book is printed on recycled, acid-free paper
containing a minimum of 50% total recycled fiber with
10% postconsumer de-inked fiber.

1 2 3 4 5 6 7 8 9 0 AGM AGM 9 0 9 8 7 6 5 4 3

P/N 004956-4

This book was set in New Century Schoolbook by Publication Services.
The editor was Eric M. Munson;
the cover illustrator was Anne Green;
the production supervisor was Richard A. Ausburn.
Project supervision was done by Publication Services.
Arcata Graphics/Martinsburg was printer and binder.

Library of Congress Cataloging-in-Publication Data

Bergin, Joseph.
   Data abstraction: the object oriented approach using C++ / Joseph
Bergin.
      p.   cm. — (McGraw-Hill series in computer science.
Fundamentals of computing and programming)
   Includes index
   P/N 004956-4
   1. Object-oriented programming (Computer science)   2. C++
(Computer program language)   I. title.   II. Series: McGraw-Hill
computer science series. Fundamentals of computing and programming.
QA76.64.B48   1994
005.7'3—dc20   93-35410

J oseph Bergin is Professor of Computer Science at Pace University in New York City. He has been teaching mathematics and computer science for over 20 years. He first looked at computing in 1972 when, with a new Ph.D. from Michigan State University, he decided to learn something practical. His first introduction to object-oriented programming was in 1985 when, while a visiting professor at Dartmouth College, he first used a Macintosh (actually a Lisa system). There was no turning back. Professor Bergin's main professional interest is language design and development, especially object-oriented languages and systems. When not at the computer, he can often be found on his bicycle or on a mountain trail (sometimes in parallel).

To my teachers,
my colleagues,
and my students.

CONTENTS

PART TWO   **THE IMPLEMENTATIONS**

The undergraduate curriculum in computing has evolved rapidly in recent years since publication of the "Computing Curricula 1991" standard. That curriculum standard encouraged innovation, especially in the design of introductory and intermediate-level courses. Dramatic changes in the subject matter of the discipline and profession of computing have also contributed to this rapid evolution. Topics like parallelism, networking, and object-oriented design have taken their place among the fundamental aspects of a modern undergraduate computer science curriculum.

At the same time, a rather interesting shift in momentum for curricular change has occurred. That is, the major impetus for change prior to the 1980s came from leading academic institutions. For example, the writings of Dijkstra and other academicians gave rise to new principles of structured programming and top-down design. However, in recent years, the forces of change have come more often from the applied side of the discipline, especially in the subject area of software methodology. Object-oriented design methodologies and programming languages have evolved largely out of the efforts of professional consultants and software corporations. The academic community is only beginning to appreciate their wisdom and assimilate this new technology into its undergraduate curriculum.

This text is one of the first effective introductions to abstraction and object-oriented design. It can be used to modernize and energize a traditional data structures course. Professor Bergin's approach to this course emphasizes abstraction in the design and implementation of objects using C++. It combines modern tools and strong fundamental concepts. It can have high impact on undergraduate programs that are looking for ways to modernize their curriculum at this critical level. The data structures course will continue to be a pivotal second or third course in an undergraduate computer science major for the foreseeable future. Instructors who are looking for graceful ways to shift to C++ and object-oriented design in that particular course should be inspired by this text. Students will find Bergin's writing style to be very accessible and unusually engaging. The examples and problems are interesting and challenging at a wide range of levels. The applications that come at the end of the text, in program translation, verification, and database normalization, provide unusual insights into the use of abstraction in various areas of computer science.

I am delighted that Professor Bergin has developed this manuscript. Not only a refreshingly up-to-date treatment of fundamental principles and topics, it also contains a most refreshing collection of examples, exercises, classes, and accompanying software to provide an especially stimulating data structures course in a wide range of undergraduate curricula.

Allen B. Tucker

When I first learned about object-oriented programming in early 1985, I was immediately excited by the effect it could have on the efficient production of high-quality software. More importantly, it was clear that the concepts of OOP could dramatically change the way that we teach programming, software engineering, and, especially, data abstraction. I knew then that I wanted to write a book to make my ideas and enthusiasm concrete. Unfortunately, good languages and tools were not widely available at the time. C++ is now changing that, with essentially one language (there are still minor differences between versions) available on a wide range of equipment from many manufacturers. The development of C++ on the Macintosh by Apple Computer and by Symantec and on the IBM/PC by Borland, by Symantec, and, more recently, by Microsoft has made C++ available on machines within the reach of all colleges and most students.

This book started as a project using Object Pascal when it became available on both the Macintosh and the IBM/PC. Although that language is quite good for the expression of many object-oriented ideas, the fact that it was not available on larger machines was definitely limiting. C++ has definitely solved that problem at the cost of using a more complex language. The overall design of the software described here was also heavily influenced by the same organizational principles embodied in the Smalltalk libraries.

PURPOSE OF THE BOOK

The goals of the book are the following, in order of importance:

1. To teach data abstraction
2. To teach object-oriented programming
3. To teach computer science

It is important to note at the outset that this is not a book designed to teach you programming in C++. Nor is its first priority to teach you object-oriented programming. It is designed to teach you principles of data abstraction. C++ is used as a tool. You are not assumed to know much about C++, except that you have a good introductory understanding of C, including C's use of pointers. Much in C++ is not discussed in this book. Also, the style of programming is not precisely the same as one often sees in commercial C++ programs, in which the purposes of the programming team lead them to develop very efficient programs. The goal here is different. It is to provide extremely general programs, programs that can be used in a large variety of situations. This goal leads us to a particular style and a particular way of using the language.

In Chapter 1 are presented only a few of the ideas that we shall need to develop the style used in this book. Novice Pascal programmers might be somewhat weak in dealing with pointers. Appendix A contains material to help in this. A book that introduces C++ concepts to skilled novices is [Graham, 1991]. Another book, especially useful for Pascal programmers, is [Pohl, 1991b].

ROAD MAP OF THE BOOK

The book has three main sections: The Fundamentals, The Implementations, and The Applications. In addition, there are two appendices.

The Fundamentals

The first part introduces the terminology of data abstraction and object-oriented programming. It also gives an overview, at the level of specification, of the landscape of useful data structures. It shows (in Chapter 5) how to use the library to build simple applications without examining the implementations of the data structures.

Chapter 1 gives some background on C++ and some background needed for study of this topic from the object-oriented standpoint.

Chapter 2 is fundamental, giving the terminology adopted in the book and introducing most of the important object-oriented concepts.

Chapter 3 introduces the top of the hierarchy of classes discussed in the book and provides the basic structuring mechanism of all of our classes.

It gives details of the object, magnitude, collection, and iterator classes. These classes are necessarily very general and somewhat abstract, so a first reading should focus on the general structuring of things rather than on the specific details. The material also forms a reference guide that may be used later for the detail, which is useful to have in one place. The exercises help to focus the abstract material.

Chapter 4 gives a reference guide to the library of classes that is discussed in the rest of the book. It should be quickly scanned. I spend about two hours of lecture on the chapter, focusing on general principles of the data structures and how they are related to each other.

Chapter 5 should be covered in detail, as it shows that the fundamental classes given in Chapter 4 can be used without having access to the implementation details. Several major projects are discussed after the exercises that may be assigned at that point or while covering later chapters that discuss the individual class implementations.

The Implementations

In this part implementations of many standard data structures and their relationships to each other are presented. Many exercises here explore alternate implementations. The most important chapters are Chapter 6, Chapter 9, and Chapter 11.

Chapter 6, on lists, is fundamental and should be covered thoroughly. Many structures shown later will use lists in fundamental ways. Program complexity is introduced here. Also, the selection-sort algorithm is developed from its loop invariant using array sections.

Sections 7.1 through 7.5 are important, but the rest of chapter 7 can be skipped. Section 7.8, on removal of recursion, should be at least skimmed, for the point that recursion can be implemented with a stack is important and is used as the basis of the development of some graph algorithms. The details of the derivation of a nonrecursive program from a recursive one may be skipped, however. These details have, in my view, some merit in general program transformation that transcends their use in removal of recursion.

Chapter 8, which treats arrays as a class, contains material on sorting, searching, and algorithm complexity and verification. All of the sorting routines are developed from the specifications of their loop invariants. Not all of the sorting routines need be covered, but some material from each of Sections 8.3 and 8.4 should be covered.

Chapter 9, on trees, is similar in style and content to Chapter 6. Binary trees are developed along with three associated classes. Binary search trees are discussed, as well as general trees. Sections 9.7 and 9.8 are less important than the rest.

Chapter 10 may be skipped altogether, or material may be selected to suit the instructor or class. Sections 10.4, 10.5, and 10.6 are independent of the earlier sections.

Chapter 11 should be covered. It may be covered any time after Chapter 6. At least sections 11.1, 11.2, and 11.5 should get serious attention. Some students get the impression from data structures courses that all data structures have to do with collections. Here we see that this is not the case. Section 11.1, which implements integers as a class, introduces hash tables as an implementation method. Section 11.5, on associations, may be skipped only if dictionaries in the next chapter are to be skipped; however, dictionaries are needed in many of our examples.

Sections 12.5 and 12.6 are less important than the rest of chapter 12. Section 12.1, on dictionaries, is important to many of our applications. Graphs are discussed in this chapter.

The Applications

The three chapters in this section present deeper applications of the material on data structures than the simple programs of Chapter 5. Many courses will not have the time to cover this material in detail, but it again demonstrates the use of data abstractions from their specifications. The chapters also explore ideas important to computer science (language translation, verification, and database internals) and some students may want to return to this material when taking other courses.

Chapters 13 and 14 form a sequence, though Chapter 13 may be studied without Chapter 14. They make use of material on trees and lists. A language is developed in Chapter 14 along with a parser for the language. A verification system for the language is built in Chapter 14.

Chapter 15 on relational databases stands alone, drawing primarily on material from sets and binary search trees.

The Appendixes

Appendix A gives a mental model of the underlying machine with its stack and heap. It also presents material on pointers that may be used as a review.

Appendix B presents additional material on C++. It discusses some material that is not essential to the exposition here but might be needed by some students.

NOTES

Each exercise in the book is labeled with the section of the chapter to which it primarily applies. It may be assigned after covering that section.

There are a number of large projects at the end of Chapter 5. They may be assigned after covering Chapter 5 or after covering the implementations of the major classes that are likely to be used. They are large projects (several weeks), and I suggest that one be assigned early and that it evolve through several cycles. Some of them make good team projects.

ACKNOWLEDGMENTS AND THANKS

I would like to thank Apple Computer and IBM for grants of equipment and the sharing of expertise in the development of this work. Apple Computer, especially, has been generous over the years in supporting my work on object-oriented systems. IBM and Borland provided fine hardware and software to aid in the preparation of the software described herein.

I want to especially thank my students of the last three years who worked with versions of this material as it was coming to life. Their suggestions have made it better. Also deserving of credit are the following reviewers who have read and commented on the several versions of this text: Doug Baldwin, SUNY Geneseo; John Gannon, University of Maryland; Harold Grossman, Clemson University; John Howland, Trinity University; Jeffrey Naughton, University of Wisconsin; Richard Reid, Michigan State; John Riedl, University of Minnesota; and, Jane Wallace Mayo, University of Tennessee. With the help of these people, the quality has been much improved.

Joseph Bergin

## PART ONE

THE FUNDAMENTALS

## CHAPTER 1

INTRODUCTION

A bstraction is the process by which we factor out some complex subset of experience and give it a name. The name then serves as a surrogate for the complexity of the experience. The name itself, as it is used, becomes a part of the complexity of our experience and thus serves as the basis for further abstractions. This book is about abstraction. Humanity has progressed from a primitive state chiefly because of this ability to form and use abstractions and to build ever more complex abstractions on the backs of simpler ones. Concepts that we use every day in the business world (corporation, loan, credit, etc.) are very abstract, based on simpler abstractions (association, value, etc.), yet we normally think of them as quite concrete.

Not only is abstraction useful to us, it is absolutely necessary. Psychologists have determined that the human mind (of most of us, at least) is limited by what I will call the Rule of Seven [Miller]. According to this rule, we are capable of simultaneously manipulating about seven independent items in our minds. For example, we may drive an automobile, listen to music, talk to the person next to us, and keep generally aware of what our friends are up to in the back seat, all simultaneously. A person learning to drive a car, however, has a much harder time integrating the various tasks needed to manipulate the controls, thinking of each of them as distinct. Each of us will eventually reach a point when we cannot add more tasks without reaching overload. Experiments suggest that overload is reached by most people when the number of independent tasks is about seven. A simple demonstration of this is that it is easier to remember telephone numbers (seven digits) than social security numbers (nine digits). Once we reach the point of overload, we need some organizational or abstractional aid to help us deal with the complexity. For example, I remember my own social security number as a sequence of three smaller numbers rather than as one long number. The hyphens normally written in the social security number seem to help in remembering the number. As an experiment of your own, think about how many telephone numbers you mentally carry around, compared with how many social security numbers you think you would be able to remember.

The limitation of the Rule of Seven is overcome by our ability to form abstractions. The ability to factor out some complexity (several independent items) and represent it by an abstraction or surrogate (a single item) automatically reduces the tendency to overload and lets us use our mental power to the maximum.

More specifically, this book is about how a programmer may use object-oriented programming techniques to build software that is maximally reusable by applying principles of abstraction. Programmers have wanted to build reusable software components almost from the beginning. The first (and nearly only successful) attempt was the FORTRAN Library, which contained numerical routines such as SIN and LOG, which freed most programmers from the need to program such subroutines in order to use them. The fact that they were widely implemented and fairly true to an abstract model of behavior increased the portability of the programs that used them. Portability, the ability of software to be moved easily from one machine to another, is only one of the goals of reusable software, however. Another is the ability to reuse components of one project in others. In nearly every field of human action, one hears the admonition "Don't reinvent the wheel" whenever attempts are made to advance the state of the art. In programming, however, it is still too often true that components are rebuilt from scratch for each new use. This contrasts sharply with the general practice in hardware design of using standardized, off-the-shelf components to build much of a new hardware system. The same practice can and should take place in software design.

Object-oriented programming offers hope of being able to provide a mechanism by which software components would be more easily reused, extended, and, especially, interchanged among practitioners. For example, Smalltalk, a small and simple language developed by Xerox in the 70s and 80s, is always furnished with a large and complex software library called the "class hierarchy." The Smalltalk class hierarchy has proved capable of providing a mechanism of reusability and extendibility over a number of years on large and small projects. A person programs in Smalltalk by exploiting the power of the class library more than the power of the language itself. There is a negative aspect to Smalltalk, however, if one is to build large, multiperson, multiyear software systems. The class library is on line in source form and easily modified. This advantage for prototyping is a disadvantage for large systems, where there is more need of stable specifications as a means of communication among the various people building the system.

Although not perfect, C++ offers many advantages, especially to the person learning how to build large, reliable software systems. It is strongly typed, providing early warning of potential errors. It has a definite modularity, permitting separate compilation of modules. It has various forms of information hiding, making it easier to control change. It is also possible to use C++ to implement object-oriented systems, thus, as we shall see, offering definite advantages when we require large, modular programs.

1.1   OBJECT-ORIENTED PROGRAMMING

Object-oriented programming (OOP) began with the language Simula, developed in Scandinavia in the mid-60s. Simula was used primarily for simulation programming, where it is natural to model external entities in the software system and to think in terms of the entities and their behavior. Simula has a syntax much like that of Pascal (which was created at about the same time, and in the same tradition), but the practitioner thinks quite differently when designing a program that will be built in Simula. Rather than deciding on the various processes that must be implemented to complete the system, the designer considers the entities (objects) that exist in the system being modeled and how they will be represented in the model. The designer then decides whether the objects are unique in the system or coexistent with other objects having the same behavior. Collections of such similar objects are called "classes," and the primary job of the designer is to determine the behavior that characterizes the class. Often these behaviors are interactions with objects of the same or other classes, so communication patterns must be established that model the interactions. These communication patterns result in objects sharing information by sending messages to each other. One object requests a service from another by sending it a message. The receiving object executes some procedure to provide the service to the sender.

A fundamental idea of OOP, introduced in Simula, is that of inheritance. Using inheritance, a programmer defines a class by extending or specializing some existing class. The description of the new class is only a description of the differences between the old and the new classes. New behaviors can be added and old ones can be modified. There are two benefits of this. The first, though less important, is that it eases the programmer's task if much of the behavior of a new kind of object is already programmed into the system. More importantly, classes organized by inheritance into a class hierarchy constitute a unifying structure around which a software system may be built and understood (as per the Rule of Seven) by its designers, programmers, and users. In effect, each class forms an abstraction on which other abstractions may be built.

In brief, the main difference in programming in the object-oriented style is that the design of the data items (objects within classes) comes before the design of the procedures (behaviors of the objects, called "methods" in OOP).

After Simula, the next generally known language to adopt support for object-oriented programming was Smalltalk, developed in the 70s at Xerox PARC (Palo Alto Research Center). The design of the language was driven by the desire to provide a rapid prototyping system on powerful, personal workstations. It was developed as an aid in the design of graphical human-computer interface systems and was originally an experiment. Smalltalk and the systems built with it, though not wildly successful in the marketplace (in fact it was purposely kept out of the marketplace for years) have been responsible for much of the evolution in desktop systems that has led to the Macintosh and to OS/2.

Both Simula and Smalltalk are elegantly designed, offering a small number of powerful concepts and a purity or uniformity that makes them easy to learn, relative to the complexity of the things that can be done with them. Although Smalltalk has a reputation for being difficult to learn, this is only due to the richness of the library of source code provided with each system, which must be learned to make full use of the language.

1.2　OTHER LANGUAGES

Object Pascal was developed at Apple Computer in the early 80s to add support for OOP to a popular and fairly standardized version of Pascal, UCSD Pascal. The language was designed by a team headed by Larry Tesler, formerly of Xerox PARC and a developer of Smalltalk, and aided by Niklaus Wirth, the developer of Pascal. UCSD Pascal (from the University of California at San Diego) already had a modular structure, permitting separate compilation of modules (called units) and separation of interface and implementation. Rather than creating a language from the ground up, Object Pascal was to be an extension of Pascal. The only changes made were those necessary to permit the creation of a class hierarchy, create classes, and implement the message-passing method of procedure execution that appears in Smalltalk and Simula. Even here the syntax changes were simple extensions of constructs already in the language, primarily the the record structure. Getting started is very easy for those who know Pascal, because the syntax is very familiar. It is only necessary to learn the OOP style of programming, which, admittedly, may be very difficult for a while. The negative side is that Object Pascal lacks the uniformity of some other languages. Integers are not objects, for example, and occasionally you would like them to behave as objects. Sometimes you have to do some extra work to overcome the lack of uniformity. A conscious effort was made to keep the number of new concepts in Object Pascal as small as possible without overly affecting the power of the language, so this is not a great problem. Also on the negative side is that most current implementations of Object Pascal have a problem in hiding information that should not be seen and used by programmers but needs to be seen by compilers. Object Pascal is one of the primary development languages on the Macintosh and was originally used to develop MacApp, the standard application development environment. MacApp has now been rewritten in C++. The International Standards Organization has begun to discuss standardization for object-oriented extensions of Pascal, based on the current standard Extended Pascal.

The object-oriented paradigm has been successfully applied to functional programming, with several extensions to Lisp and Scheme. In particular, the Common Lisp Object System (CLOS) has been used to build several commercial systems. One of the advantages of the Lisp family of languages is that it is possible to add something as sophisticated as object-oriented programming to the language without actually changing or extending the language. This is due to the great flexibility of Lisp.

In addition, a number of other languages support object-oriented programming very well. Some of the best of these are Eiffel, Trellis/Owl, Modula-3, and Beta. Each of these languages is suitable for the construction of large, complex software systems.

1.3 THE LANGUAGE C++

In the middle 80s a team at Bell Labs, headed by Bjarne Stroustrup, began development of a language to be a successor to the popular language C. At first the project was more of a research project than a real development effort. Early versions of the language were relatively simple extensions of C. Important to the design criteria was a belief that the language had to permit programs to be as efficient as possible. As in C, there are many places in which C++ gives up safety and ease of use for power and efficiency. Also important was a high degree of compatibility with existing C programs. Third, a high degree of portability was hoped for. The most important goal, however, was to strengthen C's weak support for data types, and especially the encapsulation and hiding of information that should be private to the implementation of a data type. Generally speaking, the design goals were met. Lately, however, the language has become very complex, with a multitude of features and rules. The design team at Bell Labs is proud of saying that they develop "sharp tools" for expert programmers. Like any sharp tool, C++ must be wielded with care. A standardization effort is also under way for C++, which began with Bell Labs' version 2.1 of C++. This book is based on version 2.1 of C++ [Ellis & Stroustrup].

1.4   PROGRAMMING IN C++

Unfortunately, a language is only a tool and not a panacea. Any language has advantages and disadvantages, and any language provides better support in some areas than in others. It is often useful to look at what application areas the designers of a language were interested in when you are trying to match a language to a software project. Even those languages that try to be all things to all programmers have their drawbacks, usually size and complexity. Programming in C++, as in any language, is easier if the programmer adopts a mental attitude appropriate for the language and adopts a style that complements the language and mitigates its weaknesses. This book will attempt to develop such a mental attitude and teach such a style.

C++ is a powerful tool and a very complex language. Learning to use it well will empower the programmer in several ways, of which the most important is the following: given facility with powerful tools, especially organizational tools, and ideas, it becomes easier to use all tools, even simpler ones. The reverse is not true. Thus it is worthwhile learning to program in the object-oriented way, even if ultimately you have to program in languages offering no support for OOP, because you will have learned additional important ways to organize software components that will make the task easier and the product more reliable.

1.5   INTRODUCTION TO THE ELEMENTARY IDEAS AND SYNTAX OF C++

C++ contains a subset that is very similar to, though not exactly the same as, ANSI C. (ANSI is the American National Standards Institute, part of the International Standards Organization.) This section will present some of the low-level details that a programmer needs to know to be able to read this "C subset of C++" effectively. It is assumed here that the reader is a "skilled novice" in either C or Pascal. This means that the reader is fluent in the use of the language's functions and procedures, arrays, program control statements, and structs (records in Pascal), and has had some experience programming with pointers. Appendix A has some additional material, especially on pointers.

1.5.1   Input and Output

C++ does much of its output using *streams*. These are defined in a built-in file iostream.h. When we define a new file to contain C++ statements, we generally begin with

```
#include <iostream.h>
```

This instruction to the *preprocessor* of C++ informs it that we need to use the standard file `iostream.h` and to include it in the compilation.

Once we have included `iostream`, we have access to the standard files `cout`, `cin`, and `cerr`. These three files provide easy input, output, and error reporting. Their use is very similar to that of `printf` and `scanf` of C and `write` and `read` of Pascal. One can output a variable `aVariable` of simple type by using the output operator `<<`, as in the statement

```
cout << aVariable;
```

One can even string several variables together. If we have an `int` variable named `value` and a `char` variable named `tok`, we can output a line of information with labeling as

```
cout << "The value of token " << tok << " is"
   << value << ".\n";
```

Each variable or `const` string is separated from the next by the output operator `<<`. The last item output after the period is the newline indicator `\n`, which tells the `iostream` to output an end-of-line symbol so that future output to `cout` will begin on a new line. Likewise we may use `cin` for input with the input operator `>>`:

```
cin >> anInt;
```

This reads a value from standard input and formats it as appropriate for the variable `anInt`, which is presumably an integer. The file `cerr` is an output file used for error reporting, so we may separate the normal output from error messages. Generally speaking, operating systems provide ways to interface these simple internal files with computer devices such as keyboards, screens, and file systems.

1.5.2 Operators

As it says in the C++ documentation, the language has a wealth of operators. Most of these were taken directly from C, and the basic ones will be familiar to most programmers. We expect addition, subtraction, and multiplication to use `+`,`-`, and `*`, respectively, and they do. Division uses the generally familiar `/` operator. The modulo (remainder) operator is `%`, so that `8 % 3` is 2. We may use `+`, `-`, `*`, and `/` with either `int` or `float` data, as well as the many variations on these types, such as `short` and `long` (integers) and `double` (real values).

Most of the relational operators are familiar, such as `<` and `>=`. C++ uses `==` for the equal comparison operator, however. This is discussed in the next section.

C++ has several forms of the assignment operator that are often useful. The basic assignment operator is =, so `anInt = 3` assigns `anInt` the value 3. Since constructs like `anInt = anInt + 3` are very common in programming, C++ provides a special operator, +=. Thus, we may increment `anInt` by 3 simply by saying `anInt += 3`. The other arithmetical operators are also supported in this way. For example, in `ans %= 5` the new value of `ans` is the remainder obtained by dividing its old value by 5: `ans = ans % 5`.

Another useful operator is++, which increments an item either before or after use. The operator is written after a variable if we want the variable incremented by one after use, and is written before the variable if we want the incrementing done before use. For example,

```
b = 2;
a = 5;
a = a + b++;
```

leaves a with value 7 and b with value 3. If we replace b++ with ++b, a will be given value 8 and b will again be left with value 3. We note that this operator increments in a way that depends on the type of the variable it is applied to. In particular, if x is a pointer to an array type, then x always refers to some element in the array, so that x++ makes x refer to the next element. The actual value stored in x will be changed by some amount that is likely greater than one. The companion decrement operator (--) behaves similarly.

Comments are either enclosed in the marks /* and */, as in C, or they begin with the double slash symbol, //, in which case the comment extends only to the end of the current line.

1.5.3 Statements and Expressions

C++ has retained the statement structure of C, so there are no suprises there for C programmers. Pascal programmers will need to note a few items, however.

Structured statements requiring a Boolean part, such as `if` and `while` statements, actually operate on `int` or `char` variables, because there is no built-in Boolean type. The syntax requires that the test expression be enclosed in parentheses, as in

```
while (first < last)
    doSomething ();
```

The *equal* comparison operator is ==, not =. The = is the assignment operator and is legal in the same context, although it is seldom the desired operator.

The assignment in C++, as in C, is actually an expression returning a value. It is the terminating semicolon that causes it to be treated as a command. Therefore it is legal to have

```
while (first = last)
   doSomething ();
```

but what occurs is that the variable first is given the value of the variable last, and that value is used to determine whether the loop is continued. The loop body is therefore either not executed at all or is executed infinitely often (unless doSomething () changes last). It was probably intended as

```
while (first == last)
   doSomething  ();
```

I have a sticker attached to my computer monitor that says "= != = =," which means " '=' (the assignment) is '!=' not equal to '= =' (the equality test)."

The *and* and *or* operators in C and C++ are && (*and*) and !! (*or*). Expressions in which they appear are evaluated from the left, and only enough of the expression is evaluated to determine whether the result should be treated as true (not zero) or false (zero). This is sometimes called "short circuit" evaluation. Therefore the following will work and will guarantee that we do not divide by zero as part of evaluating a test:

```
if (x != 0 && y / x < 20) ...
```

The for statement of C is very powerful. Its form, using an informal pseudocode, is

for (initializers; termination; eachstep) statement;

where often the statement is a compound statement using the brace symbols { and }. Sometimes the statement is actually empty. The initializer part is a list of statements, separated by commas, that are all executed prior to entering the loop. The loop terminates immediately if the termination condition is false. Otherwise the statement is executed. Then the *eachstep* statements (there may be several separated by commas) are all executed and the termination condition is checked again. Iteration continues until the termination condition becomes false, either initially or between executions of the statement. An example is

```
for (i = 0; i < 10; ++i) cout << i << '' << i * i;
```

It is also possible to declare the control variable i within the for statement itself, in which case it represents a new variable that will no longer exist after the loop terminates.

```
for (int i = 0; i < 10; ++i)
    cout << i << ' ' << i * i;
```

Finally, note that the switch statement is similar to but more primitive than the case statement of Pascal. It is really a structured go-to apparatus. Once we end up in some case, we will execute its statements, but we will continue to execute from that point until we reach a *break* statement, which takes us to the end. This can be very convenient, but it is a frequent source of difficult-to-detect errors.

```
switch (a) {
    case 0: doZeroStuff ();
    case 1: doOneStuff (); break;
    case 2: case 3: doTwoThreeStuff (); break;
    default: doOthers ();
};
```

If a has value 0 upon entering this switch statement, then both doZeroStuff () and doOneStuff () are executed. My general style in a situation like this is to put a comment after doZeroStuff () to indicate that this "fall through" to the next case is intended:

```
switch (a) {
    case 0: doZeroStuff (); // Continue.
    case 1: doOneStuff (); break;
    case 2: case 3: doTwoThreeStuff (); break;
    default: doOthers ();
};
```

One final note in this section. Since I like to be able to read the code I have written, I seldom abbreviate anything. Nor do I depend on magic constants or tricky constructs. In particular I declare the constants TRUE and FALSE for use in setting and testing Boolean values.

1.5.4 Pointers and Reference Parameters

As in C, pointers are heavily used in C++, much more so than in Pascal. Strings and arrays are represented by pointers, and one can do arithmetic on pointers. A string in C or C++ is an array of char variables that is terminated by the character \0 (ASCII zero, the NULL character). This array is implemented and declared as char *: pointer to char. It is possible to write a string s with the following while loop:

```
while (*s != 0) cout << *s++;
```

or even

```
while (*s) cout << *s++;
```

The test checks whether the pointer s refers to the NULL character, and the statement treats *s as a character and increments the pointer after use. Incrementing the pointer makes it refer to the next element of the array, here the next char variable. Note that the dereference operator has the same precedence as the increment operator (Appendix B.1), and both associate from the right. This means that *s++ is the same as * (s++), but that it is the original value of s that is dereferenced, not the incremented value, since ++ is the "post-increment" operator, which increments after its value is used.

The while loops above are equivalent (in processing the array) to the following:

```
int i = 0;
while (i < len(s)) cout s[i++];
```

This has the advantage of not changing the pointer s that references the beginning of the array.

Similarly, if a and b are arrays with num elements of the same type, we may copy one to the other using

```
for (i = 0; i < num; i++) *a++ = *b++;
```

which can also be done as

```
for (i = 0; i < num; i++) a[i] = b[i];
```

Note that the first form changes the pointers a and b, so if we are not careful we might not be able to find the beginning of either string after executing this code. Pointers may point to ordinary local or global data items. It is not necessary to call the operator new to create the thing that a pointer points to. For example, the string s of the above example might have been defined by the following:

```
char hiMsg[10] = "Hi there.";
char *s = hiMsg;
```

This creates hiMsg as a static string that requires 10 characters, because of the terminating NULL. It also creates the char pointer (char *) s and initializes it to point to the first char in hiMsg. Some care is required in processing such pointers in C and C++ so that you don't move your only reference to some complex data item down along its storage while processing it and thereby lose your only reference to its beginning.

We also note, for readers knowledgeable about Pascal, that C and C++ treat strings, and arrays in general, as a much more primitive type than Pascal does. It is not possible, for example, to assign one array variable to another in order to copy the contents of the first array. Only the pointer to the beginning of its storage is copied. To copy the contents requires a loop. It is also important to note that a declaration of a string as a pointer to char (char *) does not allocate any memory for the string. Using a string constant such as "Hi There.\n" does allocate memory, however. There is an extensive library of string manipulation routines available. To get access to them you must include <string.h>. See the documentation of your own C++ system for details of this library.

As an example of arrays, suppose that we have some type named element. An array of elements, values, is declared as

```
element *values;
```

If we know how large the array is to be at compile time, say 100, then we may specify it as

```
element values[100];
```

but values is still a pointer to element. To create an array of this type when using the first form of declaration, we must allocate it with a call to the operator new.

```
new values[size];
```

This creates storage for the array and makes the variable values a pointer to the first (zero-subscript) element. We may walk along the array by incrementing values with values++.

We note that C++ has added a new kind of parameter called a **reference parameter**. It is a special kind of pointer that is essentially equivalent to Pascal's var parameters. See Section 1.5.7, on function prototypes.

Finally, if p is a pointer to a struct (like Pascal's records) or a class type, and if the thing pointed to has a field (technically a *member* in the C++ language) named size, you access this field using the -> dereference operator, as in p -> size. We will use this extensively in coming chapters. Alternative syntax for this same dereferencing is (*p).size. We won't use this latter form, however. The equivalent Pascal syntax would be p^.size.

1.5.5 **Stronger Typing and** `typedef`

C++ retains C's structural equivalence of types for pointers and, hence, also for arrays. This means that two pointers to identical structures are considered to be the same type. Therefore giving a type a name with a `typedef` statement, as in

```
typedef foo *fooPointer;
```

which introduces the name `fooPointer` for the type `foo*` (pointer to `foo`), is less important in C++ than in a language like Pascal. In C++ if we declare p1 to be of type `fooPointer` and p2 to be of type `foo*`, then p1 and p2 are of the same type. Nevertheless, we shall be consistent in naming types and in using type names rather than repeat constructions. For class types, C++ uses a stronger form of type equivalence; two classes that have identical wording for their declarations, but different class names, will thus be treated as separate types, and assignment will not normally be done from one of the types to the other. C++ therefore encourages us to declare our classes in a centralized way.

1.5.6. **Type Conversions and Type Casting**

C++ does a good job of permitting you to mix arithmetic values of different types, attempting to do something sensible with expressions of mixed type. Conversions are done automatically when you combine an `int` and a `float` (you get a `float`) or an `int` and a `long` (you get a `long`). This is called automatic type conversion.

We can specify a type conversion if we wish, as in `(long) 25` which converts the `int` 25 to a `long` value. This is called type casting, and the syntax uses a type name or a type expression in parentheses before the value to be cast.

It is also possible to force C++ to treat a value of one type as if it had another type. Whether the value is modified depends on the context. We can treat a constant integer as if it were a pointer by casting `(char *) 10000`. No conversion of value is made here; the compiler just treats the result as a pointer. Whether this is meaningful or not depends on the system.

A newer syntax for user-specified type conversions is to use a name of a type as a function: `long (25)`. The effect is the same as `(long) 25`. There are circumstances in which one or the other is more convenient.

1.5.7 **Function Prototypes**

C++ has added to the safety of declaring and using functions. Generally one should declare functions that need to be used by many pieces of a program within some header file, and give the parameters and return type of the function. If we want to write a function whose purpose is to swap two integer variables, we could give its *prototype* as

```
void swap (int*, int*);
```

We indicate that the parameters are to be pointers to integers so that we may get return values back using the parameters themselves. We could name the parameters if we wish, as in

```
void swap (int *first, int *second);
```

The type `void` is used as a return type to indicate that there is to be no return value. Thus this is an ordinary procedure. A true function that returns the sum of an array of integers could be given as

```
int sumArray (int *a, int length);
```

which indicates a function that returns an `int`.

C++ has added reference parameters (`var` parameters of Pascal) to the standard value parameters of C. Therefore, in C++ it is preferable to use the following prototype for the above:

```
void swap (int &, int &);
```

In this way the user does not have to create or manipulate pointers simply to get a value back from a function via the parameters. In some implementation file the definition of `swap`, given this last declaration, might be

```
void swap (int &first, int &second) {
    int temp;
    temp = first; first = second; second = temp;
};
```

A function returns a value compatible with its return type by executing one of possibly several return statements within its body. Execution of the function terminates at that point, and the expression following the `return` keyword is evaluated and returned to the caller. A function declaring return type `void` is a pure procedure and may return via a `return` statement with no following expression or simply by reaching the end of the function body. Functions may also be defined to have optional arguments by providing default values for them. Thus, a routine `atoi` (ASCII to `int`) designed to translate from a string to an integer might have the declaration

```
int atoi (const char *s, int radix = 10);
```

Parameter `radix` has a default value supplied for it so that the user need not supply a value unless the default is not desired. Then `atoi` could be called with either

```
aValue = atoi ("10234");
```

or

```
aValue = atoi ("10234",16);
```

In the first case the radix would be assumed to be 10, the default. In the second it is supplied as 16.

Like Pascal, but unlike C, C++ requires that you declare a function before you call it. This is done sometimes by careful arranging of the declarations, but more often by giving the function prototypes that we have seen here. The actual body of the function must be given at some point in the program. For example,

```
int atoi(const char *s, int radix = 10){
   int result;
   ⋮
   return result;
};
```

1.5.8 Conditional Compilation

C++ maintains a set of user-defined names called symbols that are different from the ordinary names used in the program. These names may be used to produce very sophisticated effects, such as keeping specialized code for different computers in the same program. The mechanism for defining a name is the `define` directive, as in

```
#define goldbar
```

The name `goldbar` is entered into the symbol name space. One may then write code such as

```
#ifdef goldbar
   ⋮
#endif
```

in which any statements may appear between `#ifdef` and `#endif`. The compiler will process these statements only if the symbol `goldbar` is defined. Thus you can make great changes in a program depending on whether you say #define goldbar or its opposite, #undef goldbar, at the beginning.

1.5.9 Separate Compilation and Linkage

Large C and C++ programs are broken up into a collection of small files. Some of these files contain public declarations, usually of types and procedures, less frequently of variables. These declaration files are called headers and usually are distinguished by having file names that end in .h ("dot h"). Generally speaking, these files are meant to be *included* into other files so that we may obtain access to the declarations. Any procedures whose declarations (name and parameters) are in a header must be defined. Commonly this is done in an implementation file, which may have the same name as the header except that it ends in .cp or .cpp rather than .h. A header file may include several other headers, and an implementation file will include at least the header declaring the items it is implementing. A trivial example follows. First we show a header file, Nothing.h:

```
#ifndef __Nothing__
#define __Nothing__

void message (int);
#endif
```

This file simply declares a function of an integer argument (and no return value) named message. The corresponding implementation file nothing.cp for this header would look like

```
#include "nothing.h"

#ifndef __IOSTREAM__
#define __IOSTREAM__
#include <iostream.h>
#endif

void message (int worldNum){
    cout << "Hi World number: " << worldNum;
};
```

Here we define the function that was declared in the header.

Another file that wanted access to this function would conditionally include nothing.h to get access to the protocol for calling it, and a running program would be constructed by the linker by linking to the file `nothing.cp`. Since this file uses things declared in a system file `iostream.h`, it includes this file on the conditional that it has not been included already by some other file. The angle brackets, `<>`, around the name help the system find the file in the system library.

The C++ compiler is intended to compile these implementation files, and it will open and read each included file at the point at which the `include` directive appears. A large program will have several implementation files, one of which contains the definition of a function `main`. This is the entry point, or start point, for the program. In the above case, the main function would be in a file that has the following outline:

```
#include "nothing.h"
    ⋮
void main (void){
    ⋮
    message(365); // Call the message function
    // of "nothing.h" with a constant argument.
};
```

Each of these implementation files may be compiled separately by the C++ compiler. It is the purpose of the linker to take the compiler outputs and create a *run unit*. For it to do so, every function declared by the appearance of its prototype in a header must actually be defined (given a function body), and storage for each declared variable must be defined only once. If a variable is to be seen by more than one implementation file, it will need to be flagged as `extern` at all but one of its declarations. In this way the compiler and linker will combine to get it defined once. If other units are to see the declaration of the variable `otherWorld`, they will declare it `extern`, as in

```
extern int otherWorld;
```

informing the compiler that the name will be used to refer to an integer, but that the linker will supply the address of the integer. The declaration will appear exactly once without `extern`, such as

```
int otherWorld = 255;
```

The modularization of C and C++ is not as sophisticated as the modules of Modula-2 or the packages of Ada. If a name is in a file that is included, it can be seen and used. If a name is declared anywhere, it will be seen by the linker and must not conflict with other names appearing in other places. C++ is a bit stronger than C in this regard, but there is still much that the programmer must do to ensure that there are no name conflicts.

Generally speaking, a header file defines a symbol, such as `__Nothing__`, by which it may be known that the header has already been included. We shall have complex relationships between header files, and they must be included no more than once in any compilation, so this is important. We adopt the following convention. If a file, say `PBinaryT.h`, is used primarily to define the type `BinaryTree`, the header will define the symbol `__BinaryTree__`. There are two underscores at either end of the name, which has capitalized subwords and no abbreviations. The first statement of the header will check whether the symbol has already been defined, and if it has, the header will be skipped altogether. This can be achieved by use of the `#ifndef` directive at the beginning of the header file and the `#endif` directive at the end:

```
#ifndef __BinaryTree__
#define __BinaryTree__
: body of the header
#endif
```

Any file that needs to see the declarations in this header will include it with

```
#include "PBinaryT.h"
```

Note that we use a slightly different form for system files, since we can't be certain that they follow such a convention. To make your software as portable as possible, use the form that we used for `<iostream.h>` above for all system library files. For these we surround the `#include` directive by `#ifndef`, `#define`, and `#endif`. We will implement the declared functions of this file in another file named `PBinaryT.cp`, and the above conditional inclusion must appear there also. Note that we only include headers, and that angle brackets are used only for system library files. Other headers are included by enclosing the name in double quote marks. Also note that when we include a system library file, we also define a symbol of the same name, because we can't depend on the system to adopt our convention about symbols, nor be sure that two systems on which we might want to run our software will have adopted the same system, even if they have nearly identical libraries. This aids in the portability of the software.

1.5.10 Example

The following is a straightforward implementation of the greatest common divisor of two `long` integers.

```
long gcd (long a, long b) {
   // Precondition: b > 0, a >= 0.
      // Postcondition returns gcd of a, b.
   long r;
   if (a != 0)
      do {
         if (a < b) {
         r = a;
         a = b;
         b = r;
         };
      a = a % b;
      } while (a > 0);
   return b;
};
```

We can transform this into a simpler form if we use some facts about C++ operators and separate out the three lines of code that swap the values of a and b into a function.

```
void swap (long &x, long &y) {
   long t;

   t = x; x = y; y = t;
};


long gcd (long a, long b) {
   // Precondition: b > 0, a >= 0.
      // Postcondition returns gcd of a, b.
   long r;

   if (a) //  nothing if a = 0 (false)
      do {
         if (a < b) {
            swap (a, b);
         };
      a %= b;
      } while (a > 0);
   return b;
};
```

If we were to put these into the file gcd.cp, its header file, gcd.h, would look like

```
#ifndef __gcd__
#define __gcd__
```

```
long gcd (long a, long b);
    // Precondition: b > 0, a >= 0.
    // Postcondition returns gcd of a, b.
        // Returns the greatest common divisor
        // of its inputs.
#endif
```

The **precondition** means that the user is responsible for guaranteeing that b > 0 and a >= 0 before calling gcd. Preconditions are an important means of communication between the designer of a unit and its user because they inform the user as to her or his responsibilities at the point of call of a function. Similarly, the last comment contains a special case of a **postcondition**, which is what the implementor must guarantee to happen whenever the precondition is met. In other words, the precondition and the postcondition form a contract between a builder and a user stating the responsibilities of each.

A program that might test these is

```
#include "gcd.h"

#ifndef __IOSTREAM__
#define __IOSTREAM__
#include <iostream.h>
#endif

void main (void) {

    for (int i = 1, j = 1; j < 11 ; i++){
        cout << "gcd ( " << i << ',' << j
            << " ) is: " << gcd (i, j) << '\n';
        if (i == 10) {i = 0; j++;};
    }
}
```

Here we have written a for statement with two control variables. We therefore need double initializers, and we also want to increment both control variables for each iteration. Variable i is incremented by the for statement itself, but j is incremented when i overflows its intended bounds and is reset. This program prints the greatest common divisors of all combinations of integers between 1 and 10.

The details needed to build the above program vary from system to system. On the Turbo C++ system it is enough to choose the build command from the Compile menu. On a UNIX[1] system or on a Macintosh you may

_____

[1]UNIX is a trademark of AT&T Bell Labs.

need to create a `makefile` that describes the files to be compiled and the linker command needed. Some systems, such as the Macintosh MPW environment, will partially automate this process.

1.6   SUMMARY

Abstraction is the means by which we control information overload. In programming it is achieved by designing packages that present consistent, logical interfaces to the "clients" that utilize them. This helps programmers, and those who must understand the work of programmers, to deal effectively with the myriad details present in any software system.

Object-oriented programming helps with this in two ways. First, it provides mechanisms by which the visibility of information may be controlled. This makes it possible to hide the details of an implementation that are not needed by those who utilize it in other parts of the system. Second, object-oriented programming presents a simple model of computation that is similar to the world in which we live and that makes it easy to design data elements that present simple interfaces to the other parts of the system they are in.

EXERCISES

Each exercise in the book is labeled with the chapter section to which it primarily applies. It may be assigned after that section is covered.

1.1 (1.5.2) C++ has a wealth of operators, which fall into several precedence classes. For example, multiplication has a higher precedence than addition. Shown below are several of the operators of C++, with operators on the same line having equal precedence and those at the top having higher precedence than those below.

( ) parentheses
prefix ++, unary +, unary −, `new`, `delete`
∗ multiplication, / division, % modulo (remainder)
+ addition, − subtraction
‹‹, ›› output to and input from streams
‹, ‹=, ›, ›= size comparison
==, ! = equality testing
&& logical *and*
¦ ¦ logical *or*
=, +=, −=, etc. assignment operators
, comma operator

a. Using this order of precedence, put parentheses into the following expression to indicate the meaning.

```
a = b < c !! d = e != f, x += ++y * z
```

b. How is the above expression different from

```
a = b < c !! d == e != f, x += +y * z
```

Note that the assignment operator embedded in the middle of part a is legal and will be carried out.

Investigate the precedence and associativities of the other C++ operators. Your system documentation should help. Also see Appendix B.1.

1.2 (1.5.4) Write one program in C++ that will do both of the following:

a. Read in 10 integers from `cin`, echoing them to `cout`.

b. Write out their sum and average.

Use a `for` loop to control the program.

1.3 (1.5.4) Repeat Exercise 1.2, using a `while` loop in place of the `for` loop.

1.4 (1.5.4) Declare an array

```
int values [10];
```

Read 10 integers into this array. Write out the numbers backwards as well as their sum and average.

1.5 (1.5.4) Repeat Exercise 1.4, using an array declared as

```
int *values;
```

Be sure to allocate the array with

```
values = new int[10];
```

Why is this latter method more flexible than the former?

1.6 (1.5.7) Repeat Exercise 1.5 with the following changes. Use one procedure to read the values and another to write them. Pass the array to them by passing its pointer, and pass the array's length. Use a function to compute the sum, and pass the array and the length to this also. Use the following prototypes:

```
void readarray (int *a, int len);
void writearray (int *a, int len);
int sumarray (int *a, int len);
```

1.7 (1.5.7) Repeat Exercise 1.6 using reference parameters. Use the following prototypes:

```
void readarray (int &a, int len);
void writearray (int &a, int len);
int sumarray (int &a, int len);
```

1.8 (1.5.9) Repeat Exercise 1.6 or Exercise 1.7 separating the three function prototypes into a header and an implementation (.cp) file. Write a main function in a separate file to call these and solve the problem of the exercise.

1.9 (1.5.9) To make certain that you can use your C++ system, and that you understand multiple file linking and the calling of procedures, create the following three files and compile and link them on your C++ system. The purpose of the program is to write "Hello world." on the terminal screen.

File exe.h has only four lines.

```
#ifndef provider
#define provider
void printIt (void*msg);
#endif
```

File exe.cp has four lines.

```
#include "exe.h"
void printIt (char*msg){
   cout << msg << '\n';
};
```

The purpose of printIt is to output its parameter msg to standard output.

File test.cp has 7 lines (one of which is blank).

```
#include <iostream.h>
#include "exe.h"

void main (void) {
   char *hello = "Hello world.";
   printIt (hello);
};
```

1.10 (1.5.10) Build, run, and test the greatest common divisor program presented in this chapter.

DATA ABSTRACTION AND OBJECT-ORIENTED PROGRAMMING

How quickly Nature falls into revolt
When Gold becomes her Object!

Shakespeare, *Henry IV, Part 2*

Though this be madness, yet there is method in't.

Shakespeare, *Hamlet*

What is it that we do when we program? How shall we best accomplish that task? What tools and techniques do we have available to aid us? What constraints might there be on our behavior? What mental attitudes should we adopt to make it easiest?

These are important questions, and the answers are not obvious. If they were easy to answer, software would be cheap and simple to produce. As it is, it has taken us nearly fifty years of successive refinement of the problem to come to an approximation of the answers. In this section I will attempt to give answers to some of these questions, but it should be understood from the start that they are not the only possible answers. It is possible to give radically different answers to the questions and justify them completely.

2.1 THE PROGRAMMING PROCESS

It is advantageous to consider the programming process as a kind of modeling. Seen from a certain viewpoint a computer program is a concrete model of some system of phenomena. It is concrete because it can be manipulated directly (using a computer to execute it); it is a model because it has been created in order to give answers to some problem that exists outside the computer (or at least outside the program itself). Payroll programs model a certain form of employee/employer relationship; spreadsheets model a certain way of thinking about formulas; word processing programs model a simple, linear text creation method that existed before computers; and hypertext systems model a more sophisticated text creation/utilization method that has also been used for as long as books have been printed on separate pages, had indexes, and had been able to be flipped through. Even an operating system that controls the internal workings of a computer is a concrete expression of a simple management system (central control of scarce resources and distribution of workload among independent workers) that exists outside computers.

Creativity in programming is, then, a form of creativity in modeling. What are the fundamental features of the external system that are to be included in the model? What features are to be excluded? How are we to decompose the system to discover components of the model? How are we to compose the components of the model to construct the full model? How are we to verify that the model is "close enough" to the original system? These are more hard questions.

From a slightly different viewpoint, a computer program is a form of communication. One way to consider this is that a program is a way to communicate the needs of the programmer and his or her client to a computer. More importantly, a computer program is a form of communication between people: the programmer and the client, the programmer and the manager, the programmer and the other programmers working on the same program, and the programmer and himself or herself. It is important to realize that computers don't need programs. All they need are instructions. The problem is that people find it hard to create instructions without creating programs. Are you asking what the difference is between instructions and programs? Programs are certainly composed of instructions, but programs contain an organizational component that is not necessarily present in instructions.

In particular, computers don't need programming languages. Languages like Pascal, COBOL, C, Smalltalk, and the rest exist because of the capabilities and limitations of people, not because of the capabilities and limitations of machines. The two most important limitations of people are that we have a limited attention span and a limited short-term memory capacity, especially for detail. The most important capabilities of people are that we are adept at language and at abstraction. Our ability, in C and Pascal, to define data types and procedures aids us both in overcoming our limits and in playing to our abilities because, aided by our language facilities, we can lessen the detail load (a record may be used rather than all of its components) and build deep abstractions.

2.2   ABSTRACTION AND STRUCTURE

Webster gives several definitions of *abstract*: "disassociated from any specific instance"; "difficult to understand"; "ideal"; "expressing a quality apart from an object." The antonym of *abstract* is usually given as *concrete*. Abstraction involves discovery of some essential aspect of an object or group of objects and giving that aspect a name. For example, goodness, truth, and beauty are properties of human beings, so goodness, truth, and beauty are abstractions.

The second definition of *abstract*, "difficult to understand," derives from the fact that it is often difficult to give a definition of a particular abstraction that is not self-referential. Dictionaries define *goodness* as "the quality or state of being good." A good is "something that is good." Abstract entities are also defined in terms of other abstractions. A good is also "something conforming to the moral order of the universe." But the moral is another abstraction. In fact, definitions generally require that the user go through the same process of discovering the essential aspect that the creator of the original abstraction did. A set of concrete examples is used that embody a concept or its opposite and the user is invited to go through the process of abstraction to discover again the idea at hand. This works because people are good at abstraction.

In the first chapter we discussed the Rule of Seven, which indicates that our mental equipment is limited in its ability to retain certain kinds of detail in short-term memory. We also indicated that the ability to form abstractions largely compensates for this in practice. This is just another way of saying that we are able to discover structure and to impose structure on the world. As an example of what is meant by this, perform the following two-part experiment.

Take as long as you want to memorize the following collection of numbers: 2, 4, 6, 8, 10, 12, 14, 16, 18, 20, 22, 24, 26, 28, 30, 32, 34, 36, 38, 40. Now repeat the numbers you just memorized without looking. You will find that it is easy. Now do the same with the following numbers: 30, 40, 22, 32, 36, 20, 34, 24, 4, 18, 26, 6, 2, 38, 16, 12, 28, 8, 14, 10. This is much harder. Probably you gave up after discovering my (abstract) point that structure helps. The first set has a definite structure: it is the set of even numbers between 2 and 40. The second set has no such structure and so is harder to remember. In the first problem it is the structure that is easily discovered and remembered. This structure is a low-level abstraction.

We can use this abstraction to build higher-level abstractions, such as the sum of the first twenty positive even numbers. This sum can be easily done in the mind if we remember that because the sum of the first N positive numbers is $N(N+1)/2$, the sum of the first N even numbers is twice this (by the distributive law, which is an abstraction), or $N(N+1)$. Thus the sum of our numbers is 20 times 21, or 420. Now, if we discovered that the second collection of numbers was just a permutation (an abstraction) of the first set of numbers and the fact (abstraction) that the sum of a set of numbers is the same as the sum of any permutation of those numbers (abstraction), we discover that the sum of the second collection of numbers is also 420 (concrete fact).

Structure and abstraction as means of overcoming complexity afford another benefit. Synergy is the property by which the whole of something is more than the sum of its parts. An automobile can be described as a human-controlled, fuel-powered, ground-based transportation device, but no one of the parts out of which an automobile is constructed implies this description. The wheels imply transportation, the engine implies fuel power, and the instrument panel implies human control, but each of these components is usable in other machines, and none by itself implies the automobile. It is the combination of these things that makes an automobile. This is synergy. Synergy is also illustrated by the story of the four blind Indian wise men encountering an elephant for the first time. One exploring the flank describes an elephant as being very like a house, another feeling only the trunk describes it as very like a snake, the third at the tail exclaims that it is very like a vine, and the last, encountering only the leg, believes it to be very like a tree. In fact an elephant is more than the sum of its parts.

2.3   ABSTRACTION IN PROGRAMMING

In computer programming we would like to apply these ideas of abstraction, structure, and synergy to the creation of software systems. The need to do this arises from the fact that every nontrivial program contains a complexity of detail that is beyond our ability to understand without resorting to structure. Assembly language is more difficult to write and read than Pascal because it contains more detail and requires that the programmer keep track of more detail. This is why assembly language is considered a low-level language and Pascal a high-level language. Pascal embodies a higher level of abstraction than assembly language.

In programming we use several kinds of abstraction. In the next sections we will discuss two main forms, procedural abstraction and data abstraction. Object-oriented programming embodies both of these and goes a step beyond them.

2.4   PROCEDURAL ABSTRACTION

When we write a procedure in C++ we create a set of instructions that performs a task. Generally this task may be quite complex in detail but can be described succinctly in words. We give it a name that is a single word or short verb phrase describing what it does. We use verbs because procedures are actions. (A function is similar but is labeled by a noun phrase referring to its result.) For example, a procedure that computes the balance in an accounting system might be named `ComputeBalance`. The procedure would have an account number or name as input parameters and the balance of that account as output. The name of the procedure is an abstraction that stands for the complexity in the code itself.

> ### Procedural Abstraction
>
> Naming a segment of code so that it can be manipulated (usually just executed) by giving its name.

One important aspect of procedural abstraction is parameterization. We can separate what is fixed in a procedure from what is variable, and parameterize the variable part. Often, though not always, the data that the procedure is to manipulate constitute the variable part. By having parameters, a procedure is more useful because it can be used in more than one context.

Since procedures can be called from other procedures we have the basis for higher-level abstractions built from lower-level abstractions. For example, our ComputeBalance procedure could appear in a payroll program, which would represent a higher level of abstraction than that of ComputeBalance.

Procedures in Pascal can be nested, or defined within one another. When this is done, the local variables declared in the inner procedure are not visible to the containing procedures or the main program and are allocated on the system stack, so they have allocated storage only when the procedure is actually executing. The purpose of this is to permit and encourage a top-down hierarchical style of program design with either top-down or bottom-up programming. In C++ procedures cannot have nested definitions, but they can be called in nested fashion and thus have nested lifetimes of execution. In top-down hierarchical design one thinks of the entire programming project as a single procedure (main). The designer uses whatever creative facilities are available to decompose the overall problem into smaller subproblems having the following three properties: (1) each subproblem can be solved with a (perhaps very complex) procedure; (2) the subprocedures implied by (1) can be synthesized or composed into a whole; and (3) the resulting composition solves the original problem, or, in other words, is equivalent to the original hypothesized procedure. One then attacks the subproblems of (1) above in the same way so as to finally create the implied procedures.

The resulting program is then written down with the subprocedures conceptually nested in the procedures of their parents. If a procedure/problem has subprocedures/subproblems, the statements of the associated statement part simply express the way in which the subproblems were shown to be composed in (2). For example, if, in attacking problem P1 of Fig. 2.1, we decided that we could solve it by executing P11 three times and then executing P12 once, the procedure body for P1 would have a call to P11 in a

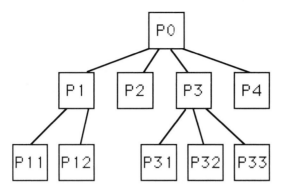

FIGURE 2.1

loop to be executed three times followed by a call to P12. Problems that can be solved directly and simply without decomposition constitute the lowest level of our hierarchy.

Pascal has nested procedures, because at the time it was created this method of program development, also called procedural decomposition, was seen to be a very important and efficient development style. C and C++ do not, because they require a more efficient implementation, but the process of program decomposition is similar even though the language doesn't support it as directly. This process is illustrated by Fig. 2.2. The "solve" step of the figure is taken to be one of simple programming if the part of the problem it deals with is simple, and a repeat of the overall process if the part of the problem it deals with is complex. This technique is often called "divide and conquer" and is a general modeling technique. To model some phenomenon P0, look at it as a collection of subphenomena P1, P2,..., interacting in some way. Model each subphenomenon, perhaps using further decompositions, and then combine the solutions or models of the subphenomena together according to the interactions discovered during the original decomposition. Note that the beginning and ending figures were not drawn to be identical, because the model always leaves out some detail deemed to be nonessential. Thus a model can be considered a faithful representation of the original only for certain purposes.

It is important to note that different languages support procedural abstraction with different degrees of completeness. Pascal's implementation of procedures is somewhat flawed because in it procedures can be used only in very limited ways. Procedures can be declared, called, and passed as arguments to other procedures. But they cannot be modified by a running program, and variables cannot have values that are procedures. (Scheme allows both of these, and Modula-2 permits the latter.) The implication of this is that in a Pascal program, except for procedure-valued parameters, at each point at which some procedure is called, the compiler knows exactly which procedure will be called. Sometimes it is desirable to postpone the decision as to which procedure to call until the program is actually running.

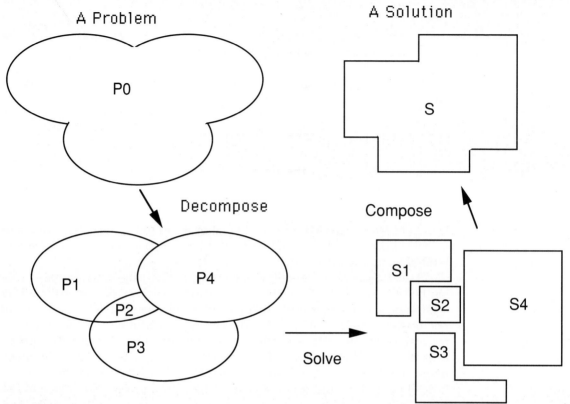

FIGURE 2.2

This *late binding* of procedures does occur in the case of procedure-valued parameters, as shown by the C++ example below.

Suppose that we have an array type in our program:

```
typedef float DataArray[size] ;
```

Then we can have several arrays of this type. Suppose that at various points in the program we need to apply some procedure to each of the float variables in one of these arrays and that at different points in the program we need to apply different procedures to one of these arrays. This process of applying some procedure to each element of some array can be abstracted out of our system by declaring a procedure as follows:

```
void Apply (DataArray &A, void (*Proc) (float &R)) {
    int i;
    for (i = 0; i < size; ++i)
        Proc (A[i]);
};
```

Note that the procedure `Apply` has two parameters, a reference to an array, A, and a pointer to a procedure, `Proc`. `Proc` has one `float` argument, and is thus compatible with any procedure having only one `float` argument. Therefore, if we had a declared array `AccountArray` and a declared procedure `Increment (float &X)` of one real argument, we could apply `Increment` to each element of `AccountArray` with the procedure call:

```
Apply (AccountArray, Increment);
```

and the effect would be the same as if we had written

```
for (i = 0; i < size; ++i)
   Increment (AccountArray[i]);
```

However, the compiler that translates this program has no way of knowing which procedure will be substituted for the formal parameter `Proc`, so the encoding of the procedure `Apply` will be generalized to permit any procedure with a single real argument to be used. Which procedure is used is determined only at run time, and not at compile time.

The above example illustrates that there is flexibility and hence power to be achieved by delaying certain decisions until late in the think-compile-test-run software development process. Delaying decisions such as what procedure to use permits them to be made in a more general way, hence more flexibly.

The flip side of this coin, however, is that there is safety in making decisions early in the cycle. In fact, if all decisions are made before the compiler translates the program into machine code, the compiler can best provide warnings of potential and actual errors and can maximize optimization. If decisions are made early, the program is more specialized and hence has more information that can be taken advantage of. This is the chief reason for Pascal's strong typing mechanism. It permits the compiler to issue warnings of type inconsistencies, which usually signify programmer errors. C has a weaker typing mechanism, in order to permit more flexibility to the programmer: decisions made late in the cycle permit a program to be more generalized.

As a final note on procedural abstraction and our divide-and-conquer methodology, note that one can divide, solve, and compose using criteria other than procedural decomposition. A problem need not be divided up according to the *processes* that will solve it. In fact, object-oriented programming uses a divide-and-conquer method but divides up the problem and creates a solution using a different decomposition, one into the objects or actors in a system rather than the actions. More on this later. Object-oriented programming also permits many decisions to be made late in the cycle, increasing flexibility.

2.5   DATA ABSTRACTION

Data abstraction exists independently of computer programming and is properly a topic of mathematics as well as computer science. The term wasn't used, however, until the need for it appeared in computer programming.

Data Abstraction

A data abstraction consists of the three following parts:

1. A set S of objects, whose representation structure is undefined.
2. A set P of operations defined on elements of S.
3. A set R of rules that define the operations and relationships between the elements of the set.

For example, by this definition, the natural numbers, $S = \{1, 2, 3, \ldots\}$, with the set of operations $P = \{+, -\}$ and the usual Peano axioms, $R = \{1$ is a natural number, every natural number has a unique successor,$\ldots\}$, is a data abstraction. I have actually given more here than is necessary, for I have given a particular representation of S, which is not required. An alternate form of S is $S = \{\{\}, \{\{\}\}, \{\{\{\}\}\}, \ldots\}$, where $\{\}$ represents the empty set, $\{\{\}\}$ is the set of one element containing the empty set, and so on.

Note that the type int i n C and C++ is an attempt to model a data abstraction, namely the integers of mathematics, though it does so imperfectly. In particular, int m odels only a bounded section of integers, $-32,768$ to $+32,767$ on many microcomputers.

In practice, the above definition of data abstraction is a bit too narrow. We will use it, however, to define a slightly richer idea called an abstract data type, or ADT.

Abstract Data Type

An abstract data type is a set of data abstractions, each with its own elements, operations, and rules, where one of the data abstractions within the ADT is specified as the principal data abstraction.

Thus an ADT is a collection of interrelated data abstractions. There are operations and rules for each individual data abstraction. There might also be rules for combining and relating elements of different data abstractions. In many cases an ADT consists only of a single data abstraction. Later we shall see many examples of the more complex case. At this point I will only give an analogy to illustrate the general idea.

Consider the situation of the business world, where there are people and corporations. People do things (perform operations) and relate to one another (follow rules). The same is true of corporations. But there are also behaviors of people and corporations toward each other, such as the buying of corporate stock (a higher-level operation), and these behaviors must obey certain laws and expectations (rules). Thus, an ADT for the business world would contain at least a data abstraction for people and another for corporations. One of these would be designated as primary, depending on the specific needs of the system.

One example of an ADT, which, as we shall see later, is closely related to computer programming, is a list, such as a shopping list. A list is a finite sequence of items of a certain kind. We can add to the list and delete from it in different places, even in the middle. For example, we might insert "Cheese" in the list "Bread," "Milk," "Eggs" just after "Milk." There may or may not be a particular ordering of the items in a list. A related data abstraction is that of a list position. This abstraction has values such as *the position of item "Milk" in the list "Bread," "Milk," "Eggs."* The two data abstractions list and list position can be bound together to form an ADT.

Another simple and useful ADT, with only one data abstraction, is that of a stack. We assume that some readers are familiar with stacks and have programmed them in the past. We shall present several ways to define and implement stacks in this and following chapters by way of introducing syntax of and ideas involved with C++. The final definition won't be given until Chapter 7. Now we simply want to discuss the stack as a data abstraction and demonstrate some simple operations it uses. We shall use a subset of C++ that is almost like C. Later in this chapter we shall examine one that uses more features of C++.

The stack is a type of data storage mechanism. Because it is a storage structure, we must be able to insert data into it and later retrieve the data inserted. The insertion into storage is a *push*, and the removal is a *pop*. No other operation modifies the storage. Objects are removed (popped) in the reverse of the order they were inserted. This is called LIFO, for "last in–first out." One accesses stored items only through reference to the top of the stack, the top being the most recently inserted item still remaining on the stack. A reference to the top of the stack is, simply, a *top* (see Fig. 2.3).

Stacks arise frequently in computer science and in applications. For example, if we were building a robot capable of walking a maze, it might be useful to organize its memory around a stack. In this way it could keep track of where it had been in the maze by pushing its coordinates onto the stack

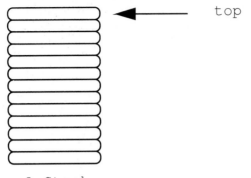

FIGURE 2.3   A Stack

each time it moved. Then it could reverse its course when it encountered a dead end by popping a coordinate off its stack and returning to it. It would always have a path back to its starting point stored in its memory.

To characterize a stack as an ADT, we must describe its one data abstraction by specifying the sets S of objects, P of operations, and R of rules. The set S contains just one element, the stack itself, and its structure is undefined. In practice it could be an array, but it need not be, and making it an array would restrict the number of elements it could contain. It is important to leave the internals of an object undefined in its specification. The set P of operations consists of at least the operations *push* and *pop*. In reality it will need at least one more operation, *initialize*, that will guarantee the existence of some specific state of the stack. Since a stack is a storage mechanism, this state is usually the empty state, representing an empty storage. It will also be useful to have an operation (actually a function) that tells us whether the stack is empty or not. This function could be named *empty*. Such a function that returns a truth value (TRUE or FALSE) is a **predicate**.

The rules R for a stack are as follows. Immediately after *initialize* we find that *empty* returns TRUE. Immediately after *push* we find that *empty* returns FALSE. Whenever *empty* is TRUE we find that *top* is an error and that *pop* is an error. Immediately after *push* has inserted X we find that *top* is X and that *pop* returns X. Finally, if the stack is in some state Y, applying *push* followed by *pop* will leave the stack in state Y.

Some additional operations are useful for stacks. One of the most common is a function, *numberOfElements*, that tells us how many data items are currently stored in the structure. To add such an operation it is necessary to define it, and we do this by adding rules. In this case the rules needed are the following: *empty* is TRUE if and only if *numberOfElements* is zero; if *numberOfElements* is N and we execute *push*, *numberOfElements* is $N+1$, but if we execute *pop* instead, *numberOfElements* is $N-1$.

It is important to remember that the operations and their rules, and not the representation of the set on which the operations act, define what a stack is. Any representation can be a stack as long as it has the required operations and that these obey the rules.

In C++ we may implement a stack (imperfectly) as follows. (Note that we are not yet taking full advantage of C++. This is almost the same as standard C. Also note that in C++, as in C, the type constructor `struct` is used to create data records, which is used in the same way in C as `record` is in Pascal.)

```
typedef struct {
      float elements[100];
      int top;
   } TStack;

void INITIALIZE (TStack &S) {
   S.top = -1 ;
};

void PUSH (TStack &S, float E) {
   if (S.top<99) {
     ++S.top;
     S.elements [S.top] = E;
   };
};

void POP (TStack &S, float &E) {
   if(S.top >= 0 ) {
      E = S.elements [S.top];
      --S.top;
   };
};

char EMPTY (TStack S) {
   return S.top < 0;
};

void TOP (TStack S, float &E) {
   if(S.top >= 0) E = S.elements[S.top];
};
```

We create an actual stack by declaring a variable to be of type `TStack` and then calling `INITIALIZE` with this variable as parameter.

A diagram of this implementation after several pushes and perhaps some pops have been performed is shown in Fig. 2.4. Note that the field `top` is an integer, here having value 7. The content of cell 7 is 4. We indicate this by an arrow to the cell with index 7. In fact it is fairly common in practice

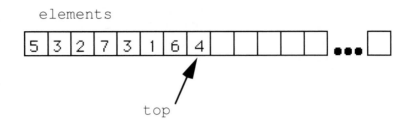

elements

FIGURE 2.4

to say "pointer" for the value of an integer index into an array, and to say that `top` "points" into the array. This should not be confused with a C or C++ pointer-valued variable, though such a variable is actually very similar to an integer array index.

Within certain limits this implementation obeys the rules that define a stack, but it is useful to catalog the ways in which it does not. The most obvious is that there is nothing in the definition of a stack that implies that no more than 100 items can be stored at one time, whereas this is clearly a property of our implementation. Thus we have actually implemented a different abstraction, a *finite* or *bounded* stack. Second, our implementation only permits `float` values to be pushed. Thus we have a *bounded stack of floats*, and not a stack per se. Finally, where the specification calls for errors we have actually implemented *no-ops*, by which no operation is performed and the call leaves the state unchanged. In order to generate errors we could remove the `if` tests in PUSH, POP, and TOP and let the run-time system halt our program when it makes a reference to an element not in the array (assuming that it would, which is not always a valid assumption). Alternatively we could provide a general error handler within our program. One way to do this would be to provide a simple procedure `error` that when called would print some message and then halt the running program. We would then modify PUSH, POP, and TOP so that if the `if` clause is FALSE we call `error`. This method is preferable.

Now we should verify that with the exceptions noted above our implementation meets the specifications. First we note that, as a storage mechanism, this implementation stores the `float` values that are in cells 0 through `top`, inclusive. What values there may be in cells of index greater than `top` is not important.

Assume that the stack is named S. INITIALIZE sets S.top = -1, and EMPTY is TRUE if and only if S.top < 0, so our first rule holds in this implementation.

No operation can make S.top less than -1, since only POP decreases it and it won't do that unless S.top was previously greater than or equal to 0. Likewise PUSH always increases S.top, so after a PUSH, S.top is always greater than or equal to zero, and thus EMPTY is FALSE and the second rule holds.

Our third rule obtains in the sense that both POP and TOP do nothing when the stack is empty (S.top < 0), and we may interpret this as a simple form of error. Including the error handler would improve our adherence to this rule.

Immediately after PUSH is executed, provided that the stack was not already full, we see that S.top contains a reference to the array element inserted by PUSH. In this case then, S.top will reference this last inserted element and POP will return it, so our fourth rule holds.

If the stack was not full before a PUSH, a POP performed immediately afterward will remove the element inserted and return S.top to the value it had before. Therefore, from a logical standpoint, the stack is in the same state that it was in before we did the PUSH. Note that it need not be in the same physical state, since there is a value in the next cell beyond S.top that was probably not the same before the PUSH. But, because this item is not logically stored in the stack, this is immaterial.

Note that in verifying the last two rules we had to provide for the exceptional case, that of a PUSH onto a full stack, after which a POP will not be a return to the original state. We could specify operations and axioms (rules) for a bounded stack that would define pushing onto a stack that held the maximum number of elements to be an error. Our implementation would then, perhaps, fully meet the definition. The reader is encouraged to make this definition and to do the necessary verification.

An *interface* is a list of type names and function prototypes annotated with information necessary to the user. One reason for providing an interface in this example is that the user of a stack should not have to depend on reading the specific code of the functions. After all, this code might need to change, either because errors are discovered or because the designer or builder discovers a more appropriate mechanism. An interface for the stack type might be something like the following:

```
TStack // A type representing a bounded
       // LIFO storage structure.
       // It is limited to containing
       // no more than 100 items
       // simultaneously.
void INITIALIZE (TStack &S) // This must be
       // called once before the stack S is
       // first utilized. It can be called
       // again to clear its storage.
void PUSH (TStack &S, float E) // Precondition:
       // S has been INITIALIZED and contains
       // less than 100 items. Postcondition:
       // E will be saved at the top of S.
```

```
void POP (TStack &S, float &E) // Precondition:
       // S has been INITIALIZED and is not empty.
       // Postcondition: The top of S will be
       // returned in E and removed from the storage
char EMPTY (TStack S) // Precondition: S has
       // been INITIALIZED. Postcondition:
       // Returns TRUE if and only if the
       // stack S is currently empty.
void TOP (TStack S, float &E) // Precondition:
       // S has been INITIALIZED. Postcondition:
       // The top of S will be returned in E
       // and the storage left unaffected.
```

A designer of this class would also communicate to the builder, who actually writes the code, that it must be an **invariant** of the type TStack that the field top within the type itself must obey the condition −1 <= top < 100 at all times after initialization. This information should not be revealed to users, however, because it has to do with the implementation of the type and not its use.

The adequacy of our imperfect implementation of the stack depends on the use to which it is to be put. If we are writing a simple program to be executed a few times by its creator, it will probably suffice, even with its flaws. If it is to go into a large software system, it may be sufficient or not depending on the specification of the overall system and its projected lifetime. If it is to be put into a library of software to be used in several projects by one or several programmers over a long period of time, it is certainly inadequate. In this situation it would be necessary to define what we mean by *error*, to implement error handling faithfully, and either remove the boundedness limitation or give rules that clearly indicate what happens when the bounds are reached.

It is instructive to compare this implementation with another based on different C-like constructs. In this case we shall use pointer variables. If you are not familiar with these, you should consult the appendixes for a discussion of pointer types and the underlying machine model that we are using, especially the information on the system heap.

Again we need to define one or more types, in order to have an implementation of the data set of the abstract data type, and we need to define several operations on this type and then verify that the rules that define a stack hold.

```
typedef struct stackNode {
      float element;
      stackNode *next;
};
```

```
typedef stackNode *TStack ;

    void INITIALIZE (TStack &S) {
       S = NULL;
    };

    void PUSH (TStack &S, float E) {
       TStack aNode;

          aNode = new (stackNode);
          aNode -> next = S;
          S = aNode;
          aNode -> element = E;
    };

    char EMPTY (TStack S) {
       return S == NULL;
    };

    void POP (TStack &S, float &E) {
       TStack aNode;
          if (! EMPTY(S)) {
             aNode = S;
             E = aNode -> element;
             S = S -> next;
             delete (aNode);
          };
    };
    void TOP (TStack S, float &E) {
       if (! EMPTY (S));
       E = S -> element;
    };
```

Again, a stack is any variable of type TStack. It is important to note that the procedures defining the operations have exactly the same parameter specification in this implementation as they did in the array-based stack given above. This implementation is also imperfect, but it does a better job than the previous example. Here there is no explicit bound, but there is an implicit one, because the heap of the underlying computer is finite. If we push often enough without popping, we will eventually exhaust the heap, and our program will probably (hopefully) crash. There are tests that would prevent this, but the method depends on the particular compiler and is not standardized.

In the previous implementation there was the implicit property that the field variable top was always greater than or equal to −1. In this

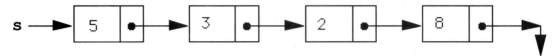

FIGURE 2.5

implementation a different property is maintained by the operations. Namely, our stack consists of zero or more nodes and either the stack variable itself, if there are no nodes, or the next field of the node that has existed for the longest time is equal to NULL. In C, NULL is not a node. It is a constant defined in the language. The run-time system has some way to set its state so that it can test for equality to NULL, but otherwise a pointer variable whose "value is NULL" does not behave like a node. In particular, when P == NULL is TRUE for some pointer variable P, it is illegal to dereference P. C programs have many tests to check for this case. Therefore, S -> element only appears inside an if statement that guarantees that S != NULL. A possible picture of our stack is shown in Fig. 2.5, where pointer variables and fields are represented by arrows and NULL is represented by a pair of arrows at right angles. Each box represents an instance of a stackNode record and each subrectangle represents one field. In this case there have been four more pushes than pops, and the top is currently 5.

If you have had little experience with pointer variables, the following pictorial trace of the stack operations may be helpful. We intersperse pictures within the program showing after each statement the effect of the statement on the state of the memory. We don't trace TOP or EMPTY, because they don't change the state of the stack itself.

```
void INITIALIZE (TStack &S) {
    S = NULL;
```
          S •——▶

```
};
```

Assume that E in the following is 5, and that the stack currently stores 2 (at the top) and 8.

```
void PUSH (TStack &S, float E) {
    TStack aNode;
```

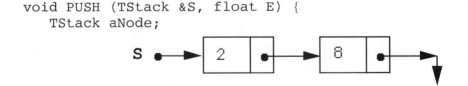

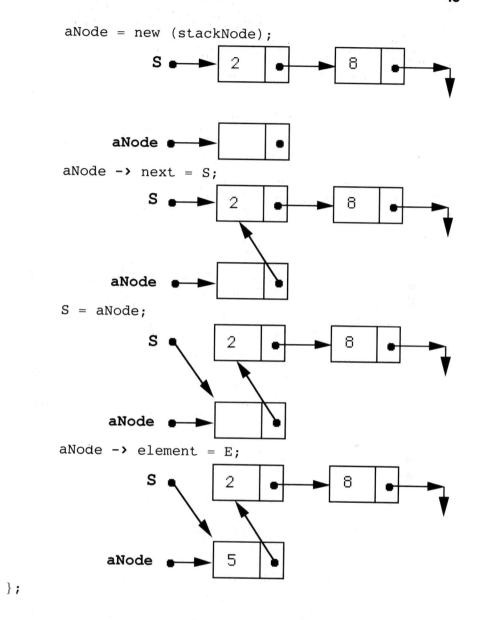

```
aNode = new (stackNode);
```

```
aNode -> next = S;
```

```
S = aNode;
```

```
aNode -> element = E;
```

```
};
```

Assume that the stack currently stores 2 (at the top) and 8.

```
void POP (TStack &S, float &E) {
    TStack aNode;
```

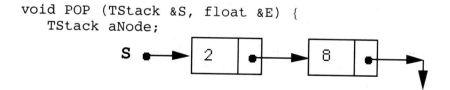

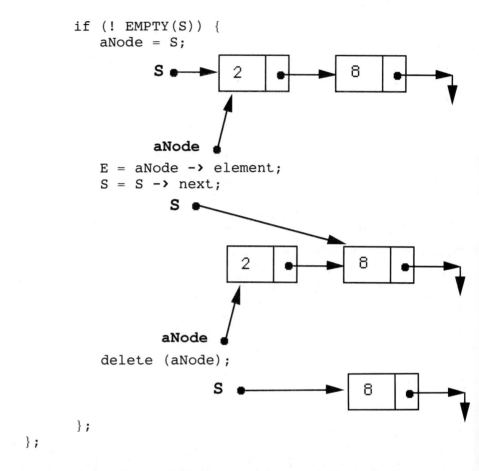

```
if (! EMPTY(S)) {
    aNode = S;
```

```
E = aNode -> element;
S = S -> next;
```

```
delete (aNode);
```

```
    };
};
```

We must again verify that the axioms that define a stack are true or discover how they are not. As mentioned above, the boundedness property of the last implementation has been relaxed, though not entirely overcome.

INITIALIZE sets the stack variable to be NULL and EMPTY tests for NULL, so the first rule holds.

PUSH always sets the stack variable to the result of a call to new, which is never NULL unless the system is out of memory. Thus, except in this case, the stack is never empty after a PUSH, and the second rule holds partially.

If EMPTY is TRUE, the stack variable is NULL and both TOP and POP are no-ops (rather than errors), which is the same as before for the third rule.

If we have just performed a PUSH, on a real value X, the stack variable is set to point to a node that contains X. POP and TOP return the value in such a node, so the fourth rule holds.

The last rule holds as well, because the PUSH operation copies the old stack variable value into the next field of the new node. The POP operation sets the stack variable to be the next field of the node pointed to originally by the stack variable.

Again, our implementation would be improved by the implementation of an error handler and by the presence of more checking, especially in the push operation to see whether the call to new su cceeds. Properly speaking, we should either make such modifications or change the specification (the rules) to describe what we have done more clearly. For example, in this case we could add a rule that an implementation on a finite machine could behave unpredictably if there is insufficient space in the memory to hold all the storage implied by the operations on the stack. This rule might be called the "cop out" rule, but it is at least a warning to users that our implementation may have holes.

2.6   OBJECT-ORIENTED PROGRAMMING

The creation of Pascal in the late 1960s was a breakthrough because the language enabled the user to create named types and use them to control access to the low-level representation (bits) of the data manipulated by a program. It also made it possible to specify types for the parameters of a procedure that would permit a form of contractual agreement between the procedure that performs a service (the server) and the procedure that needs the service (the client). Thus, programmers were freed from the necessity of continually remembering all of the details of the encodings they used to represent program data.

In FORTRAN, if you wanted to pass a procedure the information that an employee was male or female, you passed an integer parameter with the value 0 or 1 (or something similar). You had to name the parameter carefully so that a user of the procedure would not try to pass the value 55. The compiler was not able to check for valid values. Therefore, the programmer had either to verify all such low-level data by hand or encode tests into the program to check the validity of the data. Both of these methods cost time, and the latter increases the length and complexity of the code. Types permit the computer itself to carry out this task efficiently. Additionally, strongly typed systems, and compile-time-typed systems in particular, provide a maximum of information to the program author as early as possible in the development process, i.e., at compile time.

Object-oriented programming is another step in the same direction, automating low-level detail, giving the computer and the compiler additional tasks that programmers would otherwise need to perform, and making the text of the program more nearly like the high-level description of the problem it is designed to solve. In object-oriented systems there is an extra level of binding between procedures and the data they manipulate. In C++, as in Smalltalk and Object Pascal, an object is a collection of data that "knows" what procedures may be applied to it. Thus a program's author can more easily guarantee that only appropriate operations are applied to a bit of data, because she or he designed those operations when the data was defined and the object-oriented system ensures that other operations are not applied to the data object.

Object-oriented programming also offers the benefit of making it possible, and easy, to make the running program more nearly model the real situation in which the original problem arose. It is only a small leap to imagine that every program is a simulation or a model of some phenomenon.

Object-oriented programming consists of two tasks. The first is to partition the *text* of a large program into modules of a certain kind, called classes. The second task is to partition the *running program* into data elements of a certain kind, called objects. The relationship between the classes and the objects is that the classes are static descriptions of the dynamic objects. The programmer actually writes the text of the program, which is the static description, but must design both the static and dynamic aspects of the system.

Object-Oriented Programming (first version of three)

Programming methodology in which the data elements (objects) in the system form the fundamental unit of program decomposition.

2.7 CLASSES, OBJECTS, AND POINTERS TO OBJECTS

A class is a description of a collection of objects (or occasionally a single object). A class description specifies the data elements that objects use to maintain each state. These data elements are called its members, fields, or instance variables. The class description also specifies what operations can be applied to the objects of the class and, ultimately, how the data elements are changed to reflect the changed state of an object. These operations are called methods, and in C++ we have both functional and procedural methods. Procedural methods are simply functions declared to return `void`. We shall use classes to model individual data abstractions and C++ compilation units to model ADTs.

Class definitions are very similar to struct definitions. In fact the class of C++ is an extension of the struct of C. The following is the class definition of a randomized five-point star, which is a type of graphic object that might be important in a graphics application:

```
class S5PointStar {
    public:
        S5PointStar ( int imbalance, PPoint Loc,
            float Diam); // Constructor.
        void draw (SPattern fill);
        void moveTo (PPoint newLocation);
```

```
    protected:
      float fDiameter;
      PPoint fLocation;
      int fImbalance;
};
```

```
typedef S5PointStar *P5PointStar
```

If we should create and then draw such a five-point star, we might see something like Fig. 2.6.

Objects are values, and we refer to them by variables that we declare in the declaration section of the program. Almost always we shall refer to such objects using pointers. For this reason, whenever we create a class type we also create an associated pointer type:

```
typedef S5PointStar *P5PointStar
P5PointStar myNewStar;
```

A variable whose type is a pointer to a class type will be called an indirect variable. In other languages these are called reference variables, but C++ has such a named type. Objects referred to by indirect variables are sometimes called indirect objects. If they are named by ordinary variables they are direct (stack) objects. We shall generally use the term *object* to refer to indirect objects.

Indirect Variable

A variable whose type is a pointer to a class type. Indirect variables are used to refer to objects in object-oriented programming.

The essential difference between a direct object and an indirect object concerns how the object is declared and created. In C++ a direct object is created by declaring a variable with a class type, such as S5PointStar.

FIGURE 2.6

Such a declaration may be either at the global level or within a function. Such a variable represents a block of data, very much like an ordinary struct or record, except that the object knows what methods it can execute. If a constructor (a method with the same name as the class) is declared in the class of the variable, the system will ensure that a constructor is executed before the object is used. If the constructor has parameters, the programmer must supply them in the declaration statement. Thus, to declare myStar as a direct or *static* 5-point star, we could make a declaration like

```
S5PointStar myStar (5, aPoint, 7.3);
```

The object will continue to exist until the unit in which it was declared ceases to exist. Thus, if the object is global, it exists for the life of the program. If it was declared within a function, it exists only when the function executes. It is created (and constructed) each time the function is called and destructed each time the function returns. If the programmer supplies a destructor method (the name of a destructor is a tilde followed by the name of the class: ~S5PointStar), the system will automatically call it. In this way the programmer can decide what must be done to dispose of an object properly.

To create and use **indirect objects**, we declare a variable to be a pointer to a class. The declaration itself does not create the object as it does in the static case. Instead, we must call the standard operator new to create the object. The object is then created in the area of system memory known as the heap. The object exists until the operator delete is executed having as argument some pointer to the object. Therefore, to create an indirect five-point star we would declare

```
P5PointStar myStar;
```

We would then have to create the object with new. We shall, of course, have to supply appropriate parameters for some constructor. Here we have only one, so we could say

```
myStar = new S5PointStar (5, aPoint, 7.2);
```

An object created in this way will need to be explicitly deleted by the programmer when its services are no longer needed. This is done with the command

```
delete myStar;
```

At this time a destructor will be called by the system if one has been defined in the class of the object.

While it is possible to use ordinary, or direct, variables in C++, we shall not be able to achieve all of the benefits of object-oriented programming that we seek unless we use pointers. Since our style is to be quite uniform, in the use of pointers we shall intentionally say that a variable like myNewStar is an object or represents an object, even though technically it is a pointer to an object. We shall also say that the class of myNewStar is S5PointStar, or even P5PointStar, even though that is not precisely correct. Finally, we shall occasionally use the term *reference variable* rather than the more specific *indirect* or *pointer variable*. For completeness, note that most object-oriented languages reserve the word *object* for something referred to indirectly using a variable that behaves like a pointer. C++ makes a notable departure from this usage in using the term for an item allocated in the same way that local function variables are allocated. While this makes C++ more flexible and extends the benefits of the binding of procedures and data to the situation of ordinary records, it complicates the programming model.

Constructor

A method that is automatically executed when an object is created. In C++ it has the same name as the class.

A class may have many constructors, and all will have the same name as the class. They are distinguished by their parameters, not by their names, so each must have a different parameter list. (This uses a general feature of C++ called *overloading*: procedure names can be used for other procedures if the parameter lists are different.) A constructor is always called when an object (either direct or indirect) is created, even if the compiler itself has to construct one for the class. A constructor is called for a direct object when the program begins to execute the function in which it is declared, and the necessary parameters are given in the declaration itself, as shown above. For indirect objects the constructor is called explicitly as an operand of the new operator. Note that for indirect objects we don't call new or the constructor for each variable name, but only for each object that we wish to create.

There are a few special rules about constructors, most of which are implied by the fact that within a constructor the object being constructed is only partially complete. Therefore some methods cannot be called from within constructors, for they may require that the object be fully functional.

The opposite of a constructor is a *destructor*. A destructor is called by the system itself for a direct object when the procedure in which the variable was declared terminates. A destructor does not have parameters, its name is the class name preceded by a tilde, "~" The destructor of an indirect object is called when the user disposes of the object with the delete operator. Any given class has only one destructor, ~Classname.

Destructor

A method that is automatically executed when an object is deleted. In C++ it has the same name as the class preceded by a tilde.

Creation of an indirect data object requires that we allocate the object and then initialize it. However, the allocation can possibly fail, because a computer has only a fixed amount of memory. The following takes care of this:

```
myNewStar = new S5PointStar (40, ctrPt, 80.0);

failnull (myNewStar); // Halt the program if
                      // myNewStar is NULL.
```

We assume of course that the variable ctrPt was already appropriately defined. The first statement is a call to the C++ allocation operator. Thus, objects exist in the physical machine in the heap area of the memory. The method new allocates heap space for the object. The parameters indicate which of many possible constructors are called and the system will guarantee that the appropriate constructor is called. Constructors permit the designer of a class to guarantee proper initialization of our objects.

The call to failnull is a necessary safeguard, because new is occasionally unable to allocate the required space for the new object. The statement will cause the running program to halt if new is unable to find the required memory. The procedure failnull is a library procedure, as shall be seen in Chapter 3, pp. 84–99.

Because the two-statement fragment of initialization code shown above is of a very common pattern, we shall generally provide a function that contains it when we define any new class. For the S5PointStar class our function will be called new5PointStar and will appear as follows:

```
P5PointStar new5PointStar (int imbalance,
                           PPoint Loc, float Diam) {
    P5PointStar result;
    result = new S5PointStar (imbalance,
                              Loc, Diam);
    failnull (result);
    return result;
};
```

We call these functions *generator functions*, and our style shall be to call the class constructor methods only from within these generators.

This procedure will return properly initialized stars to us. A drawing application could call this function several times to populate the sky with random stars. Each call will result in the creation of a new object. Memory is allocated for our indirect objects in an area of computer memory called the heap. Unlike the local data of procedures, this memory is not automatically deallocated when a procedure returns, so it is used to create relatively long-lived items. A reference to the created object is returned by this function, and the caller will generally assign the result to some variable or otherwise ensure that some permanent reference to the object is maintained. Thus a call might be

```
anotherStar = new5PointStar (5, aPoint, 80.0);
```

Note that there is only one class description for S5PointStar and that it is used to define many objects within the class. In other words, classes are types, and objects are instances or values of the type. The application could also save the stars in some collection structure, like an array, so that the stars could be drawn, moved, and eventually destroyed.

Object-Oriented Programming (second version)

Programming methodology in which the data elements (objects) in the system form the fundamental unit of program decomposition. Objects are described by means of classes.

2.8 EXECUTING METHODS

If an object is direct and we want to execute one of its methods, we must give the name of the object followed by a period and the name and parameters of the method, as in aStar.moveTo (aPoint). To execute a method of a class on an indirect object, we give the name of an object, then an "arrow," ->, and then the name of one of the methods defined in the class of that object and any parameters it requires. In this case myNewStar is known by the compiler to be a pointer to an object in the class S5PointStar, and moveTo is one of the class's methods. Therefore the statement myNewStar -> moveTo (aPoint) is a legal statement provided aPoint is a valid PPoint. In either the direct or indirect case, the statement is called a **message**, and the message is said to be sent to the object aStar or myNewStar, respectively. In most cases the code that sends the message is part of some other method, perhaps of an object of some other class. We say that this other object sends the message moveTo to the object aStar or myNewStar. Since the draw procedure is also a method, executing it also requires sending of a message, as in

```
myNewStar -> draw (clearPat);
```

A useful mental picture of an object-oriented program in operation (using indirect objects) is that of a graph in which the nodes represent the objects and the arcs represent messages sent between the objects. The arcs are actually arrows, because messages are unidirectional, having a sender and a receiver. Functional methods, of course, return some result backward along the arrow. For example, a graphics or CAD/CAM application might have a window object that has a reference to a list object. This list object might have references to several drawable figure objects. The window might send the message draw to the list, and the list, in executing the draw method, might send the message draw to each of the figures. The picture of this is shown in Fig. 2.7.

Another possible mental picture would be a slightly different graph, much more static in concept, in which the nodes would represent objects but the arrows would represent references to other objects. This picture is similar to the ones we have used for illustrating pointer variables. In this scheme we draw arrows between objects when some class has an indirect instance variable of a class type. In S5PointStar the fLocation instance variable, whose type is PPoint, is just such a case. Such an instance variable is a reference to the other object and is represented in this picture by an arrow. At run time the instance variable contains a reference to some object of the necessary type. Actually, since the reason for maintaining a reference to another object is to send it messages, the two pictures are almost always the same. In the above case the arrows do represent messages (draw) sent, but they also represent instance variables, because a window has an instance variable of type PList. Sometimes we say that a window *contains* a list when in fact we mean that it has an instance variable of type PList, which means that it contains a *reference* to a list.

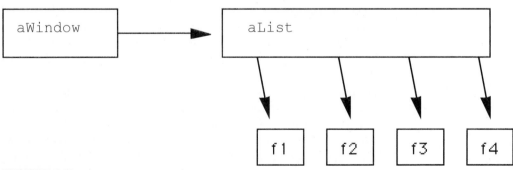

FIGURE 2.7

The two pictures may differ however, because it is possible to have global variables that refer to objects, and it is possible to use these global names to send messages to those objects. Therefore, if our list above were a global object (which is unlikely), and we sent it the message draw, we would get the picture in Fig. 2.7, but the static picture would not contain the arrow from aWindow to aList.

2.9   WHAT AN OBJECT-ORIENTED PROGRAM LOOKS LIKE

The end result of programming in C++ is very similar to the end result of programming in standard C. In both, a program consists of a collection of declarations and a main function. The major difference is that most of the important variables in the C++ program refer to objects rather than to elementary data. Also, in C++ there are usually only a few statements in the main function. These few statements generally create a master object that controls the behavior of the entire program. Usually we use elementary data items, like integers or characters, only for the fields, or instance variables, of the various objects in the system. Note that the instance variables can be of any type, including class types. They can even be pointers to the same class type as the type being defined.

Generally speaking, we shall declare our classes in header files intended to be included by other header files that need the services provided by the classes. We shall often declare several closely related classes within the same header, but we shall not declare unrelated classes within the same header. A header file therefore corresponds to an abstract data type, and the classes that it defines correspond to the data abstractions that make up the ADT. We thus employ two levels of packaging in our programming, the header level and the class level. This packaging of related things is called *data encapsulation.* C++ employs various encapsulation, or packaging, mechanisms, and these permit us to match our ideas or abstractions to our programs. For example, the C keywords { and } are used to package a group of declarations and executable statements. Likewise struct { and } encapsulate a record.

Decomposition into headers also permits various details of the definition of a class to be hidden from clients. These details are not in the headers at all but in the associated class implementation file. This makes it easier for implementors of server modules to make changes, because they know which features the implementation the clients do not utilize, and thus know what they can change without having to alter the clients' code. This is called *information hiding,* and it is a very important means of ensuring that clients do not contain code that restricts the service providers. Programs can be more easily created whose parts are relatively independent of one another. This makes changes and maintenance easier, because there being fewer relationships between parts means that fewer things need to be examined in order to discover the effects of a change and accords better with our limitations on remembering detail. If information hiding is employed, it is harder to write software in which an error in one piece will only become apparent through the failure of some other seemingly unrelated piece. It is an important way of improving the quality and understandability of software.

The header definition for our stars unit will look like the following, although many details are left out at this time.

```
#ifndef __FivePointStar__
#define __FivePointStar__

#include "PGraphic.h"
#include "PGraphSc.h"

class S5PointStar {
    public:
        S5PointStar (int imbalance,
                        PPoint Loc, float Diam);
                        // Constructor.
        void draw (SPattern fill);
        void moveTo (PPoint newLocation);
    protected:
        float fDiameter;
        PPoint fLocation;
        int fImbalance;
};

typedef S5PointStar *P5PointStar
P5PointStar new5PointStar (int imbalance,
                            PPoint Loc, float Diam);
#endif
```

The above declarations appear in the file `P5PointS.h`. Note that we have labeled a section of the declaration `public`, meaning that any client program can use the information in this part (by calling `draw`, for example). Access can also be restricted by the labels `protected` and `private`. These limit the visibility of some features of a class and will be discussed in detail in Section 2.11.

The definitions of the methods and functions appear in the companion file `P5PointS.cp`:

```
#include "P5PointS.h"

P5PointStar new5PointStar (int imbalance,
                            PPoint Loc, float Diam) {
```

```
       P5PointStar result;

       result = new S5PointStar (imbalance,
                                    Loc, Diam);
       failnull (result);
       return result;
};

S5PointStar :: S5PointStar (int imbalance,
                              PPoint Loc, float Diam) {
    fImbalance = imbalance * newRandom (1,30);
    fLocation = Loc;
    fDiameter = Diam;
};

void S5PointStar :: draw (SPattern fill) {
    :

};
// more ...
```

Note especially that the interface, contained in the header file, includes only declarations. These are the items exported by the ADT. The implementation part, in the .cp file, contains additional declarations of data private to the ADT and definitions of the procedures, functions, and methods declared in the interface.

To give a specific example, the library developed for this book consists of about 90 classes. These are defined in about 50 header files, with names like PObject.h, PList.h, and PBinaryTree.h. The methods of the classes declared in a header are all defined in a separate implementation file, such as PObject.cp and PList.cp. Therefore, in addition to the main program file, which is generally quite small, there are about 100 files used in one way or another to add functionality to the programs. This is, of course, in addition to the many files that are built into the C++ system, such as stdio and iostream.

2.10   OBJECT DESIGN

As was said above, programming involves two tasks: design of the program text (writing the program) and design of the run-time behavior (defining what the program does). The latter task is fundamental and is the place to begin. That is to say, we design the objects and their behavior and then write down descriptions of them. These descriptions are the classes. To first discover the objects, it is useful to look carefully at the problem to be solved, searching for components of the actual system that interact with other elements or are acted upon by other elements. If we think of the system to be modeled as one containing actors who provide services and require services, then we may model these actors as objects. Then we must consider how the actors are to be grouped. Usually we group actors by function, or in other words, according to services they provide. Once we have some idea of the basic actors, it is useful to think in terms of the generalization or specialization of these functions. It may be that we can think of a large class of actors/objects as being specializations of a single generalized type. For example "hourly" and "salaried" may be thought of as special kinds of a general type "employee."

Once we have an idea of what the objects are to be, we must design them. One way to design the objects is to draw the message graphs that we indicated above. A first attempt at a graphics application might result in the picture shown in Fig. 2.8. When we realize that there will be a variable number of figures drawn in the window and that we might want to segregate them into separate groupings, we might refine the picture to the one shown previously, in Fig. 2.7. We might also expand the picture so that there are several windows, each with separate figures to be drawn within each window.

Next we would discover that the figures all share some things in common since they can be drawn, like our five-point stars shown earlier. They have differences as well, such as shape, for example, rectangles having a different shape than five point stars. Therefore we decide that we want a class, SFigure, to define the common parts of all of the drawable figures, as well as an SWindow class and an SList class. The main idea is that the objects needed in the system lead us to design classes that describe those objects.

The differences between objects lead us to organize the classes in a certain way. It is a special feature of object-oriented systems that the classes

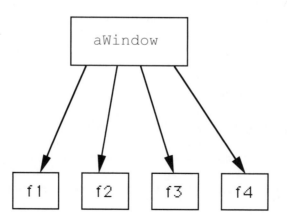

FIGURE 2.8

are related to one another and the relationship is that of a more general class to a more specific one. In most object-oriented languages the relationships are defined in a static way, within the compiler, though there are languages in which the relationships are dynamic and may be changed as the program executes. In C++ the classes form a directed graph, with each class possibly having parent classes. (The technical term for parent class in C++ is **base class**.) The general idea of a parent-child relationship is manifested in this structure in its generalization-specialization hierarchy, the parent being more general and the child being more specialized. (A child class in C++ is known as a **derived class**.)

Base Class

A class that is used as the parent in inheritance. The child class is called a derived class.

Derived Class

A class that is a subclass of another class.

In the current example we want a parent class, SFigure, that defines common properties of the drawable figures. Two appropriate subclasses of this class would be SRectangle and S5PointStar. This leads us to another picture of our system, one that is completely static and shows the relationships between classes. The root of the class hierarchy is the abstract pseudo class OBJECT, which in fact does not exist but is merely an organizational concept. You cannot declare an object to have type OBJECT. We shall create a class SObject to fulfill the function of root of our class library. In this view our system might look (in part) like Fig. 2.9.

Defining a class by giving only those features by which it differs from another class is called inheritance, and C++ has what is called multiple inheritance, for a class may have several base classes from which it is derived. Note, however, that a class inherits from all of its ancestors in the inheritance tree. The base or parent classes are also often called superclasses, though the proper C++ terminology is to call them base classes. Generally speaking, we shall restrict our attention to single inheritance. Therefore, our inheritance structure will be nearly treelike, with a single root. We shall make limited, careful use of multiple inheritance when there is a clear benefit in doing so.

The idea of inheritance as defining a generalization-specialization hierarchy has a very specific meaning. Wherever an object of a class can be used,

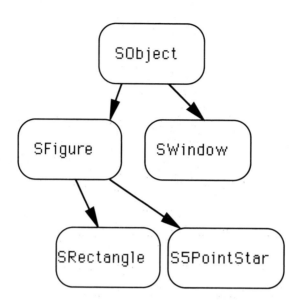

FIGURE 2.9

an object of any subclass can be substituted. To get full benefit of this, we shall need to use pointer variables to refer to objects. Thus we assume the existence of associated pointer types PFigure, PRectangle, etc. Therefore, if fig1 is a variable defined to reference an object of type PFigure, and aRect is a PRectangle, the assignment fig1 := aRect; is legal. It is legal because SRectangle is a subclass of SFigure or, speaking somewhat loosely, because PRectangle is a subclass of PFigure.

Type Specialization Principle

In any context in which an object of a given class may be used, any object of a subclass can be substituted.

The syntax for declaring that one class is a subclass of another is to put the name of the superclass after the name of the class itself in the class declaration. Therefore our declaration of S5PointStar would be changed to

```
class S5PointStar: public SFigure {
    public:
        S5PointStar (int imbalance,
                     PPoint Loc, float Diam);
                     // Constructor.
```

```
        void draw (SPattern fill);
        void moveTo (PPoint newLocation);
    protected:
        float fDiameter;
        int fImbalance;
};
```

We would need to ensure that SFigure is visible at this point in the system, probably by having the stars header include the figure header. The keyword public, which precedes the name of the base class on the first line of the declaration, indicates that it is to be public knowledge that an S5PointStar is an SFigure. Private inheritance is also possible, though it won't be used in this book.

The definition of SFigure might itself look like

```
class SFigure {
    public:
        SFigure (PPoint Loc); // Constructor.
        virtual void draw (SPattern fill);
        void free;
    protected:
        PPoint fLocation ;
};
typedef SFigure *PFigure;
```

Because SFigure defines an instance variable fLocation, it has been dropped from the definition of S5PointStar. Any such star will have such an instance variable by inheritance. Note that, since SFigure defines a draw method, it will be marked with the keyword virtual, to indicate that we intend to define new methods in subclasses of this class with the same protocol as a method defined in SFigure. The new method is said to **override** the inherited method. A five-point star will inherit the free method unchanged but will inherit only the protocol of draw, changing its actions by defining an override method. Virtual methods are very important, and their meaning is more than just that a replacement may be declared. They are actually a very important means of defining objects in such a way that they have a measure of control over what happens to them. This is discussed in detail in the next chapter.

Inheritance is thus both an organizational principle of object-oriented programming and a technique to make the work of a programmer simpler and more disciplined. Once some function has been created and tested, it can be used as part of a new system more specialized than the one from which it inherits. It is from this that object-oriented programming draws much of its power.

Object-Oriented Programming (final version)

Programming methodology in which the data elements (objects) in the system form the fundamental unit of program decomposition. Objects are described by means of classes. Classes are developed by means of successive refinement using inheritance.

The basic rule of object-oriented design is to design the objects. This means to think of your program or system as a collection of interacting objects able to communicate with each other by sending messages. Each kind of object (class) generally provides a single service or simple functionality (objects are simple). The methods of a single object tell its clients what services it provides, and they provide a means for the clients to request the services, because the method names are the names of the services. If we were designing a robot in an object-oriented way we would have classes corresponding to its various parts, such as sensor, gripper, walker, memory, and controller. We would have specializations of most of these classes, since there are different kinds of sensors and controllers. The memory would also have several parts, including a stack for remembering where the robot had been. Our design process would consider the uses of the robot and, therefore, the needed functionalities and thus the needed parts. These parts would be the objects, and the types or kinds of objects would become the classes. The generalization/specialization of the objects helps us to discover the classes.

We design the classes by designing prototypes for the services that the classes must provide and (somewhat later) by designing the actual implementation of the local state variables that the objects of the class must maintain in order to provide the services. Here it is useful to think about the parts out of which we can build an object in the class. A robot has sensors, actuators, etc. Often an object is composed of parts that are objects of different classes. Sometimes the parts are elementary data items such as integers and ordinary arrays. This phase, however, programming the classes by composition of parts, comes after the analysis of the services and the design of the prototypes of the functions that will implement the services of the class.

One possible difficulty with this approach is that although classes are defined from the top down in any system that uses inheritance, they are usually discovered from the bottom up, or even from the middle out. Therefore the design process and the programming process (the writing down of a program) do not follow the same path. One aid in designing the classes is a pack of three-by-five cards on which we write down the characteristics of our classes. The front of each card might appear as in Fig. 2.10.

The responsibilities are chiefly the services that the class is to provide to other classes. The collaborators are other classes that are needed by this one or are associated with it and whose services it requires in turn. Here

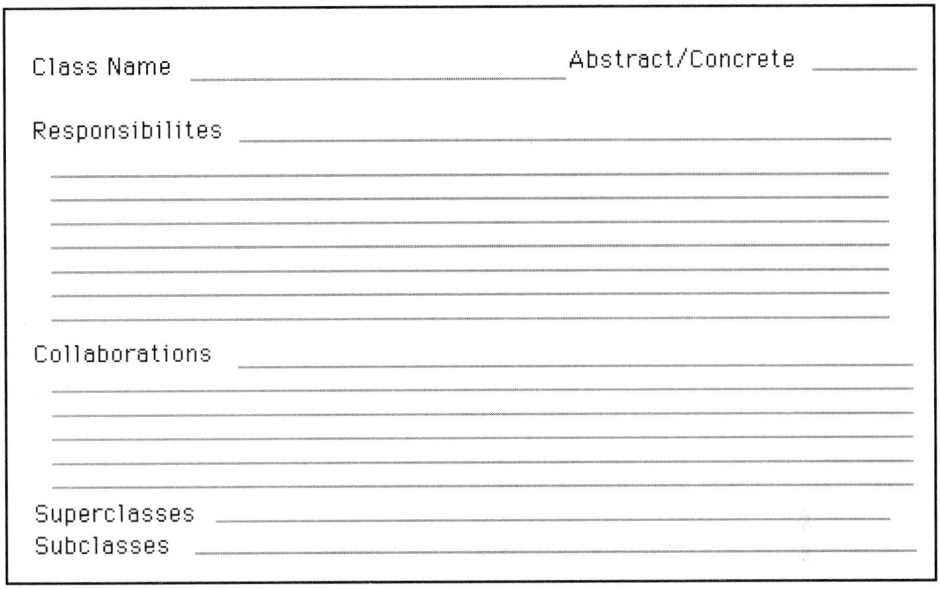

FIGURE 2.10

we write down what each class is responsible for and what other classes can assist it. The main responsibility of our SWindow class is to maintain a drawing port and to manage the objects drawn in that port. Its main collaborator is a list to keep track of the drawn objects.

The back of the card could appear as in Fig. 2.11. Here we are more specific and fill this in only when we have taken some time to consider the class responsibilities. The methods define the services that the class provides. The instance variables define the static information that objects in the class need in order to fulfill the class responsibilities: they form the internal representation of the object. To design a class, we design methods to carry out the services, and instance variables (the representation) based on the frequency with which certain services will be used. The idea is that we choose a representation so as to make frequently used services efficient. In the current example, since SWindow provides a drawing environment, it will need a draw method and, perhaps, a graphPort instance variable. These cards are called CRC cards, for class, responsibility, and collaboration.

CRC cards can be shuffled and dealt out into various geometric configurations, demonstrating different relationships and thus facilitating brainstorming. They are also disposable, so ideas that don't bear fruit can easily be discarded. CRC cards were introduced by Kent Beck and Ward Cunningham at the 1989 OOPSLA conference [Beck & Cunningham].

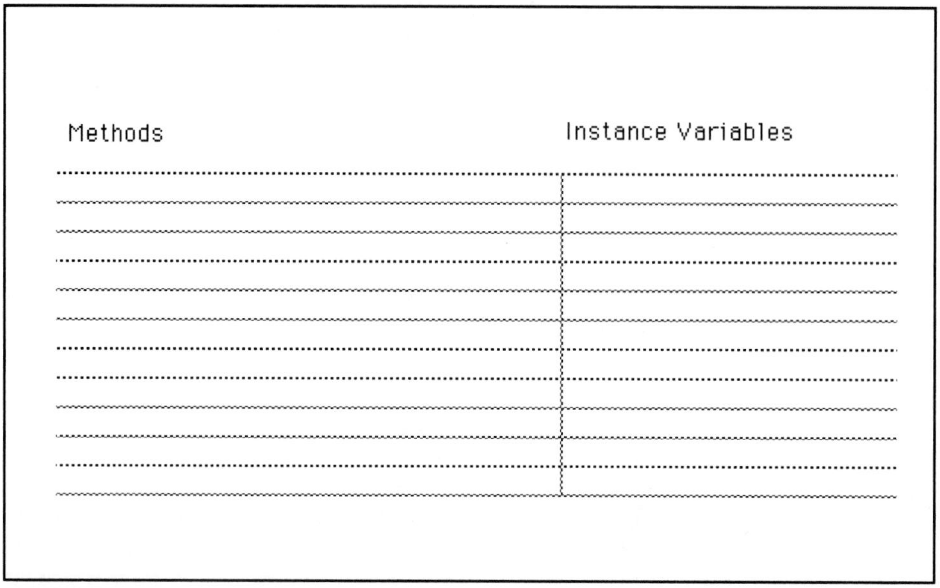

Methods	Instance Variables

FIGURE 2.11

2.11   STACKS AS A CLASS

The following declaration represents a class of bounded stacks of real numbers. The design of it could be greatly improved, but we have tried to make it agree as closely as possible with the definition given earlier.

```
class SRealStack {
    public:
        SRealStack ();
        void push (float E));
        void pop (float &E);
        char empty ();
        void top (float &E);
    protected:
        float fElements [100];
        int fTop;
    };
typedef SRealStack *PRealStack;
PRealStack NewRealStack ();
```

Note the differences between this declaration and the original `TStack` declaration of the more standard C style. First, the declarations of the procedures and functions (methods) used to manipulate these stacks are within the declaration of the stack type itself. This is called encapsulation of the methods within the data type. Next, a stack need not be named as a parameter of the methods. A message that names a method will be sent to some stack, and this stack, the receiver of the message, will be the one on whom the push or pop is performed.

Note that two protected data items (called instance variables, or IVARs) `fTop` and `fElements`, and five public methods are declared between the keyword `class` and the end of the declaration, `}`. This is perhaps the most easily recognized feature of object-oriented programming: the functions are bound up in the declarations of the data. This is perhaps the most easily recognized feature of object-oriented programming: the functions are bound up in the declarations of the data. This is more than just a notational convenience. These methods are the only means of operating on the data, which are hidden.

The CRC cards for this class might look like Fig. 2.12 and 2.13. Of course these would have been created as part of our design process for the class and would therefore exist before any of the above code.

In some ways a class declares things that are very much like structs or records, and in fact the keyword `class` of C++ is nearly interchangeable with the keyword `struct`. The difference between the ordinary structs of C and the classes of C++ is that we can use the latter as a mechanism for hiding implementation information from users.

Public Member

An instance variable or method intended for use by any user.

Protected Member

An instance variable or method intended for internal use and use by heirs in the inheritance structure.

A public member, usually a method, is the means by which a class provides a service to the clients that send its message. A protected member is an implementation detail that the class uses to help it provide the service. Usually all of the instance variables and often some methods are protected. The client should not be able to manipulate the implementation, for at least two reasons. First, the client could make it impossible to ensure that the service is provided correctly. Imagine a stack service in which any code can manipulate the top of the stack. It would be difficult for the stack to guarantee that items are produced in a last in–first out manner. The second reason for wishing to hide implementation information is that there are times when the implementation must change after the clients have been

```
┌─────────────────────────────────────────────────────────────────────┐
│                                                                       │
│                                                          Concrete     │
│   Class Name   SRealStack              Abstract/Concrete _____     │
│                                                                       │
│   Responsibilites Provide a last in – first out Storage mechanism for │
│                   real values.                                        │
│   _____ │
│   _____ │
│   _____ │
│   _____ │
│   _____ │
│   _____ │
│                                                                       │
│   Collaborations   None                                               │
│   _____ │
│   _____ │
│   _____ │
│   _____ │
│                                                                       │
│   Superclasses None                                                   │
│   Subclasses    None anticipated                                      │
│                                                                       │
└─────────────────────────────────────────────────────────────────────┘
```

FIGURE 2.12

```
┌─────────────────────────────────────────────────────────────────────┐
│                                                                       │
│                                                                       │
│     Methods                              Instance Variables           │
│                                                                       │
│    push a real                        │ top: an integer               │
│       insert into the storage         │   index of last item stored   │
│    pop a real                         │ elements: an array of reals    │
│       remove from storage             │                               │
│    top return a real                  │                               │
│       return last item pushed         │                               │
│     empty                             │                               │
│       true if nothing in storage      │                               │
│                                       │                               │
│                                       │                               │
│                                       │                               │
│                                                                       │
└─────────────────────────────────────────────────────────────────────┘
```

FIGURE 2.13

written. Sometimes this is for reasons of efficiency, and sometimes it is because the problem to be solved has changed slightly. In either case, if the clients have access only to a procedural interface to the information, the variables out of which the implementation is built can change, and often the prototypes of the procedures that the clients use will not need to change. Thus the clients will not need to be rewritten. They might not even need to be recompiled. If they have access to the variables, then, when the implementation changes and the variables of the old implementation disappear, any client using the variable will need to be redone, perhaps drastically. This drives the cost of modifying software up dramatically.

Information-Hiding Principle

Details of the implementation of a data type should not be accessible to clients of that data type.

Note that there is a separate function declaration `newRealStack` associated with the class. This function is an object generator. The generator function of `SRealStack` is intended to be the means by which we create stacks of this type. In fact it is intended that calling this function is the only way to generate a new stack. Given these declarations we could declare variables of the type in the usual way.

```
PRealStack myNewStack;
```

The variable `myNewStack` is a reference (indirect or pointer) variable and refers to an object in class `SRealStack`. We can also create the real stack itself and save a reference to it in `myNewStack` using a call to the generator.

```
myNewStack = newRealStack ();
```

Having created `myNewStack`, we could send it messages such as `push` and `pop`. A message consists of the name of an object (the receiver of the message), the name of some method of that object, and any parameters needed by that method.

```
myNewStack -> push (6.234);
myNewStack -> pop (X);
if (myNewStack -> empty())
    cout << "empty";
```

If this class were to be implemented (it won't be, but an improvement of it will), we would put the above type declaration and the declaration of the generator into a header file. In the implementation part, or `.cp` file, we would need to define all of the methods of real stacks. When we define a method of a class, we must qualify the name of the method with the name of the class because there are situations in which we need to declare more than one class in the same unit, and sometimes different classes will need to have methods of the same name. Therefore, when we define `empty()` of class `SRealStack`, we will need to call it `SRealStack :: empty()`. Look at the function definition shown below.

```
char SRealStack :: empty() {
   return fTop < 0;
};

void SRealStack::push (float E)) {
   if (top < 99 ) {
      ++fTop ;
      fElements[fTop] = E;
   };
};
```

The implementation part will also need to define the generator function `NewRealStack` that was declared in the interface part. Generators follow the pattern exhibited by this example:

```
PRealStack NewRealStack () {
   PRealStack result;

   result = new SRealStack ();
   failnull (result);
   return result;
};
```

2.12   OBJECT PROGRAMMING AND ABSTRACT DATA TYPES

Abstract data types and object-oriented programming in C++ are easily melded into a strategy for implementation. Data abstractions are modeled as classes. The collection of data abstractions making up an abstract data type form a compilation unit consisting of a header file and an implementation file. The header portion contains the class definitions and should also contain (or at least refer to) documentation giving the rules of the ADT. Thus the header provides the specifications of the ADT.

A strength of C++ is that the details (names and types) of the instance variables implementing each class can be contained in the protected section of a class definition. These are internal items, so we want to prevent clients from manipulating them directly. A program declaring a `PRealStack` named `stack` will not be able to make reference to the instance variable `stack -> fTop`. This variable is private to the stack. We can refer to the field from the methods of a class that inherits `SRealStack`, however.

C++ has a stronger form of information hiding: variables and methods can be declared `private`. The **private class features** can only be used within methods of their class or in friends of their class, as discussed in Chapter 3. They cannot be seen or used by heirs of the class. We shall not use private variables and methods, because our goals require more flexibility. We shall see that declaring some things, including all instance variables, to be protected gives us a tradeoff between security and flexibility.

Private Member

An instance variable or method intended for internal use, as an aid to implementation and not to be seen in any other class.

If one ADT is derived from another, the header implementing the derived ADT will `include` the header of the ADT it is derived from. If the derivation is a specialization, the classes implementing the data abstractions will be subclasses of classes in the ADT it is derived from.

2.13   A MENTAL MODEL FOR OBJECT PROGRAMMING

Object-oriented programming using indirect variables in C++ requires that a programmer adopt a certain mental model, or set of ideas, about the nature of the computational system that she or he is using. In many ways this model is similar to that used in standard C or Pascal, but the differences are important. Rather than thinking of a single processor, or computing mechanism (CPU), and a single memory, it is useful to think of a single processor and many memories. Each object in the system should be thought of as having its own memory. In fact, the most useful model considers each object to be composed of four parts: memory, process, sensor, and effector. (See Fig. 2.14.) An object sends messages to other objects using its effector. This is just an outward-directed communication channel. Likewise, the object receives messages through its sensor.

Within the methods of a class, the receiver of a message (which must be in the class of the method) is referred to by the standard identifier `this`.

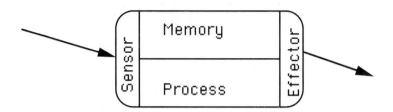

FIGURE 2.14

The model of execution is that the object itself executes the method (rather than a "computer" executing a procedure). The object currently in control is the object executing the method, and it refers to itself by the name this. Therefore, if a procedure or other message is called from within a method of SRealStack, the object, this, that is executing, can pass itself to that other procedure or method using the reference variable this.

> this
>
> The object that currently has control of the processor is known as this. When a message is sent to another object, that object becomes this while it executes a method in fulfillment of the message.

When an object receives a message via its sensor, it matches the message with some method in its own process part and then executes that method. By executing the method it can change some values in its memory part and can also use its effector part to send messages to other objects, or even to itself. Thus a system in execution might be depicted statically as in Fig. 2.15.

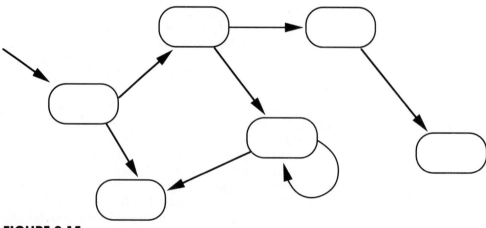

FIGURE 2.15

Here we have several objects in the system. The arrows indicate messages that have been sent at some time. This picture can be refined in order to have a more dynamic aspect and resemble a program in execution more closely. Recall that our model has only a single processor, or CPU. At any given time some object in our system has control of this processor. Suppose that we indicate the object that has control by a filled oval, as in Fig. 2.16. When the object in control sends a message to another object, it passes control of the CPU along the message path to the other object. This might leave us in the situation of Fig. 2.17. Eventually, all messages directly and indirectly sent because of our sending the message that just took us from Fig. 2.16 to Fig. 2.17 will finish. At this point the processor will have been passed back along the message path, and we will again be in the situation of Fig. 2.16. However, each of the objects that received messages as a result of this one message will have had control of the CPU, executed methods, and, perhaps, changed its own memory variables as a result. The object in control of the CPU is this. Note that a simple modification of this model would permit there to be several CPUs. Therefore, the object-programming model can be used as a simple way of thinking about parallel programs.

A slightly more accurate picture of a single object is shown in Fig. 2.18, which indicates a possible implementation of objects. The effector is nothing more than the presence of instance variables in an object whose types are class types. Here two such variables are indicated, though there could be any number of them. An object gets access to another object, enabling it to send messages to that other, by maintaining a reference to it. Therefore the effector is, in reality, just part of the memory. The memory can also contain values that are not references to other objects. These values might be integers, arrays, or whatever else is appropriate to the class of the object.

An object gets access to its process part by maintaining a reference to a class descriptor stored in the running computer. This descriptor contains

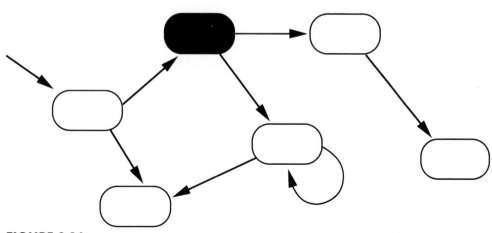

FIGURE 2.16

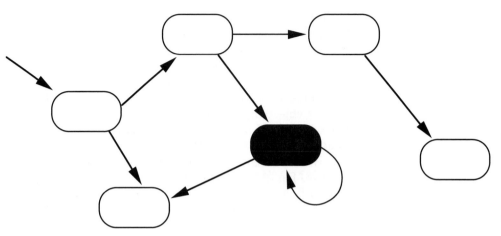

FIGURE 2.17

all of the methods defined in a given class. When an object is created within a class, it is given a reference to this descriptor, and it can never change it. Thus an object, once created within a class, is always a member of that same class. Inheritance is implemented by giving each class descriptor a reference to the descriptor of the parent class. Therefore, an object has access to the methods of its own class and its ancestor classes.

In the next chapter these ideas will be considered much more deeply.

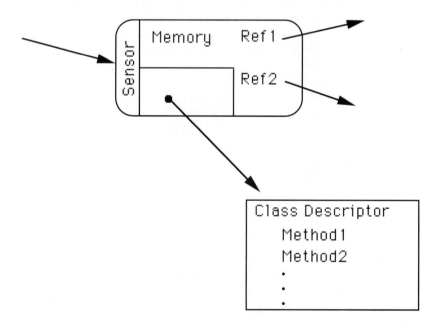

FIGURE 2.18

2.14   SUMMARY

Procedural abstraction permits us to encapsulate processes, name them, parameterize them, and then ignore the details of their implementation. It forms the basis of some software development methodologies and is an important secondary technique of object-oriented programming.

Similarly, the technique of data abstraction permits us to encapsulate data, specify their properties and actions, and ignore the details of their implementation. It is the fundamental decomposition technique of object-oriented programming. Object-oriented programs are created by designing the data that they use and assigning actions to the data.

A data abstraction is a description of a collection of objects and the properties and behaviors of those objects. An abstract data type (ADT) is a set of interacting data abstractions of which one is primary. If an ADT provides more than one data abstraction, the primary one usually obtains services from the others.

In object-oriented programming a class is a description of the data objects of a data abstraction. The description specifies the components of the data (instance variables) as well as behaviors (methods). Classes also provide a visibility mechanism by which interfaces of objects can be separated from implementation details.

Classes are organized according to a specialization structure in which parent classes describe part of the structure of child classes and child classes extend and specialize the capabilities of the parent classes.

Objects in C++ may be referred to either directly or (by means of pointers) indirectly. These two mechanisms offer a tradeoff between efficiency and flexibility, the use of indirect objects causing a small loss of efficiency (in most programs) and a large gain in flexiblility.

The model of programming appropriate to object-oriented languages is one of autonomous objects that send messages to each other. These messages request services from their receivers. The control of a computation follows the path of the messages, so that at any given time some object has control of the computation and hence of the computer on which it is running.

EXERCISES

2.1 (2.5) Build and test a linked list implementation of the class SRealStack similar to the ordinary implementation discussed in Section 2.5. Put the type declarations in the header file RealStaP.h. Put the implementations of all of the methods in the file RealStaP.cp. Build a separate test file that will exercise the package. The next field of each object should be of type PRealStack, which is SRealStack*. Omit the call to failnull unless you implement such an ordinary procedure yourself. It should print its parameter string and then halt the program.

2.2 (2.5) A fundamental problem with the stack class of Problem 2.1 is that a stack as a whole is represented in the same way as a node in the stack. Improve on this in the following way. Rename the stack class of Problem 2.1 to `SStackNode` (use the editor to change all occurrences of `RealStack` to `StackNode`). Now build another class `SRealStack` whose single instance variable is a `PStackNode`. Now an object of this new class represents the stack as a whole and the `SStackNode` class represents the nodes out of which we build a stack. You now have an ADT with two data abstractions.

2.3 (2.5) Design test data to test our implementation of `TStack`. You should have one or more tests for each of the rules in the definition of a stack. For example, the rule that states that `empty` must return TRUE immediately after initialization can be easily checked by creating a stack and immediately calling `empty`.

2.4 (2.5) Give rules defining a bounded stack similar to those we gave for a stack. Verify that our first implementation of `TStack` obeys your rules, or show specifically how it does not.

2.5 (2.9) What is it about the information hiding principle that, when it is used, makes it easier to modify existing software? Is there anything about it that makes it harder to modify existing software? How is information hiding related to the Rule of Seven discussed in the last chapter?

2.6 (2.10) What is it about inheritance that might make it possible to build software faster? What is it about inheritance that might make it possible to build better software (software having fewer bugs)?

2.7 (2.11) Build and test the `SRealStack` class as discussed in Section 2.11. Put the type declarations in the header file `RealStaA.h`. Put the implementations of all of the methods in the file `RealStaA.cp`. Build a separate test file that will exercise the package. Omit the call to `failnull` unless you implement such an ordinary procedure yourself. It should print its parameter string and then halt the program.

2.8 (2.11) Pick a board game such as checkers or chess with which you are familiar. Suppose that you wanted to write a program that would take the part of one player and manage the board and game pieces as well, showing the state of the game (a diagram of the board showing the positions of the pieces) on the screen. Name three or four classes that you would consider when designing this program. For each of them give a few methods. Which of these methods will need to request services from objects in one of the other classes? Add additional methods to those classes, if necessary, to represent those services. Create CRC cards for your design up to this point.

FUNDAMENTAL IDEAS AND THE CLASS HIERARCHY

Lovliest vision far of all Olympus' faded hierarchy!
All the better; their fraction is more our wish than their faction:
but it was a strong composure a fool could disunite.

    Shakespeare, *Troilus and Cressida*

This was a merry message.

    Shakespeare, *Henry V*

This chapter and the two that follow will lay the foundation for the development and use of a large library of general-purpose software that can be used in virtually any development project to shorten development time and help ensure the correctness of the code. They will describe a number of classes of objects arranged into compilation units that can be used by programs or other classes and compilation units. Later chapters will describe the implementation of the classes. Chapter 5 will present two examples of the use of the classes: one creating a simulator for deterministic finite automata, the other creating a simple translator of infix expressions to postfix.

3.1   CLASSES AND OBJECTS

In object-oriented programming a running program is a collection of communicating objects that carry out the computation task collectively by requesting services from and providing services to other objects in the system.

The objects are usually thought of as having some form of existence and a large degree of autonomy. An object is more than just a block of data like a record. One object, procedure, or program block (called a client) requests service from another object by sending it a message naming the service required. The object receiving the message interprets it and performs the requested service by executing a method using the parameters provided by the client. In general, the client is not permitted to modify the other object.

The following declaration of a class called SFiniteStack should solidify these ideas. From this point on we shall use the following useful naming convention. A class name is formed of the letter S followed by a noun descriptive of the class. An instance variable (field) name is formed of the letter f followed by a noun descriptive of the concept modeled by the variable. This convention helps class names and instance variable names stand out in certain contexts. Every class has an associated type definition for pointers to the class object. The name of this type is the same as the class name except for the initial letter, which is to be P instead of S. The name of a method that is a function is a noun or short noun phrase that describes the returned result. The name of a procedural method is a verb or verb phrase describing what the procedure does. One exception is for a function that returns a Boolean result, which is given a name that is an adjective describing the condition it tests. Note also that abbreviations are seldom used, that capitalization is consistent, and that when two words are joined to form a compound word, the first letters of the second and subsequent words are capitalized, as in SFiniteStack. The following declaration is an improvement on the declarations at the end of the last chapter but it is able to be improved further. See the exercises for hints. The following declarations would be put into a file named PFiniteS.h. We shall keep the names of our files to eight or fewer characters, because some operating systems cannot accommodate longer names. Generally, the filename is a truncation of the name of the principal type declared in the header.

```
// Contents of PFiniteS.h.
#ifndef __FiniteStack__
#define __FiniteStack__

#include "PObject.h"

const int sSize = 20;

class SFiniteStack;
typedef SFiniteStack *PFiniteStack;

PFiniteStack newFiniteStack ();

class SFiniteStack: public SObject {
   public:
         SFiniteStack ();
         // Construct new finite stacks.
```

```
virtual void          push(PObject d);
   // Insert d into the storage.
   // No op if the structure is full.
virtual PObject       top (void);
   // Return a reference to the last object
   // inserted into the storage.
   // If the storage is empty NULL is returned.
virtual void          pop (void);
   // Remove the most recently inserted object.
   // No op if empty.
virtual char          empty (void);
   // TRUE if there are no objects in storage.
virtual char          full (void);
 · // TRUE if there is no room for additional
   // objects to be stored.
```
```
/* Objects are inserted into the finite stack using
push. They are removed and retrieved with pop
and top, respectively. The behavior is last in-first
out (LIFO), meaning that the most recently pushed
object will be the next popped. NULL will be
returned if the client attempts to pop an empty
finite stack, and attempting to push onto a full
one results in no operation (no op) */
```
```
    protected:
    int fTop;
    PObject fElements[sSize];
};
```
```
/* FORMAL RULES
    1. Initialization must be done once for every
stack object. This is done correctly by newFiniteStack.
    2. Immediately after initialization, empty returns
TRUE and full returns FALSE. Pop is illegal and results
in a no op, and top, while also illegal, returns NULL.
    3. Immediately after push, empty returns FALSE
and full may return TRUE.
    4. If full would return TRUE, push is illegal
and results in a no op. However if push fails to
insert X by reason of executing when full is TRUE,
the stack may not properly be LIFO.
    6. newFiniteStack returns a new allocated and
initialized (empty) stack.
    7. At most sSize elements can be stored at any
time. If the stack currently holds sSize elements,
full returns TRUE.
*/
#endif
```

This declaration is illustrated in the *class photo*, shown in Fig. 3.1, which indicates that the methods are to be public, and that the instance variables, enclosed within the boundary, are to be private. The keyword *virtual* that marks five of the methods will be explained later when the consequences of inheritance are examined.

Having made the above declaration, we may want a finite stack object called ExpressionStack from class SFiniteStack to be available when the program executes. Usually we will want to refer to this object indirectly using a pointer. Therefore the declaration would be

```
PFiniteStack ExpressionStack;
```

The variable ExpressionStack is called a reference variable because it is used to refer to an object within some class. Its actual value will not be an object, however. This declaration states that ExpressionStack is to be an object, but a declaration alone is not quite enough to create the ExpressionStack. Objects are created dynamically, so in some code block in which the above declarations are visible we will need to execute

```
ExpressionStack = new (SFiniteStack ());
```

Now the ExpressionStack is a properly created object and available for providing services like push, top, and pop.

The constructor SFiniteStack is shown below. It merely guarantees that the stack is empty. This and all the other method definitions will appear in the implementation file associated with the finite stack header file. This file will be named PFiniteS.cp.

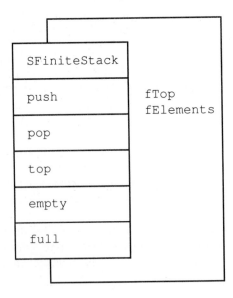

FIGURE 3.1

```
SFiniteStack :: SFiniteStack () {
   fTop = -1;
};
```

Because safe creation of an object depends on executing both the call to the standard new routine and checking that the call succeeded, we always include one or more object generator functions, which return properly initialized instances of the associated class. In this case we use the object generator function newFiniteStack, shown below. Note that it merely calls the ordinary procedures new and failnull.

```
PFiniteStack newFiniteStack () {
   PFiniteStack result;

   result = new SFiniteStack ();
   failnull (result);
   return result;
};
```

We then safely create and initialize the reference variable ExpressionStack simply with

```
ExpressionStack = newFiniteStack ();
```

Generator

A function that returns a newly created and initialized indirect object in some class. Sometimes this is an ordinary function, and sometimes it is a method of another class. In this library objects are always created with generators.

At some point in the system, within some client, we may wish to push an expression CurrentExpression onto this stack. When ExpressionStack was created its type was declared to be SFiniteStack so that it would have access to the method push. The client then sends the message

```
ExpressionStack -> push (CurrentExpression);
```

The object will receive this message and will execute the method push with parameter CurrentExpression. As executed by ExpressionStack, this method will modify the internal state of the ExpressionStack object so that the stack protocol will be maintained. In this case the instance variable fTop will be increased and then used as an index for the other instance variable, fElements. The insertion is at location fTop of fElements.

```
void SFiniteStack :: push (PObject d) {
   if (fTop < sSize) {
      ++fTop;
      fElements[fTop] = d;
   };
};
```

Then if this or some other client immediately sends the message

```
SomeExpression = ExpressionStack -> top ();
```

to ExpressionStack, it will produce the thing most recently pushed, which here would be CurrentExpression.

```
PObject SFiniteStack :: top (void) {
   if (fTop > -1)
      return fElements[fTop];
   else
      return NULL;
};
```

We remove an item from the stack with pop, which does not return a value:

```
void SFiniteStack :: pop (void) {
   if (fTop > -1)
      fTop--;
};
```

We have learned that an *object* is just a variable whose type is a *class type*, and that a *class* is just a type defined by using the class keyword. We normally access objects using pointer variables. The class definition declares instance variables and methods. Some methods are procedures and some are functions that produce a value that can be used in assignment statements or elsewhere. The Class SObject has not been described, although it has been used to help declare finite stacks. It was defined in the header PObject.h. It will be described below in the section on inheritance.

In object-oriented programming it is important to adopt the attitude that the objects are autonomous and responsible for their own behavior. An object behaves by executing a method defined within its class. The instance variables are changed only by the methods, not by other procedures. When a method is executed, it is said to be executed by the object itself. This view is very important for understanding object-oriented programming. An object is like an actor whose "part" consists of a few methods. It is given cues (messages) by other actors (objects), and each cue makes it perform (execute a method).

> ### Object Principle
>
> Objects are autonomous actors. They respond to messages by executing methods. The execution of a method may require the sending of additional messages.

Objects are defined by means of classes. A class describes both the implementation (instance variables) and the interface or protocol (methods) of the objects that belong to it. A class is like a factory, because it can create objects according to a plan.

> ### Class Principle
>
> Classes are both collections and descriptions of objects. A class provides a template, or factory, for the creation of objects of the same kind.

Within one system we may have several finite stacks, each receiving messages and each executing its own methods. All may belong to the same class. When a finite stack executes push or pop, its fTop instance variable will change, but otherwise no change will be made to fTop. This control over changes to fTop will let us guarantee to users of SFiniteStack that it will indeed behave as a stack, using LIFO protocol. If the clients could modify fTop directly we could not make the guarantee. The finite stack header file and the SFiniteStack type (class) definition are supposed to constitute the complete description of the behavior of a finite stack. Only the methods declared are to modify an object in this class.

If we had not declared the instance variables to be protected (or private), the language would not prohibit clients or others from having both read and write access to them. Thus a client could indeed say

```
ExpressionStack -> fTop = 99;
```

which would cause a lot of trouble. This ought not to be possible, because the creator of SFiniteStack should have better control over changes made and would want to ensure that it behaves in a LIFO manner. Therefore we make our instance variables protected.

The implementation file for finite stacks is shown below:

```
// PFiniteS.cp follows
#include "PFiniteS.h"
```

```
// ************** FiniteStack ********************

PFiniteStack newFiniteStack () {
   PFiniteStack result;

   result = new SFiniteStack ();
   failnull (result);
   return result;
};

SFiniteStack :: SFiniteStack() {
   fTop = -1;
};

void SFiniteStack :: push (PObject data) {
   if (fTop < sSize) {
      ++fTop;
      fElements[fTop] = data;
   };
};

PObject SFiniteStack :: top (void) {
   if (fTop > -1)
      return fElements[fTop];
   else
      return NULL;
};

void SFiniteStack :: pop (void) {
   if (fTop > -1)
      fTop--;
};

char SFiniteStack :: empty (void) {
   return fTop < 0;
};

char SFiniteStack :: full (void) {
   return fTop >= sSize;
};
```

Excerpts from a client program are shown below. Details of the expression class type have been left out for simplicity. However, it is important that the expression type have SObject as an ancestor so that expressions can be pushed onto a stack.

```
// stacktest;
#include "PObject.h"
#include "PFiniteS.h"
#include "PExpress.h"

PFiniteStack ExpressionStack AuxiliaryStack;
PExpression left, right; // Left and right operands
                         // of an operator.

void main (void) {
  ExpressionStack = newFiniteStack ();
  ⋮
  expressionStack -> push (left);
  ⋮
  AuxiliaryStack -> push (ExpressionStack -> top ());
    /* Push the top of ExpressionStack.
    onto AuxiliaryStack */
  ⋮
  right = AuxiliaryStack.top ();
  right -> writeIt (); // Output the right operand.
  ⋮
};
```

3.2   OBJECT REFERENCES

When we declare a variable to be a pointer to a class type, we say that it is a reference to an object. Thus the above ExpressionStack is a reference to an object. The object itself was created with the call to new and the execution of the class constructor. Objects are created only in this way. However, several variables can reference the same object. For example, in the program excerpt shown at the end of the last section one could have

```
AuxiliaryStack = ExpressionStack;
```

It is very important to note that this statement does not create a new stack. It simply makes AuxiliaryStack reference the same stack that ExpressionStack does. The names ExpressionStack and AuxiliaryStack are said to be **aliases**. If we use either alias in a push or a pop, the stack that it references will be affected. If we push using one of the names and top with the other, the object pushed will be retrieved.

There are two very different ideas about what we might mean to say that two objects are the same. On the one hand, we might mean that two objects are the same if they have the same type and the instance variables in them have the same values. This is called *identity by value*, and it is not what we generally want to mean by sameness. A stronger notion, *object identity*, holds only when the two objects are, in fact, one and the same. Said another way, if we have two references to objects, we say that they are the same provided that they reference the same object.

This use of references rather than direct variables is very important and intimately bound up with our ideas of abstraction and object independence. It is also the normal thing that C (ordinary C) does in assignments using variables having simple types. If `counter` has `int` type, then

```
counter = 0;
     :
counter = counter + 1;
```

first makes `counter` a reference to the integer 0 and then makes it a reference to some other integer, perhaps 1. Importantly, the first statement does not create a new zero. Zero is a mathematical concept in the first place and a bit pattern in the second. We might put a copy of this bit pattern in a new place, but we don't create a new bit pattern or a new integer. The second statement does not change zero, and it does not create a new integer. It simply makes `counter` reference a different integer, one computed from the integer currently referenced.

Notice how different things are when we use C's structured types, like arrays and structs. If `scores` and `backup` have the same array type, such as `char[100]`, then

```
for (i = 1; i < n; ++i)
   backup[i] = scores[i];
```

does not make `backup` a reference to the same array that `scores` references. The entire array is copied into the new location, so two arrays currently contain the same data. If we modify one of them, say with

```
scores[5] = xxx;
```

then one of the arrays is changed, but the other is not. Structured types are like little blocks of data that can be moved around and copied and changed *from the outside*. Neither simple types nor objects behave that way. In this regard, and others, objects are more like simple types than like structured types.

There is an important difference, though, between objects and simple types. If an element is of a simple type, as 5 is an element of `int`, it cannot be changed. Five is five. Variables referencing it can be changed to reference other things, but five cannot be changed.

Objects can be changed, but ideally they cannot (or at least should not) be changed from the outside. An object can be changed only by sending it a message, using some name that currently references it. Any name that references it will do. If `currentScore` and `lastValue` were pointers to objects, the assignment

```
lastValue = currentScore;
```

would produce `lastValue` as an alias of `currentScore`, and the assignment

```
currentScore[5]  =  xxx;
```

would be illegal because it is an attempt directly to modify `currentScore`. Instead we would say

```
currentScore.atPut  (5,xxx);
```

sending the `atPut` message to `currentScore`, and the change would be effective for the object and hence affect all names that referenced it. Figure 3.2 shows an object and two references (`aName` and `anAlias`) by which we may access it. These two references are aliases of each other.

In some way we can think of objects as being "out there," living quiet lives, going about their business. And we can think of names as being distinct from them but giving us a handle by which we can send them messages. They will respond to our messages, changing their state or behavior, but not, hopefully, disrupting it.

In a certain way objects are like people. People are distinct from their names, and may have several names (aliases); they respond to messages but are not directly modified from without; and they provide and require services.

Programming with aliases may take a bit of getting used to, and there are some problems associated with it. For example, if something destroys the object `Foo`, by using the standard operator `delete`, as in `delete Foo`, any aliases of `Foo` will be invalid. Thus control over the destruction of objects is important. There are many conceptual advantages to aliases

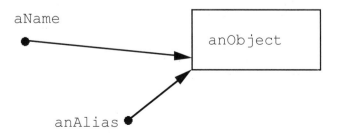

FIGURE 3.2

however, and this is the reason that they have become a fundamental technique in object-oriented programming.

For example, suppose we consider ExpressionStack again, and suppose the expressions we push onto the stack are algebraic expressions. Also suppose that such expressions have a method, simplify, by which they simplify themselves. The operation of the method changes the internal state of an expression object so that its new representation is an algebraic simplification of its former representation. Suppose we execute the following:

```
anExpression = ExpressionStack.top ();
anExpression -> simplify ();
```

Because we are using aliasing, the object anExpression is actually still in the stack (we haven't removed it), but we have caused that very object to become simplified. If the assignment operator simply copied the representation of an object to a new location, the simplify would be performed on the data at the new location and the object in the stack would not be modified. Instead, with aliases, we operate on a single object. Therefore we don't need to put the object back into the stack after performing simplify, because it was never removed.

Objects can even send messages to themselves. Often a method for some class will want to execute another method in the same class. It does this by sending a message to itself using just methodName (), with any required parameters. It is understood that the message is being sent to object this, as in this -> methodName (); however, the prefix this should not be written.

3.3   INHERITANCE: START AT THE TOP

In defining the class SFiniteStack above, we did not show the details of the SObject class on which it depends. The declaration of this class is contained in the header PObject.h shown below.

```
#ifndef __Object__
#define __Object__

#ifndef __STDLIB__
#include <stdlib.h>
#define __STDLIB__
#endif

#ifndef __IOSTREAM__
#include <iostream.h>
#define __IOSTREAM__
#endif
```

```
const char FALSE = 0;
const char TRUE = (!FALSE);

typedef enum { object,  magnitude,  collection,
               iterator,  position,  list,
               listnode,  listposition,
               listiterator,  stack,  integer,
               string,  pair,  association,
               character,  queue,  set,
               setiterator,  fraction,  bag,
               bagnode,  bagiterator,  bagposition,
               heap,  heapposition,  graph,  edge,
               vertex,  graphposition,
               graphiterator,  array,  arrayiterator,
               Boolean,  dictionary,  interval,
               buildtree,  expressionnode,
               intervaliterator,  expressiontree,
               arrayheap,  arrayqueue,
               priorityqueue,  dequeue,
               priorityqueueiterator,  largeinteger,
               tree,  treenode, treeposition,
               bstset,  fdset,  dynamicarray,
               dynamicarrayiterator,  hashdictionary,
               hashdictionaryiterator, dfanode,
               infix,  multilist,  multilistnode,
               multilistposition, multilistiterator,
               binarytree,  binarytreenode,
               binarytreeposition,
               binarytreeiterator,
               binarysearchtree,
               binarysearchtreeposition,
               registrationtree,
               registrationtreeposition,
               sortedlist,  sortedlistposition,
               functionaldependency,  recursivelist,
               recursivelistposition,
               recursivelistiterator,
               recursivetree,  recursivetreeposition,
               recursivetreeiterator,  statement,
               nonterminal, expression,  assertion,
               ifstatement,  concatenation,
               assignment,  elsepart,
               whilestatement, invariant,  sum,
               product,  quotient,  difference,
               identexpression,  paramexpression,
               intlitexpression
             } classtype;
```

```
class SObject;
typedef SObject *PObject;

class SObject { /* Abstract root class. */
   public:
      virtual char      member (classtype);
         // TRUE if this is in classtype.
      void              Error (char *);
         // PRINT error message and halt.
      virtual void      writeIt (void);
         // Produce a textual representation on cout.
      virtual char      equal (PObject o)
         {return (this == o);};
      virtual PObject   Clone();
         // Produce a bitwise copy of the object
         // and return a pointer to the copy.
      virtual long      hash (void);
         // Return an integer so that the object
         // can be inserted into hash tables.
      virtual char      less (PObject)
                           {Error ("not defined");
                            return FALSE;};
         // Used only by magnitude classes.
   protected:
      virtual int sizeOf (void)
         {return (sizeof (SObject));};
         // WARNING: Implement sizeOf ()
         // in every class.
      virtual PObject   ShallowClone ();
         // DO NOT OVERRIDE except to disable.
         // Produce a bitwise copy of the object
         // and return a pointer to the copy.
};

void failnull (PObject); // Fail if the object
                         // is NULL.
#endif
```

The enumeration type definition shows the names of all of the classes in the library that will be discussed. These names are provided here so that any object can be tested for its type. We shall occasionally need to do this, and because the facility was left out of C++, we need to provide it. The method member is used to check whether an object is in some class. The methods declared in this class are all virtual (except Error) because we shall need to override them in all of the classes that we build. The method sizeOf is needed so that we may provide a fully functional Clone method in each class, again because of the lack of support from C++.

The following is the associated implementation file PObject.cp.

```
#include "PObject.h"

void failnull (PObject obj) {
   if (obj == NULL) {
      cout << "NULL object \n";
      exit (1);
   };
};

void classAssert (PObject o, classtype c) {
   if (o == NULL) {cout << "The object is NULL
                     in classAssert"; exit (1);}
   if (!o -> member (c)) o ->
      Error ("classAssert failure");
};

void SObject :: Error (char *s) {
   cout << s << "\n";
   exit (1);
};

void SObject :: writeIt (void) {
   cout << "An Object \n";
};

long SObject :: hash (void) {
   return (labs (((long) this))/3);
      // Treat the pointer this as if it were a
      // long integer. Divide it by three and take
      // its integer absolute value.
};

PObject SObject :: ShallowClone () {
   // To be used only in Clone methods.
   // Do not override.
   PObject result;
   int n;
   n = sizeOf ();
   result = (PObject) malloc (n);
   memcpy (result, this, n);
   return (result);
};

PObject SObject :: Clone() {
    return (ShallowClone ());
};
```

```
char SObject :: member (classtype c) {return
                       (c == object);};
```

These methods will be discussed shortly. Some of them are merely templates for expansion. All classes in this library except the special class SMagnitude will be descendants of SObject, for two reasons. The first is that we can thereby ensure that every object will have some basic functionality, such as that provided by writeIt, which writes out some representation of the object, and that of hash, which produces an integer for each object that can be used by some storage structures. The second and more important reason is that we will thus be able to form lists, sets, trees, and so on having other lists, sets, trees, etc. as contents. We will be able to construct lists of trees as easily as we can lists of integers. This will be brought up again in the discussion of SCollection.

The class SObject was used in two different ways in SFiniteStack. First it was used as an ordinary type: some of the methods of SFiniteStack had parameters or return values declared to be of this type. Thus we can say that a finite stack is a stack of elements of type SObject. Second, and more importantly, the SFiniteStack class itself was defined to be a subclass of the SObject class. This was done by the occurrence of SObject in the header of the declaration (p. 74):

```
class SFiniteStack: public SObject {
  ⋮

};
```

We say that SFiniteStack *inherits* from SObject, or that it is derived from SObject, and by that we mean that every object in SFiniteStack is automatically a member of SObject. It also means that every pointer to SFiniteStack is compatible with a pointer variable to SObject. Inheritance provides a mechanism by which an object can belong to more than one class. Thus it provides a way for the sets represented by the classes to overlap. If SFiniteStack inherits from SObject, all objects of class SFiniteStack are objects of class SObject, and SFiniteStack is thus contained in SObject.

Inheritance

The use of one class to define another by declaring only the new features. Defines a subclass relationship between the original (parent) class and the new class. All objects in the new class are members of the old class.

Note that SObject has no instance variables and that it has a few methods, most of which don't do much. It is not intended that any name will be given the type SObject or that any objects will be created with the type, so SObject is an example of what is called an *abstract class*. If it were not an abstract class, the special class constructor SObject would have been included in the class declaration. The ordinary generator function newObject () would also have been provided so that such objects would be easy to create.

Abstract Class

A class that is the union of all of its subclasses. It has no object that is not also an object of some subclass. It can be recognized by the presence of pure virtual functions (discussed later). In our library it can also be recognized by the absence of a generator function.

Concrete Class

A class that can contain objects not in any of its subclasses. It can be recognized by the presence of a generator function.

The class SFiniteStack (which is *concrete*, as evidenced by its generator function and its constructor method) is called a subclass of SObject. Things become objects in an abstract class like SObject only by being created within some concrete subclass like SFiniteStack. If we declare a new class to be a subclass of SFiniteStack, objects in the new class will be instances of that class as well as instances of SFiniteStack and SObject. Each class can declare itself to be a subclass of one or more other classes (or no class at all, but for us only SObject and SMagnitude will declare no ancestor), so classes in C++ form a hierarchical structure defined by inheritance. The structure is that of a graph whose edges are arrows pointing to ancestors. The arrows form no loops or cycles, so the graph is called a directed acyclic graph, or DAG. For example, we shall define SFraction below as another subclass of SObject, and we could (but won't) define SInteger as a subclass of SFraction. SFraction will treat fractions, using numerators and denominators as objects. SInteger would treat ordinary integers as objects. We would then have the hierarchy shown in Fig. 3.3.

Alternatively we can show subclasses in the same way that we ordinarily show subsets, as in Fig. 3.4.

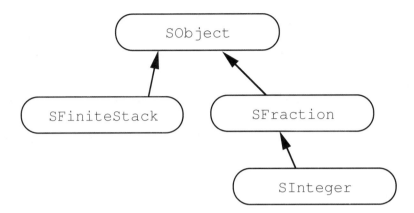

FIGURE 3.3

Figure 3.4 demonstrates the general conception of objects in class SFraction
as just special types of objects of type SObject, and objects in class
SInteger as just special types of objects of type SFraction.

Because we can directly inherit from several classes, we say that C++ is
a multiple-inheritance language. By contrast, Object Pascal and Smalltalk
are single-inheritance languages, in which a class may declare only one
immediate ancestor. With single inheritance the structure of the classes
is hierarchical, or treelike, with some class being the root of the tree, or
the ultimate ancestor of all classes. If multiple inheritance is possible, the
inheritance structure is a directed graph with no cycles, rather than a tree.

Note that inheritance is transitive, so SInteger being a subclass of
SFraction, and SFraction a subclass of SObject, it follows that
SInteger is a subclass of SObject. The ancestors of a given class form

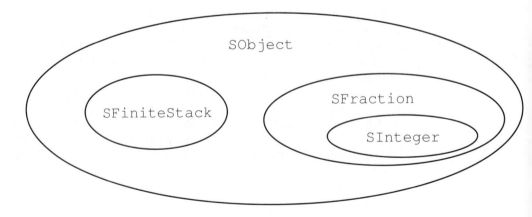

a chain back to SObject, and the descendants of class form a tree or directed acyclic graph spreading out from it.

When one class (the subclass) inherits (directly or indirectly) from another (the superclass), the objects of the class obtain methods and instance variables from the superclass and hence from all of its ancestors. Thus if SObject declared an instance variable ident, all objects in class SFiniteStack would have such an instance variable as well. Likewise, objects in SFiniteStack have the methods writeIt, Error, etc. Therefore, we could have implemented push so that an attempted push onto a full stack would have resulted in passing the Error message, which would halt the program. To do this, the object executing the method would have to send the error message to itself. This can be accomplished from within any method of any class descendant from SObject by

```
Error ("SFiniteStack.push: Stack overflow");
```

Then the same object, this, an SFiniteStack, would execute the error method, printing the string shown and then halting the execution of the program.

It is possible that an inherited method (one declared by some ancestor) provides inappropriate action in the current class. This is the case here with the writeIt method. If we have

```
ExpressionStack.writeIt ();
```

the stack would execute the method it had inherited, and we would see the string

```
An Object
```

appear in the output. When a method is inherited it is possible to redefine the action that it carries out when executed by an object of the new class. In this case we would redeclare writeIt in the SFiniteStack class definition and redefine it in the implementation file of its definition as follows.

```
class SFiniteStack: public SObject {
    :
    virtual void writeIt();
    :
};
:
```

```
void SFiniteStack :: writeIt () {
   int i;

   for (i = fTop; i >= 1; --i )
      fElements[i] -> writeIt ();
      cout << ' ';
};
```

We now send the `writeIt` message to each object in the stack, writing the stack from top to bottom. Note that we process it from the top down, as is more in keeping with the idea of what a stack is. This cannot be overemphasized. There is a key principle here:

Principle of Abstraction

The processing provided by a class should always be in accord with the nature of the abstraction on which the class is based.

Note the new keyword, `virtual`, which indicates that a method can be overridden in a subclass. Although the keyword need only be used in the class in which the method is first defined, we shall repeat it, using the same expression at the first introduction and at every redefinition. Our style will be to have all methods virtual.

Inheritance is very powerful if we combine the above ideas with the ideas of indirect, or reference, variables. Suppose that we have declared and defined the `SFraction` and `SInteger` classes discussed above and declared the associated pointer types `PFraction` and `PInteger` as usual. We shall see below that `SFraction` will declare a method named `add`. Assume that `SInteger` has a method `isPrime` that returns a Boolean TRUE if the integer is a prime number. Updated (but simplified) class photos are shown in Fig. 3.5, with inheritance indicated by arrows between the classes. Note that as we descend the hierarchy, we don't lose the public methods of the ancestors, although we may add additional ones. The deeper we get in the inheritance structure, the more sophisticated our classes, and hence the objects, become.

Suppose that we have declared two reference variables, `myFraction` and `myInteger` as in

```
PFraction myFraction;
PInteger myInteger;
```

The properties of reference variables, the nature of object identity, and the fact that subclasses are like subsets together imply that it is possible to make the assignment

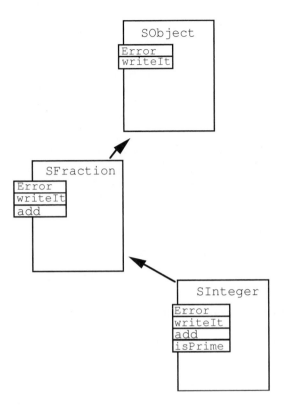

FIGURE 3.5

```
myFraction = myInteger;
```

and so make myFraction, even though it is declared to be a name associated with class SFraction, now a reference to an SInteger. Note that
we are assuming that this integer object was properly created in the first
place, with a call to new and proper initialization.

This integer object, masquerading under the name myFraction,
ought to behave as any integer. Therefore, if writeIt was redeclared in
SFraction and then redeclared again in SInteger, and if we next say

```
myFraction -> writeIt ();
```

Virtual Method

A method of a class that, when used with an indirect variable,
is interpreted in the most specific way possible. The method executed is the method associated with the object itself and not
necessarily the name associated with the class of the variable
used to refer to the object.

then the method executed is the one known to the object itself, which is an SInteger, not the one in class SFraction. Thus the object is seen to be autonomous in a very real sense. We can't get it to behave improperly even if we reference it with a name associated with an ancestor class. See Exercises 3.11 and 3.12.

The reason we have chosen to program with indirect variables when using objects is that they grant this autonomy of objects. Direct variables do not do so. When we assign a variable of type SInteger to a variable of type SFraction, only that part of the SInteger that is also an SFraction is assigned. Any additional fields or methods of the SInteger are lost. With pointers to objects, however, we simply create a new alias to the existing object.

Likewise, when referred to by an indirect variable, the object should be able to respond to the message ...isPrime, but here we have a difficulty. C++ is very strongly typed, much more so than standard C, and is typed by the compiler, which means that the names are typed. Thus if we try to say myFraction − > isPrime, the compiler will complain that myFraction is a reference to type SFraction and there is no such method in that class. The compiler has no way to know that we have made an assignment *up the hierarchy* and that myFraction will reference an SInteger at this spot at run time. If the *programmer* can verify that in every execution of the program myFraction will reference an SInteger at this spot, we can get the object to respond to isPrime by *type casting* the name, as in:

```
PInteger (myFraction) -> isPrime;
```

Note that the type name is used as a prefix to the object name and returns a pointer to an object of that type. Type casting is more complex in C++ than in ordinary C, because the value of the reference variable may be changed. Type casting reassures the compiler that the programmer knows what is best and can verify externally that myFraction always represents an SInteger. In fact, type casting does more, as will be discussed shortly. Note that if you use type casting (we will, in important ways) and you are wrong, myFraction holding a reference to something not in SInteger, at run time you will get an error. It will probably not be caught by the run-time system and your program will wind up crashing. Type casting must be used carefully and only when one can prove that it is valid. Type casting can never make a correct program incorrect, nor an incorrect program correct. It can hide errors, resulting in programs that are harder to debug. It puts the compiler's type-checking mechanism to sleep, which can be dangerous. It must be used only when the programmer is willing to take on the burden of ensuring correctness. The reason why C++ is unlikely to help us with errors of this kind is that in order to check for them a certain amount of overhead must be built into programs, which increases the size of objects.

The designers of C++ were unwilling to make all programs pay for what only some will need.

SFiniteStack is used to hold, in a structured way, references to objects of other classes. Therefore it is an example of a *collection class*. Often we shall want to push objects from several classes onto a single stack. This is why the element type for the elements array was declared to be a pointer to the most general class, SObject. When we pop the objects off the stack we get things whose class is not known to the compiler other than as pointers to SObject. We shall need to type cast them so that the compiler will let us operate on them after they are removed. To aid in doing this we build in the function member. It takes one argument, a type name, one of the names declared in the enumeration type classtype within PObject.h. Method member returns a Boolean TRUE if the object is in that class. For example, we might say something like

```
if (myFraction -> member (integer))
    myInteger = myFraction;
```

where myInteger was declared to be of type PInteger. Of course the compiler will complain about this, because we are assigning *down the hierarchy*, which is not valid. The syntax has to be changed slightly by using type casting:

```
if (myFraction -> member (integer))
    myInteger = PInteger (myFraction);
```

The type casting done here (down the hierarchy) has a meaning very different from that of the assignment up the hierarchy. In fact, the compiler does more than relax its vigilance about types. In some situations it modifies the reference pointer so that what is assigned to myInteger is a pointer to a location such that the original pointer (myFraction) references that part of an integer object that represents a fraction object. This needs to be done because the inheritance that C++ uses embeds a superclass object within each of its subclass objects. Therefore, every subclass object (SInteger) contains a part that is a complete superclass object (SFraction). Because classes can inherit from more than one other class, there may be several such embedded objects. By doing this adjustment, the references are always valid. The opposite adjustment is made when you assign up the hierarchy. Thus, if myInteger is a reference as shown in Fig. 3.6 and we make the legal assignment myFraction = myInteger, then myFraction will be as shown in Fig. 3.7. If we later typecast as in myInteger = PInteger (myFraction), the compiler will know how to find the right value of myInteger from the value of myFraction.

This ability to use a single name, such as myFraction, to reference different kinds of things is a special kind of strong typing. Standard strong typing (such as found in Pascal) is very strict about every name, with

myInteger

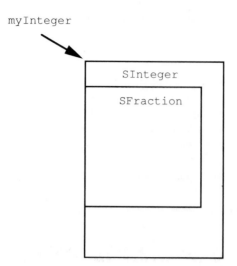

FIGURE 3.6

everything having only a single type. The same is true here, but in C++ the types are not disjoint. A pointer to class type consists of all objects in a class and in all pointers to subclasses of that class. Assignment compatibility is consistent with this view. If a name is declared to be associated with a class type, it can refer to any object in that class or in any subclass of that class. We say that C++ introduces *type polymorphism* into the language, for we may associate many forms, or types, with a name.

Type Polymorphism

The ability of a name to refer to objects of many different types.

myFraction

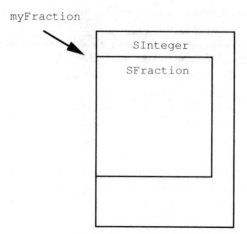

FIGURE 3.7

It is important to note that both names and objects have types. The type of a name is established by the programmer in a declaration. The compiler sees this declaration and associates a type with the name. From then on, that name may be associated only with that type (or a subtype). Importantly, *the typing of names occurs at compile time*. Objects are given a type when they are created by new. The type of the name of the parameter used with new is assigned to the newly created object. From then on, the object can be referred to by many different names (aliases), but its type never changes. An object always has a single type. The names that refer to it are names associated with its own type (creation type) or the types of superclasses of that type. Importantly, *the typing of objects occurs at run time*.

Continuing the discussion of SObject, some of its methods are specifically included for no other purpose than to be overridden. The method writeIt is such a method. Normally every class should override writeIt, and so (because we never directly create objects of type SObject) we should never execute the method. It is here to provide a *protocol*, which other inheriting classes will use in a consistent way. If every class declared a method to show an external representation of the object, but all used different names, it would be difficult to remember what name was used in what class. We are thus programming here according to the Rule of Seven discussed earlier. Other methods, especially here in the root class, are intended never to be overridden. These are Error and ShallowClone. Note that they were defined using a capital letter as the initial letter of their names; this is just a simple style convention to indicate their special nature. The method Clone is provided so that we may override it as necessary to create objects identical to the one that executes the method.

The sizeOf method is protected, which means that it can be called only by methods of the class and methods of heirs. It is used for implementing the ShallowClone method, which itself is used to implement all the Clone methods of the various classes. For everything to work right, sizeOf must be implemented in every class. It has the same implementation in every class except for the type of one variable. We shall see that we can create it with a template in each class. It will be mentioned again after we discuss the dynamic binding principle later in this chapter.

There is only one other method to discuss here. It is called hash and is used by other classes that need to represent objects with a (not unique) nonnegative integer. The typical use is in the creation of special storage structures called hash tables. These will be extensively discussed later when we look at the implementation of SInteger and SHashDictionary. The hash method must always return a nonnegative long integer for use by these clients. We implement it by taking the address at which the object itself is stored, treating it as a number, and doing a bit of arithmetic on it.

The file PObject.h also declares a public function that is not a method, failnull. This procedure is here because a call to new may fail. It is used within generator functions as

```
result = new (SStack);
failnull (result);
```

and causes a structured shutdown of the program rather than a crash if the heap is out of room. Note that it can't be a method, because it is called in situations in which there might be no object to execute it. We similarly provide the ordinary function classAssert, which checks whether its first parameter is a member of a class whose code name is the second parameter. If it is not, the string is printed and the program is halted. It is called Assert because of the halt. We are asserting that the object has a certain type and wish the computation to halt if we are wrong.

Finally, in this section we look at just what is inherited and what is not. In C++ what is inherited is the physical structure of the instance variables, the method declarations, and, for those methods not overridden, the code of the inherited methods. It is neither possible to omit an instance variable or a method name in a subclass nor change the type of an instance variable or any parameter of an inherited method. We can add something new or redefine the code for a method. That is all.

The above description is very physical and could be misleading to a user attempting to develop a good style of object-oriented programming. Conceptually we want to think that we are inheriting much more than code and bits. Specifically, when we define an SFiniteStack class, we declare that it exhibits a LIFO protocol and we are careful to specify how that is interpreted in terms of the actions of push and pop. If we create a subclass of SFiniteStack, the subclass is supposed to be "like a subset" of SFiniteStack, or in other words, a specialization of SFiniteStack. This means in particular that subclasses of SFiniteStack should still be LIFO and because the name is SFiniteStack, they should also be finite. Another way to say this is to say that the relationship between a subclass and its superclass is *is-a*, pronounced "is a." Thus, in the above, SInteger *is-a* SFraction, and a mathematician would agree. Nothing in the C++ language definition or implementation enforces this, however. It is necessary for the programmer to be aware of what he or she is doing when using inheritance and, generally speaking, to ensure that a subclass is a specialization of its superclass.

---

is-a

The normal relationship between a subclass and its superclass (other relationships are possible). An object of a subclass *is-a* (is an) object of its superclass if it exhibits all of the properties of a superclass object. The relationship implies that the subclass is a specialization of the superclass.

Occasionally it is useful and even necessary to program as if *is-a* weren't the norm. In these cases it is important to be clear in the documentation of a class that it is only like its superclass. Sometimes when we need to create some software in a hurry, we look at that which we already have and find that some class does most of what we want. We might need to examine the code to determine this, although the specifications should be adequate. Then, to create the new software, it is tempting and useful to subclass the existing class, ignoring the intent and the specification of the original and only taking advantage of the code. In such a case the subclass objects are only similar to the superclass objects, and we say that the relationship between the subclass and the superclass is *is-like* rather than *is-a*. For example, a queue (first in–first out, FIFO, structure) can be implemented by subclassing a stack, but queues aren't specialized stacks, but only similar to stacks. The programmer needs to recognize when each relationship is being used. The relation *is-a* is more important, on account of the Rule of Seven: the more similarities there are, the less has to be remembered. If our class hierarchy is a specialization hierarchy, with each class adding behavior but not changing it, we achieve a conceptual unity that will help us use what we have and avoid the errors that come from misunderstanding what we do.

---

is-like

A relationship between a class and its superclass, weaker than *is-a*, which implies that the subclass is a modification of its superclass. It is used only for code reuse rather than as an abstraction mechanism.

3.4   COLLECTIONS AND ITERATORS

The class `SFiniteStack` discussed above is an example of a general type of class called a collection. The idea of a collection is that it is a container of some sort for objects (or data). Sets, lists, stacks, arrays, and dictionaries are examples of collections. What we shall be collecting in our collections will be references to objects. Since we can have several references (pointers) to the same object, one object can be a member of several collections simultaneously. An object can be processed by some function while it is a member of a collection, so we don't need to remove elements from sets or lists in order to manipulate them. An implication of this is that removal of an object from a collection never implies its destruction; it can still be referenced from other places in the program. Since the collections store references to objects rather than copies of objects, we don't have to update all the copies of some item when one copy changes. Since we permit several aliases, the owner of an object need not give up access to it when inserting it into a list or stack.

Since a collection is a general idea, it can be specialized. And since classes are a way to implement specialization, it will be useful for us to create a class SCollection. Most of the classes that we discuss in this book are either subclasses of SCollection or of another major grouping, SMagnitude, which is discussed in the next section. Since collections store objects we shall need ways to get objects into a collection, ways to get them out, and ways to find out what information is in the collection. Different subclasses will use different methods, with different names, for their primary insertion and deletion operations. For stacks the operations are traditionally push and pop, and for queues they are enqueue and dequeue. But all collections exhibit an adding and a removing behavior. Therefore the class SCollection will need the method insert and the method remove, which will be inherited by all subclasses and will be overridden by most of them.

The things to be inserted into our collections will always be of type PObject, or references to objects in this hierarchy. This has a benefit and a cost. The benefit is that we may have lists or stacks of anything that we build here, since they will all derive from SObject. We can have stacks of lists or lists of stacks, or heterogeneous collections, such as a stack that simultaneously contains fractions and lists. We need not be limited to some particular type, since the types are extendible by inheritance. The cost is that if we wish to collect something that is not part of this hierarchy, we will have to build a special class that derives from SObject to serve as a package of the thing that we really want.

```
class SCollection;
typedef SCollection *PCollection;

class SCollection: public SObject {
  public:
    virtual char        member (classtype c);
    virtual void        insert (PObject) = 0;
    virtual void        remove (PObject) = 0;
    virtual char        empty (void) {return (TRUE);}
    virtual PIterator   newIterator (void);
    virtual void        writeIt (void);
        // Write out all members
        // of the collection.

  protected:
    virtual int sizeOf (void);
};
```

Note that the insert and remove methods are defined to be = 0. This is how C++ indicates a *pure virtual function*, a function having no body and intended entirely to be overridden in subclasses. The presence of such functions indicates that SCollection is abstract. C++, in fact, will not let us create such objects directly; we can create objects only of subclasses in which all of the pure virtual functions have been redefined. Also note that there is no newCollection generator function. No object in this class is not also in some subclass. That doesn't mean that the class is useless. It serves two important purposes. First, it defines a protocol of method/message names that will be preserved by all subclasses. For example, if we were to improve upon the SFiniteStack class as given above, we would make it a subclass of SCollection. Then we would implement insert within SFiniteStack as a call to push. In that way we would get the advantage of the generality of an insert method while strictly maintaining the LIFO protocol of a stack.

Pure Virtual Function

A method declared to have a statement part =0. A class with such a method is abstract. A descendant of such a class either is abstract or must override all pure virtual functions, giving them statement parts.

The second purpose served by the class SCollection is that it can include some very useful code, which will be inherited and probably not overridden, and which all subclasses will find useful. For example, writeIt can be written here to guarantee that any collection will write out all of its elements. The method empty could also be implemented in this way, but we shall just pass on the responsibility for this to all subclasses. However, before the implementation can be described, another fundamental idea must be discussed.

Collections being containers of many things, it is often necessary to process all of the elements of a collection in some way. For example, to count or write the objects in a collection, we need to access them as a whole, without disturbing the contents of the collection. An *iterator* makes this possible.

Iterator

A mechanism for processing the elements of any collection sequentially. Iterators generalize the operation of for loops on array structures.

Iterators are the means of processing the elements of a collection one at a time until all have been processed. Usually this means sending some message, such as `writeIt`, to each element in the collection, or possibly sending each object of a collection as a parameter to some processing procedure. This idea is embodied in the abstract class `SIterator`. Each subclass of `SCollection` (`SList`, for example) will have an associated iterator class (in this case `SListIterator`) that is a subclass of `SIterator`. The declaration of the iterator protocol is as follows:

```
class SIterator;
typedef SIterator *PIterator;

class SIterator: public SObject {
    public:
            SIterator(PCollection);
        virtual char    nextItem (PObject&) = 0;
        virtual void    reset (void)= 0;
            // {fDone = fCollection -> empty();};
        virtual void    Short (void) {fDone = TRUE;};
        virtual char    done (void);
        virtual char    member (classtype c);

    protected:
        char            fDone;
        PCollection     fCollection;
        virtual int     sizeOf (void);
};
```

Within any collection class is a method, `newIterator`, that creates and initializes an iterator of the appropriate kind for that class. This is the only appropriate way to create an iterator. Interestingly, the `SIterator` constructor code is all the initialization necessary for some iterators, and it is simply

```
SIterator :: SIterator (PCollection c) {
    fCollection = c;
    fDone = c -> empty ();
};
```

An iterator will always produce the objects the collection mentioned in its initialization and saved in its instance variable. Remember that only a reference is saved. The collection is not copied by this code. The instance variable `fDone` remembers whether any more elements remain; if the collection is empty, `fDone` will be TRUE initially. Note that an iterator cannot operate correctly if a collection is changed after an iterator is initialized (or reset). Thus it is not safe in general to use an iterator as a mechanism for modifying the collection over which it iterates. See Section 10.5 for some ideas about how this requirement may be relaxed. The method `reset` will permit an iterator to be reused.

The objects in a collection are accessed by calling an iterator's `nextItem` method. It is used in the following way in virtually all cases. Suppose that `SList` is a subclass of `SCollection` (`SList` is described briefly in Chapter 4 and completely in Chapter 6) and that `SListIterator` is a subclass of `SIterator`. Suppose that `aList` has type `PList` and has been created, initialized, and used, so that it contains some objects. Assume that `IT` is declared to be of class `PIterator`, but that it has not been created. Finally, assume that `aValue` is a pointer variable declared to be of type `PObject`. Then to write all the objects in `aList` we could write

```
IT = aList -> newIterator ();
    // Creates a list iterator.
while (IT -> nextItem (aValue))
    aValue -> writeIt ();
delete IT;
```

The repeated sending of the `nextItem` message will yield successive elements of the list `aList`, and the function return value will be TRUE as long as there is more to yield. This is very much like the way that a `for` loop is used to iterate over an array (actually over the subscripts of the array, which form a primitive type of collection). This is a situation in which type casting comes to our aid. If we had been storing only objects in some class `SExpression` in the list, and if such objects respond to the `simplify` message, we could simplify all of them in the list with

```
IT = aList -> newIterator ();
    // Creates a list iterator.
while (IT -> nextItem (aValue))
    PExpression (aValue) -> simplify ();
```

The type cast is needed because `aValue` has a declared type of `PObject`, which does not have a `simplify` method. Note that it doesn't help to declare `aValue` as type `PExpression`, because then it conflicts with the parameter type of `nextItem`.

The `nextItem` method of `SIterator` is an example of the use of a reference parameter. It is used to pass information back from the routine `nextItem` to its caller. This means that the value of the pointer variable passed in to `nextItem` will be changed and a new value passed back out. The caller can make use of this new value. Thus, `nextItem` gives us access to a new item from a collection each time it is called. We do not return this item as the function result because we want to use the function result for loop control, returning FALSE only when nothing can be returned for the reference parameter.

Note that in the definition of `SIterator` we have an instance variable `fCollection` which has the type of a pointer to class. We can say that an iterator *has-a* collection. This is yet another relationship between classes. An object in one class *has-a* object in another if one of its instance variables is in that other class.

---

has-a

A relationship between classes such that A *has-a* B is true if B is used to implement A. A component of A is an element in B. Sometimes we choose between *is-a* and *has-a* when designing a new class.

Because the class `SCollection` is abstract, it has no instance variables to implement a collection. The subclasses will create these. Therefore the `insert` and `remove` methods cannot be implemented here and will be defined in the declaration of the class to be pure virtual functions:

```
virtual void    insert (PObject) = 0;
virtual void    remove (PObject) = 0;
```

The system then guarantees that if we create a subclass of `SCollection` we won't forget to implement the `insert` method. This declaration would catch the error immediately. Many of the methods in `SCollection` and in `SIterator` are implemented in the same way.

So far `SCollection` and `SIterator` have been described as useless in themselves but capable of being made useful through the creation of subclasses. The following will show how the virtual method `writeIt` can be implemented even though we don't know how an actual collection, such as a list, stack, or binary tree will be implemented.

```
void SCollection :: writeIt (void) {
    PIterator IT;
    PObject item;

    IT = newIterator ();
    while (IT -> nextItem (item)) {
        item -> writeIt ();
        cout << '';
    }
    cout << '\n';
    delete IT;
}
```

This writes a list, separated by spaces, of the objects in any collection. Note that all objects inherit or override `writeIt`, because this method was first declared in SObject. There is a very subtle but extremely important point to be made about this code. Suppose that writeIt is not overridden in some subclass, say SList, of SCollection and that a client sends the writeIt message to aList in class SList. Then aList will be the object executing the method above and the one sending itself the newIterator message that appears there. Note that SList will override newIterator (it is a method that msut be overridden). Therefore, when it executes newIterator, aList will execute its own version, not the version (error version) in SCollection. This is in spite of the fact that the code above is from the class SCollection. This is an instance of the important dynamic binding principle, one of the things that make object-oriented programming special.

> ## Dynamic Binding Principle
>
> Every virtual message that is sent is interpreted in the context of the object executing the method.

Because of this principle we can create a method in a superclass and mention other methods that will be called at run time even though they haven't been created yet. All that is required is that we establish in this class (or a superclass) the protocol for the method, that is, its name and parameter list. If an object in some subclass executes this method, it will interpret all messages in the method in light of its own definition, taking into account any overrides of the methods known to the class that contains the method being executed. This is very useful. Also, the dynamic binding principle on which it is based is very simple and easy to remember. It must be emphasized, however, that the dynamic binding principle applies only to virtual methods of C++ objects referred to indirectly. Again, this is the reason we use indirect objects almost exclusively. To get the benefits of the dynamic binding principle it is necessary to use virtual methods. Therefore we use them uniformly, except for the method Error of class SObject. It is this principle on which everything in this book depends. It is also fundamental to the idea of object-oriented programming that the objects should be autonomous and in control.

An illustration of the dynamic binding principle is provided by the method sizeOf, which was originally declared in SObject and will be redefined in every class. The dynamic binding principle assures us that if we send some object a sizeOf message, the object will respond with its own true size, even if that object is currently being referred to by a name associated with one of its superclasses. In turn, this will ensure that ShallowClone works properly, and thus that Clone does also. We say that this makes sizeOf polymorphic, as it works on many types.

3.5   MAGNITUDES

The class SMagnitude embodies our ideas of size and quantity. It has many subclasses, like SFraction, SComplex, and even SInteger, which treats ordinary integers as if they were objects. The key to magnitudes is the comparison of objects by methods like less and equal. The abstraction on which magnitudes are built is the idea of the partial ordering of a set.

Partial Order

A set is in partial order if between the elements of the set there is a relation, $\leq$, that satisfies the following rules.

    a. reflexivity ($a \leq a$ for any a)
    b. transitivity ($a \leq b$ and $b \leq c$ implies $a \leq c$)
    c. antisymmetry ($a \leq b$ and $b \leq a$ implies $a = b$)

A partial ordering is called total if, in addition to the above,

    d. for any pair of elements a and b, either $a \leq b$ or $b \leq a$.

The integers are in total order with the usual $\leq$. A hierarchical structure, like our class structure (if we consider only inheritance from SObject), represents a partial order (but not a total order) if we let $\leq$ stand for the ancestor-descendant relationship. That is, we say class $A \leq$ class B if B is an ancestor of A or is the same class.

The class protocol for SMagnitude is as follows:

```
class SMagnitude;
typedef SMagnitude *PMagnitude;

class SMagnitude {
  public:
    virtual char      member (classtype c);
      // TRUE if this is in classtype.
    virtual char      less (PObject m) = 0;
      // Not implemented here.
    virtual char      equal (PObject o) = 0;
      // Not implemented here.
    virtual char      greater (PObject o);
      // TRUE if not less(o) and not equal(o).
```

```
    virtual  char        notEqual (PObject m);
    virtual  char        lessEqual (PObject m);
    virtual  char        greaterEqual (PObject m);
    virtual  char        between (PObject m, PObject n);
    virtual  PObject     max (PObject m, PObject n);
    virtual  PObject     min (PObject m, PObject n);

  protected:
    virtual    intsize Of (void);
};
```

This is again an abstract class and will only have objects that are created in some subclass. All subclasses must implement less and equal, but most of the others are implemented here using these two. They are often overridden by subclasses for efficiency. The most important thing to notice about SMagnitude is that it does not inherit SObject. It is also the top or root of a hierarchy. It will be used in the following special way. Some classes, like SInteger, will inherit both SObject and SMagnitude, through multiple inheritance. In his way the features of SMagnitude are mixed into other classes that inherit from SObject. Therefore there will be no objects of type SMagnitude unless they are also members of some class that inherits from SObject. Our design criteria for classes is that except for mixin classes, we shall use only single inheritance. Mixin classes are used to add functionality to other classes, but they do not themselves inherit from other classes unless those are also mixins. Classes may inherit several others, but at most one of the parents derives from SObject. If none derive from SObject, the class is a mixin. We shall not create objects in a class that is a mixin. Rather, we shall use mixins as heirs in multiple inheritance schemes that involve some descendant of SObject. We shall have variables and values (objects) only of descendants of SObject.

One way to describe mixin classes is that they describe properties of objects rather than objects themselves. Magnitude is a property possessed by objects, therefore we make SMagnitude into a mixin class. Note that the methods of SMagnitude operate on members of SObject, not on members of SMagnitude. In fact, the objects they operate on will be heirs both of SObject and SMagnitude. Since objects in SInteger have this property, they can be compared using less, etc.

SObject implemented an equal method. In that class objects are equal only if they are the same object (aliases). In magnitudes, we have a fundamentally different idea. Magnitudes are equal if they have the same "size," according to the law of antisymmetry. For this reason equal and less are implemented here as pure virtual methods.

```
virtual char equal (PObject o) = 0;
virtual char less (PObject m) = 0;
```

Because the parameter of `equal` is required to be in the same class as the receiver, it is generally possible to compare magnitudes only if they are in the same class or if one of the objects is in a subclass of the class of the other. In the latter case the `equal` message must be sent to the object in the superclass, the other object being used as the parameter.

The method `greater` can be implemented in terms of the required `less`.

```
char SMagnitude :: greater (PObject m) {
    return (!less (m) && !equal (m));};
```

The others are similar. For example:

```
char SMagnitude :: between (PObject m, PObject n) {
    return (greaterEqual (m) && lessEqual (n));
};
```

The typical use of these methods is in `if` and `while` statements, as in

```
if (anExpression -> less (aLeftHandSide)) {
    ⋮

}
```

which assumes that `anExpression` and `aLeftHandSide` are both pointers to objects in some subclass of `SMagnitude`.

It is important to note that objects are compared using `less` and `lessEqual`, not `<` or `<=`, which work only on a restricted subset of the built-in data of C++. These functional methods extend the idea of comparison to a large class of objects. We can compare not only integers, characters, etc., but also fractions, geometric figures, and whatever else we choose to make a subclass of `SMagnitude`. Finally, C++ does allow us to redefine the meaning of built-in operators like `<` and `<=` within classes. We can use this feature of the language to permit more natural-looking comparisons between magnitude objects. The interested reader can look up operator overloading in C++ reference books.

3.6   ANOTHER SIMPLE EXAMPLE: FRACTIONS

This section will present an implementation of the magnitude subclass `SFraction`. Because they can be compared, fractions are magnitudes. But they are more than this. They are a member of an important set of subclasses of `SMagnitude`, called numeric classes because they can also be operated on with the usual arithmetic operators. We could implement the following numeric class, but we shall not. If we did then `SFraction` would be a subclass of SNumeric. Note that SNumeric would be a mixin if implemented.

```
class SNumeric ;
typedef SNumeric *PNumeric;

class SNumeric: public SMagnitude {
    // Abstract mixin class.
  virtual PObject   add (PObject b);
    // Return the "sum" of this and b.
    // Meaning depends on class of this.
  virtual PObject   subtract (PObject b);
  virtual PObject   multiply (PObject b);
  virtual PObject   divide (PObject b);
};
```

This class won't exist except in our documentation, because its use as an abstract class requires that too many type casts would need to be given in its concrete subclasses. Because it doesn't exist, we call it a *pseudoclass*. Since SNumeric is a pseudoclass, SFraction is actually a subclass of SMagnitude.

> **Pseudoclass**
>
> A purely conceptual class used to convey details of a protocol, not actually declared or implemented, and recognized by its complete absence, except in documentation.

```
class SFraction;
typedef SFraction *PFraction;

PFraction newFraction (long numerator,
                            long denominator);
    // Return a new fraction with given numerator
    // and denominator. If denominator = 0, return 0.

class SFraction: public SMagnitude, public SObject {
    // INVARIANT: Denominator positive, lowest terms.
    public:
        SFraction (long N, long D);
            // Initialize a fraction with N as numerator
            // and D as denominator. If D = 0
            // return the fraction 0.
        virtual PFraction   add (PFraction);
```

```
                // Sum of two fractions.
        virtual PFraction    subtract (PFraction);
        virtual PFraction    multiply (PFraction);
        virtual PFraction    divide (PFraction);
            // Fraction division.
            // Error if the argument is zero.
        virtual char         less (PObject m);
            // m must be a PFraction.
        virtual char         equal (PObject m);
            // m must be a PFraction.
        virtual char         member (classtype c);
        virtual void         writeIt (void);
    protected:
        long                 fNumerator, fDenominator;
        virtual int          size Of (void);
    friend void reduce (PFraction f);
};
```

Note that we include the required overrides for SMagnitude and a consistent reworking (but not inheriting) of SNumeric. C++'s strong typing won't let us redefine less as

```
virtual char   less (PFraction m);
```

because it doesn't permit redefinitions of the types of parameters in virtual methods when we create a new version in a subclass. This would be unsafe in any case. Therefore we include the restriction as a precondition that must be observed by clients and subclasses and state it as part of the declaration. There is no system enforcement of this requirement, other than that the system can crash if it is not fulfilled. We shall, however, program defensively, making less safe to use when clients try to compare fractions to other magnitudes.

We have also included a class invariant as part of the documentation of the class. An *invariant* is a statement than can be guaranteed to be always true. In this case it means that to an external observer (client or subclass) the numerator and denominator will always appear in lowest terms: any common factors will have been divided out of both. While methods of this class execute, there will be short periods of time when the invariant will not be true, but all methods will restore the truth of the statement before they exit, or they must fail.

Class Invariant

A statement guaranteed by the implementor to be always true when observed from outside the class.

The implementation of the class SFraction depends on the following three support procedures, which are defined entirely within the implementation file PFraction.cp.

```
long sgn (long a) {
    if (a > 0) return 1;
    else if (a == 0) return 0;
    else return -1;
};

long gcd (long a, long b) {
    // Precondition: b > 0, a >= 0.
    // Postcondition: returns gcd of a, b.
    long r;

    if (a != 0)
        do{
            if (a < b) {
                r = a;
                a = b;
                b = r;
            };
            a %= b;
        } while (a > 0);
    return b;
};

void reduce (PFraction f) {
    // Precondition: denominator != 0.
    // Postcondition: f in lowest terms, denom>0.
    long r;

    r = gcd (labs (f -> fNumerator),
             labs (f -> fDenominator));
    f -> fNumerator /= r;
    f -> fDenominator /= r;
    if (f -> fDenominator < 0) {
        f -> fDenominator = -f -> fDenominator;
        f -> fNumerator = -f -> fNumerator;
    };
};
```

Both gcd and reduce list *preconditions*, which any user (in this case just the routines in this implementation part) must guarantee before calling the procedure, and *postconditions*, which the code itself will guarantee, if the precondition is true on entry. This listing of preconditions and postconditions is entirely within the spirit of programming by implementing abstractions, and forms a guide to the programming.

Precondition

A fact that the user of a method or procedure must guarantee before calling the method or function. This is the user's responsibility.

Postcondition

A fact that the implementor will guarantee will be true after the routine finishes if all of its preconditions were true at the time of call.

The method `reduce` is a very special function for the class `SFraction` Note that it makes reference to the fields of its parameter `f`. Normally this is not permitted because all the instance variables are protected. However, anticipating this need, we have indicated in the class declaration of `SFraction` that `reduce` is to be a class `friend`. This means that `reduce` can see and manipulate the protected (and private) instance variables and methods of `SFraction`. A class can give friendship status to an ordinary function or to an entire class, as we shall see. This facility must be used sparingly to avoid serious problems in the software library. Every function (or class) granted friendship status must be rebuilt whenever the implementation of the class granting friendship changes. We strive for a high degree of independence between the components of our library, and friends get in the way of this. It would be extremely unusual to grant friendship to anything declared outside a single compilation unit.

Initialization is the key method in this class. Note that it implements the class invariant and respects the precondition of `reduce`, which it calls.

```
SFraction :: SFraction (long N, long D) {
    if (D != 0) {
        fNumerator = N;
        fDenominator = D;
        reduce (this);
    }
    else {
        fNumerator = 0;
        fDenominator = 1;
    };
};
```

The class generator function newFraction is entirely typical. All generator functions look like this, differing only in the type of the result local variable and the constructor called.

```
PFraction newFraction (long numerator,
                               long denominator) {
    PFraction result;

    result = new SFraction (numerator, denominator);
    failnull (result);
    return result;
};
```

The other methods are similar to add, using initialization to do the hard work:

```
PFraction SFraction :: add (PFraction b) {
  PFraction result;

  result = newFraction (fNumerator * b ->
       fDenominator + fDenominator * b -> fNumerator,
       fDenominator * b -> fDenominator);
  return result;
};
```

The method writeIt will produce a formatted fraction, putting parentheses around the number.

```
void SFraction :: writeIt(void) {
   cout << " ("<<fNumerator<<"/"<<fDenominator<<") ";
};
```

Note that methods like add as shown above are likely to overflow because of the extensive arithmetic done, even when the result, reduced to lowest terms, is easily represented. One can use more sophisticated methods to avoid this. A good (but not perfect) version of equal is shown below.

```
char SFraction :: equal (PObject m) {
  // Lessen possibility of overflow.
  long r, n, p;

  if (m -> member (fraction)) {
    r = gcd (((PFraction) m) -> fDenominator,
                           fDenominator);
    p = fDenominator / r;
    n = ((PFraction) m) -> fDenominator / r;
```

```
      return (fNumerator * n) == (p *
                                 ((PFraction) m)
                                 -> fNumerator);
   }
   else
     return FALSE;
};
```

If overflow were not an issue (it is, of course) we could just compare the cross products of the numerator of each fraction and the denominator of the other. Note that we must type cast each occurrence of the parameter m, since it is required to be declared of type PObject.

Once we have finished this class definition, we can do simple arithmetic on fractions. In fact, if we had a calculator program that correctly worked on integers, it would be a matter of a few minutes' work to turn it into a fraction calculator, because integers as objects (the class is SInteger) have nearly the same protocol as this class. The calculator program would work by creating and manipulating integers through the SInteger protocol. To make the transformation, we need only change a few type declarations and call the fraction generation function instead of the integer generator as appropriate. This is the power of programming with abstraction.

3.7   SUMMARY

Classes can be concrete, abstract, or mixin. A class of which SObject is an ancestor and that is not itself abstract is a concrete class. An abstract class is intended to form the common parent of classes needing the same interface. Mixin classes do not derive from SObject and are intended to add independent properties to other objects.

A class can be thought of as the set of its objects and is defined by description of the features of each object within it. The class features are instance variables and methods. In C++ these features are called members. The visibility of members can be controlled by marking them *public*, *private*, or *protected*. The extendibility of the methods of a class can be controlled by marking them as *virtual* or not. Virtual methods provide flexibility at the cost of efficiency and security. These costs are small in most systems.

In C++ constructors can be defined for a class to guarantee safe initialization of any object created. Likewise, destructors can be defined to guarantee that the cleanup is done properly when an object is no longer needed.

The combination of indirect objects and virtual methods leads to the fundamental dynamic binding principle, which guarantees that objects are permitted to act autonomously. Each indirect object will determine precisely how it will interpret any virtual message sent to it. It will do so in accordance with its own personal type, the class it was given when it was created by the new operator.

This text describes a specific class structure, described in the next chapter, designed to illustrate data abstraction techniques and the object-oriented style of programming. The class structure emphasizes flexibility whenever possible.

The class SObject describes the basic functionality of all objects considered in this text. This functionality derives from a mechanism for determining the actual type of an object at run time, a facility for cloning an object, and a means of writing a representation of the object on standard output.

The principle of inheritance implies that all objects in this system will be able to use and extend this basic functionality.

The class SCollection, which inherits from SObject, is the root of a large subhierarchy of classes, all of which provide a data collection service to their clients. Subclasses of SCollection will handle lists, stacks, queues, and other specialized storage mechanisms. SCollection provides insert and remove as well as an associated iteration mechanism. All collection classes have associated iterator classes.

SMagnitude provides a means of creating classes with a partial order relationship between objects by creating a comparison interface (less, greater, etc.). This relationship will be "mixed in" to other classes, such as SInteger and SString, that also derive from SObject.

EXERCISES

3.1 (3.1) Build and test the finite stack unit discussed in Section 3.1. To test it you may push and pop any objects from any classes derived from SObject. Characters are a good choice. To use characters, you must include the header PCharact.h in your main program file and initialize the character unit by calling initCharacters () at the beginning of your main routine. Character objects can be generated by the generator function asCharacter (char). Note that characters won't work correctly without the initialization step, which should be performed only once during the run of any program using characters.

3.2 (3.2) Build and test an implementation of stacks that is like SFiniteStack but uses pointers to nodes containing references to objects in order to implement the storage for a stack that need not be finite.

3.3 (3.4) Give the header file that defines a class SFiniteStack as a subclass of SCollection. Be sure to include all methods required for stacks, all methods that are inherited and must be overridden, and the associated class SFiniteStackIterator with all of its required parts. Give definitions of all of the methods used. For example, what is the meaning of SFiniteStack :: insert? Also be certain to define the appropriate generator functions and the usual associated pointer types.

3.4 (3.4) Apply the dynamic binding principle to the following situation. Suppose you have built a graphical figure class that includes a method draw. Its implementation begins by calling another method, vertices, that returns a list of the vertices (points) of the smallest rectangle with horizontal and vertical sides containing the figure. Then draw draws lines from each vertex to the next in the returned list, finishing by drawing a line from the last vertex to the first. Thus, `draw` always draws a rectangle: the boundary rectangle of a figure. Next, suppose you build a new subclass, called five-point star, of the graphical figure class. You give it a new `vertices` method that returns the 10 points, in order, representing the five outer and the five inner intersections of the edges of a five-point star. You do *not* implement a new `draw` method.

Now, suppose that you create a five-point star and send it a `draw` message. Which version of `vertices` will be called by `draw`, the one originally created in the class in which the `draw` method was created, or the one created in the new class that inherits the `draw` method? What will be drawn?

3.5 (3.4) a. How does the dynamic binding principle increase the *flexibility* of an implementor of a class?

b. The dynamic binding principle must be wisely used so that software becomes easier to build and use rather than harder. In light of this, what must implementors of override methods consider and what must they do?

c. Discuss the importance of stating preconditions and postconditions. Discuss the importance of adhering to preconditions and postconditions when you program.

3.6 (3.4) Explain the relationship between virtual functions and the dynamic binding principle.

3.7 (3.5) In C++ it is possible to overload the comparison operators, such as `<` and `>=`. We have not done so, in order to lessen the number of concepts discussed in this book. Investigate this area and add the required capability to `SMagnitude`. Remember, however, that most of our usage will be in comparing things that are pointers to C++ objects and not the objects themselves.

3.8 (3.5) Implement the methods of class `SMagnitude` except `equal` and `less`. Use these two methods in your implementations.

3.9 (3.6) When we have a class B that *is-like* another class A rather than *is-a* A we prefer *not* to implement B as a subclass of A but to implement B using an instance variable whose type is A or A*. This is true even when we must write more code to do it this way. Why is this? To make the question more concrete, consider that a set *is-like* a list since they are both storage classes (collections) and that anything that we want to do with sets, we can do with lists. Why don't we want to implement sets as a subclass of lists, but to implement sets using an instance variable that is a list?

3.10 (3.6) a. Implement `SFiniteStack` from this chapter.

b. Now, build `SFraction` as discussed in this chapter.

c. Create some `PFractions` and one `PFiniteStack`, and push the fractions onto your stack.

d. Write out the stack using `writeIt`.

3.11 Build and test the following. It uses class `SStack`, which is discussed in Sections 4.35 and 7.1. It creates a class `SExpression` of data objects to insert into a stack.

```
#include <iostream.h>
#include "PObject.h"
#include "PStack.h"
```

```
class SExpression: public SObject {
   public:
      SExpression (int a = 0, int b = 0)
         {left = a; right = b;};
      virtual void writeIt (void) {
         if (left == 0) {cout << right;}
         else if (right == 0) {cout << left;}
         else {cout << left << " + " << right;}
      };
      virtual void simplify (void) {left += right;
                                    right = 0;};
   private:
      int left, right;
};

typedef SExpression *PExpression;

PExpression newExpression (int a = 0, int b = 0) {
   PExpression result;
   result = new SExpression (a, b);
   failnull (result);
   return result;
};

PStack s;
PExpression e1, e2, e3;

void main (void) {
PIterator IT;
PObject o;
   initLists (); // required for stacks
   e1 = newExpression (1, 2);
   e2 = newExpression (3, 4);
   e3 = newExpression ();
   s = newStack ();
   s -> push (e1);
   s -> push (e2);
   s -> push (e3);
   s -> writeIt ();
   cout << '\n';

   IT = s -> newIterator ();
      // Simplify all the expressions in s.
   while (IT -> nextItem (o)) {
      PExpression (o) -> simplify ();
         // Typecast required.
   };
   s -> writeIt ();
   delete IT;
};
```

3.12 Build and test the following modification of the code of Exercise 3.11. It derives
the class SExpression from a simpler class STerm. It also pushes three of
these objects onto a stack and manipulates them while they are in the stack.
Be sure you understand which simplify and writeIt methods are being
called. You might want to output the name of the class whenever a simplify
or writeIt method is called. You can put a line like

```
cout << "STerm :: simplify";
```

into the simplify method of STerm and a similar one into that of SExpression.

```
#include <iostream.h>
#include "PObject.h"
#include "PStack.h"

class STerm: public SObject {
   public:
      STerm (int a = 0) {left = a;};
      virtual void writeIt (void) {cout << left;};
      virtual void simplify (void) { }; // Nothing.
   protected: // May be seen by subclasses.
   int left;
};
typedef STerm *PTerm;
PTerm newTerm (int a = 0) {
   PTerm result;
   result = new STerm (a);
   failnull (result);
   return result;
};

class SExpression: public STerm {
   public:
      SExpression (int a = 0, int b = 0):
                  STerm (a) {right = b;};
      virtual void writeIt (void) {
         if (left == 0) {cout << right;}
         else if (right == 0) {cout << left;}
         else {cout << left << " + " << right;}
      };
      virtual void simplify (void) {left += right;
                                    right = 0;};
   protected:
      int right; // We inherit member left.
};
typedef SExpression *PExpression;
PExpression newExpression (int a = 0, int b = 0) {
   PExpression result;
   result = new SExpression (a,b);
```

```
      failnull (result);
      return result;
   };

   PStack s;
   PTerm e1, e2, e3; // Note the change of type
                     //   from Exercise 3.11.
   void main (void) {
   PIterator IT;
   PObject o;
      initLists (); // Required for stacks.
      e1 = newExpression (1, 2);
      e2 = newExpression (3, 4);
      e3 = newTerm (6);
      s = newStack ();

      s -> push (e1);
      s -> push (e2);
      s -> push (e3);

      s -> writeIt ();
      cout << '\n';

      IT = s -> newIterator ();
      while (IT -> nextItem (o)) {
         PExpression (o) -> simplify ();
      };
      s -> writeIt (); // Write the entire stack.
      cout << '\n';
      IT -> reset (); // Reuse the same iterator.
      while (IT -> nextItem (o)) {
         // Write the stack by iterating over its contents.
         PExpression (o) -> writeIt ();
            // Note: we don't call writeIt from SObject.
         cout << '\n';
      };
      delete IT; // Dispose of the iterator.
   };
```

3.13 This exercise is a real challenge at this point. It will be very easy if done
later. The finite stack discussed in this chapter can't be used like the stack
in Exercises 3.11 and 3.12 unless we build an iterator class to go with it. If
that is done, then SFiniteStack could be rebuilt so that it inherits from
SCollection, which is more appropriate. A stack iterator should work from
the top of the stack toward the bottom. It needs a nextItem method that
will yield each item once and return FALSE thereafter. Implement this class
and make the corresponding changes to SFiniteStack. Then redo Exercise
3.12 with this new stack type in place of SStack. Hint: For an internal state
variable, an SFiniteStackIterator needs only an integer to keep track
of the next item that has not yet been yielded. Initially this should be the
index of the top of the stack.

THE COLLECTION AND MAGNITUDE CLASSES

He had a very curious collection of scarabees.

Evelyn, *Diary (1827)*

A great man ... even in the magnitude of his crimes, finds a rescue from contempt.

Junius, *Letters*

In this chapter will be described the classes in our class hierarchy. Implementations of the classes will not be discussed, but only the abstractions on which the classes depend and the protocol of each class. These classes can then be used to build sophisticated programs even without examination of the details of the class implementations. The reader can proceed from this chapter immediately to the applications later in the book or examine the implementations as they are discussed in following chapters. In the next chapter two applications will be discussed that illustrate both collection and magnitude classes. These classes will be discussed in detail beginning in Chapter 6.

The main idea on which each class depends and the major methods that the class provides to its clients will be discussed. Because the implementations are not discussed here, the class declarations will be incomplete, and most of the instance variables won't be shown at this time. Some methods that are private to the implementation will not be shown or discussed because they are not properly part of the specification and are of little help in learning to use these classes.

This chapter contains a lot of detail. It is probably better browsed than read completely from end to end. It serves as a collection of the protocols of the various classes for a user of the library.

The complete hierarchy is shown in Fig. 4.7, at the end of this chapter.

4.1   OBJECTS

Every class used to create objects is a subclass of SObject, which is abstract. As shown below it implements the basic capability that we always want. The major subclasses of SObject are SCollection and those classes that mix in SMagnitude. There are a number of others, though most of them are associated in one way or another with either some collection class or some magnitude class.

The methods of SObject are included here for reference. They are discussed in the previous chapter. Here note only that method less is implemented here to aid us in some things we intend to do and discuss later.

```
typedef SObject *PObject;

class SObject {  /* Abstract root class.*/
    public:
        virtual char      member (classtype c);
            // TRUE if this is in classtype.
        void              Error (char*);
            // Print error message and halt.
        virtual void      writeIt (void);
            // Produce a textual representation
            // on cout.
        virtual char      equal (PObject o)
                              {return (this == o);};
        virtual PObject   ShallowClone ();
            // DO NOT OVERRIDE except to disable.
            // Produce a bitwise copy of the object
            // and return a pointer to the copy.
        virtual PObject   Clone();
            // Produce a bitwise copy of the object
            // and return a pointer to the copy.
        virtual long      hash (void);
            // Return an integer so that the object
            // may be inserted into hash tables.
        virtual char      less (PObject)
                              {Error ("not defined");
                               return FALSE;};
            // Used only by magnitude classes.
    protected:
        virtual int sizeOf (void) {return (sizeof
                                    (SObject));};
            // WARNING: Implement sizeOf ()
            // in every class.
};
```

4.2　MAGNITUDES

Magnitudes provide a notion of size. Magnitudes can be compared by `less` and its siblings. Most of the major subclasses of SMagnitude are familiar: characters, strings, and various numeric types. They are all created by mixing in this class to another class that inherits from SObject. Additionally, there is the important subclass, SAssociation, which is built on the idea of a key-value pair. The class SMagnitude has public protocol:

```
class SMagnitude { // Abstract mixin class.
    public:
        virtual char       member (classtype c);
            // TRUE if this is in classtype.
        virtual char       less (PObject m) = 0;
            // Not implemented here.
        virtual char       equal (PObject o) = 0;
            // Not implemented here.
        virtual char       greater (PObject o);
            // TRUE if not less(o) and not equal(o).
        virtual char       notEqual (PObject m);
        virtual char       lessEqual (PObject m);
        virtual char       greaterEqual (PObject m);
        virtual char       between (PObject m,
                                    PObject n);
        virtual PObject    max (PObject m, PObject n);
        virtual PObject    min (PObject m, PObject n);
};
```

4.2.1 Characters

The first subclass of SMagnitude to be discussed is SCharacter. It gives us a way of treating elements of the built-in type char as if they were objects. This is often useful and is necessary when we want to use collections of objects to collect simple things. For example, in our class SFiniteStack, defined above, we have a stack of objects. In many applications we shall want to stack characters (or integers, or strings, etc.), and the class SCharacter gives us the means to do this. The essence of characters is that they can be displayed as ordinary text and can be composed into strings. They also form an ordered type, so their sizes can be compared using `less`. Since SCharacter is a subclass of SMagnitude, we must override the required methods `less` and `equal`. We also want to include a `writeIt` method that will write out the value of an SCharacter.

```
class SCharacter;
typedef SCharacter *PCharacter;
```

```
// WARNING: Do not create new Character objects
// directly. Do not declare objects of type
// SCharacter and do not call "new SCharacter."
// Call the access function
// "asCharacter(char)" instead.

class SCharacter: public SMagnitude, public SObject {
    public:
        virtual char      value (void);
            // Return ordinary char equivalent.
        virtual PObject   ShallowClone (void);
        virtual PObject   Clone (void);
        virtual char      less (PObject m);
            // ASCII comparison
        virtual char      equal (PObject m);
            // TRUE if this and m represent same char.
        virtual void      writeIt (void);
            // Output just the char equivalent.
        virtual char      member (classtype c);
};

PCharacter asCharacter (char);
    // The generator for characters.
void initCharacters (void);

// REQUIREMENTS For Use: Execute the following
// at program startup
//    initCharacters ();
```

Notice that there is no public constructor method SCharacter ().
The implication is that SCharacters are not to be created directly. The
generator function asCharacter (rather than newCharacter) returns
an SCharacter equivalent to the parameter that it is sent. This dis-
crepancy is caused by the fact that the characters form a fixed set. We
don't create characters. They exist. We simply get a reference to one of the
standard characters with a call to asCharacter. Two separate calls of
asCharacter ('A') will return two references to the same object. As
there is only one character *A*, there should be only one SCharacter equivalent to it. The method value is the inverse of asCharacter, returning
a character value for the object.

The requirements comment at the bottom of the protocol informs us
that in order to use the class we must perform a one-time initialization. This
need arises from the implementation details of the class. In order to use
this class or those classes, like SString, that depend on it, it is necessary
to call the initialization procedure initCharacters () exactly once.
A means of achieving this initialization easily is discussed in Chapter 6
(p. 205), when lists are examined which need a similar class initialization.

4.2.2 Strings

The next class, SString, is more standard. An SString represents a catenation of characters, like a word, sentence, or paragraph. We create new strings as we need them and we require the ability to insert characters into existing strings as well as the ability to remove characters. SStrings will inherit from both SMagnitude and SCollection, so they will have the behavior of both magnitudes and collections. In order for this to occur, we need to reimplement all methods, from either of the parents that were defined as pure virtual functions.

```
class SString;
typedef SString* PString;

PString newString (char* = "");

class SString: public SMagnitude,
               public SCollection {
    public:
        SString (char* = "");
        virtual              ~SString (void);
        virtual char          member (classtype c);
        virtual char          less (PObject m);
            // Lexical ordering.
        virtual char          equal (PObject o);
            // Same string (characterwise).
        virtual void          insert (PObject);
            // Append a PCharacter on right.
        virtual void          remove (PObject);
            // Remove leftmost copy of object
            // (a PCharacter) if present.
        virtual PCharacter    first(void);
            // Return first character in string
        virtual void          removeFirst (void);
            // Remove first character in string.
        virtual char*         value ();
            // Return an ordinary string
            // (a new string).
        virtual void          writeIt (void);
            // Output the string.
        virtual char          empty (void);
            // True if no characters.
        virtual PObject       Clone (void);
};
// REQUIREMENTS For Use
//     initCharacters ();
```

We include methods for construction, the required magnitude methods, and the required collection methods `insert` and `remove` that let us treat members of the class `SString` as if they were collections. We provide a default parameter for calls to the constructor and the generator function so that we can easily get the empty string. If the constructor call mentions no parameter, the empty string, `""`, will be used. The class encapsulates C's usual string methodology, using a pointer to `char`. The members of `SString` are character strings of variable length.

4.2.3 Associations

The next class implements the abstract notion of a key and an associated value. Within any system keys are considered to be unique. The purpose of a key is to give access to the associated value. An example of a key-value pair is a social security number (key) and a person's employment information (value). If the keys within a system are not unique, we will not access a single data value but a collection. Associations are used as the basis of a dictionary, which is just a set of associations. Dictionaries (see the collection class `SDictionary`) give a way to store information simply and to retrieve it efficiently. We shall use dictionaries when we build finite automata, in Chapter 5. The public protocol of `SAssociation` follows. We inherit from `SMagnitude` and the class `SPair`, which implements the idea of an ordered pair of values. The idea is that association adds magnitude to an ordered pair.

```
PAssociation newAssociation (PObject k, PObject v);

class SAssociation: public SMagnitude, public SPair {
   public:
        SAssociation (PObject k, PObject v);
      virtual char      member (classtype c);
      virtual PObject   value (void);
         // "Value" in this association.
      virtual char      less (PObject m);
         // TRUE if key of this is less than key of m.
      virtual void      setValue (PObject);
         // Force a value into this.
      virtual char      equal (PObject o);
         // TRUE if keys are equal.
      virtual void      writeIt (void);
         // Write key and value.
};
```

One use of a dictionary would be to create a graph (a geometric figure composed of vertices connected by arcs). Each vertex in the graph could maintain a dictionary in which each key represents an arc incident at that vertex and the associated value is a reference to the vertex at the other end of that arc. The keys could either be some natural feature of the application or, artificially, be just a numbering of the arcs emanating from the vertex. Such a representation would have both advantages and disadvantages. It is important to note that this representation distributes the information about the graph to the vertices, rather than holding it all in one place. The information about the neighbors of a vertex is stored at that vertex, rather than having global information about the entire graph held centrally. This is illustrated in Fig. 4.1.

The usual generator function newAssociation returns to us a fresh, properly initialized association of the given key and value. It uses the SAssociation constructor method. We also see the usual magnitude methods. We also have methods to get the key and the value of any association or to set a value, but these are inherited from SPair and so are not shown here. Note that changing the key of an association will not change its identity.

It is important to note that the comparison methods of associations depend only on the keys stored in them; the values are completely ignored for purposes of comparison. Thus, if two associations have the same key, they will be equal though they will not be related by the operator ==. Thus,

```
if (anAssociation == anotherAssociation) . . .
```

is different from

```
if (anAssociation -> equal (anotherAssociation)) . .
```

To emphasize this further, if A and B are two object reference variables, A == B will be true only when A and B are aliases of the same object. However, the truth of A -> equal (B) depends on the meaning of the method equal in the class of A. The default meaning of equal is ==, however, because this is how equal is defined in SObject.

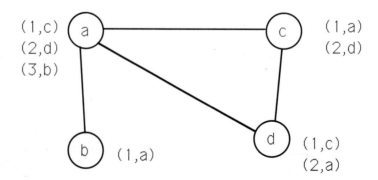

FIGURE 4.1

The second form above is nearly always the correct one. The first one is true only if the two names are aliases or references to the same object. This is sometimes called for when collections of associations are implemented but not often used otherwise. The key idea to remember is that the class itself is supposed to know what it means for its elements to be equal, and so the programmer most often uses the second form, letting the class be the judge.

4.2.4 Pairs

Pairs, though not magnitudes, are shown here for completeness. They are like associations, except that the keys are not assumed to be unique. For this reason equality of pairs is dependent on both the key and the value. Pairs are just the ordered pairs of mathematics. The class SPair encapsulates this. Two members of the class are equal if their keys as well as their values are related by the operator == (recall that == means identical). A set of pairs can be used to implement a relation, whereas a set of associations (a dictionary) implements a function. Here are methods for obtaining the key and the value.

```
PPair newPair (PObject k, PObject v);

class SPair: public SObject {
    public:
          SPair (PObject k, PObject v);
       virtual char      member (classtype c);
       virtual PObject   key (void);
          // Return the key in this.
       virtual PObject   value (void);
          // Return the value in this.
       virtual char      equal (PObject);
          // Equal if keys are equal
          // and values are equal.
       virtual void      writeIt (void);

    protected:
       PObject       fKey;
       PObject       fValue;
       virtual int   sizeOf (void);
};
```

4.2.5 Numeric Classes

The next class, SNumeric, will not be implemented and is therefore a pseudoclass. We include it here to show the protocol of all of the numeric classes

SInteger, SFraction, SReal, SComplex, and SLargeInteger. If C++ were not strongly typed, requiring typing of all method parameters, we would include this class. As it is, we exclude it, except from our documentation, because doing so will give us more control over types. The numeric classes all have arithmetic operations in addition to the comparisons of magnitudes.

```
class SNumeric;
typedef SNumeric *PNumeric;

class SNumeric: public SMagnitude {
    // Abstract mixin class.
    PObject add (PObject b);
        // Return the "sum" of this and b.
        // Meaning depends on class of this.
    PObject subtract (PObject b);
    PObject multiply (PObject b);
    PObject divide (PObject b);
};
```

The above methods implement the ordinary arithmetic operations. In pseudo-subclasses of this pseudoclass, the parameters will always be elements of the specific subclass. In addition to these methods, each class will also provide a means of dealing with information specific to that numeric type. For example, SComplex could provide a method, imaginaryPart, to return the imaginary part of objects within it.

4.2.6 Fractions

We have seen SFraction above. The class implements ordinary fractions reduced to lowest terms. It provides all of the SNumeric and the SMagnitude methods.

```
class SFraction;
typedef SFraction *PFraction;

PFraction newFraction (long numerator,
                       long denominator);

class SFraction: public SMagnitude, public SObject {
    public:
            SFraction (long N, long D);
        virtual PFraction    add (PFraction);
        virtual PFraction    subtract (PFraction);
        virtual PFraction    multiply (PFraction);
        virtual PFraction    divide (PFraction);
        virtual char         less (PObject m);
```

```
            virtual char          equal (PObject m);
            virtual char          member (classtype c);
            virtual void          writeIt (void);

        protected:
            long fNumerator, fDenominator;
            virtual int sizeOf (void);
        friend void reduce (PFraction f);
};
```

4.2.7 Complex Numbers

A complex number class won't be shown in this book but will be left as an exercise. Its protocol is suggested by the above, and its implementation is similar to that of SFraction.

4.2.8 Integers

The integer class, SInteger, is like SCharacter in that it implements a fixed set of integers. A member of SInteger is a 32-bit (or larger) integer stored as an object. It is a member of SMagnitude and is a numeric class. We won't create new SIntegers with new but will generate references to the standard set of integers instead. Integers aren't created; they must be considered to exist outside the software. The implementation will need to be clever so as not to store all four billion or so possible values and yet behave as if they were all available.

```
class SInteger;
typedef SInteger *PInteger;

// WARNING: Do not create new Integer objects
// directly. Do not declare objects of type SInteger
// and do not call "new SInteger." Call the access
// function "AsInteger(long)" instead.
// REQUIREMENTS For Use
//    initLists ();
//    initIntegers ();

class SInteger: public SMagnitude, public SObject {
    public:
        virtual char          member (classtype c);
        virtual long          value (void);
        virtual PObject       ShallowClone (void);
        virtual PObject       Clone (void);
```

```
      virtual char        less (PObject m);
      virtual char        equal (PObject m);
      virtual PInteger     add (PInteger a);
      virtual PInteger     subtract (PInteger a);
      virtual PInteger     multiply (PInteger a);
      virtual PInteger     divide (PInteger a);
      virtual void        writeIt (void);
};

void initIntegers (void);
```

All of the methods should be familiar. As usual with a class that implements a fixed collection, our generator procedure, `asInteger`, doesn't create an integer object but returns a reference to a standard object equivalent in value to the parameter of the `asInteger` function.

4.2.9   Real Numbers

Another class that we won't build here is `SReal`. The idea is the same as that of `SInteger`, and its implementation could be similar as well. The protocol, except for the type names, would be the same as that of `SInteger`, unless special methods were needed. The details are left to the exercises.

4.2.10   Large Integers

The last magnitude class to be discussed is `SLargeInteger`. It is like `SInteger`, except that as implemented it permits the use of forty-digit integers. A different implementation could easily (if slowly) permit even larger integers to be represented.

```
class SLargeInteger;
typedef SLargeInteger *PLargeInteger;

PLargeInteger newLargeInteger (char sign = positive,
                               int p9=0, int p8=0,
                               int p7=0, int p6=0,
                               int p5=0, int p4=0,
                               int p3=0, int p2=0,
                               int p1=0, int p0=0);

class SLargeInteger: public SObject,
                     public SMagnitude {
```

```
public:
    SLargeInteger (char isPositive);
    virtual char        less (PObject) ;
    virtual char        equal (PObject);
    virtual char        sign (void);
      // Positive == TRUE.
    virtual PLargeInteger add (PLargeInteger);
    virtual void         increment (PLargeInteger);
      // Add a large integer to this.
    virtual void         decrement (PLargeInteger);
      // Subtract a large integer from this.
    virtual PLargeInteger negated (void);
      // Return value of this negated.
    virtual void         negate (void);
      // Change sign of this.
    virtual PLargeInteger subtract (PLargeInteger);
      // Return difference.
    virtual PLargeInteger multiply (PLargeInteger);
    virtual PLargeInteger divide (PLargeInteger);
    virtual PLargeInteger rem (PLargeInteger);
      // Remainder.
    virtual char         isZero (void);
      // TRUE if this represents zero.
    virtual char         member (classtype c);
    virtual PObject      Clone (void);
    virtual void         writeIt (void);
};
```

Most of these methods and the constructor, SLargeInteger, should be familiar. Note that increment changes the object that receives the message, whereas add does not, simply returning the sum. Finally, negated returns a new large integer equal to the negative of the receiver, and negate changes the sign of the receiver.

The implementation of this class is as base-10000 integers stored in an array. There are additional protected methods, such as At and atPut, that let us directly manipulate the representation, as is needed to implement the arithmetic operations. When in the exercises you are asked to change the implementation from arrays to lists, you may need to change these private methods and even their protocols. This is why they are protected. Any client code that used them directly would possibly need to be rewritten if we changed the implementation. All other methods should have a protocol that is insensitive to changes in implementation.

4.3   COLLECTIONS AND THEIR ITERATORS

We saw the collection and iterator classes above when we looked at finite stacks. Collections are one of the richest of abstractions. In fact, most of them require us to develop groups of abstractions, because collections are linked to iterators. Collections differ in the amount of structure internal to the collection as well as in the type of object that can be collected. Some classes, for example, only permit us to collect magnitudes. SSortedList is an example of this, as is SBinarySearchTree. Sometimes an imple mentation imposes restrictions. An SSet, for example, can hold any sort of object and imposes no structure on the objects in it. A similar class ex ternally is SBSTSet, which also implements a set, but its implementation although more efficient, requires that the objects in it be in some subclass of SMagnitude.

Some collection classes, for example, SList and all tree classes have a well-defined notion of position in the collection. These classes are called indexed collections and are subsumed in the pseudoclass SIndexedCollection. We shall also have another matched abstrac tion SPosition, for all such classes. In arrayed collections position is ordinal position: first, second, etc. The ordered collections, such as SBinarySearchTree, impose an order on the contents that is derived from the values of the contents themselves. They require that their contents be in SMagnitude. If the physical order within the collection is the same as the natural order of the contents then the collection is an SSortedCollection, as is SSortedList. Seeing the entire hier archy at once is instructive, so it is presented below. Indentation shows inheritance here; a DEQueue is a Queue that is a List that is a Collection. (Note that there are a few inaccuracies in the list below. Our implementations will be a little different, with some of the classes using an implementation dependent on some of the others.)

```
SCollection
    SSet {finite set of objects}
        SDictionary {set of associations
                    -- key-value pairs}
        SHashDictionary {hash table implementation}
    SBag {a multi-set -- multiple inclusion possible
    SIndexedCollection {collection with position
                        -- pseudoclass}
        SList
            SQueue
                SDEQueue {double-ended queue}
            SStack
            STree {a general tree}
                SBinaryTree
            SArrayedCollection {position is an integer
                            -- pseudoclass}
                SDynamicArray {very large arrays
                            -- dynamic arrays}
                SString {shown above with magnitudes}
```

```
        SFixedSizeCollection {not expandable
                                    -- pseudoclass}
            SInterval
            SArray
      SOrderedCollection {pseudoclass}
          {collection of magnitudes,
           kept partially ordered}
          SHeap
          SBinarySearchTree
          SAVLTree
          S234Tree
          SBTree
          SBSTSet {a binary search tree
                    implementation of a set}
          SSortedCollection {imposes total
                              order on contents
                              -- pseudoclass}
            SSortedList
```

All of these classes are associated with corresponding iterator classes. Iterators provide generalized repetition operators for any collection class. Most iteration classes have the same protocol. A few provide several different forms of repetition. Thus, parallel to the hierarchy shown above there is a hierarchy that matches an iteration class to every collection class. The following two classes are defined in PCollect.h, which also defines the SPosition class.

```
class SCollection: public SObject {
  public:
    virtual char      member (classtype c);
    virtual void      insert (PObject) = 0;
    virtual void      remove (PObject) = 0;
    virtual char      empty (void) {return (TRUE);};
    virtual PIterator newIterator (void);
    virtual void      writeIt (void);
};

class SIterator: public SObject {
  public:
      SIterator (PCollection);
    virtual char  member (classtype c);
    virtual char  nextItem (PObject&) = 0;
    virtual void  reset (void) = 0;
      // {fDone = fCollection -> empty ();};
    virtual void  Short (void) {fDone = TRUE;};
    virtual char  done (void);
```

```
  protected:
    char           fDone;
    PCollection    fCollection;
    virtual int    sizeOf (void);
};
```

Additionally, all subclasses of the pseudoclass SIndexedCollection are associated with a corresponding position class. Thus there is a class SListPosition and another SBinaryTreePosition. The class SPosition forms the head of the hierarchy of position classes. It doesn't do much, because the details of a position depend too much on the nature of the indexed collection that they correspond to.

```
class SPosition: public SObject {
  public:
      SPosition (PCollection c): fCollection (c) {};
    virtual char    member (classtype c);

  protected:
    PCollection     fCollection;
    virtual int     sizeOf (void);
};
```

4.3.1 Sets

The simplest collection is a set. We are striving for a mathematician's idea of a set. Sets contain objects. An object can be an element of a set or not. Multiple inclusion is not meaningful or possible. Inserting an object into a set that already contains it is a no-op (no operation is performed). Sets can also be heterogeneous and contain objects of different types.

```
PSet newSet ();

class SSet: public SCollection {
    public:
      SSet (void);
    virtual              ~SSet (void);
    virtual void         insert (PObject);
        // Insert object into this.
    virtual void         remove (PObject);
        // Remove object if present.
    virtual PSet         setUnion (PSet);
    virtual PSet         intersection (PSet);
    virtual PSet         allBut (PObject);
        // Return a copy with object removed.
    virtual char         subset (PSet);
```

```
          // TRUE if this is a subset of parameter.
    virtual int         cardinality (void);
       // Number of elements in this.
    virtual char        element (PObject);
       // TRUE if object is in this.
    virtual PIterator   newIterator (void);
    virtual char        member (classtype c);
    virtual void        writeIt (void);
    virtual PObject     Clone (void);
};
```

4.3.2   Bags, or Multisets

A bag is one of the most general collection mechanisms. It is called a multiset by mathematicians. A bag is like a set except that multiple inclusion is possible. Therefore, when an object is removed from a bag it can still be in the bag. A bag must somehow account for the cardinality of each element that it contains and should be able to report it. Otherwise, a bag's protocol is like that of a set.

```
PBag newBag (void);

class SBag: public SCollection {
   public:
        SBag (void);
        virtual           ~SBag (void);
        virtual char      element (PObject);
           // TRUE if object is in this.
        virtual void      insert (PObject o);
        virtual void      remove (PObject);
        virtual PBag      intersection (PBag);
        virtual PBag      bagUnion (PBag);
        virtual PBag      allBut (PObject);
           // Returns a copy of this but with one
           // copy of parameter removed (if present
           // in this at all).
        virtual char      subset (PBag);
        virtual char      empty (void);
        virtual PObject   Clone (void);
        virtual int       cardinality (void);
           // Number of elements (counting repetitions).
        virtual int       cardinalityOf (PObject);
           // Number of times object appears in this.
        virtual PIterator newIterator (void);
        virtual char      member (classtype c);
        virtual void      writeIt (void);
};
```

4.3.3   Dictionaries

Dictionaries were discussed above when associations were introduced. A dictionary is just a set of associations, or key-value pairs. Thus a dictionary is a simple data base, maintaining information (value) for us that is retrievable at will (via the key). A hash dictionary is similar, differing in the implementation. Another way to think of a dictionary is that it implements a function whose domain is the keys and range is the values.

```
class SDictionary: public SSet {
    // A set of associations.
    // Each key only appears once.
  public:
      SDictionary (void);
    virtual char      member (classtype c);
    virtual void      insert (PObject o);
    // Insert an association in the dictionary.
    // If there is already an association with
    // the same key then just change its value
    // to match o's value.
    virtual void      atPut (PObject k, PObject v);
    // Creates a new association if necessary,
    // with key k and value v. If there is
    // already an association with key k this
    // just changes its value.
    virtual PObject   at (PObject k);
    // Returns the value of the
    // association with key k or NULL of no
    // such present.
    virtual void      removeKey (PObject k);
    // Removes the association with this
    // key if present.
    virtual PObject   keyAtValue (PObject o);
};
```

The method atPut is the basic insert operation into a dictionary. It sees to the creation of an association that will store the key and the value. In fact, no creation may be necessary. If the key is already contained in the dictionary, atPut simply changes the value of the stored association to the new value given. Likewise, at is the method by which we access the value from the given key. Note that it does not remove anything from the dictionary; only removeKey will do that, removing the association with the given key. If an association was created externally, insert can be used to insert it into a dictionary. Note that if it has a key equal to the key of any association already in the dictionary, this is a replacement operation.

4.3.4   Lists and List Positions

The class SList is one of the more complex classes in the entire hierarchy, because it is linked to three other classes: SListNode, which implements the storage of a single datum; SListPosition, which gives us an abstract notion of position in the list; and SListIterator, which lets us operate on every element of a list. The fundamental idea of a list is that of a linear or sequential structure that has a first member and in which every member except the last member has a successor or next member. Each member of the list except the first and last is thus "related" to two others, the next item and the previous item. There is no necessary relationship between the values of the data in the list and the position in the list. There is no necessary relationship between the order of insertion and the position. Multiple inclusions of the same object are possible.

There are two ways to think about lists. The first is that a list is a collection of data connected together into a linear structure. This view, if refined, distinguishes between the values in the list and the nodes that hold the values. Conceptually it is a list of values, as shown in Fig. 4.2. From the implementation point of view, it is a list of special objects called nodes, and the nodes hold the data. See Fig. 4.3. This is how we shall implement lists. Lists, values, and nodes all have their own behaviors, designed into their protocols. We shall permit the lists to contain any objects and shall not restrict the values in a list to one kind. Applications that use lists often do impose such a restriction, but nothing in the idea of a list itself requires all of its data to come from the same general class of items.

The second way of looking at lists is to consider that a list is either empty or composed of a data value (val) and another list (rest). This definition is recursive: a list is defined in terms of a (sub-) list. The statement that a list can be empty prevents the definition from degenerating into an infinite loop of definitions, which doesn't define anything. This idea is illustrated in Fig. 4.4.

We shall prefer the first definition of lists, but the second will be defined and implemented in Chapter 10. The language LISP is built on the second idea of lists.

The design we use here utilizes nested classes. We use nodes to implement lists, but they are not seen by clients, who are encouraged to think of lists as containing data, not nodes. Therefore we include the declaration of SListNode in the protected section of the declaration of SList.

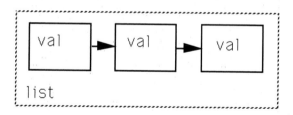

FIGURE 4.2

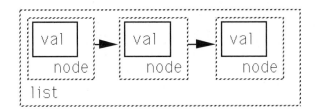

FIGURE 4.3

SListNode is completely private to an implementation. SListIterator and SListPosition will be defined outside the class declaration of SList, though they could reasonably be nested in the public part of SList. Here we show the actual structure of lists but have not included some of the protected details.

```
// REQUIREMENTS For Use
//    initLists ();

class    SList;
class    SListIterator;
class    SListPosition;

typedef SList              *PList;
typedef SListIterator      *PListIterator;
typedef SListPosition      *PListPosition;

enum WhereFound {IsHere, IsNext, NotFound};

PList newList (void);

class SList: public SCollection {
  public:
      SList (void);
    virtual                    ~SList (void);
    virtual char               member (classtype c);
    virtual PObject            first (void);
        // Return object at beginning of list.
```

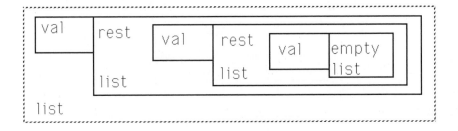

FIGURE 4.4

```
        virtual void             insert (PObject);
          // Insert object at head of list.
        virtual void             remove (PObject);
          // Remove object (once) if present
        virtual void             removeFirst (void);
          // Remove first object in list if any.
        virtual PIterator        newIterator (void);
        virtual PListPosition    newPosition (void);
          // Return a new position initialized to head.
        virtual PObject          Clone (void);
          // Return a new list with same elements
          // as receiver.
        virtual char             empty (void);
          // TRUE if list has no elements.
        virtual char             element (PObject);
          // TRUE if object is in list.
        virtual void             selectionSort (void);
          // Sort the list in order of its elements.
          // Precondition: All elements must
          // be magnitudes.
        virtual PList            merge (PList);
          // Merge this and parameter and return result.
          // Precondition: All elements of both lists
          // must be magnitudes.
        virtual int              length (void);
          // Length of the list.
        virtual void             writeIt (void);
          // Write all elements in order,
          // starting at head.

    protected:
      class SListNode;
    public:
      typedef SListNode *PListNode;
    protected:
      virtual PListNode newNode (PObject, PListNode);
      virtual PListNode lastNode (void);

  // nested protected class SListNode
  class SListNode: public SObject {
    public:
        SListNode (PObject);
        SListNode (PObject /* value */,
                 SListNode* /* next */);
        virtual char        member (classtype c);
        virtual PObject     value (void);
          // Value stored in the node.
```

```
    virtual void          writeIt (void);
       // Write the value in the node.
    virtual PListNode      next (void);
       // Return the next node after this one.
    virtual void          setNext (PListNode);
       // Set the next node after this one.
}; // End list node class.
};
```

```
void initLists (void);
```

As usual, not all of the details are shown here, for example, the fact that a
node references a value, the data, and a list references a node, its first node
The protocol is designed so that the user can easily ignore the nodes and
treat the list as if it is a list of values rather than nodes. The user doesn'
create or destroy the nodes directly; they are created implicitly when the
user uses insert or insertFirst to add a data item to the list. The
myth being maintained is that only the values matter. Therefore atFirst
and atLoc return values, not nodes. The method remove names a value
and that value is removed from the list. The value is not destroyed (there may
be other references to it in the system), but the node that held it is destroyed

  Note that there isn't much here to let us manipulate a list other than
at its beginning. There are two ways that such manipulation can be done
First, like all collections, lists have iterators, which can be used for operating
on the list as a whole. The protocol for a list iterator is as follows:

```
class SListIterator: public SIterator {
   public:
        SListIterator (PList L);
      virtual char       member (classtype c);
      virtual char       nextItem (PObject&);
         // Return the next item in the list if any
      virtual void       reset (void);
         // Set to first item in the list.
      virtual PObject    Clone (void);
};
```

  The second way to operate on a list is to create and use a list position
Because lists are examples of the pseudoclass SIndexedCollection
we must create an abstraction for position in a list and then implemen
the abstraction. A list position is a reference to some item (data value
stored in the list. Positions can move forward or backward in the linea
list structure, and operations can be applied at the current location of a
position. The protocol is as follows:

```
class SListPosition: public SPosition {
   public:
        SListPosition (PList L);
```

```
      virtual char         member (classtype c);
      virtual void         next (void);
         // Move this to next position.
      virtual void         insertFirst (PObject);
         // Insert object at head of list
         // then move there.
      virtual void         insertAfter (PObject);
         // Insert object after current position.
      virtual PObject      at (void);
         // Return object at this position.
      virtual void         atPut (PObject);
         // Put object into this position.
      virtual char         last (void);
         // TRUE if at last position in list.
      virtual char         afterLast (void);
         // TRUE if after last position in list.
      virtual void         toFirst ();
         // Move to first position.
      virtual void         deleteFirst (void);
         // Remove first item in list and move
         // to new first.
      virtual void         deleteNext (void);
         // Remove item after the current location.
      virtual PObject      atNext (void);
         // Return object in next position
         // (may be NULL).
      virtual WhereFound   search (PObject);
         // Search for object starting at current
         // location. If object is in this
         // location return isHere. If object is not
         // in list at or after this location, return
         // not Found.  Otherwise move to
         // location prior to location of object and
         // return isNext.
      virtual void         moveTo (PListPosition);
         // Move to same location as parameter.
      virtual void         exchangeValues
                              (PListPosition);
         // Swap values with loc of parameter.

   protected:
      virtual PListNode nodeAt (void);
};
```

Except for the protected method, which has *node* as part of its name, all of these methods maintain the view that the list is one of values. The instance variables indicate that a position is a position in a particular list and that it is implemented by a reference to a particular node in that list. The protocol includes position movement methods, such as `toFirst`, and `next`, and includes `last` for determining whether the end is reached. Note that `next` won't take us past the end. The methods `at` and `atNext` retrieve data from the list, and `atPut`, `insertFirst`, and `insertAfter` insert values. The method `insertAfter` creates a new node to hold the data and changes the relative positions of all following nodes, increasing their ordinal positions in the list by one. We can delete values (and their nodes) with `deleteFirst` and `deleteNext`, which also change the ordinal positions of the values in the list. The method `moveTo` permits us to easily set the location of one position to the current location of another, which is useful in complex list manipulations, and `exchangeValues` exchanges the values in the nodes at two positions (that of the receiver of the message and that of the parameter) while leaving the nodes in place. The `nodeAt` method is used for internal processing. Because it breaks the myth of lists of values, it must be used carefully. If the user calls `nodeAt` and then `removeFirst`, the node returned by the first message can be destroyed by the second.

The user must also be somewhat careful in using positions while otherwise changing a list. There are two ways to remove the first value in a list. One is with a message sent to a position, and the other is with a message sent to the list itself. The former method is safer if positions are active, because it permits the position to update its internal data. Generally, deletions from and insertions into a list in which positions are active must be carefully thought out. If the method `toFirst` is sent to a position in a list whose first element has just been deleted, the position will be properly updated. The user should also be careful to delete any positions when their lists are deleted.

4.3.5   List-Like Structures

Stacks, queues, and double-ended queues (dequeues) are related to lists. They all have sequential structure and are all collections of objects. They differ in the protocol for insertion and deletion. Stacks, as we have seen before, implement a LIFO protocol for insertions and deletions. The easy way to handle this is to keep the elements in the stack in a list and permit insertions and deletions only from one end. The definition of `pop` has changed, for it now returns an object as well as removing that object from the list. Queues implement a FIFO structure, in which the next item to be removed is the one that has been in the queue for the longest time. This is easily done by inserting at one end of a list and deleting at the other end. A dequeue (pronounced "deck," as in *deck of cards*, which is an example of a dequeue, in fact) permits insertions and deletions at either end of a list but not elsewhere. The formal rules for stacks have been discussed. The rules for queues and double-ended queues will be discussed in Chapter 7.

```
class SStack: public SCollection {
  public:
       SStack (void);
    virtual            ~SStack (void);
    virtual PObject     pop (void);
       // Remove object at top if any.
    virtual void        push (PObject o);
       // Push object o onto this.
    virtual PObject     top (void);
       // Return object at top (may be NULL).
    virtual PIterator   newIterator (void);
    virtual char        empty (void);
    virtual void        writeIt (void);
    virtual void        insert (PObject);
       // Same as push.
    virtual void        remove (PObject);
       // Disabled.
    virtual char        member (classtype c);
    virtual PObject     Clone (void);
};

class SQueue: public SList {
  public:
       SQueue (void);
    virtual PObject   Dequeue (void);
       // Remove object at front and return it.
    virtual void      enqueue (PObject);
       // Insert object at rear.
    virtual void      insert (PObject);
       // Same as enqueue.
    virtual PObject   atFront (void);
       // Return object at front.
    virtual void      insertFirst (PObject);
       // Insert at front (needed for safety; see Ch. 7).
    virtual void      remove (PObject);
       // Remove object of present.
    virtual void      removeFirst (void);
       // Remove object at front.
    virtual char      member (classtype c);
    virtual PObject   Clone (void);
};

class SDEQueue: public SQueue {
  public:
       SDEQueue();
    virtual PObject   atRear (void);
       // Return object at rear of this.
```

```
virtual PObject    DequeueRear (void);
   // Remove object at rear and return it.
virtual void       removeRear (void);
   // Remove object at rear.
virtual char       member (classtype c);
};
```

Note that, as collections, these classes have access to iterators. Queues and dequeues inherit their access to list iterators and positions without defining new classes, though perhaps a queue should be given a new iterator which would change the order in which it yielded the elements in the queue. Note that a dequeue is a queue, and so most of the important methods are inherited. We must consider how to provide the iterator capability to stacks.

Stacks are used extensively to process any data that occurs in a nested manner. This permits us to handle a nested item (by pushing) and then return to the item that contained it (by poping). Again, pop has a different meaning here than in Chapter 2, since it is a function returning a value. Queues are used when items might be encountered in processing other items and we want to be sure that we get around to processing the newly encountered ones without interrupting the current processing. We enque an item when it is encountered and dequeue it when we are ready to handle a new one. Queues are also used in service systems, such as simulations, where we may need to process items repeatedly and cyclically, providing equal opportunities for service to all of the objects.

4.3.6 Sorted Lists

Sorted lists keep their data in order. This requires special insert methods and requires that the data all be in SMagnitude, for it is from here that we get the ability to compare sizes. The protocol won't be shown here, because it is similar to what we have seen.

4.3.7 Binary Trees

Trees are important both because they arise naturally in a number of important application areas and because they offer an efficient implementation mechanism in many others. The syntax of a computer program is usually described by a tree, the parse tree, which offers an abstract representation of the static program. Compilers often construct this tree as part of translation. Even if they don't construct it directly they implicitly visit the nodes of the tree to determine whether the program is valid. Trees can also be an efficient implementation mechanism for sets, especially sets of magnitudes.

Trees are indexed collections and so have both positions and iterators. Trees also hold data in nodes. Unlike the nodes of lists, the nodes here will be treated more as first-class citizens, partly because the shape of the tree, independent of the data, often carries important information. The simplest sort of tree is a binary tree, and we shall implement the class SBinaryTree. Binary trees are made up of nodes and links. Each node internal to the tree has exactly two children, the left child and the right child, who are also binary trees. The node is called the parent of those children. We normally think of the children as being below the parent. A node that is not internal is called external and has no children. The node with no parent is called the root of the tree. A binary tree is illustrated in Fig. 4.5. The solid circles are internal nodes, and the squares external nodes.

We must be able to create trees and their nodes, insert, retrieve, and remove data, move about in the tree, and process the tree as a whole. Movement must be provided both upward, toward the root, and downward along the many paths from a node to the external nodes (leaves) below it. For the same reasons for which we nested the class SListNode within SList, we shall nest SBinaryTreeNode within SBinaryTree. The protocols are shown separately for convenience.

```
class SBinaryTreeNode: public SObject {
    public:
            SBinaryTreeNode (PObject);
        virtual void        recursiveDestruct (void);
            // Destroy child nodes then this.
        virtual PObject     value (void);
            // Return value in this.
        virtual char        member (classtype c);
        virtual void        writeIt (void);
        virtual void        recursiveWriteIt (void);
            // Output value in this node then,
            // recursively output values in child nodes.
        virtual PObject     Clone (void);

        PBinaryTreeNode            fLeft;
        PBinaryTreeNode            fRight;
        PObject                    fValue;
        virtual PBinaryTreeNode leftChild (void);
            // Return node to left.
        virtual PBinaryTreeNode rightChild (void);
            // Return node to right.
```

FIGURE 4.5

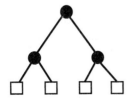

```
        virtual int sizeOf (void);
     friend void initBinaryTrees (void);
     friend SBinaryTreePosition;
}; // End binary tree node.
```

The tree class itself is as follows:

```
class SBinaryTree: public SCollection {
  public:
        SBinaryTree (void);
     virtual              ~SBinaryTree (void);
     virtual char         empty ();
     virtual void         writeIt (void);
        // Write the values in this in preorder.
     virtual PIterator    newIterator (void);
     virtual PBinaryTreeIterator
        newInOrderIterator (void);
     virtual void         insert (PObject);
        // Insert as leftmost descendant.
     virtual void         remove (PObject);
        // Remove object if present.
     virtual char         member (classtype c);
     virtual PObject      Clone (void);
     virtual PBinaryTreePosition  newPosition (void);
                  // Return a new position
                  // initialized to root of this.

  protected:
        /* Nested protected class. */
class SBinaryTreeNode: public SObject {
  :
}; // End binary tree node.
}; // End binary tree.

void initBinaryTrees (void);
  // Call once to initialize the class.
```

Tree positions let us move about in trees and do complex manipulations. They are similar to list positions except that the processing is complicated by the two children that follow any given node. We must be able to move to either child and to the parent. There are methods for movement, checking position, insertions of nodes and data, removals, retrievals, and searching.

```
class SBinaryTreePosition: public SPosition {
  public:
        SBinaryTreePosition (PBinaryTree);
```

```
virtual void        setToRoot (void);
  // Move location to root.
virtual PObject     at (void);
  // Return value at current loc.
virtual void        atPut (PObject);
  // Put object into current loc.
virtual PObject     atLeftChild (void);
  // Return value at left child.
virtual PObject     atRightChild (void);
  // Return value at right child.
virtual void        exchangePositions
  (PBinaryTreePosition);
  // Swap locations of this and parameter.
virtual void        exchangeValues
  (PBinaryTreePosition);
  // Swap values of this and parameter.
virtual void        find (PObject);
  // Search for object and move there if found.
virtual char        leaf (void);
  // TRUE if this loc has no children.
virtual char        noLeft (void);
  // TRUE if this has no left child.
virtual char        noRight (void);
  // TRUE if this has no right child.
virtual char        oneChild (void);
  // TRUE if this has exactly one child.
virtual char        isFull (void);
  // TRUE if this has exactly two children.
virtual void        moveTo (PBinaryTreePosition);
  // Move to loc of parameter.
virtual void        moveLeft (void);
  // Move to left child position.
virtual void        moveRight (void);
  // Move to right child.
virtual void        moveToParent (void);
  // Move to location of parent if not at root.
virtual char        isAtRoot (void);
  // TRUE if currently at root.
virtual void        insertLeft (PObject);
  // Only if left is empty.
virtual void        insertRight (PObject);
  // Only if right is empty.
virtual char        member (classtype c);
virtual void        writeIt (void);
  // Output value at current loc
  // (and note it is a position).
```

```
protected:
  virtual void    findNode (PBinaryTreeNode);
  virtual void    insertLeftNode (PBinaryTreeNode)
    // Replace left node with param.
  virtual void    insertRightNode (PBinaryTreeNode
    // Replace right node with param.
  virtual void    truncateLeft (void);
    // Remove a node and its children.
  virtual void    truncateRight (void);
    // Remove a node and its children.
  virtual PBinaryTreeNode nodeAt (void);
};  // End binary tree position.
```

Users must exercise caution when inserting a node into a tree. When the node is already in the tree, the result is not a tree but a graph. Possibly the resulting graph will even have cycles, so repeatedly moving to a child will eventually bring you back to where you began. A structure with this property is not a tree at all, and such an insert will make iterators fail. In fact they may loop infinitely. The protected node routines are intended primarily for internal use, and the use must be carefully thought out. It is possible to protect against such misbehavior, but the resulting programs run much more slowly due to the extra checking that needs to be performed. When such protection is necessary, you can write a procedure, containsNode, to check whether a given node is already present in a given tree. You can also write a function, safeToInsert, that would let you know whether an insertion would create a cycle.

Tree iterators are more complicated than other iterators since it is often necessary to be specific about the order in which the iterator yields the nodes of a tree. For our purposes the two most important protocols are preorder and inorder, and methods will be provided so that an iterator may operate in either way. The preorder protocol requires that a node be yielded prior to its children, and that the left child be yielded before the right. This is called top-down traversal. With inorder protocol the left child of a node is yielded before the parent and the right child after the parent. Because this is applied recursively, the first node yielded in inorder traversal is one far down the left side of the tree. A third protocol, postorder (bottom-up), yields the parent last but our iterators don't have a bottom-up protocol. As usual, we get a tree iterator by sending the newIterator message to a tree. The method executed returns a properly initialized preorder iterator. The message newInOrderIterator returns an iterator initialized for inorder traversal.

```
class SBinaryTreeIterator: public SIterator {
  public:
        SBinaryTreeIterator (PBinaryTree);
```

```
                    virtual           ~SBinaryTreeIterator (void);
                    virtual char      nextItem (PObject&);
                        // Return next item in preorder.
                    virtual char      nextItemInOrder (PObject&);
                        // Return next item in inorder.
                    virtual char      nextNode (PBinaryTreeNode&);
                        // Return next node in preorder.
                    virtual void      reset(void);
                        // Reset to root.
                    virtual void      resetInOrder (void);
                        // Reset to first inorder node.
                    virtual void      iterateFrom
                        (PBinaryTreePosition);
                        // Prepare to iterate in preorder from
                        // location of parameter.
                    virtual char      member (classtype c);
                    virtual void      writeIt (void);
                        // Output "A binary tree iterator."
                    virtual PObject   Clone (void);
            }; // End binary tree iterator.


            // REQUIREMENTS For Use
            //    initLists ();
            //    initBinaryTrees ();
```

4.3.8   General Trees

Sometimes binary trees are not adequate for the application being developed. For this we need general trees, which permit an arbitrary number of children, as in Fig. 4.6.

All the tree operations (movement, retrieval, insertion, and deletion) are complicated by the possible presence of many children. Our implementation of the general tree utilizes binary trees, but the protocol must permit referencing of the numerous children that a node may have. It also nests the node class. The parts are shown separately here.

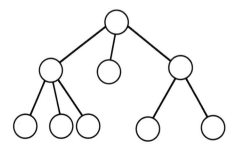

FIGURE 4.6

```
class STree: public SCollection {
   public:
         STree ();
      virtual                 ~STree (void);
      virtual void            insert (PObject);
         // Insert as far to left as possible.
      virtual PTreePosition   newPosition (void);
         // New position initialized to root.
      virtual char            member (classtype c);
      virtual PObject         Clone (void);
      virtual void            remove (PObject);
         // Remove object of present.
      virtual char            empty (void);
         // TRUE if tree has no values stored.
      virtual PIterator       newIterator (void);
      virtual void            writeIt (void);
         // Write tree in preorder.
};

class STreePosition: public SBinaryTreePosition {
   public:
      virtual void       moveToChild (int);
         // Move to child numbered by parameter
         // if any.
      virtual void       insertChild (PObject);
         // Insert a new first child.
      virtual void       moveToParent (void);
         // Move to parent of current loc.
      virtual PObject    atChild (int);
         // Return value stored at first child.
      virtual void       insertLeft (PObject) {};
         // Disabled.
      virtual void       insertRight (PObject) {};
         // Disabled.
      virtual char       member (classtype c);
};

class STreeNode: public SBinaryTreeNode {
   public:
      virtual char       member (classtype c);
      virtual PObject    Clone (void);
   protected:
      PTreeNode    fParent;
         // A reference to the parent
         // of current node.
};
```

Note that nothing new is added to the tree itself. We get the new capability by changing the position abstraction. Here we can add a new child independently of how many exist. The children are not ordered in any fixed way. The method `moveToChild` sets the position to the child currently in the ordinal position given by the parameter. The method `atChild` returns the data in the current nth child. Inserting a new child will change this ordinal position.

4.3.9   Binary Search Trees and Heaps

A Binary search tree is a binary tree in which the data in the left child of any node is less than the data at that node, and the data in the right child is greater. This requires that the data all be in SMagnitude so that we can apply the ordering operations. AVL trees, 234Trees, and BTrees are variations on the same theme. They form efficient ways to store sets of values and are useful in database applications. A heap is a similar structure, except that the ordering relationship is weaker. All that is required in a heap is that the data in any node be less than the data in its children. Thus size increases as you go down a tree and decreases as you go up. Heaps are very useful in implementing efficient sorting routines for data that will ultimately be held in sequential structures, as their smallest item of all is in the root. Note that if we repeatedly remove the root of a heap while maintaining the heap property, we gain access to the data in sorted order.

4.3.10   Dynamic Arrays

One of the major difficulties with arrays is that they take up a lot of room even when only a few of their elements are needed. A mechanism is needed that would be like an array that can be created one element at a time. This is our SDynamicArray class. Dynamic arrays have a protocol similar to that of standard arrays, except that they don't take up much more space than is required for the data actually stored. We must be able to insert and retrieve data at arbitrary index positions.

```
class SDynamicArray: public SCollection {
    public:
         SDynamicArray ();
    virtual              ~SDynamicArray (void);
    virtual void         insert (PObject);
        // Disabled. Use atPut.
    virtual void         remove (PObject);
        // Disabled. Use atPut(NULL).
    virtual void         atPut (int, PObject);
        // Put object at loc of int.
```

```
        virtual PObject      at (int);
            // Return object at loc of int
            // (may be NULL).
        virtual char         empty (void);
            // TRUE if the array is empty.
        virtual PIterator    newIterator (void);
        virtual char         member (classtype c);
        virtual void         writeIt (void);
            // Not currently implemented.
        virtual PObject      Clone (void);
};
```

The implementation is as a list of nodes each of which includes an index at which the data is considered to be located. The key methods in SDynamicArray are at and atPut, each of which take an integer argument that is the ordinal position in the large array that we wish to reference. We don't need a position class for these because a position is just the integer index of a datum. We need, of course, an iterator class for these, as we do for all collections.

4.3.11   Intervals

An interval is a finite algebraic sequence of integers, such as 1, 4, 7, 10. This interval goes from 1 to 10 by 3. Intervals are useful in array processing when we want to process some but not all elements in an array. They are equally useful in similar situations that do not involve arrays. An interval is a collection of fixed size that cannot be added to or removed from once it is created. An iterator over the interval will yield the elements of the sequence in order. The protocol is as follows.

```
class SInterval: public SCollection {
   public:
        SInterval (int from, int to, int by);
        virtual int          at (int);
            // Return value at loc of param.
        virtual int          size (void);
            // Size of the collection.
        virtual void         insert (PObject)
                             {Error ("SInterval :: \
                             insert: Fixed size \
                             collection");};
        virtual void         remove (PObject)
                             {Error ("SInterval :: \
                             remove: Fixed size \
                             collection");};
        virtual char         empty () {return (FALSE);};
```

```
        virtual PIterator     newIterator (void);
        virtual char          member (classtype c);
        virtual void          writeIt (void);

protected:
        int fFrom;
        int fTo;
        int fBy;
};


// REQUIREMENTS For Use
//    initLists ();
//    initIntegers ();
```

The iterator is completely standard. It yields the next item as an SInteger. The interval method at gives us the value at a relative position. For example, in 1, 4, 7, 10, the 7 is at position 2 (assuming we start counting with zero). The method size gives us the number of elements in the collection. In the above example it should be four.

4.4   ABSTRACTION AGAIN

The previous sections briefly described a number of classes and their protocols. This set of classes was chosen because they illustrate techniques of data structuring and, more importantly, because they have been shown to be useful in a wide variety of programming situations. If object-oriented programming is to meet its promise it should be possible to use this class library without examining the implementations of most of the methods. It should also be possible to use inheritance to extend the capabilities of the above classes. For example, the discussion of binary trees did not include a method for putting new data into the left child of the current position. If such a method were needed it could be added by modification of the existing class SBinaryTreePosition or by creation of a new class that inherits from this one and provides the new capability. Ideally, if the base class hierarchy is sound, it should not need to be modified. Nor should it be necessary to override methods frequently in order to correct behavior. Overriding should be used to extend the class to new capabilities and when new instance variables need to be properly handled in a subclass.

This is the basic idea of abstraction at this level: Create a collection of ideas (stack, queue, largeInteger, etc.), construct classes to implement the ideas, and implement the ideas consistently and faithfully. Understand the classes by reference to the ideas, not by reference to the code, which contains too many details for us to remember effectively. Build complex ideas on the backs of simpler ideas. Use inheritance to implement the complex ideas using previously implemented classes. Proceed primarily from the general to the specific as you design and build.

4.5   SUMMARY

This chapter has presented the interfaces of the main subclasses of SMagnitude and SCollection as well as classes associated with collections. It also gives the ideas underlying each class. These classes form a lattice or directed acyclic graph, in which a lower element in the graph inherits protocol and some capability from those above it. We thus obtain a high degree of reusability in the system, with many components of ancestor classes being reused in the descendant classes.

Figure 4.7 summarizes the relationships between most of the classes discussed in the book. It contains a number of classes here that are not discussed in this chapter, which has focused on only the main classes.

EXERCISES

4.1 (4.2.7) Give a header file for the class SComplex.

4.2 (4.2.8) In the last chapter you were asked to implement methods such as lessEqual and greater from the class SMagnitude. If you implement SInteger and build appropriate less and equal methods, will your inherited lessEqual and greater work in SInteger? Keep in mind that SMagnitude implemented some methods as errors. Keep the dynamic binding principle in mind. Do you need to give different answers if our use of these classes involved direct rather than indirect variables? That is to say, if we declare a variable to be of type SInteger rather than type PInteger, do the methods greater and lessEqual have the same standing?

4.3 (4.2.9) Give a header file for the class SReal.

4.4 (4.2.9) Give the protocol for SReal and SComplex.

4.5 (4.3.5) Give a critique of the design and implementation of the real stack class discussed in Chapter 2 and implemented in the exercises of that chapter. In what ways (if any) is the finite stack class discussed in Chapter 3 an improvement on it? In what ways is the stack class discussed in this chapter an improvement on both of those? Is there a tradeoff? That is to say, have we given up anything to gain the advantages you cite?

4.6 (4.3.10) Give the proper protocol for a dynamic array iterator. Give the proper protocol for a dynamic array position. Be sure to permit movement of position by ordinal position in the list. What does it mean to move to the thirty-third item? What does it mean to move to the item in array slot 33? Should we permit movement using both ideas if they are different?

4.7 (4.3.10) We could easily add the two key methods of our dynamic array class to the list class:

```
virtual void       atPut (int, PObject);
virtual PObject    at (int);
```

The first puts an object into a given ordinal position in a list and the second retrieves the object at an ordinal position. Why is this not the same as a dynamic array? That is, why would the behavior still not be "array-like"?

4.8 (4.4) Consider the classes in Fig. 4.7. Are there any that you would like to include? Try to think of one or two additional classes that might be developed as subclasses of SMagnitude or SCollection. Design protocols for your classes. How would they be used? What do your methods do? Give preconditions and postconditions where appropriate. Are there other major classifications (such as magnitude or collection) that have been omitted?

4.9 (4.4) Reevaluate your answer to Exercise 3.8.

FIGURE 4.7

## CHAPTER 5

USING THE FUNDAMENTAL STRUCTURES

Lend me an arm; the rest have worn me out
With several applications

    Shakespeare, *All's Well That Ends Well*

Now it is time to deliver on the promise. We have seen a lot of protocol and the implied promise that it would be useful. Two applications will now be presented that build on the above framework and do some things that every student of computer science should see. Our methodology will be to create a new class to form the framework for the solution of our problem. In each case the instance variables of the new class will have types that come from the hierarchy discussed in Chapter 4. We shall use these instance variables directly, without needing to rebuild the classes from which they come. The new class can be thought of as a director ensuring that the messages are sent to the instance variables at the right time. In a certain sense we will be writing high-level application-oriented code in the methods of these new classes, drawing on the low-level classes of the hierarchy.

    The first application will be a simulator for deterministic finite automata. The deterministic finite automaton (DFA) is a simple abstract computing machine, simpler than a computer but capable of carrying out some simple computations. We shall utilize dictionaries and the classes `SString` and `SCharacter`.

    The other application is the translation of arithmetic expressions from the standard *infix* form, which people are used to, into the *postfix* form, which is very suitable for computers. This is called operator precedence translation and is a very important compiler technique. The fundamental data structure here is the stack, though we shall also use the classes `SString` and `SInteger`. A variation will use a form of `SBinaryTree`.

5.1   DETERMINISTIC FINITE AUTOMATA

A finite automaton is a simple model of computation that is sufficient for some tasks but inadequate for others. Finite automata also have great theoretical importance, due to their equivalence to a class of languages called regular languages. Simply, a DFA is a machine that has input but no output. It has a fixed number of internal states, and at any given time it is in one of these states. It runs a fixed program, and when it reaches the end of its input, announces whether the input was accepted or not, depending on what its internal state is at the time. A program is just a table of the transitions it must make from state to state. A schematic of a DFA is shown in Fig. 5.1.

One of the states is the start state, and one or more are final states. If the machine reaches the end of the input and is in a final state, the input is accepted; otherwise it is rejected. The operation of the machine is as follows. The (finite) input is written on a tape and the machine is set with its read mechanism over the leftmost symbol on the tape. The symbols on the tape come from some fixed finite alphabet. The state of the machine is its initial state. When started, the machine reads the current input symbol and moves the read mechanism one symbol to the right. Then, depending on the current state and the symbol just read, the machine changes its state according to its program. When the end of the tape is reached, the machine accepts its input if it is in a final state; otherwise it rejects the input. If the

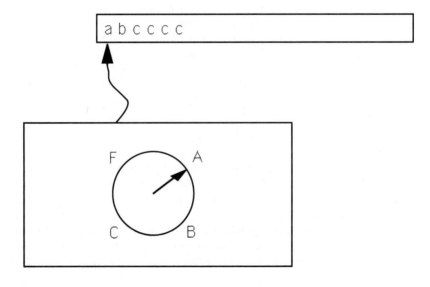

FIGURE 5.1

machine is in some state and its program has no instruction corresponding to the current symbol, the machine halts in error and rejects the input.

Deterministic Finite Automaton

A DFA consists of five parts:

1. A finite tape alphabet.
2. A finite set of states.
3. A specification of the start state.
4. A specification of the final states.
5. A program that consists of a finite set of triplets (s, r, t) where s is the current state, r is the read symbol, and t is the state that the machine should move to if it reads r while it is in state s.

A DFA program is a partial function whose domain is the Cartesian product of the states and the alphabet and whose range is the set of states. We can model a DFA by modeling its program function. A tabular presentation of the function is adequate for some purposes. The following example of a DFA has four states, A, B, C, and F, and an alphabet of the three letters a, b, and c. The initial state is A, the single final state is F, and the transition function is as follows.

```
(A, a) -> B
(A, b) -> C
(B, b) -> F
(C, a) -> F
(F, c) -> F
```

Another simple way to model a DFA is with a directed graph having one node for each internal state. The arcs in the graph represent the various triplets (s, r, t) of the program: we draw an arc from s to t and label it with r. Final states are drawn as double circles, and the initial state is marked with an arc arriving from no node. The above DFA is shown in Fig. 5.2.

This DFA will accept any string that consists of an a followed by a b followed by zero or more c's. It will also accept strings consisting of ba followed by zero or more c's. All other strings will be rejected. A set of strings is called a language, and a language for which there is a DFA accepting exactly the strings in that language is a *regular language*. Regular languages have both theoretical and practical value. Their practical importance comes from the fact that the words and symbols we use to express the programs

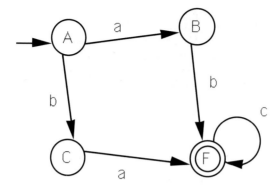

FIGURE 5.2

in most programming languages form regular languages. In C these basic symbols, such as the keyword `struct`, the identifier `VAT37`, and special symbols such as `/=` and `==`, form a regular language. Individually these symbols are called **tokens**. The scanner within a compiler has the job of translating the stream of characters in the program text file into a stream of tokens in order to make the rest of the translation easier. A scanner is often nothing more than a simulator of some DFA equivalent to the token language. In this section we want to develop a simulator for DFAs. We shall do it in a general way, permitting a user to construct a DFA, give it an input, and then determine whether that DFA accepts that input string.

Scanning Problem

Separation of the characters of a file into meaningful words and symbols, called tokens. If the words and symbols form a regular language, a DFA can solve the scanning problem.

We take our own advice above and model the DFA as a graph. Now we need to figure out how to model the graph. Let us model the nodes directly, creating the new class `SDFANode`. This new class will do little more than package up capability provided by our other classes. Other than a constructor it will only need two methods to do the work of a DFA. A DFA will be some collection of these nodes. We could create some class to handle this collection, or we could use some existing class like `SSet`, but there is an even easier way. If each node knows who its neighbors are in the graph, the graph as a whole is modeled in a distributed way, there being no central collection of information about the graph.

A way to effect this is to partition the transition function into a collection of functions by projection onto each state. In other words, we put two transitions into the same function in the partition if they map the same state. In this way we get a function for each state rather than one function for the whole DFA. This set of functions will model the DFA. For the DFA discussed above, we get four partial functions, one for each state. We first select all mapping pairs that start at the same state.

State *A*:

```
(A, a) -> B
(A, b) -> C
```

State *B*:

```
(B, b) -> F
```

State *C*:

```
(C, a) -> F
```

State *F*:

```
(F, c) -> F
```

Then we project these onto the states to get the required functions.

State *A*:

```
a -> B
b -> C
```

State *B*:

```
b -> F
```

State *C*:

```
a -> F
```

State *F*:

```
c -> F
```

When we initialize a node, we should indicate whether it is a final state. We also need a way to store the information about the neighbors and the labels on the arcs to those neighbors. A dictionary is especially suited for this, because a dictionary represents a function as does the DFA program. A dictionary is a set of association pairs of which each key is a magnitude and appears no more than once in the dictionary. We can build associations in this case by using the characters in the input alphabet as the keys. (This is a restriction. The definition of a DFA permits more general sets of symbols.)

The value in the association will be the state at the other end of the arc
Note that only the state at the tail of an arc needs to store the arc.

Finally, we must determine how to represent the tape and how to sim
ulate the DFA's reading of the tape. The answer to the former question is
simply to use elements of SString, because these are finite sequences o
characters, as our tape is. The tape can be read by sending the origina
string to some state (the initial state) as a parameter to the run message
The state node removes the first character from the string, looks it up ir
its own dictionary, and, if it gets a match, puts the DFA into the corre
sponding state by sending the string (with its first character removed) tc
that state as a parameter to another run message. If a state doesn't have
an association for a given input character, it halts the run with an erroi
message but doesn't pass on the run message. Also, if a state is sent ar
empty string, it announces "accept" if it is a final state but "reject" other
wise.

Required Classes

```
SObject
    SDFANode
    SMagnitude
        SAssociation
        SCharacter
    SCollection
        SList
        SSet
            SDictionary
        SString
    SListNode
```

The protocol for our class follows.

```
PDFANode newDFANode (char isFinal);

class SDFANode: public SObject {
    public:
        SDFANode (char final = FALSE);
    virtual             ~SDFANode (void);
    virtual char        member (classtype c);
    virtual void        writeIt (void);
    virtual void        addNeighbor (PDFANode nbr,
                            PCharacter
                            transition);
    virtual void        run (PString tape);
    virtual PObject     Clone (void);
```

```
    protected:
        PDictionary fNbrs;
        char        fIsFinal;
        virtual int sizeOf (void);
};
```

```
// REQUIREMENTS For Use
//    initLists ();
//    initCharacters ();
```

Generation of new nodes is standard:

```
PDFANode newDFANode (char isFinal) {
    PDFANode result;

    result = new SDFANode (isFinal);
    failnull (result);
    return result;
};
```

This gives us a properly initialized DFANode, as always. Initialization itself must create a new empty dictionary for its instance variable and mark itself as final or not.

```
SDFANode :: SDFANode (char final) {
    fNbrs = newDictionary ();
    fIsFinal = final;
};
```

The method addNeighbor creates a new arc in the DFA by insertion into its own dictionary. The state to assume if we see the character transition is nbr. We call atPut from SDictionary to make the insertion.

```
void SDFANode :: addNeighbor (PDFANode nbr,
                                      PCharacter transition) {
    fNbrs -> atPut (transition, nbr);
};
```

The run method does all of the work. With a parameter that is a PString, it is sent to a state. It assumes that the nodes have been created and initialized and that each node has been given its complete list of neighbors.

```
void SDFANode :: run(PString tape) {
    PCharacter aChar;
    PDFANode aTrans;
```

```
    if (tape -> empty ()) {
      if (fIsFinal) { // If the tape is empty,
                      //   quit and report.
        cout << "Accepted\n";
        }
      else {
        cout << "Not Accepted\n";
        };
    }
    else { // If tape is not empty, then lookup
           //   the first symbol and
      aChar = tape -> first ();
      aTrans = PDFANode (fNbrs -> at (aChar));
      if (aTrans != NULL) { // If we find a match,
                            //   pass the remaining t
        tape -> removeFirst ();
        cout << ".";
        aTrans -> run (tape); // to the next node.
      }
      else // If no match, then quit.
        cout << "Not accepted -- Halted\n";
    };
};
```

We begin by checking whether the string is empty, and if it is, we make the
proper announcement. Otherwise we extract the first character from the
string and use the method at to determine whether there is a corresponding
association in our dictionary, fNbrs. If there is, at will return the value
in the association rather than the association itself. If we get a non-NULL
value, we remove the first character from the string and pass the run
message on to the new state.

To create the DFA given in the example above and test it on the tape
abccccc, we would use the following code. The result should be accepted.

```
A = newDFANode (false);
B = newDFANode (false);
C = newDFANode (false);
F = newDFANode (true);
A -> addNbr (B, 'a');
A -> addNbr (C, 'b');
B -> addNbr (F, 'b');
C -> addNbr (F, 'a');
F -> addNbr (F, 'c');
A -> run (newString ("abccccc"));
```

Extensions   There are many variations of DFAs. A finite-state transducer
which is simple to implement, is like a DFA except that it produce

some output when it makes a state transition. A program consists of quadruples (s, r, t, o) where o is produced when we move to state t if we are in state s and read symbol r. We would store keys in our dictionary just as before, but in modification of the above we would construct pairs for the values. The pairs would consist of the output symbols and the transition states, and SDictionary :: at would return one of the pairs. Alternatively, we could create a new class to hold the pair of items and use these for the values. We would have to add a new addNbrs routine and would need to override run to accomplish this.

Another, more complex variation is a Turing machine, named for Alan Turing, one of the pioneers of computation theory. A Turing machine can both read and write its tape and can move its tape head in either direction. Thus it can use the tape as a sort of changeable memory. It turns out that a Turing machine is exactly equivalent to what we think of as a computer. There is a conjecture, Church's thesis, that anything that can be computed can be computed with a Turing machine. Thus a Turing machine is the most powerful sort of abstract machine; not powerful in the sense of fast or easy to use, but powerful in the sense of being able to compute the most things.

An intermediate machine is called a push-down automaton (PDA). In such a machine there is a single stack onto which we can push or pop symbols. Transitions depend on the current state, the symbol at the read mechanism of the tape, and the symbol on top of the stack. The machine makes a transition from some state s by reading the next input symbol r, popping the top of the stack p, and, if there is a transition for this combination of input symbol and stack top, moving to a new state and pushing some symbols (several, perhaps) onto the stack. Termination generally requires that the stack be left empty. We could build this by treating the stack in the same way that we treated the tape in a DFA: just pass it on to the next state. Another way is to create a separate class for the PDA as a whole and let it store the stack. Actually, a PDA can be a specialization of SStack and therefore inherit from SStack. An object in PDANode will then be told what PDA it is part of when it is initialized and will store this as an instance variable. When it comes time to pop, it just sends the pop message to that instance variable.

```
class SPDANode;
typedef SPDANode *PPDANode;
class SPDANode: public SDFANode {
   public:
        SPDANode (PStack myPDA);
      virtual void   transition (PPDANode NBR,
                                 char *pushing,
                                 char trans,
                                 char top);
      virtual void   run (PString aString);
      virtual void   writeIt (void);
```

```
    protected:
       PStack   fPDA;
};
class SPDA: public SStack {
    public:
          SPDA (void);
       virtual void   run (PPDANode from,
                           PString aString);
};

PPDANode newPDANode (PStack myPDA);
PPDA newPDA (void);

// REQUIREMENTS FOR USE
//    initLists ();
//    initCharacters ();
// Create a stack externally, push "asCharacter('$')
// onto it, and pass it to each node in the same PDA
// when initializing.  Initializing a PDA and
// passing it will be sufficient.
```

In SPDA the method run is also sent a node as the initial state. In SPDANode, transition must somehow use both trans and top as the key and construct a value with the rest of the information. We can put trans and top into a pair for the key (a pair is not a magnitude, so there is a problem, which we discuss below). We also put NBR and pushing into another pair for the value (pushing will need to be stored as an SString). The method run will need to extract and decode this information from the dictionary and will have to push all of the characters of the push string onto the stack. We show run below. The rest is an exercise. Note that an empty stack is one with just the $ character, which is initially pushed. Note also that a pop is always performed, so if $ is ever popped, it must be pushed.

The problem mentioned above is that, because dictionaries require associations and pairs are not associations, we cannot insert pairs into a dictionary. Nor do we want the normal equal comparison of associations when we construct the key and value as described above. We shall therefore need a new class, SIdentityAssociation, that is like an association except that it has a more appropriate equal method. We can insert these into an ordinary dictionary. Note that this dictionary will have pairs of pairs for its contents: the key as well as the value of each member is an IdentityAssociation.

```
void SPDANode :: run (PString aString) {
    PCharacter aChar, topChar;
    PDFANode aTrans;
    PIdentityAssociation key, value;
    PString pushString;
```

```
        PIterator IT;
        PObject aValue;
    if (aString.empty)
        if (fIsFinal && (fPDA -> top () ==
            asCharacter ('$')))
            cout << "Accepted";
        else
            cout << "Not Accepted";
    else if (fPDA -> empty ()) {
        cout << "Not Accepted--underflow in stack";
    }
    else {
        aChar = aString -> first ();
        aString -> removeFirst ();
        key = newIdentityAssociation (aChar,
                                      fPDA -> top ());
        value = PIdentityAssociation (fNBRs -> at (key));
        if ( value != NULL) {
            pushString = PString (value -> getKey ());
            fPDA -> removeFirst ();
            IT = pushString -> fString -> newIterator ();
            while (IT -> nextItem (aValue))
                fPDA -> push (aValue);
            delete IT;
            aTrans = PPDANode (value -> getValue ());
            aTrans -> run (aString);
        }
        else
            cout << "Not Accepted--halted";
        delete key;
        };
    };
```

5.2   EXPRESSION TRANSLATION

In the final section we show how to translate ordinary arithmetic expressions, which may or may not involve parentheses, into postfix form, which is useful for computation. In fact, the Hewlett-Packard company has built a very successful line of calculators around the idea of postfix expressions. In this section we shall use stacks, dictionaries, strings, characters, and integers.

The standard form of arithmetic expressions is called infix: the operator is between its operands, as in A + B. In postfix form the operator comes after its operands, as in A B +. There are a number of advantages of postfix, the most important being that parentheses are not necessary, as they are in the infix form. For example, the infix expression A + B ∗ C is ambiguous without a special rule that informs us that the multiplication is to be done first, which means that the expression is treated as equivalent to A + (B ∗ C) rather than (A + B) ∗ C. If we intend the latter expression, we need to use the parentheses. In postfix notation A + (B ∗ C) would be written A B C ∗ +, and (A + B) ∗ C would be A B + C ∗, removing any ambiguity and not needing parentheses. Postfix expressions can also be easily evaluated while reading the expression from left to right if there is a stack available to hold intermediate results. The rule is simple: If you have an operand, push it. If you have an operation, pop the correct number of operands for that operation, perform the operation and push the result. For the expression 3 4 + 5 ∗ we would push first 3 then 4. We then see the +, so we pop the 4 and 3, add them, and push the resulting 7. The next symbol is 5, so we push it, and the last is ∗, so we pop 5 and 7, multiply them, and push 35. This is the end of the input, so the result is at the top of the stack: 35.

A translator must do several things. First, if the input is a character stream, it must solve the scanning problem. Second, it must solve the parsing problem. That is to say, it must determine whether its input can be formed into a correct token stream. It must verify that the sequence of tokens is valid. (An example of an incorrect token string is an unclosed parenthesis.) For many languages this is accomplished using a push-down automaton, and we will use something similar here. Finally, the translator must produce some correct output: the translation. Here we will just output a postfix string that is equivalent to the input string and assume that the input was correctly formed.

The Parsing Problem

Determination of whether the tokens of a language form a correct sequence. If the language is *context free*, a push-down automaton can be used to solve the parsing problem (see Chapter 13).

We want to write a program to translate infix expressions into an equivalent postfix form. The idea for this section came from [Teague, 1972], a book worth having even if you never program in FORTRAN. The translation technique is called operator precedence translation. It has been in use for a long time and is still used in many C compilers. The basic idea is to assign numeric values indicating precedence to each kind of symbol. These precedences determine how a symbol will be handled. A stack holds symbols that have been seen in the input but have not yet been transferred to the output. There are separate precedences for symbols in the stack and in the input. Suggested values are as follows.

Character	Input	Stack	Use
;	0	0	Marker of end of input
=	1	1	Assignment operator
)	2	0	
+,−	3	4	
*,/	5	6	
letter	7	8	
digit	7	8	
(	9	2	

Note that = is the assignment operator. We would like to translate something like

```
A = (B + C) * (D + E);
```

into

```
A B C + D E + * =
```

The protocol of our system is shown below. We create an enumerated type for the various token types and a class to manage the translation. The class will maintain its own stack and its own input string as instance variables.

Required Classes

```
SObject
    SInfix
    SCollection
        SList
        SStack
        SSet
            SDictionary
        SString
        SBinaryTree
    SMagnitude
        SCharacter
        SInteger
        SAssociation
    SListNode
    SBinaryTreeNode
```

```
enum TTokenType {lparen, rparen, ident, digit,
    addop, mulop, assign, endmark, notoken};

class SInfix;
typedef SInfix *PInfix;

PInfix newInfix (void);

class SInfix: public SObject {
    public:
            SInfix (void);
        virtual                 ~SInfix(void);
        virtual char            member(classtype c);
        virtual void            writeIt(void);
        virtual PString         translate(const PString);
        virtual PObject         Clone(void);

        protected:
            PStack              fExpressions;
            PString             fValue;
            virtual int         sizeOf (void);
            virtual PToken      getToken (void);
            PDictionary         svalues, ivalues;
            PInteger            lookupTop (TTokenType t);
            PInteger            lookupInput (TTokenType t);
};

// REQUIREMENTS For Use
//    initLists ();
//    initCharacters ();
//    initIntegers ();
```

Once we have built the above class, we can use it as in the following excerpt from a main program. The variables x and y have type PString, and opt has type PInfix.

```
cout << "Operator Precedence Translation";
opt := newInfix ();
x = newString ("a=b/(c+d)*F");
cout << "postfix";
y = opt -> translate (x);
y.writeIt ();
```

The output from this is

```
Operator Precedence Translation
postfix
a b c d + / F * =
```

The translation proceeds by reading the inputs from left to right. When we need a new input symbol, we call `getToken` and it returns an object to us corresponding to the next significant symbol in the input. We maintain a stack. The rules for its use are as follows.

Operator Precedence Translation

1. If the next input token has precedence greater than the precedence of the top stack token, push the input (removing it from the input by calling `getToken`).
2. If the input precedence is the same as the stack precedence, discard the input and pop the stack, discarding the top value as well.
3. If the input precedence is less than the stack precedence, pop the stack top and append the result to the output, but leave the input as it is.

[Floyd, 1963]

This simple rule forms the basis of our translation routine. However, we also need to represent the tokens, store the precedences, and manage the stack. For tokens we want objects so that we can push them onto stacks, but otherwise they are just like records. We won't even give them any methods. We need not rebuild stacks, as we may just use `SStack` without change.

```
struct SToken: public SObject {
    TTokenType fToken;
    PCharacter fCharValue;
    char fOperator;
};

typedef SToken *PToken;
```

The precedences can be held in two dictionaries, `ivalues` for the input precedences and `svalues` for the stack precedence values. These are best saved as instance variables of an operator precedence translator. They are created and filled with their lookup tables when the translator is constructed. The constructor must also create a stack to hold the intermediate information.

```
SInfix :: SInfix (void) {
    ivalues = newDictionary ();
    svalues = newDictionary ();
    fExpressions = newStack ();
    fValue = NULL;
```

```
      ivalues -> atPut (asInteger ((endmark)),
                        asInteger (0));
      ivalues -> atPut (asInteger ((assign)),
                        asInteger (1));
      ivalues -> atPut (asInteger ((rparen)),
                        asInteger (2));
      ivalues -> atPut (asInteger ((addop)),
                        asInteger (3));
      ivalues -> atPut (asInteger ((mulop)),
                        asInteger (5));
      ivalues -> atPut (asInteger ((ident)),
                        asInteger (7));
      ivalues -> atPut (asInteger ((digit)),
                        asInteger (7));
      ivalues -> atPut (asInteger ((lparen)),
                        asInteger (9));

      svalues -> atPut (asInteger ((endmark)),
                        asInteger (0));
      svalues -> atPut (asInteger ((assign)),
                        asInteger (1));
      svalues -> atPut (asInteger ((rparen)),
                        asInteger (0));
      svalues -> atPut (asInteger ((addop)),
                        asInteger (4));
      svalues -> atPut (asInteger ((mulop)),
                        asInteger (6));
      svalues -> atPut (asInteger ((ident)),
                        asInteger (8));
      svalues -> atPut (asInteger ((digit)),
                        asInteger (8));
      svalues -> atPut (asInteger ((lparen)),
                        asInteger (2));
    };
```

The procedure getToken, though long, is quite simple. Recall that it simulates a certain DFA, which is shown in Fig. 5.3. Unfortunately, it has 68 transitions (52 letters, 10 digits, etc.). We also need to know what final state the DFA is in when it halts. Exercise 5.11 provides some hints on how to extend a DFA to build a getToken. The getToken procedure models the DFA directly. Its case statement is its way of determining a state transition.

```
PToken SInfix :: getToken (void) {
    PToken theToken;
    TTokenType tok;
```

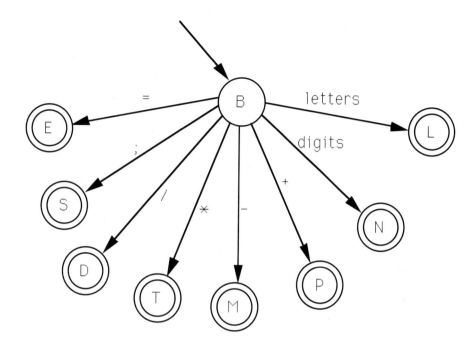

FIGURE 5.3

```
PCharacter chVal;
char isOperator;

theToken = NULL;
theToken = new SToken;
failnull (theToken);
if (!fValue -> empty ()) {
   while (!fValue -> empty ()
        && (fValue -> first ()) -> equal
            ((PObject) asCharacter (' '))) {
      fValue -> removeFirst ();
   };
   chVal = fValue -> first ();
   isOperator = FALSE;
   fValue -> removeFirst ();
   switch (chVal -> value ()) {
      case '(': tok = lparen;
         break;
      case ')': tok = rparen;
         break;
      case '0': case '1': case '2': case '3':
      case '4': case '5': case '6': case '7':
      case '8': case '9':
         tok = digit;
         break;
```

```
            case 'a': case 'b': case 'c': case 'd':
            case 'e': case 'f': case 'g': case 'h':
            case 'i': case 'j': case 'k': case 'l':
            case 'm': case 'n': case 'o': case 'p':
            case 'q': case 'r': case 's': case 't':
            case 'u': case 'v': case 'w': case 'x':
            case 'y': case 'z':
                chVal = asCharacter (toupper (chVal ->
                                    value ()));
            case 'A': case 'B': case 'C': case 'D':
            case 'E': case 'F': case 'G': case 'H':
            case 'I': case 'J': case 'K': case 'L':
            case 'M': case 'N': case 'O': case 'P':
            case 'Q': case 'R': case 'S': case 'T':
            case 'U': case 'V': case 'W': case 'X':
            case 'Y': case 'Z':
                tok = ident;
                break;
            case '+': {
                tok = addop;
                isOperator = TRUE;
            };
                break;
            case '*': {
                tok = mulop;
                isOperator = TRUE;
            };
                break;
            case '/': {
                tok = mulop;
                isOperator = TRUE;
            };
                break;
            case '=': {
                tok = assign;
                isOperator = TRUE;
            };
                break;
            case ';': tok = endmark;
                break;
            default:
                Error ("SInfix :: getToken:
                        not defined.");
        }
    }
    else {
```

```
        tok = endmark;
        chVal = asCharacter (';');
    };
    theToken -> fToken = tok;
    theToken -> fCharValue = chVal;
    theToken -> fOperator = isOperator;
    return theToken;
};
```

The routine is just a string processor, getting characters from the input and comparing them against various possibilities. At the end it returns the desired information.

The `translate` method is the main engine of the class, of course, but it needs two additional functions for easy access to the precedence values that we stored in the dictionaries in the constructor. These two functions, `lookupTop` and `lookupInput`, search the stack and input dictionaries for the precedences of the current stack top and input token, respectively. The key searching is handled by a call to `at` of the dictionary class.

```
PInteger SInfix :: lookupTop (TTokenType t) {
    return PInteger (svalues -> at (asInteger (t)));
};

PInteger SInfix :: lookupInput (TTokenType t) {
    return PInteger (ivalues -> at (asInteger (t)));
};
```

The translation routine compares the top of the stack with the next input token. When a new token is needed, we call `getToken`. Whenever we are done with the top of the stack, we can pop.

The initialization guarantees that the stack is in a known state before we start by we pushing a special marker onto it. It also appends the semicolon character to the input to be certain to recognize its end.

```
PString SInfix :: translate (const PString s) {
    PString result;
    PToken aToken, stackTop;
    PInteger topVal, inputVal;
    char transError;
    PToken marker;

    marker = new SToken (); // Mark the stack.
    failnull (marker);
    marker -> fToken = endmark;
    marker -> fCharValue = asCharacter (';');
        // And mark the input.
```

```
        fExpressions -> push (marker);
        transError = FALSE;
        fValue = s;
        fValue -> insert (asCharacter (';'));
        result = newString ();
        aToken = getToken (); // Start the processing.
        while (aToken -> fToken !=
               endmark && !transError) {
            if (fExpressions -> empty ())
                transError = TRUE;
            stackTop = PToken (fExpressions -> top ());
                // Get precedence values of top and input.
            topVal = lookupTop (stackTop -> fToken);
            inputVal = lookupInput (aToken -> fToken);
            if (topVal -> greater (inputVal)) {
                // If top is greater, append top to result.
                if (fExpressions -> empty ())
                    transError = TRUE;
                stackTop = PToken (fExpressions -> pop ());
                result -> insert (stackTop -> fCharValue);
                result -> insert(asCharacter (' '));
            }
            else if (topVal -> less (inputVal)) {
                // If input is greater, push it.
                fExpressions -> push (aToken);
                aToken = getToken ();
                }
            else { // If both are equal, discard both.
                aToken = getToken ();
                if (fExpressions->empty())
                    transError = TRUE;
                fExpressions -> removeFirst ();
            }
        };
        while (!fExpressions -> empty ()) {
            // At end empty stack to result.
            aToken = PToken (fExpressions -> pop ());
            if (aToken -> fToken != endmark) {
                result -> insert (aToken -> fCharValue);
                result -> insert (asCharacter (' '));
            };
        };
        delete marker;
        return result;
    };
```

The main part of the `translate` method compares the precedence, `topVal`, of the top of the stack to the precedence, `inputVal`, of the current input. If `topVal` is greater, we pop the stack and append the result to the output, `theResult`. If `topVal` is less than `inputVal`, we push the input token. Finally, if they are equal, we discard both by popping and calling `getToken`. When the input string has been completely processed, we append any remaining contents of the stack to the output.

This class can be extended quite easily to permit the creation of an expression tree representing the expression as the translation proceeds. An expression tree is a specialization of `SBinaryTree`, which we have seen.

> ### Expression Tree
>
> A tree with the property that interior nodes represent operations. The children of a node represent operands of the operation at that node. Composite operands are represented by subtrees. Elementary operands are represented by values in external nodes.

A new method, `createExpressionTree`, in the class `SInfix`, will create such a tree while translating. The logic of `createExpression-Tree` is the same as that of `translate` except for the handling of the output. Instead of just appending an item to the output when the stack precedence is greater, we create a new tree node to hold the item just popped. In addition, if the item popped is an operator, like +, we pop the appropriate number of operands for that operator from the stack (they will be at the top), attach them as children to the tree node just created, and push the tree node back into the stack. The details are left as an exercise. An expression tree is illustrated in Fig. 5.4.

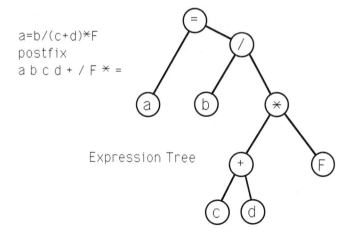

```
a=b/(c+d)*F
postfix
a b c d + / F * =
```

Expression Tree

FIGURE 5.4

Another extension that can be readily made is to turn the translator into an evaluator. The idea here is to evaluate expressions on the fly rather than merely transform the output. Suppose that our input consists of infix expressions with single-digit (numeric) operands rather than symbolic names. Then, in the `translate` method, instead of simply outputting symbols to the output string we can do the following. If the symbol to be output is an operand, we push it, as a `PInteger`, onto another stack, the evaluation stack. If the symbol is an operator, we pop the correct number of operands for the operator off the evaluation stack and apply the operator to them using methods of `SInteger`. The operand furthest down in the stack is the leftmost operand. The result of applying the operation should be pushed back into the evaluation stack. When the input is exhausted, the result of the expression should be at the top of the evaluation stack.

5.3   SUMMARY

A class can be utilized without understanding its implementation. All that is necessary is to understand its protocol, which consists of its interface and the specifications of the procedures defined by the interface.

The method of solving problems with such a class library is to create a new class (or a small collection of classes) that will orchestrate the usage of the class hierarchy. This new class behaves much like the director of an orchestra, who does not make music so much as help the individual musicians coordinate their efforts toward a common end.

Our DFA class simulated the actions of a deterministic finite automaton using the existing capabilities of dictionaries, associations, and strings, adding only the specific code necessary to the DFA itself.

EXERCISES

5.1 (5.1) Complete the implementation of the PDA and test it. The following test code may be used for a partial test. Note that a transition occuring on the character $ at the top of the stack must include replacement of the $, which is popped to check it. The $ is actually a bottom-of-stack indicator.

```
aPDA = newPDA ();
sA = newPDANode (aPDA);
sB = newPDANode (aPDA);
sA -> becomeFinal ();
sA -> transition (sB, "$a", 'a', '$');
sB -> transition (sA, "", 'a', 'a');
sB -> transition (sA, "$", 'a', '$');

aPDA -> runString (sA, "aaaaa");

aPDA -> writeIt ();  // Should be empty if
                     // the string is accepted.
```

5.2 (5.1) A better implementation of push-down automata uses a list in a PDA object that holds references to all the states making up the PDA. One creates states using a message passed to a PDA, which creates the required state, inserts it into its list, and, perhaps, returns a reference to it. Discuss the desirability of this, and implement it.

5.3 (5.2) Provide better error correction in the translator of Section 5.2. Unless we modified the translator as suggested in Exercise 5.4, we would get garbage if we tried to translate the string A=MM but we would not get an error message. We should either quit processing when we have seen a complete expression just before an illegal character, or we should complain about the violation.

5.4 (5.2) Modify the translator of Section 5.2 to accept long names for identifiers. Names should be permitted to be in class `SString`. This requires that we extend `getToken` and modify the token class.

5.5 (5.2) Modify the translator of Section 5.2 by adding an evaluator of infix expressions whose operands are integer constants and whose operations are those currently implemented.

5.6 (5.2) Modify the translator of Section 5.2 by adding an evaluator of infix expressions that consist of any constants or identifiers and operations. Implement storage for the identifiers as a dictionary of name-value associations. When a name is given a value, enter the name-value association into the dictionary. When a name is used, retrieve the association corresponding to the name in order to access the value.

5.7 (5.2) Modify the translator of Section 5.2 by turning it into a translator of infix fractions to postfix. Input of fractions should be in the same form that `SFraction :: writeIt` uses to output them. This will require modifying `getToken` so that it looks for the character [.

5.8 (5.2) Create a fraction calculator by combining Exercises 5.5 and 5.7.

5.9 (5.2) Complete the implementation of `SInfix` by providing for the creation of expression trees as suggested at the end of the Section 5.2.

5.10 (5.2) Discuss the validity of the claim that the operation of `SInfix ::` `translate ()` is merely the operation of a particular PDA.

5.11 (5.2) This exercise is quite long, almost a project. Create a scanner for the `SInfix` class using the ideas about SDFAs in Section 5.1. In particular,

    a. We need to return a token from `run` (rather than print a message) so that the caller will know which token was in the input. Method `run` must be a function returning a `PToken`.

    b. A scanner needs to be called several times to retrieve several tokens, not just one. The best way to do this is to consider the input string as a sequence of tapes rather than a single one, with each tape being terminated by the beginning of the next rather than by a marker. This requires a change in the definition of acceptance. We scan until we have no possible transition from some state. If this state is a final state, we consider the string so far to be accepted; if it is not final, no token is accepted. If we halt and accept, we should return a token whose `fValue` has been set so as to indicate what was seen in the part of the input: an element of `TTokenType`. If we halt and reject the input, we set `fValue` to be `notoken`.

    c. Each call of `run` will consume only part of the input string, so it should return the remaining portion so that the next call to run can begin at that point. Since elements of `SString` keep the string they represent internally, this will happen automatically.

d. When a state is constructed, it should be told what value of `TTokenType` it should return if `run` halts in that state. States that are not final must return `notoken`, and others must return a token indicating what has been seen in the input.

PROJECTS

The following represent larger projects that can be undertaken, or at least begun, now. They can also be delayed until the implementations and further details of the classes in our hierarchy have been discussed in the following chapters. Expect to spend at least a few weeks developing these programs. Some of them are intended to be rather open-ended.

1. Relational Databases

A relational database consists of a set of *relations*. A relation consists of a set of *tuples* over a set of *attributes*. A tuple can be thought of as a dictionary in which the keys are exactly the set of attributes and the values are arbitrary. You can think of a relation as a two-dimensional table with the attributes labeling the columns and the tuples forming the rows. In the following example, taken from Chapter 15, the attributes are <Name>, <Address>, etc., and one tuple, expressed as a dictionary, is { (<Name>, <Fein, Jacob>), (<Address>, <10 Oak>), ...}.

Name	Address	Home Phone	Business Phone
Fein, Jacob	10 Oak	555-1234	555-2234
Hai, Sari	3 First	555-4312	555-3312
Low, Judith	22 Elm	555-2314	555-3314
Ng, Lai	92 Third	555-2134	555-1134
Ng, Mary	92 Third	555-2134	555-4434
Smith, John	52 Maple	555-3214	555-2214

Define a class, `STuple`, whose objects are single tuples, and another class, `SRelation`, whose objects are sets of tuples over the same set of attributes. Be sure that you include the attribute set as well as the tuples themselves in this class structure. You will need to be able to insert tuples into a relation and remove them. The attribute set of a relation is fixed when the relation is created and is not changed afterward. In this last class, implement the *natural join* operation, which is described below. Define a class, `SRelationalDatabase`, whose objects are sets of relations.

The natural join of two relations A and B is a third relation, J, that satisfies the following:

1. The attribute set of J is the union of the attribute sets of A and B.
2. Let X represent the intersection of the attribute sets of A and B. If each of A and B has a tuple whose values on the attributes in X are identical, J has a tuple formed by the union of the dictionaries of those tuples from A and B.

A consequence of rule 2 is that if the attribute sets of A and B are disjoint (the intersection is empty), J consists of the Cartesian product of A and B: each tuple of A unioned with each tuple of B.

2. Grocery Warehouse Problem

a. Design an inventory system for a grocery warehouse. The *inventory* is a list of *products*. A product consists of the product description ("beans") and a list of *items*. An item consists of a supplier ("Shurfine") and the quantity on hand. You need to be able to create new products and new items, adjust the quantities up and down as items are bought and sold, and remove items when the supplier of an item is discontinued. Decide what classes need to be designed, which classes the above suggested methods properly belong to, and how everything is to be implemented.
b. Discuss your design with someone else. Modify it as necessary.
c. Build the final design.

3. Maze-Walking Robot Problem

A *maze* can be built as a two-dimensional array of which some cells are occupied by *obstructions*. The obstructions can be used to build walls and rooms. You will want to be able to create a new maze, place and remove obstructions, and inquire as to the presence of an obstruction in a cell. You will also want to be able to write a maze to a file and read it back in, since mazes are tedious to build. Note that all cells outside the maze boundary are treated as obstructed.

One cell is marked as the *goal*. A *robot* occupies a cell of a maze, being placed at some cell when created. Its purpose is to seek the goal by moving to it without passing through any obstructions. To do this, the robot must be able to move from one cell to any adjacent cell (north, east, south, or west) that does not contain an obstruction. The robot will need some *memory*. One way to organize the memory is to keep a set of the cells that it has already visited so that it doesn't wind up going around in circles, and two stacks. The first stack contains the cells of a path leading back to the starting point. This current path stack will be used if the robot reaches a dead end in the maze and needs to back out of it and resume at the most recent crossing point. The other stack, the trials stack, contains hints about where the search should be continued, if necessary, as described below. The robot should also know which direction it is facing.

An algorithm for searching for the goal is as follows.

Empty the memory of the robot.
Push the current cell onto the current path.
Enter this cell into the set of cells visited.
If more than one of the four directions is not obstructed, push the
    adjacent cell in all but one of the free directions onto the trials
    path (it now has zero to three items). Push the current cell onto the
    trials path. Push the cell in the remaining direction onto the trials
    path.
Otherwise, if only one direction was free, push the adjacent cell in
    that direction onto the trials path.
While the trials path is not empty and we are not at the goal, do the
    following.
Pop a cell from the trials path.
Push it into the current path and move to that cell.
Enter this cell into the visited set.
If this is the goal, quit; the goal has been found.
Otherwise, if more than one of the three directions to its left, front,
    and right are not obstructed and have not been visited, push all but
    one of them onto the trials stack and push the current cell on top of
    them.
Otherwise, if exactly one is free and not visited, simply push it onto
    the trials path (i.e., push the cell in that direction).
Otherwise, if none of these directions are free and not visited, back
    up by popping the current path and moving to the corresponding
    cell until the top of the current path matches the top of the trials
    path. Leave this cell in the current path, then pop the trials path.

A *mapper* is a specialized robot whose purpose is not to find the goal but to traverse every reachable cell in the maze and create a *map* of the maze as it goes. A map is like a maze except that its cells are labeled initially "unknown" and eventually "reachable," "goal," or "obstructed."

A *seeker* is a specialized robot that has a map of the maze in its memory and uses the map to find the goal as efficiently as it can.

Build a maze class and one or more of the robot classes. Try to improve the searching algorithm.

4. Simulation Problem

Many situations can be simulated by a set of queues that interact with each other. College registration is one system that is easily modeled by this technique. A collection of queues will be called a queuing system. Each queue is named or numbered and represents a service provided to one client at a time. If a client arrives for service when another is being served, the new arrival waits by being inserted into the queue. The server dequeues an item (client) when it finishes serving it, which can take a variable amount of time. Each client arrives at the queuing system with a list of the queues it must visit in the order that they must be visited, and it leaves the system when it has received service from every queue in its list. Each time it receives service from one server, it presents itself to the next one on its list.

The purpose of the simulation is to determine certain statistics on the time behavior of the system. The total time taken to process a given client or set of clients is one such statistic.

A clock controls the simulation. A clock is an object that responds to the following two messages.

AdvanceTime (advance the clock by some fixed amount).
GetTime (return the current clock time).

The queuing system simulation proceeds by executing the following algorithm.

While there are still clients in the system, do
   Advance the time.
   For each queue do
     ServeClient

A node serves a client by executing the following algorithm repeatedly:

If we are serving a client, then
   Check the clock against the termination time of this client.
   If time is up, release the client.
If now free and queue is not empty, then
   Dequeue one client from the queue.
   Compute the finish time for this client as a random number between the limits appropriate for this server.

When a client is released from a server, it executes the following.

If the list of queues to be visited is not empty, remove the next queue and
   enqueue on it.
Otherwise, mark the completion time by consulting the clock and wait on
   (insert self into) a list so that termination statistics can be computed
   when all clients finish.

Build such a system and test it.

5. Huffman Encoding and Decoding Problem

Often we want to compress a text file of some kind so that it will take up as little space as possible. This occurs, for example, when we want to reduce storage space or charges or send the file over an expensive phone link.

You probably know that computers use some sort of numeric encoding to represent characters—EBCDIC and ASCII are the two most popular ones. These encodings all have the property that every legal character is represented by the same number of bits (7 bits in ASCII, 8 in EBCDIC). Such encodings are convenient to use, but also somewhat redundant: if we could come up with an encoding that used fewer bits for frequently used characters, like E or T, it would more than make up for the corresponding increase in the number of bits required for rarely used letters, like X or Q.

One way to think about character encodings is to consider a tree structure in which 0 means "go left" and 1 means "go right." If we are interested only in the letters $ABCDEFGH$, we could assign them three-bit codes as follows:

A	000	E	100
B	001	F	101
C	010	G	110
D	011	H	111

This corresponds to the tree structure in Fig. 5.5, where a letter's code is represented by the path from the root to the letter.

If we know that E occurs much more often than G, we might want to distort this tree so that E is fewer steps from the top and G correspondingly more. The tree in Fig. 5.6 is the best tree possible given the frequencies of these eight letters in English. This gives the following encodings:

A	11	E	01
B	00000	F	0001
C	100	G	00001
D	001	H	101

One thing to notice is that the numerical order is no longer the same as the alphabetical order. However, since E is about eight times as common as G, we can see that we will use much less space. The word $GEEEEEEEE$ required 27 bits before and only 21 now. (In practice, compression of better than 50% is common.) If we know the expected frequencies of characters in the file, we can use the encoding that gives us the smallest expected file length. Such an encoding is called a Huffman encoding, and the tree that summarizes such an encoding is called a Huffman tree.

We can use a table or dictionary of Huffman codes to compress a file. For instance, if the file consists of the word $CHAFED$, we could look up C

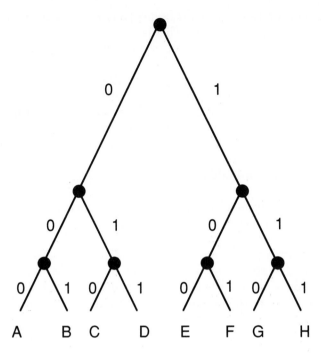

FIGURE 5.5

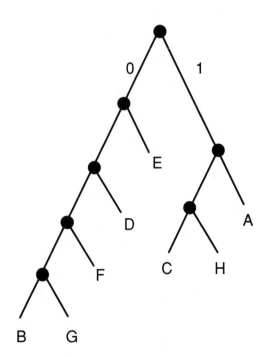

FIGURE 5.6

and output 100, look up H and output 101, and so on, producing the output file 10010111000101001. This is slightly compressed, requiring only 17 bits in contrast to the 18 needed if we used fixed-length codes, or 42 if we used ASCII.

To decompress the compressed file, it is convenient to use the tree. We start at the root and look at the first bit of the compressed file. Since it is 1, we move down to the right and read the second bit. Since this is 0, we move left. The third bit is 0, so we move left again, which brings us to the C. Thus the first letter is C; we output it and start over at the root again.

Huffman's tree-building algorithm.

1. Collect all the characters you want to encode and assign a weight to each, based upon the expected frequency of each character in a typical input file. Frequencies are given below.
2. Create a list of one-node binary trees with these weights and characters. The list should be in increasing order of the weights.
3. Repeat until there is only one node left in the list ($n - 1$ times):
   a. Remove the two nodes having the smallest weights and connect them to a common parent.
   b. Assign the weight of the parent to be the sum of the weights of the two children.
   c. Insert this new tree into the list of trees.
4. The remaining tree is the Huffman tree.

Here are the relative frequencies of allowed character set:

73	9	30	44	130	28	16	35	74	2
A	B	C	D	E	F	G	H	I	J
3	35	25	78	74	27	3	77	63	93
K	L	M	N	O	P	Q	R	S	T
27	13	16	5	19	1				
U	V	W	X	Y	Z				
2	2	9	15	258	20				
(	)	,	.	space	eoln				

Note: End-of-line (eoln) is not treated as a character in many systems. It is present here because we want our compressed files to record the locations where line boundaries appear so that we can restore those line boundaries when we decompress the files. The easiest way to do this is to choose some character not shown above (e.g., $) to stand in for eoln in the Huffman tree. When an end-of-line condition is detected on input, it should be encoded with the compressed code. When the compressed code for eoln is detected during the decode operation, start a new line of decoded output.

Here is the beginning of an example of this. After performing step three for the first time, we have

```
2   2   3   3   3   5   9   9  and so on until   130   258
(   )   °   K   Q   X   B   ,                     E    space
       /\
      Z   J
```

After performing it the second time, we have

```
3   3   3   4   5   9   9   and so on until   130   258
°   K   Q   °   X   B   ,                      E    space
/\         /\
Z   J     (   )
```

And after performing it the third time, we have

```
3   4   5   6   9   9  and so on until   130   258
Q   °   X   °   B   ,                     E    space
   /\     /\
  (   )  °   K
         /\
        Z   J
```

After you have built the tree, you must traverse it recursively to extract the encodings. An abstract version of this part might look like this:

```
void ExtractCodes (node p, path fromroot) {
// fromroot contains the path from the root to node p.

   if (p is a leaf node) {
     Announce that the code for character in p is fromroot.
   }
   else {
     ExtractCodes (LeftChild (p), fromroot extended with 0);
     ExtractCodes (RightChild (p), fromroot extended with 1);
   };
};
```

Even though this doesn't show how to implement a node or a path, it is the correct algorithm for extracting the codes. The action announce might mean simply printing the code found or adding it to a table or dictionary. Once the encoding table is built, encoding simply involves a table lookup for each character.

Huffman Decode: To decode an encoded file, one must examine the bits of the file and use the Huffman tree. An algorithm follows:

1. Initialize p to the root of the Huffman tree.
2. While the end of the message has not been reached
    Let x be the next bit in the string.
    If $x = 0$,
       set p to LeftChild (p)
    Else set p to RightChild (p)
    If p is a leaf, then
       Display the character associated with that leaf.
       Reset p to the root of the Huffman tree.

Build and test a program or set of programs to do the following.

a. Using the frequencies given above, construct a Huffman tree using the algorithm described above.

b. Traverse the Huffman tree to make a table of the Huffman codes.

c. Use the table of Huffman codes to translate an input file into compressed form. Use any input text you like, but make sure that it contains only those characters you have codes for. This input file should be at least ten lines long.

d. Use the Huffman tree to translate the compressed file back into normal text.

Your program should print the codes assigned to the alphabet above and display the original file in character form, the Huffman encoded file in binary form (that is, as zeroes and ones), and the decompressed file in character form. The decompressed file should, of course, be identical to the original. Your program should also print the length (number of characters) of the original message the length compressed file (number of bits). Since the alphabet we are using has 32 characters, we would ordinarily need five bits per character. How does this compare with the translation done according to your Huffman codes?

Notes

1. Since you need to make insertions into and deletions from the list of partial trees, it may be helpful to organize the partial trees into a list ordered by weight; that is, when you initially build it, use an `InsertInOrder` procedure. If you then keep it in order, all deletions will occur at the front of the list and insertions done by `InsertInOrder`.

2. Because the zeroes and ones you write out to create the compressed file will be ASCII or EBCDIC, the output file will be considerably larger than the original file. To create a truly compressed file requires knowledge of how values are stored in memory and written to a file and knowledge of the use of low-level bit manipulations.

3. As you build the tree, the important data for the interior nodes is the *weight*, while in the leaves the only important data is the *character*. It's easiest to make all values inserted into the tree to be objects with fields for weight and character and use whichever is appropriate. Even better is to use two different object types. In the initial list of trees each tree would consist of a single node with both a weight and a character.

4. You should implement `writeIt` for the new object types so that it will be easy to write out the Huffman trees.

5. A more sophisticated version of this, which is appropriate for long, unusual files, is to scan the file to be compressed, determining the actual frequency of the characters, and then make a Huffman code tailored to that file. Then, before the file is sent using this encoding, the code itself (or equivalently the frequency distribution used to build it) is sent in the clear (unencoded). For a file that is long and contains character distributions significantly different from English prose, this can represent a large savings.

(Thanks to David Wall, of Digital Equipment Corporation, for this assignment.)

6. Simulation of a Simple Computer System

A simple computer system consists of a processor capable of processing one job at a time and its associated peripherals. However, a processor can be made to share, or multiplex, its time among the various jobs so that when a process requests input or output (I/O), the processor can execute another process while waiting for the I/O request to finish. I/O is much slower than the processing; if the processor simply waited without processing another job, much time would be wasted and system throughput would be reduced to the speed of the slowest device. Thus a processor contains a job queue that holds jobs ready to be executed but not currently being executed.

We want a simulator of such a system so as to get statistics on the time required to complete a job or a certain mix of jobs. The simulated processor will provide two services to the jobs, `execute` and `processIO`. While a job is being executed the system advances a clock. Each job is given by the system a certain amount of time, and when the job currently being executed exceeds its allotted time, it is temporarily halted and placed on the job queue. It is resumed when it reaches the head of the queue. A job is also halted and placed on the queue when it requests I/O by executing `processIO`. The processor always knows which job is current, and when it puts a job on the queue it extracts a new current job from the queue. The processor is also responsible for placing new jobs on the queue when the time comes for them to be executed.

Each job has a job number, a start time, and an expected time require-ment, the average time the job would take to execute if it were not interupted for I/O and had exclusive use of the processor. The time needed by a job when it runs always exceeds this time requirement, because delays are inevitable if the job does any I/O and very likely even if not. Another parameter of the job is the probability that it will do I/O in a fixed time interval, or *clock tick*. The job must provide the processor with its job number and parameters. It should also permit a processor to reduce its time requirement toward zero so that as the clock runs the processor will know when the job is finished.

A job's access to the processor can be thought of as execution of the following program.

```
while (timeRequirement > 0) {
    processor -> execute ();
    if (randomNumber () < I_OProbability)
        processor -> processIO;
};
```

The function `randomNumber` is assumed to return a random real number in the range of zero to one. Random integers can be obtained from the system function `rand` in `<stdlib.h>`. Suitable processing transforms them into the required `float` values.

The processor can be assumed to execute the following pseudocode pro-gram.

```
do {
    advanceClock;
    if (new_job_waiting) enter_it_into_queue;
    if (no_current_job) dequeue_a_current_job;
    if (current_job_finished) terminate_it; continue;
    if (current_job_requesting_IO) queue_it; continue;
    advance_time_of_current_job;

} while (any_jobs_in_queue);
```

When a job is terminated, its statistics can be printed. The `continue` statement in C++ restarts the loop without execution of the statements that follow it.

The following refinement of the above makes the I/O processing more realistic. When an I/O request is submitted, the time required for comple-tion of the request is also submitted. Then, when the processor removes a job from the queue, it can check whether that job's previous I/O request is finished, and if it is not, it can reinsert the job on the queue and process another. You must be careful here that you don't create an infinite loop by checking without advancing the clock.

Here are some sample test data:

Job Number	Execution Time	IO Prob.	Entry Time
1	5	.6	1
2	1	.2	2
3	10	.1	4
4	4	.4	5
5	3	.2	7
6	8	.3	9
7	2	.5	10
8	9	.9	12
9	6	.2	13
10	5	.4	15

THE
IMPLEMENTATIONS

## CHAPTER 6

LISTS AND LINEAR STRUCTURES

On paine of death, no person be so bold as to touch the listes, Except the Marshall.
Shakespeare, *Richard II*

Now she is in the very Lists of love, Her champion mounted for the hot encounter.
Shakespeare, *Venus & Adonis*

In this and the next few chapters, some of the collection classes are going to be examined in detail. In each case the header files from the library will be presented, which contain the interfaces shown in the earlier chapters and the protected parts of the implementation. Then possible implementations of most of the major methods will be discussed. Since this is the first of the chapters discussing implementations, some methods, such as sizeOf and writeIt, that are implemented in every class will also be discussed.

First, our focus will be on classes that have a linear structure. Such structures have a fundamental notion of "next" and "previous," as if the data were lined up for inspection. The general idea is that of a finite sequence of data having an associated notion of position. There are many different kinds of linear structures. A one-dimensional array is an example of a linear structure, but it has certain additional properties that distinguish it. In particular, it is of fixed finite size and it is stored densely in memory so that arbitrary positions (subscripts) in the structure can be accessed very quickly. Other linear structures have other properties. For example, a list is a linear structure of finite, but not fixed, size in which new elements can be inserted between others, making, for example, the fifth position into the sixth. Other linear structures such as stacks and queues are like lists except that the positions at which one can insert new items are restricted. In contrast, trees, graphs, and sets are nonlinear storage structures. Linear collections are a special case of a more general kind called ordered collections. Ordered collections have a notion of position. For lists this is determined by our ideas of the first and next in a list. Trees are ordered collections with a different type of ordering. By way of contrast, a set is a collection, but it is not ordered.

Because the classes which we shall examine are all subclasses of `SCollection`, they hold references to objects of some kind: they are used for storage. Therefore, we need to be able to insert into and remove from them. We also want to be able to access the elements stored, perhaps without removing them. This is called retrieval. We may want to change or modify the data stored at some location in the structure. It is also sometimes necessary to put the data into some particular order to make retrieval more efficient. This is called sorting.

A Partial Taxonomy of Linear Structures

Array: Arrays have a fixed, finite size. As a consequence of the fixed size, there is no insertion or removal; an element can only be modified. They use dense storage, meaning that the elements of the array make efficient use of the memory and can be addressed and retrieved quickly.

Sorted Array: These have all of the properties of arrays, and, additionally, the order of the elements is determined by their values. This order depends on the nature of the elements and the needs of the application. For example, if the elements are magnitudes, the order can be given by the notion of *less*.

List: Lists are of finite size but can grow or shrink. The storage is linked, so an element is accessed only from the beginning of the list or from another element. Elements can be inserted or removed anywhere in the list.

Sorted List: A sorted list has all of the properties of a list and a well-determined ordering of its elements.

Sequence: Sequences are of finite size and usually use dense storage. They permit insertion only at the rear, or end, of the sequence, which is normally called `append`. They permit no removals except `removeAll`. The standard type `file` of Standard Pascal is generally implemented as a sequence.

Stack: Stacks are of finite size and can grow and shrink. They permit insert or removal at only the front. The front is called the top.

Queue: Queues are of finite size and can grow and shrink. Insertion can occur only at the rear and removal only at the front.

The difference between dense storage and linked storage is that dense storage allows global, external computation of the position and location of any element. Generally speaking, this makes it fast (hence cheap) to use the structure for a random access storage mechanism: if data is to be accessed nonsequentially, that is, if the position of each required item bears no necessary relationship to the last one used, a dense structure is very helpful. Each position in linked storage maintains a reference to (at least) one other position. These references, or links, are the only way to access any given position, and there may be no way to access a given item other than to start at the first item and examine each item in turn, following the link at each position until the desired item is found. Thus it is cheap to process the structure using an order consistent with the links and expensive otherwise. We shall see later that tree-based storage (Chapters 9 and 10) and hashing techniques (Chapters 11 and 12) provide mechanisms intermediate in cost between dense storage and linked linear storage.

6.1   LINKED ACCESS

For the rest of this chapter we shall examine linked lists and some other classes that can be derived from them. Lists will serve two functions for us. The first is as a structure in its own right, because lists of objects are very useful in many programming contexts. The second function is to help us implement other things that are not list-like. For example, sets can be implemented using lists, even though sets do not have a sequential structure and have restrictions that lists themselves do not have (like the fact that an item can appear in a set only once, whereas an item in a list can appear several times).

Lists are collections; as such, their use is to hold references to objects of any type. The user of a list should merely need to declare a variable to be a list, create and initialize a particular list, and then utilize the methods of lists, such as insertion and removal. The user should not need to be concerned with the type of objects inserted. We shall treat a list as a sequence of nodes such that each has a reference to an object that the user has inserted into the list. The external picture that the user has is that a list is a sequence of objects, as in Fig. 6.1.

The internal picture is more complex. A node will also keep a reference to the node that refers to the next object in the list. Using arrows to indicate references to objects, we shall implement the above list as shown in Fig. 6.2. The special zed node will be discussed shortly.

Each node will have a reference to the object inserted and a reference to some following node. Lists will be terminated by the special node we have named zed, which will have special properties, which are described later. It is frequently useful and not difficult to think of the objects in the

FIGURE 6.1

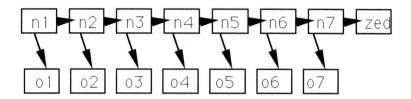

FIGURE 6.2

above picture as if they were contained within the nodes. This was how we pictured them in Chapter 4.

Since we are dealing with collections, we need to create iterators. A list iterator operating on the above list would be able to yield each of the objects o1,...,o7 in the list so that the client could use each to perform some task. Because the list is treated as a sequential structure, an iterator should respect the structure and return the objects in the order of the list.

Insertions into and removals from lists must be possible at any point in the list, for example, between the objects at positions 5 and 6. For this reason we find it useful to create an abstraction corresponding to position within a list, allowing us to make insertions in some sense at a position and to manipulate positions, primarily by moving or changing them.

To summarize the above, we need to create a compilation unit for the list abstract date type and to declare within it the four classes that correspond to our four ideas. The classes will be SListNode, SList, SListPosition, and SListIterator. We shall also need a generator function for lists. Nodes, positions, and iterators are constructed by methods of the list class. Although we shall use a slightly more complex form, an outline of this C++ header file could be as follows.

```
#ifndef __List__
#define __List__

#include "PCollect.h"
#include "PMagnitu.h"

// REQUIREMENTS For Use
//     initLists ();

class SList;
class SListIterator;
class SListPosition;
class SListNode;
typedef SList             *PList;
typedef SListIterator     *PListIterator;
typedef SListPosition     *PListPosition;
typedef SListNode         *PListNode;

enum WhereFound {IsHere, IsNext, NotFound};
```

```
PList newList (void);

class SListNode: public SObject {
    public:
        SListNode (PObject);
    ⋮
}; // End list node class.

class SList: public SCollection {
    public:
        SList (void);
    ⋮
};

class SListPosition: public SPosition {
    public:
        SListPosition (PList L);
    ⋮
};// End SListPosition.

class SListIterator: public SIterator {
    public:
        SListIterator (PList L);
    ⋮
};

void initLists (void);
#endif
```

In our more complex form the declaration of SListNode is nested inside
the declaration of SList, indicating that the idea of a list node is subor-
dinate to the idea of a list. Besides doing other things, this will allow us to
treat the nodes out of which we build a list as being hidden entities, to be
used by the implementation only.

```
#ifndef __List__
#define __List__

#include "PCollect.h"
#include "PMagnitu.h"

// REQUIREMENTS For Use
//    initLists ();
```

```
class SList;
class SListIterator;
class SListPosition;

typedef SList                *PList;
typedef SListIterator        *PListIterator;
typedef SListPosition        *PListPosition;

enum WhereFound {IsHere, IsNext, NotFound};

PList newList (void);

class SList: public SCollection {

    public:

            SList (void);
        virtual                 ~SList (void);
        virtual char            member (classtype c);
        virtual PObject         first (void);
        virtual void            insert (PObject);
        virtual void            remove (PObject);
        virtual void            removeFirst (void);
        virtual PIterator       newIterator (void);
        virtual PListPosition   newPosition (void);
        virtual PObject         Clone (void);
        virtual char            empty (void);
        virtual char            element (PObject);
        virtual void            selectionSort (void);
        virtual PList           merge (PList);
        virtual int             length (void);
        virtual void            writeIt (void);
            // The next two methods test recursion
            // removal.  Code is in file ListWrit.cp.
        virtual void            RWriteIt (void);
        virtual void            RWriteReverse (void);

    protected:
        class SListNode;

    public:
        typedef SListNode *PListNode;

    protected:
        friend SListNode;
        friend SListPosition;
```

```
        PListNode fFirstNode;
        virtual int sizeOf (void);
        virtual PListNode newNode (PObject, PListNode);
        virtual PListNode lastNode (void);

    // Nested protected class SListNode.
    class SListNode: public SObject {
        public:
            SListNode (PObject);
            SListNode (PObject, SListNode*);
        virtual char        member (classtype c);
        virtual PObject      value (void);
        virtual void         writeIt (void);
        virtual PListNode    next (void);
        virtual void         setNext (PListNode);
        SListNode            *fNext;
        PObject              fValue;
        virtual int          sizeOf (void);

        friend SListPosition;
        friend SList;
        friend void initLists(void);

            // The following is used
            // by recursion removal.
        friend void doWrite (SList :: PListNode x);
        friend void doReverseWrite (SList :: PListNode x);

    }; // End list node class.
        friend void doWrite (SList :: PListNode x);
        friend void doReverseWrite (SList :: PListNode x);
        friend void initLists (void);

        protected:
            static PListNode zed;
    }; // End list class.

    class SListPosition: public SPosition {
        public:
            SListPosition (PList L);
        virtual char         member (classtype c);
        virtual void         next (void);
        virtual void         insertFirst (PObject);
        virtual void         insertAfter (PObject);
        virtual PObject      at (void);
        virtual void         atPut (PObject);
```

```
            virtual char          last (void);
            virtual char          afterLast (void);
            virtual void          toFirst ();
            virtual void          deleteFirst (void);
            virtual void          deleteNext (void);
            virtual PObject       atNext (void);
            virtual WhereFound    search(PObject);
            virtual void          moveTo (PListPosition);
            virtual void          exchangeValues
                                  (PListPosition);

        protected:

            SList :: PListNode fHere;
            virtual SList :: PListNode nodeAt (void);
            virtual int sizeOf (void);

        friend SListIterator;
    }; // End SListPosition.

    class SListIterator: public SIterator {
        public:
            SListIterator (PList L);
            virtual char          member (classtype c);
            virtual char          nextItem (PObject&);
            virtual void          reset (void);

            // For use by friends and their heirs only
            virtual char          nextNode (SList ::
                                      PListNode &);
            virtual PObject       Clone (void);

        protected:
            PListPosition      fPosition;
            virtual int        sizeOf (void);
    };

void initLists (void);
#endif
```

This header, PList.h, will define all we need in order to create and use lists of objects. It will also form the basis for the implementation of other classes, which access these classes by including this header and linking to its implementation file PList.cp. This unit corresponds to our list abstract data type, which is composed of the four data abstractions for nodes, lists, positions, and iterators.

Note the following things about this declaration. First, declarations can be nested within the various visibility classes (public, protected, and private) of a class declaration. Second, declarations of things other than classes can be nested including types and functions. Once we have nested the pointer type PListNode within SList, its full name becomes SList :: PListNode. The qualifier SList :: doesn't need to be used if we are inside the class SList, but otherwise it does. (See the note at the end of this chapter.) We have also declared a special list node **z e d** to be a *static* member of SList, meaning that there will be only a single such node, and that zed is not an instance variable of lists. It is simply a global variable to which all lists shall have access. It is protected so that only lists and their friends can see and manipulate it; it would be a disaster if it were modified inadvertently. We shall use it to terminate all lists. The purpose of the (friend) procedure initLists () is to create and initialize this node properly and thereby make all lists behave correctly. Also note that SListNode is nested inside the protected part of SList but that it has a completely public interface, including all of its instance variables. This will permit lists and heirs of list to see the details of list nodes but will prevent clients of the list class from manipulating the nodes directly. We use the visibility control of SList rather than that of SListNode to prevent access from outside this abstraction. Within it we shall have more flexibility.

6.2   PROPERTIES OF LIST NODES

The nodes of a list are, in a sense, just an implementation detail. The client will not need to deal with the nodes of a list, though some subclasses of SList may need to. For most uses client programs will best treat lists as if they were made up of data, not of nodes, in keeping with the model of Fig. 6.1. On the other hand, the list that contains the nodes must be able to manipulate the nodes of which it is composed and treat them somewhat physically, as in the model of Fig. 6.2. The following protocol, extracted from the above, is suitable for list nodes:

```
class SListNode;
typedef SListNode *PListNode;
class SListNode: public SObject {
    public:
            SListNode (PObject);
            SListNode (PObject /* value */,
                       SListNode* /* next */);
        virtual char        member (classtype c);
        virtual PObject     value (void);
        virtual void        writeIt (void);
        PListNode           fNext;
```

```
        PObject              fValue;
        virtual int          sizeOf (void);
        virtual PListNode     next (void);
        virtual void         setNext (PListNode);
     friend SListPosition;
     friend SList;
     friend void initLists (void);
};
```

There is no ordinary `newListNode` function defined for this class. Instead, the method `newNode` of `SList` will be used instead. The instance variables `fValue` and `fNext` hold references to the objects stored in the node and the next node, respectively. A very interesting feature of this class is that the `fNext` instance variable is a pointer to the same class as the class being defined. Such a data structure is called recursive, meaning that the structure is defined in terms of itself. Defining a class in this way has the important consequence that it often makes it easy to process this class using recursive methods, that is, methods that send messages having the same name as the methods themselves. This is discussed in some detail in the next chapter.

Recursive Data Structure

A structure that has a component that is of its own type. These are normally used for structures of expandable size. In C++ these need to be implemented using pointers.

The constructor `SListNode` sets `fValue` as part of node initialization. The method `writeIt` sends the `writeIt` message to the object stored in `fValue`. The methods `next` and `setNext` are used to retrieve and modify the value of field `fNext`. The other methods are standard methods that we implement in every class and are discussed below.

6.2.1 The Special Node zed

There are a number of ways to terminate lists, but termination is required. The field `fNext` of the last node in any list must have a definite value. It is not valid to leave it uninitialized, because then it would have no definite value and we could not test for the last node. There are at least three ways of assigning a value to the `fNext` field of the last node.

First, we could assign it to be NULL. This is a common solution, but we shall not use it, because if we have any variable, `fNext` in particular, whose type is `PListNode`, we would like to be able to make reference to its fields, `fValue` and `fNext`. We would also like to be able to utilize it in a message statement, such as fNext -> writeIt (). However, if the value of the variable is NULL, all of these are illegal, because NULL is not a list node. In fact, NULL is not an entity. Therefore, we would have to precede every occurrence of such references by a test as to whether the value is NULL.

The second solution is to make the last node in a list self-referential. This would be done by making the fNext instance variable of the last node refer to that same node. This will generally work, but it requires special code for inserting into an empty list and adding elements to the end of a list, and therefore it requires tests for an empty list and for the end of a list.

The third method, and the one we shall use, is to create a special, terminator node, that will be physically last in every list and will appear on empty lists. This node is self-referential, and its fNext field refers to the node itself. This node is named zed and is unique in our system: we shall create only one and be careful not to dispose of it. It is created as part of the unit initialization. List initialization inserts this node onto the newly created, empty list. We also don't want this variable to be used outside this abstraction or its name to be generally known to clients. Therefore, inside the SList class declaration we have said

```
static PListNode zed;
```

This declares but doesn't define it and gives it the full name SList :: zed. To define it, we must also say somewhere outside the class declaration

```
SList :: PListNode SList :: zed;
```

We also need to create and initialize this node. This is the purpose of the public procedure initLists ().

```
void initLists (void) {
   SList :: zed = new SList :: SListNode (NULL);
   failnull (SList :: zed);
   SList :: zed -> fNext = SList :: zed;
   SList :: zed -> fValue = NULL;
};
```

We must also guarantee that this procedure is called. For this reason we provide a special header file, initClass.h, that includes initialization segments for every class that needs such initialization. Every main program that uses any of these classes includes this header and then simply executes the procedure initClasses, as in

```
initClasses ();
```

FIGURE 6.3

NULL

The file `initClass.h` looks something like the following.

```
void initClasses (void) {

#ifdef __List__
initLists ();
#endif

#ifdef __Integer__
initIntegers ();
#endif

   .
   .
   .


};
```

In diagrams NULL will be indicated by the electrical grounding symbol shown in Fig. 6.3. The `zed` node, which refers to itself but whose `fValue` is NULL, is shown in Fig. 6.4.

It is important to realize that this means of list termination does not free us of the burden of testing for the end of the list. It simply permits somewhat more flexibility in the way we test and changes the failure mechanism to one more under the programmer's control.

6.2.2   Using Generator Methods and Functions

Given the existence of `zed`, we create a new node using the generator method `newNode (PObject, PListNode)`, of class `SList`, which returns a new initialized node to us. Generator functions exist for most concrete classes, and their code always follows the same pattern: construct the node, initializing it, check whether the initialization was successful, and then return the object. Occasionally a class has more than one generator function, and occasionally, as here, the generator function is a method of another class. If an object from the class can be initialized in more than one reasonable way, there will be several generator functions.

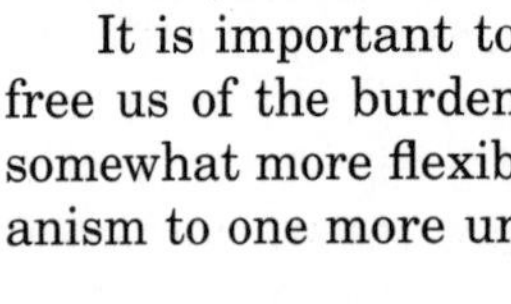

zed

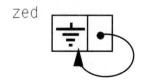

FIGURE 6.4

The list node class itself is internal to the list class, and a node is always within a particular list. Therefore, in order to create a node, we must use a method of lists; that is, we must send a message to an individual list. Also, clients of this unit do not create nodes directly. They are created automatically when we apply certain methods of SList and SListPosition.

```
SList :: PListNode SList :: newNode (PObject o,
                                            PListNode n) {
    SList :: PListNode result;

    if (n == NULL) n = SList :: zed;
    result = new SListNode (o, n);
    failnull (result);
    return result;
};
```

If initialization requires parameters, the generator generally has the same parameters, as is the case here. Generation functions differ in the type of the object returned, which is always an object in the class associated with the generator. They also differ in the type of the result local variable and in the constructor executed. Otherwise their form is the same for all classes, whether the generator is a method or an ordinary function. After calling newNode, we have a pointer to an object whose essence is shown in the oval in Fig. 6.5: its fValue refers to (points to) some object, of any kind whatever, and its fNext refers to another node, perhaps zed.

For the class SListNode, as for most, the constructor method that provides initialization must give appropriate values to the instance variables. Initialization of fValue uses the parameter of the generator, and fNext is set to the second parameter or to zed, in order to give it a definite value that can be tested in an if or while statement.

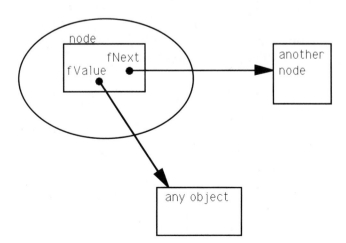

FIGURE 6.5

```
SList :: SListNode :: SListNode (PObject o
                                 /* value */,
                                 SListNode *n
                                 /* next */) {
    if (n != NULL)
        fNext = n;
    else
        fNext = SList :: zed;
    fValue = o;
};
```

List nodes have another constructor for use when we don't know what value fNext should be given. It sets fNext to be zed.

```
SList :: SListNode :: SListNode (PObject o) {
    fNext = SList :: zed; fValue = o;
};
```

The writeIt method of SListNode is very simple.

```
void SList :: SListNode :: writeIt (void) {
    if (fValue != NULL) fValue -> writeIt ();
};
```

The writeIt method was originally implemented in SObject, and is thus available for all objects. It will be reimplemented in every class that needs to provide a more specific version than the one inherited. Thus fValue -> writeIT () will do the right thing no matter what class fValue belongs to. The if statement prevents writeIt messages from being sent to NULL, which is not an object.

Finally, the methods member () and sizeOf () are needed in every class. The latter is needed because it provides a virtual object size function instead of the one built into C++, which is not virtual. We need this for the proper behavior of ShallowClone () in SObject. The code is always the same, except for the type of the argument sent to the built-in version of sizeof, which should always be the name of the class in which it is being defined.

```
int SList :: SListNode :: sizeOf (void) {return
    (sizeof (SList :: SListNode));};
```

The presence of this as a virtual method means that when the code in SObject :: ShallowClone () is executed, we get the proper size of the actual object, not the size of the variable by which the object is referred.

The function member allows us to test an object for its membership in a particular class and then take action depending on its type. We most often use it when we have put some object into a collection, such as a list. When we retrieve the object, we may not know what class it was from, especially when our collection holds references to many kinds of objects. Most frequently we will use member to verify that an object is in a class and then use a type cast to access the special features associated with that class, such as its methods. Again, the form of the implementation of member is always the same, except for the types. In PObject.h we defined the enumeration classtype to be a list of about 90 code names that represent all of the classes in this hierarchy. One of these names was listnode. When we ask whether a variable, foo, of type PObject represents a member of class SListNode, we do it by asking

```
foo -> member (listnode);
```

The code below will return TRUE if it is. Note that if we ask whether the object is in SObject with

```
foo -> member (object);
```

then we should also get TRUE, because every list node is an object. The second clause in the return statement ensures that member returns TRUE.

```
char SList :: SListNode :: member (classtype c) {
   return ((c == listnode) || SObject :: member (c));
};
```

In general, the code for member is to return a result formed as a disjunction, that is, a sequence of *or* clauses. The first clause is always a comparison of the parameter c with the code name of the class as defined in classtype. The others each execute the inherited member function of one of the direct ancestors of the class. Since SListNode inherits only from SObject, the only other clause is SObject :: member (c). This executes the member method that was inherited from SObject, rather than being a recursion on the SListNode member function itself. For comparison, the following is the corresponding method from class SList, which inherits from SCollection:

```
char SList :: member (classtype c) {
   return ((c == list) || SCollection :: member(c));
};
```

6.3   LISTS

The class SList corresponds to our abstract notion of a list as a whole. We insert data into the list and may remove it, and there is the idea that there exist items that come before or come after any given item in the list. In order to get a full picture of lists and their properties, we must also examine the

two related classes SListPosition and SListIterator. SList
needs the iterator class, since it is a collection. It needs the position class,
since it is an ordered collection, with order determined by the physical
position of the data within the list. This idea of an ordered collection is
slightly different from that of a sorted collection, in which the ordering has
something to do with the values of the included items rather than their
physical positions. The methods of SList are those that can be said to operate on a list as a whole, or to refer to well-defined positions in a list, such
as the head or the tail. We shall see that the methods of SListPosition
provide additional capabilities for lists.

The only instance variable of an object in SList is fFirstNode,
which represents the implementation of the list itself, represented as a
reference to an SListNode. That node, of course, refers to another node,
and so on until some node in the list refers to zed. Following is the class
declaration of SList with all nested type definitions removed so that we
can focus on the details of lists themselves.

```
class SList: public SCollection {
    public:
            SList (void);
        virtual                      ~SList (void);
        virtual char                 member (classtype c);
        virtual PObject              first (void);
        virtual void                 insert (PObject);
        virtual void                 remove (PObject);
        virtual void                 removeFirst (void);
        virtual PIterator            newIterator (void);
        virtual PListPosition        newPosition (void);
        virtual PObject              Clone (void);
        virtual char                 empty (void);
        virtual char                 element (PObject);
        virtual void                 selectionSort (void);
        virtual PList                merge (PList);
        virtual int                  length (void);
        virtual void                 writeIt (void);

    protected:
        PListNode                    fFirstNode;
        virtual int                  sizeOf (void);
        virtual PListNode            newNode (PObject,
                                         PListNode);

        virtual PListNode            lastNode (void);
    friend SListPosition;
    friend SListNode;
    public:
        static    PListNode zed;
};
```

We construct a new list with SList, which simply sets the value of fFirstNode to the special zed node. The generator function newList will use this constructor to create and return a list on which the other methods will work properly. After a list has been created and a number of insertions have been performed, we might picture it as the contents of the oval in Fig. 6.6. Its fFirstNode points to some list node, which itself points to another, until we reach zed. The nodes are drawn inside the oval, since conceptually they are part of the list, even though they are actually distinct objects. A client creating a list would deal only with the list and not with the nodes of which the list is composed.

Because SList implements the idea of a list as a whole rather than as composed of parts (which SListPosition does), our insertion and removal operations work only on the beginning of the list. Insertions and removals elsewhere will be handled by objects of type SListPosition. The method insertFirst inserts an object at the beginning of an existing list, including an empty list. The instance variable fFirstNode of our list refers to the first node. We need to create a new node and attach it to the list at the beginning. The new node can be created and initialized by the protected method newNode, discussed above. It is a protected method of SList because a node itself is private. Nodes should be created only by their lists; therefore, newNode should be called only from within a list.

Upon insertion of the new node, the current first node becomes the second node, or the successor (fNextNode) of the new first node. Since we are dealing with references, it is important that the two operations,

1. Make the old first node the successor of the newly created first node.
2. Make the new node the first node.

be performed in the order given. The reason for this is that the current first node, fFirstNode, is obtained *only* by means of the reference variable fFirstNode. If we change the value of this variable first, we will have lost all references to the current first node. In the following, passing

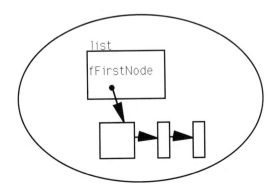

FIGURE 6.6

fFirstNode to the method newNode accomplishes the first task. The other statement handles the second.

```
void SList :: insert (PObject o) {
    PListNode aNode;

    aNode = newNode (o, fFirstNode);
    fFirstNode = aNode;
};
```

Note that the reference to the method newNode is the sending of a message. However, we are within a method of class SList, and this is a method of SList, so the receiver of the newNode message is the pointer this, which represents the object currently executing. The receiver is implicitly given by the context.

In general, pointer variables are very sensitive to the order in which operations are done on them. The basic rule for such variables is that you must guarantee that you always maintain at least one reference to each allocated object. Before you change the last reference, make certain that you create another. In the current context fFirstNode is our last (and only) reference to the node at the head of the list. In the last statement above, because fFirstNode is on the left-hand side of an assignment, it will change the reference. Therefore, just before the assignment we create another reference to the same object, by saving the reference as aNode -> fNext. Note that we have a reference to aNode and hence one to aNode -> fNext.

Reference Maintenance Rule

Before you change your last reference or pointer to an entity created with new, make certain that you create another reference or pointer to the entity.

Removal of the first item in a list is the reverse of the above. We must, however, guarantee that we never remove the zed node from our physical list. The auxiliary variable aNode and the first statement in the body are an application of the reference maintenance rule.

```
void SList :: removeFirst (void) {
    PListNode aNode;

    aNode = fFirstNode;
    fFirstNode = aNode -> fNext;
    if (aNode != zed)
        delete aNode;
};
```

The second statement removes the first node (and its value) from the list, and the last disposes of the node. Note that we dispose of the node with `delete`, but we do not dispose of the value that the node refers to. The idea in the user's mind when using this method is not that the object is destroyed but that it is merely no longer in the list. The user of our list somehow created this object and will expect its continued existence. In fact, it could be in several lists simultaneously. This is the beauty of using reference variables. The node, on the other hand, was not created directly by the user, and it should therefore be destroyed invisibly (to the user) by some method of this class. This is just an application of the abstraction principle.

Similarly, the destructor ~SList, which is used to dispose of a list entirely when it is no longer needed, must be certain to dispose of all of the nodes in the list but preserve its data. Again, the data are external and might be of any type, such as integers (`SInteger`) or other lists, or whatever. Destroying a list should mean only that they are no longer listed and not that they are destroyed. But the nodes are internal to the implementation of lists and so should be destroyed. One way to accomplish this is shown here. Refer again to Fig. 6.2. The nodes, n1..., are destroyed, but not the objects, o1....

```
SList :: ~SList (void) {
   PListNode next, item;

   item = fFirstNode;
   while (item != zed) {
      next = item -> fNext;
      delete (item);
      item = next;
   };
};
```

The `while` loop uses `delete`, which automatically calls the `SListNode` destructor and destroys the nodes. It finishes when the list is empty (`item == zed`). Note that before it calls `delete`, it obtains a reference to the `fNext` field of the node that is about to be deleted. Destruction of lists will be discussed again in Section 6.10.

The rest of the methods of `SList` are either trivial to implement (see the exercises at the end of the chapter) or depend on list positions and iterators. We shall return to them after discussing these other classes.

6.4   LIST POSITIONS

We treat a position in a list as an abstract idea. A list embodies the notion of a linear sequence of data. A position is a location in the sequence. It is not a datum contained in the list though there is a datum "at" a position.

It is not a node; it is not an integer. It is simply a position. A position may be the first position (an ordinal number, of course), or it may be the next or the previous position to a given position. Since a list is a finite sequence, we should also be able to refer to the last position. We shall also need to refer to the position of a certain datum, and shall sometimes want to refer to a position ordinally, such as in the fifth position.

A position is always a position in a particular list. When a position is created, it is (forever) associated with this list. Initialization of a list position automatically sets its position to the first item in the list. From a given position we can insert data into or retrieve it from the list and make whatever other modifications can be thought of as being local to some place in the list. By contrast, `SList` implements behaviors of the list as a whole, and `SListIterator` implements individual access to the components of a list.

An object of `SListPosition` is simply a way of saying "here" in a list. The implementation is a pair of instance variables: `fCollection` is inherited from the parent class, `SPosition`, and refers to the list of which this is a position, and `fHere` is a reference to a particular node in that list. Since `fHere` might be the zed node, we will need to take special precautions when manipulating a list through its positions, in order to be certain that we never modify or destroy `zed`.

```
enum WhereFound {IsHere, IsNext, NotFound};

class SListPosition: public SPosition {
    public:
            SListPosition (PList L);
        virtual char        member (classtype c);
        virtual void        next (void);
        virtual void        insertFirst (PObject);
        virtual void        insertAfter (PObject);
        virtual PObject     at (void);
        virtual void        atPut (PObject);
        virtual char        last (void);
        virtual char        afterLast (void);
        virtual void        toFirst ();
        virtual void        deleteFirst (void);
        virtual void        deleteNext (void);
        virtual PObject     atNext (void);
        virtual WhereFound  search (PObject);
        virtual void        moveTo (PListPosition);
        virtual void        exchangeValues
                            (PListPosition);

    protected:
        SList :: PListNode fHere;
        virtual SList :: PListNode nodeAt (void);
```

```
        virtual int sizeOf (void);
    friend SListIterator;
} ;
```

Constructing a list position requires setting its two instance variables. The list of which it is to be a position is provided as a parameter. The position is always set to the beginning. Of course, the list's first node might be the zed node.

```
SListPosition :: SListPosition (PList L):
    SPosition (L) {fHere = L -> fFirstNode;};
```

Note the special syntax for executing the required constructor of the parent class. After the parameters but before the statement body we give a constructor, SPosition, and its own required parameter, a collection, here a list. Refer to the constructor of SPosition in PCollect.h to see what is required for it:

```
SPosition (PCollection c) {fCollection = (c);};
```

Constructors in classes that are subclasses of other classes that themselves have constructors with parameters must always specify one of the parent class constructors in this way. Calling a constructor or separately initializing instance variables from within the constructor body is not sufficient, because the construction itself depends on having access to the parameter values.

The ordinary generator function, newListPosition, is not present, but the newPosition method of SList serves the same purpose. Note that the only proper way to get a position is to have a list already and ask that list for a new position within itself. This emphasizes the tight binding between positions and their lists. After executing the generator method and using a list position for a while, we can picture the list position as the contents of the oval in Fig. 6.7. Its fHere instance variable references a

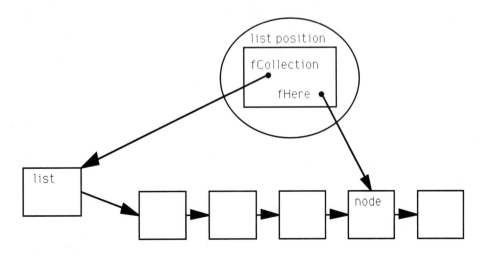

FIGURE 6.7

node in the same list that is referenced by the inherited `fCollection` variable. Upon creation `fHere` always references the first node of the list `fCollection`.

6.4.1   Checking and Moving Positions in a List

Sometimes we need to know whether a list position refers to the beginning or end of a list. The class `SListPosition` provides two Boolean functions (**predicates**) for this, `first` and `last`. When these are sent to a list position, they return TRUE or FALSE depending on whether the current position is or is not the corresponding position. They will both return TRUE if the list is empty. Note that `last` returns TRUE both when the position is at the last node of the list and when we have somehow moved past this node to the `zed` node. The function `first` is left as an exercise, and `last` is shown below:

```
char SListPosition :: last(void) {
   return (fHere -> fNext == SList :: zed);
};
```

There is another method, `afterLast`, that returns TRUE only if the position references the `zed` node. Recall that `zed` is not known to clients, so we need an equivalent way to check for its location as the target of a position.

```
char SListPosition :: afterLast (void) {
   return (fHere == SList :: zed);
};
```

`SListPosition` also provides four methods for changing the current position. Sending `toFirst` to a list-position object makes it refer to the first position in its list; `next` makes a list position object move down one position in the list unless it is already the last position; `prev` causes backward movement; and `toLast` causes a list-position object to refer to the last position in a list. They must be carefully programmed so that they accord with our idea of a list and the internal nature of the `zed` node. In some situations these methods should do nothing at all. Because its declaration was in PCollection, `toFirst` must typecast the `fCollection` instance variable as it actually refers to an `SList`. We need to extract information about the `fFirstNode` of this list. We also need `SListPosition` to be a friend of `SList` so that the reference to an instance variable of a list is legal from a list position.

```
void SListPosition :: toFirst () {
   fHere = PList (fCollection) -> fFirstNode;
};
```

```
void SListPosition :: next (void) {fHere = fHere ->
                                    fNext;};
```

We leave the others as exercises.

We sometimes need to use more than one position at a time or set a position variable to refer to the same position as another. Assuming that both positions have been initialized to refer to the same list, we can send moveTo to the position we want altered, using the other position as a parameter. Note carefully that we are looking into the physical representation of the parameter and creating an alias of its fHere instance variable. This is possible only because C++ is somewhat loose about references to objects of the same type. Note also that we are not changing this variable but only reading it. We have thus respected its autonomy if not its privacy.

```
void SListPosition :: moveTo (PListPosition p) {
   fHere = p -> fHere;
};
```

The method exchangeValues is somewhat similar. It is sent to one position, with another position as parameter. The data at the two positions are exchanged, but the nodes and positions are left unchanged. This is used in sorting and otherwise rearranging data in a list. Here we are a bit more careful about being object-oriented and only operate on the parameter using its public methods at and atPut, which are discussed below.

```
void SListPosition :: exchangeValues
                      (PListPosition p) {
   PObject o;

   o = at ();
   atPut (p -> at ());
   p -> atPut (o);
};
```

6.4.2 Getting and Modifying Data in a Given Position

All collections for which positions are meaningful should implement two methods in their position class for the purposes of retrieving or changing the data at a given position. Referring to them by their standard names, at retrieves data, and atPut puts data into a given position. The method at is a function and returns the data as the function result. The method atPut is a procedure that passes the data to be inserted as a parameter. The latter method should perform no operation if the position is not legal, so, in the case of list positions, we do not attempt to insert data into the zed node, which was initialized to contain a NULL reference in place of its data.

```
PObject SListPosition :: at (void) {
    return(fHere -> value());
};

void SListPosition :: atPut (PObject o) {
    if (fHere != SList :: zed) fHere -> fValue = o;
};
```

6.4.3 Searching in a List for a Given Datum

Suppose we have a datum that might be in some list. We would like to set a position so that we can manipulate the item or the list. Searching for items in collections of all kinds is a general problem, but with lists the solution is natural: to search for a datum you must set some list position so that it refers to it if found. One problem with this general idea is that we don't know for certain how the user will manipulate the data item if it is found or what the user will want to do if it is not found. Another problem is that the item may appear in the list (or general collection) more than once. Therefore, our solution must be general enough to cover the possible needs and must return sufficient information so that the user can take appropriate action in the various possible cases.

Normally a search starts with a position that references the beginning of a list. However, if an item can occur several times in a list, the user should not have to start at the beginning, but rather be able to continue a successful search after dealing with a found item. Since the user may want to insert the data item into the list if it can't be found, the position should be left in such a state that the insertion is easy. This means leaving it so that the insertAfter method may be used. Finally, since the user may search for an item intending to remove it, the position should be left pointing to the node just before the node that contains the data item, if possible. This isn't always possible, however, since we may find it in the very first position.

For the reasons discussed above, we treat our search method as a function. We pass it to some position with the object searched for as a parameter. The position then moves down the list from its current position attempting to set itself at the node previous to the one containing the data. The method returns a value telling the caller what the outcome of the search is. There are three possible values for this. If the object is found at the original position, search returns IsHere, a value of type WhereFound that we use for just this purpose. If the object is not at or after the starting position, search returns NotFound. Otherwise, the position refers to the node just before the one containing the data, and search returns IsNext. If the list is empty or the item searched for is NULL, search returns NotFound.

```
WhereFound SListPosition :: search (PObject o) {
    WhereFound result;

    result = NotFound;
    if (! fCollection -> empty () && o != NULL) {
```

```
            if (fHere -> value () == o) {
               result = IsHere;
            }
            else {
               while ((result == NotFound) && (! last ())) {
                  if (fHere -> fNext -> value () == o)
                     result = IsNext;
                  else
                     next ();
               };
               if (fHere -> value () == o)
                  {result = IsHere;};
            };
         };
      return result;
   };
```

6.4.4 Inserting New Data into a List and Removing Data from a List

The normal mode of inserting a new value into a list is either to insert it at the head of the list or to insert it between two existing values. Insertion at the end of the list can be thought of (and is implemented as) a special case of insertion between two values. The standard list operation insert will handle the first case, but a method should be included equivalent to it in the list position class. It can be called insertFirst and be implemented by sending the insert message to its own fCollection. If insertFirst is implemented this way, the position that receives the insertFirst message is not changed, though it might be desirable for this position to reset itself to the head of the list, which is the location that it just caused to be inserted.

```
void SListPosition :: insertFirst (PObject o) {
   fCollection -> insert (o);
   fHere = PList (fCollection) -> fFirstNode;
};
```

Insertion into a list at a location other than the beginning takes a bit more work. To insert a new value between two existing values, we must first set some position to the first of these two existing values. This is represented, of course, by using a reference to a particular node in the list. Then this position is sent the message insertAfter. This method first creates the new node with the required value and then makes the fNext field of the new node refer to the node that is to follow it, which is just fHere -> fNext, the fNext field of the node of the current position. Finally, the node at the current position is updated to refer to the new node as its own fNext field. These steps must be carried out in this order, or the list structure itself will be destroyed. The transitions are shown in Fig. 6.8

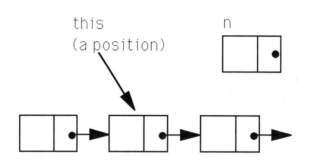

After creating the new node

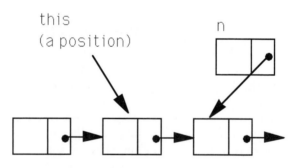

After setting fNext of the new node

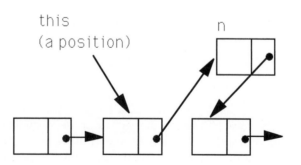

FIGURE 6.8   After setting fNext of the current node

```
void SListPosition :: insertAfter (PObject o) {
    SList :: PListNode aNode;
```

```
    if (fHere != SList :: zed) {
       aNode = PList (fCollection) -> newNode
                (o, fHere -> fNext);
       fHere -> fNext = aNode;
    };
};
```

Removal of a node within the list requires that we set some position so that it refers to the node just before the node to be deleted. Of course, this prevents us from deleting the first item in this way, but deleteFirst does that. The usual way to establish this position is to begin at the beginning of the list and walk down the list using next within a while loop, checking for some condition that indicates the node to be removed. For example, if we wanted to delete the first item in the list equal to the object someObject, we would say

```
aPosition= aList -> newPosition ();
while (! (aPosition -> atNext ()) ->
      equal (someObject))
   aPosition -> next ();
```

Of course, this requires that we know that someObject is in the list and that it is not first. To be more general, the above code must be more complicated. In particular, an if statement should be used to check whether the item is first. The situation in which the object may not appear in the list is best handled by using an auxiliary Boolean variable, found. (We again assume a special check for the first location.)

```
aPosition = aList -> newPosition ();
found = (aPosition -> at ()) -> equal (someObject);
   // Is it the first item?
while (! aPosition -> isLast () && ! found )
   if ((aPosition -> atNext ()) -> equal (someObject))
      found = TRUE;
   else
      aPosition -> next ();
```

At this point we can check found to determine whether the object is in the list or not.

Once we have established the location and checked that it isn't the first, we use deleteNext to remove the item from the list. It is important that we also delete the node that contains the item but that we not delete the item. Recall that list operations created the node but did not create the data item. Also, we must never try to free the zed node, so we provide a special check for this.

```
void SListPosition :: deleteNext (void) {
    SList :: PListNode n;

    n = fHere -> fNext;
    fHere -> fNext = n -> fNext;
    if (n != SList :: zed)
        delete (n);
}
```

Note that the code slightly breaks one key idea of pure object-oriented programming. The reference fHere -> fNext is one object, this, looking at an instance variable of another object. The reference fHere is a reference to another object (a list node). Thus fHere -> fNext is one of that object's instance variables. Furthermore, to refer to its fNext field is to treat the object as if it were transparent. One reason for the style convention we use of starting all instance variable names with the lower case letter *f* is to make such transgressions obvious in our code. See Exercise 6.10. Many object-oriented languages (for example, Smalltalk) do not permit this style of programming. They require that we provide functions in each class that return references to instance variables that must be seen by other objects. This provides an important measure of insulation between classes, making it possible to change the implementation details of one class (its instance variables) without affecting the behavior of another. However, in C++, using friends and following our programming style, we have chosen to create and implement all of these classes (SList, SListPosition, SListIterator, and SListNode) together by including them in one compilation unit. Classes that must be implemented together are called **friend classes**. A change in one might naturally imply a change in another. Therefore we permit such impure code, but we are careful to limit it. If we are too free about letting one object access the details of another, we cause problems for ourselves in large projects. Situations can easily arise where a seemingly simple change in the implementation of some class requires very extensive changes in the implementations of many others. Additionally, it

---

Friend Class

A class that is permitted to see the protected and private features of the class granting the friendship. Generally this is used only for classes that are defined together and that must be implemented together. Objects in such classes can be transparent to one another. A friend can see and even modify the instance variables of the class granting friendship.

might be difficult even to find all of the points that need changing, leading to software failure. With only slight exaggeration we may say that a synonym for friend classes is "dangerous classes." They must be used sparingly and carefully.

Several examples of the use of positions will be seen in the next two sections. The merge and selectionSort methods discussed in Sections 6.7 and 6.8 are especially helpful.

6.5   LIST ITERATORS

Like all iterator classes, SListIterator defines objects associated with a specific collection, here a list, that can generate or yield the elements of the collection in an order specific to the collection so that an operation can be performed on each element. In the case of a list iterator, the order is the same as the list order, from first to last. The public interface of list iterators is standard, except that we shall also provide a special nextNode method so that implementations can work directly on the nodes. It returns nodes rather than the data items in the list. The only instance variable that we need to add to the ones inherited is a position so that we can remember the item that is to be returned next. Subsequent calls to the method SListIterator :: nextItem return the item at this location and then move it to the next location. Recall that SListIterator inherits instance variables fCollection and fDone.

```
class SListIterator: public SIterator {
  public:
      SListIterator (PList L);
    virtual char      member (classtype c);
    virtual char      nextItem (PObject&);
    virtual void      reset (void);

      // For use by friends and their heirs only.
    virtual char      nextNode (SList :: PListNode&);
    virtual PObject   Clone (void);

  protected:
    PListPosition    fPosition;
    virtual int      sizeOf (void);
};
```

A list iterator is created by sending the message newIterator to a list object. This method is discussed in the next section. It constructs a list iterator using the following constructor method. This is a standard template for iterator initialization: construct the parent iterator class and then initialize the instance variables of this iterator class. The reference

`SIterator (L)` in the following guarantees that the iterator is associated with the proper collection and that it is marked as not being done or finished. This method was discussed in Chapter 3 when collections were discussed. It initializes `fCollection` and `fDone`.

```
SListIterator :: SListIterator (PList L):
                SIterator (L) {
  fPosition = (PListPosition) L -> newPosition ();
};
```

Part way through an iteration we might picture a list iterator as the contents of the oval in Fig. 6.9. Note that the position object is referred to by the variable `fPosition`.

A list Iterator works by maintaining information internally about the state of an iteration: which elements of the list have been returned already and which need to be returned still. All that is needed is a reference to the next node to be returned, since the list iterator produces items in the order of the list itself. Iterators are used by including calls to `nextItem` as the test expression in a `while` loop. This method returns a Boolean value as its function return value, which causes an exit from the loop if everything in the collection has already been generated. If more remains to be generated, the method returns the next value as the value of its reference parameter. The method must first test whether its iterator has already finished, so we immediately look at `fDone` and set the function result accordingly.

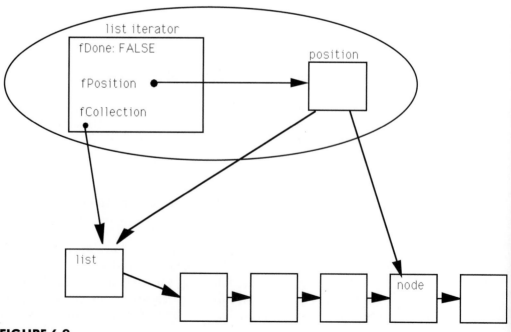

FIGURE 6.9

Otherwise we must determine the next object and return it. For lists we simply walk along the list using the position, fPosition, maintained by the iterator. Note that the object this (a list iterator) has its own life-time and the variable fPosition is stored in the iterator itself, rather than being local to some procedure. Therefore, the value of fPosition is maintained across several calls of the nextItem method.

Keep in mind that when nextItem is called for the first time, we have not yet yielded any items from the list, but the instance variable fPosition has been initialized with respect to the list and so refers to the first item in the list. Therefore our method of yielding items (assuming we have checked fDone to be sure that something will be yielded) will be the following: return the item at the current position and then attempt to move fPosition to the next location, setting fDone to TRUE if it is not possible. Generally speaking, the implementation of iterators is easiest if they maintain enough state information so that between calls of nextItem they represent the location of the next item to be returned rather than that of the one most recently returned. Some iterator classes are exceptions, but list iterators follow the preferred plan. This leads to the following imple-mentation.

```
char    SListIterator :: nextItem (PObject &o) {
char    result;

result = !fDone;
if (result) {
   o = fPosition -> at ();
   if (fPosition -> last ()) {
      fDone = TRUE;
   }
   else {
      fPosition -> next ();
   }
};
return (result);
};
```

The special iteration method nextNode is very similar to nextItem. It has the same structure but uses nodeAt rather than at to obtain a reference to return. Resetting an iterator to the beginning so that it can be reused is also quite standard. We must set the instance variables to the state they were in just after initialization.

```
void SListIterator :: reset (void) {
   fPosition -> toFirst ();
   fDone = fCollection -> empty ();
};
```

We shall see an example of the use of list iterators in the next section when we consider the `Clone` method of lists.

The method `Short` is inherited from `SIterator`. It exits a loop being driven by an iterator when we decide that its purpose has been served and that further iteration would be fruitless. It is often used to short-circuit a search after the item sought has been found. We show it here for completeness.

```
void SIterator :: Short (void) {
    fDone = TRUE;
};
```

6.6   MORE ON LISTS: METHODS THAT USE POSITIONS AND ITERATORS

We can treat a list as a variable-length array if we are willing to ignore the time inefficiency of searching for an item by ordinal position. The method `atLoc` illustrates the idea. It retrieves an item based on its ordinal position in the list. Interestingly, it uses a list position to find the ordinal position. Note that it returns NULL if there is no corresponding position in the list. It uses a simple `for` loop to walk the list using a position and repeatedly sending the message `next`. Note that our implementation of `next` makes this safe, though slow, if the parameter n is larger than the length of the list. The details are left to be done in Exercise 6.14.

The method `element` tells us whether its parameter is an element of the list. It uses an iterator to search for the required object and shorts the iterator if it finds it.

```
char SList :: element (PObject o) {
    char result;
    PListIterator IT;
    PObject item;

    result = FALSE;
    IT = newIterator ()
    while (IT -> nextItem (item))
    if (item -> equal (o)) {
        result = TRUE;
        IT -> Short ();
    };
    delete IT;
    return result;
};
```

We use a `PListIterator` here, since `nextItem` is a virtual method. Therefore, if another class is derived from `SList`, and implements its own

newIterator method, this code will work correctly, and the iterator referred to by IT will belong to a subclass of the one we are currently building.
One of the major problems in C++ when we don't use virtual methods or
when we use static objects that can't take advantage of virtual methods is
that we have to predict that we will never want this code interpreted in a
wider context. Often we are wrong. It would be a mistake of design to use
a static object here for IT (i.e., using class SListIterator rather than
a pointer). Most of the design changes I had to make to this library as the
book was being developed were forced on me because I had made the code
too restrictive, often by using static objects instead of dynamic ones. The
only advantage of static objects is that they are more efficient. However, efficiency only matters when you need it, and you seldom know that you need
it until you are fairly far along in development and can get a feel for what
the performance is and can determine where the program is wasting time
or space and thereby degrading performance. In general, it is advantageous
to seek code as flexible as possible, not as efficient as possible, during the
design process.

The method remove is complex because its argument is the item to be
removed from the list and might appear several times in the list or not be
in the list. The following implementation searches for the first occurrence of
the item in the list, using a technique called *sequential search*, and removes
this item and destroys its node if it is found. This method is most easily
implemented using a list position to walk the list searching for a match
with the parameter. We first test for occurrence of the parameter at the
beginning of the list. Afterward we use the position to walk the list. Note
the compound condition in the while loop. It would not be valid without
the original test for the first location. When we exit the while loop we
don't know which condition caused exit, so we must test again whether the
item was found.

```
void SList :: remove (PObject o) {
   PListPosition p;

   p = newPosition ();
   if (p -> at () != NULL) {
      if (p -> at () -> equal (o))
         removeFirst ();
      else {
         while (!(p -> atNext () -> equal (o))
               && !(p -> last ()))
            p -> next ();
         if (p -> atNext () -> equal (o))
            p -> deleteNext ();
      };
   };
   delete (p);
};
```

Note that the delete operation is at the same nesting level as the call to newPosition that created the object p.

The newIterator method of SList is different from a generator only in that it is a method rather than an ordinary procedure. The advantage of this is that it emphasizes that an iterator works with only a single list and, therefore, is created by that list. The generator method needs no parameter even though the constructor that will be called does, because the list will send itself as the list over which to iterate.

```
PIterator SList :: newIterator (void) {
    PListIterator result;

    result = (new SListIterator (this));
    failnull (result);
    return result;
};
```

Cloning a list involves first creating a shallow clone, then creating clones of all of the nodes in the list, and finally making sure that these nodes refer to values identical to the values in the original list (this, actually). Note that the nodes are cloned, because these are what hold the list together, making it into a collection. The data is not cloned, because we want a new collection of the same things, not a new collection of new things that are like the old things. Having cloned a list, we can insert into one of the two clones and not the other. Once one of the lists is changed, they are no longer collections of the same items.

The easiest way to access all of the elements of the original list is to use an iterator. The associated while loop is used to insert the items into the new list. We also utilize a list position, which walks the new list so that insertAfter can insert the items in the same order as the original list. This shows the classic use of iterators to drive a while loop.

```
PObject SList :: Clone (void) {
    PList result;
    PListPosition p;
    PIterator IT;
    PObject anItem;

    result = PList (ShallowClone ());
    result -> fFirstNode = zed;
    IT = newIterator ();
    p = result -> newPosition ();
    while (IT -> nextItem (anItem)) {
        if(p -> afterLast ()) {
            p -> insertFirst (anItem);
        }
```

```
            else {
                p -> insertAfter (anItem);
                p -> next ();
            }
        }
        delete p;
        delete IT;
        return (result);
    };
```

6.7   SORTING LISTS

The final two methods we shall consider for lists require that all of the elements of the list be in some SMagnitude subclass. Sorting puts the items in a list in order depending on the size or magnitude of the items. SMagnitude items can be compared by their method less. Merging creates a single sorted list from the elements of two sorted lists. Our implementation of merge will use the list this as one of the inputs, so it merges another list and itself to produce the output list.

The idea of selection sort is to divide the list into two parts of which the first is sorted and the second unsorted. The first part also contains the smallest values in the entire list. Fig. 6.10a indicates that from index first to index p-1 the array is sorted and contains the smallest items in the entire array, and that from index p to index last the array is undetermined. It is assumed that the elements currently in the array are the same elements that were originally in the array before sorting started.

Initially all of the list is in the second, unsorted, part. We achieve this immediately when we create a position p, since a newly created list position references the beginning of its list.

```
void SList :: selectionSort (void) {
    PListPosition p;
    p = newPosition ();

// Move p to the right end and keep Fig. 6.10a true.
    delete p;
};
```

We now need to move position p down the list while ensuring that keeping Fig. 6.10a remains true for each step. If we can do so, p will reference the right end of the list and the sorted part will be all of the list, and we will have finished. If we can find the smallest value in the right part and move it to location p before we move p, we will have achieved our goal of keeping the picture true:

sorted smallest values	

FIGURE 6.10a   first   p   last

```
void SList :: selectionSort (void) {
    PListPosition p;
    p = newPosition ();

    while (!p -> last ()) {
        if (!p -> at() -> member (magnitude)) return;
            // Bail out if we find something not a
            // magnitude. Find the smallest value
            // in the right part & put it into
            // location p.
        p -> next();
    };
    delete p;
};
```

Starting at p, we scan the unsorted part for its smallest item, and when we find it, we move it to the end of the first sorted part. This makes the sorted part bigger and the unsorted part smaller. To do this scan, we use another PListPosition, q, and additional variables to hold our place. The local variable where tells us where we have found the smallest value yet on the current scan.

```
void SList :: selectionSort (void) {
    PListPosition p, q, where;
    PObject min;
    p = newPosition ();
    q = newPosition ();
    where = newPosition ();

    while (!p -> last ()) {
        if (!p -> at() -> member (magnitude)) return;
            // Bail out if we find something
            // not a magnitude.
        q -> moveTo (p);
        min = q -> at ();
        where -> moveTo (q);
        do { // Set "where" to the smallest value
             // in the right part.
```

```
        } while (!q -> last ());
        p -> exchangeValues (where);
        p -> next ();
    };

    delete p;
    delete q;
    delete where;
};
```

Eventually the unsorted part is empty and the entire list is the sorted part. Three positions keep track of the state of the algorithm. The position p represents the first location in the unsorted part, q is used to scan the unsorted part looking for the smallest value, and where is used to remember the location of the smallest yet found. See Fig. 6.10b.

The auxiliary variable min remembers the smallest magnitude seen on each scan. It is initialized with the value at location p. We can ensure that Fig. 6.10b is true initially by setting positions q and where to be the same as position p. Examining just this part, we have the following.

```
q -> moveTo (p);
min = q -> at ();
where -> moveTo (q);
do {
    q -> next ();
    val = q -> at ();
    if ((val) -> less (min)) {
        min = val;
        where -> moveTo (q);
    };
} while (!q -> last ());
```

Combining all of this, we get the final code for selectionSort.

```
void SList :: selectionSort (void) {
    PListPosition p, q, where;
    PObject min, val;
```

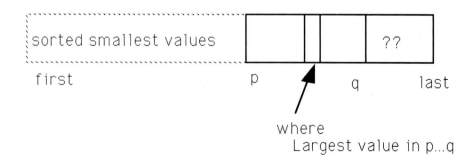

first   p   q   last

                                      where
                                   Largest value in p...q

FIGURE 6.10b

```
    p = newPosition ();
    q = newPosition ();
    where = newPosition ();
    while (!p -> last ()) {
        if (!p -> at () -> member (magnitude)) return;
        q -> moveTo (p);
        min = q -> at ();
        where -> moveTo (q);
        do {
            q -> next ();
            val = q -> at ();
            if ((val) -> less (min)) {
                min = val;
                where -> moveTo (q);
            };
        } while (!q -> last ());
        p -> exchangeValues (where);
        p -> next ();
    };
    delete p;
    delete q;
    delete where;
};
```

The outer while loop in the above code advances the sorted part. The inner do-while loop searches for the smallest value in the unsorted part, which starts at location p. Note that we use the list-position method exchangeValues, so we leave the nodes intact and in their original order. We move only the references to the items in the list. Also, we use the member function to make sure that the items in the list are indeed in SMagnitude.

6.7.1   Verifying that the Selection-Sort Program Is Correct

In the above discussion of selection sort, Fig. 6.10 was fundamental. Its two parts serve both as a description of how to proceed and as a key to the proof that the method does indeed sort its list. Figure 6.10a can be thought of as a Boolean statement, which can be either true or false for a list, that we would like to keep true. We would also like to advance p so that eventually the entire list is sorted. The Boolean statement the figure defines is called the loop invariant of the outer loop of the program we eventually developed. A loop invariant is a logical statement that has a few properties. If associated with a while loop, it must obey three laws.

1.   A loop invariant must be such that we can make it true before we enter the loop. Initialization takes care of this, usually in a trivial way. In

the above we achieve this by setting p to be at the beginning of the list. Since there is nothing before p, our condition is satisfied.

2. If a loop invariant is true before the body of the loop is executed, it must also be true after it is executed. This is why it is called an invariant: its truth doesn't change if we stay in the loop. In the above method, this was achieved by the combination of moving p (p -> next ()) and moving the smallest item in the unsorted part to p.

3. The truth of the invariant combined with the falsity of the while condition must imply that the problem has been solved. In our example, when the outer loop's condition is FALSE, p must be at location last, and hence there is only one item in the unsorted part; but the other part is sorted and contains the smallest items. Therefore the entire list is sorted.

We must do one other thing to guarantee that a program containing a loop is correct. We must guarantee that the loop exits. This was achieved by moving p once each iteration of the loop. Thus, each loop iteration made progress toward the exit in a situation in which we could prove that only a finite number of such steps was possible, since lists are finite.

Likewise, Fig. 6.10b represents the loop invariant for the inner loop of the program. The purpose of the inner loop was to find the smallest item in the unsorted part. The reader is encouraged to demonstrate that the three requirements hold for this loop as well and to verify that the loop exits. These ideas will be discussed again in detail in Chapter 14.

6.7.2   The Time Efficiency of the Selection Sort

Again consider Fig. 6.10a. Finding the smallest item so that it can be moved to position p requires a linear scan of the unsorted part. Once we have performed this, we no longer need to operate on that location. In other words, a linear scan of the unsorted part of the list permits the elimination of one item from further consideration. An algorithm with this property operates in an amount of time proportional to the square of the original length of the list. Thus, if the length of a list to be sorted is doubled, the time required to sort it will be increased four times. If it takes a second to sort 10 items, it takes 10 days to sort 10,000 items. The reason such an algorithm requires time proportional to n^2 when the length of the list is n comes from the solution of the following recurrence relation, which simply states that the time necessary to solve a problem of size n is n (the time required for the linear scan) plus the time required to solve a similar problem of size $n - 1$, since we have eliminated one item.

$$T_n = n + T_{n-1} \qquad \text{if } n > 1 \text{ and } T_1 = 1$$

The solution of this equation is not difficult and can be done by repeated substitution of the right-hand side for the recursive term on the right.

$$T_n = n + T_{n-1}$$
$$T_n = n + (n - 1 + T_{n-2})$$
$$T_n = n + n - 1 + (n - 2 + T_{n-3})$$
$$\vdots$$
$$T_n = n + n - 1 + n - 2 + \cdots + 2 + T_1)$$
$$T_n = n + n - 1 + n - 2 + \cdots + 2 + 1) = \tfrac{1}{2}n(n + 1)$$

For the program with which we represent this algorithm, the same result can be had in another way, of course. The loops are nested: the outer one processes the entire list, and the inner one executes once for each iteration of the outer one and processes, on the average, half of the entire list. Thus we again see that the running time is proportional to n^2 for n items.

In fact, it isn't precisely correct to say that the algorithm's processing time is proportional to n^2 for all values of n. This is true only for large n, because every implementation spends some fixed amount of time on initialization. To be careful, we say that the time is proportional to n^2 for large n.

Often we are interested only in obtaining a worst-case estimate, or upper bound, of the running time of an algorithm for increasing input size n. The mathematical notion of the order of a function is helpful in this situation. We say that an algorithm A has running time that is $O(g)$, read "big O of g," for some function $g(n)$, if for all large n the running time of A on an input of size n is less than some constant C times $g(n)$. Said concisely: there is a constant C and a value N such that $A(n) \leq C \cdot g(n)$ whenever $n > N$.

The above discussion of selection sort says that it is $O(n^2)$. This is not the kind of algorithm that we would like to use to sort a lot of data, say 1000 items, since 1000^2 is one million. That would likely take an inordinate amount of time on nearly any computer. We shall see in Section 8.4 that it is possible to sort 1000 items in only a few tens of thousands of steps.

There is a related, though not identical notion of a lower bound on the running time of an algorithm. The running time of an algorithm A for an input of size n is $\Omega(h)$, "big omega of h," for a function $h(n)$ provided that there is a constant C such that for any value N, $A(n) \geq C \cdot h(n)$ for at least one $n \geq N$. This is just another way of saying that $A(n) \geq C \cdot h(n)$ for infinitely many values of n.

Thus the selection sort is also $\Omega(n^2)$, indicating that the time to do a selection sort increases with the square of the size of the problem.

6.8   MERGING TWO LISTS INTO ONE

Merging produces a single sorted list from the elements of two nonempty sorted lists. Here we simply merge the elements of the parameter list 1 into the elements of this. However, we create a new list to hold the elements of the lists being merged. We use three positions. Position p is used to walk list this, position q walks list 1, and current always refers to the last item in the newly created list result. See Fig. 6.11. We do not modify the two input lists, but we do require that they both be nonempty sorted lists. First, we pick the lesser of the first elements of the two input lists, in order to get the result list started. Each time we insert an item into the new list, we send next () both to the position it had in its original list and to current. This guarantees that it is always a reference to the last node. Eventually one of the input positions will reach the end of its list. At this time all of that list has been copied to the new list, but the other list still has some elements not yet copied. We must then process the rest of that other list.

```
PList SList :: merge (PList 1) {
PListPosition p, q;
PListPosition current;
PObject aValue;
PList result;

p = newPosition ();
q = 1 -> newPosition ();
result = newList ();
aValue = p -> at ();
if ((aValue) -> less (q -> at ())) {
    result -> insert (aValue);
    p -> next ();
}
else {
    result -> insert (q -> at ());
```

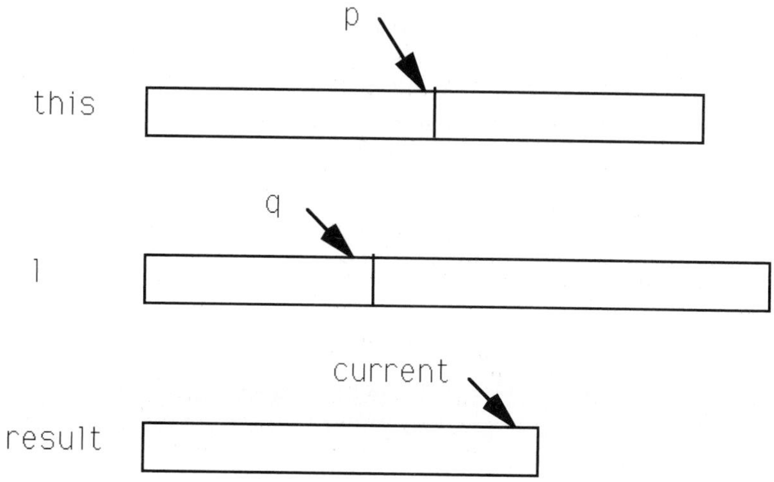

FIGURE 6.11

```
      q -> next ();
   };
   current = PListPosition (result -> newPosition ());
   while (!(p -> afterLast () !! q -> afterLast ())) {
      aValue = p -> at ();
      if ((aValue) -> less (q -> at ())) {
         current -> insertAfter (aValue);
         p -> next ();
      }
      else {
         current -> insertAfter (q -> at ());
         q -> next ();
      };
      current -> next ();
   };
   while (!q -> afterLast ()) {
      current -> insertAfter (q -> at ());
      q -> next ();
      current -> next ();
   };
   while (!p -> afterLast ()) {
      current -> insertAfter (p -> at ());
      p -> next ();
      current -> next ();
   };
   delete current;
   delete p;
   delete q;
   return result;
};
```

Note that when we create a newPosition for the resulting list, we must give a type cast, or *type assertion* so that we can assign the result to a variable of type PListPosition. This is normally an illegal assignment, because SListPosition is lower in the class hierarchy than SPosition, and the declaration of newPosition only promises to return a PPosition. We know, however, that sending newPosition to a list always results in a PListPosition, so we use the type assertion to assure the compiler that we know the actual class of the returned value.

Type Assertion

A statement by the programmer that a variable associated with some supertype refers to an object of one of its subtypes at run time.

To make this type cast or type assertion, we say

```
current = PListPosition (result -> newPosition ());
```

The use of the type name indicates that the expression that follows in parentheses is a pointer to an `SListPosition`. If such a type cast is wrong, the program is certain to fail, usually bizarrely, because the compiler does not build in code to check whether we are correct; it trusts us. If we are wrong, we will be using data in some context that should not be used there.

6.9   THE CLONING PROBLEM

Every class must somehow implement the ability to clone its members. Frequently a faithful copy of an object is desired rather than an alias. C++, with its complicated model of objects, has two types of clones that we might consider: the clone of a static object, or an object of direct class type, and the clone of an indirect object, or a pointer to a class type. The former can be achieved by overloading the assignment operator = so that the assignment `anObject = anotherObject` is handled by a programmer-defined function. We shall not do that here, because we don't need to assign such direct objects (see Section 4 of Appendix B). We want to clone objects that pointers refer to. Remember that a pointer assignment statement, assigning an object to a reference variable, creates an alias, but not a new object. Therefore, if `Foo` and `Bar` are pointers to a class type,

```
Foo = Bar;
```

does not result in two objects. It results in two names or references to the same object: the object that `Bar` referred to before this assignment was executed. Creating a new object that is a copy of another is called cloning, and the copy is a **clone**. One normally obtains a clone of an indirect object by sending it the `Clone` message, which is implemented as a function that returns a faithful copy.

A major difficulty when discussing cloning is that the term "faithful copy" is not very well defined. In practice it can mean various things. For example, suppose that we want to clone a set A. We want to get set B that is not the same set as A so that if we later insert something into B, it won't be inserted also into A. Note that if B is an alias for A, every operation applied to B applies to A as well. (It is more truthful to say "nearly every" operation. There is a problem with the dispose operation, which is discussed in Section 6.10.) We also want B to "contain the same elements" as A. The problem that arises depends on what we mean by "the same elements." Do we mean that "the same objects" are in both sets, or do we mean that the sets contain different actual objects, but the corresponding objects have the same values? For sets the answer is clear from the abstraction principle. When we say that two sets contain the same elements, we mean that if a thing is in one of the sets it must also be in the other. Therefore we mean that the objects themselves are the same in both sets. Note that this is one of the principal advantages of using pointer variables to denote objects in C++: we can duplicate references quite freely by creating aliases. Our clone operation for sets should not, therefore, clone the elements of the set as well. It should insert aliases of the elements in the original set into the new set. The usual way of implementing a set is to create a class that has some instance variables that represent the elements of the set. Typically these instance variables are pointers to a class type. The implication of the above discussion is that these pointer-to-class–type instance variables should not be cloned, but rather aliased.

This brings us to two different types of cloning. The first is called shallow cloning and the other deep cloning. In practice, something intermediate between these is needed. A shallow clone is a copy of an object in which the pointer-to-class–type instance variables of the clone refer to the same objects as do those of the object cloned; i.e., aliasing is used for instance variables. A shallow clone is easily created in C++. We create a new object of the required class and then simply assign it instance variables using the instance variables of the object cloned. Simple assignment creates the required aliases. Even simpler is to execute our virtual `sizeOf` function to determine at run time the size of our object, use the low level heap management routine `malloc` to obtain storage of the required size, do a low-level block transfer, `memcpy`, of the bits from the old object to the new, and then to type-cast the result to the required type. This is what our `SObject :: ShallowClone ()` does. The advantage of it is that it is generic and works in every class that implements `sizeOf`.

Deep cloning requires that pointer-to-class–type instance variables also be cloned. The question arises as to what type of cloning is required for them, shallow or deep. In deep cloning the instance variables are deep-cloned as well. If the object cloned has pointer-to-class–type instance variables, they are deep-cloned, and if they themselves have pointer-to-class–type instance variables, they are deep-cloned, etc., until we reach a stage (we must) where some objects are implemented only in terms of primitive types. Intermediate levels of cloning between shallow and deep cloning require cloning of some intermediate levels but do not go as far as deep cloning.

All of our classes will implement shallow cloning. Only those that need more will be required to implement some deeper cloning. The standard functional method `ShallowClone`, implemented in `SObject`, creates these copies. No other class needs to implement `ShallowClone`. The only reason it has been made virtual is to permit a class to disable it and therefore prohibit cloning of the members of that class. We shall need to do this when we implement our integer class, `SInteger`, in Chapter 11.

For abstraction purposes each class should provide a `Clone` method that is appropriate to its nature. This method is called simply `Clone`, and `SObject` provides a standard implementation of it, which is just a call to `ShallowClone`. This method can be overridden as necessary to provide the necessary fine tuning required by a class. For list nodes, the default behavior is appropriate, so we do not need to do anything, using the inherited method automatically. We have seen that for lists we needed to do more. We needed to clone all of the nodes, but not the data within the nodes. This was an example of an intermediate level of cloning between shallow and deep. It is the natural thing to do for a list, so it is called just Clone. We emphasize that clients don't generally call ShallowClone. It is just a means of implementing Clone, which is the method that is called when we want a copy.

6.10   THE DISPOSAL PROBLEM

Similar to the cloning problem is the problem of disposing of indirect objects that have been created, either by cloning or by calling a generator function. Similarly, there are a number of types of disposal that might be required in different circumstances. Since indirect objects are dynamically created by new, they are dynamically disposed of by delete. When delete is called, a destructor method is called by the system if it has been provided in the class of the object being deleted. If you don't define a destructor, the system executes a generic one. Generally speaking, if your class requires a Clone method, it requires a destructor. If the object has instance variables that are (references to) other objects, these objects are left as they are by the standard delete. This is generally the correct behavior. When we destroy a set, for example, we don't generally destroy its elements; those elements have independent existence. We can provide various levels of deeper disposal in a class by having our destructor delete some or all of the pointer-to-class–type instance variables as appropriate. For this reason SList has a destructor:

```
virtual ~SList (void);
```

Most destructors should be virtual. They do not take parameters or return any result. The implementation of this one must see that the nodes are destroyed, but not the data in the nodes, just as Clone saw to cloning the nodes, but not the data. We have seen this destructor before but repeat it here.

```
SList :: ~SList (void) {
    PListNode next, item;

    item = fFirstNode;
    while (item != zed) {
        next = item -> fNext;
        delete (item); // Destruct the node item.
        item = next;
    };
};
```

Note that it is dangerous to call virtual methods of the class of the object in a destructor, because the object is in the process of being destroyed. Various parts of the object come from various levels in its class hierarchy and are destroyed in turn. If a part is destroyed and then is required by a virtual method, there will be serious trouble.

There is another question about disposal, however: that of when and by what an object should be destroyed. There are two considerations, one physical and the other logical. The easier is the former, or physical, consideration. If an object is created in a function or method using a local variable or value parameter as a reference variable, either that object must be destroyed before the procedure returns, or some alias must be used that passes a reference to the object outside the procedure. This can be a non-local variable or a reference or pointer parameter. The reason for this is that the local storage of functions is reclaimed at the time the function completes, but dynamically created data is not. Thus, if we don't adhere to this rule, the object would take up dynamic space (called heap space), but all references to it would be destroyed; we would not have any access to it.

The problem as to what code should be responsible for executing the `delete` operator on an object no longer needed is more subtle. The basic principle is that the destroyer of an object should be at the same level as the creator. If an object is created by client code directly, the client code should be responsible for its disposal. If an object is created by some method of a class, that method or another method of the same class should be responsible for its disposal.

In the present situation, list nodes are treated as internal to the notion of lists and are created by methods of `SList` when objects are inserted into lists. List nodes should therefore be destroyed by the methods of `SList`, probably when objects are removed from lists. In particular, a client should not have to dispose of list nodes in order to use lists.

6.11   SETS IMPLEMENTED AS LISTS

Sets of objects are an attempt to model the mathematicians' idea of sets by implementing the simple operations of ordinary set theory. Sets are composed of elements. One can form unions and intersections of sets to obtain other sets. Sets have size. If an element is already in a set, inserting it yields the same set. Sets can be heterogeneous, containing elements of different kinds, or homogeneous, all elements being of the same kind.

An easy way to implement sets is to create a subclass of `SList`. Iterators and positions of lists can be used without alteration. The key thing is to reimplement `insert` so that an item cannot be inserted twice. We must also provide for the normal set operations.

```
class SSet: public SList {
    public:
            SSet (void);
```

```
        virtual void        insert (PObject);
        virtual void        remove (PObject);
        virtual PSet        setUnion (PSet);
        virtual PSet        intersection (PSet);
        virtual PSet        allBut (PObject);
        virtual char        subset (PSet);
        virtual int         cardinality (void);
        virtual char        member (classtype c);
        virtual void        writeIt (void);
        virtual PObject     Clone (void);

    protected:
        virtual int   sizeOf (void);
};
```

However, there are subtle reasons why we don't want to do this. The most important is that what we should inherit is some sort of meaning from the parent class. But the meaning of a list is not very consistent with the meaning of a set. In particular, sets don't have position, but lists do. Therefore it is better to implement sets from scratch as a subclass of SCollection. We must provide an iterator type for it, but generally we do not open ourselves to as many problems if we do a little more work here.

```
class SSet: public SCollection {
    public:
            SSet (void);
        virtual             ~SSet (void);
        virtual void        insert (PObject);
        virtual void        remove (PObject);
        virtual PSet        setUnion (PSet);
        virtual PSet        intersection (PSet);
        virtual PSet        allBut (PObject);
        virtual char        subset (PSet);
        virtual int         cardinality (void);
        virtual char        element (PObject);
        virtual PIterator   newIterator (void);
        virtual char        member (classtype c);
        virtual void        writeIt (void);
        virtual PObject     Clone (void);

    protected:
        virtual int sizeOf (void);
        PList fElements;
    friend SSetIterator;
};
```

The most important method is insert, because it maintains the idea of set. It first checks that the item to be inserted is not already in the set.

```
void SSet :: insert (PObject o) {
   if (!fElements -> element (o))
      fElements -> insert (o);
};
```

The method element merely applies the element() method to its fElements, which is a list.

```
char SSet :: element (PObject o) {
   return fElements -> element (o);
};
```

The other set operations are quite easy and are left as exercises.

The set iterator class can work easily by holding a reference to a list iterator as its implementation:

```
class SSetIterator: public SIterator {
   public:
      SSetIterator (PSet);
      virtual            ~SSetIterator (void);
      virtual char       member (classtype c);
      virtual char       nextItem (PObject&);
      virtual void       reset (void);
      virtual PObject     Clone (void);

   protected:
      PListIterator fIterator;
      virtual int    sizeOf (void);
};
```

When a set iterator is constructed, it constructs fIterator in turn:

```
SSetIterator :: SSetIterator (PSet s): SIterator (s)
   fIterator = PListIterator (s -> fElements ->
                              newIterator ());
};
```

The other methods of SSetIterator pass a message on to fIterato For example, here is nextItem.

```
char SSetIterator :: nextItem (PObject &o) {
   return fIterator -> nextItem (o);
};
```

The rest are left as an exercise.

6.12   WHAT DO WE INHERIT?

The previous section brings up important points that should be considered in general. When is it appropriate to inherit, or use *is-a*, when should we use the weaker form of inheritance *is-like*, and when should we use *has-a*? Object-oriented languages generally don't distinguish well between the first two forms. The first possible implementation of sets in the last section appears good at first, because very little needs to be built. We get nearly the entire implementation of sets just by using inheritance. However, further reflection reveals that what we are using here is *is-like*.

There are at least three ways to think of what is obtained from inheritance. The weakest is that the code of the parent classes is inherited, which certainly makes programming easier, because we don't have to rebuild things that we already have. The next stronger is that the protocols (or type) of the parents are inherited. Sets need a method void insert (PObject). Lists already have such a prototype method. Therefore we inherit from SList to get access to its prototype methods, implementing as necessary the ones whose function bodies in SList are not appropriate in SSet. This level of meaning of inheritance is enforced by C++ and by many other object oriented languages.

The third conception of inheritance is that what is inherited is the *meaning* of the parent class. The meaning has to do with what the class is, not with how it is implemented. The advantage of this conception is that it makes it easier to think about what is in the class library and to be able to infer things about a class by knowing its position in the library, without examining its code. The disadvantage is that it requires us to build a few more things along the way, but only a few more things, and they are usually simply built. In the present example, if we build SSet as a subclass of SList, decide to ignore the extra non-setlike protocol, and then build a subclass of SSet, the question arises as to how to treat this extra protocol in the new class.

Here is another example. For insertion into a list, a node can be built by building a subclass of the thing intended to be inserted and giving it another instance variable, link, that is a pointer to this new subclass. Since we build this as a subclass, the nodes are the things inserted. Thus, given our class SInteger, we could build a class SIntegerNode by making SInteger the parent class, providing an additional instance variable link of type PIntegerNode, and providing additional methods to manipulate the link field. At first this seems advantageous, but it has serious side effects. The most important problem is that such objects need to be treated fully as if they were members of SInteger in all contexts in which members of SIntegers might arise. There is also an implication that the client must remember to create one of these new things rather than an ordinary SInteger if it is anticipated that it might need to be inserted into a list, or alternatively, there must be a means of transforming an ordinary SInteger into an SIntegerNode.

The best solution to the above problems is to build most classes using inheritance only when we intend to specialize some deep meaning of the parent class. In other situations we use instance variables of various types (*has-a*) to implement new meaning. This was our solution for building sets. We used an instance variable of type `PList` to hold the elements of our list. A set is not a list, but it has the use of a list.

There are exceptions to the above rule. Sometimes we do use the *is-like* form of inheritance. Generally speaking this is only done when we expect that the class we are building will never have any subclasses. Still, be careful even then. It is possible to be wrong.

6.13   INFORMATION HIDING AND HOW TO ACHIEVE IT

C++ has powerful means of hiding implementation details. Class declarations can have both protected and private sections. Ordinary variables, types, and other classes can be defined in these sections as well as instance variables and methods. These tools generally work very well for a single class and its ancestors and heirs. They don't work as well when there is a tightly bound set of classes, as in the list abstraction, in which nodes, lists, positions, and iterators all contribute to the abstraction. In this section some rules of the various visibility classes and the consequences of the rules will be given.

There are at least three different types of programmers who have some need of the declarations in a class definition. The first is the client, who wants the capability of the class and expects to call its public methods. The second is the person who must implement the methods of the class. The third is a programmer who wants to extend the capability of a class by using it as the ancestor of another class.

Instance variables are not made public, even though that seems to be convenient for clients, because the implementor might decide that the capability is best provided by using different instance variables than those first devised. If clients had seen and used them, their code, and not only the code of the class, would need to be changed following such a reimplementation. For this reason, recognizing that the third type of programmer, the *extender*, is really a client of a different sort, it is often suggested that all instance variables should be private, not just protected. Heirs cannot see private instance variables; only the class methods themselves can manipulate them or call private methods. (There is a major hole in C++. An object that has a reference to another object in the same class (not a subclass), can in fact manipulate the private instance variables of that other object. Objects are given special rights to their *siblings*.) As an aid to inheriting classes, one can (should) provide some protected methods to gain at least limited, logical, access to the private features. Thus, if in class `SIterator` we had made the instance variable `fCollection` a private variable, we would need some way to set it (the constructor will do it) and some way to access it from an heir like `SListIterator`. We could use a protected method, `itsCollection`, to return a reference to it. This style has not been adopted in this book because we have been building base classes whose implementation should be stable. If we were building higher-level user-interface or application code, however, we would certainly adopt this style. In those situations we should present an abstract interface to all of our clients, even our heirs. If our code changes, we don't want to have to cascade changes to the code of others.

Problems arise in C++ when a class must be designed along with another class, such as list nodes and lists. The difficulty is that it is often necessary for one class to have access to the other in ways that normal clients should not. Lists need to be able to have the `fNext` fields of list nodes modified. They should not be modified by a public method of the list node, because clients should not be able to do this. Only lists should. To fill this need, C++ provides the `friend` construct. A class (or function) can be declared to be a friend of a class, thereby being granted the right to see and manipulate the private features of the grantor. List nodes grant this privilege to lists and to list positions. Methods of either can see and manipulate the fields of a node. There are two problems with this approach. The first is that it is too general and the second that it is too restricted. The first problem, generality, arises from the fact that any class can grant friendship to any other. This leads to complex linkages between sections of programs that lead to too much work needing to be done when anything changes.

Friendship in C++ can also cause difficulties because friendship is not inherited. If class A grants friendship to class B and C is an heir of B, then class C cannot see the private, or even the protected, features of A. This is both a philosophical and a practical problem. Any object of class C is supposed to be in B. However, B has some capabilities that C does not have (for example, B sees A). The practical problem comes from the fact that the friend class B is often a service provider for A, and the subclass C a provider of a more specialized service that requires special information from A. You must either provide additional protected methods in B to access the features of A, requiring anticipation of the need when B is built, or build a subclass of A that does nothing new except grant friendship to C, which is wasteful.

Thus we have made `SListNode` a protected nested class of `SList`, but with a completely public interface. This gives heirs of `SList` more visibility than friendship alone does.

Establishing the correct visibility of the features of a class requires that we think hard about the various uses to which the class definition will be put. It is a mistake to make some feature public just because some class needs to use it. Sometimes a cleaner solution involves subclasses, sometimes friendship. Sometimes, however, it requires that you take a step back from your work and rethink your pieces carefully, perhaps leading to a different design.

6.14   WHAT IS VERIFICATION, AND WHY DO WE NEED IT?

Section 6.7.1 discussed a proof that the selection sort program is correct. At this point in your career, you may wonder why we want to do this, rather than just test the resulting program on some test data. The difficulty is that a sophisticated program might work well on some sets of data and exhibit errors (bugs) only on others. For example, a sorting routine that has an error might not work correctly on a file that has data all of the same value, or only a single value, or some values equal to the largest possible value, and so on. Since our testing will not, in general, be able to consider all possible combinations of data, it might not be able to discover all potential errors.

It needs to be stressed that nontrivial programs cannot be verified simply by testing them. If a program is as simple as a single `while` loop that iterates a number of times dependent on the input, the program has a potentially infinite number of execution paths. Testing is a finite process. By the nature of the complexity of programs, testing is a necessary, but totally inadequate means of gaining confidence in the correctness of our work. We need more powerful tools. These tools come from our own ability to form logical hypotheses and to prove them true or false.

> **Rule of Testing**
>
> Testing only reveals the presence of errors. It does not prove the absence of errors.
>
> > Paraphrase of a quote by Edsger Dijkstra.

Programming is a two-step process. We need to reason out what we are to do, and we must do it. It is possible to make errors in either part of this, but if we reason carefully, then we lessen the chance of error in the reasoning part. We are still faced with the fact that we may make errors in the execution of our ideas. Testing will catch at least most of the errors of this sort. An error in reasoning is the hardest to find and is the sort of error with which our compilers help the least. Errors of reasoning (bugs) don't fly into our programs: we put them there. We would like to stop doing that.

We need to be able to reason about our programs both as we are developing them and after we are finished and are looking them over to convince ourselves or others that we have got them right. Since reasoning is a logical process, we must apply a form of logic to the development and verification of programs.

6.15   WHAT IS EFFICIENCY, AND HOW DO WE MEASURE IT?

The time efficiency of the selection sort was discussed in Section 6.7.2. It may seem strange that a lot of emphasis is put on the efficiency of algorithms when the power of computing equipment is increasing so fast. Even desktop computers now have the power that mainframe computers had only a few years ago. The problem is that an increase in computer power cannot make up for a truly inefficient algorithm. One reason for this is that as computers become more powerful and have more memory, people naturally want to solve larger problems with them. For many algorithms (most) the time it takes to solve a problem increases as the size of the data increases. Also, most algorithms do not have a linear relationship between the size of the data and the time. Many don't even have a linear relationship between the required storage and the size of the input data. If the time and space requirements of a program grow faster than the size of the problem to be solved, computer advances (speed and memory capacity) can't keep pace with the needs.

Consider the following thought experiment. Suppose you have a certain budget for computing (say 1000 "Koplars"), you can buy a certain amount of computing power with that budget, and you need to solve a certain problem. Suppose now that your budget increases by a factor of 100 (to 100,000 Koplars) and the size of the problem to be solved also increases. If the nature of the algorithm that you are using is quadratic, $O(n^2)$, the new problem can only be 10 times as large as the old one, even though the budget has increased by a factor of 100. And yet the expectation of the people paying the bills would likely be much greater than this. It would be even worse for a cubic algorithm, $O(n^3)$. In this case we would be able to solve a problem only about 5 times as large. For an exponential algorithm, $O(2^n)$, we could add only about 7 items to the data before our budget was exhausted. If the original size of the problem was a few hundred items, this would indeed be a tiny increase in power for a large increase in cost.

The efficiency of an algorithm has very little to do with the precise statements used to implement it or with whether the programmer avoids repeating calculations done previously. It has nearly everything to do with the depth of nesting of loops and the number of repetitions of a recursive program. In order to determine these things we must look at a program as a whole, rather than with a microscope, and we must perform a formal, mathematical, analysis of the work that it does. This is the purpose of the recurrence relation that we saw above. The big-O notation gives us a convenient way to express the results that doesn't depend too much on the details of a particular machine. In fact, when we buy a faster machine (assuming that it is uniformly faster over all instructions) and run an old program on it, the real effect is simply to decrease the constant C implicit in the big-O notation. For an algorithm that is superlinear in its growth, this is the smallest part of the efficiency problem.

For completeness note that even though many problems have different solutions that exhibit different efficiencies, most problems have a certain mathematical limit on how fast they may be solved by any algorithm. For example, sorting random data is fundamentally a problem that requires approximately $O(n \log_2(n))$ time. A large class of problems require algorithms of exponential running time. The search for more and more efficient algorithms needs to be guided by such considerations; otherwise a programmer could waste time and effort in the search for an algorithm that might not even exist. These topics are covered in detail in courses on computer science theory, especially those on computability and automata.

6.16   SUMMARY

The list classes are fundamental to this software library and to many projects. Lists are used extensively, both as a superclass of other, more specialized, classes and as instance variables in classes that need a simple and flexible storage mechanism.

Lists by themselves are not extremely useful, however. We also need the important notion of position within a list. Sometimes lists are built so that no distinction is made between the implementation of a list and that of a position of the kind we have made here. It is an important conceptual idea in any case, and errors are occasionally made in software because designers forget the distinction.

Lists also need iterators, as all collections do, so that we can apply some process to all of the elements in the list. The process to be applied is unlikely to be known by the designers of the list abstraction, because it is more properly in the client's domain.

Lists can be built out of nodes or otherwise. In Chapter 10 we shall see lists built without nodes. There the lists, rather than the nodes, will form a recursive data structure. It is important in any case that the user of a list should not be burdened with the job of creating and destroying nodes. The picture that lists should present to the client is one of a list of data, even though the implementation is one of nodes holding references to data.

Occasionally we need to sort the data in a list. We have shown selection sort for lists, which is fundamentally inefficient but doesn't perform too badly when lists are short. The expected performance is proportional to the square of the number of items sorted. Sorting algorithms are inherently complex. To develop one that does not contain errors requires careful stating of specification as well as attention to developing the program in accordance with the specification. We shall visit sorting again in Chapter 8.

EXERCISES

6.1 (6.3) Implement a method `writeReverse` in lists. The easiest way to do this is to build a method into list nodes that help us write the list. That method is easiest to build if it is recursive, sending the same message to the node `fNext`. Two parts are required: sending `writeIt` to `fValue` and sending `writeIt` to `fNext`. The trick is to perform the two parts in the right order.

6.2 (6.3) Suppose an application creates a list of lists. That is to say, suppose that we create a list, `ListOfLists`, in which the values stored in the nodes are also lists. What is the effect of `ListOfLists -> writeIt`? What is the effect of `ListOfLists -> writeReverse`?

6.3 (6.3) Implement and test the list generator function `newList`. Implement `SList :: writeIt`.

6.4 (6.3) Implement and test `SList :: insertFirst` by making it a synonym for `SList :: insert`. Why should we *not* make `remove` a synonym for `removeFirst`?

6.5 (6.3) Implement `SList :: empty` and `SList :: atFirst`. Implement `SList :: newNode`.

6.6 (6.3) Suppose `SList` has an instance variable, `fLength`, that always contains the current length of the list. What methods must be modified to maintain `fLength` correctly? Does implementing `SList :: atLoc` using a simple `for` loop make sense in the current implementation? If we add the `fLength` field, does it make more sense? Discuss the trade-offs in space and time efficiency of maintaining this length component.

6.7 (6.4) Implement and test the generator method `newPosition` and the method `SListPosition :: atNext`.

6.8 (6.4) `SListPosition` can be given methods that act on the nodes themselves independently of the data in them. They have to behave differently with the `zed` node than with other nodes, because the `zed` node must never be modified or deleted. Discuss the desirability of implementing the three methods `lastNode`, `nodeAt`, and `attachNodeAfter`. The method `lastNode` returns a reference to the last node in a list (not the `zed` node, but the one before it), `nodeAt` returns a reference to `fHere`, and `attachNodeAfter`, given a node as a parameter, inserts it in a manner similar to the way `insertAfter` inserts data after the current position. These methods could be used internally by methods of this compilation unit that must operate on lists physically. Could they be used outside this unit? Should they be? How can you make them useful internally but prevent their use from elsewhere?

6.9 (6.4) Implement a new method of `SListPosition`,

```
void toNth (int n);
```

that is to set the position to the ordinal position n, if such exists. Be certain to define what should occur if the position does not exist. Give this situation careful thought.

6.10 (6.4) At the end of Section 6.4, the danger of treating objects as transparent was discussed. In the code for `deleteNext` note the reference `fHere -> fNext` appearing on the left side of an assignment statement. Discuss why this reference is even more dangerous than what occurs on the right side of the same statement. Consider that `this` is a list position but `fHere` is a list node and therefore clearly a different object.

6.11 (6.5) Implement a method `SList :: removeAll` that removes all occurrences of its argument rather than just the first one.

6.12 (6.5) Explain how the iterator method `Short` can be useful in using an iterator for searching for an object within a list.

6.13 (6.5) Investigate an alternate method of terminating lists. Instead of having a single node `zed` to terminate all lists, suppose that we simply let the last node on any list refer to itself as its `fNext`. This is illustrated in Fig. 6.12. Using this idea, reimplement the method `SListNode :: last`. What else

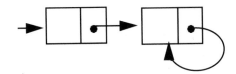

FIGURE 6.12

needs to be changed in the code of the list unit? What else might need to be changed in client code? Discuss the benefit of hiding the declaration of the node zed.

6.14 (6.5) Several methods of the list abstraction were suggested but not built, including

```
PObject SList :: atLoc (int);
void SListPosition :: prev (void);
```

Implement and test these additional methods.

6.15 (6.5) All of our classes have generator functions. Some of these functions are ordinary functions (newList ()), and others are methods of other classes (SList :: newPosition ()). These make it easy for the user to create objects without errors. In detail, what are the differences between

```
x = L -> newPosition ();
```

and

```
x = new SListPosition (L);
```

assuming that x is an SListPosition object and L is an SList?

6.16 (6.8) The method SList :: merge requires a precondition that the input lists be nonempty. Rebuild merge so that this can be relaxed. The rules should be as follows. If both lists are empty, return a new empty list. If self is empty, return a clone of the parameter. If the parameter is empty, return a clone of self. Otherwise return the merger of the two nonempty lists.

6.17 (6.8) In SList :: merge an if statement is used to insert the first item into the new list, result. After the appropriate insertion is made, we send next () to the position from which the item was retrieved. What bug is introduced if we replace SListPosition :: next with the following?

```
void SListPosition :: next (void) {
    if (fHere -> fNext != SList :: zed)
        fHere = fHere -> fNext;
}
```

Why are we unlikely to find this bug by testing? How could we find and repair such a bug? (It is time for honesty: I first wrote SList :: merge using this version of next and didn't find the bug by testing, but rather found and repaired it using the techniques to be discussed in the chapter on program verification.)

6.18 (6.11) Implement the set method `setUnion` by using an iterator over each of the sets partaking in the union. You must create a new set and return it. Determine the time efficiency of your algorithm.

6.19 (6.11) Implement the set method `intersection` by iterating over one of the sets and checking membership in the other with `element`. The method `subset` is nearly the same. Implement it also. Determine the time efficiency of your algorithm.

6.20 (6.11) `SSet :: allBut` returns a set with all of the elements of `this` except the parameter (`this` is unmodified). Implement it using the set intersection model of Exercise 6.19. Determine the time efficiency of your algorithm.

6.21 (6.11) In implementing sets we gave no rules that the implementation must obey. (See `SFiniteStack` for an example of such rules.) What are the appropriate rules for sets, especially as they relate to the insertion methods? Is it possible to break the rules given the first suggested implementation of sets shown in this chapter? (Yes, it is.) How can list positions be used to break the rules? How should we implement set positions to solve the problem? Do set positions make any sense? How about set iterators? Do they make sense? With that implementation we inherit iterators. Is the inherited iterator adequate?

6.22 (6.11) Finish the implementation of `SSet` as a subclass of `SCollection`. Most of your methods can simply pass an appropriate message to the `fElements` instance variable. Don't forget to deal with the fact that sets need iterators. One way to do this is to implement a class `SSetIterator`. The other is to be clever about what the method `newIterator` does. Note that `newIterator` is inherited from `SCollection`.

6.23 (6.12) The method `element` was implemented for the first time in `SList`.
   a. Discuss the conceptual and technical feasibility of moving this method to `SCollection`. What are the consequences of such a move?
   b. If you would recommend this move, act on your recommendation. Answer the same question for the `cardinality` method.

6.24 (6.15) Algorithms whose running times are $O(n)$, $O(n^2)$, $O(n^3)$, or $O(2^n)$ are called linear, quadratic, cubic, or exponential, respectively. Show that the methods `SList :: remove`, `SList :: merge`, and `SListPosition :: search` are all linear. We saw that `selectionSort` was quadratic. Can you think of any cubic operation on lists? What would it mean to be $O(1)$? Name some $O(1)$ methods of `SList` and `SListPosition`.

6.25 (6.15) Verify the estimates on problem size that we saw in Section 6.15. Hint: Use the equation that relates the size of a problem to its cost for a given algorithm. If the algorithm is $O(f(n))$ for some function f, the cost of the program, in terms of its inputs, is $cf(n)$, where c is some constant and n is the size of the data set. Use this and an equation that says the new budget is 100 times the old budget.

Note on versions of C++. At the time of this writing, not all versions of C++ being sold conformed to the latest standard, which was AT&T's version 2.1. The one important difference that affects us is the usage of qualified names for nested items. We should, and do, refer to list nodes by their full name `SList :: SListNode`. However, the version 2.0 compilers that were common in 1993 treat this as an error in some contexts. Thus the software supplied may have the qualifiers set in comments in order to permit compiling by a 2.0 compiler. You will see `/* SList :: */ SListNode`. When this is seen by a version 2.1 compiler, it generates a warning that you should use the qualified name. To avoid these warnings, just delete the comment brackets. Note that this book uses no features specific to version 3.0.

## CHAPTER 7

MORE LINEAR STRUCTURES

They came not out ... in the morning til their hair was queued.

Dalrymple, *Travels in Spain & Portugal*

The Indians (I mean the Sect of their Wise Men) lay Themselves quietly upon a Stacke of Wood and so Sacrifice themselves by Fire.

Bacon, *Essays: Custom & Education* (Arber) 1625

In this chapter we shall examine some specialized linear structures. Some of the implementations given here will be subclasses of SList of the last chapter. Most of them will use lists as instance variables. Using lists as the foundation for stacks and queues will give us a great deal of flexibility in the use of these structures, because of the easily extendible length of lists. We shall need to be somewhat careful so that we don't wind up with inefficient implementations, but for the structures discussed here, this is not a large problem. We have seen stacks before. They are linear structures that have LIFO (last in–first out) protocols for insertion and removal. Queues are similar except that insertions are at one end of the structure (the rear) and deletions are at the other end (front). Their protocol is FIFO, or first in–first out. The item next removed is always the one that has been stored for the longest amount of time. Double-ended queues, called dequeues (dequeue is pronounced "deck") are a combination of stacks and queues. They have two ends, and insertion and removal can be at either the front or rear. Finally, sorted lists are lists in which the elements are always magnitudes and are kept in order at all times. They do not need sort procedures, but their insertion routines need to be designed so that items are inserted in order.

7.1   STACKS

The class SFiniteStack that we examined in Chapter 3 is flawed, because we compiled the maximum size of the stack into it. Doing that requires us, in most projects, to overestimate the probable maximum size required and accept the fact that some space will be wasted. In the next chapter we shall examine arrayed linear structures in which the size is determined at run time, giving more flexibility. The size of an array-like structure can even be extended after it has been allocated; we shall study this later, also.

Here is our final implementation of stacks. The new class is called SStack and is a subclass of SCollection. We therefore have access to iterators and must provide one. The header of our new unit is

```
#ifndef __Stack__
#define __Stack__

#include ''PList.h"

class SStack: public SCollection {
    public:
            SStack (void);
        virtual              ~SStack (void);
        virtual PObject      pop (void);
        virtual void         push (PObject o);
        virtual PObject      top(void);
        virtual PIterator    newIterator (void);
        virtual char         empty (void);
        virtual PObject      Clone (void);
        virtual void         writeIt (void);
        virtual void         insert (PObject);
        virtual void         remove (PObject);
        virtual void         removeFirst ();
        virtual char         member (classtype c);
    protected:
        virtual int     sizeOf (void);
        PList           fElements;
};

typedef SStack *PStack;
PStack newStack (void);
```

```
// REQUIREMENTS For Use
//    initLists ();
#endif
```

We implement the stack using an instance variable that is a PList. We can therefore say that a stack *has-a* list, but not that it *is-a* list.

Stack generation using the function newStack is standard, but it is shown here to emphasize its similarity with other generator functions shown in previous chapters. In the future the details of generators will not be shown.

```
PStack newStack (void) {
   PStack result;
   result = new SStack ();
   failnull (result);
   return result;
};
```

Stack initialization is exactly the same as list initialization. We simply have to call the list generator to initialize the instance variable.

```
SStack :: SStack () {
   fElements = newList ();
};
```

Pushing onto a new stack is just a synonym for insertFirst and so may be implemented by passing insertFirst to fElements.

```
void SStack :: push (PObject o) {
   fElements -> insertFirst (o);
};
```

We have changed the protocol of pop in this class. Here pop not only removes the top of the stack, but it also returns the value stored in that location. The list operation first can retrieve the top item, and removeFirst can delete it.

```
PObject SStack :: pop (void) {
   PObject     result;
   result = fElements -> first ();
   fElements -> removeFirst ();
   return (result);
};
```

The method `top` returns a reference to the top item in the stack, as was done before. The method `first` from lists can achieve this.

```
PObject SStack :: top (void) {
    return fElements -> first ();
};
```

Most of the other methods are similar. Even `newIterator` works this way, since the list iterator that is returned iterates over the contents of the stack. We pass a message to the instance variable, `fElements`, which does the work. The method `Clone` from `SList` is adequate to clone `fElements` here because it returns a faithful copy when `fElements` is cloned. The following is a fairly standard method for cloning a class that has an instance variable of a different class type.

```
PObject SStack :: Clone (void) {
PStack result;
    result = PStack (ShallowClone ());
    result -> fElements = PList (fElements ->
                                    Clone ());

    return result;
};
```

To create a stack abstraction that fits the ideas in the purest way possible, we should remove a few methods from the stack class, because methods such as `remove` have no place in the idea of stacks. The following will work for this situation.

```
void SStack :: remove (PObject o) {
    Error (''SStack :: remove not implemented.");
};
```

There are other situations in which it is necessary to remove methods declared in one class from a subclass as it is being developed. One can easily override the offending method and provide a method body that is either empty or is a call to the inherited error method.

7.2   QUEUES

A queue (pronounced like the letter *q*) simulates a waiting line such as the line at a ticket window. Queues have a rear where new items are inserted and a front where removals occur. The formal protocols will be discussed shortly. Queues are easily implemented as lists with an extra instance variable to keep track of the item (actually the node) at the rear. The front and the first item (node) are identical. Insertion is called enqueue and deletion dequeue (pronounced "de-queue"). The method dequeue also returns a reference to the front-most item, the one removed.

The rules of a queue are harder to state than those of a stack, because FIFO is a more difficult concept than LIFO. The rules are as follows.

Queue Protocol

1. Immediately after creation, empty returns TRUE.
2. Immediately after enqueue, empty returns FALSE.
3. Whenever empty is TRUE, removeFirst, remove, atFront, and dequeue are errors.
4. Suppose we enqueue an object x to a queue. If the queue was originally empty, dequeue will return x and leave the queue empty; if it was not originally empty, dequeue will return the same item that would have been returned had we not inserted x.
5. If we enqueue x to a nonempty queue and then dequeue, the queue will be left in the same state as if we first dequeued an item and then enqueued x.

Our implementation must respect these rules.

Queues are used extensively in simulations of systems in which waiting lines are common. For example, an airport simulation will have queues of aircraft arriving and needing to land on a runway, queues of aircraft waiting to take off, and queues of customers buying tickets. More importantly, the simulation will have queues of events, such as the arrival of planes over the airport, that have occurred at some clock tick and that the program must handle.

```
class SQueue;
typedef SQueue *PQueue;
PQueue newQueue (void);
class SQueue: public SList {
    public:
            SQueue (void);
        virtual PObject    Dequeue (void);
        virtual void       enqueue (PObject);
        virtual void       insert (PObject);
        virtual PObject    atFront (void);
        virtual void       insertFirst (PObject);
```

```
    virtual void       remove (PObject);
    virtual void       removeFirst (void);
    virtual char       member (classtype c);
    virtual PObject    Clone (void);

  protected:
    PListNode      fRear;
    virtual int    sizeOf (void);

};

// REQUIREMENTS For Use
//    initLists ();
```

At first it seems as though we have included a number of methods here that were defined in SList and that don't need to be overridden. They seem to provide the same functionality. removeFirst is such a method. However, we must ensure that the new instance variable fRear is updated properly by all methods. See Fig. 7.1 for a view of the implementation of a queue. Only the nodes are shown, but they have references to the data in the queue. Note that if there is only a single item in the queue, fFirstNode and fRear refer to the same node. Also, when the queue is empty, both fFirstNode and fRear are references to the zed node. The constructor must implement this rule. The constructor for the parent class SList handles fFirstNode before this is called.

```
SQueue :: SQueue (void) {
   fRear = fFirstNode;
};
```

The method enqueue can insert into an empty queue using insert-First, but it must also set the fRear variable to reference the newly inserted node. For a nonempty queue it should insert the new item in a new node directly after the current rear and then adjust the rear to refer to the new node.

```
void SQueue :: enqueue (PObject o) {
   PListNode n;
```

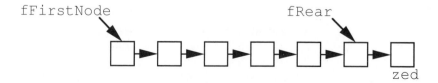

FIGURE 7.1

```
    if (empty ()) {
       insertFirst (o);
       fRear = fFirstNode;
    }
    else {
       n = newNode (o, NULL);
       fRear -> setNext(n);
       fRear = n;
    };
};
```

Removal using `dequeue` requires an initial check as to whether the queue is empty; if it is not, we return the first item and then remove it. We must be careful that when we remove the last item, `fRear` is set to refer to the same location as `fFirstNode`, which is actually the `zed` node, which is always left in place.

```
PObject SQueue :: Dequeue (void) {
    PObject result;

    result = atFront ();
    if (!empty ())
       if (fRear == fFirstNode) {
          removeFirst ();
          fRear = fFirstNode;
       }
       else {
          removeFirst ();
       };
    return result;
};
```

We provide `atFront` as a synonym for `first` in keeping with our idea that the design should match the concept as closely as possible. Likewise, the required and inherited collection method, `insert`, is made a synonym for `enqueue`. The method `removeFirst`, which is also inherited, must take care of the situation in which we happen to remove the last node, in which case we must also update `fRear` appropriately.

```
void SQueue :: removeFirst (void) {
    if (fRear == fFirstNode) {
       SList :: removeFirst ();
       fRear = fFirstNode;
    }
```

```
    else {
       SList :: removeFirst ();
    };
};
```

Here we use the inherited method of the same name. We say SList :: removeFirst () in this context. Note that we would like to factor out the call to the inherited method so that it appears once, before the if statement, but in this case that isn't possible, since that would change the test of the if itself.

The method remove is inherited from SList. It removes an object named as a parameter, from the list. The item can occur anywhere in the list or not at all. Because it is not part of the queue concept, we could choose to implement it here as a no-op or an error call, but if we think it might be useful, we must reimplement it, because the inherited version will not properly update fRear. In the following code two special cases are factored out immediately. If the object to be removed is not the one at the rear, it is not the only item, and so the inherited version will suffice. If the item is at the rear and is the only item, we can use removeFirst. Otherwise we must find the position just before the rear, so that we can remove the rear and then update the rear to point to this position. We can use an iterator for this to walk through the list, but because we must match nodes and not values, we need to use the nextNode method of SListIterator instead of the usual nextItem. Thus we specify the iterator as a PListIterator rather than simply as PIterator (which usually suffices). This requires a type assertion on the object returned from newIterator, which we know is a list iterator even though the declaration names only PIterator. Note that we have chosen here to work with the nodes directly rather than using the positions that we have also inherited from SList.

```
void SQueue :: remove (PObject o) {
    PListNode prev,last;
    PListNode v;
    PListIterator IT;

    if (o != fRear -> value ()) {
       SList :: remove (o);
    }
    else if (fRear == fFirstNode) {
       removeFirst ();
    }
    else {
       IT = PListIterator (newIterator ());
       while (IT -> nextNode (v)) {
```

```
                if(v -> next() == fRear) {
                    prev = v;
                    IT -> Short ();
                };
            delete IT;
            last = fRear;
            prev -> setNext (fRear -> next ());
            fRear = prev;
            delete last;
            };
        };
    };
```

Another method that doesn't belong in the concept of a queue is `insertFirst`, but it is inherited from `SList`, and so we must do something with it, at least reimplement it to be a no-op or an error. Here we build it so that it works properly, requiring that we handle `fRear` when inserting into an empty queue.

```
void SQueue :: insertFirst (PObject o) {
    if (empty ()) {
        SList :: insert (o);
        fRear = fFirstNode;
    }
    else {
        SList :: insert (o);
    };
};
```

7.3   PRIORITY QUEUES

The priority queue is a modification rather than an extension of the queue. Each object inserted into a priority queue is associated with a priority, usually a natural number. Smaller numbers generally represent higher priority. The `dequeue` operation returns the saved item of highest priority. If several items in the priority queue have the same priority, the one that has been in the priority queue for the longest time is the one returned. The item is also removed from the structure. Priority queues are used in operating systems to keep track of processes in need of services from the system, and in many simulation programs to maintain information about events that the system must handle.

Since this is a modification of the queue concept, it will not be implemented as a subclass of `SQueue`, but as a subclass of `SCollection`. In order to implement `insert`, which does not allow the naming of a priority, we shall introduce the concept of the *current priority;* an ordinary insert causes insertion at that priority. We shall need ways to set the current priority. We shall also provide enqueue, which will specify both an item to be inserted and the priority it is to have.

To implement the priority queue, we use an array of queues. The idea is that if an item is to be inserted at priority *K*, we enqueue the item onto the *K*th ordinary queue. See Fig. 7.2. Our implementation assumes that the lowest priority (largest value) is known in advance (at the time the priority queue is created). More specifically, here we assume that priorities between 0 (the highest) and 5 (the lowest) are possible. For greatest flexibility in this implementation, we shall use a pointer to our class SArray rather than ordinary arrays. The class SArray is discussed in the next chapter.

```
class SPriorityQueue;
class SPriorityQueueIterator;
typedef SPriorityQueue *PPriorityQueue;
typedef SPriorityQueueIterator
        *PPriorityQueueIterator;

PPriorityQueue newPriorityQueue (int max);

class SPriorityQueue: public SCollection {
    public:
            SPriorityQueue (int max);
    virtual             ~SPriorityQueue (void);
    virtual void        setPriority (int);
    virtual void        enqueue (int, PObject);
    virtual PObject     Dequeue (void);
    virtual void        insert (PObject);
    virtual void        remove (PObject);
    virtual char        empty ();
    virtual PIterator   newIterator (void);
    virtual char        member (classtype c);
    virtual PObject     Clone (void);
    virtual void        writeIt (void);
```

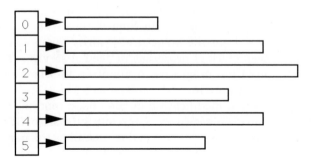

FIGURE 7.2

```
       protected:
          int            fMax;
          int            fPriority;
          PArray         fElements;
          virtual int    sizeOf (void);
       friend SPriorityQueueIterator;
};

class SPriorityQueueIterator: public SIterator {
   public:
          SPriorityQueueIterator (PPriorityQueue);
       virtual            ~SPriorityQueueIterator (void);
       virtual char       nextItem (PObject&);
       virtual void       reset (void);
       virtual char       member (classtype c);
       virtual PObject    Clone (void);

       protected:
          int            fLevel;
          int            fMax;
          PArray         fIterators;
          virtual int    sizeOf (void);
};


// REQUIREMENTS For Use
//    initLists ();
```

Construction and initialization of a priority queue require that we create a new PArray and that we set the default priority to a sensible value. It makes sense to set it to zero, the highest priority. Initialization should also create new queues so that the array fElements is properly initialized and ready for use.

```
SPriorityQueue :: SPriorityQueue (int max) {
   fMax = max;
   fElements = newArray (max+1);
   fPriority = 0;
   for (int i = 0; i <= max; ++i) {
      fElements -> atPut (i,newQueue ());
   };
};
```

Note that the new array has one more element than the lowest-priority value, because our priorities begin with zero. The array fElements itself is given values that are newly created queues.

The method `setPriority` merely sets `fPriority` to its argument. The method `insert` sends enqueue to the ordinary queue at index `fPriority`.

```
void SPriorityQueue :: insert (PObject o) {
  PQueue(fElements -> at (fPriority)) -> enqueue (o)
};
```

The method enqueue is similar. The call `enqueue (i, o)` sends enqueue `(o)` to the ordinary queue whose index in `fElements` is the first parameter, *i*. Note that two different methods in our class hierarchy now share the name enqueue, but the classes they belong to are not related by ancestry, though they have a common ancestor, `SCollection`. In this case they can have different numbers and types of parameters. `SQueue :: ` enqueue has only a single parameter, the item to be inserted. `SPriorityQueue :: ` enqueue has two parameters, of which one is the priority associated with the other.

The dequeue method is more interesting. We must search for a nonempty queue, starting at level 0. If we find such a queue, we dequeue from it and return the result as the result of `SPriorityQueue :: ` dequeue. In the case that all of the queues in `fElements` are empty, NULL is returned as the function result. A `while` loop controls this search process. The control variable `done` represents a complex exit condition. We exit if either we have found a nonempty queue or all queues are empty. Also, setting the result to be NULL before we search for a value guarantees that we return something properly even if the following search fails.

```
PObject SPriorityQueue :: Dequeue (void) {
    int i;
    char done;
    PObject result;
    result = NULL;
    done = FALSE;
    i = 0;
    while (!done) {
        if(!PQueue(fElements -> at (i)) -> empty ()) {
        result = PQueue (fElements -> at (i))
                          -> Dequeue ();
        done = TRUE;
    };
    if (i == fMax)
        done = TRUE;
    else
        ++i;
    };
```

```
      return result;
};
```

The structures of remove and empty are essentially similar to the above. The writeIt method should send writeIt to each of the queues in fElements. It may also do some additional formatting. This class needs a destructor, of course, so that the array fElements and its queues, can be deleted when the priority queue that used it is deleted.

```
SPriorityQueue :: ~SPriorityQueue (void) {
   for (int i = 0; i <= fMax; ++i)
      delete fElements -> at (i);
   delete fElements;
};
```

The priority queue iterator class presents a few interesting problems since we are not going to implement priority queue positions. There are a number of possibilities here, but using what we have already built is better than building an iterator from scratch. We shall use an array (PArray) of iterators, one iterator for each of the queues in the associated priority queue. The instance variable fLevel is the priority level that we are currently scanning as the iteration progresses. Iterator initialization involves creating the array of iterators and setting the level to 0, as well as the standard iteration initialization carried out by the initialization of SIterator. The order in which the items should be produced by a priority queue iterator is the same order in which they would be dequeued.

```
SPriorityQueueIterator :: SPriorityQueueIterator
                    (PPriorityQueue q): SIterator (q) {
   fMax = q -> fMax;
   fLevel = 0;
   fIterators = newArray (fMax+1);
   for (int i = 0; i <= fMax; ++i){
      fIterators -> atPut (i, PQueue
                             (q -> fElements
                              -> at (i))
                              -> newIterator ());
   };
};
```

The iteration is controlled by nextItem. Between calls of nextItem we need to maintain enough state information in the iterator so that the next call will produce the next item. The instance variable fLevel remembers which of the iterators we are currently using and that iterator maintains its own internal state. Since we defer some of the state information to a

contained object (the iterator), we must also defer the check on comple-
tion until we look at some iterator in fIterators. We maintained earlier
that if an iterator is finished, it should not modify its reference parameter. In the following code the variable done enables us to establish a
complex condition for exiting the loop. The loop is to be exited both if an
object is returned by one of the iterators and if the last iterator is finished. When an iterator other than the last is finished, we need to check
the next by increasing fLevel by one and continuing the loop. However,
we must be careful to give fLevel only legal values. The iterator variable IT holds a reference to the iterator currently being scanned, and an
object variable anObject maintains a reference to any object returned
by IT. Note that setting anObject originally to be NULL enables us to
avoid changing the parameter o in case nothing can be found to return.
All of this leads to the most complex nesting of structures that we have yet
seen.

```
char SPriorityQueueIterator :: nextItem
                                (PObject& o) {
    char done;
    PObject anObject;
    PIterator IT;

    anObject = NULL;
    if (!fDone) {
        IT = PIterator (fIterators -> at (fLevel));
        done = FALSE;
        while (!done) {
            if (IT -> nextItem (anObject))
                done = TRUE;
            else {
                if (fLevel == fMax) {
                done = TRUE;
                fDone = TRUE;
                }
                else {
                    ++fLevel;
                    IT = PIterator (fIterators ->
                                    at (fLevel));
                    IT -> reset ();
                };
            };
        };
    };
    if (anObject != NULL)
        o = anObject;
    return !fDone;
};
```

Notice that we must set the instance variable fDone to TRUE when we exhaust the last iterator.

As usual, reset sets the state of the iteration back to the beginning. Because the state is determined both by fLevel and by the state of the queue iterator fIterators[fLevel], we must set both of these back to the beginning. Not all of the iterators in the array need to be reset, because they are reset during the iteration as we finish with one and move to the next. Of course, fDone must also be set to a valid value: FALSE, unless the collection itself is empty.

```
void SPriorityQueueIterator :: reset (void) {
  fLevel = 0;
  PIterator (fIterators -> at (fLevel)) -> reset ();
  fDone = fCollection -> empty ();
};
```

The destructor ~SPriorityQueueIterator is provided so that a priority queue iterator can free all of the individual iterators that it uses as well as the PArray that held the iterators. The logic is similar to that of the destructor in SPriorityQueue.

Finally, it should be noted that the term priority queue is occasionally used in a different sense altogether. Sometimes a requirement is made that the items to be inserted be magnitudes and that enqueue inserts them consistently with their size. In other words, their size (sometimes the size is the value itself) is used as the priority. *Dequeue* has the same sense that we have used: the item of highest priority (value) that has been in the priority queue for the longest time is dequeued.

7.4   DOUBLE-ENDED QUEUES

A double-ended queue is a queue that permits removals at the rear as well as insertions at the front: we can insert and remove at either end. It is therefore easily implemented as a specialization of a queue. Note that insertFirst is already implemented within SQueue. We only need to handle the removals at the rear. The implementation is very similar to what we have seen for queues and is left as an exercise. The only trick is to handle both fRear and fFirstNode properly, especially when the last item is being removed.

```
PDEQueue newDEQueue (void);

class SDEQueue: public SQueue {
    public:
          SDEQueue ();
        virtual PObject    atRear (void);
        virtual PObject    DequeueRear (void);
```

```
        virtual void        removeRear (void);
        virtual char        member (classtype c);

    protected:
        virtual int    sizeOf (void);

};
```

7.5   SORTED LISTS

SList has a method, selectionSort, that can order the elements of a
list, provided of course that all of the elements are in some magnitude class.
SSortedList has the same structure and methods of SList except that
its elements must be in some magnitude class and be kept ordered at all
times. That its elements be in increasing order is an *invariant* of the class.
Its insert method maintains this invariant by inserting an object into
the proper location in the list. To implement the class, we can subclass
SList, since the structure is the same, but we must override any method
that inserts elements, including methods of the associated position class,
so that the insertions maintain the invariant.

```
class SSortedList;
typedef  SSortedList  *PSortedList;
PSortedList newSortedList (void);

class SSortedList: public SList {
    public:
            SSortedList ();
        virtual void            insert (PObject);
        virtual char            member (classtype c);
        virtual PListPosition   newPosition (void);

    protected:
        virtual int    sizeOf (void);

};

class SSortedListPosition: public SListPosition {
    public:
            SSortedListPosition (PSortedList S);
        virtual void  insertFirst (PObject);
        virtual void  insertAfter (PObject);
        virtual void  atPut (PObject);
```

```
        virtual void   exchangeValues (PListPosition);
        virtual char   member (classtype c);

   protected:
        virtual int    sizeOf (void);


};
```

   The standard method `insertFirst` must be drastically modified. Either it should be a no-op (at least when the argument greater than the current first element), or it must insert its parameter in the appropriate location, which is not likely to be the first position. Our implementation is to make `insertFirst` a synonym for `insert`, which does the insertion at the appropriate place. The overridden methods in the position class could be implemented by sending the `insert` message to their `fCollection` instance variable, the list of which they are positions. Then, if `SSortedList :: insert` is implemented correctly, all insertions will maintain the sort order of the sorted list. We shall not do this, however, but rather implement the `insert` methods of the position class as errors. The same needs to be done to `exchangeValues`, which would destroy the ordering.

   There are two simple cases for `insert`. Insertion into an empty list and insertion of a new minimum value both involve insertion at the beginning of the list. Simply calling `insertFirst` is not sufficient, however, because that method is being redefined as a synonym for `insert`. We must instead call the inherited version of `insertFirst`, `SList :: insertFirst`. This implementation has two complications. The first is that, for this method, `SSortedListPosition` is worthless. We actually need to perform the insertion physically at the place we determine. We could perform the three steps required to update a list manually, but a cleaner way is to create an ordinary list position, whose method `insertAfter` will work. However, to do this we cannot merely call `newPosition ()`, because, according to the dynamic building principle, that is designed to return a sorted list position. Instead, we must call `SList :: newPosition ()`, which is the method of the parent class, `SList`, and therefore get back a `PListPosition`. This is a very subtle problem, though it does crop up somewhat frequently. We are defining a new level of functionality that has more structure built into it, but in order to achieve it we need the old functionality, which has less structure but more control. This is what access to the inherited methods is used for.

   The second complication is that our search loop for the location in which to insert the new value has a complex exit criterion. We should exit the loop the first time that the value in the position following the one we are at is greater than or equal to the value to be inserted. We must also exit when we reach the end of the list, whether we have found an appropriate position or not, and we must halt before our position runs onto the terminator node so that we can employ `insertAfter` from that spot. Our test condition for the loop will be provided by the Boolean variable `found`, which we repeatedly recompute depending on what we learn. After each recomputation we immediately check it again. As soon as `found` becomes TRUE, we don't need to modify it again (and must not), for we then know that the loop should be exited.

```
void SSortedList :: insert (PObject o) {
    PObject val;
    PListPosition p; // Not a sorted list position.
    char found;

    if (o -> member (magnitude)) {
        if (empty ()) SList :: insert (o);
        else if (o -> less (fFirstNode -> value ()))
                            SList :: insert (o);
        else {
            p = (PListPosition) SList :: newPosition (
            found = p -> last ();
            if (!found) {
                val = p -> atNext ();
                found = o -> less (val);
            };
            while (!found){
                p -> next ();
                found = p -> last ();
                if (!found) {
                    val = p -> atNext ();
                    found = o -> less (val);
                };
            };
            p -> insertAfter (o);
            delete p;
        };
    };
};
```

7.6   LARGE DYNAMIC ARRAYS

This section is somewhat specialized and may be skipped on first reading. It discusses a method for making lists behave like arrays. From the client's viewpoint there is an array into which one can insert data at arbitrary index positions. The data can later be retrieved by using the same index.

Retrieval from a cell that has not been initialized yields NULL; this could be defined alternatively as an error. One advantage is that this "array" has dynamic size. Another is that no more space is used than is required for the data actually stored. The disadvantage is that retrieval can be slow if the structure contains a lot of data. The key to the idea is to store values and their indices in list nodes and keep the nodes in order of the array indices. We shall not create a place for an item until we know the item and its index. This method is most useful for storing a very large array in which almost every cell is empty, called a *sparse* array. The class is SDynamicArray. It is somewhat complex, so for the sake of clarity the related iterator class will not be developed. The rest may be implemented as an exercise.

We create SDynamicArray as a simple list. It has ordinary list nodes, but the data they contain are objects of the new class SDynamicData. An object of the SDynamicData class is implemented as a value and a location; the location is the subscript of the item represented by the value. These objects are the data physically stored in the nodes; a value stored in the dynamic array is stored in one of these dynamic data cells. The cells are kept on the list in order of their location fields. If data are stored in cells 15, 17, and 31, three nodes, and three cells, are needed to hold the list that represents the array. The dynamic data class is not defined in the header, PDynamic.h, because it is private to the dynamic array class. Instead it is defined within PDynamic.cp.

Within the header we declare SDynamicArray and its associated iterator. There is no position class; because this list is arraylike, ordinary integers can indicate position.

```
class SDynamicArray;
class SDynamicArrayIterator;
typedef SDynamicArray *PDynamicArray;
typedef SDynamicArrayIterator *PDynamicArrayIterator;

PDynamicArray newDynamicArray (void);

class SDynamicArray: public   SCollection {
    public:
        SDynamicArray();
    virtual                 ~SDynamicArray (void);
    virtual void            insert (PObject);
    virtual void            remove (PObject);
    virtual void            atPut (int, PObject);
    virtual PObject         at (int);
    virtual char            empty (void);
    virtual PIterator       newIterator (void);
    virtual char            member (classtype c);
    virtual void            writeIt (void);
    virtual PObject         Clone (void);
```

```
    protected:
      PList          fElements;
      virtual int    sizeOf(void);
    friend SDynamicArrayIterator;
};

class SDynamicArrayIterator: public    SIterator {
   public:
       SDynamicArrayIterator (PDynamicArray);
      virtual          ~SDynamicArrayIterator (void)
      virtual char     nextItem (PObject&);
      virtual void     reset (void);
      virtual char     member (classtype c);
      virtual PObject  Clone (void);

   protected:
      PListIterator    fWhere;
      virtual int      sizeOf (void);

};

// REQUIREMENTS For Use
//    initLists ();
```

Within the implementation file we define the dynamic data class:

```
struct SDynamicData: public SObject {
   int fLocation;
   PObject    fValue;
};

typedef SDynamicData *PDynamicData;
```

We use the simpler struct mechanism here so that all the features of an object in this class can be public. This is the default for objects defined using struct, whereas the features of objects defined using class are private by default. This is used only for implementation within dynamic arrays, so it can safely be public. It has no methods, because we shall manipulate it directly, as an ordinary struct. Note, however, that it does declare objects, and in fact objects that inherit from SObject.

The dynamic array insertion method atPut is passed an integer index and an object. The object is to be inserted in the cell whose logical position is the index; thus, atPut must determine the position of that cell within the currently stored data. This is similar to insertion into a sorted list, except that the index determines the position. For an empty list, a new cell is created and inserted into the first position; otherwise an ordinary list position is used. Note that if a cell with the same index as the one searched for is found, the value stored there is merely updated.

```
void SDynamicArray :: atPut (int i, PObject o) {
   PListPosition here;
   PDynamicData newItem, anItem;

   if (empty ()) {
      newItem = new SDynamicData;
      failnull (newItem);
      newItem -> fLocation = i;
      newItem -> fValue= o;
      fElements -> insert (newItem);
   }
   else {
      here = PListPosition (fElements ->
                                 newPosition ());
      anItem = PDynamicData (here -> at ());
      if (anItem -> fLocation == i)
         anItem -> fValue = o;
      else if (anItem -> fLocation > i) {
         newItem = new SDynamicData;
         failnull (newItem);
         newItem -> fLocation = i;
         newItem -> fValue = o;
         fElements -> insert (newItem);
      }
      else {
         while ((!here -> last ())
                 && PDynamicData (here -> atNext ())
                    -> fLocation <= i)
            here -> next ();
         anItem = PDynamicData (here -> at ());
         if (anItem -> fLocation == i)
            anItem -> fValue = o;
         else {
            newItem= new SDynamicData;
            failnull (newItem);
            newItem -> fLocation = i;
            newItem -> fValue = o;
            here -> insertAfter (newItem);
         };
      };
      delete here;
   };
};
```

The method at is the companion retrieval method. It must also search the list for the required cell. The method returns NULL if there is no data with the requested index.

```
PObject    SDynamicArray :: at (int i) {
   PObject    result;
   PIterator IT;
   PObject    o;

   result = NULL;
   IT = fElements -> newIterator ();
   while (IT -> nextItem (o)) {
      if (PDynamicData (o) -> fLocation == i) {
         result = PDynamicData (o) -> fValue;
         IT -> Short ();
      };
   };
   delete IT;
   return result;
};
```

It is possible, of course, to treat a list as an array by adding methods that insert and remove by ordinal position. Our atLoc method in SList did this. The disadvantage of this is that an insertion in the middle leaves all subsequent values having higher subscripts. We avoid that here by storing the subscript within the cell.

In closing this section, note that it is possible to be a bit more sophisticated with this class. Instead of holding only a single array element in our dynamicData items, we could hold a small array of data. The fLocation value would be a segment number and the array offset within the segment would be used to compute a relative subscript for the data item stored. Consider Fig. 7.3, which shows two segments, 3 and 6, with some data stored (the x's) and some empty array positions (NULL's). With five elements in each segment, logically fifteen elements belong to the left of segment 3, even though they have not been stored, nor space for them been allocated. Thus, the first object in segment 3 is the subscript 15. Similarly the first object in segment 6 is the subscript 30, since there are ten additional elements associated with the two segments 4 and 5 between the two shown. Note that the segment number is just the array index divided by the segment size, and the location within the segment is the remainder: index modulo segmentsize.

Such an implementation is advantageous when the data cluster in an otherwise sparse array, with several items having approximately equal subscripts, long gaps appearing between the clusters. We use a listlike imple-

FIGURE 7.3

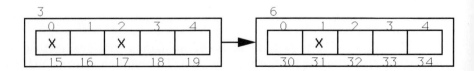

mentation between the clusters and an arraylike implementation within a cluster, a tradeoff between size and speed.

There are other situations in which you need a dense, rather than sparse, array (few gaps or none) but cannot say in advance how much data there will be. In a situation like this the segments should be made quite large so that there are only a few of them. This is especially true if the processing is expected to be relatively local; that is, if once you are operating on elements in a segment, it is likely that you will continue to operate on nearby elements. In the next chapter we shall see an alternative method of implementing dynamic array structures.

7.7   DOUBLY LINKED STRUCTURES

Our list structures have all been singly linked. Each node has a single reference field, fNext, that is used to keep a linked chain of values. This is adequate if backing up frequently in the list structure is not necessary. Our list positions did provide a method prev backing up, but it was relatively inefficient, especially for long lists. If moving to previous positions is to be frequent, a more suitable implementation is the doubly linked list (or the circular list discussed in the exercises). Double linking involves providing another reference variable in each node called fPrev. See Fig. 7.4. The prev method of the position class can then back up by following the references. Of course, the extra instance variable will have to be updated in all of the methods that insert or remove nodes, generally adding two statements to each method. Here we are trading the extra time to update the nodes in the list when they are created against the time needed for executing the prev method. If it is infrequently needed, the extra complexity is not worth the effort, and can cause the entire program to run more slowly.

This class should have two zed nodes, one for the front of every list and the other for the rear. Note that if a position references one of these nodes, calls of next and prev will not return to the list proper.

7.8   REMOVAL OF RECURSION

In this section we shall take a short side trip and examine program transformations. Using some rules and some creativity, we shall transform a program in one form into a different form. More specifically, we shall create nonrecursive procedures equivalent to two procedures that use recursion.

FIGURE 7.4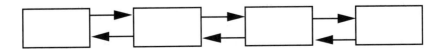

We shall use two methods that might be added to SList and that in themselves aren't very useful, since we have other ways to do the same things.
They each write out the contents of the list, one in forward order, the other
in reverse order.

```
void SList :: RWriteIt (void) {
   doWrite (fFirstNode);
};

void SList :: RWriteReverse (void) {
   doReverseWrite (fFirstNode);
};
```

Each of these calls an ordinary procedure that does the work. These procedures must be friends of the list node class, because they must see the
private instance variables of the nodes.

```
void doWrite (SList :: PListNode x) {
   if (x != SList :: zed) {
      x -> fValue -> writeIt ();
      cout << " ";
      doWrite (x -> fNext);
   };
};

void doReverseWrite (SList :: PListNode x) {
   if (x != SList :: zed) {
      doReverseWrite (x -> fNext);
      x -> fValue -> writeIt ();
      cout << " ";
   };
};
```

Examining these is instructive. The essential difference between them is
that in the former a value is written before the procedure calls itself. In
the latter the recursion comes before the value is written. The effect of the
latter method is to write the tail of the list before its head, thereby writing
it backwards. As in all recursion, we must test whether recursion should be
done at all, and in the case that we are at the zed node, there is nothing
left to do.

   The form of recursion in the procedure doWrite is tail recursion. It
is so named because the recursion is the last thing executed in the procedure. After the recursive call returns, nothing remains for the containing
procedure to do but to return. We shall see that this form of recursion is
particularly easy to remove. It is also generally advisable to do so, because

the resulting version will be more efficient without being more complicated, as we shall see.

The method `doReverseWrite` is more complicated because it does not use tail recursion. After the recursive procedure returns, more must be done, since `writeIt` must be sent to the value of `x`. We shall see that such recursion is more difficult to remove cleanly. We shall also see that the removal of tail recursion almost always speeds up the execution of a procedure without complicating its code. Non-tail recursion is a more difficult matter to evaluate. Removing it is sometimes beneficial but generally gives us a more complex program.

There are four reasons for examining recursion removal. First, seeing an alternative formulation helps in the understanding of recursion. Second, the program transformations we shall make are useful in their own right, even in other contexts. Third, these specific transformations occasionally improve efficiency. The fourth reason will have to wait until the end of Section 7.8.2.

7.8.1 Removal of Tail Recursion

We consider the removal of the tail recursion in `doWrite` first.

```
void doWrite (SList :: PListNode x) {
    if (x != SList :: zed) {
        x -> fValue -> writeIt ();
        cout << " ";
        doWrite (x -> fNext);
    };
};
```

We shall see, by constructing a proof, that this procedure is exactly equivalent to the nonrecursive version shown below.

```
void doWrite (SList :: PListNode x) {
    while (x != SList :: zed) {
        x -> fValue -> writeIt ();
        cout << " ";
        x = x -> fNext;
    };
};
```

When a program like the first version executes the recursive call, the executing computer must do three things. First, it must ensure that when the recursion is executed, the new parameters of the call are properly set up. Second, it must ensure that all of the code in the recursive procedure (with the new parameters) is faithfully reexecuted. Finally, it must guarantee that the recursion finishes properly.

In the case of tail recursion this is very simply arranged. Since the code of the recursion is merely the code of the current procedure, we need only reexecute it with the new values of the parameters. This is simple using the `goto` statement of standard C. If we just remove the recursive call but assign the parameter its new value using

```
x = x -> fNext;
```

and then return by a `goto` statement to the beginning of the procedure, we will be almost correct. The small flaw is in the ending condition. We must guarantee that the procedure properly exits whenever a `zed` node is encountered. This can be arranged by reversing the value of the `if` statements test expression and using `goto` to get to the end of the procedure when this new test fails. Combining these ideas, we get a new version of `doWrite`.

```
void doWrite (SList :: PListNode x) {
start:
    if (x == SList :: zed) goto finish;
    x -> fValue -> writeIt ();
    cout << " ";
    x = x -> fNext;
    goto start;

finish:;
};
```

This is not to suggest, however, that `goto` statements should be used. In a language like Modula-2, these labels and `goto` statements are not even available. The purpose here is to show a structure and a transformation technique. In fact, we aren't yet finished, because we want a nicely structured program. Following the execution path of procedures like the current version of `doWrite` is difficult, which is one of the principal reasons why Pascal and C were developed with the structured statements that they have.

If we examine the code carefully, we see that we have a loop. We start at the top, and later a `goto` statement takes us back to that spot. Note that immediately after the label a test appears, which if passed will take us to a point beyond the statement that completed the loop. In other words, the test takes us out of the loop. Its placement at the beginning makes the loop equivalent to a `while` loop. However, jump logic, the logic of `goto` statements, is precisely the opposite of Boolean logic. When we say `if (e) s;` we mean to execute s when e is TRUE. With jump logic we say `if (e) goto END; s; END:`, which means execute s when e is FALSE. Therefore, to transform our structure of `doWrite` into a loop, we must change the sense of the test. Our final version of `doWrite` is as follows, with all labels removed because they are no longer needed.

```
void doWrite (SList :: PListNode x) {
   while (x != SList :: zed) {
      x -> fValue -> writeIt ();
      cout << " ";
      x = x -> fNext;
   };
};
```

A side effect of the above transformation is that any tail recursion is easily made into a single loop. This is so easy to do that many optimizing compilers carry it out automatically. Some languages, like Standard ML, were designed to take advantage of this phenomenon. The improvement in performance comes from the fact that the overhead of testing a loop is much less than the overhead associated with calling a procedure. (Procedures have two kinds of overhead: the time it takes to set up the procedure call and return and the space requirements needed for the local data of the called procedure. There is a discussion of this in Appendix A, Section A.9). Note that the code of our final version is about as complex as the original.

7.8.2 Removal of Non-Tail Recursion

The original version of doReverseWrite was recursive but not tail recursive. Removal of its recursion is difficult, because more remains to be done after any recursive call returns. Usually this involves the original parameters; therefore, before we reset these parameters to new values, we must save the old values somewhere. Because the recursion will continue, we must store the current values where they cannot be overwritten by another recursion. Since the lifetimes of recursive activations are nested, one finishing entirely before an earlier one is resumed, a stack is the appropriate place to save the parameters. The last one started is the first one that finishes, so the last parameters stored should be the first ones reused. Hence a stack.

```
void doReverseWrite (SList :: PListNode x) {
   if (x != SList :: zed) {
      doReverseWrite (x -> fNext);
      x -> fValue -> writeIt ();
      cout << " ";
   };
};
```

To manage the recursion removal, we must create a new stack at the beginning of doReverseWrite and free it at the end. Then, to remove the recursive call, we must save the current parameter x in the stack, set the parameter to the new value, x -> fNext, and finally reexecute all of the current code (not the stack generation, however).

```
    s = newStack ();
start:
    if (x == SList :: zed) goto ???;
    s -> push (x);
    x = x -> fNext;
    goto start;
???:    // Label for previous goto.
    ⋮
```

Just after the current recursive call we need to mark the resume point, since after any recursive call we must finish the current code. This is the location of the x -> writeIt () statement. At this point we must restore the parameter x, by popping the stack. For this we must test whether the stack is empty and exit the entire procedure if it is.

```
resume:
    if (s -> empty ()) goto finish;
    x = PListNode (s -> pop ());
    x -> fValue -> writeIt ();
    cout << " ";
```

The last wrinkle in our transformation is that we must ensure that every path in the current code that leads to the exit takes us to the resume point in the transformed code. The two ways out of the recursive version are to fail the original test or to pass it and then execute all the body of code indicated by the if statement. The new version will be exited only when the stack is empty at the resume point. This gives us the following code, which needs three labels, one for the top so that we can reexecute, one for the resume point, and finally, one for the exit point.

```
void doReverseWrite (SList :: PListNode x) {
    PStack s;

    s = newStack ();
start:
    if (x == SList :: zed) goto resume;
    s -> push (x);
    x = x -> fNext;
    goto start;
resume:
    if (s -> empty ()) goto finish;
    x = PListNode (s -> pop ());
```

```
    x -> fValue -> writeIt ();
    cout << " ";
    goto resume;

finish: delete s;
};
```

Now we can easily notice that the code from the label `resume` to label `finish` is a simple `while` loop. Removing the labels and replacing the `goto` logic with structured logic gives us

```
void doReverseWrite (SList :: PListNode x) {
    PStack s;

    s = newStack ();
start:
    if (x == SList :: zed) goto resume;
    s -> push (x);
    x = x -> fNext;
    goto start;
resume:
    while(!s -> empty ()) {
        x = PListNode (s -> pop());
        x -> fValue -> writeIt ();
        cout << " ";
    };

delete s;
};
```

Now we note that from the label `start` to the label `resume` is another `while` loop. Replacing it with structured code gives the final version.

```
void doReverseWrite (SList :: PListNode x) {
    PStack s;

    s = newStack ();

    while (x != SList :: zed) {
        s -> push (x);
        x = x -> fNext;
    };
    while (!s -> empty ()) {
        x = PListNode (s -> pop ());
        x -> fValue -> writeIt ();
        cout << " ";
    };
```

```
        delete s;
};
```

In this case we wind up with two loops. Because they are not nested, this procedure is relatively efficient compared to a recursion. However, we also have to take into consideration the fact that we have a stack to manage, which takes both space and time. In fact, the push and pop operations are performed frequently because they are carried out in these loops. If the stack implementation is extremely fast this version could provide an overall improvement of time efficiency. It might even be a space improvement, depending on the overhead of procedure call for the particular compiler. In effect, we have just simulated here what a compiler does when it translates a procedure call, whether recursive or not. The only simplification we have here is that there is only one possible return point from the call, the point we marked resume.

Notice that the code shown here in the final version of doReverse-Write is more complex than the original version. It is probably more difficult to understand than the original, as well.

We are now in a position to discuss a final reason why recursion removal is important to know about. Sometimes a useful algorithm is discovered by removing recursion from a recursive algorithm, and then replacing the recursion stack with a queue. The resulting algorithm is certainly not likely to be a solution to the same problem as the original algorithm, but it is often a useful solution to a related problem. We shall see a specific example of this in Chapter 12 in the discussion of graphs.

7.9   APPLICATIONS

The classes discussed in this chapter are extremely common in practice and occur in many programs of different types. Here will be given a few ideas from the range of possibilities.

We have already seen postfix expressions (Chapter 5). A stack can be used to evaluate postfix expressions in the following way. Read the postfix expression from left to right. If the symbol is an operand, push it onto the stack; if it is an operation, pop the needed number of operands for that operation off of the stack, apply the operation to those operands, and push the result back onto the stack. If the postfix expression was well formed, the result will be at the top of the stack when you finish. This is exactly the process used by a Hewlett-Packard reverse-Polish-notation calculator, although the maximum height of its stack is only four.

Message systems of all kinds (computerized or not) use queues and priority queues. When messages arrive they must be handled, but other messages may have arrived first. Arriving messages are put into a queue for handling in the order received. Sometimes the queue is a priority queue so that important messages can be handled before others that have arrived earlier.

Simulation programs are similar to message queues. Many simulations involve objects that must receive service at one or more stations. The stations are connected in some network so that the output of one station is the input to one or more others. When a station is busy, the objects are enqueued for service when the server becomes free. An example is an airport, where the main server is the runway used by the planes. There are, in fact, two queues with different priorities: the planes in the air waiting to land and those on the ground waiting to fly. Hospital waiting rooms are another example of priority queues.

We also saw how a stack controls the operation of a push-down automaton. In fact, Pascal programs are often translated into assembly code using a similar technique. One of the problems in language translation is discovering whether an input program is correct, and, if it is, discovering its structure: the parsing problem. The following technique is more general than the one described in Chapter 5. Program structures are defined using a form called BNF (Backus-Naur form), which is a way of defining a collection of terms simultaneously and recursively. A BNF is also sometimes called a grammar. The following is an example of a BNF for algebraic expressions.

```
<expression>    ::= <term> <addopTerm>
<addopTerm>     ::= empty
<addopTerm>     ::= + <expression>
<addopTerm>     ::= - <expression>
<term>          ::= <factor> <mulopFactor>
<mulopFactor>   ::= empty
<mulopFactor>   ::= * <term>
<mulopFactor>   ::= div <term>
<factor>        ::= identifier
<factor>        ::= number
<factor>        ::= (<expression>)
```

The names in angle brackets, called *nonterminals,* are all being defined, and the first one, <expression>, is the main symbol. It is assumed that the other symbols, like * and number, either stand for themselves explicitly or are known from other sources. These other symbols are called *terminals,* or *tokens.* Each line is called a *production,* and each production is a possible definition of the name on its left. The form on the right gives the form of the definition.

Using such grammar, you write a legal program in the following way. Start by writing down the principal symbol, always a nonterminal. Any nonterminal can be replaced with all of the right-hand side of any production whose left-hand side is that nonterminal. You stop when only tokens are left. Any string of tokens defined in this way is a legal string in the language defined by the grammar.

Here is how to use a stack to determine whether a given string is valid according to a given grammar. Start with the principal symbol on the stack.

Repeat the following until the stack and the string to be tested are simul-taneously empty.

1. Compare the symbol on top of the stack with the symbol at the begin-ning of whatever is left of your string.
2. If the symbol on the stack is a token and matches the symbol in your string, eliminate both and cycle.
3. Otherwise, if the symbol on the stack is a token that doesn't match your string's head, the string is not legal in the language, and you can quit.
4. Otherwise, if the symbol on top of the stack is a nonterminal, find a production in the grammar whose left-hand side is that nonterminal and whose right-hand side begins with the first symbol of the rest of your string. Pop the nonterminal from the stack and replace it with the right-hand side of that production, pushing on the symbols of the production from right to left so that its first symbol is left on the top of the stack. (In this case do not discard any symbols from your string). Then cycle.

If you don't empty the stack and the string simultaneously, the string is not in the language.

The above technique doesn't work for all grammars, but the class for which it does is very large. They are called LL (left-left) grammars, because the program string can be scanned or read, and translated from left to right. Pascal does not have such a grammar, but it is close enough that this technique is used on most of the language. Also it is sometimes difficult to determine whether a production starts with your string's beginning token, especially when the right sides of many productions start with nontermi-nals, as happens in the above grammar. In any case, a Pascal compiler can use a stack like this to translate your program. A course on compiler the-ory or design or on automata and computability will take these ideas much farther.

7.10   SUMMARY

We have seen that lists can be used in a variety of ways to build other struc-tures. Queues use lists as a parent class, and stacks and priority queues are clients of lists and have instance variables of the list type. The exercises involve reusing the methodology of lists to build circular structures.

Note that at this point the class lattice is starting to get deep as well as broad. Double-ended queues inherit from queues, which are lists, and so on. We are starting to achieve a high degree of reuse of software previously written. In particular, the positions and iterators of lists have been useful in all of these structures.

Recursion removal should be known by a working computer scientist, not because it is often done by hand, but because the transformation technique is sometimes useful in other circumstances. It also occasionally helps in the discovery of other algorithms. It is important to note that recursive procedures have nested lifetimes, with the called procedure beginning after and ending before the caller does. The stack we use to simulate recursion has a similar property, in that the lifetimes of the elements on the stack are nested within the lifetimes of those below them. It is this that makes stacks and recursion fit together so well.

EXERCISES

7.1 (7.1) Restate the stack rules of SFiniteStack so that they apply to the SStack of this chapter, given that we have made pop into a function here.

7.2 (7.3) Class SPriorityQueue was implemented as an array of queues. Discuss the feasibility and desirability of implementing it as a list of queues instead. What are the trade-offs? Design a protocol for such a class. Write the header file.

7.3 (7.3) Another implementation of SPriorityQueue is to maintain a single list in which the priorities of the items are maintained as well as the references to the data. The dequeue method removes and returns the front of this list. The enqueue method involves a search for the last item of the same or higher priority as the item to be inserted. A list insertion is done after this location. Define and implement SPriorityQueueNode as a subclass of SListNode so that it has room for a priority. Define and implement SPriorityQueue as a subclass of SList or SQueue using the idea above. Do you need to build new positions and iterators for this class, or will the inherited methods apply?

7.4 (7.3) Our implementation of priority queues did not include an associated position class. Design and implement such a class. Having done so, would it make sense to rebuild SPriorityQueueIterator? In particular, what would nextItem look like in such a reimplementation?

7.5 (7.3) Implement SPriorityQueue :: remove and SPriorityQueue :: empty.

7.6 (7.4) Implement the class SDEQueue.

7.7 (7.5) Our discussion of insert for SSortedList made reference to the three steps needed to insert a value into a list. What are the three steps?

7.8 (7.6) Implement an SDynamicArrayIterator class. Be sure to give SDynamicArray a newIterator method so that the iterators may be constructed.

7.9 (7.6) Note that there is no remove operation for large arrays. This is because an array is logically a dense structure and one can't remove from such a structure, but only replace one value by another, perhaps NULL. However if we put a NULL value at a location, it is desirable to actually remove the cell from the list for efficiency. What method should be added or modified to make this happen? Implement it.

7.10 (7.3 and 7.6) Refer to Exercise 7.3. An alternate method of building a priority queue is to use an ordinary list, but to construct a special data class to hold a value and its priority. These new items are inserted into the list, usually in priority order. Implement this idea.

7.11 (7.7) Reimplement SList so that it is doubly linked. You may implement two zed nodes, each with fNext and fPrev, that refer to the node itself. One of these nodes can follow the last non-zed node in the list and the other precede the first non-zed node. Note that if you ever set a position to this node, both next and prev will take you nowhere.

7.12 (7.7) An alternative to double linking that is sometimes used is to link the list circularly by connecting its end to its beginning. You can make zed complete a loop, so that the last node refers to zed and zed refers to the first node. This is called circularly linking the list. There is a serious flaw in this idea; be sure that you find it. A technique similar to this that does work is to create a new *lock* node for each list. Think of our list as an iron chain, and think of the new node as a padlock that joins the first and last links to form a circle of the chain. The problem is that we need to be able to distinguish this special node when we find it, even though it is not unique in the system, but only unique in each circular list. Devise a scheme so that this node can be found regardless of the data that a client program may want to store in the list.

7.13 (7.7) Another way to build a circular list is to avoid the terminator node altogether. Each node refers to the next in the circular list, and all nodes are active. This is sometimes precisely what you want to do, especially if your problem has data that are naturally circularly linked (e.g., people around a table) and there is no natural first position. Design, build, and test such a circular structure. It will be especially helpful to keep a reference to the logical last node in the list, rather than the first. Draw some pictures illustrating inserts at the front and rear of such a list to convince yourself of this.

7.14 (7.7) Discuss the desirability and feasibility of modifying SList to contain a method insertLast. Discuss the desirability and feasibility of implementing SList with both fFirstNode and fLastNode instance variables.

## CHAPTER 8

ARRAYS AS OBJECTS

Pharoh arrayed him in vestures of fine linnen.

Genesis 41:42

To sort our nobles from our common men.

Shakespeare, *Henry V*

You are already familiar with arrays in C. In this chapter we shall develop a class, called SArray, that turns ordinary arrays into objects. This has two advantages. The first is that it will let us develop arrays as an ADT, using the encapsulation and data-hiding principles that we have already seen. It will permit us to package sorting and searching procedures with the objects that they operate on. The second advantage is more practical. In many situations we want arrays to behave as if they were objects rather than as a low-level C++ construct. In effect, all we are going to do is build a layer of packaging around ordinary arrays.

8.1   THE ARRAY CLASS

We want to create an ADT consisting of two data abstractions. The first will represent arrays themselves, and the second will be iterators over the arrays. The iterators will give us a convenient way to operate on the data stored in the arrays. We shall do this in such a way that the user may decide at the time of creating an actual array object how big the array should be. In other words, we shall treat arrays as dynamically sized objects. We shall even permit a user to expand the size of an array previously created.

Shown below is the header part of the class SArray.

```
class SArray;
typedef SArray *PArray;

PArray newArray (int size);

class SArray: public SCollection {
    public:
            SArray (int n);
        virtual                 ~SArray (void);
        virtual void        insert (PObject);
        virtual void        remove (PObject);
        virtual void        atPut (int, PObject);
        virtual char        empty () {return (FALSE);};
        virtual PIterator newIterator (void);
        virtual PObject    at (int);
        virtual void        extend (int);
        virtual int         physicalSize (void);
        virtual void        swap (int,int);
        virtual void        bubbleSort (void);
        virtual void        selectionSort (void);
        virtual void        insertionSort (void);
        virtual void        ShellSort (void);
        virtual void        quickSort (int L, int U,
                                    char avoid);
        virtual void        mergeSort (int L, int U);
        virtual char        sequentialSearch (PObject t,
                                            int &Loc);
        virtual char        binarySearch (PObject t,
                                        int &Loc);
        virtual char        recursiveBinarySearch
                            (int L, int U, PObject t,
                             int &Loc);
        virtual void        randomArray (void);
        virtual PObject    Clone (void);

        virtual char        member (classtype c);
        virtual void        writeIt (void);

    protected:
        PObject             *fElements;
        int                 fLength;
        virtual int         sizeOf (void);
```

```
            virtual void     insertionSortSubArray (int L,
                                                    int U);
            virtual void     merge (int L, int M, int U);
            friend SArrayIterator;
    };

    class SArrayIterator;
    typedef SArrayIterator *PArrayIterator;

    class SArrayIterator: public SIterator {
        public:
                SArrayIterator (PArray);
            virtual char     nextItem (PObject&);
            virtual void     reset (void);
            virtual char     member (classtype c);
            virtual void     writeIt (void);

        protected:
            int              fPosition;
            virtual int      sizeOf (void);

    };
```

As mentioned before, our primary data abstraction and primary class is SArray. Its instance variables are fElements, which is nothing but a pointer to an ordinary array, and fLength, which keeps track of the current size of the array fElements. The element type of this array is PObject, permitting us to store any objects in the array. An array could consist of integers if we use objects in class SInteger, sets if we use SSet, or even other arrays. In fact, the array could be hetereogeneous, with each element an object of a different kind.

As usual, a constructor, SArray, creates the internal storage, fElements, and sets all of the references to NULL. The first part of its code is a call to the new operator, indicating how large the allocated array of PObjects is to be. The last part of the code is a for loop that iterates over the range from 0 to the length, setting the components to be NULL. Note that we guarantee to allocate at least one cell.

```
SArray :: SArray (int n) {
    if (n <= 0) n = 1;
    fElements = new PObject[n];
    if (fElements == NULL)
        Error ("System Heap exhausted.");
    fLength = n;
    for (int i=0; i<n; i++)
        fElements[i] = NULL;
};
```

The destructor must delete fElements, of course, which was allocated in the constructor. It may seem strange at first, but the standard insert and remove methods are overridden and implemented as error calls. Because an array is a collection of fixed size, we do not insert or remove data. The positions, or cells, always exist and always have some data stored in them, even if it is just NULL. Our initialization set all of the cells of fElements to NULL, and we can replace the contents of any cell at any time, but we cannot remove a cell.

```
void SArray :: insert (PObject) {
    Error ("SArray :: insert: Fixed-size collection")
};
```

The inherited version of insert, SCollection :: insert, generates an error already. This reimplementation just permits a more informative message to be sent to the user. A similar implementation of remove is appropriate.

The most important methods of this class are at and atPut. The method atPut inserts an object into a position in the array, and at returns a reference to the object at a given position. These are the exact equivalents of using an ordinary array subscript reference on the left-hand side of an assignment (in the case of atPut) or in an expression (in the case of at). In fact, the code for atPut could be simply

```
fElements[i] = o;
```

It will be advantageous, however, to do a little more. One of the common errors made with arrays is to attempt to reference a subscript that is not in the valid range. We can make such subscripting safe (from crashes, not from errors) by testing in these methods. If the reference is out of bounds, atPut can be either an error or a no-op and at can return NULL. We could also automatically extend the array when such a reference is made, but this would be very dangerous. (Why?)

```
void SArray :: atPut (int i, PObject o) {
    if (i < fLength && i >= 0)
        fElements[i] = o;
    else Error ("Array out of bounds");
        // Or nothing.
};

PObject SArray :: at (int i) {
    if (i < fLength && i >= 0)
        return fElements[i];
    else Error ("Array out of bounds");
        // Or return NULL.
};
```

Similarly, the fact that arrays are of fixed size means that the empty functional method should always return FALSE. An array is never empty, even though it may contain only references to NULL. Be careful with this idea, however. If you fail to initialize every cell with a valid value, errors can occur, since the initialization only sets the values to NULL. There are some uses of arrays for which you want empty to return TRUE if all references in the array are NULL, and some uses in which an array is only partially "filled." In such a case a subclass of the array class should be created and given a new instance variable, fCount, that would keep track of the number of non-NULL references. The empty method of such a subclass could return TRUE when this variable has value zero. The atPut method would need to be overridden in this new class to maintain a valid value for this new variable.

The discussion in the previous paragraph brings up an important point of object-oriented programming. The question often arises, "Should I modify an existing class or create a new subclass?" Usually the question is asked because some method is not what is wanted in the application. The answer to the question depends on circumstances. Generally speaking, a class should be changed only if the user perceives that the existing definition or implementation is in error. Otherwise, creating a new class that either subclasses the existing class or uses an object of its type as an instance variable is better. The reason for preferring a new class is that a library might be used in several applications and should be stable. A change in a class might be inconsistent with the use in some other program previously written. If that program is modified, it won't work with the modified library, which would have to be changed back to its original form. It will work with the extended library, however, and with a few changes in its own declarations can even take advantage of the new functionality.

This brings us to the question of what is the minimum amount of code necessary to create a subclass of an existing class. The answer is that we need a class definition with at least one new method, and perhaps some additional instance variables. If the class is not an abstract class, we also need to provide a constructor and a generator function so that objects in the class can be properly created.

We can extend an existing array by reallocating fElements and copying all of the old elements into the new storage. This is time consuming and so should be used only where it is essential. Accurately determining what the maximum size must be at the time the array is first allocated is better.

```
void SArray :: extend (int n) {
   PObject *newElements;
   if (n > 0) {
      newElements = new PObject[fLength + n];
      if (newElements == NULL) Error ("System Heap
                                      exhausted.");
      for (int i = 0; i < fLength; ++i)
         newElements[i] = fElements[i];
```

```
    for (i = fLength; i < fLength + n; ++i)
        newElements[i] = NULL;
    // Delete old elements but not the data.
    delete []fElements;
    fLength += n;
    fElements = newElements;
  };
};
```

ARRAY ITERATORS

An array iterator is implemented by means of an instance variable, fPosition, that represents the location in the array of the next item to be yielded. This variable is initialized to zero, since it is appropriate for any array iterator to yield the items in order starting at zero.

```
SArrayIterator :: SArrayIterator (PArray a):
                  SIterator (a) {
    fPosition = 0;
};
```

Subsequently sending nextItem to this iterator yields us the contents of cell zero, and further calls yield the other elements sequentially. The variable fPosition keeps track of where we are in the iteration. When we have given up all of the elements, we must set fDone to be TRUE. The code for nextItem is as follows:

```
char SArrayIterator :: nextItem (PObject& o) {
    char result;

    result = !fDone;
    if (result) {
        o = PArray (fCollection)
            -> fElements[fPosition];
        ++fPosition;
        fDone = fPosition
            >= PArray (fCollection) -> fLength;
    };
    return result;
};
```

It first determines whether it has finished by consulting its fDone instance variable. If it has finished, it does nothing else except return FALSE as its function value. Otherwise, it sets the parameter to the contents of cell fPosition, the next item not yet returned, increments fPosition, and sets fDone to be TRUE or FALSE appropriately.

We use this method in contexts such as

```
IT = PictureArray -> newIterator ();
while (IT -> nextItem (aPic))
   PPicture (aPic) -> draw ();
```

We need to make type assertions about `aPic`, because `nextItem` expects to be sent an object in the root class but `draw` is not known in that class. Therefore, `aPic` is best declared to be in `PObject` and the `draw` statement typecasted as in `PPicture (aPic) -> draw ()`. This is a common problem with all collection classes. Because collection classes are defined so as to be able to hold any kind of data, the class of the data retrieved from is difficult to determine. Generally the programmer keeps track of this, although the `member` function can help if the collection holds items from a variety of classes. The `member` function was discussed in Chapter 3 (p. 95).

8.3   SIMPLE SORT ROUTINES FOR ARRAYS

We saw sorting before in the chapter on lists. We want to arrange the contents of some structured collection so that the elements are in order according to their magnitudes. Of course, the contents of the collection must be in some subclass of `SMagnitude`. We examined the selection sort, which repeatedly looks for the smallest item in the unsorted portion of the list and moves that value to the end of the sorted portion, eventually sorting the entire list. That same sort can be performed on an array, but many other sort routines are also feasible since within an array we have quick access to any of the elements. In this section we shall look at a number of simple sort routines. They all work but are less efficient on large arrays than the methods to be discussed in the next section.

Before we begin to develop the sorting methods, we need to take a short side trip. We shall express the final sorting algorithms in terms of `for` loops, but our development will use `while` loops. We need to transform `while` loops into `for` loops simply. Some such transformations are trivial, of course. For example, the following two loops are equivalent, and the first can be taken as the definition of the `for` loop that follows it. `S` can be any statement and can depend on `i`.

```
i = a;
while (i < b) {
   S;
   ++i;
};

for (i = a; i < b; ++i) S;
```

Slightly more complex is the following `while` loop, which increments the control variable at the beginning instead of the end.

```
i = a;
while (i < b) {
    ++i;
    S;
};
```

This is not equivalent to the loops above, because it executes S with slightly different values of i. To make an equivalent `for` loop, we first transform it into a `while` loop that increments at the end. Noting that this loop executes S first when i = a+1 and last when i = b, we get

```
i = a+1;
while (i <= b) {
    S;
    ++i;
};
```

This loop is then equivalent to the `for` loop

```
for (i = a+1; i <= b; ++i) S;
```

This is also equivalent to

```
for (i = a+1; i < b+1; ++i) S;
```

With this in mind, we can go directly from the preincrement form to this `for` loop without the middle steps.

For each sort method that we discuss we shall develop a picture of the process in action. The pictures are called array sections; we used a similar picture when we discussed `SList :: selectionSort`. For example, Fig. 8.1a indicates an array whose lowest and highest indices are 0 and Max. Let k be an index such that the elements from k+1 to Max are the largest in the array and are sorted. This sorted section has exactly i values. The elements in cells 0 through k are arbitrary. The purpose of such an array is to show the idea behind a sort method. It is also a way to verify that a loop used to implement the sort is correct. If we could keep reducing k but still keep the picture accurate, eventually k would equal -1 and the entire array would be in order.

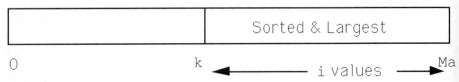

FIGURE 8.1a

8.3.1 Bubble Sort

Figure 8.1a can be taken as the definitional picture of the bubble sort, so called because large items "bubble up" to their final positions. The description at the end of the last paragraph leads to the following overall program structure. Define i to be the size of the sorted portion of the array. Then k is Max - i, and for us Max is fLength-1.

```
i = 0; // Make the picture true because the right
       // part is empty.
while (i < fLength) {
   // Increase i but keep the i values to the right
   // sorted and >= anything in the other cells.
};
```

When we exit, i will be the size of the array, and the array will all be sorted. This task can be accomplished if we find the largest item in the left part and move it to cell k just before finally incrementing i. The item currently in cell k will need to be moved elsewhere in the left part to make room. This leaves us with modified pseudocode:

```
i = 0; // Make the picture true because the right
       // part is empty.
while (i < fLength) {
   // Move the largest item in the left part to
   // cell k = fLength-1 - i, moving other
   // cells there as appropriate.
   ++i;
};
```

In order to find and move this largest value we shall use another index j and another loop controlled by j. When this loop is in operation, the index j in the array is the cell index of the largest item in cells 0 . . . j. In other words, we keep the largest item in 0 . . . j in the rightmost cell of this section. This is illustrated in Fig. 8.1b. When j is 0, cell j automatically contains the largest value in section 0 . . . j, which is just 0 . . . 0. Therefore the initialization of this inner loop is just j = 0.

We now increase j and compare the content of cell j with that of the one to its left. If the two cells are out of order, we swap their contents using the following method.

```
void SArray :: swap(int i,int j) {
   PObject temp;
   if (i >= 0 && i < fLength && j >= 0
       && j < fLength) {
      temp = fElements[i];
      fElements[i] = fElements[j];
      fElements[j] = temp;
```

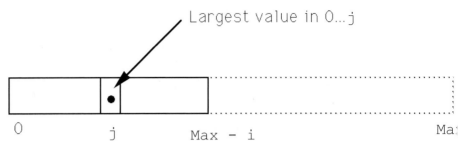

FIGURE 8.1b

```
      }
   else
      Error ("SArray :: swap: subscript violation");
};
```

After the above step the largest element in cells $0 \ldots j$ (for the newly incremented j) is in cell j itself. We stop when j reaches $k = \text{Max} - i = \text{fLength} - 1 - i$. At any given time during this scan, the situation in Fig. 8.1b is TRUE, and as the scan continues we shall eventually encounter the largest element in the left part of the array. Once we do, it will be bigger than any other item and so will keep being swapped to the right. It will eventually come to rest in slot k.

When j reaches $k = \text{fLength} - 1 - i$, the largest value in the entire section is in that rightmost cell. This will increase the size of the right portion of Fig. 8.1a, so we can safely increment the control variable i of the outer loop. This process should replace the comment that forms the body of the While loop above. If we write this out in C++, we get

```
j = 0;
while (j < fLength -1 - i) {
   ++j;
   if (fElements[j] > fElements[j-1])
      swap (i,j);
};
```

This leads to the following code, which is implemented with for loops such that i is increased (thereby decreasing k) and, for each increment of i, j is used to scan the left portion.

```
void SArray :: bubbleSort (void) {
   for (int i = 0; i < fLength; i++)
      for (int j=1; j < fLength-i; j++) {
         if ((fElements[j]) -> less (fElements[j-1])
            swap(j, j-1);
      };
};
```

Sorted & Smallest	

0   i   Max

FIGURE 8.2a

8.3.2 Selection Sort

The bubble sort of the last section does a lot of exchanging (swapping) of data. Selection sort eliminates much of this. We saw the selection sort before, when we discussed lists. Its array section is shown in Fig. 8.2a. The section between 0 and $i-1$ is sorted and contains the smallest items in the entire array, so the idea is to increase i until it is equal to Max. It doesn't need to exceed Max, because when it is equal to Max, the largest value in the array is in cell Max.

Note that i is initialized to be 0, so the portion to the left of i is empty and is thus sorted, by default. Therefore, our overall strategy is expressed in the following:

```
i = 0;
while (i < fLength -1) {
    // Find the smallest value in i ...  Max
    // and move it to cell i.
    ++i;
};
```

To increase i correctly, keeping this invariant true, we use another index, j, to search for the smallest item beyond i. See Fig. 8.2b. An index s is used to remember the location of the smallest item between locations i and j. The indices j and s are initialized to be i also. The purpose here is to increase j so that when it reaches Max, s points to the smallest item beyond i. Then we just swap the contents of cells i and s, increasing the size of the left part in Fig. 8.2a.

Using an auxiliary variable, small, to hold an alternate reference to the contents of cell s, we get the following code for this inner loop, the replacement of the comment in our *strategy program* above.

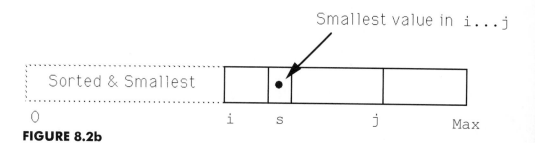

FIGURE 8.2b

```
s = i;
small = fElements[s];
j = i; // Figure 8.2b holds now.
while (j < fLength-1) {
    ++j;
    if (fElements[j] -> less (small)) {
        s = j; // s is the location of the smallest
               // value in i... j
        small = fElements[s];
    };
};
```

If we now rewrite this using `for` loops, we get the following.

```
void SArray :: selectionSort (void) {
    int s;
    PObject small;

    for (int i = 0; i < fLength-1; ++i) {
        s = i;
        small = fElements[s];
        for (int j = i+1; j < fLength; j++)
            if ((fElements[j]) -> less (small)) {
                s = j;
                small = fElements[s];
            };
        fElements[s] = fElements[i];
        fElements[i] = small;
    };
};
```

8.3.3 Insertion Sort

The insertion sort is almost the opposite of the selection sort. Instead of selecting the next item and appending it to an already sorted subarray, we take an arbitrary element from the unsorted part of the array and insert it into its proper place in an already sorted subarray. The idea is one of a box of sorted index cards. You grab the next item from an unsorted box and then run through the cards in the sorted box, moving them aside in order to see the values, and make an opening into which the new card can be dropped when you come to its proper position. In this case the portion of the array from 0 to i−1 is sorted, as shown in Fig. 8.3a.

Since an array of one item is sorted, we begin with i equal to one. Our outer loop in the insertion sort is

Sorted	Unexamined

```
0                              i                    Max
```

FIGURE 8.3a

```
for (i = 1 ; i < fLength; ++i) {
   // Keep 0...i-1 sorted.
};
```

The strategy for keeping the section sorted is to grab the item from cell i and call it T, making the slot from which it came temporarily available for holding some other item. We then shift items to the right by one cell until we find the slot into which T should be placed. At any given time we have just moved an item to the right, freeing a cell which we call j. We decrease j until we reach 0 or find the slot into which T should be placed. See Fig. 8.3b.

We can therefore refine our strategy to the following.

```
for (i = 1; i <= fLength -1; ++i) {
   // Make T a copy of slot i.
   // Slide values to the right until the next one
   // is less than or equal to T, or slide them all.
   // Put T into the empty slot.
};
```

The code implementing this is as follows.

```
j = i;
T = fElements[j];
while (j > 0 && T -> less (fElements[j - 1])) {
   fElements[j] = fElements[j - 1];
   --j;
};
fElements[j] = T;
```

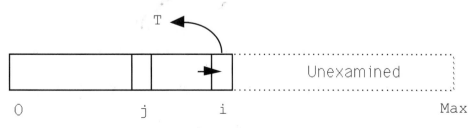

```
0              j         i                    Max
```

- values in j+1...i are > T.
- j is empty.

FIGURE 8.3b

Note that when $j = 0$, the short-circuit nature of the operator && takes us out of the loop before we attempt the evaluation of fElements[j-1], which is illegal when $j = 0$. Combining the inner and outer loops, we get the following.

```
void SArray :: insertionSort (void) {
    int i, j;
    PObject T;

    for (i=1; i < fLength; ++i) {
        j = i;
        T = fElements[j];
        while (j > 0 && T -> less (fElements[j-1])) {
            fElements[j] = fElements[j-1];
            --j;
        };
        fElements[j] = T;
    };
};
```

8.3.4 Shell Sort

The last of the simple sorts is quite a bit more complicated but also much more efficient. It is called the Shell sort, after its inventor, D. L. Shell. In effect, it is a series of passes over the array, of which each effects a partial insertion sort on part of the array. With each pass the part of the array affected by the sort increases in size until it is all sorted. It sounds complex, and it is, but it is fast, because the insertion sort is very fast on very small lists and also on nearly sorted lists. Therefore, sorting sublists actually speeds it up, even though there may be many passes. In fact, the code is misleading. The three nested loops would seem to take a long time.
  Consider a sequence of numbers such as the following:

$$1, \ 6, \ 31, \ 156, \ \ldots$$

Each term is generated by starting at one and repeatedly computing

$$h := 5 * h + 1;$$

Take the last item in the series that is less than or equal to the size of the array. For example, this is 31 for an SArray with 100 elements. Consider the array to be a collection of h small arrays, each composed of elements that are h ($=31$) cells apart in the original array; i.e., every hth cell. These subarrays are numerous, but each has only three or four elements. The two inner loops in the following code perform insertion sorts on these subarrays. Then we reduce h to the next smaller value in the series, which is 6 for these arrays, and repeat the process. This time the subarrays have only about 16 elements (100/6), and their order has already been improved by the first pass. Also there are fewer of these subarrays, since h is smaller. This is repeated until the final pass, in which $h = 1$ and the entire array is sorted. Compare the inner loops with the code for insertion sort; the only difference is that the slots are h cells apart instead of 1 cell apart.

```
void SArray :: ShellSort (void) {
    int h, i, j;
    PObject T;

    h = 1;
    do {
        h = 5 * h + 1; // This does not generate an
                       //     optimal sequence!!!
    } while (h < fLength);
    do {
        h = h / 5; // Get the previous value in the
                   //    sequence of h's.
        for (i = h; i < fLength; ++i) {
            j = i;
            T = fElements[j];
            while (j >= h && T -> less
                    (fElements[j-h])) {
                fElements[j] = fElements[j-h];
                j -= h;
            };
            fElements[j] = T;
        };
    } while (h > 1);
};
```

If the `for` loop in the above code incremented by h instead of by one, the code would be that of a single insertion sort with "1" replaced by "h." However, the increment is by one, so the above code represents h insertion sorts interspersed with one another rather than carried out sequentially. Such interspersion saves us a lot of loop overhead, because one loop construct manages all of the various smaller sorts that the Shell sort carries out for each value of h. Figure 8.4 will help to visualize the process. If the array size is ten and h is four, we can consider the array to be divided into four subarrays whose elements are separated by four cells. The first subarray consists of cells 0, 4, and 8, the next of cells 1, 5, and 9, and so on. If we sort each of these four subarrays, we have improved the order of the array of which they are a part, having generally moved small items to the left and large ones to the right. If we then let $h = 2$, we have only two subarrays, each twice as large as the ones here.

8.4   MORE SOPHISTICATED SORTING

In this section two sorts are discussed that, although more complex than the preceding ones, are much more suited to the task of sorting large arrays.

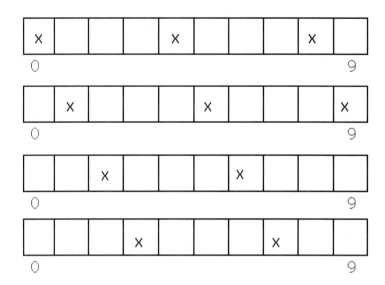

FIGURE 8.4

The difficulty with the simpler sorts is that, except for the Shell sort, the algorithms all take time proportional to the square of the size of the array we are sorting. This means that there is some constant C, generally determined by the number of statements in the inner loop of the program, such that the time required to sort an array of n random items is approximately equal to Cn^2. This time is not extreme for small arrays, but if you double the size of the array, you quadruple the time involved. The Shell sort is not quite as good as the methods in this section, but is much better than the quadratic-time sorts. Both of the algorithms discussed here, the quick sort and the merge sort, take time proportional to the size of the array times its logarithm (base 2). Since the logarithm of a large positive number is much less than that number, we get a huge savings in time. For $n = 1024$, the difference is that between $n \log_2(n) = 10,240$ and $n^2 = 1,048,576$. Ten thousand is only one percent of a million. In fact, the difference is not this large, because the constants of proportionality are different. But they are still just constants, and so the bigger the array to be sorted, the bigger the effect.

Each of these sorts is based on an idea from which the algorithm is developed. Here the ideas are recursive. We solve large problems in terms of the solutions of smaller problems. The general idea is this. If we know how to solve some simple problems and also how to combine the solutions of simple problems to get solutions of larger problems, then we can solve large problems. In particular, assume that we can solve all extremely simple sorting problems, say those with only one or two elements, that a sorting problem of any size can be expressed as a collection of problems with strictly fewer elements, and finally that we know how to combine the solutions of the simpler problems, once we have them, into a solution of our harder problem. Then we can solve any sort problem.

This is the general idea behind recursive programming. Give explicit solutions (code) for all simple cases of the problem. Then for complex problems give solutions in terms of combinations of the solutions to the strictly simpler problems. A more explicit description of this is as follows.

1. If it is possible to solve a problem with a computer program, we imagine that the solution exists, even if we haven't written down a solution yet.
2. We name the solution imagined in part 1 and give a complete specification (in ordinary language) of the solution. This amounts to a definition of the name.
3. We now write down a description of the solution/name given in part 2. We use programming terminology for this description.
4. Since the program exists and has a name, we can use the name when writing down the description in part 3. When we use the name, the program called meets the specification created in part 2.
5. However, a description that is entirely circular is no description at all, so the description must not be self-referencing for simple cases, and must express complex cases in terms of solutions to simpler cases.

8.4.1 Quick Sort

The `quickSort` method can be developed according to the above principles. If the array has only one element, sorting it is trivial: do nothing, for it is already sorted. A larger array is split into two portions, both strictly smaller than the entire array, and such that every element in the left portion is smaller than every element in the right portion. We then sort the two smaller portions similarly. Having sorted the smaller portions we have finished, because we had previously put the smaller elements to the left of the larger ones. The general outline is as follows:

```
quickSort (all) IS
    IF all has more than one element THEN
        Split the array into two smaller parts.
        Move the small elements to the left part
            and the larger elements to the right part.
        quickSort (left part);
        quickSort (right part);
```

Because we need to express the sorting of the whole in terms of the sorting of parts, we must pass information to `quickSort` about what part of the array it is to sort. We pass it the two indices that indicate the lower and upper cells in the array that it should work on. Therefore, the message `theArray -> quickSort (4,20)` indicates that it should sort the portion of `theArray` from cell 4 to cell 20 inclusive. The declaration will use L and U for the lower and upper indices, respectively.

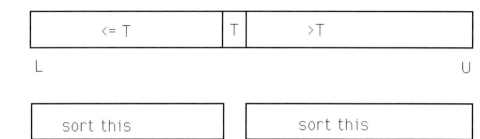

FIGURE 8.5a

One small problem is ensuring that both parts are strictly smaller than the entire array. Splitting the array into one part that is empty and the other part comprising the entire array is too easy, and in such a case the above process does not terminate. We therefore make a small refinement. We pick some item in the array such that all smaller items are to its left, all larger items are to its right, and its value is intermediate between the items in the two parts. We then interpret the left part to be the portion strictly left of our central, pivot, element, and the right part is the portion strictly to the right of it. These parts are less than the whole, because neither includes the pivot. See Fig. 8.5a.

A second problem concerns the second step, moving the small and large items. We first divide the array into three parts. The first part consists of a single value in the very first position, slot L. The second part comprises those values less than or equal to that first value. These are between the second location and a location named `lastLow`. The third part of the array comprises all values larger than the first, and these are in locations from `lastLow+1` to the end, which is cell U. See Fig. 8.5b.

Once the array is in this form, we can swap the first and `lastLow` elements, making the required division.

The final problem is achieving the division described above, with the value T being in the first slot, smaller (and equal) values just beyond it, and larger values to the far right. For this an array picture will help (Fig. 8.5c). We scan the entire array with an index i, which starts in the first position, L. Each time we increase i, we test whether the element it refers to is greater than T. If it is, we do nothing, the section containing values greater than T has been enlarged. If it is not greater than T, we increase `lastLow` by one and swap the contents of cells at i and the new `lastLow`. This enlarges the section containing values less than or equal

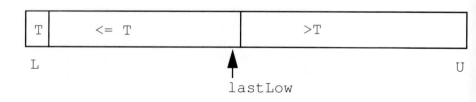

FIGURE 8.5b

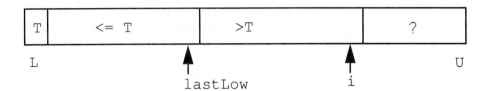

FIGURE 8.5c

to T. Eventually i > U, so the entire array is partitioned as required. We then make the final swap described at the end of the last paragraph.

This process can be carried out as follows:

```
T = fElements[L];
lastLow = L;
i = L; // Third section is initially empty.
while  (i < U) {
    ++i;
    if (fElements[i] -> less (T)) {
        ++lastLow;
        swap (lastLow, i);
    };
};
```

When this ends we swap locations L and lastLow to get the required partition, with the pivot in a centralized position. Changing the while loop into an equivalent for loop, we get the following.

```
void SArray :: quickSort (int L, int U, char avoid) {
    int i, lastLow;
    PObject T;

    if (L < U) {
        if (avoid) {}; // An exercise.
        T = fElements[L];
        lastLow = L;
        for (i = L+1; i <= U; i++)
            if ((fElements[i]) -> less (T)) {
                ++lastLow;
                swap (lastLow,i);
            };
        swap (L, lastLow);
        quickSort (L, lastLow-1, avoid);
        quickSort (lastLow+1, U, avoid);
    };
};
```

The `avoid` parameter in the `quickSort` procedure solves a small but perplexing problem. The algorithm may not be as efficient as was suggested earlier. If you apply `quickSort` as described above to an array that is already sorted, the time behavior is quadratic. Because the `<=T` section remains empty, each time we reduce the size of the problem, one of the parts is empty, and the other part is only one cell smaller than the original. This is equivalent to a pair of nested loops, each iterating a number of times dependent on the size of the array. The algorithm is slowest when the array is already sorted. To avoid this case and speed up the algorithm, we can randomly choose the pivot value from the contents of the array by swapping the element `fElements[L]` and the element in a randomly determined cell. The method does this when the parameter `avoid` is TRUE. If the array might be already sorted, this parameter should be set to TRUE when `quickSort` is called.

8.4.2 **Validating the** `while` **Loop in** `quickSort`

We shall validate the loop in `quickSort` using the version of it that appeared just before we substituted a `for` loop for the `while` loop. There are two major steps to validating a loop. The first is ensuring that the loop eventually exits. This is guaranteed here because in each iteration of the loop we increment `i` and test it for large values. The second step involves showing that when the loop exits, it does what we need done: that it meets its specification.

The purpose of the `While` loop in the `quickSort` method is to establish the truth of Fig. 8.5b. To do this we need to construct a loop invariant. This is given in this case by Fig. 8.5c. This step consists of three parts. First, we must guarantee that the loop invariant is TRUE before we enter the loop. The two initialization statements just before the `while` loop establish this by emptying the `<=T` and `>T` sections of the figure. Therefore, everything is in the `?` section. Next, we must ensure that what we have called the invariant is, indeed, invariant. In fact, the first statement might make the Boolean expression implied by the figure FALSE (it will if `fElements[i]` `<` `T`). The following `if` statement repairs the truth of it in this case. Therefore, if the statement is TRUE before executing the body, it is TRUE after. The third required part concerns what we know to be TRUE when we exit. Because of the initialization and the loop invariant, we know that the loop invariant is TRUE after exit. But we also know that `i` `=` `U`. Therefore the `?` part is now empty, and we have established the truth of Fig. 8.5b.

8.4.3 **Merge Sort**

Like `quickSort`, the merge sort is recursive and is applied to subarrays. Therefore it has a pair of parameters, L and U, to give the lower and upper subscripts of the subarray to which it is being applied. The mergeSort method also divides the array into two parts. If the number of items is even, it makes an exact division at the midpoint. If the number of items is odd, it leaves one fewer element in the left part than the right. If the array has more than two elements, mid = (L + U) / 2 is strictly between L and U, so L . . . mid and mid+1 . . . U are proper subsets of the indices of the array. The mergeSort method divides the L . . . U portion of the array into two parts at point mid and (recursively) sorts the two parts. The recursions return two sorted lists.

```
void SArray :: mergeSort (int L, int U) {
    int mid;

    if (L+1 == U) {
        if ((fElements[U]) -> less (fElements[L]))
            swap(L,U);
    }
    else if (L+1 < U) {
        mid = (L + U) / 2;
        mergeSort (L, mid);
        mergeSort (mid+1, U);
        merge (L, mid, U);
    };
};
```

Now the two sorted lists must be combined into a single sorted array. The process for this step is called merge. We consider the two portions of the original array as if they were separate arrays. If there are more than two elements, merge scans each array, one cell at a time, comparing an item from each array. The smaller of the two items is output to the leftmost free slot in a temporary array. Then the scan variables of the source of the item and the temporary array are incremented. This process was illustrated in Fig. 6.11 in the discussion of the merging of lists. When one of the two input arrays becomes empty, we copy the remainder of the other into the remaining free slots of the temporary array and copy all of the temporary array back to the original array. If there are two or fewer elements, a sort is trivial, being mere comparison; thus the recursion eventually ends.

```
void SArray :: merge (int L, int M, int U) {
    int toWhere, left, right, i;
    PArray temp;

    toWhere = L;
    left = L;
    right = M + 1;
    temp = newArray (fLength);
```

```
      while (left <= M && right <= U)
         if ((fElements[left]) ->
             less (fElements[right]))
            temp -> atPut (toWhere++,
                               fElements[left++]);
         else
            temp -> atPut (toWhere++,
                               fElements[right++]);
      if(left>M)
         for (i=right; i <= U; ++i)
            temp -> atPut (toWhere++, fElements[i]);
      else if (right > U)
         for (i = left; i <= M; ++i)
            temp -> atPut (toWhere++, fElements[i]);
      for (i=L; i <= U; ++i) fElements[i] = temp -> at
      delete temp;
   };
```

An alternative merger stores the temporary data in an ordinary array rather than in an element of SArray. Since we can make fElements a reference to this newly allocated array after disposing of the current fElements, we can avoid copying the temporary array back into the original array.

```
void SArray :: merge (int L, int M, int U) {
   int toWhere, left, right, i;
   PObject *temp;

   toWhere = L;
   left = L;
   right = M+1;
   temp = new PObject[fLength];
   while (left <= M && right <= U)
      if ((fElements[left]) ->
          less (fElements[right]))
         temp[toWhere++] = fElements[left++];
      else
         temp[toWhere++] = fElements[right++];
   if (left > M)
      for (i = right; i <= U; ++i)
         temp[toWhere++] = fElements[i];
   else if (right > U)
      for (i = left; i <= M; ++i)
         temp[toWhere++] = fElements[i];
   delete []fElements;
   fElements = temp;
};
```

8.4.4 Why These Sorts Are Faster Than the Simple Sorts

The methods bubbleSort, selectionSort, and insertionSort all must linearly scan the data to remove one item from further consideration. Thus their running times are quadratic functions of the size of their inputs, obeying the recurrence relation discussed in Section 6.7.2. A quadratic algorithm has the interesting property that if the set of data over which it operates is divided into two equal portions and the algorithm is then applied to the two parts, the total time required is less than the time required to process the original data. This is the converse of the fact that doubling the size of the data quadruples the time. Processing both halves of the original data takes only half the time required to process the original, because each half takes only one quarter of the time. If combining the two solutions into a solution for the original data takes less than the other half of the time, the sort will have been accelerated. These algorithms achieve an even greater speedup because the halves of the original are themselves redivided by the recursive step, leading to more saved time if the combinations can be accomplished quickly enough. This is the case here, because in both quickSort and mergeSort the combination step (partitioning for quickSort and merging for mergeSort) can be done with a single scan of the data.

In mergeSort, for example, the merge step is linear in the number of inputs, since the merging of two halves of the data requires us to examine each item in the data only once. Also, the data is split in half once for each such merge step. (Actually it is split before the merger, but the order is not important.) Therefore, each recursion of mergeSort splits the data into two equal parts, each of which must be similarly handled, and linearly scans the data. The resulting recurrence relation is

$$T_1 = 0, \qquad T_n = n + 2T_{n/2} \quad \text{if } n > 1$$

T_1 is zero because a list with one item needs no sorting. In order to solve this recurrence relation, let us make the substitution $n = 2^k$ and assume that n is some power of 2. Thus k is $\log_2(n)$. Making this substitution we see that

$$T_{2^0} = 0, \qquad T_{2^k} = 2^k + 2T_{2^{k-1}} \quad \text{if } k > 0$$

If we apply the same repeated substitution to this that we employed in Chapter 6, we see that when $n > 1$,

$$T_{2^k} = 2^k + 2T_{2^{k-1}}$$

$$T_{2^k} = 2^k + 2^k + 4T_{2^{k-2}}$$

$$\vdots$$

$$T_{2^k} = 2^k + 2^k + 2^k + \cdots + 2^k + 2^k T_{2^0}$$

There are exactly $k + 1$ terms in the last expression, of which the last is zero, so the result is $k2^k$, which, in terms of n, is $n \log_2(n)$.

Finally, note that recursion can be removed from these more sophisticated sorting methods by the techniques used in Chapter 6. Thus, even expressed nonrecursively, the algorithms achieve these relatively fast running times, because the work they do is still defined by the above recurrence relations.

8.5   SEARCHING IN ARRAYS AND THE EFFICIENCY OF SEARCH

8.5.1   Sequential Search

If an array (or a list or other sequential structure) is not sorted, it is best searched sequentially. Start at the beginning and look for the item sought, one cell at a time, until you have either found it or examined every item. The following implementation assumes nothing about the order of the elements in the array or even their class. In general, the items might not be able to be ordered since they might not be in SMagnitude. We implement a function that indicates the success or failure of the search by a returned Boolean value and returns the location in which the object is found by a reference parameter. It uses the equal comparison implemented in SObject, and therefore implemented in every class whose elements might be compared rather than the == comparison of standard C, because some classes require implementation of a meaning of equal different from ==. The magnitude classes, for example, require a special meaning for equal. We must make a special case for NULL, which we might wish to search for. Since NULL is not an object, it cannot be the target of the equal message, and so requires ==.

```
char SArray :: sequentialSearch (PObject t,
                                 int &Loc) {
    char result, done;
    int i;

    result = FALSE;
    done = FALSE;
    i = 0;
    while (!done) {
        if (fElements[i] == NULL || t == NULL) {
            if (t == fElements[i]) {
                Loc = i;
                done = TRUE;
                result = TRUE;
            };
        }
```

```
        else if (fElements[i] -> equal(t)) {
            Loc = i;
            done = TRUE;
            result = TRUE;
        };
        ++i;
        if (i >= fLength) done = TRUE;
    };
    return result;
};
```

Note that Loc does not change unless the item is found. This may be important to a caller.

8.5.2 Binary Search

Sequential search takes time proportional to the size of the array, since potentially it must examine each element in the array. Binary search can be much faster, but it applies only to sorted arrays. Therefore, it requires that the elements of the array be magnitudes. The binary search is probably the method you use to search a dictionary or phone book, each of which is a sorted list. You start in the middle somewhere. If you don't find the target there, you know from the data there, and the fact of the sort, which half to look in next. The binary search is also the basis of the game in which you are asked to guess a number between 1 and 100 and are told whether the guess is too high or too low. If you are clever, you can always succeed in a small number of guesses. (How many are required? Suppose the numbers are between 1 and 1000? Suppose they are between 1 and a million?)

Binary search proceeds by first examining the middle position of the array by computing mid = (low+high) / 2. If the target is not at this location, either low is set to mid+1 or high is set to mid−1, depending on whether the target is greater or smaller than the entry at location mid. This proceeds until either the targets found or high becomes less than low. See Fig. 8.6. If the target is not in the array, high must eventually become less than low, because each time we change high we make it strictly smaller, and each time we change low we make it strictly larger. Also, since the section of the array being searched is divided in half at each step, the entire array can be searched in time proportional to the

not here			not here

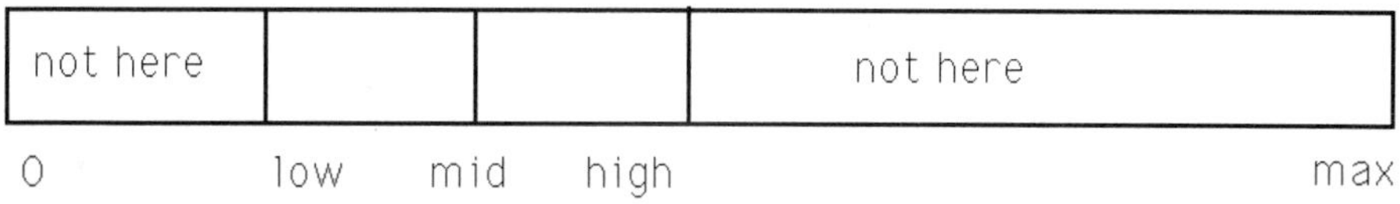

FIGURE 8.6   0   low   mid   high   max

logarithm of the size of the array, which for large arrays is much less than the size of the array.

```
char SArray :: binarySearch (PObject t, int &Loc) {
   char result;
   int low, high, mid;

   low = 0;
   high = fLength - 1;
   mid = (low + high) / 2;
   while (low < high && ! t -> equal
           (fElements[mid])) {
      if (fElements[mid] -> less (t)) low = mid+1;
      else high = mid - 1;
      mid = (low + high) / 2;
   };
   result = (fElements[mid] -> equal (t));
   if (result) Loc = mid;
   return result;
};
```

The binary search can be carried out recursively, of course. After all, half of the array is searched by the same process as the entire array. We do need to provide parameters to the routine specifying the index bounds of the search.

```
char SArray :: recursiveBinarySearch (int L, int U,
                                      PObject t,
                                      int &Loc) {
   char result;
   int mid;

   mid = (L + U) / 2;
   if (L >= U && !fElements[mid] -> equal (t))
      result = FALSE;
   else if (fElements[mid] -> equal(t)) {
      Loc = mid;
      result = TRUE;
   }
   else if ((fElements[mid]) -> less (t))
      result = recursiveBinarySearch (mid+1,
                                      U, t, Loc);
   else
      result = recursiveBinarySearch (L, mid-1,
                                      t, Loc);
   return result;
};
```

8.6 TESTING THE SORTS

Testing the sort routines requires consideration of several cases. Some that seem simple but often help us discover bugs are (1) an already sorted array; (2) an array with all values equal; and (3) a reverse-sorted array. Some of our routines perform badly on some of these arrays; the time required for sorting can be greater for some of these simple cases than for more unsorted data.

Testing the sort routines also requires generation of random data, for which a standardized set of routines is helpful. ANSI C has a function, rand, that produces random integers.

The method randomArray can easily generate data with which to test the sort and search routines. Here we generate integer data in a fairly large range.

```
void SArray :: randomArray (void) {
   for (int i = 0; i < fLength; i++)
      fElements[i] = asInteger (rand() % 1000);
};
```

8.7 OTHER SIMILAR CLASSES

A number of other linear structures can be implemented with arrays. We have seen the class SFiniteStack already. A bounded queue class can be similarly implemented. The queue will be capable of holding only a fixed number of items, so a new method, full, will be needed by which a user can test whether the queue is full before trying to insert an object. Otherwise the protocol of the class is the same as that of SQueue. The implementation uses an array of objects and references to two cells of the array, fFront and fRear.

```
PAQueue newAQueue (int size);

class SAQueue: public SCollection {
   public:
         SAQueue (int size);
      virtual            ~SAQueue (void);
      virtual void       insert (PObject);
      virtual void       remove (PObject);
      virtual PObject    Dequeue (void);
      virtual void       enqueue (PObject);
      virtual PObject    atFront (void);
      virtual void       insertFirst (PObject);
      virtual void       removeFirst (void);
      virtual char       empty ();
      virtual char       full ();
      virtual PIterator  newIterator (void);
```

```
          virtual char          member (classtype c);
          virtual PObject       Clone (void);
          virtual void          writeIt (void);

      protected:
          PObject               *fElements;
          int                   fFront;
          int                   fRear;
          int                   fSize;
          virtual int           sizeOf (void);

  };
```

The variable fFront is the cell number of the object that has been in the queue the longest time (however, insertFirst is actually implemented, and it treats the object inserted as if it were the oldest). This cell contains an object unless the queue is empty; fRear, on the other hand, is always an empty cell. It is the location into which the next item will be enqueued, unless the queue is full. If fFront == fRear, the queue is empty. Therefore queue initialization sets both these instance variables to zero. The enqueue method first checks whether the queue is full (more later), and if it is not it inserts its parameter into the empty slot at fRear and then increments fRear. However, if fRear is already at the maximum value, fSize-1, the value of fRear should "wrap around" to zero. The arithmetic for incrementing the rear is just modular arithmetic: fRear = (fRear + 1) % fSize. See Fig. 8.7.

Dequeue is similar. If the queue is not empty, fFront refers to a valid cell, whose contents are returned. Then fFront is incremented, again by modular arithmetic. Now we can examine the condition for fullness. A queue is full if enqueue cannot be carried out properly, meaning that it is full if fRear is one less (modulo the size of the array) than fFront, because trying to enqueue at this point would increase fRear to equal fFront, leaving the queue in the empty state.

```
char SAQueue :: full () {
    return (fRear+1) % fSize == fFront;
};
```

FIGURE 8.7

Why not implement this class with an instance variable of type SArray rather than an ordinary array? It could certainly be done, but there is no need to do it. We don't require the implementation to have object character, with the ability to use subtypes, or even the functionality provided by the array classes. Therefore, we build SAQueue out of simpler stuff: ordinary arrays.

8.8   SUMMARY

Because of their ability to access any stored item very rapidly, arrays have some advantages over lists as a storage mechanism. We have seen in this chapter that it is possible to package low-level language constructs, such as C++ arrays, into a class. Such array classes fit better into the overall object-oriented framework.

Given a structure with a fast lookup of an individual item, the construction of sophisticated sorting and searching mechanisms, some of which we have examined, becomes feasible. Some, such as insertionSort, although being generally slow on large sets of data, perform well on certain kinds of data. Others, such as quickSort, behave well in general, but badly in specific circumstances. The designer and the user must be aware of these limitations; the designer so that she or he can mitigate them as much as possible, and the user so that she or he can choose an algorithm best to fit the needs of a problem.

Again, we have seen that sophisticated routines need to be developed methodically. Loop programs and recursive programs are especially prone to bugs. An important technique for developing such programs is to develop them from Boolean specifications, as we did with our array pictures in this chapter. The reader who wants to go into depth in this area should consult *The Science of Programming* [Gries, 1981]. We used the verification technique to motivate the design of the algorithms and to verify the validity of the programs written from them. A more powerful variant of the technique, however, lets you actually discover the invariant, and hence the algorithm, from a statement of the specification. For example, by this technique we can discover the loop invariant expressed by Fig. 8.5c by examining the Boolean statement implied by Fig. 8.5b. This technique is beyond the scope of this book.

EXERCISES

8.1 (8.2) Read the article by Peter J. Denning entitled "Saving All the Bits" in the September–October, 1990, issue of *The American Scientist*. Implement genetic memory as described in the article. Figure 2 of the article is especially helpful. A list of arrays is a good data structure for this problem.

8.2 (8.3) Why is insertion sort fast for nearly sorted arrays? Is the same true for selection sort? Why or why not? How about our bubble sort? Can you improve bubble sort so that it doesn't try to sort an already sorted array? Hint: First replace the inner `for` loop with something equivalent.

8.3 (8.4) In `quickSort` implement the body of the `if (avoid) {}` block by swapping a random location with cell L.

8.4 (8.4) Validate `bubbleSort`. Each of the two loops will require a separate part. The loop invariants are illustrated in Figs. 8.1a and 8.1b. The model of validation used for `selectionSort` in Chapter 6 can be followed.

8.5 (8.4) The partition procedure used in `quickSort` can also be the basis of a method for finding the median of a set of data. The median of a set, A, of values, is the value, A[k], that is larger than or equal to half of the data and less than the other half. If the data were to be sorted, it is the value whose position is in the middle. Sorting is an expensive way to find the median, however, unless sorting needs to be done anyway. Note that the partition step results in a pivot in a central position, but it might not be the median. However, if the pivot is to the left of the middle position, the median must be to the right, and conversely. We can then (recursively) partition the portion that we know must contain the median to eventually find it.

8.6 (8.4) Prove that for random data the algorithm for the median-finding process described in the previous exercise is of linear running time. Hint: The algorithm requires a linear pass over the data to eliminate half of the data from further consideration. Demonstrate also that this median process behaves badly in the same situations in which `quickSort` behaves badly.

8.7 (8.5) Test each of the above sorting methods on data that are already sorted, on data that are all identical, and on data that are in reverse order. Examine the code to determine whether any of these cases should be particularly good or particularly bad for each of the routines. Make and test hypotheses about the running time of the sorts under various input conditions.

8.8 (8.5) Implement a method, `sequentialSearchSorted`, in the array class that requires that the elements be in `SMagnitude` and that the array be sorted. Exit the search when the first match is found, as we have done, or if an item is found whose value is larger than that of the target. Discuss the efficiency of this if the data consist of sorted random integers. Also discuss the efficiency if we are far more likely to search for small values than large ones and far more likely to search for data actually stored in the list rather than arbitrary data.

8.9 (8.5) The *expected value* of a random variable is the sum of a collection of products, where each product is that of a value of the random variable and the probability that it occurs. The sum is over all such products. Discuss the efficiency of `sequentialSearchSorted`, of Exercise 8.8, by computing the expected number of probes in the array if the order of the items and the nature of the target of the search have the following properties. The array has 100 elements. The probability that the item sought is the first item is .75. The probability that it is among the first two is .9; among the first three it is .95; among the first four it is .98; and all of the other 96 values are equally likely to occur.

8.10 (8.5) The maximum number of probes in a binary search is the logarithm (base 2) of the number of items in the array. The average number is only one less than that. Explore the reason for this by drawing a binary tree, such that each node in the tree has two children, and the tree is completely filled up to a depth of five. If we store data at every vertex in such a tree, how many values are there in the tree? How many of those values are at leaves of the tree? How does this relate to binary search? Generalize your findings.

8.11 (8.5) Our sequential search finds the first match of the target but it has a problem if we want to find several occurrences. Implement a `sequentialSearch-From` method in the array class that is passed the index it is to use as the beginning of its search. Explain how this could be used to find all the occurrences of some target.

8.12 (8.5) Suppose we wish to search a sorted array for values using binary search. Suppose, however, that many duplicates of values are possible. Devise a strategy for repeatedly returning references to values equal to `target` so that we can be assured that each duplicate is returned once.

8.13 (8.5) Explore the following refinement of the idea of Exercise 8.12. Suppose we replace our array of values with an array of lists in which duplicate values can be stored. Thus an array cell is associated with a single value, and duplicates of that value are saved in the same list. Suppose the array is sorted in order of the values stored in the lists it contains. How difficult is it to sort such an array in the first place? Given that we can do it effectively, answer Exercise 8.8 again for this structure.

8.14 (8.7) Complete the implementation of the bounded queue discussed in the last section. Enqueuing into a full queue should be a no-op or an error. Dequeuing from an empty queue should return NULL or be an error. Be careful when you implement `insertFirst`. You must decrease `fFront` before storing the new item. Note that the modulo operator does not always work properly. In particular, (−1 % 5) yields −1 on many compilers, although to a mathematician it should be four. Bounded queues need iterators, of course.

## CHAPTER 9

TREES AS NODES
AND ARCS

He that hath suffer'd this disorder'd spring
Hath now himself met with the fall of leaf:
The weeds which his broad-spreading leaves did shelter
That seem'd in eating him to hold him up,
Are pluck'd up root and all by Bollingbroke:
I mean the Earl of Wiltshire, Bushy, Green.

Shakespeare, *Richard II*

I think that I shall never see
A poem lovely as a tree

Joyce Kilmer

If it weren't for our ability to abstract,
we'd still be swinging from the trees.

Joseph Bergin

Trees, especially binary trees, can be extremely useful both as an organizational aid for complex collections of data and for increasing the
efficiency of the implementations of many algorithms. One common way of
managing the user-defined names within a compiler is to maintain a tree,
of which the nodes represent identifiers and their associated information.
Searching for a name can be very fast (if the tree is properly built), because
one needs only search along a single path from the root toward a leaf. The
number of nodes that must be examined can be very small compared to the

total number in the tree. In a properly built tree containing a thousand nodes, it might be necessary to examine a maximum of only ten.

Any hierarchical system is, of course, easily modeled as a tree. Similarly, any block-structured system in which items are nested completely within other items or appear in sequences is naturally modeled as a tree, with nested blocks being children, and sequences of blocks being siblings. Figure 9.1a might represent procedures B through P nested within a Pascal program A or statements nested within a block of a C program. The equivalent tree representation is shown in Fig. 9.1b.

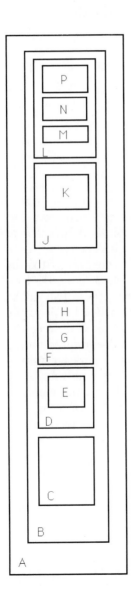

FIGURE 9.1A

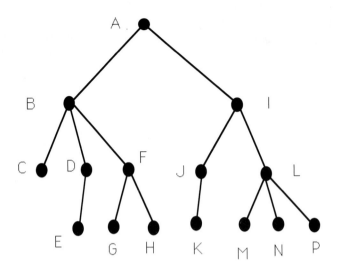

FIGURE 9.1B

9.1   DEFINITIONS

A tree or, in general, a graph, is composed of a set of *nodes*, or *vertices*, and a set of *links*, or *arcs*. Nodes are primitive and abstract. They are often represented graphically by points. A link is a pair of nodes from the node set. Sometimes we say that a link *connects* its nodes. A link is either ordered (ordered pair of nodes) or unordered. If A and B are nodes, (A,B) is a link. If the links are ordered, the link (A,B) is different from the link (B,A), but if the links are unordered, these two links are the same. A link is often represented graphically as a line between the points representing its nodes, and a directed (ordered) link is represented as an arrow whose head represents the second node of the ordered pair.

The foregoing describes graphs. A general graph has unordered links, and a directed graph (digraph) has ordered links. A *path* in a graph or tree is a subset of the links such that the second element of one link matches the first element of some other link. A *path from A to B* is a minimal path having the property that A is the first element of some link and B is the second element of some link in the path. Minimal here means that no link can be removed from the set and the set still be a path from A to B. (It doesn't mean minimum length.) The length of a path is the number of links of which it is composed. The distance between two nodes in a connected graph is the length of the shortest path between them. In a general graph, a path from A to B is also a path from B to A, but this is not the case in digraphs. See Fig. 9.2 and Fig. 9.3.

A graph is connected if every pair of nodes in the graph is connected by at least one path. A *cycle* is a path from some node to itself with at least one link. A cycle can consist of just a single link, provided some node is

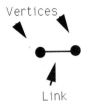

Vertices

Link

FIGURE 9.2A

both the first and second element of the link. The graph shown in Fig. 9.2c has a cycle from B to B. In a digraph paths are formed in the order of the links, and cycles have to be defined accordingly. The digraph shown in Fig. 9.3 b has a (clockwise) cycle from the lower left node to itself.

> **Tree**
>
> A tree is a connected graph with no cycles.

A tree is a connected graph with no cycles. See Fig. 9.4. Usually, and in all of the following, some node of the tree is singled out and is called the *root* of the tree. If a root exists, any nonroot node connected to only one other node is a *leaf*; the other nodes (nonroot, nonleaf) are *interior*. Also, if the tree has a root, the links are often considered to be ordered, with all paths pointing toward the root. Thus, there is a path from every nonroot node to the root but no paths in the other direction. (Sometimes it is convenient to reverse the order of all of the links, so that all paths point away from the root.) Trees are usually drawn with the root at the top and the leaves below. The set representation of the tree in Figure 9.4 is

Nodes = {A, B, C, D, E, F}
Links = {(C, A), (B, A), (D, B), (E, B), (F, B)}

A node X is a *child* of a node Y if (X,Y) is a (root-pointing, directed) link of the tree. Thus E is a child of B in the above tree. B is called the *parent* of E. The analogy is to family trees, of course. A node Z is a *descendant* of a node Y if there is a path from Z to Y; Y is then called an *ancestor* of Z. A *binary tree* is a tree in which the root has either 0 or 2 children, and every interior node has exactly two children. A tree is of order n if the root and every interior node have at most n nodes. (Thus a tree of order 2 is not necessarily a binary tree, although the converse is true.)

The *height of a node* is the length of the (unique) path from that node to the root. The height of the tree is the height of the highest (leaf) node. In the example of Fig. 9.4, A is at height 0, B is at height 1, F is at height 2, and the height of the tree is 2.

Every pair of nodes in a tree share a lowest common ancestor, which is one of the two nodes if it is an ancestor of the other, and otherwise is the

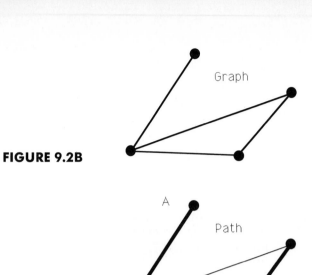

FIGURE 9.2B

Graph

FIGURE 9.2C

A

Path

B

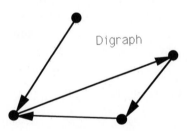

FIGURE 9.3A

Vertices

Ordered Link

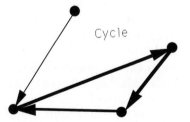

FIGURE 9.3B

Digraph

FIGURE 9.3C

Cycle

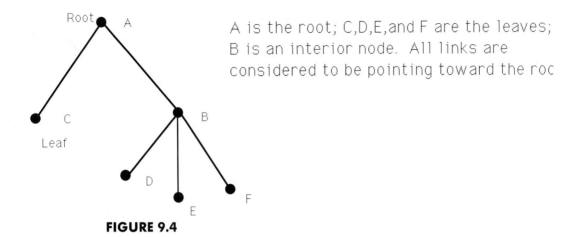

A is the root; C,D,E,and F are the leaves;
B is an interior node. All links are
considered to be pointing toward the roc

FIGURE 9.4

node that is a common ancestor of both nodes (as is the root of the tree) and such that no descendant is also a common ancestor of the two nodes.

Nothing said above rules out an empty tree, a tree with no nodes and no links. Generally this is admissible, though usually a binary tree is required to consist of at least a root node.

For more on trees and graphs, consult the excellent book *Combinatorial Optimization,* by Papadimitriou and Steiglitz [1982].

So far we have considered trees to be composed of nodes and links. There is another way to think of them, however. Since each node in a tree can be considered to be the root of a tree consisting of that node and all of its descendants, we can consider a tree to be made up of (sub) trees, leading to the following definition.

Tree
    A tree is either

a.   empty, or
b.   a node, called the root, and a collection of trees, called the children of the root.

This definition is recursive. A tree is defined in terms of trees. Like every recursive definition it needs a part that is not recursive. If trees need not be empty, an alternate definition is useful:

A tree is either

a.   a node, or
b.   a node, called the root, and a collection of trees, called the children of the root.

In our example tree above, F is a tree (it is a node); likewise D and E are trees. Thus B, D, E, and F form a tree (a node and children that are trees). Also since C is a tree, A, B, C, D, E, and F form a tree. We then just say that the root represents or is the tree, although the language is a bit sloppy. Therefore, A is a tree. We mean, of course, that A and its children are a tree.

Here the idea of a link has disappeared, though we may consider the children to be linked to the parent. This way of looking at trees is considered fully in the next chapter. For the remainder of this chapter we shall consider trees to be composed of nodes and links.

9.2   BINARY TREES AS A COLLECTION OF NODES AND LINKS

In this implementation, a tree is a construct of nodes and links (vertices and arcs) with certain properties (no cycles). Instead of designing only one class, we create four, similar to what we have already done with the class SList. The four classes correspond to four ideas. The first class, SBinaryTree, corresponds to the idea of the tree as a whole, and contains methods that treat the tree as an entirety. The second class, SBinaryTreeNode, corresponds to the node of a tree, or, more exactly, to the node and its links to child nodes. This class contains methods that manipulate individual nodes. The third idea is that of position in a tree. The idea of a position is simply that as we "walk about" within a tree, stepping from node to node, we are at any given moment "at" some particular place or position in the tree. The class SBinaryTreePosition implements this notion, having methods for changing position and for modifying a tree locally. Most of the tree insertion methods are methods of SBinaryTreePosition, as insertions are made "somewhere," i.e., at a position. Finally, we need the class SBinaryTreeIterator to provide the iteration abstraction for this collection class. We use nested class declarations here, as we did for SList and its associated classes. The main declarations of the header file for our classes is as follows.

```
// REQUIREMENTS For Use
//     initLists ();
//     initBinaryTrees ();

class SBinaryTree;
class SBinaryTreePosition;
class SBinaryTreeIterator;

typedef SBinaryTree *PBinaryTree;
typedef SBinaryTreePosition *PBinaryTreePosition;
typedef SBinaryTreeIterator *PBinaryTreeIterator;

PBinaryTree newBinaryTree (void);
```

```
class SBinaryTree: public SCollection {
  public:
      SBinaryTree (void);
    virtual                  ~SBinaryTree (void);
    virtual char             empty ();
    virtual void             writeIt (void);
    virtual PIterator        newIterator (void);
    virtual PBinaryTreeIterator     newInOrder
                                    Iterator (void);

    virtual void             insert (PObject);
    virtual void             remove (PObject);
    virtual char             member (classtype c);
    virtual classtype        Member (void);
    virtual PObject          Clone (void);
    virtual PBinaryTreePosition     newPosition
                                    (void);
      // The following is for testing
      // recursion removal.
    virtual void             writeInOrder ();

  protected:
    class SBinaryTreeNode;
  public:
    typedef SBinaryTreeNode *PBinaryTreeNode;
  protected:
    friend SBinaryTreeNode;

    PBinaryTreeNode fRoot;
    virtual int sizeOf (void);
    virtual PBinaryTreeNode newNode (PObject o);
    virtual void removeNode (PBinaryTreeNode);

/* Nested protected class. */
class SBinaryTreeNode: public SObject {
  public:

      SBinaryTreeNode (PObject);
    virtual void             recursiveDestruct (void);
    virtual PObject          value (void);
    virtual char             member (classtype c);
    virtual classtype        Member (void);
    virtual void             writeIt (void);
    virtual void             recursiveWriteIt (void);
    virtual PObject          Clone (void);

    PBinaryTreeNode fLeft;
    PBinaryTreeNode fRight;
```

```
        PObject fValue;

        virtual PBinaryTreeNode leftChild (void);
        virtual PBinaryTreeNode rightChild (void);

        virtual int sizeOf (void);
        friend void initBinaryTrees (void);
        friend SBinaryTreePosition;
          // For recursion removal.
        friend void doInOrder(PBinaryTreeNode x);
    }; // End binary tree node.

        friend SBinaryTreePosition;
        friend SBinaryTreeIterator;
        friend void doInOrder (PBinaryTreeNode x);
        friend void initBinaryTrees (void);
      protected:
        static PBinaryTreeNode zed;

    }; // End binary tree.

    class SBinaryTreePosition: public SPosition {
      public:
        SBinaryTreePosition (PBinaryTree);
        virtual void        setToRoot (void);
        virtual PObject     at (void);
        virtual void        atPut (PObject);
        virtual PObject     atLeftChild (void);
        virtual PObject     atRightChild (void);
        virtual void        exchangePositions
                              (PBinaryTreePosition);

        virtual void        exchangeValues
                              (PBinaryTreePosition);
        virtual void        find (PObject);
        virtual char        leaf (void);
          // Both children are missing.
        virtual char        noLeft (void);
          // The left child is missing.
        virtual char        noRight (void);
          // The right child is missing.
        virtual char        oneChild (void);
          // Has only one child.
        virtual char        isFull (void);
          // Has both left and right children.
        virtual char        missingNode (void);
          // TRUE when at the special
          // terminator zed.
```

```
        virtual void          moveTo
                                (PBinaryTreePosition);
        virtual void          moveLeft (void);
          // Move to left child if any.
        virtual void          moveRight (void);
          // Move to right child if any.
        virtual void          moveToParent (void);
          // Move to parent if not at root.
        virtual char          isAtRoot (void);
        virtual void          insertLeft (PObject);
        virtual void          insertRight (PObject);

        virtual char          member (classtype c);
        virtual classtype     Member (void);
        virtual void          writeIt (void);

    protected:
      SBinaryTree :: PBinaryTreeNode fHere;
      PBinaryTree fTree;
      virtual int     sizeOf (void);
      virtual void    findNode (SBinaryTree ::
                                PBinaryTreeNode);
      virtual void    insertLeftNode (SBinaryTree ::
                                PBinaryTreeNode);
      virtual void    insertRightNode (SBinaryTree ::
                                PBinaryTreeNode);
      virtual void    truncateLeft (void);
      virtual void    truncateRight (void);
      virtual SBinaryTree :: PBinaryTreeNode
                              nodeAt (void);

    friend SBinaryTreeIterator;
    friend SBinaryTree;
  }; // End binary tree position.

  class SBinaryTreeIterator: public SIterator {
    public:
        SBinaryTreeIterator (PBinaryTree);
        virtual               ~SBinaryTreeIterator (void)
                              ;
        virtual char          nextItem (PObject&);
        virtual char          nextItemInOrder (PObject&);
        virtual char          nextNode (SBinaryTree ::
                                PBinaryTreeNode&);
        virtual void          reset (void);
        virtual void          resetInOrder (void);
```

```
        virtual void            iterateFrom
                                (PBinaryTreePosition);
        virtual char            member (classtype c);
        virtual classtype       Member (void);
        virtual void            writeIt (void);
        virtual PObject         Clone (void);
    protected:
      PBinaryTreePosition fPosition;
      virtual int sizeOf (void);

}; // End binary tree iterator.

void initBinaryTrees (void);
  // Call once to initialize the class.
```

SBinaryTreeNode has methods only for initializing a node and for writing the value in it. It has the field fValue because data is stored in the nodes of the tree. It also has the fields fLeft and fRight for implementing the links to child nodes that hold the tree of which it is a part together. For some applications SBinaryTreeNode should include an additional field, fTree, that would reference the SBinaryTree of which the node is a part. This field would contain the address of the tree to which to send messages from the node. Thus, the node would know the tree of which it was a part and could access instance variables in the tree structure. A similar idea might lead us to implement a field, fParent, that would reference the parent of a node from within the node. This would permit us to move upward in the tree easily.

We also declare SBinaryTreePosition to be a friend class of SBinaryTreeNode, opening the implementation of the nodes to methods of SBinaryTreePosition. Positions need to look at, and perhaps manipulate, fLeft and fRight to carry out their tasks. We also declare the protected methods leftChild and rightChild to get references to the left and right children, though SBinaryTreePosition still must be a friend to call these functions.

SBinaryTree has the collection methods we have seen before, but note that many of the methods we might expect for tree manipulation are missing. The only methods here are those that reference the tree as a whole (writeIt) or are required by our position in the class hierarchy (insert, remove). The additional functionality will be provided by tree positions. SBinaryTree must declare SBinaryTreePosition to be a friend so that an empty tree can be made nonempty, as we shall see below.

SBinaryTreePosition has most of the useful methods. An SBinaryTreePosition has instance variables that hold references to its SBinaryTree and has an SBinaryTreeNode that represents the current position. The parameter of the constructor of SBinaryTree-Position must be a PBinaryTree so that the SBinaryTree-

Position can be properly associated with a particular SBinaryTree. Once initialized, an SBinaryTreePosition can refer to various places in one tree but never to a position in another tree. Several positions can be active in the same tree at any given moment once they are declared and initialized.

SBinaryTreePosition has the methods for moving in the tree and for creating new vertices of the tree. The notion of a subtree as well as that of a position in a tree is implemented through SBinaryTreePosition. Also, SBinaryTreePosition declares SBinaryTree to be a friend, though this is mostly for efficiency. The justification for implementing the classes together is that we are designing them together.

The SBinaryTreeIterator class is standard except that it allows us more than one order of production of nodes. The two most useful ways to iterate over a tree are *pre-order* and *in-order*. An iterator can be used in either way, depending on its initialization and the messages it is sent.

We have also included a unit initialization routine, initBinary-Trees, which needs to be called once by every program that uses these classes. The initBinaryTrees procedure creates the special terminator node, SBinaryTree :: zed, which is used to represent the leaves in our trees. That is to say, the nodes we consider to exist in our trees are, from the viewpoint of graph theory, only the interior nodes. What we shall call leaf nodes are actually interior nodes with both children equal to this zed node. They represent the lowest level of visible nodes. There is a bit of extra flexibility in this, since if one child is the zed node and the other is not, we may consider that the node has one child without implementing a special case.

We begin the implementation file of this abstract data type by declaring zed and creating it in initBinaryTrees.

```
SBinaryTree :: PBinaryTreeNode SBinaryTree :: zed;

void initBinaryTrees (void) {
   // Call once to initialize the class.
   SBinaryTree :: zed =
      new SBinaryTree :: SBinaryTreeNode (NULL);
   failnull (SBinaryTree :: zed);
   SBinaryTree :: zed -> fLeft = SBinaryTree :: zed;
   SBinaryTree :: zed -> fRight = SBinaryTree :: zed
};
```

9.3   TREE NODES

Most of the methods of SBinaryTreeNode are simple and obvious, but note that the constructor SBinaryTreeNode initializes a nonempty node. The node zed, which looks similar, is an empty node. The method writeIt merely writes its data. The method `recursiveWriteIt` will be discussed later.

```
SBinaryTree :: SBinaryTreeNode :: SBinaryTreeNode
                                      (PObject o) {
    fValue = o;
    fLeft = SBinaryTree :: zed;
    fRight = SBinaryTree :: zed;
};

void SBinaryTree :: SBinaryTreeNode
                  :: writeIt (void) {
    if (fValue == NULL) cout << "NULL";
        else fValue -> writeIt ();
};
```

The node class implements links as well as nodes, so a binary tree is cloned by passing a `Clone` message to the node at its root. This node will be responsible for cloning the subnodes, which represent subtrees. `Clone` must not only clone the nodes recursively but also construct a tree with the results. Knowing that we never clone `zed` and that the leaves of every tree are all `zed`, we know how to end the recursion.

```
PObject SBinaryTree :: SBinaryTreeNode
                  :: Clone (void) {
    SBinaryTree :: PBinaryTreeNode result;

    if (this == SBinaryTree :: zed)
        return SBinaryTree :: zed;
    else {
        result = SBinaryTree :: PBinaryTreeNode
                                  (ShallowClone ());
        result -> fLeft = SBinaryTree
                        :: PBinaryTreeNode
                        (fLeft -> Clone ());
        result -> fRight = SBinaryTree
                        :: PBinaryTreeNode
                        (fRight -> Clone ());
        return result;
    };
};
```

In a certain sense destructors are the opposite of cloning methods. We need a special destruct method here that gives us more control over the process of deleting a tree as a whole. We can't depend on the standard destruct method ~`SBinaryTreeNode` because of the danger of deleting the `zed` node, which would make all of our trees invalid. We need `recursiveDestruct` so that when a tree is being deleted it can see to the deletion of its nodes. An iterator or position won't work properly in this situation because the tree is being destroyed. Note that `recursiveDestruct` recursively operates on the subtree of `fLeft` just before deleting `fLeft`. Thus the tree is destroyed from the bottom up, from the leaves toward the root.

```
void SBinaryTree :: SBinaryTreeNode
                        :: recursiveDestruct (void) {
   if (fLeft != SBinaryTree :: zed) {
      fLeft -> recursiveDestruct ();
      delete fLeft;
   };
   if (fRight != SBinaryTree :: zed) {
      fRight -> recursiveDestruct ();
      delete fRight;
   };
};
```

9.4   THE BINARY TREE CLASS

Initializing an `SBinaryTree` involves setting the reference to its root to be the zed node, indicating an empty tree. The destructor sends `recursiveDestruct` to its root if the root is not zed.

```
SBinaryTree :: SBinaryTree (void) {
   fRoot = zed;
};

SBinaryTree :: ~SBinaryTree (void) {
   if (fRoot != zed) {
      fRoot -> recursiveDestruct();
      delete fRoot;
   };
};
```

Testing for an empty tree requires checking the root reference:

```
char SBinaryTree :: empty () {
   return fRoot == zed;
};
```

The inherited `insert` method inserts its parameter at the root of an empty tree and as the leftmost leaf, first searching for its location, in a tree that is not empty. Note that we insert data; the method takes care of creating a new node to hold the data. The method `newNode` is a standard generator for nodes, implemented as a method of `SBinaryTree`.

```
void SBinaryTree :: insert (PObject o) {
   PBinaryTreeNode aNode, aLoc;

   aNode = PBinaryTreeNode (newNode (o));
   if (fRoot == zed) {
      fRoot = aNode;
   }
   else {
      aLoc = fRoot;
      while (aLoc -> fLeft != zed) aLoc = aLoc
                                             -> fLeft;
      aLoc -> fLeft = aNode;
   };
};
```

The method `removeNode` removes a node from a tree and is a bit trickier, because it must first find the node. It is to remove the node and all of its descendants. It can use the position method `findNode` to search for the node to be deleted and then apply `moveToParent` to find its parent, but this process will not find the node at the root, so a special check is needed. In the model of the tree as nodes and links, the root node can be removed. Such removal leaves an empty tree. Removal of the root node is harder in the model of the tree as a tree of subtrees, which we shall consider in the next chapter.

```
void SBinaryTree :: removeNode (PBinaryTreeNode n)
   PBinaryTreePosition p;

   if (fRoot == n) fRoot = zed;
   else {
      p = PBinaryTreePosition (newPosition ());
      p -> findNode (n);
      p -> moveToParent ();
      if (p -> fHere -> fRight == n)
         p -> truncateRight ();
      if (p -> fHere -> fLeft == n)
         p -> truncateLeft ();
      delete p;
   };
};
```

The `findNode` method of `SBinaryTreePosition` maintains an iterator for carrying out the search. It searches only from the current position. If it doesn't find the node, it doesn't change its own position. A special method, `iterateFrom`, of our iterator class permits starting the iteration at a point other than the root of a tree.

```
    void SBinaryTreePosition :: findNode
                              (SBinaryTree
                               :: PBinaryTreeNode o) {
        PBinaryTreeIterator IT;
        SBinaryTree :: PBinaryTreeNode anObject, aNode;

        aNode = fHere;
        IT = PBinaryTreeIterator (fTree ->
                                   newIterator ());
        IT -> iterateFrom (this);
        while (IT -> nextNode (anObject))
           if ((anObject) -> equal (o)) {
              aNode = o;
              IT -> Short ();
           };
        fHere = aNode;
        delete IT;
    };
```

We need removal methods for data parallel to those for nodes. In fact,
removal of data is generally more useful than node removal in applications.
Generally speaking, trees manage the creation and deletion of nodes internally, whereas the above methods give responsibility for nodes to clients.
The remove method removes at most one value from the tree and removes
the node that contained it. It does not remove the children of the node. Thus
it is more complex, especially because it must be able to remove a value that
has two children in the tree.

```
    void SBinaryTree :: remove (PObject o) {
        PBinaryTreePosition p,q;
        PBinaryTreeNode n;
        PObject aValue;

        p = PBinaryTreePosition (newPosition ());
        p -> find (o);
        aValue = p -> at ();
        if (o -> equal (aValue)) {
           q = PBinaryTreePosition (newPosition ());
           q -> moveTo (p);
           while (!q -> leaf ()) {
              q -> moveLeft ();
              while (! q -> noRight ()) q -> moveRight ();
           }
           p -> exchangeValues (q);
           n = q -> fHere;
           q -> moveToParent ();
           if (q -> fHere -> fLeft == n) {
```

```
              q -> truncateLeft ();
          }
          else if (q -> fHere -> fRight == n) {
              q -> truncateRight ();
          }
          else {
              fRoot = zed;
          }
          delete q;
      };
      delete p;
  };
```

The `remove` method uses two tree position objects. The first is moved by `find` to the node to be deleted. If `find` is successful, the other position object takes over the search from the location of the first, searching for a leaf below the node to be removed. Once the leaf is found, the data values are exchanged and the leaf is removed. Note that the node with the data itself will be removed if it is a leaf. The nested loops are required because in order to find a leaf we must continue downward in the tree as long as the node we are at has either a left or a right child.

Binary trees have the usual generator methods for positions, nodes, and iterators. The only special method here is the one that creates an in-order iterator because the standard iterator is pre-order. More will be said about pre- and in-order in a moment. An in-order iterator is the same object as a pre-order iterator except that it has been initialized differently, using a special method of the iterator class.

```
PBinaryTreeIterator SBinaryTree ::
                    newInOrderIterator (void) {
    PBinaryTreeIterator result;

    result = PBinaryTreeIterator (newIterator ());
    result -> resetInOrder ();
    return result;
};
```

All that is left to implement is the `writeIt` method, which can use either the pre-order or the in-order protocol. Several implementations of `writeIt` will be shown. The first is simple, recursive, and pre-order. The second is an equivalent in-order version. The third version is similar to the second but is implemented without aid from the node class. The final is a reworking of the third, recursive in-order version, but it is not recursive and uses a stack to manage the subtrees. This version requires access to `SStack` and its methods and requires every program using it to initialize lists as well as trees, because of the implicit usage.

To walk a tree, we imagine ourselves as an ant standing on the base of the tree, the root. We want to travel up and down the branches of the tree so that we visit each leaf of the tree exactly once. In doing so we must traverse each branch, or link, in the tree twice, once going downward and again going upward. We pass through each internal node several times, depending on the number of children the node has. We agree that we shall *visit* each internal node on one of the passes through it. Thus we visit each node of the tree exactly once. If we visit each internal node the first time we come to it, we call our walk a pre-order walk. If the visit of internal nodes is done at the last traversal, we call the walk a post-order walk. If the tree is a binary tree and we visit the internal nodes between visiting the nodes in the left subtree and those in the right subtree, we call the walk in-order. To walk the tree in Fig. 9.4 we could visit the nodes in the following orders:

Pre-order: A, C, B, D, E, F
Post-order: C, D, E, F, B, A

In-order is not defined for this tree (it is not a binary tree) unless we extend the definition so that in-order means visiting a node immediately after its left child has been walked. With this definition we get

In-order: C, A, D, B, E, F

The writeIt routines shown here implement pre-order protocols and use the `recursiveWriteIt` method of `SBinaryTreeNode`. The recursive version is the following.

```
void SBinaryTree :: writeIt (void) {
   cout << "A binary tree \n";
   fRoot -> recursiveWriteIt ();
};

void SBinaryTree :: SBinaryTreeNode
                :: recursiveWriteIt (void) {
   if (this != SBinaryTree :: zed) {
      if (fValue == NULL) cout << "NULL";
         else fValue -> writeIt ();
      cout << " ";
      fLeft -> recursiveWriteIt ();
      fRight -> recursiveWriteIt ();
   };
};
```

In terms of the data-structuring techniques we have used, it is the nodes that are defined recursively. Therefore our recursion must involve the nodes. The procedure that does this, `recursiveWriteIt`, itself represents the root of some subtree and is recursive as long as it is not itself an empty tree.

Since the recursion is over subtrees, it is guaranteed to halt, because we eventually meet empty subtrees as we proceed down the tree. We write the value of each node before walking (hence visiting and writing) the subtrees. This visiting of the node first makes this pre-order. The change to an in-order version is trivial: simply reverse the relative positions of the output statements and the first recursion.

```
void SBinaryTree :: SBinaryTreeNode
                :: recursiveWriteIt (void) {
   if (this != SBinaryTree :: zed) {
      fLeft -> recursiveWriteIt ();
      if (fValue == NULL) cout << "NULL";
         else fValue -> writeIt ();
      cout << " ";
      fRight -> recursiveWriteIt ();
   };
};
```

An alternate in-order version of `writeIt` is shown below, renamed `writeItOrder`. It uses an ordinary procedure, rather than a method of `SBinaryTreeNode`, to write the values in the nodes. In fact, the standard `writeIt` method inherited from `SCollection` works in this class, because it uses iterators generated by the `newIterator` method of the class it is in, and `newIterator` is implemented here. When returned, the iterator (discussed later) causes the data in the tree to be listed according to pre-order protocol because the iterator returns the data in that order. A `writeIt` method for listing the data according to in-order protocol would use an in-order iterator. However, constructing this method recursively and then using recursion removal will demonstrate the effect of recursion removal and so be instructive. A simple recursive version is shown below. Note that the `doInOrder` procedure is recursive, rather than the method. Also, the `writeIt` message is sent to the node x between two recursive calls, thus implementing in-order protocol. Finally, note that we have one tail recursion, the second, and one non-tail recursion.

```
void SBinaryTree :: writeInOrder () {
   doInOrder (fRoot);
};
```

This ordinary procedure `doInOrder`, a friend of the tree class, simply effects recursion over the left and right children of the node it receives as its parameter. It sends the `writeIt` message to this node between these recursions. The `writeIt` method of `SBinaryTreeNode` writes the data in the node itself, without any additional actions.

```
void doInOrder (SBinaryTree :: PBinaryTreeNode x) {
   if (x != SBinaryTree :: zed) {
```

```
            doInOrder (x -> fLeft);
            x -> writeIt ();
            cout << " ";
            doInOrder (x -> fRight);
        };
    };
```

In the last version of `SBinaryTree :: writeIt`, this function `doInOrder` is transformed so that it creates a stack at the beginning and disposes of it at the end. In between, it pushes nodes onto the stack and pops them in an order appropriate to an in-order walk of the tree. We shall use the general recursion removal method discussed in Chapter 7.

First we remove the tail recursion, introducing two labels. Then we shall attack the second, harder, recursion. We shall not simplify the program in between because leaving the labels in place from the first removal will provide more flexibility in structuring the code when we finish. In the first less recursive version of `doInOrder`, the tail recursion is removed by assigning the parameter to the value used in the call and then branching back to the beginning of the procedure rather than starting the recursion. The `if...then` structure is replaced with an `if...goto` equivalent to make the start and exit points more visible.

```
void doInOrder (SBinaryTree :: PBinaryTreeNode x) {
    start:
        if (x == SBinaryTree :: zed) goto finish;
        doInOrder (x -> fLeft);
        x -> writeIt ();
        cout << " ";
        x = x -> fRight;
        goto start;
    finish:;
};
```

Now we must attack the second, internal recursion. As usual, we first mark the `resume` point in the code. Because it is the point to which we return after any recursion is finished, it is just after the recursive call. We mark it with a new label.

```
void doInOrder (SBinaryTree :: PBinaryTreeNode x) {
    start:
        if (x == SBinaryTree :: zed) goto finish;
        doInOrder (x -> fLeft);
            // Next remove this recursion.
    resume:
        x -> writeIt ();
        cout << " ";
        x = x -> fRight;
```

```
        goto start;
    finish:;
};
```

Now we are ready to remove the recursion. We must create a stack to hold intermediate results, as before. At the point of the recursion, we push the current parameter, x. We then assign x a new value according to the parameter passed in the recursion. Finally we branch back to the beginning. We must also handle the resume spot, however. At that point we must check whether the stack is empty and exit altogether if it is. If the stack is not empty, we pop x from the stack and execute the rest of the code. After executing all of the rest of the code we must also return to the resume point, but note in what follows that this branch is redundant since the last statement is already a goto statement. Finally, the target of the goto of the first if statement must be made the resume label so that what would have been an exit to a previous recursion takes us to the resume point of this nonrecursive version.

```
void doInOrder (SBinaryTree :: PBinaryTreeNode x) {
    PStack s;

    s = newStack ();
    start:
        if (x == SBinaryTree :: zed) goto resume;
                            // Step 6.
        s -> push (x);      // Step 1.
        x = x -> fLeft;     // Step 2.
        goto start;         // Step 3.
    resume:
        if (s -> empty ()) goto finish; // Step 4.
        x = PBinaryTreeNode (s -> pop ()); // Step 5.
        x -> writeIt ();
        cout << " ";
        x = x -> fRight;
        goto start;
    finish: delete s;
};
```

Between the start label and the resume label is a simple while loop. We can replace it and get rid of the resume label, but we must keep the start label since there is another branch to it.

```
void doInOrder (SBinaryTree :: PBinaryTreeNode x) {
    PStack s;
```

```
    s = newStack ();
start:
    while (x != SBinaryTree :: zed) {
        s -> push (x);
        x = x -> fLeft;
    };
    if (s -> empty ()) goto finish;
    x = PBinaryTreeNode (s -> pop ());
    x -> writeIt ();
    cout << " ";
    x = x -> fRight;
    goto start;
finish: delete s;
};
```

How to structure the remaining code is not obvious. Careful examination of the positions of the labels and jumps discovers a loop, but it is neither a while loop nor a repeat loop because the test is in the middle. We turn such a loop into a while loop by the following general trick. There are two steps. First, the statements before the exit test are removed from their current position at the beginning of the loop. One copy of them is placed outside the loop, just before the start label, and another copy is placed at the end of the loop, just before the branch to the beginning. A little thought shows that the execution path of the transformed code is the same as that of the original in all situations.

```
void doInOrder (SBinaryTree :: PBinaryTreeNode x) {
    PStack s;


    s = newStack ();
    while (x != SBinaryTree :: zed) { // Copy 1.
        s -> push (x);
        x = x -> fLeft;
    };
start:
    if (s -> empty ()) goto finish;
    x = PBinaryTreeNode (s -> pop ());
    x -> writeIt ();
    cout << " ";
    x = x -> fRight;
    while (x != SBinaryTree :: zed) { // Copy 2.
        s -> push (x);
        x = x -> fLeft;
    };
```

```
        goto start;
   finish: delete s;
};
```

The transformation above left us with a `while` loop because the test is now at the initial label. Replacing the `goto` statements and the labels with this loop gives us the final version.

```
void doInOrder (SBinaryTree :: PBinaryTreeNode x) {
   PStack s;

   s = newStack ();
   while (x != SBinaryTree :: zed) {
      s -> push (x);
      x = x -> fLeft;
   };
   while (!s -> empty ()) {
      x = PBinaryTreeNode (s -> pop ());
      x -> writeIt ();
      cout << " ";
      x = x -> fRight;
      while (x != SBinaryTree :: zed) {
         s -> push (x);
         x = x -> fLeft;
      };
   };
   delete s;
};
```

This code is considerably more complex than the original version. It also has nested loops, although the original did also, implicitly. Finally, that the code solves the problem at all is not so entirely obvious from looking at it. However, our transformation technique assures us that it does. A little testing helps, too. If we were programming in a language, such as an early version of FORTRAN, that does not permit recursion, the transformation yielding the final version would provide a solution to an otherwise difficult problem.

9.5   TREE POSITIONS

A tree position corresponds to the notion of pointing to a location in a tree. The location to which we point can change, moving up or down the various branches of the tree. Once we have referenced a position, we might want to change the tree at that position. We might want to utilize several positions simultaneously to restructure the tree or find complex patterns represented by the tree or the data it contains. Without positions we are unable to do much with trees as we have constructed them here, having little control over where insertions are made.

An object of the class `SBinaryTreePosition` has an instance variable that refers to a particular tree, which is set at initialization and not changed for the life of the object, and an instance variable that refers to a particular position, a tree node. Since trees can be empty, a tree position might refer to the zed node. The method `setToRoot` resets the position to the root of its tree. Often we must send this message after modifying a tree. If a position references the root, as it does after a call to the constructor, `SBinaryTreePosition`, modifying the tree can make the position invalid.

```
SBinaryTreePosition :: SBinaryTreePosition
                    (PBinaryTree t): SPosition (t) {
   fHere = t -> fRoot;
   fTree = t;
};
```

```
void SBinaryTreePosition :: setToRoot (void) {
   fHere = fTree -> fRoot;
};
```

Assuming that a tree position has a valid position, we can use `moveLeft`, `moveRight`, and `moveToParent` to navigate the tree.

```
void SBinaryTreePosition :: moveLeft(void) {
   // But not if zed.
   if (fHere -> fLeft != SBinaryTree :: zed)
      fHere = fHere -> fLeft;
};
```

Note that `moveLeft` and `moveRight` do not cause us to reference a zed node, which in the external view of `SBinaryTree` is just a missing node. Because parent nodes are not represented directly, execution of `moveToParent` requires a search for the parent. It uses an iterator to access the nodes, and for each node received, it checks whether the node we are moving from is the child. If it is, `moveToParent` halts the search and sets its own internal position to this node.

```
void SBinaryTreePosition :: moveToParent (void) {
   PBinaryTreeIterator IT;
   SBinaryTree :: PBinaryTreeNode aNode;
   IT = SBinaryTreeIterator (fTree -> newIterator ());
   while (IT -> nextNode (aNode))
```

```
    if (aNode -> fLeft == fHere !!
        aNode -> fRight == fHere) {
      fHere = aNode;
      IT -> Short ();
    };
    delete IT;
  };
```

Since the movement routines moveLeft and moveRight do not move
to the zed node, we need to determine whether one is present. The methods
noLeft and noRight make this determination.

```
char SBinaryTreePosition :: noLeft (void) {
    return fHere -> fLeft == SBinaryTree :: zed;
};
```

The nodeAt method returns a reference to the node at the current position. It is normally used only for implementing things in this compilation
unit. The user is only interested in the data.

```
SBinaryTree :: PBinaryTreeNode SBinaryTreePosition
              :: nodeAt (void) {
    return fHere;
};
```

The methods truncateRight and truncateLeft set the corresponding subtree to the zed node. They do not destroy anything. Thus you
have to be careful not to leave garbage in the heap; if you are truncating
things that will not be reattached later, you should delete the truncated
nodes.

```
void SBinaryTreePosition :: truncateLeft (void) {
    fHere -> fLeft = SBinaryTree :: zed;
};
```

The insertion methods, insertLeftNode and insertRightNode,
insert a new node in the tree. They also both insert at the root of an
empty tree automatically. Because positions are not allowed to reference
the zed node except in an empty tree, the guard provided here is sufficient.

```
void SBinaryTreePosition :: insertLeftNode
              (SBinaryTree :: PBinaryTreeNode n) {
    if (fTree -> fRoot == SBinaryTree :: zed) {
      fTree -> fRoot = n;
      fHere = n;
```

```
    }
    else
        fHere -> fLeft = n;
};
```

The methods `insertLeft` and `insertRight` perform a similar function but are passed data instead of nodes. The node creation is handled internally.

```
void SBinaryTreePosition :: insertLeft (PObject o) {
    SBinaryTree :: PBinaryTreeNode n;

    if (fTree -> fRoot == SBinaryTree :: zed) {
        n = SBinaryTree :: PBinaryTreeNode (
                                    fTree -> newNode (o)
                                            );
        fTree -> fRoot = n;
        fHere = n;
    }
    else if (fHere -> fLeft == SBinaryTree :: zed) {
        fHere -> fLeft = SBinaryTree :: PBinaryTreeNode
                                    (fTree -> newNode (o));
    }
};
```

Finally, `moveTo` makes one `PBinaryTreePosition` reference the same position as another, assuming that both have been properly initialized for the same tree. The assignment of one `PBinaryTreePosition` to another does not have the same effect, but rather creates two references to the same `SBinaryTreePosition`, so that moving one of them in the tree will move the other as well. `Clone` could be used, but it would create a new `SBinaryTreePosition`, which is often more than we need.

```
void SBinaryTreePosition :: moveTo
                            (PBinaryTreePosition p) {
    fHere = p -> fHere;
};
```

Next we need the methods in `SBinaryTreePosition` that permit us to manipulate the data in the referenced tree. The first of these is `find`, which uses an iterator to cycle through the nodes until we achieve a position at which the data matches the parameter. If the data is not in the tree, the position is left unchanged. Note that `find` searches only at and below the current position. If the entire tree is to be searched, the position can be set to the root before `find` is invoked. The logic is the same as that of `findNode`, which was shown earlier.

```
void SBinaryTreePosition :: find (PObject o) {
  PBinaryTreeIterator IT;
  SBinaryTree :: PBinaryTreeNode anObject, aNode;
  aNode = fHere;
  IT = PBinaryTreeIterator
                           (fTree -> newIterator ());
  IT -> iterateFrom (this);
  while (IT -> nextNode (anObject))
    if (((anObject) -> value () -> equal (o)) {
    aNode = SBinaryTree :: PBinaryTreeNode
                           (anObject);

    IT -> Short ();
    };
  fHere = aNode;
  delete IT;
};
```

The remaining methods, exchangeValues, at, atPut, atLeft-
Child, and atRightChild retrieve or set the data in the current position. exchangeValues swaps the data values of two positions in the
tree, and the three methods beginning with *at* report the values stored in
the nodes at the positions.

```
void SBinaryTreePosition :: exchangeValues
                            (PBinaryTreePosition p) {
    PObject temp;


    if (this -> fHere != SBinaryTree :: zed
        && p -> fHere != SBinaryTree :: zed) {
      temp = at ();
      atPut (p -> at ());
      p -> atPut (temp);
    };
};

PObject SBinaryTreePosition :: at (void) {
   return fHere -> value ();
};

void SBinaryTreePosition :: atPut (PObject o) {
   if (fHere != SBinaryTree :: zed)
      fHere -> fValue = o;
};
```

```
PObject SBinaryTreePosition :: atLeftChild (void) {
    return fHere -> fLeft -> value ();
};
```

9.6   TREE ITERATORS

Binary tree iterators have some functionality beyond that of most iterator classes, because the order in which the nodes are yielded by the iterator must sometimes be specified. We have only one kind of iterator here, but it can yield the nodes either in pre-order or in in-order protocol. In-order protocol implies that the root of any subtree is visited after visiting the nodes in the left subtree and before visiting the nodes in the right subtree. In the pre-order protocol, first the node is visited, then all of its left heirs, and then all of its right heirs. In the post-order protocol the node is visited after all the heirs are visited. These protocols are shown in Fig. 9.5.

The tree-walking code here is interesting because it must implement an incremental walk of the tree, with a single step taken for each call to nextItem. From some position in the tree, the iterator must calculate which node is next in the current protocol (in-order or pre-order) and set the position to that node after yielding the contents of the current position. The iterator must then return to its caller and await the next call. Walking a tree is much easier if done recursively and all at once instead of incrementally, but that doesn't work for iterators that are fundamentally incremental.

Because pre-order iterators start at the root, the standard initialization sequence is sufficient. In-order iterators must first yield the node that is reached from the root by following the chain of left children as far as possible. (Following a chain of left children to the end is called moving to the leftmost descendant.) Therefore, to initialize an in-order iterator, construct it and then send it the resetInOrder message.

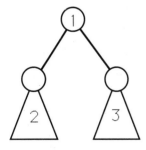   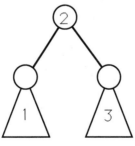   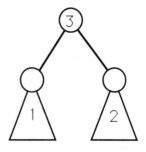

Pre-Order   In-Order   Post-Order
root-left-right   left-root-right   left-right-root

FIGURE 9.5

```
SBinaryTreeIterator :: SBinaryTreeIterator
                      (PBinaryTree t): SIterator (t) {
    fPosition = PBinaryTreePosition (t ->
                                    newPosition ());
};

void SBinaryTreeIterator :: resetInOrder (void) {
    fPosition -> setToRoot ();
    fDone = fCollection -> empty ();
    if (!fDone)
        while (!fPosition -> noLeft ())
            fPosition -> moveLeft ();
};

void SBinaryTreeIterator :: reset (void) {
    fPosition -> setToRoot ();
    fDone = fCollection -> empty ();
};
```

A pre-order iterator's nextItem method is called either when the data at the current position has not yet been yielded or when no data remain to be yielded. Therefore, we give the data at the current position and set the position to the next pre-order node. This node is the left child of the current one if there is a left child. If we have just yielded node 2 in Fig. 9.6a, we should set the position so that it refers to node 4.

If there is no left child, the next node is the right child if there is one. In Fig. 9.6b we would move from node 2 to node 5. If we start at a leaf, the next node is the right child of the nearest ancestor that has a right child not yet yielded. If there is no such ancestor, we have finished. If we move up to a node from the right side, we know we have already yielded the node. In Fig. 9.6c we would move to node 5 after node 4. Moving up to node 2 from the left, we find that it has a right child, and so we move to it.

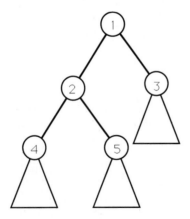

FIGURE 9.6A

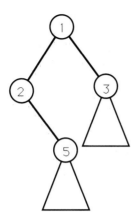

FIGURE 9.6B

However, we move up to node 2 also from node 5, but it is from the right. We therefore keep moving upward. We move to node 1 from the left, find that it has a right child, and so move to node 3, which will be the next node after node 5.

```
char SBinaryTreeIterator :: nextItem (PObject& o) {
   SBinaryTree :: PBinaryTreeNode here;
   char doneClimbing;
   char result;
   result = !fDone;
   if (result) {
      o = fPosition -> at ();
      if (fPosition -> fHere -> fLeft
         != SBinaryTree :: zed)
         fPosition -> moveLeft ();
      else if (fPosition -> fHere -> fRight
              != SBinaryTree :: zed)
         fPosition -> moveRight ();
      else {
         here = fPosition -> fHere;
         doneClimbing = FALSE;
```

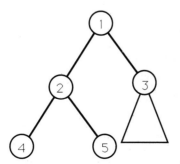

FIGURE 9.6C

```
        while (!doneClimbing) {
            if (fPosition -> fHere == fPosition
                -> fTree -> fRoot)
                doneClimbing = TRUE;
            else {
                here = fPosition -> fHere;
                fPosition -> moveToParent ();
                if (fPosition -> fHere -> fRight
                    != here &&
                    fPosition -> fHere -> fRight
                        != SBinaryTree :: zed)
                    doneClimbing = TRUE;
            };
        };
        if (fPosition -> fHere -> fRight != here &&
            fPosition -> fHere -> fRight
            != SBinaryTree :: zed)
            fPosition -> moveRight ();
        else
            fDone = TRUE;
    };
};
    return result;
};
```

An in-order iterator behaves differently, of course. When an in-order iterator is called, either it has yielded the entire tree previously and its fDone field has been set to TRUE, or it is at a node that has not yet been yielded. In the latter case it yields this item and calculates the position of the next node according to the in-order protocol and moves there. In the in-order protocol, if you are at a node that has a left child, that left child and all of its descendants have already been visited. If we start at a node that has a right child, the next node is the leftmost descendant of the right child. In Fig. 9.6a we would move from node 2 to the leftmost node in the tree below node 5. If there is no right child but if we are at the left child of some node, the next node is the parent. In Fig. 9.7a, from node 2 we would move to node 1.

Otherwise (that is, if there is no right child, and the current node is not the left child of its parent) we continue to move up the ancestor chain until we stop at a node whose left child we were just at. If one is not found, we eventually reach the root and finish. In Fig. 9.7b, the node following node 5 is node 1; we move up to the parent from the right, then up to the parent from the left, and quit.

```
char SBinaryTreeIterator :: nextItemInOrder
                            (PObject& o) {
    SBinaryTree :: PBinaryTreeNode here;
```

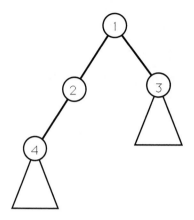

FIGURE 9.7A

```
char doneClimbing;
char result;
result = !fDone;
if (result) {
    o = fPosition -> at ();
    if (fPosition -> fHere -> fRight
        != SBinaryTree :: zed) {
        fPosition -> moveRight ();
        while (fPosition -> fHere -> fLeft
                != SBinaryTree :: zed)
            fPosition -> moveLeft ();
    }
    else if (fPosition -> isAtRoot ())
        fDone = TRUE;
    else {
        doneClimbing = FALSE;
        while (!doneClimbing)
            if (fPosition -> isAtRoot ())
                doneClimbing = TRUE;
            else {
                here = fPosition -> fHere;
                fPosition -> moveToParent ();
```

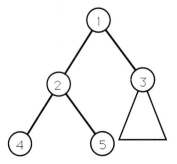

FIGURE 9.7B

```
            if (fPosition -> fHere -> fRight
                 != here)
              doneClimbing = TRUE;
            else if (fPosition -> isAtRoot ()) {
              fDone = TRUE;
              doneClimbing = TRUE;
            };
          };
        };
      };
    return result;
};
```

We also permit an iterator to yield the nodes rather than the data, though the uses of this are rather specialized. The logic here is the same as that of a pre-order iterator.

```
char SBinaryTreeIterator :: nextNode
                          (PBinaryTreeNode& o) {
    SBinaryTree :: PBinaryTreeNode here;
    char doneClimbing;
    char result;

    result = !fDone;
    if (result) {
        o = fPosition -> nodeAt ();
        if (fPosition -> fHere -> fLeft
            != SBinaryTree :: zed)
          fPosition -> moveLeft ();
        else if (fPosition -> fHere -> fRight
                 != SBinaryTree :: zed)
          fPosition -> moveRight ();
        else {
            here = fPosition -> fHere;
            doneClimbing = FALSE;
            while (!doneClimbing) {
                if (fPosition -> fHere == fPosition
                    -> fTree -> fRoot)
                  doneClimbing = TRUE;
                else {
                    here = fPosition -> fHere;
                    fPosition -> moveToParent ();
                    if (fPosition -> fHere -> fRight
                        != here &&
                        fPosition -> fHere -> fRight
                           != SBinaryTree :: zed)
                      doneClimbing = TRUE;
                };
```

```
            };
            if (fPosition -> fHere -> fRight
                   != here &&
                fPosition -> fHere -> fRight
                   != SBinaryTree :: zed)
                fPosition -> moveRight ();
            else
                fDone = TRUE;
        };
    };
    return result;
};
```

Finally we permit a partial iteration. The following method initializes an iterator to some predetermined position. Iteration then proceeds from the node at that position. The iteration can be either in-order or pre-order.

```
void SBinaryTreeIterator :: iterateFrom
                            (PBinaryTreePosition p) {
    fPosition -> fHere = p -> fHere;
    fDone = p -> fHere == SBinaryTree :: zed;
};
```

9.7   BINARY SEARCH TREES

A typical use of trees is to keep a collection in order efficiently. A binary search tree is a special kind of binary tree that contains sequenceable data (subclass of SMagnitude) at its nodes such that, for each node, every value in the left subtree is less than the value in the root, and every value in the right subtree is greater than the value in the root. If the same value must be held several times in the tree (i.e., maintaining a bag rather than a set), it is common (but not always desirable) to put the copies down the right subtree (or at least to be consistent, always using the left subtree or always using the right). See Fig. 9.8. Binary search trees lead to the subclass SBinarySearchTree of SBinaryTree. The purpose of a binary search tree is to make the find routine more efficient.

FIGURE 9.8

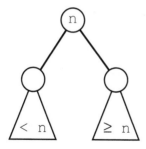

We must guarantee that no insertions or deletions can destroy the binary search tree properties. Therefore we have to modify the `insert`, `insertData`, and `remove` methods of `SBinaryTree`, and the `insertLeft`, `insertRight`, and `exchangeValues` methods of `SBinaryTreePosition` so that they do not destroy the binary search tree property. The easiest way of so modifying is to make them into either no-ops or error routines. Alternatively, we could make `insertLeft` and `insertRight` call `insert` on their own `fTree` instance variable. This won't have the effect implied by their names, however, and should be avoided. We should, of course, modify `find` to take advantage of the other changes. If the item is not in the tree, `find` should not change the current position. We therefore add an additional method, `seek`, that is like `find` except it leaves us where we could add the data item if we wish. This results in the following.

```
class SBinarySearchTree;
typedef SBinarySearchTree *PBinarySearchTree;

PBinarySearchTree newBinarySearchTree (void);

class SBinarySearchTree: public SBinaryTree {
   public:
         SBinarySearchTree (void);
      virtual void                insert (PObject);
      virtual void                remove (PObject);
      virtual PBinaryTreePosition newPosition
                                  (void);
      virtual char                member (classtype
                                          c);
      virtual classtype           Member (void);
      virtual void                writeIt (void);


   protected:
      virtual int    sizeOf (void);
};

class SBinarySearchTreePosition;
typedef SBinarySearchTreePosition
   *PBinarySearchTreePosition;

class SBinarySearchTreePosition:
   public SBinaryTreePosition {
   public:
         SBinarySearchTreePosition (PBinarySearch
                                    Tree);
      virtual void      find (PObject);
      virtual char      seek (PObject);
```

```
        virtual void            exchangeValues
                                (PBinaryTreePosition);
        virtual char            member (classtype c);
        virtual classtype       Member (void);

    protected:
        virtual int    sizeOf (void);
      friend SBinarySearchTree;
};
```

```
// REQUIREMENTS For use
//     initLists();
//     initBinaryTrees();
```

We shall look at the position class first, because we need it for insert and remove of the tree class. The data insertion methods insertLeft and insertRight should be overridden also to provide no-ops, because physical insertions by a client could destroy the order.

The seek method searches from the current position for the item, using the binary search tree property to guide the search. If the search is unsuccessful, the position is left where the data can be inserted while maintaining the property. The seek method also tells us whether the search was successful.

```
char SBinarySearchTreePosition :: seek (PObject o) {
    char done;
    char result;

    done = FALSE;
    while (!done) {
        if (leaf ()) {done = TRUE;}
        else { if (o -> equal (at ())) {done = TRUE;}
            else {
                if (o -> less (at ()))
                    if (noLeft ()) done = TRUE;
                    else moveLeft ();
                else
                    if (noRight ()) done = TRUE;
                    else moveRight ();
            };
        };
    };
    if (missingNode ()) result = FALSE;
    else {
        result = o -> equal (at ());
```

```
      };
   return result;
};
```

Given this method, find is extremely simple, requiring only that we remember the original position so that we can return to it.

```
void SBinarySearchTreePosition :: find (PObject o) {
   SBinaryTree :: PBinaryTreeNode thisNode;

   if (o -> member (magnitude)) {
      thisNode = fHere;
      if (!seek (o)) fHere = thisNode;
   }
   else
      Error ("SBinarySearchTreePosition
             :: find: not a magnitude.");
};
```

In seek the objects o and at (result of the method call) are compared not using the built-in comparison == but using the method equal. This is important, because at is unlikely to return the same object even if they are of the same magnitude. Thus o == at () would be the wrong test here.

The insert method in SBinarySearchTree is now relatively simple, because we can use a position object to do most of the work:

```
void SBinarySearchTree :: insert (PObject o) {
   PBinarySearchTreePosition p;

   if (o -> member (magnitude)) {
      if (empty ()) SBinaryTree :: insert (o);
      else {
         p = PBinarySearchTreePosition (newPosition ())
         if (!p -> seek (o)) {
            if (o -> less(p -> at ()))
               p -> SBinaryTreePosition :: insertLeft (o
            else p -> SBinaryTreePosition :: insertRight
         };
         delete p;
      };
   }
   else
      Error ("SBinarySearchTree :: insert:
             not a magnitude.");
};
```

All that is left is the `remove` method. It is rather tricky, because we must remove the node that contains the parameter `o`, and yet preserve the descendants of that node. We could have `remove` leave most of the data nodes intact and just move the contents around, but this contradicts our basic idea about what constitutes a tree. A tree is composed of trees. External references to some of the subtrees are possible, though unlikely (why?), and we would like these references to remain valid. Therefore, `remove` should involve surgery on the tree, pruning and grafting the nodes as appropriate. We first must learn whether the item is in the tree, so we search for it from the root. If it is at the root, we set the variable `target` to the root and set `found` TRUE; otherwise, we use an iterator that sets both the target and its parent. We represent both the target and the parent by references to nodes. Once we are sure that the item is in the tree, we construct a new node to replace the target and, finally, pin this new node into the tree either as the root or as the correct child of the parent of the original target. The work is in building the replacement node. The target is to be replaced by the largest item in the left subtree of the target. If no such subtree exists, the target can be replaced by its right subtree. This latter case is shown in Fig. 9.9a. The target's left tree is missing, so the variable `anewNode` is set to be the right subtree, resulting in the tree of Fig. 9.9b.

```
void SBinarySearchTree :: remove (PObject o) {
    char found;
    SBinaryTree :: PBinaryTreeNode target, aNewNode,
                    leaf, p;
    PBinaryTreeIterator IT;
    PObject aValue;


    p = fRoot;
    found = FALSE;
    if (!empty ()) {
```

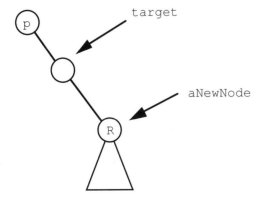

FIGURE 9.9A

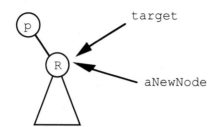

FIGURE 9.9B

```
aValue = p -> fValue;
if (aValue -> equal (o)) { // Remove root.
   target = p;
   found = TRUE;
}
else {
   IT = PBinaryTreeIterator (newIterator ());
   while (IT -> nextNode (p)) {
      if (p -> fLeft != SBinaryTree :: zed)
         if ((p -> fLeft -> value ())
               -> equal (o)) {
            found = TRUE;
            target = p -> fLeft;
            IT -> Short ();
         };
      if (p -> fRight != SBinaryTree :: zed)
         if ((p -> fRight -> value ())
               -> equal (o)) {
            found = TRUE;
            target = p -> fRight;
            IT -> Short ();
         };
   };
   delete (IT);
};
};
if (found) {
   aNewNode = NULL;
   if (target -> fLeft == SBinaryTree :: zed)
      aNewNode = target -> fRight;
   else {
      leaf = target -> fLeft;
      if (leaf -> fRight == SBinaryTree :: zed)
         aNewNode = leaf;
         aNewNode -> fRight = target -> fRight;
      }
```

```
        else {
            while (leaf -> fRight -> fRight
                    != SBinaryTree :: zed)
                leaf = leaf -> fRight;
            aNewNode = leaf -> fRight;
            leaf -> fRight = aNewNode -> fLeft;
            aNewNode -> fLeft = target -> fLeft;
            aNewNode -> fRight = target -> fRight;
        };
    };
    if (p == target)
        fRoot = aNewNode;
    else if (p -> fLeft == target)
        p -> fLeft = aNewNode;
    else
        p -> fRight = aNewNode;
    };
};
```

If `target` has a left child node, there are two additional cases to consider. First, the right child of the left child might be missing, as in Fig. 9.10a. In this case `anewNode` might be the left child itself, because no larger data can be in this left tree. Moving this node up to the target position yields Fig. 9.10b. Note, though, that we must pin this right child to L as its (new) right child in order not to lose the right child of the target.

Second, if the left child of the target has a right child, we must follow the chain of right children to the end, as shown in Fig. 9.11a. When we reach the end, we have `anewNode`, but we have to worry about a possible left child of `anewNode` (it can have no right child) as well as the left and right children of the target. We simply attach the left child to the parent

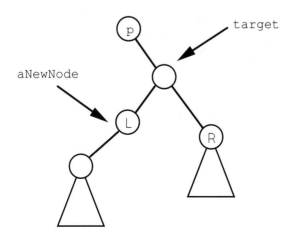

FIGURE 9.10A

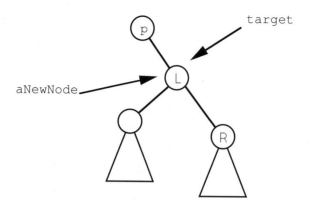

FIGURE 9.10B

of anewNode because we are about to move newNode anyway. Then both children of anewNode are free, and we attach the target's left and right children to it. (Why doesn't this break the binary search tree property?) Now we are ready to reattach anewNode in the tree in the proper position, and after doing so, we have the situation in Fig. 9.11b.

9.8   GENERAL TREES

Now that we have a rich class for binary trees, we need to look at the situation in which a tree can have more than two children at each node.

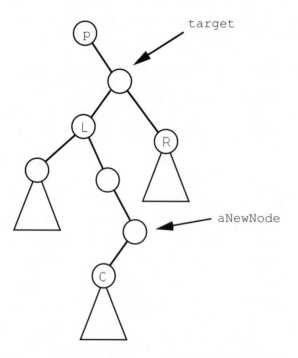

FIGURE 9.11A

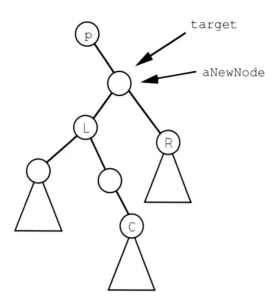

FIGURE 9.11B

Instead of a pair of children (ordered pair, actually), we need a collection of children. The collection could take almost any form, such as a list or a set, and implementations would be built from whatever was chosen. Since a tree is itself a collection, we could even store the children of a node in a tree. A remarkably simple implementation results if we adapt this last idea, using an ordinary binary tree as an instance variable. The children do not form a tree, but the descendants do. We also need to build new classes for general tree nodes and for general tree positions.

```
class STree;
typedef STree *PTree;
class STreePosition;
typedef STreePosition *PTreePosition;

PTree newTree ();

class STree: public SCollection {
    public:
          STree ();
      virtual                  ~STree (void);
      virtual void             insert (PObject);
      virtual PTreePosition    newPosition (void);
      virtual char             member (classtype c);
      virtual PObject          Clone (void);
      virtual void             remove (PObject);
      virtual char             empty (void);
      virtual PIterator        newIterator (void);
```

```
        virtual void                writeIt (void);
    protected:
        PBinaryTree      fElements;
        virtual int      sizeOf (void);
        virtual PBinaryTreeNode      newNode (PObject o)

        class STreeNode; // Nested.
    public:
        typedef STreeNode *PTreeNode;
    protected:

    class STreeNode: public SBinaryTreeNode {
        public:
            virtual char        member (classtype c);
            virtual PObject      Clone (void);
        protected:
            PTreeNode        fParent;
            virtual int      sizeOf (void);
        private:
                STreeNode (PObject);
        friend STree;
        friend STreePosition;
    }; // End STreeNode.
        friend STreePosition;
    }; // End STree.

    class STreePosition: public SBinaryTreePosition {
        public:
            virtual void        moveToChild (int);
            virtual void        insertChild (PObject);
            virtual void        moveToParent (void);
            virtual PObject      atChild (int);
            virtual void        insertLeft (PObject) {};
                // Disabled.
            virtual void        insertRight (PObject){};
                // Disabled.
            virtual char        member (classtype c);
        protected:
            virtual int      sizeOf (void);
        private:
                STreePosition (PBinaryTree t);
        friend STree;
    }; // End STreePosition.

    // REQUIREMENTS For Use
    //     initLists ();
    //     initBinaryTrees ();
```

In STreeNode, fParent is a reference to the parent of the given node in the tree of which the node is a part. The root node of a general tree has a NULL parent (not zed). The constructor STreeNode sets fParent to NULL, so it is always valid.

In STreePosition we want to be able to move to a given child of the current position, as indexed by the parameter. We also want to be able to insert a node as a child of the current position, to move to the parent, and to retrieve the data at a node. In fact, a number of other methods are very useful and have been left as exercises.

We shall implement general trees by what is known as the first child–next sibling representation. It can represent any tree, indeed any forest (collection of trees), as a single binary tree. For example, consider the general tree shown in Fig. 9.12.

Suppose we erase the links connecting a parent to children other than the left-most child and replace them with horizontal links connecting all the children of that parent. We get the picture shown in Fig. 9.13. Note that it is, indeed, a tree, as it is connected and has no cycles. Another way to think about the same picture is that a node always has a pointer to the first child and that this child maintains a linked list of its siblings.

Next, suppose we stretch the horizontal lines down so that they become slanted. The linked lists become chains of right children of successive nodes. We get Fig. 9.14, which is just a topological transformation of Fig. 9.13. Note that this is just a binary tree. Also, the root of the binary tree has no right child. In the binary tree a right child corresponds to a sibling of the general tree that it represents, and a left child represents a reference to the first

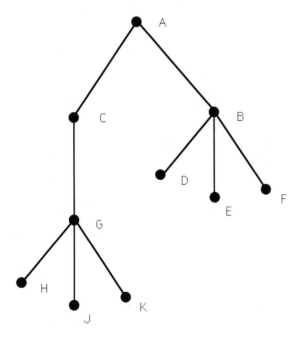

FIGURE 9.12

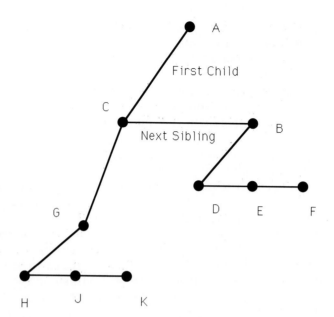

FIGURE 9.13

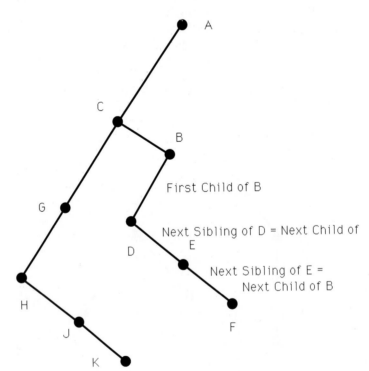

FIGURE 9.14

child of a chain of perhaps many. (In the representation of a forest, the right child of the root is the next tree.)

Now we need to override moveToParent since, in STree, moveTo-Parent moves from E to B, but the inherited method moves only to D. Also, a parent node is physically distant from its child. If we include the instance variable fParent in our general tree nodes, we can directly access the parent, avoiding a lengthy search. In fact, a double loop would be required to find the parent without this. (Why?)

The insert method of STree illustrates the concept. It adds a new descendant of the root of a nonempty tree or replaces the root of an empty one.

```
void STree :: insert (PObject o) {
   PTreePosition aLoc
   PTreeNode aNode, parent;
   aLoc = PTreePosition (newPosition ());
   aNode = PTreeNode (newNode (o));
   if (empty ()) {
      aLoc -> insertLeftNode (aNode);
   }
   else {
      while (!aLoc -> noLeft ()) {
         aLoc -> moveLeft ();
      };
      aLoc -> insertLeftNode (aNode);
      parent = PTreeNode (aLoc -> nodeAt ());
      aNode -> fParent = parent;
   };
   delete aLoc;
};
```

The insertChild method creates the nearest, or first, child of the current position. Note that the current first child (fPosition -> fLeft) is made into the child following the new first child, which is the node inserted. If the node is missing, the zed node is appended, exactly as we want.

```
void STreePosition :: insertChild (PObject o) {
   STree :: PTreeNode n;
   PBinaryTreeNode here;

   n = STree :: PTreeNode (PTree (fCollection)
                                 -> newNode (o));
   if (fCollection -> empty ()) {
      insertLeftNode(n); // Replaces root.
      setToRoot ();
   }
```

```
   else {
      here = nodeAt ();
      n -> fRight = here -> fLeft;
      here ->fLeft = n;
      n -> fParent = /* STree :: */ PTreeNode (here
                        ;
   };
};
```

A method for inserting data rather than nodes could call this method after creating a node to hold the data. The new moveToParent becomes very simple, and the retrieval of data from a child is very much like moving to a child given the index, except that a PTreePosition manages it.

```
void STreePosition :: moveToParent (void) {
   PBinaryTreeNode here;

   if (!isAtRoot ()) {
      here = nodeAt ();
      toNode (PTreeNode (here) -> fParent);
   };
};

PObject STreePosition :: atChild (int i) {
   PObject result;
   PTreePosition P;
   int j;

   P = PTreePosition (Clone ());
   P -> moveLeft ();
   for (j=2; j <= i; ++j)
      P -> moveRight ();
   result = P -> at ();
   delete P;
   return result;
};
```

Note that if you ask for the data in the fifth child of a node that has only three, you will get the data from the third. What happens if there are no children?

9.9   SUMMARY

We may think of a tree as a generalization of a list. In fact, between the root and a given leaf is a list. A tree is an advantageous storage structure if items need to be searched for quickly. When a tree is arranged carefully, the number of steps required for finding data is the logarithm of the number of nodes. This is most important when there are a lot of data.

We have implemented strict binary trees, but since all the leaf nodes were physically implemented as a single zed node, the user of trees sees a more general tree in which a node may have zero, one, or two children.

Like all collection classes, trees need iterators. Since trees are a form of ordered collection, they also have positions. Tree iterators are more complex than list iterators, because they must work upward in the tree at certain times, and list iterators only need to work forward.

General trees were not implemented as a subclass of binary trees, but as a subclass of SCollection using an instance variable of type SBinaryTree.

EXERCISES

9.1 (9.6) Implement pre-order and post-order searching in binary trees.

9.2 (9.7) Consider a binary search tree of height n in which every leaf is at height n and no nodes are missing. How many nodes are there? How many nonleaf nodes are there? What is the proportion of leaf nodes to total nodes? Given this information, state why the average search for a random item in such a tree requires only one less probe than the worst case.

9.3 (9.4) The implementation of binary trees given in Section 9.2 could, perhaps, be improved if we merged the classes SBinaryTreeNode and SBinaryTree-Position into a single class. Design such a combined class and comment on whether it is an improvement or not.

9.4 (9.4) Refer to Exercise 9.3. It might also be possible to make SBinaryTree-Position into a subclass of SBinaryTreeNode. Try to do this, and comment.

9.5 (9.4) Transform the recursive pre-order writeIt method into the nonrecursive form as shown in Section 9.4. Use the method shown in the transformation of writeInOrder.

9.6 (9.6) Modify class SBinaryTreeIterator so that each iterator has a private stack. Use this stack to speed up the searching for the next item to be produced, by keeping in it the nodes that have been passed in our walk but not yet been produced. Hint: See the nonrecursive tree writing procedure given in this chapter.

9.7 (9.6) As an alternative to the stack suggested in Exercise 9.6, consider giving each SBinaryTreeIterator an fParent field in which to maintain a reference to the parent of the current position. Can this be made to work efficiently? What can be done? Should it be done?

9.8 (9.6) Our binary tree iterator permitted a partial iteration. We can set an iterator to a given position in the tree from which it will then iterate. When we do this, does the iterator restrict itself to a subtree of the starting position? Why or why not?

9.9 (9.6) The find method in SBinaryTree could definitely be improved by using the concepts employed in SListPosition :: search. We would prefer to be left at the parent of the node we are searching for, if possible, since this leaves us the maximum flexibility for manipulating the tree. Can we use the same type WhereFound as a return type? Implement such a method.

9.10 (9.7) In SBinarySearchTree the remove method inherited from SBinary-Tree is not safe to use. Why not? Give an example in which its use on a binary search tree would result in a tree that fails to have the binary search tree property.

9.11 (9.8) Complete the implementation of the class STree and its associated classes.

9.12 (9.8) Implement a new method of STreePosition that moves to the *j*th child of any node. Note that moveToChild (j) moves left once and then right *j* − 1 times.

## CHAPTER 10

RECURSIVE STRUCTURES AND OTHER ADVANCED IDEAS

My father, mother, and brother Recurse unto my thought, and straight plucke downe The resolution I had built before.

Cowley, "Love's Riddle"

For even now the axe is laid at the root of the trees; every tree therefore that is not bringing forth good fruit is to be cut down and thrown into the fire.

Matthew 3:10

In the first three sections of this chapter we shall examine an alternate way of defining lists and trees. Some of what we do will be similar to our previous treatment, but because we start with a different concept of what lists and trees are, the means of working with them and the mental state to adopt when programming with them must be quite different. In previous chapters lists and trees were indirectly recursive structures. Each of these structures was composed of nodes, and the nodes were recursive, themselves having nodes as components. Now we shall let lists and trees be directly recursive. Lists will have lists as components, and trees will have trees as components. There will be no nodes at all in our model. Some things will be quite different, as you can't add a root node to an existing tree and think of the result as being the "same tree" as the original. What we shall build may be used in a way similar to the way one uses data structures in functional programming languages, such as Lisp or ML.

In the latter part of the chapter we shall return to the nodes and links model and show how to implement sets using binary search trees, and also consider some advanced ideas about trees, such as balanced trees.

10.1   LISTS AS car AND cdr

The programming language Lisp is built on an efficient implementation and powerful primitives for manipulating lists. In Lisp a list can either be empty (nil) or consist of a value, called car, and a list, called cdr. Lists are always finite. (1, 2, 3, 4, 5, 6) is a list whose car is 1 and cdr is (2, 3, 4, 5, 6). We are not using precise Lisp syntax. The terms car and cdr (pronounced could-er, or cud-er) originated as the names of the two internal registers used in the original implementation of Lisp on the IBM 704 computer. car was contents of the address register, and cdr was contents of the decrement register. The names stuck. In Lisp one forms a list using a function, cons, that takes a value and a list as input and produces a list with that value as car and that list as cdr. For example, cons (3, (1 3 5 6)) is the list (3, 1, 3, 5, 6). Speaking informally, we might represent the nil list by ( ), and the list of the first three positive integers as (1 2 3), to emphasize the inserted elements, or as (1 (2 (3 ( )))), to emphasize the car and the cdr of each list and its sublists. This notation is not acceptable to C++, though it is similar to the notation in Lisp.

To summarize,

> List
> > A list is
>
> a.   nil, or
> b.   a value, called car, and a list, called cdr.

A list whose car is the integer 5 might be pictured as in Fig. 10.1, where the cdr is pictured as another rectangle, which can be nil or another list.

Figure 10.2 shows a refinement of the structure. Here the car is any value, and the cdr is another list. A list itself is made up of its car and its cdr. This is the idea we wish to implement in our new class SRList. The *R* is for recursive, of course. We shall implement much more than car, cdr, and cons, because we would like these lists to fit in with our other structures. We shall give a protocol quite similar to that of SList, including positions, SRListPosition, and iterators, SRListIterator.

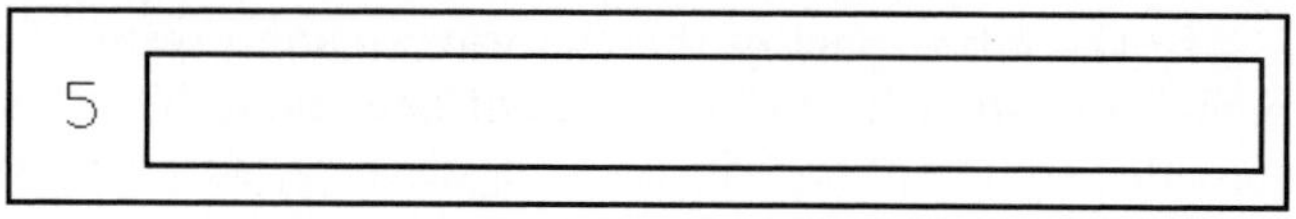

FIGURE 10.1

5 [   ]

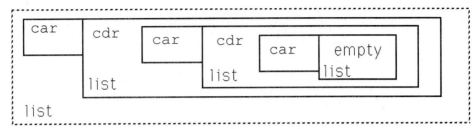

FIGURE 10.2

```
class SRList;
typedef SRList *PRList;
class SRListPosition;
typedef SRListPosition *PRListPosition;
class SRListIterator;
typedef SRListIterator *PRListIterator;

PRList newRList (); // Returns the "nil" list.
PRList newNonEmptyRList (PObject o);

class SRList: public SCollection {
    public:
          SRList (PObject o);
      virtual              ~SRList (void);
      virtual void         insert (PObject); // Error.
      virtual void         remove (PObject);
         // Will not remove the first item.
      virtual char         empty (void);
      virtual int          length (void);
      virtual void         selectionSort (void);
      virtual PRList       merge (PRList);
      virtual PObject      atLoc (int n);
      virtual PRList       cons (PObject);
      virtual PObject      car (void);
      virtual PRList       cdr (void);
      virtual PIterator    newIterator (void);
      virtual char         member (classtype c);
      virtual PObject      Clone (void);
      virtual void         writeIt (void);
      virtual void         writeReverse (void);

    protected:
      PObject         fCar;
      PRList          fCdr;
      virtual int     sizeOf (void);
```

```
        friend SRListPosition;
        friend void initRLists (void);
    };


    PRListPosition newRListPosition (PRList L);

    class SRListPosition: public SPosition {
        public:
                SRListPosition (PRList L);
            virtual void           next (void);
            virtual void           prev (void);
            virtual void           insertAfter (PObject);
            virtual PObject        at (void);
            virtual void           atPut (PObject);
            virtual char           last (void);
            virtual char           first (void);
            virtual char           isNil (void);
            virtual void           toFirst (void);
            virtual void           toLast (void);
            virtual void           deleteNext (void);
            virtual PObject        atNext (void);
            virtual WhereFound     search (PObject);
            virtual void           moveTo
                                   (PRListPosition);
            virtual void           exchangeValues
                                   (PRListPosition);
            virtual char           member (classtype c);
            virtual PObject        Clone (void);
            virtual void           writeIt (void);


        protected:
            PRList          fList;
            PRList          fPosition;
            virtual int     sizeOf (void);

    };

    class SRListIterator: public SIterator {
        public:
                SRListIterator (PRList L);
            virtual            ~SRListIterator (void);
            virtual char       nextItem (PObject&);
            virtual void       reset (void);
            virtual char       member (classtype c);
            virtual PObject    Clone (void);

        protected:
```

```
          PRListPosition      fPosition;
          virtual int         sizeOf (void);

};


PRList nil; // Do not modify this list.
void initRLists (void);

// REQUIREMENTS For Use
//     initRLists ();
```

The variable nil is a pseudoconstant. It must never be changed. It is very much like the zed node of SList, except that it is intended to be a public item rather than a private one. It is created by initRLists, which must be called exactly once, before anything else in this unit is used. Because nil will terminate our lists and stand for the empty list, we must never modify it. The implementations shown below are careful about this, but clients will need to treat it as a constant also.

Recursive lists (RLists) are implemented with a field for the value, called fCar, and a field for the rest, called fCdr, to match Lisp usage. The value is any data, and the rest is another list, which may or may not be the nil list. The implementation is directly recursive. We shall see that processing such lists through recursive procedures and functions is extremely easy. The general form of such a procedure is as follows.

```
void SRList :: Foo () {
   if (this == nil)
      whatever_for_nil ();
   else {
      handle_fCar_somehow ();
      fCdr -> Foo (); // Recursion on the rest.
   };
};
```

This template exactly matches the definition of a list (as nil or a value and a list), and the else clause exactly matches the implementation of a non-nil list.

The positions in this ADT are implemented using a position variable and a list variable. The position refers to the current location, and the list is the list of which this is a position. However, each of these is implemented as an SRList. When a position is in use, its fPosition is a sublist of its fList.

The iterators use positions for their implementation. The code used here is essentially the same code as that used in SList (except for the classes of the variables), so we shall not further discuss SRListIterators.

The class initialization procedure creates the nil list that appears as part of every other list. It is the (only) empty list.

```
void initRLists (void) {
   nil = new SRList (NULL);
   failnull (nil);
   nil -> fCdr = nil;
};
```

The generator function `newRList` returns a reference to `nil`. It doesn't create a new list, but rather returns a reference to an empty `RList`. In fact there is only one empty `RList`, `nil`. Therefore we need another generator, `newNonEmptyRList`, that returns a list that is the `cons` of the argument and `nil`. In other words, it returns an `RList` comprising a single value followed by the `nil` list. The class constructor for `RLists` need only be for non-empty lists, so we need a parameter that will be inserted as the `car` of the list being initialized. `SRList` then also makes `fCdr` `nil`.

```
SRList :: SRList (PObject o) {
   fCar = o;
   fCdr = nil;
};
```

Our destructor has an especially difficult job, since it must guarantee that it never deletes the `nil` list. This is difficult to manage without halting the entire computation.

```
SRList :: ~SRList () {
   if (this != nil && fCdr != nil) delete fCdr;
   if (this == nil) Error ("deleting nil list.");
};
```

The `writeReverse` method illustrates our general recursive technique. We want to write a list in reverse. If it is `nil`, there is nothing to do. Otherwise, through recursion we reach the tail of the list and then write the value of the `car`. Since we do it in this order, and since the recursion also writes its tail before its head, we get the list in reverse.

```
void SRList :: writeReverse (void) {
   if (fCdr != nil) fCdr -> writeReverse ();
   if (this != nil) {fCar -> writeIt ();
                     cout << " ";};
};
```

The `RList` versions of `insert` and `remove` are special. The `insert` method is implemented as an error since other and better methods are provided for these lists. In particular, if a new value is inserted at the head of a list, the modified list cannot be considered to be the same list as the original. This is because the object that represents the list also represents the `car` of the list, and to insert a new value before the head of a list would leave us with the inconsistency of trying to represent by one thing both the list as a whole and its second item, which was its former head. This seems like a flaw in the structure, but in fact it is not. The solution to the dilemma is to make insertion a function rather than a procedure. This way the insertion process returns to us a list, constructed from the old, that has the new value as *its* head, leaving the original list intact, though it is a sublist of the returned list. This is the method `cons`, which is discussed below.

The `remove` method is also special, since it is impossible to delete the head of a list, for the same reasons why it is impossible to insert a new head. The item to be deleted is sent to `remove` as a parameter. If it is the head of the list, the procedure does nothing. Otherwise it locates the target object and removes it. It uses an `RList` position to walk the list in a standard way and the `deleteNext` method of the position class to delete the item if it is found. Note that the function `cdr` serves as a functional `delete` for the head of a list.

```
void SRList :: remove (PObject o) {
   PRListPosition p;

   p = newRListPosition (this);
   while (! p -> atNext () -> equal (o)
          && ! p -> last ())
      p -> next ();
   if (p -> atNext () -> equal (o))
      p -> deleteNext ();
   delete p;
};
```

An alternate version of `remove` that is functional and removes the head of a list is the following function, `allBut`, which returns a new list.

```
PRList SRList :: allBut (PObject o) {
   PRList result;

   if (this == nil) return nil;
   else if (o -> equal (fCar)) return fCdr;
   else {
      result = newNonEmptyRList (fCar);
      result -> fCdr = fCdr -> allBut (o);
      return result;
   };
};
```

The method `cons` can be thought of as a constructor, since it is a function. It constructs a new list from its parameter and itself and returns it. Note that `this` is a sublist of the list returned.

```
PRList SRList :: cons (PObject o) {
   PRList result;
   result = newNonEmptyRList (o);
   result -> fCdr = this;
   return result;
};
```

The implication of returning sublists is that freeing lists is dangerous
in general, especially when it is difficult to tell whether a list no longer
needed is a sublist of a needed list. A method can be written to determine
whether one list is a sublist of another and whether two lists have a common
sublist. If two lists have the same last element (other than nil), they have
a common part. If the head of one list is in the other, it is a sublist of the
other.

The methods car and cdr are the reverse of cons. They tear a list
into its parts and return them to us. Note that cdr returns a sublist of
this.

```
PObject SRList :: car (void) {
   return fCar; // This returns NULL if empty ().
};
```

```
PRList SRList :: cdr (void) {
   return fCdr;
};
```

Clone can take the same recursive approach or be implemented
using positions or even iterators. Here we show a recursive version of
Clone, which illustrates the general technique. A number of important
things should be noted. First, nil should never be cloned. Second, the
recursion on the tail handles the cloning of the rest of the list. The
call to the ShallowClone method creates a proper list object of the
same type as the object executing this method even if that is in a subclass of this one. Finally, we send ShallowClone only to this. The
correct message to send to any other object is Clone. The purpose of
ShallowClone is only to begin the construction of a clone of this, handling allocation of an object of the correct type and copying of all static data
values.

```
PObject SRList :: Clone (void) {
   PRList result;
   result = this == nil? nil: PRList (ShallowClone (
   if (fCdr != nil)
      result -> fCdr = PRList (fCdr -> Clone ());
   return result;
};
```

Selection sorting and merging can follow exactly the same logic that was seen in SList. Only a few names must be changed.

```
void SRList :: selectionSort (void) {
    PRListPosition p, q, where;
    PObject min, val;

    p = newRListPosition (this);
    if (p -> at () -> member (magnitude)) {
        q = PRListPosition (p -> Clone ());
        where = PRListPosition (p -> Clone ());
        while (!p -> last ()) {
            q -> moveTo (p);
            if (q -> at () -> member (magnitude))
                min = q -> at ();
            else Error ("SRList :: selectionSort:
                        Not a magnitude.");
            where -> moveTo (q);
            do {
                q -> next ();
                if (q -> at () -> member (magnitude))
                    val = q -> at ();
                else Error ("SRList :: selectionSort:
                            Not a magnitude.");
                if (val -> less (min)) {
                    min = val;
                    where -> moveTo (q);
                };
            } while (!q -> last ());
            p -> exchangeValues (where);
            p -> next ();
        };
        delete q;
        delete where;
    };
    delete p;
};
```

See the exercises for an interesting variation of this method.

10.1.1 SRList **Positions**

The positions of SRLists are quite standard and easily implemented. Note the absence of methods to insert and remove the first elements in RLists. The instance variable fList represents the list of which we are a position, and fPosition, which is a sublist of fList, represents the current location.

The initialization method must set both of these to the list itself, which is passed as a parameter. Otherwise, only `insertAfter` and `deleteNext` need to be considered. The logic of insertion is the same as that of node insertion, seen in Chapter 6. The only difference is that we are creating `RLists` rather than nodes. The current `cdr` becomes the `cdr` of the new node and the new node becomes the `cdr` of the current position. Deletion is essentially the reverse of this.

```
void SRListPosition :: insertAfter (PObject o) {
    PRList n;

    if (fPosition != nil) {
        n = newNonEmptyRList (o);
        n -> fCdr = fPosition -> fCdr;
        fPosition -> fCdr = n;
    };
};

void SRListPosition :: deleteNext (void) {
    PRList n;

    n = fPosition -> fCdr;
    fPosition -> fCdr = fPosition -> fCdr -> fCdr;
    n -> fCdr = nil;
    delete n;
};
```

We have not included a search method in the class, though it could easily be done. Its protocol could be the same here as in `SList`:

```
virtual WhereFound search (PObject);
```

The code can be the same as that of `SList :: search`, except for the change of a few names.

10.1.2   An Extension of the Position Class

The positions of `RLists` can be extended by providing methods that insert or remove the first elements of the lists to which the positions refer. These extended positions of `SRLists` behave quite differently from those described above. In the previous model, a position is always a position in a given list, and that list never changes, although the contents of the list do. In this new model, a list position can become a position in another list, though only in two ways. If a position is used to append a value to the head of a list or remove the head of a list, the position automatically becomes a position in the new list. Otherwise, positions do not change lists. We have not included these methods in `SRListPosition` because of this anomalous behavior. However, if we wanted such methods, we might proceed as follows:

```
void SRListPosition :: insertFirst (PObject o);
void SRListPosition :: deleteFirst (void);
```

The difficulty is that within a method of a class we don't have a way to change this. This is why we didn't implement insertFirst in SRList. Here we are in an associated class and can therefore create a new list. However, we must be able to return this list outside the procedure, or creating it does no good. Our protocol for insertFirst was established in the original SList class. Although we could change it, since we are not inheriting from there, we do not, for cons in the RList class does the same thing. Therefore we extend the meaning of a position in this case so that the position automatically becomes a position in the new list. Thus a user will access the new list only by having access to the position itself.

```
void SRListPosition :: insertFirst (PObject o) {
    PRList n;

    fPosition = fList;
    n = newNonEmptyRList (o);
    n -> fCdr = fPosition;
    fPosition = n;
    fList = n; // Important---the list of this
               // has changed.
};
```

```
void SRListPosition :: deleteFirst (void) {
    PRList n;

    n = fList;
    fPosition = n -> fCdr;
    n -> fCdr = nil;
    if (n != nil) delete n;
    fList = fPosition; // The list of this has changed.
};
```

10.1.3 Functional Programming

Lisp introduced a form of programming called functional programming. The tradition has been carried on in more modern languages, such as Standard ML. The idea of functional programming is to program without variables, procedures, statements, loops, or an underlying model of changeable memory. "What else is there?" you ask. Expressions, functions, and constants, called values, are about all that is left. One programs functionally by defining and evaluating functions and naming their return results. The result is closer to mathematical purity than we can get in C or Pascal programming, which use a paradigm called imperative programming, or even than we get in C++, in which we have been using object programming. To a mathematician, a variable isn't something that can vary. It is a name for a definite value, though it can be unknown. Mathematicians also make functions and evaluate them in more and more complicated contexts. SRList provides a framework for functional programming if we are careful about modifying our lists and use car, cdr, and cons for most of our work. For example, a list with a few odd numbers in it would be the following (note that we have neglected to surround the integers with asInteger(), for the sake of brevity).

```
odds = cons (1, cons (3, cons (5, cons
              (7, cons (9, nil))))));
```

We could throw in a few negatives with

```
moreOdds = cons (-5, cons (-3, cons (-1, odds)));
```

The values in moreOdds are (in order) -5, -3, -1, 1, 3, 5, 7, and 9. We would get away from functional programming if we did some surgery on one of these lists, such as removing the 5 from odds. Note that we would change both lists if we did so, since odds is a sublist of moreOdds. However, such surgery is seldom necessary, since we can use an iterator to walk the list and construct a new list with the values desired, avoiding those we do not want. We could also construct such a list by evaluating a recursive function whose argument was odds. For example, the following works:

```
PRList butFive (PRList L) { // L is a list
                           // of SIntegers.
   if (L == nil)
      return nil ;
   else
      if (L -> car () -> equal (asInteger (5)))
         return butFive (L -> cdr ());
      else
         return cons (L -> car (),
                     butFive (L -> cdr ()));
};
```

This function returns with the same elements list as the original except that all the fives have been removed. Note that butFive is recursive and always operates recursively on a proper sublist of its input. This fact together with the fact that the empty list, nil, is separately provided for ensures that the recursion terminates. It is no accident that so many of our methods of this class are functions rather than procedures and that most of them return an SRList or a Boolean.

Using C++ functionally, we still need variables, of course (at least a few), but it is surprising what you can do with only function value parameters and return results. In particular, you can program without loops, using recursion to effect repetition. The example above shows this clearly. The next section applies the functional programming approach to binary trees.

Instead of `car` and `cdr` we have `root`, `leftTree`, and `rightTree`. We also have a `cons` but its protocol has been changed to allow for two children rather than the single part that we have called the rest.

10.2 THE BINARY TREE AS A TREE OF TREES

In this section we shall give an alternate, recursive, view of trees and implement them according to the new view. We define a nonempty tree as being composed of trees. This definition makes some things easier and some things more difficult. For example, subtrees are more easily discussed in this conceptualization. Deleting the root from a tree without invalidating external references to the tree or its parts, however, is harder. Distinguishing between a tree as a whole, and a tree as a part of another is also harder, though positions help in this. Also, disposing of these trees with the `delete` operator is rather dangerous, because other trees might be active subtrees or even supertrees of the tree we would like to free.

We saw earlier, in the discussion of lists, that a variety of abstract viewpoints can lead us to a variety of protocols for abstract data types, and from there to a variety of implementations. The same is true here.

Using the ideas from Section 9.1, we can make the following definition.

Binary Tree
   A binary tree is either

a.   empty, or
b.   a node, called the root, and a pair of binary trees, called, respectively, the left and right children of the root.

We shall see shortly that this definition presents us with some difficulties both in creating a suitable abstraction and in the implementation. In general, one wants to save data at some of the nodes of the tree. In various applications one uses the root, the interior nodes, or the external nodes to store data. As before, we shall store data at only the internal nodes and the root. The word *node* used here is different from our previous usage. Here it means the root of a tree or of one of its subtrees.

Here we need to implement the tree class, here called `SRTree`, a class for associated positions, and an associated iterator class. The nodes are incorporated into the tree abstraction.

```
class SRTree;
typedef SRTree *PRTree;
class SRTreePosition;
```

```
typedef SRTreePosition *PRTreePosition;
class SRTreeIterator;
typedef SRTreeIterator *PRTreeIterator;

PRTree newRTree ();
PRTree newNonEmptyRTree (PObject);

class SRTree: public SCollection {
    public:
         SRTree (PObject);
     virtual              ~SRTree ();
     virtual void         insertSubTree (PRTree);
     virtual char         subTree (PRTree);
     virtual char         isNil (void);
     virtual char         isLeaf (void);
     virtual PRTree       cons (PObject o,
                              PRTree right);
     virtual PObject      root (void);
     virtual PRTree       leftTree (void);
     virtual PRTree       rightTree (void);
     virtual PRTree       findParentOfHeir (PRTree);
     virtual PRTree       search (PObject);
     virtual PRTree       findParentOfRightmost
                              (void);
     virtual void         setLeftTree (PRTree);
     virtual void         setRightTree (PRTree);
     virtual void         insert (PObject);
     virtual void         remove (PObject);
     virtual char         empty (void);
     virtual PIterator    newIterator (void);
     virtual char         member (classtype c);
     virtual PObject      Clone (void);
     virtual void         writeIt (void);
     static PRTree         nil;

    protected:
       PObject fValue;
       PRTree fLeft;
       PRTree fRight;
       virtual int sizeOf (void);
    friend SRTreePosition;
    friend SRTreeIterator;
    friend void initRTrees (void);
};

PRTreePosition newRTreePosition (PRTree T);
```

```
class SRTreePosition: public SPosition {
   public:
           SRTreePosition (PRTree T);
       virtual PObject      at (void);
       virtual void         setToRoot (void);
       virtual void         moveLeft (void);
       virtual void         moveRight (void);
       virtual void         moveToParent (void);
       virtual void         insertLeft (PObject);
       virtual void         insertRight (PObject);
       virtual void         insertLeftTree (PRTree);
       virtual void         insertRightTree (PRTree);
       virtual char         member (classtype c);
       virtual PObject      Clone (void);
       virtual void         writeIt (void);

   protected:
      PRTree fTree;
      PRTree fPosition;
      virtual int sizeOf (void);
   friend SRTreeIterator;
};

class SRTreeIterator: public SIterator {
   public:
           SRTreeIterator (PRTree T);
       virtual              ~SRTreeIterator (void);
       virtual char         nextItem (PObject&);
       virtual void         reset (void);
       virtual char         member (classtype c);
       virtual PObject      Clone (void);

   protected:
      PRTreePosition fPosition;
      virtual int sizeOf (void);

};


void initRTrees (void);
// REQUIREMENTS For Use
//     InitRTrees
```

The instance variables are fLeft and fRight, which are the children, and fValue, which is the data held in the root. Because fLeft and fRight are of PRTree, the declaration is recursive, matching the recursive definition of a binary tree. There is a hidden implication here. The tree and the root of the tree are the same thing. If we modify the tree by changing its root, all external references to the tree as a whole become invalid. In addition, clients have the responsibility of keeping a reference to the tree as a whole when changing position in the tree.

The method subTree tells whether the SRTree provided as a parameter is a subtree of the receiver of the message. When the message insertLeft or insertRight is received, an SRTreePosition attaches an SRTree, with data provided as a parameter, as the left or right child subtree, respectively. The methods insertLeftTree and insertRightTree are similar, except that the tree to be inserted, rather than data for a new tree, is supplied. The methods leftTree and rightTree return the left and right children, respectively. Thus, to move about in a tree T, use a form such as

```
T = T -> leftTree ();
```

If T references some PRTree before this is executed, it will reference the left subtree of that PRTree afterward. If there is no left subtree, the reference T is not changed. Here we see the client's responsibility to maintain a reference to the tree as a whole. If T were our only reference to the tree before the above move to leftTree, all reference to the tree as a whole would have been lost.

All external nodes will be represented by a single tree, called nil. We shall think of this tree as being the only empty tree, similar to nil in SRList. Thus the initRTrees class initialization procedure and the SRTree constructor will look like the following. Because the generator function newRTree returns a reference to the empty tree, nil, we provide another generator for a nonempty RTree.

```
void initRTrees (void) {
    SRTree :: nil = new SRTree (NULL);
    failnull (SRTree :: nil);
    SRTree :: nil -> fLeft = SRTree :: nil;
    SRTree :: nil -> fRight = SRTree :: nil;
};

SRTree :: SRTree (PObject o) {
    fValue = o;
    fLeft = nil;
    fRight = nil;
};

PRTree newRTree () {
    return SRTree :: nil;
};
```

```
PRTree newNonEmptyRTree (PObject o) {
   PRTree result;

   result = new SRTree (o);
   failnull (result);
   return result;
};
```

As in `SRList`, we must not allow the destructor to delete the special tree `nil`.

```
SRTree :: ~SRTree () {
   if (this != nil && fLeft != nil) delete fLeft;
   if (this != nil && fRight != nil) delete fRight;
   if (this == nil) Error ("Deleting nil tree.");
};
```

We also must be able to check whether a tree is only an external node or, equivalently, whether the tree is empty, and whether a tree is only a leaf node. Therefore, `empty` returns TRUE only if it is sent to the `nil` tree. The `isLeaf` method serves a similar function, telling whether a tree represents a leaf of the tree it is in. A tree is a leaf if both of its children are `nil`.

```
char SRTree :: empty (void) {
   return this == nil;
};
```

```
char SRTree :: isLeaf (void) {
   return fLeft == nil && fRight == nil;
};
```

A binary tree whose children are all empty trees is called a leaf node. All such empty trees (definition *a*) are represented by the single value `nil`. A single value suffices for all because we do not intend to put data in the external nodes. A tree with two children (definition *b*) is called an internal node. One child of an internal node can be empty and the other a nonempty tree. One way of thinking of the `nil` tree when it is a child of some tree is that it represents a missing child of that tree.

Given this representation, the creation of a new tree from two given trees is easy. The primary creation method is `cons`, which is similar to the generator for `RList` except that when it is sent to a tree as a message it has two parameters: the data for the root of the new tree, and another tree that will become the right child of the new tree. The receiver, `this`, is the new tree's left child.

```
PRTree SRTree :: cons (PObject o, PRTree right) {
   PRTree result;

   result = newNonEmptyRTree (o);
   result -> fLeft = this;
   if (right != this)
      result -> fRight = right;
   else
      result -> fRight = nil;
   return result;
};
```

One way to picture a member of SRTree is to look at the individual instance variables of the tree and its subtrees. Suppose Atree is a PRTree whose right and left subtrees are the external nodes Y and Z, respectively. This tree might be defined as

```
Atree = newNonEmptyRTree (asCharacter('A'));
```

The tree might be depicted as in Fig. 10.3. If we then create and insert children of tree A with the following,

```
Z = newNonEmptyRTree (asCharacter('Z'));
Y = newNonEmptyRTree (asCharacter('Y'));
Atree -> setLeftTree (Z);
Atree -> setRightTree (Y);
```

we get the situation shown in Fig. 10.4. If we use arrows to point to the nodes referenced, we have Fig. 10.5.

The methods leftTree and rightTree are like the cdr method of lists, though we need two of them. Their implementation is trivial. That of leftTree is shown here:

```
PRTree SRTree :: leftTree (void) {
   return fLeft;
};
```

Note that if the left is a missing node, a reference to nil is returned.

The writeIt method performs a recursive walk of the tree and visits each node in the tree once. We must decide in which order to walk the tree, i.e., in which order the subtrees are to be processed. We shall use the in-order walk, in which the left subtree (if any) is processed first, then the tree or node itself, and then the right subtree (if any). This is carried

FIGURE 10.3

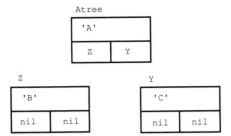

FIGURE 10.4

out recursively, so when a tree's left subtree is processed, that subtree's left subtree is processed first, etc. Thus for the tree shown in Fig. 10.6, the order of processing would be D, G, B, A, E, C, F. If we indicate by a lowercase *x* the positions in which the missing (nil) nodes would appear, we get x, D, G, B, x, A, E, C, F.

Because the tree itself is defined recursively in terms of its subtrees, the writeIt method is written naturally and best recursively. This is an application of our general principle that a recursive data structure to be processed as a whole can most easily be handled using recursion that parallels that of the definition. A pre-order version of writeIt is the following.

```
void SRTree :: writeIt (void) {
    if (this == nil) cout << "nil ";
    else {
        fValue -> writeIt (); cout << " ";
        if (fLeft != nil) fLeft -> writeIt ();
        if (fRight != nil) fRight -> writeIt ();
    };
};
```

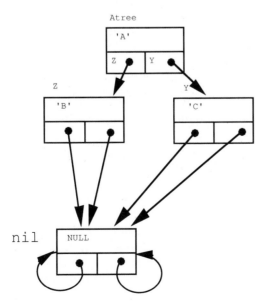

FIGURE 10.5

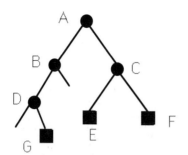

FIGURE 10.6

Note that `writeIt` is recursive in the sense that it sends the `writeIt` message to its subtrees. As usual in recursion, we need to guard against infinite recursion, so we are careful to send the `writeIt` message only when we know there is a subtree. Another way to say this is that we must allow recursion only on *proper* subtrees of the given tree. If `nil` sent `writeIt` to its children and no tests were done, we would iterate forever, since those children are `nil` themselves. An internal node sends `writeIt` to any of its children, but it walks the left subtree before it writes its own value, and it ends by walking the right subtree.

In another sense of the meaning, `writeIt` is not recursive. The original message `writeIt` is sent to some tree. In carrying out `writeIt`, that tree sends `writeIt` messages to two other trees, actually its children. Thus, the context in which `writeIt` is executed is different for each execution. In class `SBinaryTree`, the `writeIt` method from which we removed the recursion was recursive in the normal sense, as discussed in Section 9.4.

Consider the following test code. Note that `root` is needed to remember the root of the original tree so that we always maintain a reference to it.

```
PRTree r, s, root, t;

// Tree test.
r = newNonEmptyRTree (asCharacter ('F'));
r = nil -> cons (asCharacter ('C'), r);
s = newNonEmptyRTree (asCharacter ('D'));
t = newNonEmptyRTree (asCharacter ('E'));
t = s -> cons (asCharacter ('B'), t);
root = t -> cons (asCharacter ('A'), r);
root -> writeIt ();
```

This code generates the tree of Fig. 10.7 and should produce an in-order listing of the nodes, D, B, E, A, C, F.

For testing purposes (and for some applications) we can declare a global (hence static) integer variable `Level` and initialize it to −1. We can add a new method, `walk`, to `SRTree` that recursively writes out the current value of `Level` (instead of or in addition to the data in the node).

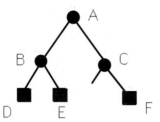

FIGURE 10.7

```
void SRTree :: walk () {
   ++Level;
   if (fLeft != nil)
      fLeft -> walk ();
   cout << Level;
   if (fRight != nil)
      fRight -> walk ();
   --Level;
};
```

Then, each time we call walk on some subtree, the Level is increased by one, and each time we return to the parent, Level is decreased. Thus the height of each node in the tree is printed out when it is visited. For the above test code we get

2 1 2 0 1 2

which are the heights of the nodes according to in-order protocol.
 We now must deal with the inherited methods needing to be overridden. Being a subclass of SCollection, SRTree needs insert and remove. We can implement insert as an error call as we did in SRList, or we may choose to insert the node anywhere. The method remove should find the data and remove it if present. Note that insert and remove reference data. A parallel method, insertSubTree, inserts an arbitrary tree into another. It is used by insert. Note that it is recursive and seeks a left-most missing node. The insertion can be made where the recursion eventually ends since at that point Left == nil is TRUE.

```
void SRTree :: insert (PObject o) {
   insertSubTree (newNonEmptyRTree (o));
};

void SRTree :: insertSubTree (PRTree t) {
   if (this != nil)
      if (fLeft == nil)
         fLeft = t;
      else
```

```
            fLeft -> insertSubTree (t);
};
```

To remove a subtree, we need a reference to its parent, because the tree must be modified at that point. We provide a recursive method, findParentOfHeir, to aid in this. It is passed to a tree, the heir, and it seeks the parent of that tree within the tree this. It returns nil if it is passed to an empty tree or if it seeks the parent of a tree that is not an heir or subtree of this. This function is difficult to understand if you try to trace it. It is an example of a case in which in order to believe that the recursive process does what is asked of it on a recursion, it is necessary to rely on its specifications. The specifications must be carefully implemented. In this case the specification is the following: If T is a subtree of this, but not the entire tree, findParentOfHeir returns a reference to the parent of T. Otherwise, it returns a reference to nil. If a tree is nil or if it can be immediately determined that T is a child of this, findParentOfHeir returns this (which might be nil). Otherwise, the tree is nonempty and T is neither the left or right child, though it can be an heir. Suppose we perform recursion on both child trees. One of the recursions returns nil by the specification. The other can return nil also or a reference to the parent of T. The recursion does not have to occur twice in all cases, for we might find what we want on the first recursion. We save the result of the first recursion. If it is nil, we perform the second recursion; otherwise, we return the result of the first. Setting the local variable o to this is a way of initializing o and thereby guaranteeing a testable value.

```
PRTree SRTree :: findParentOfHeir (PRTree T) {
    PRTree o;

    if (this == nil !! fLeft == T !! fRight == T)
        return this;
    else if (isLeaf ()) return nil;
    else {
        o = this;
        if (fLeft != nil)
            o = fLeft -> findParentOfHeir (T);
        if (fRight != nil && (o == this !! o == nil))
            o = fRight -> findParentOfHeir (T);
        return o;
    };
};
```

We need another auxiliary method to help in removal. It searches down the right branch of any tree until it can move no further to the right. Thus it is searching for nil as a right descendant. This is needed because we want to operate on a right child that has an open slot as *its* right child.

```
PRTree SRTree :: findParentOfRightmost (void) {
   PRTree result;

   result = nil;
   if (! (this == nil !! fRight == nil))
      if (fRight -> fRight == nil)
         result = this;
      else
         result = fRight -> findParentOfRightmost ();
   return result;
};
```

We now turn to the remove method of SRTree. This implementation does not permit us to remove the root node. See the implementation of binary search trees in the next section for a discussion of that problem. The many cases in the following were discussed in Chapter 9. The whole trick is to rearrange the nodes. A node with at most one child is needed so that we can find places to attach the (potential) two children of the node being removed. We don't need a leaf (no children) because when we prune a node with one child, the node's parent gets a free slot in which we can attach the child. (This promotes a grandchild to the position of a child.) Also, we could use an iterator to find the parent of the node being removed.

```
void SRTree :: remove (PObject o) {
   PRTree t, p, pr, r;
   if (o != NULL && !fValue -> equal (o)) {
      t = search (o);
      if (t != nil) {
         p = findParentOfHeir (t);
         if (t -> isLeaf ())
            if (p -> fLeft == t)
               p -> fLeft = nil;
            else
               p -> fRight = nil;
         else if (t -> fLeft == nil)
            if (p -> fLeft == t)
               p -> fLeft = t -> fRight;
            else
               p -> fRight = t -> fRight;
         else if (t -> fRight == nil)
            if (p -> fLeft == t)
               p -> fLeft = t -> fLeft;
            else
               p -> fRight = t -> fLeft;
```

```
        else if (t -> fLeft -> fRight == nil)
            if (p -> fLeft == t) {
                t -> fLeft -> fRight = t -> fRight;
                p -> fLeft = t -> fLeft;
            }
            else {
                t -> fLeft -> fRight = t -> fRight;
                p -> fRight = t -> fLeft;
            }
        else {
            pr = findParentOfRightmost ();
            r = pr -> fRight;
            r -> fRight = t -> fRight;
            pr -> fRight = r -> fLeft;
            r -> fLeft = t -> fLeft;
            if (p -> fLeft == t)
                p -> fLeft = r;
            else
                p -> fRight = r;
        };
    };
};
}; // See Exercise 10.13.
```

We do not dispose of the nodes removed, for a reason that is fundamental to our entire approach. We have not created these subtrees in methods of this class. They were created by clients by calling cons or some similar operation. Therefore, they should be disposed of by clients. After all, the client will often be depending on them.

10.2.1 SRTree **Positions**

As expected, the position class provides a means of operating on an SRTree at some location. It is much less useful here than with our original binary trees, since we have recursive methods of SRTree to do most of what is necessary. Sometimes, though, the surgery of inserting a subtree at some location is necessary. This class provides methods for insertions of both data and subtrees. In the case of data, the subtrees are created automatically. We should provide varying degrees of protection within these methods. Otherwise, for example, a tree that is already a subtree could be inserted into another. Worse, two trees could be inserted into each other. If this happens, all of our recursive procedures and most of the others are likely to run for a long time, causing the program to fail. A naive insertLeftTree is the following:

```
void SRTreePosition :: insertLeftTree (PRTree t) {
   if (fPosition != SRTree :: nil
       && fPosition -> fLeft == SRTree :: nil)
      fPosition -> fLeft = t;
};
```

We can improve on it by having it check whether either tree is a subtree of the other.

```
void SRTreePosition :: insertLeftTree (PRTree t) {
   if (! fPosition -> subTree (t)
       && ! t -> subTree (fPosition))
      fPosition -> fLeft = t;
};
```

This is a check only against inserting a node that would create a circular reference (such as in the case of two nodes of which each is the left child of the other). Such circularity would make the walk into an infinite recursion. We can still create a structure that is not a tree, as in the following

```
t = newNonEmptyRTree (asCharacter ('B'));
t1 = newNonEmptyRTree (asCharacter ('C'));
r = t -> cons (asCharacter ('A'), t1);
s = r;
r = r -> left;
rp = newRTreePosition (r);
rp -> insertLeftTree (t1);
```

The last insertLeftTree inserts a node t1 into r and hence into s. The insertion will not be prevented. t1 is not in the tree rooted at r, because we changed the reference r, but it is in the tree rooted at s. Therefore s is no longer a tree, since it has two references to t1.

Theorem: In the new versions of insertRightTree and insertLeftTree, if T1 appears as a descendant of T0 in some tree, T0 does not appear as a descendant of T1. Thus circularity is prevented.

Proof: Assume the contrary. In this case, T0 must have been made a descendant of T1 either after T1 was made a descendant of T0 or before. The two cases are symmetric, so assume the former. In this case, when we attempt the insertion, say Tx -> insertLeftTree (T0) (for some Tx, either T1 or a descendant), the guard (! t -> subTree (this)) replies FALSE (because t = T0 contains this == Tx as subTree at this time, since it contains T1, which contains Tx). Thus, the guard prevents the insertion.

Note however, that T1 could be a descendant of several nodes of the tree, destroying the tree property.

10.2.2 SRTree **Iterators**

Iterators of this class are similar to those of the ordinary SBinaryTree. As before, we must return the item at the current position and then move to the next pre-order or in-order position. Here we shall see only a pre-order iterator. Note that the next pre-order position of a tree is well defined. We just need to be certain that when we finish the left branch of any subtree, we correctly climb to the top node in the right branch of that tree. This requires that we know whether we are climbing up the left or the right branch of the tree. Note that if we are to use iterators extensively in large trees, we need a better way to move upward. Providing a reference in each node to its parent would be such a way. Providing a stack of ancestors is another. In this case moveToParent would take a single step, rather than a scan of the tree.

```
char SRTreeIterator :: nextItem (PObject o&) {
    PRTree here;
    char result, doneClimbing;

    result = !fDone;
    if (result) {
        o = fPosition -> at ();
        if (fPosition -> fPosition -> fLeft
            != SRTree :: nil)
          fPosition -> moveLeft ();
        else if (fPosition -> fPosition -> fRight
                != SRTree :: nil)
          fPosition -> moveRight ();
        else {
            here = fPosition -> fPosition;
            doneClimbing = FALSE;
            while (!doneClimbing) {
                if (fPosition -> fPosition ==
                    fPosition -> fTree)
                  doneClimbing = TRUE;
                else {
                    here = fPosition -> fPosition;
                    fPosition -> moveToParent ();
                    if (fPosition -> fPosition -> fRight
                        != here
                      && fPosition -> fPosition -> fRigh
                        != SRTree :: nil)
                      doneClimbing = TRUE;
                };
            };
            if (fPosition -> fPosition -> fRight
```

```
                    != here
                    && fPosition -> fPosition -> fRight
                        != SRTree :: nil)
                    fPosition -> moveRight ();
                else
                    fDone = TRUE;
            };
        };
        return result;
    };
```

<h2>10.3   THE BINARY SEARCH TREE AS A SPECIAL CASE OF SRTREE</h2>

Just as we may define binary search trees as a subclass of SBinaryTree, we could define them as a subclass of SRTree.

```
class SRBinarySearchTree;
typedef SRBinarySearchTree *PRBinarySearchTree;

PRBinarySearchTree newRBinarySearchTree ();

// INVARIANT: In every subtree the
// data in the left subtree must
// be less than the data in the root,
// and the data in the right
// subtree must be greater.

class SRBinarySearchTree: public SRTree {
    public:
            SRBinarySearchTree ();
        virtual void        insert (PObject);
        virtual void        remove (PObject);
        virtual PRTree      search (PObject);
        virtual char        member (classtype c);
        virtual PObject     Clone (void);
        virtual void        writeIt (void);

    protected:
        virtual int     sizeOf (void);

};
```

The constructor, SRBinarySearchTree, is just a call to SRTree. The insertion can be done in a number of ways, and we shall show a simple one here. It involves always inserting at a missing position. First, we determine that the data item o is not in the tree (this) already. This determination requires a search. The structure of the tree, however, guarantees that we need only search a single path from the root to some leaf or external node, because if o is not in a node, its value relative to the value in that node tells us whether we should continue the search down the left or the right subtree. If we haven't found o by the time we reach a leaf or a missing node, we must create a new child of that leaf or create a node in place of the missing node.

```
void SRBinarySearchTree :: insert (PObject o) {
    if (o -> member (magnitude)) {
        if (o -> less (fValue))
            if (fLeft -> empty ()) fLeft
                = newRBinarySearchTree (o);
            else fLeft -> insert (o);
        else // Greater or equal.
            if (fRight -> empty ()) fRight
                = newRBinarySearchTree (o);
            else fRight -> insert (o);
    };
};
```

The code is recursive, of course. If o is less than fValue but we are not at a leaf or the parent of a missing node on the left, we begin another recursion by sending insert to the left subtree. If the item is greater than or equal to the value at the current location, we insert into the right subtree, either by recursion or by replacing a missing tree directly. We cannot insert into an empty SRBinarySearchTree or insert at the root of an existing one, for the same reason that we cannot insert at the head of an empty SRList: such insertion would change the structure itself, and the fact of the change would not be communicated back to the user holding a reference to the current root.

We implement a new search method because it will be much more efficient here than in SRTree, because the magnitudes of the elements can guide us down the tree. From any node we only need to search one branch.

```
PRTree SRBinarySearchTree :: search (PObject o) {
    if (this == nil !! fValue -> equal (o))
        return this;
    else if (o -> less (fValue))
        return fLeft -> search (o);
    else
        return fRight -> search (o);
};
```

The remove method is rather tricky, because we must remove the node that contains o but preserve the descendants of that node. Our solution could be to leave most of the data nodes intact and just move the content, fValue, but this would contradict our basic idea about what constitutes a tree. The tree is composed of trees, and external references to some of the subtrees are likely here. In the last chapter we had an entirely different situation than we have here, because the nodes there were private entities. Here the nodes are just other trees. We want these references to subtrees to remain valid. Therefore our solution involves surgery on the tree, pruning and grafting the subtrees as appropriate. In this implementation we cannot prune the root, because it represents the whole tree. We cannot destroy this in a method. Thus we compromise, avoiding removal of the root. (Again, the alternate abstraction/implementation shown in Chapter 9 is an improvement on this.) We can also make remove into a function that returns a reference to the tree with the removed item. Generally this is a reference to the former root. However, if we remove the root itself, the returned reference is to the new root. Our strategy is simply to avoid removing the root. However, since our trees may contain the same data several times, and since we insert multiple items to the right in insert, we shall also attempt to remove the item from the right subtree if we find it at the root.

```
void SRBinarySearchTree :: remove (PObject o) {
   PRTree t, p, r, target;

   if (this != nil)
      if (fValue -> equal (o))
         fRight -> remove (o);
      else {
         t = search (o);
         if (! t -> empty ()) {
            p = findParentOfHeir (t);
            if (t -> isLeaf ()) target = newRTree ();
            else if (t -> leftTree () -> empty ())
               target = t -> rightTree ();
            else if (t -> rightTree () -> empty ())
               target = t -> leftTree ();
            else if (t -> leftTree () -> rightTree ()
                        -> empty ()) {
               t -> leftTree () -> setRightTree
                  (t -> rightTree ());
               target = t -> leftTree ();
            }
            else {
               r = t -> leftTree () ->
                  findParentOfRightmost ();
               target = r -> rightTree ();
               r -> setRightTree (r -> rightTree ()
                                     -> leftTree ());
               target -> setRightTree
```

```
                     (t -> rightTree ());
            };
            if (p -> leftTree () == t)
                p -> setLeftTree (target);
            else
                p -> setRightTree (target);
        };
    };
};
```

First we locate the tree t, which is the node containing o, as well as its parent, p, being careful about our implementation of missing nodes. We want to prune t from the tree, so first we calculate the node, target, that will appear where t now appears in the pruned tree. If t is an external node, there will be no new node when we finish, so the parent, p, will reference nil; thus we now make target a reference to newRTree. Otherwise, we must replace t with another node while preserving the binary search tree property. We choose a node with one or more missing children to replace the target, because such a node has fewer children to worry about. To maintain the binary search tree property, we want a node whose data is greater than that in its left subtree and less than that in its right subtree. A suitable node is the node with the largest data in the left subtree of the current location t. This node is always one step to the left and zero or more steps to the right from t, where we cannot step any further without stepping out of the tree. Thus we have a node with a missing right subtree. Therefore we check whether there must be any right steps after a single left step. If not, we just promote the left child of the target, being careful to preserve the right subtree of t, if any exists. If we must take right steps, we do so until we can take no more and then replace t with this node while again maintaining the right subtree of t and the left subtree of the node promoted.

10.4   AN IMPLEMENTATION OF SETS USING BINARY SEARCH TREES

We have seen that a set can be designed using instance variables in SList. Here we will give a different implementation and, in fact, a different implementation strategy. The notes at the beginning of Section 10.3 suggest that SSet can be made a subclass of SRBinarySearchTree, and indeed this is so. SSet can also be implemented using a binary search tree as an instance variable. The following is nearly our original declaration of SSet. The most significant difference is that we use an instance variable, fElements, in class PBinarySearchTree. Here we are using our first implementation of binary search trees from Chapter 9, rather than the one of the last section.

Our reason for demonstrating a new class is that it is advantageous to have both kinds of set implementations available and to be able to compare them within one library. In fact, this is just a different implementation of SSet.

```
class SBSTSet;
typedef SBSTSet *PBSTSet;

PBSTSet newBSTSet ();

class SBSTSet: public SCollection {
    public:
            SBSTSet ();
        virtual              ~SBSTSet ();
        virtual void         insert (PObject);
        virtual void         remove (PObject);
        virtual PBSTSet      setUnion (PBSTSet);
        virtual PBSTSet      intersection (PBSTSet);
        virtual PBSTSet      allBut (PObject);
        virtual char         subset (PBSTSet);
        virtual int          cardinality (void);
        virtual char         element (PObject);
        virtual PIterator    newIterator (void);
        virtual char         member (classtype c);
        virtual PObject      Clone (void);
        virtual void         writeIt (void);

    protected:
        PBinarySearchTree fElements;
        virtual int sizeOf (void);

};


// REQUIREMENTS For Use.
//     All inserted elements are in some subset
//     of SMagnitude. initBinaryTrees ();
```

Initialization requires creation of a new binary search tree in which to hold the data.

```
SBSTSet :: SBSTSet () {
    fElements = newBinarySearchTree ();};
```

Most of the other methods just pass on some message to fElements, as in

```
void SBSTSet :: insert (PObject o) {

    if (!element (o))
        fElements -> insert (o);
};
```

The `element` method can use the `find` method of a binary search tree position.

```
char SBSTSet :: element (PObject o) {
   char result;
   PBinarySearchTreePosition P;
   result = FALSE;
   P = fElements -> newPosition ();
   P -> find (o);
   if (o -> equal (P -> at ())) result = TRUE;
   delete P;
   return result;
};
```

The code for union and intersection can be as we have seen before, utilizing the already implemented `insert` method and iterators to obtain the values of one of the operands.

10.5   POSITIONS REVISITED: ENSURING SAFE DELETIONS

Our implementation and use of iterators in lists and trees has a small flaw. Iterators are good for many things, but they are dangerous for removing data (and nodes) in these structures. The iterator automatically changes positions, and it usually changes position to the next item to be returned just before returning from the method call that produces the current item. An iterator used to delete items will fail if the item returned is used to find the item to be removed and if that removed item happens to be the item at the position currently being saved within the iterator. In this section a method for making such changes safe will be outlined.

The problem is with the positions rather than the iterators themselves. Therefore we shall modify the position class, using binary trees to illustrate the method. We could incorporate these changes into `SBinaryTree`, but we prefer to create a new subclass to contain these enhanced facilities. This is in line with the philosophy that the system should be extended by subclassing rather than modification; the modification of a class could cause some earlier client of the hierarchy to fail. The new class is called `SRegistrationTree`, because it requires every position created to be registered with the tree it is a position of. The tree then knows about all of its positions. Thus, when a tree is modified by deletion of a node, it can inform all registered positions that the node is about to be destroyed so that they can take defensive action. Only the methods required for our purposes are shown. We need a number of others, such as clone and insert.

```
class SRegistrationTree;
class SRegistrationTreePosition;

typedef SRegistrationTree *PRegistrationTree;
```

```
typedef SRegistrationTreePosition
  *PRegistrationTreePosition;

PRegistrationTree newRegistrationTree (void);

class SRegistrationTree: public SBinaryTree {
  public:
        SRegistrationTree ();
     virtual char     member (classtype c);
     virtual void     notifyAll (SBinaryTree ::
                                    PBinaryTreeNode);
     virtual void     Register
                         (PRegistrationTreePosition);
     virtual void     DeRegister
                         (PRegistrationTreePosition);
     virtual void     remove (PObject);
     virtual PBinaryTreePosition     newPosition
                                        (void);
  protected:
     PList fRegisteredPositions;
     virtual int sizeOf (void);
};

class SRegistrationTreePosition:
  public SBinaryTreePosition {
  public:
        SRegistrationTreePosition
           (PRegistrationTree);
     virtual          ~SRegistrationTreePosition
                         (void);
     virtual char     member (classtype c);
     virtual void     notify (SBinaryTree
                                 :: PBinaryTreeNode);

  protected:
     virtual int   sizeOf (void);

  friend SRegistrationTree;
};

// REQUIREMENTS For Use
//    initLists ();
//    initBinaryTrees ();
```

An SRegistrationTree has a list of the positions that are registered with it. Initialization therefore requires creation of this list.

```
SRegistrationTree :: SRegistrationTree () {
   fRegisteredPositions = newList ();
};
```

When a new position is created it registers itself. SRegistration-Tree provides this registration service.

```
void SRegistrationTree
   :: Register (PRegistrationTreePosition p) {
   fRegisteredPositions -> insert (p);
};
```

All that is required of positions is that they use the service when they are created.

```
SRegistrationTreePosition
   :: SRegistrationTreePosition (PRegistrationTree t)
   SBinaryTreePosition (t) {
      t -> Register (this);
};
```

Also, when a position is notified of the destruction of a node, it must do something sensible if it is referencing that position. Otherwise, it can ignore the notification. Here we just set the position to the root, though that is not the best method if iterators use positions. (Why?)

```
void SRegistrationTreePosition
   :: notify (BinaryTree :: PBinaryTreeNode n) {
      if (fHere == n) setToRoot ();
};
```

An SRegistrationTree notifies all of its positions when it is about to destroy a node.

```
void SRegistrationTree :: notifyAll
                          (PBinaryTreeNode n) {
   PIterator IT;
   PObject anItem;

   IT = fRegisteredPositions -> newIterator ();
   while (IT -> nextItem (anItem))
      if (anItem -> member (registrationtreeposition))
         PRegistrationTreePosition (anItem)
            -> notify (n);
      else
         Error("Not a registration position.");
```

```
        delete IT;
    };
```

All the removal methods of this class and associated classes (such as SRegistrationTreePosition itself) must send the notifyAll message to the tree just before destroying any node. For example, in remove we see the call just before execution of removeNode.

```
void SRegistrationTree :: remove (PObject o) {
    PRegistrationTreePosition p, q;
    PBinaryTreeNode n;
    PObject aValue;

    p = PRegistrationTreePosition (newPosition ());
    p -> find (o);
    aValue = p -> at (); // Bug.  Position p
                            // can be NULL;
    if (o -> equal (aValue)) {
        q = PRegistrationTreePosition
            (newPosition ());
        q -> moveTo (p);
        while (! q -> leaf ()) {
            q -> moveLeft ();
            while (! q -> noRight ())
                q -> moveRight ();
        };
        p -> exchangeValues (q);
        n = q -> fHere;
        notifyAll (n); // We are about to modify
                        // the tree.
        removeNode (n);
        delete q;
    };
    delete p;
};
```

Finally, an SRegistrationTree provides a deregistration service so that a position will be able to deregister when it frees.

10.6   **SOME ADVANCED IDEAS: BALANCED TREES**

The main reason for using binary search trees, rather than lists, for implementing sets is the (potential) difference in efficiency in the element method. In list implementations, the expected number of probes into the collection to determine whether an item is a member is about half the size of the set. For large sets this can be costly in time. In implementations using binary search trees, the expected number of probes is about equal to the length of the path in the tree that would contain the data item. If the data is inserted into the tree in random order, this length is about $\log_2 N$ (often written $\mathrm{Lg}(N)$), where N is the number of nodes in the tree. Of course, if the data are inserted in order of their magnitude, the tree degenerates into a list. The difference between N and $\mathrm{Lg}(N)$ is dramatic for large N. When N is 1,000,000, $\mathrm{Lg}(N)$ is about 20. Users are likely to notice the time difference between half a million probes and 20 probes.

We can ensure that the storage tree does not degenerate into a list by keeping it balanced as we insert. A tree is balanced if every leaf is of the same height. There are various definitions of degree of balance, but all require that the minimum height of a leaf (or missing node) and the maximum leaf height are not too dissimilar. Two standard techniques are AVL trees and 2-3-4 trees. An AVL tree (named for the creators, Adel'son-Vel'skii and Landis) is a binary search tree in which the left and right subtrees differ in height by no more than one and are themselves AVL trees. A 2-3-4 tree is a tree in which every leaf is of the same height, each node is a leaf or has 2, 3, or 4 children, each of which is a 2-3-4 tree, and more than one item is stored. In fact, as in a binary tree node, there is one less item than there are children. Thus a node with four children will store three values. In both AVL trees and 2-3-4 trees the tree property is maintained by complicating the `insert` as well as `delete` algorithms, and in each case the trade-off is in speeding up the lookup algorithm.

Theorem: Globally, no leaf in an AVL tree is of more than twice the height of any other.

Proof (by induction on the height, k, of the tree T): The theorem is certainly true for any AVL tree of height 0 or 1, as enumeration will show. So assume that $k > 1$ and that the theorem is true for all AVL trees of height less than k. Let T be an AVL tree of height k. Then T $\rightarrow$ fLeft and T $\rightarrow$ fRight are AVL trees, and their heights differ by no more than 1, so their heights are either $k - 1$ or $k - 2$, and one of them, say T $\rightarrow$ fLeft, is of height $k - 1$. We won't discuss the case where T $\rightarrow$ fRight is of height $k - 1$, because it is easier than the other. Thus, assume that T $\rightarrow$ fRight is of height $k - 2$. Then no node in T $\rightarrow$ fLeft is of height (in T) less than $\frac{1}{2}(k - 1) + 1 = \frac{1}{2}(k + 1)$, and no node in T $\rightarrow$ fRight is of height (in T) less than $\frac{1}{2}(k - 2) + 1 = \frac{1}{2}k$. So no node in the tree is of height less than $\frac{1}{2}k$. Because k is the maximum height, so the theorem is proved. (Note the need for two base cases, 0 and 1, because we reduce the induction by 1 or 2 to $k - 1$ or $k - 2$. We are thus guaranteed in the induction to hit one of the base cases in either situation.)

An AVL tree can have a node at twice the height of another. For example, in the AVL tree of Fig. 10.8, the leftmost leaf is of height 4 and the rightmost

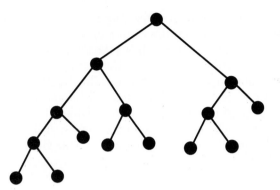

FIGURE 10.8

only of 2. Still, even though some nodes are much farther from the root than others, none are very far, as we needed fifteen nodes to construct the example, and its height is only 4. The height of an AVL tree with N nodes is no greater than $2 \log_2 N$. Therefore, the nearest leaf to the root is at a height, greater than or equal to $\log_2 N$. An AVL tree, then, has good, but not perfect, balance.

Balance is maintained in an AVL tree by storing in each node the difference in height between the left and right subtrees (always 0, +1, or −1). Then, when `insert` or `delete` is performed at some position, that information is used to adjust the tree, if necessary, by rotating the data about some node. Rotations can be to either the left or the right; a leftward rotation is shown in Fig. 10.9. We want to rotate leftward about the node named g in the first picture. The result is shown at the right, where the g node has moved down the tree to the left, the p node has been promoted,

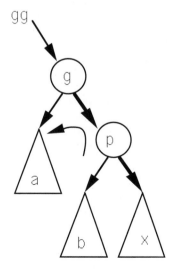
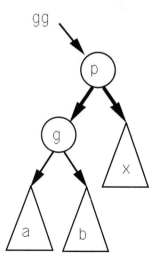

FIGURE 10.9

and the former left child of p has become the new right child of g. Note that the tendency is to shorten the right side while lengthening the left, usually improving the balance. (It may leave the degree of balance unaffected. Why?) The trick is to perform such a rotation, or a slightly more complicated one, at the right place in the tree to maintain the AVL property.

A 2-3-4 tree is defined to be perfectly balanced; every leaf is of the same height. The height of the tree is somewhere between $\log_2 N$ and $\log_4 N$, and the search time is similar to that of an AVL tree, the shorter height being made up for by the complication of searching each node for the given value. To learn more about balanced trees consult [Sedgewick, 1988] or [Manber, 1989].

10.7   SUMMARY

Trees and lists can be considered to be built either from nodes and arcs or from other trees and lists. In this chapter we adopted the latter view. The structure is nearly parallel to the earlier development in Chapter 6 and Chapter 9, except that the new concept imposes a few constraints; namely, constraints on what happens at the location representing the structure as a whole. The root of an SRTree cannot be removed, for example.

We also examined tight linkages between trees and tree positions in our registration tree class. Objects in one class can be given detailed knowledge about other objects that must coordinate with them. This registration and signaling facility is very useful in many software projects.

Finally, more advanced algorithms can do a lot to keep a tree's height balanced, thereby making searching for individual items much faster than in the general case.

EXERCISES

10.1 (10.1) Using only car, cdr, and cons, and if statements and recursive procedures but no loops, devise a list reversal function. This method takes a list as input and produces the reverse of the list as output. Hint: First write a recursive function that moves the head of a list to its last position. Also, think about lists of zero, one, and two elements. They might be special cases, and their correct handling might prevent your recursion from running forever.

10.2 (10.1) Using only car, cdr, and cons, and if statements and recursive procedures but no loops, devise a selection sort method for SRList. Hint: Write a function that returns the minimum of a list. Then write another function that returns the contents of a list with its minimum removed. Build selection sort out of these two functions.

10.3 (10.1) (Harder) Try an insertion sort using the same limitations as in the previous two problems.

10.4 (10.1) Implement a Boolean functional method sublist in class SRList that tells whether this is a sublist of the argument (another SRList).

Implement a Boolean functional method, `intersect`, in `SRList` that tells whether `this` and the argument have any common elements.

10.5 (10.1) Write a recursive `Clone` method for `SRList`. Make sure you don't clone `nil` but just return a reference to it if asked to clone it. Write a nonrecursive version that uses an `SRList` position to walk the list being created and an `SRList` iterator to get the data out of the list being cloned (which is `this`, of course).

10.6 (10.1) Another challenge. Write a `merge` method using `car`, `cdr`, and `cons` rather than members of `SRListPosition`. The protocol is

```
PRList merge (PRList l); // Merge this and l into
                         //       single list.
    //Pre-elements in both lists are in SMagnitude
    //and sorted by less.
```

Use a synonym for `this`, such as s (s = `this`). Don't be afraid to say l = l -> cdr () to move down the list. The parameter l is just a local variable. Don't try to free anything in this method. In effect, l and s are like positions. You will need to write a new (recursive) method, `insertLast`, that takes an object and returns a new list with that object in the last position. The rest of the list should be a copy of the elements of `this` in their original order. For example, `insertLast` (5) sent to the list (1, 3, 4) should return (1, 3, 4, 5). (Again we have used ordinary integers as data, but of course we need objects.)

10.7 (10.1) Implement a `search` method in the class `SRList`. Its input is an object, and it produces the sublist of which that object is the `car` if the object is in the list and `nil` otherwise. The method should be a recursive function.

10.8 (10.2) Write a method that finds the lowest common ancestor of two nodes in a binary tree. What class should the method be in? What is its protocol? How can we best implement it?

10.9 (10.2) Rebuild the `insert` method of Section 10.2 so that it does indeed add the node if there is no node in the tree with the same data. Why might it be important to preserve a node, especially a node that was created outside the tree? What about possible children of the node? What conditions should be imposed on a node inserted into a binary search tree?

10.10 (10.2) Use `findParentOfRightmost` and its companion `findParentOf-LeftMost` to permit removals of the root. Since `this` can't be destroyed, find an appropriate value, swap the values without swapping the nodes (which are trees here), and remove the node from the bottom of the tree that had the value now in the root. The value you want is either the largest value in the left subtree or the smallest in the right. If a tree is just a single node you are stuck. `remove` cannot remove it.

10.11 (10.3) Add the rest of the needed methods to the class `SRBinarySearch Tree`, its position class, and, if needed, an iterator class. What form of iterator is needed? Will the pre-order iterator suffice?

10.12 (10.3) Our strategy for removing an object found at the root of a recursive binary search tree is not very good. Why not? Consider the case in which we have initialized such a tree with 5 and then immediately inserted a 7 followed by another 5. What will our method do if we try to remove 5? Suppose we inserted the second 5 before we inserted the 7?

10.13 (10.5) `SRegistrationTree :: remove` has a bug. Correct it.

10.14 (10.6) Refer to Exercise 6.2. Demonstrate that in such a (balanced) tree the running time of `SBinaryTree :: find` is $O(\log_2 n)$. Such an algorithm is called logarithmic. Does this imply that `find` is $O(\log_2 n)$? Why or why not? What is the order of the running time of `SBinaryTreeIterator :: nextItem`, linear, logarithmic, quadratic, or other?

10.15 (10.6) Use the theorem on AVL trees to prove the corollary that the height of an AVL tree with N nodes is less than or equal to $2\log_2(N + 1)$.

10.16 (10.6) Define a Fibonacci-like sequence, $FIBP(k)$, by the following: $FIBP(k) = 1$ if $k < 0$, and $FIBP(k) = 1 + FIBP(k - 1) + FIBP(k - 2)$ otherwise. Show by induction that the minimum number of nodes of an AVL tree with height k is $FIBP(k)$.

10.17 (10.6) Implement AVL trees by creating a subclass of `SBinarySearchTree`. (See [Manber, 1989].)

## CHAPTER 11

THE MOST IMPORTANT MAGNITUDE CLASSES

Hush, never tell me; I take it much unkindly
That thou, Iago, who hast had my purse
As if the strings were thine, shouldst know of this.

    Shakespeare, *Othello*

Thou that didst bear the key of all my counsels,
That knew'st the very bottom of my soul,

    Shakespeare, *Henry V*

In this chapter we shall develop implementations for a number of important magnitude classes, such as integers and associations. Magnitudes are objects that in some sense have size. Their sizes are compared with the sizes of other objects (in their own classes) using the method less. Objects in this class interpret the equal message differently from other classes. In SObject equal is implemented to mean object identity. Two objects are equal only if they are really one object, perhaps referred to by aliases. Among magnitudes equal means of equal size. In particular, two members of SAssociation can be different objects and still be equal. The class SMagnitude, on which these classes are built, is a special kind of abstract class called a mixin. SMagnitude is used only by building another class that inherits both from it and from SObject or one of its subclasses.

11.1　　　　　　INTEGERS AS OBJECTS

One of the fundamental difficulties of C++, and of any language such as Object Pascal in which objects have been incorporated into another language, is that not every datum is an object. Ordinary `int`, `char`, and `struct` variables still occur in C++ just as in C. The situation is different in Smalltalk, where everything is an object, including the methods themselves. Occasionally built-in values must be treated as if they were objects. For example, we might want to push some integers onto an object in class `SStack`. This section shows how to make integers behave like objects. Said another way, it shows how to make a class of objects behave like integers. The class is called `SInteger`. As magnitudes, the objects of `SInteger` must implement some comparison operators, such as `less` and `equal`. In order to behave like integers, such objects must also respond to integer operations, such as addition.

An important consideration in class `SInteger` is that if its objects are to model the integers accurately, we must deal with the fact that there is only one integer 5, and only one 52. If we ask whether 5 `==` 5, the answer must be yes regardless of how we arrived at the 5 on each side of the comparison. Five is a unique concept, representing the size of a certain class of sets: the sets with five elements. If we were only to create an object, `FirstFive`, with an instance variable `fValue`, set to 5, and then repeat the process, creating another object, `otherFive`, with `fValue` set to 5, we would not achieve the desired effect. We would not get `firstFive` `==` `otherFive`. We could get `firstFive` `->` `equal` `(otherFive)` if we build the `equal` method correctly, but because these other objects are magnitudes `equal` compares the sizes and not their identities. We would like to ensure that integer objects that have the same values are identical.

The solution is to implement `SInteger` in a way that gives us more control over the creation of the objects and expresses to the users of this class the idea that the objects are special. When they ask for an object for 5, they get a reference to the unique object that represents that value, and no matter how the object that is to represent a 5 is generated it must be a reference to the standard object. Part of our communication to our users is to use a different generator function for this class from the one used in most other classes. We do not call the generator function `newInteger`, because the name implies creation of a new thing. We want another name that has no such implications. The name we use is `asInteger`. The implication of the name is that we consider an ordinary integer as an `SInteger`. Therefore, `asInteger` `(5)` returns a reference to the unique object representing the integer 5. Similarly,

```
asInteger (2) -> add (asInteger (3))
```

which is one way to add two such objects, should return a reference to that same object 5. Our specification of the class hints that something strange is going on by requiring that lists be initialized before the class is. Otherwise, the methods of the class are not remarkable.

```
class SInteger;
typedef SInteger *PInteger;

// WARNING: Do not create new Integer objects
// directly. Do not declare objects of type SInteger
// and do not call new SInteger. Call the access
// function asInteger(long) instead.

class SInteger: public SMagnitude, public SObject {
    public:
        virtual char        member (classtype c);
        virtual long        value (void);
        virtual PObject     ShallowClone (void);
        virtual PObject     Clone (void);
        virtual char        less (PObject m);
        virtual char        equal (PObject m);
        virtual PInteger    add (PInteger a);
        virtual PInteger    subtract (PInteger a);
        virtual PInteger    multiply (PInteger a);
        virtual PInteger    divide (PInteger a);
        virtual void        writeIt (void);
    protected:
        long fValue;
        virtual int sizeOf (void);
        SInteger (long v);
    friend PInteger asInteger (long);
    friend PInteger createIt (int where, long i);
    friend char findIt (PInteger o, long i,
                        PInteger &aValue);
};

void initIntegers (void);

// REQUIREMENTS For Use
//     initLists ();
//     initIntegers ();
```

The trick we shall use to achieve our goals for SInteger is to create an integer object with a given value only once, and to remember that we have done so. If the same integer is required in the future, we look it up and return a reference to the one created earlier. Thus we must save all such objects, in some collection mechanism. However, we shall be more sophisticated than simply to store them in a list, because of the long time it can take to search a list for a value if there are many values. Instead, we shall use the specialized lookup mechanism called a hash table.

11.1.1   Implementing Integers Using Hash Tables

A hash table is a storage mechanism that is optimized for lookup. If possible, we want a lookup to take a small fixed time independent of how much data is in the storage structure. One possibility for this is an array, but then we are limited by the size of the array. What we use instead is an array of lists, giving us a good trade-off between the speed of lookup and the amount of information we can store. See Fig. 11.1.

Since we have an array of lists, we need a well-determined way to find the particular list an object should be inserted into. This is where hash comes in. The idea of hash comes from high diner cuisine. Take a bunch of food, onions and corned beef and whatever else is lying around the counter, chop it finely so that it is barely recognizable, and throw it into the skillet. The chopping, which is the key step in hash, is not so much to hide the details as to achieve uniformity in the product with the individual elements thoroughly interspersed. More will be said about this shortly.

All of our objects know a method named hash that returns an ordinary nonnegative long integer. There doesn't need to be any sense at all about the value returned, except that the same object should always return the same value. (Don't implement it with a randomizer.) It is better if the value is unrelated to the object itself, for reasons that will be made clear shortly. If

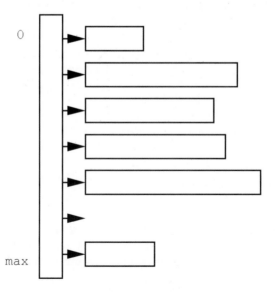

FIGURE 11.1

we look back at SObject, we see that we take a simple approach and just use the address of the object itself with a minor arithmetic transformation. The variable this is a pointer, and we type-cast it to a long integer, in effect using it as an address.

```
long SObject :: hash (void) {
    return (labs (long (this)) / 3);
};
```

The set of objects that yield the same result as a given hash function is called a hash bucket, though sometimes that term is reserved for only those objects actually in use rather than the larger set of potentially used objects. The above hash function will not be used with SInteger because we need to be able to hash an ordinary long integer as well as an object in order to make this system work. It will be used in the next chapter when hash dictionaries are discussed.

Within our implementation file PInteger.cp we declare the following constant and variable.

```
const int size = 68;

PList Integers[size];
```

The purpose of initIntegers is to initialize this array, which cannot be seen or used outside this file. We also need to initialize lists somewhere, because of the element type of the array. We don't do that here, though, because it should be done only once, and the user of a list unit will expect to have to do that elsewhere anyway. We don't even create new lists for the array. We just set all the elements to NULL. The constant value of size is arbitrary in this case. In the following discussion we use max for the constant (size − 1).

```
void initIntegers (void) {
    int i;

    for (i = 0; i < size; ++i) Integers[i] = NULL;
};
```

The array Integers is called a bucket table, and each list stored in the array holds the members of one hash bucket that appear in a given program. Now that the array of lists has been initialized, we are ready to accept requests for SIntegers via asInteger.

```
int index (long m) {
    int result;
```

```
      result = int (m);
      return (abs (result) %size);
   };

char findIt (PInteger o, long i, PInteger &aValue) {
   char result;

   result = FALSE;
   if (o -> fValue == i) {
      result = TRUE;
      aValue = o;
      };
   return result;
};

PInteger createIt (int where, long i) {
   PInteger what;

   what = new SInteger (i);
   failnull (what);
   Integers[where] -> insert (what);
   return (what);
   };

PInteger asInteger (long i) {
   int where;
   PInteger aValue;
   char found;
   PIterator IT;
   PObject nextValue;

   where = index (i);
   if (Integers[where] != NULL) {
      found = FALSE;
      IT = Integers[where] -> newIterator ();
      while (IT -> nextItem (nextValue) && !found) {
         found = findIt (PInteger (nextValue),
                             i, aValue);
         };
      delete IT;
      if (!found)
         aValue = createIt (where, i);
      };
   else {
      Integers[where] = newList ();
      aValue = createIt (where, i);
   };
```

```
        return aValue;
};
```

The function `asInteger` needs three functions to help it. The one named `index` is our hash function for this class. Given a long integer, it returns a value between 0 and `max`.

When we ask `asInteger` for a `PInteger`, it first looks up the long integer supplied as an argument in the hash table `Integers` to see whether there is an object with the required value. If the object can be found, `asInteger` returns a reference to it. If it can't be found, `asInteger` creates a new object, inserts it into one of the lists, and returns a reference to it. The key to making it all work quickly is to be able to decide which of the many lists the object is in. This is the purpose of hashing. With each possible value we associate an integer, `hash`, between 0 and `max`. We then guarantee that if the object is in the list, it is in the list numbered `hash`. Thus we need to search only one list out of many, and if the objects created are about uniformly distributed among the lists, all of the lists have about the same size, or about the fraction 1/`size` of the total number of elements stored. This is why we want our hash function to produce a uniform distribution of the values in its range when applied to all values in its domain. Also, making the output value as unrelated as possible to the input value helps prevent clustering. The function `asInteger` is passed a long integer that is to be the value of the `PInteger`. We go through a process of computing a hash value in the range of valid indexes for our array, from 0 to `max`. Modulo arithmetic works for this. We provide the function `index`, which performs both computations and returns the result. Since this computation is identical for identical input, we can guarantee that we always look on the same list.

When `index` is called from within `asInteger`, it returns a location, `where`, that is the number of the list that should contain the desired `PInteger`, whether it is currently stored or not. If that list is NULL, the object is not stored, so we create a new list for that array index, and we create a new `PInteger`, initialize it with the correct value, and insert it on the newly created list. The function `createIt` helps with the creation and insertion. It returns the created object so that it can be returned as the value of `asInteger`.

If the list `where` is not NULL, the list `Integers[where]` must be searched for an object with the required value. We use a list iterator for this, but we have doctored its loop somewhat so that we don't need to keep searching after we have found the item. The Boolean `found` signals the exit from the loop. The body of the loop is a call to a Boolean function, `findIt`, that determines whether the item returned by the iterator is a match, and if so it sets `found` to TRUE. However, it also sets the variable `aValue`, which is both local to `asInteger` and is a reference parameter to `findIt`, and which will be returned to the caller of `asInteger`. It is important to say that if we don't set this value in findIt, we *will* exit the loop, but the value of the item returned by the list iterator at that time will most likely be the one following the one we found, because nextItem is executed one additional time while we are checking the value of found. Therefore, setting aValue after exit would be an error.

Finally, if the iterator fails to find the value in the list, the value must be created and inserted into that same list.

Some of the other methods in this class are extremely easy. However, note that the constructor SInteger is a protected method, so it can't be called by clients.

```
SInteger :: SInteger (long v) {fValue = v;};
```

The only way to create an SInteger is by calling asInteger. Clone must be made into a functional no-op, returning a reference to this rather than creating a copy. The method writeIt just writes out its fValue. In some of the methods we need only be careful about the types of our operands. For example, less just compares the value of this with the value of the parameter, but it must be sure that the parameter is a PInteger. Note that an object of any subtype of SInteger will both make sense and be valid as a parameter. The other comparison operators, including equal, are implemented similarly. Note the very different meanings of equal here and in SObject.

```
char SInteger :: less (PObject m) {
    if (m -> member (integer))
        return fValue < PInteger (m) -> value ();
    else
        Error ("SInteger :: less not defined.");
};
```

SInteger inherits from both SObject and SMagnitude, the protocols of both the parent classes are inherited. It also means that the common methods, less and equal, must be implemented here so that their names won't be ambiguous. The methods inherited from SMagnitude have no function bodies in any case and so specify no actions. The relation equal is special here, and in all magnitudes. It compares the sizes or magnitudes of the objects, not the object identities.

```
char SInteger :: equal (PObject m) {
    if (m -> member (integer))
        return fValue == PInteger (m) -> value ();
    else
        Error ("SInteger :: equal not defined.");
};
```

The only other structural issue is to be certain that we use the ideas in the class consistently, which means we never return a new object when we already have one with the same value. Thus the arithmetic operators must be something like the following. We easily compute the value to be returned, but we must call `asInteger` to transform it, rather than create a new object, because the result may already exist as an `SInteger`.

```
PInteger SInteger :: add (PInteger a) {
    return (asInteger (fValue + a -> value ()));
};
```

Of course we could do more. We could check the inputs into our arithmetic methods to watch for overflows, such as those that occur when we try to add two integers close to the maximum. We could check whether the value to be returned is too big by subtracting the value of `this` from the largest possible value. Of course, that subtraction causes an error if `this` is negative. The proper check would start by comparing the signs of the two values. If they are different, addition is not a problem. If they are the same, one of them can be added or subtracted from the maximum (or minimum) long integer. Then the question arises as to the proper course of action to take when we do get overflow. One possibility is to halt the program by calling `Error`. Another possibility is to give this class an exported Boolean variable, named `IntegerOverflow`, that is set or cleared by the arithmetic operations and can be checked by clients after each such operation to see whether overflow has occurred.

11.1.2 Hash Tables in General

The hash table strategy we employed in `SInteger` is called separate chaining. The purpose of hash tables is to achieve fast lookup of stored items. If each bucket is of size one, we achieve the ideal of a short, fixed time for each lookup, since the lookup time is the time to compute the hash function plus the overhead of accessing the single item in that bucket. If all the buckets are small, performance is good, but if even a single bucket grows the performance on the average can degrade quite badly. Imagine that the bucket that stores zero is growing and that all insertions are done at the head of the list. Since zero is likely to be used often in most programs, it takes longer and longer to find the item in its bucket. The implementation strategy works for `SInteger` because in most uses of objects of `SInteger`, one expects the lists holding the object references to be uniformly short. However, a case can be imagined in which this is not true, even if only a relatively small number of different elements of `SInteger` appear in a given program. For example, if all the integers used were multiples of the size of our bucket table, only one list would be nonempty, and searching would degenerate to searching a list. Thus the size of the bucket table must sometimes be tailored to the problem at hand. Note also that the hash buckets don't need to be implemented as lists. They can be implemented as any storage structure. In certain situations a specialized hash table that has specialized storage mechanisms for the buckets might be advantageous. Sorted lists are an obvious possibility, as are binary search trees.

We can use the hash table as a general collection technique. The idea is to execute a hash function using any object that is to be stored. The result will tell us which bucket the item belongs in. We can think of the hash function as a machine that hashes the object uniformly. It outputs the index of the bucket in which the object belongs. See Fig. 11.2. The function is required to yield the same index upon different lookups of the same object or lookups of objects that are `equal`.

Another possibility for the construction of a hash table is circular hashing. In this implementation we don't build each bucket individually. Suppose we can guarantee that no more than some maximum number of values will ever be stored in our hash table. We might not know what they are, but we know the maximum size of the hash table. Then a hash table can be implemented as an array [0...someMax] of PObject. Instead of an array of lists, it is an array of objects. If this array is initialized to have NULL contents, we can insert into the table by computing `hash` for the object to be inserted, reducing this to the appropriate range using the modulo operator, `%,` and attempting to insert the item into that cell of the array. If the cell is NULL, the insertion is made. Otherwise we must search for the first empty slot following the desired cell, being careful to try cell 0 after cell `someMax`. If `someMax` is larger than or equal to the number of items to

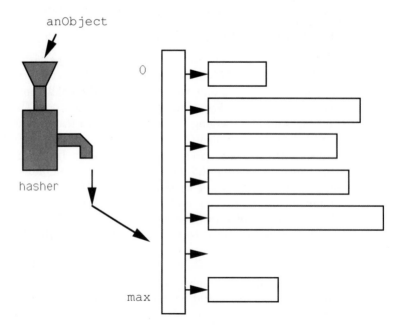

FIGURE 11.2

be inserted, there will always be some open slot. The search for an object is the same process except that a match is checked for rather than an empty cell. If removals are not done, the search can stop whenever an empty cell is reached (or a match is found).

If objects can be removed from the hash table, either the search must proceed beyond empty cells until all possible cells have been searched (why?), or we need to keep more information in the structure about the contents of the cells. Suppose we keep another array, of the same size as our storage array, in which the values stored are unused, empty, and full. Initialization sets all cells to unused. Insertion sets a cell to full when the corresponding cell in the primary array is filled, and removal similarly sets it to empty. Subsequent insertions can use cells marked unused or empty. Searching proceeds until a match or an unused cell is found.

11.2   CHARACTERS AS OBJECTS

Characters have many of the properties of integers. They are magnitudes and are uniquely defined, but they are not numeric. We could use the same strategy that was used for SInteger, but we shall employ a slightly simpler scheme since there are such a small number of possible characters. Our new class, SCharacter, will ensure that every use of a character will refer to the same object, but we shall not need lists. In fact, we can predefine all the characters, since there are only 128 of them. (Extension to 256 characters would allow access to special graphics characters, implemented in most microcomputers. This extension isn't made here since such characters are not uniformly defined.)

```
class SCharacter;
typedef SCharacter *PCharacter;
// WARNING: Do not create new Character objects
// directly. Do not declare objects of type
// SCharacter and do not call new SCharacter.
// Call the access function asCharacter (char)
// instead.

class SCharacter: public SMagnitude, public SObject {
    public:
        virtual char        member (classtype c);
        virtual char        value (void);
        virtual PObject     ShallowClone (void);
        virtual PObject     Clone (void);
        virtual char        less (PObject m);
        virtual char        equal (PObject m);
        virtual void        writeIt (void);
```

```
    protected:
        char fValue;
        virtual int sizeOf (void);
        SCharacter (char v);
    friend PCharacter asCharacter(char);
    friend void initCharacters (void);
};

PCharacter asCharacter (char);
void initCharacters (void);

// REQUIREMENTS For Use
//     initCharacters ();
```

The effect of most of these should be obvious, and many shall not be shown here. The implementation is not unlike the circular hashing scheme discussed in the last section.

The variable Characters is an array of PCharacter objects indexed by the ordinary ASCII values. The initialization procedure for the class creates all the objects and stores each one in the appropriate cell.

```
const int charsetsize = 128;

PCharacter Characters[charsetsize];

void initCharacters (void) {
    for (int i = 0; i < charsetsize; ++i)
        Characters[i] = new SCharacter (i);
};

PCharacter asCharacter (char c) {
    return Characters[c];
};

SCharacter :: SCharacter (char v) {fValue = v;};
```

Then asCharacter (c) returns the object in the cell c of Characters. The comparison methods compare the ordinary characters stored in the objects, after checking that their parameters are also members of SCharacter. Clone needs to be implemented similarly to the corresponding method of SInteger. It returns a reference to this rather than creating a new object.

The array Characters is, in fact, a hash table for which we know in advance the objects to be stored and can therefore use a specially tailored hash function, the ASCII value, and a specially sized structure.

11.3   STRINGS AS OBJECTS (COLLECTIONS AND MAGNITUDES)

In this section, string data treated as an object will be discussed. Strings can be considered as both collections of characters and as magnitudes. As collections, strings require insertion and removal of characters. As magnitudes, they are to be compared to other strings. In fact, using multiple inheritance, we shall declare the class SString to be a subclass of both SCollection and SMagnitude.

Multiple inheritance presents a number of problems, especially in the implementation of a specialization hierarchy. A common example is that of the class STruck and class SToy. You can obtain the class SToyTruck by inheriting from both. The problem is that a toy truck really is a toy, but it isn't a truck. Questions such as "What is its mileage?" have no meaning. Many of the problems of multiple inheritance go away if you use it only to inherit from abstract classes. There are a number of syntactical issues that must be dealt with, such as the question of what happens if both parent classes have a method with the same name but different protocols or different meanings, but most of these can be dealt with using clever language design. Some more of the problems go away if you don't think of the hierarchy of classes (now a network rather than a hierarchy) as a specialization hierarchy, but then you open a large class of new problems because the meanings of classes become too variable to be used as an abstraction mechanism. The language Trellis-Owl has multiple inheritance and controls its use so that most of the negative side effects can be avoided. Other languages, such as Modula-3 and Beta, don't permit multiple inheritance because of the difficulties with the concept rather than the difficulty of implementation. Of the languages permitting multiple inheritance, C++ is perhaps the one with the fewest restrictions and safeguards. This means that it must be used wisely and carefully if we are to avoid problems.

Our solution to the problems of multiple inheritance has been to make magnitudes special. They are not only abstract, but they also represent only a specific attribute of an object. In particular, SMagnitude is used only as a parent class of some class that also inherits directly or indirectly from SObject. A class such as SMagnitude is called a mixin class to indicate that it is intended only to mix some functionality (here size) into some other group of classes. Therefore, we give the strings the comparison methods of magnitudes and the insertion and removal methods of collections. The protocol for the new class SString is quite long, since it needs the methods of SCollection as well as additional comparison methods of the SMagnitude class. It also needs an iterator class, as does every collection.

```
class SString;
typedef SString *PString;

PString newString (char * = "");
```

```
class SString: public SMagnitude,
               public SCollection {
   public:
          SString (char * = "");
      virtual                 ~SString (void);
      virtual char            member (classtype c);
      virtual char            less (PObject m);
      virtual char            equal (PObject o);
      virtual void            insert (PObject);
      virtual void            remove (PObject);
      virtual PCharacter      first (void);
      virtual void            removeFirst (void);
      virtual char            *value ();
      virtual void            writeIt (void);
      virtual char            empty (void);
      virtual PObject         Clone (void);
   protected:
      char            *fValue;
      int             fLength;
      virtual int     sizeOf (void);
};

class SStringIterator: public SIterator {
   public:
          SStringIterator (PString);
      virtual char    nextItem (PObject &);
      virtual void    reset (void);
      virtual char    member (classtype c);
   protected:
      int             fNextChar;
      virtual int     sizeOf (void);
};

// REQUIREMENTS For Use
//     initCharacters ();
```

The implementation shown here uses an instance variable that is an ordinary C string, or pointer to char. It also stores the current length for efficiency. Note that fLength is the logical size of the string. The allocated storage is one more than this to allow for the NULL character that C++ requires. The strings in this class do not actually save SCharacter objects, but logically they can be treated as if they do. The iterators, for example, return objects in PCharacter, and insert expects to insert a PCharacter as well. A PString is created by sending an ordinary C string to newString. The initialization step sets the fValue field to be this string. Notice that a copy is made of the string passed in. The object manages its own storage for the characters. If we used the storage that is referred to by the input parameter, the value of a string could be changed from outside by manipulating that same pointer externally. Note also that there is a default empty string value for the string passed in.

```
PString newString (char *s ) {
   PString result;

   result = new SString (s);
   failnull (result);
   return result;
};

SString :: SString (char *s) {
   fLength = strlen (s);
   fValue = new char[fLength + 1];
   if (fValue == NULL) Error ("System heap
                                 exhausted.");
   strcpy (fValue, s);
};
```

The inherited `insert` method inserts characters (PCharacter) by appending the new character to the right of the current value. The built-in function `strcpy` can be easily used. We must check the type of the input parameter, of course. We must allocate space in this method, because the size of our stored string will grow. We must therefore also deallocate the old storage.

```
void SString :: insert (PObject o) {
   // o must be a PCharacter.
   char *newValue;

   if (o -> member (character)) {
      newValue = new char[fLength + 2];
      if (newValue == NULL)
         Error ("System heap exhausted.");
      strcpy (newValue, fValue);
      newValue[fLength] = PCharacter (o) -> value ();
      newValue[fLength+1] = '\0';
      delete []fValue;
      fValue = newValue;
      fLength++;
   }
   else
      Error ("SString :: insert: Not a character.");
};
```

We could also append one `PString` to another with the method append, which has been left as an exercise.

```
virtual void append (PString s);
    // Append s to the right of this.
```

Removal of a `PCharacter` requires that we find the position in the existing string at which the character to be removed appears. Once again we must check the type of the input parameter, and once again we have a built-in function, `strchr`, that finds one ordinary `char` in a string. If `strchr` cannot find the target string in the source, it returns zero. Once we find the character, we must move all following characters one slot to the left and then reduce `fLength`. We could use similar logic to remove a substring from within another string.

```
void SString :: remove (PObject o) {
    char ch, *where;

    if (o -> member (character)) {
        ch = PCharacter (o) -> value ();
        where = strchr (fValue, ch);
        if (*where != '\0') {
            while (*where != '\0') {
                *where = * (where + 1);
                where++;
            };
            fLength--;
        };
    };
    else
        Error ("SString :: remove: Not a character.");
};
```

The method `empty` just checks the `fLength` of the string. The `first` method returns the `PCharacter` equivalent of the first character in `fValue`, unless `fValue` is empty, in which case it returns NULL.

Since `strcmp` can compare ordinary strings, we can use it to implement the comparison methods. Because, we are subclassing `SMagnitude`, we need only implement `less` and `equal`, the other comparisons being inherited.

```
char SString :: less (PObject m) {
    if (m -> member (string))
        return strcmp (fValue, PString (m) ->
                        fValue) < 0;
    else
        return FALSE;
};
```

```
char SString :: equal (PObject o) {
   if (o == NULL) return FALSE;
   if (o -> member (string))
      return (strcmp (fValue, PString (o)
                              -> fValue) == 0);
   else
      return FALSE;
};
```

The iterator class is standard. An ordinary integer references the in-dex in fValue of the next character to be returned by nextItem. This position variable is initialized to zero by SStringIterator. No position class is necessary, since ordinary integers or elements of SInteger serve quite well as positions. The nextItem method follows a standard pattern of checking whether the iterator has finished and, if not, setting up the character to be returned and setting fDone if that character is to be the last item.

11.4   GENERAL PAIRS OF DATA ITEMS

This class implements the mathematician's idea of an ordered pair of values. An object in class SPair is conceptually a pair of members of PObject. The first object in the pair is called the key, and the other is called the value. Two pairs are considered equal if their keys are related by the operator == and their values are related by the operator ==. This time we do not say equal for either of these comparisons. We require identity here, which gives us a class similar to the ordered pairs of math-ematics. Pairs are used in geometry of course, as points in the Euclidean plane. They are also used as the basis of mathematical functions and relations.

```
class SPair;
typedef SPair *PPair;

PPair newPair (PObject k, PObject v);

class SPair: public SObject {

   public:
         SPair (PObject k, PObject v);
      virtual char      member (classtype c);
      virtual PObject   key (void);
      virtual PObject   value (void);
      virtual char      equal (PObject);
      virtual void      writeIt (void);
```

```
     protected:
        PObject          fKey;
        PObject          fValue;
        virtual int      sizeOf(void);
};
```

The equality method compares the keys and the values using ==.

```
char SPair :: equal (PObject o) {
   if (o -> member (pair))
      return (fKey == PPair (o) -> key () &&
               fValue == PPair (o) -> value ());
   else
      return FALSE;

};
```

We have methods to retrieve the key and value of these objects, and our initialization sets them. Our most important use of them, however, is in building the next class, SAssociation, which is needed for dictionaries.

11.5   ASSOCIATION: A SPECIALIZED PAIR WITH A KEY AND DATA

An association is a pair of objects of which the first, called the key, comes from a magnitude class and the other, called the value, comes from any subclass of SObject. Two associations are to be considered equal if they have equal keys. Note that we said equal keys, not the same key. In the magnitude classes these two concepts are distinct. The chief use of associations is in building dictionaries, which are sets of associations. Dictionaries will be discussed in the next chapter. We used dictionaries and therefore associations when we built our DFA class in Chapter 5. An association is itself a magnitude, with the magnitude determined by the magnitude of the key. Therefore our class inherits from both SPair and SMagnitude.

```
class SAssociation;
typedef SAssociation *PAssociation;

PAssociation newAssociation (PObject k, PObject v);

class SAssociation: public SMagnitude, public SPair
      public:
          SAssociation (PObject k, PObject v);
         virtual char       member (classtype c);
         virtual PObject     value (void);
         virtual char       less (PObject m);
         virtual void       setValue (PObject);
```

```
        virtual char        equal (PObject o);
        virtual void        writeIt (void);

    protected:
        virtual int     sizeOf (void);
};
```

We create a new association by giving it a key and an associated value. Two associations with the same key are `equal`, but they are not `==`. Insertion of an association into a set already containing an association with the same key results in there being only a single association in that set with that key, because sets check their members for equality with the items that we try to insert.

The `set` and `get` methods, inherited from `SPair`, set and get the instance variables. Providing these methods makes it unnecessary for clients to deal directly with the instance variables and thus allows us to change the implementation without changing the client code, as long as we also reimplement the methods to make them consistent with the new definitions. If clients were setting or even referring to instance variables of classes outside themselves, they would have to be rewritten when those classes were altered. Many object-oriented languages prevent clients from seeing instance variables and so require methods such as these for each case in which instance variables need to be visible. Here, of course, clients must be able to set the keys and values of associations, because this is the purpose of the class.

Equality testing is the special feature of the association class. Two associations are treated as `equal` if their keys are `equal`. But since the keys are magnitudes, the keys need not be identical. The meaning of `equal` for a magnitude depends on the class and is generally related to the size of the object. As usual, equality is defined only within the class of the receiver.

```
char SAssociation :: equal (PObject o) {
    if (o -> member (association))
        return ((fKey) -> equal (PAssociation (o)
                                    -> key ()));
    else
        return FALSE;
};
```

Similarly, `less` is implemented in terms of a comparison of keys.

```
char SAssociation :: less (PObject m) {
    if (m -> member (association))
        return (fKey -> less (PAssociation (m)
                                    -> key ()));
    else
        return FALSE;
};
```

As we shall see in the next chapter, associations form the basis of dictionaries, which are a way to implement mathematical functions and a way to save certain kinds of databases.

11.6   LARGE INTEGERS: WHEN 32 BITS AREN'T ENOUGH

Now we shall take a little excursion into an area that is only occasionally useful but from which something can be learned. Sometimes ordinary integers and even long integers are not sufficient for holding the values we need. Real values give us larger size but less precision. Sometimes we need forty-digit integers or even larger. For example, expression of the U.S. national debt in dollars now requires more than 12 digits. This class will implement larger integers. In effect, we shall build 40-digit base-10 integers implemented as 10-digit integers using base 10,000. To do this, we need an array of 10 ordinary integers to hold a single value of our large integers. See Fig. 11.3.

```
const positive = TRUE;
const negative = FALSE;

extern char overflow;

class SLargeInteger;
typedef SLargeInteger *PLargeInteger;

PLargeInteger newLargeInteger (char sign = positive,
    int p9 = 0, int p8 = 0, int p7 = 0, int p6 = 0,
    int p5 = 0, int p4 = 0, int p3 = 0, int p2 = 0,
    int p1 = 0, int p0 = 0);

class SLargeInteger: public SObject,
    public SMagnitude {
    public:
        SLargeInteger (char isPositive);
    virtual char          less (PObject) ;
    virtual char          equal (PObject);
```

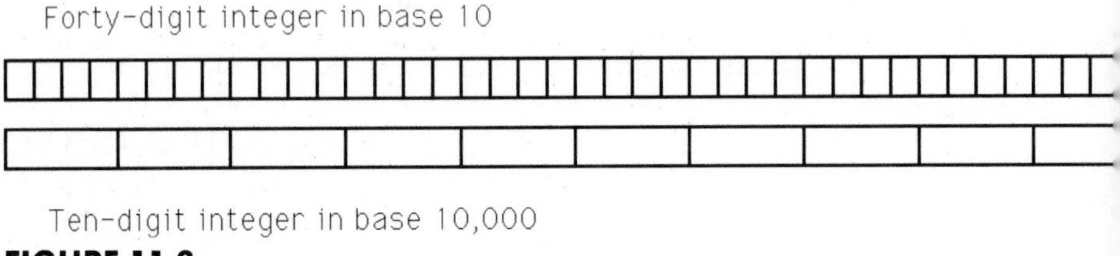

Forty-digit integer in base 10

Ten-digit integer in base 10,000

FIGURE 11.3

```
        virtual char              sign (void);
                                  // positive == TRUE
        virtual PLargeInteger     add (PLargeInteger);
        virtual void              increment
                                  (PLargeInteger);
        virtual void              decrement
                                  (PLargeInteger);
        virtual PLargeInteger     negated (void);
        virtual void              negate (void);
        virtual PLargeInteger     subtract
                                  (PLargeInteger);
        virtual PLargeInteger     multiply
                                  (PLargeInteger);
        virtual PLargeInteger     divide
                                  (PLargeInteger);
        virtual PLargeInteger     rem (PLargeInteger);
        virtual char              isZero (void);
        virtual char              member (classtype c);
        virtual PObject           Clone (void);
        virtual void              writeIt (void);

    protected:
        static const size;
        static const baseLessOne;
        int *fValue; /* [SLargeInteger :: size]*/
        char fIsPositive;
        virtual int at (int);
        virtual void atPut (int w, int v);
            // w in 1...size, v in 0...baseLessOne
        virtual void iMult (int m, PLargeInteger r);
            // r=this times m
        virtual int sizeOf (void);

    friend
        PLargeInteger newLargeInteger (char sign,
        int p9, int p8, int p7, int p6, int p5, int p4,
        int p3, int p2, int p1, int p0);
};
```

Note first that an object of this type is not quite the same as an integer as implemented in SInteger. Here the value of an object can change as a program proceeds. We can negate an object or increase it by the value of another, for example. The stronger semantics could be implemented, of course, but the protocol would have to be revised and the increment, decrement, and negate methods removed.

A large difference in implementation is that in `SInteger` we can use ordinary long-integer arithmetic. Here we need to implement the ordinary algorithms of arithmetic within our methods.

We also define and export two constants, `positive` and `negative`, that are just synonyms for the Boolean values but make the code read better. We define and export a variable, `overflow`, as well that enables the user to check the result of the most recently performed arithmetic operation on large integers.

These integers are most easily thought of as having a sign, either positive or negative, and forty ordinary digits. Another view is that they have a sign and 10 super-digits that can have any one of 10,000 different values. Another way to think of the objects in `SLargeInteger` is that they are arrays of 10 cells, any one of which can hold a value between 0 and 9999. This is, in fact, our implementation. In this implementation view we shall think of cell 9 as being on the left and cell 0 as being on the right, so that values of higher significance are stored in cells with larger subscripts.

```
SLargeInteger :: SLargeInteger (char isPositive) {
    fValue = new int[SLargeInteger :: size];
    overflow = FALSE;
    for (int i = 0; i < SLargeInteger :: size; ++i)
        fValue[i] = 0;
    fIsPositive = isPositive;
};
```

The standard constructor yields a large integer of value 0; its sign is provided as a parameter, and all its digits are zero. A generator function is provided that has eleven arguments, all of which are optional and have default values. Any large integer can be negated by the method `negate`, which changes the instance variable `fIsPositive`. Given a large integer, the method `negated` returns a new large integer whose value is the negative of the receiver. It uses the `Clone` method to get a copy, changes the sign of that copy, and returns it. The sign of any large integer can be determined by sending it the `sign` message.

Although both +0 and −0 can be encoded, the method `isZero` returns TRUE for both representations. It checks every cell in the array as to whether it is zero. The `equal` method also considers both encodings of zero to be the same.

```
char SLargeInteger :: equal (PObject o) {
    char result;
    int i;

    if (o -> member (largeinteger)) {
        result = (isZero () && PLargeInteger (o)
            -> isZero ()) || (sign ()
```

```
                == PLargeInteger (o) -> sign ());
        i = SLargeInteger :: size - 1;
        while (i >= 0 && result) {
            if (fValue[i] !=
                    PLargeInteger (o) -> fValue[i])
                result = FALSE;
            --i;
            }; // while
        }
        else {
            result = FALSE;
        };
    return result;
};
```

The signed magnitude form with which we encode these large integers complicates many of our operations. For example, less needs several cases, for the possible combinations of signs of its arguments. The same is true of most of the arithmetic operations. Most of the checks are simple, requiring computation only when the signs are the same. In less we check the number from the most significant portion (the rightmost digits) down to the least significant portion until we observe a difference. At this point we can determine the relative sizes of the two values.

```
char SLargeInteger :: less (PObject o) {
    char result, stillEqual;
    int i;

    if (o -> member (largeinteger)) {
        if ((fIsPositive && ! PLargeInteger (o)
            -> sign ()) !! (isZero ()
            && PLargeInteger (o)
                -> isZero ())) result = FALSE;
        else if (! fIsPositive && PLargeInteger (o)
                -> sign ()) result = TRUE;
        else {
            result = TRUE;
            stillEqual = TRUE;
            i = SLargeInteger :: size - 1;
            while (stillEqual && i >= 0) {
                if (fValue[i] > PLargeInteger (o)
                    -> fValue[i]) {
                    result = FALSE;
                    stillEqual = FALSE;
                }
                else if (fValue[i] < PLargeInteger (o)
```

```
                              -> fValue[i]) {
                    stillEqual = FALSE;
                };
                --i;
            };
            if (stillEqual) result = FALSE;
            else if (!fIsPositive) result = !result;
        };
    }
    else {
        Error ("SLargeInteger ::
                less: Not a large integer.");
        result = FALSE;
    };
    return result;
};
```

The method `writeIt` uses some formatting to make sure that non-significant zeros are written. For example, a 3 stored in some cell must be written as 0003 if there are any nonzero cells with more significance.

```
void SLargeInteger :: writeIt (void) {
    int i, it;

    if (fIsPositive) cout << " +";
    else cout << " -";
    for(i = SLargeInteger :: size - 1; i >= 0; --i) {
        it = fValue[i];
        if (it > 999) cout << it;
        else if (it > 99) cout << '0' << it;
        else if (it > 9) cout << "00" << it;
        else cout << "000" << it;
    };
    cout << '\n';
};
```

Additional hidden methods aid in the computations of the arithmetic methods. The method `at` returns the integer value in cell i of `fValue` and `atPut` stores a new value in a specified cell. These methods have no arithmetic meaning and are therefore `protected`. Multiplication is aided by the `protected` method `iMult`, which multiplies `this` by an ordinary integer (in the range from $-$ `baseLessOne` to `baseLessOne`) and returns the value in its other parameter. Note that the other parameter is not created by this routine, but must be created externally and passed in as an input parameter. This routine needs only a single loop to perform the multiplication. The process should be familiar from your earliest school days. We start multiplying at the right, carrying to the next digit as necessary to avoid writing down a number larger than or equal to the base. A property of the algorithm is that we can carry only into the next position, because the carry can never be as big as the base. Within the method the arithmetic is carried out using long integer values in order to avoid overflow.

```
void SLargeInteger :: iMult (int m, PLargeInteger r) {
    long mpr, partial;
    int i, carry, big = SLargeInteger :: baseLessOne;
    mpr = abs (m);
    if (mpr <= big + 1) {
        overflow = FALSE;
        r -> fIsPositive = fIsPositive;
        carry = 0;
        for (i = 0; i < SLargeInteger :: size; ++i) {
            partial = carry + mpr *fValue[i];
            r -> fValue[i] = partial % (big + 1);
            carry = partial / (big + 1);
        };
        if (m < 0) r -> negate ();
        overflow = carry !=0;
    };
};
```

Most of the main arithmetic methods are very similar to each other. One case is computed directly and the other cases are computed using this case or other methods. For example, if this is not positive, add can be calculated by performing a subtraction. On the other hand, if this is positive and the parameter b is not, addition can be done by creating the negative of b and then performing a subtraction. Since subtract will sometimes call add, we must be careful to avoid a situation where each of these calls the other for the same case. However, if the case handled is the positive-positive case in both methods, such a situation will not arise. Again, the algorithm should be familiar. It is the same one you have used for years. Start at the right, adding values in the same position. Write down the rightmost digit and carry the rest. Here the digits are values in the range from 0 to baseLessOne. Both add and subtract return a newly created large integer.

```
PLargeInteger SLargeInteger :: add (PLargeInteger b) {
    int i, carry, big = SLargeInteger :: baseLessOne;
    PLargeInteger result, temp;

    if (!fIsPositive) {
        temp = PLargeInteger (Clone ());
        temp -> negate ();
        result = b -> subtract (temp);
        delete temp;
    }
```

```
    else {// this is positive.
       if (b -> sign ()) {// b is positive.
          overflow = FALSE;
          result = newLargeInteger (positive);
          carry = 0;
          for (i = 0; i < SLargeInteger :: size;
               ++i) {
             if (fValue[i] <= (big - b -> fValue[i])
                  - carry) {
                result -> fValue[i] = fValue[i] +
                   b -> fValue[i] + carry;
                carry = 0;
             }
             else {
                result -> fValue[i] = fValue[i] -
                   big + b -> fValue[i] + carry - 1;
                carry = 1;
             };
          };
          result -> fIsPositive = TRUE;
          if (carry == 1) overflow = TRUE;
       }
       else {// b is negative.
          temp = PLargeInteger (b -> Clone ());
          temp -> negate ();
          result = subtract (temp);
          delete temp;
       };
    };

    return result;
};
```

Subtraction is similar except that we borrow rather than carry. Borrowing involves reducing the value to the left. In other words, borrowing is the same as carrying a negative value.

```
PLargeInteger SLargeInteger :: subtract
                              (PLargeInteger b) {
   PLargeInteger result, temp;
   int carry, i, big = SLargeInteger :: baseLessOne;

   if (fIsPositive) { // this is positive.
      if (less (b)) {
         result = b -> subtract (this);
         result -> negate ();
      }
```

```
          else {
             overflow = FALSE;
             carry = 0;
             result = newLargeInteger (positive);
             for (i = 0; i < SLargeInteger :: size;
                   ++i) {
                if (fValue[i] - carry >=
                     b -> fValue[i]) {
                   result -> fValue[i] = fValue[i] -
                      carry - b -> fValue[i];
                   carry = 0;
                }
                else {
                   result -> fValue[i] = big - b ->
                      fValue[i] - carry + 1 + fValue[i];
                   carry = 1;
                };
             };
             if (carry == 1) overflow = TRUE;
          };
       }
       else { // this is negative.
          if (b -> sign ()) {
             temp = PLargeInteger (Clone ());
             temp -> negate ();
             result = temp -> add (b);
             result -> negate ();
             delete temp;
          }
           else { // b is negative.
             temp = PLargeInteger (b -> Clone ());
             temp -> negate ();
             negate ();
             result = temp -> subtract (this);
             negate ();
             delete temp;
          };
       };

    return result;
};
```

The methods increment and decrement, which modify this, may be encoded using add and subtract.

```
void SLargeInteger :: increment (PLargeInteger b) {
   PLargeInteger temp;
```

```
    temp = add (b);
    fIsPositive = temp -> fIsPositive;
    for (int i = 0; i < SLargeInteger :: size; ++i)
        fValue[i] = temp -> fValue[i];
    delete temp;
};
```

Multiplication and division are somewhat more complicated. Multiplication uses a familiar algorithm. In both we need only compute the case where both operands are positive and use negation to adjust the signs in the other cases. We need two loops to perform multiplication, one for each operand. The second loop is hidden inside iMult. We also perform the additions as we go along, using increment. Likewise, we use a simple shift loop to take care of the fact that multiplication by a single digit of the multiplier is actually multiplication by that digit times a power of the base.

```
PLargeInteger SLargeInteger :: multiply
                                (PLargeInteger b) {
    PLargeInteger result, temp, adder;
    int i, j, size = SLargeInteger :: size;
    char sawOverflow;

    sawOverflow = FALSE;
    overflow = FALSE;
    if (fIsPositive) {
        if(b -> sign ()) {
            result = newLargeInteger (positive);
            temp = newLargeInteger (positive);
            adder = newLargeInteger (positive);
            for (i = 0; i < size; ++i) {
                if (fValue[i] > 0) {
                    b -> iMult (fValue[i], adder);
                    if (overflow) sawOverflow = TRUE;
                    temp -> increment (adder);
                };
                result -> fValue[i] = temp -> fValue[0];
                for (j = 1; j < size; ++j) temp ->
                        fValue[j - 1] = temp -> fValue[j];
                temp -> fValue[size - 1] = 0;
            };
            overflow = temp -> fValue[0] != 0 ||
                sawOverflow;
            delete temp;
            delete adder;
        }
        else {
```

```
                    temp = PLargeInteger (b -> Clone ());
                    temp -> negate ();
                    result = multiply (temp);
                    result -> negate ();
                    delete temp;
                };
            }
        else {// Negative.
            if (b -> sign ()) {
                result = b -> multiply (this);
            }
            else {
                temp = PLargeInteger (b -> Clone ());
                temp -> negate ();
                result = multiply (temp);
                result -> negate ();
                delete temp;
            };
        };
        return result;
    };
```

Division employs a common algorithm modified only in that it carries
out its subtractions in place rather than down the page. It repeatedly finds
a trial divisor and subtracts the trial divisor times the divisor from the
dividend. It chooses a trial divisor guaranteed to be small enough, though
it frequently chooses one that is too small. Rather than increase the trial
divisor, it just reduces the dividend with it and iterates again. In the following the divisor is called subr. The shifting, done by for loops, makes
the computation of subscripts easier. In effect, we line things up each time
before we start. The algorithm could be sped up if we avoid these shifts.

```
PLargeInteger SLargeInteger :: divide
                               (PLargeInteger b) {
    PLargeInteger result, temp, dvnd, subr;
    int i, m, n, trial, size = SLargeInteger :: size;
    int base = SLargeInteger :: baseLessOne + 1;
    long current, carry;

    if (b -> isZero ()) {
        overflow = TRUE;
        result = NULL;
    }
    else if (fIsPositive) {
        if (b -> sign ()) {
            overflow = FALSE;
            result = newLargeInteger (positive);
```

```
            dvnd = PLargeInteger (Clone ());
            subr = PLargeInteger (b -> Clone ());
            temp = newLargeInteger (positive);
            m = size - 1;
            while (subr -> fValue[m] == 0) --m;
            m = size - m - 1;
            for (i = size - 1; i >= m; --i) subr ->
                fValue[i] = subr -> fValue[i-m];
                //Sic.
            for (i = m - 1; i >= 0; --i) subr ->
                fValue[i] = 0;
            n = size - 1;
            carry = 0;
            while (m >= 0) {
                current = dvnd -> fValue[n] +
                    carry * base;
                while (subr -> fValue[n] < current) {
                    trial = current / (subr ->
                                        fValue[n] + 1);
                    result -> fValue[m] = result ->
                        fValue[m] + trial;
                    subr -> iMult (trial, temp);
                    dvnd -> decrement (temp);
                    if (n < size - 1) carry = dvnd ->
                                            fValue[n+1]
                    else carry = 0;
                    current = dvnd -> fValue[n] +
                        carry * base;
                };
                while (dvnd -> greaterEqual (subr)) {
                    dvnd -> decrement (subr);
                    result -> fValue[m] = result ->
                                            fValue[m] + 1;
                };
                carry = dvnd -> fValue[n];
                for (i = 1; i < size; ++i) subr ->
                                fValue[i-1] =
                                subr -> fValue[i]
                subr -> fValue[size - 1] = 0;
                --m;
                --n;
            };
            delete temp;
            delete subr;
            delete dvnd;
        }
        else { // pos div neg
```

```
            temp = PLargeInteger (b -> Clone ());
            temp -> negate ();
            result = divide (temp);
            result -> negate ();
            delete temp;
        };
    }
    else {
        negate ();
        result = divide (b);
        negate ();
        result -> negate ();
    };
    return result;
};
```

The remainder of two large integers can be computed with the same formula used for ordinary integers: a % b = a - (a / b) * b.

```
PLargeInteger SLargeInteger :: rem
                                (PLargeInteger b) {
    PLargeInteger result, quot, temp;
    quot = divide (b);
    temp = quot -> multiply (b);
    result = subtract (temp);
    delete quot;
    delete temp;
    return result;
};
```

11.7   SUMMARY

Collections are not the only abstractions around which to build classes. We have seen integers, characters, and strings, all of which have low-level counterparts in C++ and in most languages. We have also seen ordered pairs and associations, which are seldom represented directly in computer languages, though they are frequently used in applications. We shall see associations again in the next chapter when we study dictionaries.

Integers and characters were carefully implemented so that the uniqueness of the values was maintained. Since there is only one number 9, there is only one SInteger that means 9, whether we create the object directly or generate it as a result of arithmetic operations.

Strings were built more simply. In effect, we simply packaged the low-level C++ construct, making it possible to push strings onto stacks and make them keys of associations.

We also studied an additional collection mechanism, the hash table, that is optimized for fast lookup. In the best case, both insertion and lookup take time independently of the number of items stored, though in practice this is not always achieved.

EXERCISES

11.1 (11.1 and Section B.6) Reread the discussion of asInteger, especially what regards use of the iterator to search for the item. Of course, the list-position method search could carry out this task. We could also do the following. The problem in search is that the exit condition for the loop is compound. We want to exit if the iterator is exhausted or the item is found. In class SListIterator implement the new method

```
char nextItemWhich (PObject &o, char (*condition)
                            (PObject O, void *Link), void *Link)
```

which returns the next item in the list that meets the condition, where condition is a (pointer to a) Boolean function that returns TRUE for some objects and FALSE for others. The purpose of the Link parameter is to pass some extra information from the caller of nextItemWhich into the actual condition tester. The iterator will only return an item v from this method if condition (v) is evaluated TRUE. The usage here would be to create a Boolean function isEqual inside the scope of asInteger:

```
char isEqual (PObject O, void *Link) {
return 0 -> fValue == (int*)*Link
// Link is a pointer to an integer.
};
```

The use of the iterator in asInteger where we are searching for an integer i would be

```
IT = Integers[where] -> newIterator ();
if (IT -> nextItemWhich (aValue, isEqual, *i))
    // Found it.
else
    // Didn't find it; must create it.
```

11.2 (11.1) Taking the ideas expressed in our implementation of SInteger, build a new collection class, SHashTable, that implements a general storage structure implemented as a hash table. It needs the usual SCollection methods and an associated iterator class. The bucket table should be an instance variable of this class rather than a global variable. (Why?) You can depend on using the hash method of all objects.

11.3 (11.1) One possibility for implementing hash tables does not involve using an ordinary array for the bucket table. Suppose an object in class SDynamicArray as modified at the very end of Section 7.6 serves as the bucket table. Also suppose that the size of a segment is to be a power of 2, such as 32. When we create the hash table, we use a single segment, giving us 32 buckets, all in one segment. If at some point we decide that the buckets are getting too large, we can double the number of segments, doubling the number of buckets. We would then scan the entire contents of the hash table, recomputing the bucket numbers for each element stored. If we use simple modular arithmetic as the last step in our hash function, as we did when implementing SInteger (see index in asInteger), every object belongs either in its original list or in one of the new lists. In the latter case the node it occupies can be moved from one list to the other. On the average, each bucket will have only half as many objects. Verify that what we have said about hash functions is true, and implement hash tables as we suggest.

To decide when to expand the size of the bucket table, you can somehow keep the lengths of each list and of the longest list. These are updated on insertions and removals. When the length of the longest list exceeds some predetermined size, you trigger the reorganization. The reorganization is best written as a separate private method. Implement the test of the need to reorganize as a Boolean functional method.

11.4 (11.1) Implement a hash-table storage mechanism for the storage of arbitrary objects that employs circular hashing. If the structure is to be general, it needs to deal with the removal problem. If it is to be limited to problems not needing removals, the inherited method remove should be disabled.

11.5 (11.1) Fractions were implemented in Chapter 3 as a subclass of SMagnitude. Investigate the desirability and the feasablity of reimplementing them as a subclass of SInteger. You could let fValue represent the numerator in such a fraction and use another instance variable for the denominator. Consider how fractions should fit into a *specialization* hierarchy that includes integers. How would you deal with the problem of adding a fraction to an integer?

11.6 (11.1) C++ (as well as C) provides a floating type, called double, that provides for real numbers with about 15-digit accuracy and exponents in the range of about -300 to 300. Implement the class SFloat to encapsulate this type. Use a strategy like the one used for SInteger. Note that the extra overhead of using objects justifies the common use of the larger real sizes. Storage of real variable type double requires eight bytes. Give special thought to what you mean by equal for floating numbers. For example, if you add 1.2 and 4.6 do you get 5.8? Many systems won't get exactly 5.8 for the sum, but it should equal 5.8.

11.7 (11.2) Design a class, SBoolean, to implement the ordinary Booleans as a class.

11.8 (11.2) Design a class, SFuzzy, to implement fuzzy logic as a class. Fuzzy logic is similar to ordinary Boolean logic, except that there are three values, TRUE, FALSE, and UNKNOWN. You must extend the ordinary Boolean functions to handle the new value. For example, TRUE **and** UNKNOWN is UNKNOWN, and TRUE **or** UNKNOWN is TRUE. Investigate whether this class should be a subclass of your class SBoolean.

11.9 (11.3) Design a class, SComplex, to implement complex numbers. You can store either rectangular coordinates (real and imaginary parts) or spherical coordinates (distance from origin and angle from the real axis). Your methods should permit all common arithmetic as well as transformations between rectangular and spherical forms. If you store rectangular coordinates, you need functions to get the spherical ones. If you use spherical coordinates, you should consider our implementation of fractions, where we used a representation in lowest terms. A similar thing is required here. Are complex numbers magnitudes? If so, then how do you compute `less`, and what does it mean? Explore the mathematics of partial (as opposed to total) order.

11.10 (11.3) Implement the method `append` of class `SString` as discussed in Section 11.3. Implement a method that removes a substring from a given string.

11.11 (11.3) Implement the `SStringIterator` class.

11.12 (11.3) Rather than store strings in their underlying representation, it is sometimes advantageous for the programmer to implement a different storage structure. A string can be represented within a string object as a pair of integers, the first being an index into a spelling buffer and the second being the length of the string itself. The spelling buffer is a large global array (say 64 kilobytes) into which we put every new string. This array is shared by all string objects but is not visible to clients of the strings unit. The advantage of the structure is that, in some applications, it allows us to share storage for strings, searching among the already stored strings for the new string rather than allocate space for a new copy of it. If an application needs lots of string space and the strings are long lived and don't change, this can be useful. Of course, we need to implement a search for strings within the buffer to take advantage of this. Implement such a class.

11.13 (11.5) Discuss how a function can be considered to be a set of associations. Why is this true of associations even though it is not true that a function is a set of general pairs? Implement a finite factorial function with the integers between 0 and 10 for domain: $f(n) = n!$, $n = 0 \ldots 10$.

11.14 (11.6) Explore and implement a complement form of our large integer class. Instead of storing signed magnitudes, having separate signs, store the array of 10 ordinary integers and encode the negatives within it. Mimic the scheme called two's complement that is used on many computers. Since the base is 10000, the super-digits are between 0000 and 9999. If the leftmost of these is 5000 or larger, treat the number it is part of as a negative integer. If it is 4999 or less, treat it as nonnegative.

To negate a number, perform the following process. Replace each of its super-digits by subtracting the current value from 9999. After this is done for all ten entries, add 1 to the total result. Thus, negating the positive number

$$1234567890123456789012345678901234567890$$

the first step leaves us with

$$8765432109876543210987654321098765432109$$

The final step, adding 1, gives

$$8765432109876543210987654321098765432110$$

which is negative, having an 8 in the leftmost position (or an 8765 if you think of super-digits) If you do this again, you get the original number back, as expected. When adding 1 as part of this negation process, if you would normally carry left out of the leftmost position, ignore that carry. With this scheme addition needs no special cases (try it) and subtraction can be implemented as negation followed by addition.

## CHAPTER 12

MORE COLLECTIONS

For this they have engrossed and piled up
The canker'd heaps of strange-achieved gold;

   Shakespeare, *Henry IV*

A wealthy foole doth in vain hope by all his bagges to purchase wisedome.

   Bishop Hall, *Hard Texts*

In this chapter we shall examine six additional collection classes. A dictionary is a set of associations. An ordinary (book) dictionary associates keywords with definitions. A phone book associates names with phone numbers. We shall see that because of the definition of the equality of associations, a dictionary implements the mathematician's idea of a function. A hash dictionary is an ordinary dictionary, except that its implementation uses hash tables rather than sets. This means that we can achieve faster lookup times than we can with objects in SDictionary. A heap is a type of binary tree that imposes a special ordering on its contents. The ordering requires that we store only magnitudes, but a heap is a useful implementation mechanism for priority queues and can implement the sorting of lists.

   A graph is composed of nodes and arcs. It is a collection that is a generalization of a tree. In a graph it may be possible to follow a path along the arcs, moving from node to node, and come back to your starting place without retracing any arcs. This isn't possible in a tree. In a directed graph the arcs have a direction or orientation. We shall see one implementation of directed graphs, which is sufficiently general to be used in most graph problems.

An interval is nothing more than a finite arithmetic progression, such as 1, 3, 5, 7, 9, 11, which can be described as every second number between 1 and 11, inclusive or "from 1 to 11 by 2." This is the kind of collection that for loops in many languages are designed to use. In fact, a for loop is a kind of iterator over an interval. Finally, a bag is like a set and has similar operations, except that one item can appear in a bag more than once. The name is meant to suggest a bag of marbles, which can contain several identical objects.

12.1   DICTIONARIES

A dictionary is a (usually sorted) set of associations. An ordinary dictionary (the book kind) is such a set, of which the associations are keyword-definition pairs and the set of them is sorted. The keys and the definitions are strings. Some (book) dictionaries use pairs rather than associations, collecting the separate definitions of a word under separate but identical keywords. We won't generally permit that in this class, however. A dictionary is actually a (finite) function from a magnitude class to an arbitrary class, because of the rule that equal associations are those that have equal keys, and therefore a dictionary can have only one association with a given key. One way to say this is that the keys are unique. Another way is to say that a dictionary implements a function.

```
class SDictionary;         // A set of associations.
typedef SDictionary *PDictionary;

PDictionary newDictionary (void);

class SDictionary: public SSet {

    public:
            SDictionary (void);
        virtual char        member (classtype c);
        virtual void        insert (PObject o);
                            // Requires o in PAssociat:
        virtual void        atPut (PObject k,
                                PObject v);
                            // Requires k in PMagnitude
        virtual PObject     at (PObject k);
        virtual void        removeKey (PObject k);
        virtual PObject     keyAtValue (PObject o);

    protected:
        virtual int     sizeOf (void);
};
// REQUIREMENTS For Use
//    initLists ();
```

Our dictionary class is implemented as a subclass of SSet, which itself is implemented using SList. We won't sort our dictionaries, however. The constructor returns a new empty dictionary. We insert into the dictionary either by creating associations externally and inserting them or by calling the specialized insertion method atPut, which creates a new association to hold the supplied key and data. Both forms of insertion ensure that the set property is maintained, but they behave differently. If we try to insert a given association and there is already an association with this key, the new association is not inserted. Somewhat differently, atPut (aKey, aValue) inserts a new association if there is none with key equal to aKey, but if such exists, it changes the value of the one found to aValue.

```
void SDictionary :: insert (PObject o) {
   if (o -> member (association)) {
      SSet :: insert (o);
   }
   else
      Error ("SDictionary :: insert:
            Not an association.");
};

voidSDictionary :: atPut (PObject k, PObject v) {
   PObject o;
   PIterator IT;
   PAssociation newItem;
   PAssociation aPair;
   PObject anObject, aKey;

   newItem = NULL;
   IT = fElements -> newIterator ();
   while (IT -> nextItem (o)) {
      aPair = PAssociation (o);
      anObject = aPair -> key ();
      aKey = (anObject);
      if (k -> equal (aKey)) {
         newItem = PAssociation (o);
         IT -> Short ();
      };
   };
   delete IT;
   if (newItem != NULL) {
      newItem -> setValue (v);
   }
   else{
      newItem = newAssociation (k, v);
      if (newItem == NULL) Error ("NULL association \n");
```

```
        insert (newItem);
    };
};
```

The methods `at` and `keyAtValue` are our lookup methods for dictionaries. The method `at` returns the unique value associated with a given key (or NULL if there is no such item), and `keyAtValue` returns some key for a supplied value. Several different keys may have the same value. We are certain only to get back one valid key (or NULL of course, if there is no such item). Both of these methods require a search of the dictionary. Since our implementation is sequential, we do a sequential search. Iterators are inherited and can be used easily. The method `removeKey` is similar to these. It searches for the supplied key and, if such an association is found, calls (the inherited) `remove` to remove the association.

```
PObject SDictionary :: at (PObject k) {
    PObject o;
    PIterator IT;
    PAssociation newItem;

    newItem = NULL;
    IT = fElements -> newIterator ();
    while (IT -> nextItem (o)) {
        if (k -> equal (PAssociation (o)
                            -> key ())) {
            newItem = PAssociation (o);
            IT -> Short ();
        };
    };
    if (newItem != NULL)
        return newItem -> value ();
    else {
        return NULL;
    };
    delete IT;
};

PObject SDictionary :: keyAtValue (PObject o) {
    PObject item;
    PIterator IT;
    PAssociation newItem;

    IT = fElements -> newIterator ();
    while (IT -> nextItem (item)) {
        if (o -> equal (PAssociation (item) ->
                            value ())) {
```

```
                newItem = PAssociation (item);
                IT -> Short ();
            };
        };
        if (newItem != NULL)
            return (newItem -> key ());
        else {
            return NULL;
        };
        delete IT;
    };
```

12.2   HASH DICTIONARIES

Conceptually there is no difference between our original dictionary class and the class SHashDictionary. Only the implementation is different. We have presented a new class here only so that the two may coexist in the same library. We are seeking better performance when we look up a key in the dictionary. To achieve the performance, we shall give each dictionary a hash table rather than a list of associations. A hash table is an array of lists, one for each possible value of an internal hashing function. When we insert an association into the dictionary, we evelute the hash function of the key of the association in order to obtain an index and then store the association in the list with the same index value.

```
class SHashDictionary;
class SHashDictionaryIterator;
typedef SHashDictionary *PHashDictionary;
typedef SHashDictionaryIterator
    *PHashDictionaryIterator;

PHashDictionary newHashDictionary (int hashsize);

class SHashDictionary: public SCollection {
    public:
            SHashDictionary (int hashsize);
        virtual             ~SHashDictionary ();
        virtual void        atPut (PObject k,
                                PObject v);
        virtual PObject     at (PObject k);
        virtual void        removeKey (PObject k);
        virtual PObject     keyAtValue (PObject o);
        virtual void        insert (PObject);
        virtual void        remove (PObject);
        virtual char        empty (void);
```

```
        virtual PIterator     newIterator (void);
        virtual char          member (classtype c);
        virtual PObject       Clone (void);
        virtual void          writeIt (void);

    protected:
        PList *fDictionary;
        int fSize;
        virtual int sizeOf (void);
        virtual int index (PObject m);
        friend SHashDictionaryIterator;
};

class SHashDictionaryIterator: public SIterator {
    public:
            SHashDictionaryIterator
            (PHashDictionary h);
        virtual            ~SHashDictionaryIterator ();
        virtual char       nextItem (PObject&);
        virtual void       reset (void);
        virtual char       member (classtype c);
        virtual PObject    Clone (void);


    protected:
        int fRow;
        PList fList;
        PIterator fIterator;
        virtual int sizeOf (void);



};

// REQUIREMENTS For Use
//     initLists ();
```

Initialization of a hash dictionary involves initializing all of the lists in its hash table. It should call newList in a loop, setting the contents of the array to the results of the calls.

```
SHashDictionary :: SHashDictionary (int hashsize) {
    fSize = hashsize;
    if (fSize < 1) fSize = 1;
    fDictionary = new PList[hashsize];
    if (fDictionary == NULL) Error ("System heap
                                    exhausted.");
```

```
    for (int i = 0; i < fSize; ++i) {
       fDictionary[i] = newList ();
    };
};
```

The index method, which is our internal hashing function, uses the public hash method of every object. It then reduces the returned value using the remainder function so that it represents a valid index into our hash table.

```
int SHashDictionary :: index (PObject m) {
   long result;

   result = m -> hash ();
   result %= fSize;
   return result;
};
```

The atPut method must check whether the key parameter is already stored. If it is, atPut must adjust the associated value; otherwise it must insert a new association into the proper list.

```
void SHashDictionary :: atPut (PObject k,
                                PObject v) {
   PAssociation a;
   PIterator IT;
   int where;
   PObject o;
   a = NULL;
   where = index (k);
   IT = fDictionary[where] -> newIterator ();
   while (IT -> nextItem (o))
      if (k -> equal (PAssociation (o) -> key ())) {
         a = PAssociation (o);
          IT -> Short ();
       };
   if (a == NULL) {
      a = newAssociation (k, v);
      fDictionary[where] -> insert (a);
   }
   else
      a -> setValue (v);
   delete IT;
};
```

Most of the rest of the methods of SHashDictionary are similar. The iterator class is complicated by the fact that many of the lists in a hash dictionary may be empty. It must skip over these when it is iterating. Once it has a nonempty list for some index, it creates a new iterator for that list and uses it until that list is finished. If there are more lists, it needs to delete this iterator and generate a new one for the next nonempty list.

```
SHashDictionaryIterator :: SHashDictionaryIterator
                            (PHashDictionary h):
                            SIterator (h) {
    if (!fDone) {
       fRow = 0;
       while (PHashDictionary (fCollection) ->
          fDictionary[fRow] -> empty () && fRow <
          PHashDictionary (fCollection) -> fSize)
             ++fRow;
       fList = PHashDictionary (fCollection) ->
          fDictionary[fRow];
       fIterator = PListIterator (fList
                                   -> newIterator ());
    }
    else {
       fRow = 0;
       fList = NULL;
       fIterator = NULL;
    };
};

char SHashDictionaryIterator
    :: nextItem (PObject &o) {
    char result, ok;

    result = !fDone;
    if (result)
       if (!fIterator -> nextItem (o)) {
          delete fIterator;
          if (fRow == PHashDictionary
             (fCollection) -> fSize) {
             fDone = TRUE;
             fIterator = NULL;
          }
          else {
             ++fRow;
             while (PHashDictionary (fCollection)
                    -> fDictionary[fRow]
                    -> empty () && fRow <
```

```
                    PHashDictionary (fCollection)
                       -> fSize) ++fRow;
               fList = PHashDictionary (fCollection)
                  -> fDictionary[fRow];
               fIterator = PListIterator
                  (fList -> newIterator ());
               ok = fIterator -> nextItem (o);
               };
         };
     return result;
  }; // See Exercise 12.1.
```

12.3   HEAPS

A heap is a kind of binary tree, specialized in three ways. First, it is generally, though not essentially, stored in an array structure. Second, it imposes a certain kind of ordering on its elements, which are therefore required to be magnitudes. Finally, it must obey a certain restriction on which nodes have children, which makes the array storage particularly efficient. We shall examine each of these requirements in turn.

Suppose we store a binary tree in an array in the following way. The root is stored in cell 1 (we leave cell 0 empty for now). The left and right children, if there are any, of cell N are stored in adjacent cells $2N$ and $2N + 1$, respectively. There can be no conflict in this; the children of no other cell will be stored in either of these. For example, the children of cell 5 are stored in cells 10 and 11, those of cell 4 are stored in cells 8 and 9, and those of cell 6 are stored in cells 12 and 13. In general, this method of storage is not very efficient. For example, a tree that had a right child whose right child had a right child, and so on, with only right children to a great depth, would have relatively few nodes but would require a large array for its storage. The root would be in cell 1. The only node of height 1 would be in cell 3. The only node of height 2 would be in cell 7. If there were 12 nodes, the last one would be in cell 4095. The purpose of the third restriction on heaps is to improve the density of storage in the array; in fact, to maximize it.

The second restriction on heaps is that the children of a cell store only values that are smaller than or equal to the value stored in the parent. Thus the largest value stored in a heap is always at the root. The heap as a whole is not necessarily sorted, and there is no necessary relationship between the sizes of the values stored in the left and right children of a node, as long as they are both not larger than the value stored in their parent.

Heaps are useful in building a sorting routine, as we shall see. Another use of heaps is as an implementation of priority queues. Suppose we build associations whose keys are priorities. If we insert these associations into a heap, the one with the largest priority is always at the root (cell 1). We shall also build efficient methods for removing the root, so that we have, in effect, efficient methods for performing the dequeue operation of priority queues.

The third restriction on heaps, and the one that makes the storage strategy efficient, is that they be complete binary trees. A binary tree is called *complete* if two conditions hold. First, the height (distance from the root) of every leaf differs by no more than one from the maximum leaf height. For example, if the tree is of height 5, then 1 cell, the root, is at height 0, exactly 2 cells are at height 1, exactly 4 are at height 2, exactly 8 at height 3, exactly 16 are at height 4, and between 1 and 32 are at height 5. Notice that all of the levels whose heights are less than the height of the tree are completely full. The second requirement of complete binary trees deals only with the lowest (leaf) level. All of the leaves on the lowest level are as far to the left as possible. This means that if a node in the tree has a descendant of a given height, all the nodes to its left on the same level also have descendants of that same height, and that if a node has a right child, it also has a left child.

A heap is shown as a binary tree in Fig. 12.1. If this same heap were stored in an array, the size would be 10 and the contents would be 8, 7, 3, 5, 2, 2, 1, 3, 4, 1, in that order. The children of the 5 in the fourth cell are in the eighth and ninth cells, which hold the the adjacent 3 and 4. This ordering of a tree is also called *level order*.

The *completeness* of a heap is what makes the storage in an array efficient. In the array implementing the heap, the cells from index one to some

FIGURE 12.1

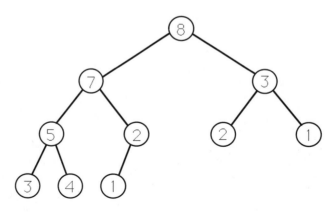

maximum index, called the size of the heap, are completely filled with objects. In a heap of height 5, 31 cells are filled by objects of levels less than 5, and between 1 and 32 cells are filled by objects of the last level, and these also have cell numbers as small as possible. If there are 9 leaves at level 5, the entire heap will occupy cells 1 through 40 of our array.

Our new class, SHeap, is built as a collection. An array of pointers to objects holds the elements in the heap. When we create a heap we must know the maximum number of elements that we will store in it so that we may allocate this array. This requires knowledge of the uses of the heap and an assumption that we won't need to store more than some fixed number of values in any such heap. If this is not a valid assumption, we will need methods that permit extensions of the size of the storage array as we saw in class SArray. See the exercises for other possibilities. We need one instance variable, fMax, to store the current allocated size and another, fSize, for the current active size, since a heap will occupy only a portion of the array. Our array classes are defined with a cell zero. We use this cell but not as a container for an object in the heap; therefore, a heap occupies cells from 1 to fSize. Thus, initialization needs to set fSize to be zero, indicating that there are no elements.

```
class SHeap;
typedef SHeap *PHeap;
PHeap newHeap (int max);

class SHeap: public SCollection {
    public:
                SHeap (int max);
        virtual                 ~SHeap ();
        virtual void            insert (PObject);
        virtual void            remove (PObject);
        virtual PObject         removeMax (void);
        virtual PObject         replaceMax (PObject);
        virtual void            filterUp (int);
        virtual void            trickleDown (int);
        virtual void            doHeap (void);
        virtual void            heapSort (void);
                        // Destroys the heap property.
        virtual char            empty (void);
        virtual char            full (void);
        virtual PIterator       newIterator (void);
        virtual char            member (classtype c);
        virtual PObject         Clone (void);
        virtual void            writeIt (void);

    protected:
        int fSize; // Current active size,
```

```
                    // cells 1 ... fSize.
        int fMax; // 0 <= fSize <= fMax
        PObject *fElements;
        virtual int sizeOf (void);
};
```

The methods `filterUp` and `trickleDown` maintain the heap property while insertions and removals are performed. They are not intended to be called by clients. It is also possible that we shall destroy the heap property occasionally. Both `insert` and `remove` maintain it, but the sorting method, `heapSort`, certainly destroys it, since it leaves the smallest element in cell one. The purpose of `doHeap` is to restore the heap property. It need only be called after `heapSort`, because that is the only method that breaks the property. The methods `removeMax` and `replaceMax` are somewhat nonstandard, since they are both procedures (they modify the heap) and functions (they return a value). Note that `replaceMax` might return the same object that it is sent as a parameter, since it effectively inserts the parameter into the heap and then removes and returns the maximum value.

If a datum is inserted into a heap, a new cell becomes occupied. This cell is on the bottom level of its tree and farthest to the left. If we were to insert a new object into that location, we might destroy the ordering of the heap. The method `filterUp` works from this last leaf of the heap upward, moving data downward and the value at the new leaf upward until the heap property is restored. Note that the parent of cell M is stored in the array at location $M/2$. First `filterUp` copies a reference to the data in the last cell, and then it walks up toward the root until it finds an ancestor larger than the data saved. For each upward step taken, the data moves downward, occupying the lower cell. When it is impossible to move upward any farther, the saved data is stored in the last cell vacated by the downward move. Note that if the data is larger than the content of some cell in a heap, it is larger than the contents of the children, and so it will be legal to put the larger data in that cell, provided that it shouldn't go higher.

```
void SHeap :: filterUp (int k) {
    PObject aValue;
    int where;
    char done;

    if (k <0 !! k > fSize) Error ("SHeap :: filterUp:
                                    Illegal parameter."
    where = k;
    done = FALSE;
    aValue = fElements[where];
    while (where > 1 && !done) {
        if (PMagnitude (aValue) -> lessEqual
            (fElements[where / 2]))
```

```
                done = TRUE;
            else {
                fElements[where] = fElements [where / 2];
                where /= 2;
            };
        };
        fElements[where] = aValue;
    };
```

The method `trickleDown` proceeds in the opposite direction. It starts at some point in the structure and works downward, moving data upward, until the heap property is restored. It is used primarily in removals, which may be at the root or elsewhere. The root is removed by first copying a reference to the root so that it can be returned at the end, copying the data in the last cell to the root, almost certainly breaking the heap property, and then calling `trickleDown` to restore the property. When we work downward we need to consider both children. If a node is in cell M, its children are in cells $2M$ and $2M + 1$. We want the largest of the values of these three cells to occupy cell M. If one of the two children must be moved to achieve this, we continue to work down that branch. We stop when no further move is necessary or when we reach a node that has no children. Note that if $2M > $ fSize, there can be no child.

```
void SHeap :: trickleDown (int k) {
    PObject aValue;
    int j;
    char done;

    if (k < 0 !! k > fSize) Error
        ("SHeap :: trickleDown: Illegal parameter.");
    done = FALSE;
    aValue = fElements[k];
    while (k <= fSize / 2 && !done) {
        j = 2 * k;
        if (j < fSize && fElements[j]
            -> less (fElements[j + 1]))
            ++j;
        if (PMagnitude (fElements[j])
            -> lessEqual (aValue))
            done = TRUE;
        else {
            fElements[k] = fElements[j];
            k = j;
        };
    };
    fElements[k] = aValue;
};
```

If trickleDown is executed in a state in which the structure is a heap except for cell k, meaning that the value in cell k is less than or equal to the value in its parent and that *some* replacement value would make the structure into a heap, then the post-condition is that the structure is a heap. Likewise, if filterUp is executed in a state in which the structure is a heap from cell k downward, the structure is a heap when filterUp (k) finishes.

Given filterUp, insert is easily built. Similarly, removeMax, which removes and returns the root, is easy. We need only copy the last cell to the root and then have trickleDown restore the heap property. Of course, the size of the heap must also be adjusted in both of these operations.

```
void SHeap :: insert (PObject o) {

    if (o -> member (magnitude) && fSize < fMax) {
        ++fSize;
        fElements[fSize] = o;
    };
    filterUp (fSize);
};

PObject SHeap :: removeMax (void) {
    PObject result;

    if (fSize > 0) {
        result = fElements[1];
        fElements[1] = fElements[fSize];
        --fSize;
        trickleDown (1);
        return result;
    };
    else
        return NULL;
};
```

The remove method must find and remove the parameter object. It can copy the last object to the slot vacated and then call either filterUp or trickleDown. It is not enough to assume that trickleDown will always work. (Why?)

```
void SHeap :: remove (PObject o) {
    int i;
    char found;

    i = 1;
    found = FALSE;
```

```
        while (! found && i <= fSize)
            if (fElements[i] -> equal (o))
                found = TRUE;
            else
                ++i;
    if (found)
        if (i == fSize)
            --fSize;
        else {
            fElements[i] = fElements[fSize];
            --fSize;
            if (i == 1)
                trickleDown (i);
            else if (PMagnitude (fElements[i])
                        -> greater (fElements[i / 2]))
                filterUp (i);
            else
                trickleDown (i);
        };
};
```

The method `replaceMax` could work by inserting and then removing the maximum. A trick is possible, however. Cell 0 is free, $2 \cdot 0$ is also 0 and $2 \cdot 0 + 1$ is the root of the heap. Thus `trickleDown` can work from cell 0 as well as from any other. It will move the largest element into cell 0, from which it can be returned, and place the others in the normal heap cells.

```
PObject SHeap :: replaceMax (PObject o) {
    fElements[0] = o;
    trickleDown (0);
    return fElements[0];
};
```

The method `doHeap` restores the heap operation. It repeatedly calls `trickleDown`, working upward toward the root. Since it works upward, it can depend on the heap condition's being met below it. This greatly improves the efficiency of the process. We only need to work from cells that might have children, so we begin the process in cell `fSize / 2`.

```
void SHeap :: doHeap (void) {
    for (int k = fSize / 2;k > 0; --k)
    trickleDown (k);
};
```

12.3.1 Heap Sort

The `heapSort` process uses the heap property to repeatedly obtain the largest cell of a collection efficiently. In effect, we swap the root of a heap

and its last cell. We then *artificially* reduce the size of the heap by one
so that we don't include the maximum just moved. Then we restore the
heap property on the smaller heap, obtaining a new maximum, the second
largest of the original data, at the root. We then repeat the process until
only the smallest is left. Note that this destroys the heap property, and to
carry it out we also change the size of the heap. The size is restored at
the end, but the data are left in a sorted state rather than a heap state.
The heap property may later be restored by the user with doHeap. The
invariant that we attempt to maintain is shown in Fig. 12.2. The left portion
of the active section is maintained as a heap. The right portion is sorted
and contains the largest of the original objects. We advance the sort by
swapping cell 1, which contains the largest value in the heap, and cell
fSize. We then decrease fSize, increasing the size of the sorted portion.
A trickleDown operation restores the heap property on the segment 1
...fSize.

```
void SHeap :: heapSort (void) { // Destroys the
                                // heap property.
    int M;
    DObject aValue;

    M = fSize; // A trick. It will be restored.
    do {
        aValue = fElements[1];
        fElements[1] = fElements[fSize];
        fElements[fSize] = aValue;
        --fSize;
        trickleDown (1);
    } while (fSize > 1);
    fSize = M;
};
```

12.3.2 Efficiency of the Heap Operations

Most of the heap operations operate on a single path from root to leaf.
The notable exception is remove, which uses a linear search through the
array. If a heap contains about 1000 items, its height is about 10. Therefore,
the length of the longest path in a large heap is much shorter than the
length of the array, which is the number of items. In fact, the lengths are
logarithmically related, making heap operations extremely efficient both in
space and in time.

HEAP	Sorted/Largest

FIGURE 12.2   1   fSize   M

12.4   GRAPHS

Graphs were discussed in Chapter 9. In this section we shall see one method of implementing directed graphs and see a few of the things that might be done with them. This is just an introduction to a very deep and complex topic, however. Our implementation can be easily extended to ordinary (undirected) graphs and is sufficiently general to solve most problems. In many problems, however, a specialized implementation would increase efficiency.

A graph is a collection of vertices and edges. The vertices are primitive in the mathematical model, though they can be used to hold data. We model the vertices as objects that hold data and that know about their edges. An edge is a pair of vertices. In a directed graph, an edge is an ordered pair of vertices, usually with the first element of the pair called the tail and the second called the head. Data can be stored along the edges as well as at the vertices, but that will not be stressed. We model a directed edge as an object stored in a list associated with a vertex, its tail end. Such an object can contain a data field, which would store values. An edge object has an instance variable that represents the vertex at the head of the edge. Its tail is not directly represented. The tail of an edge is represented indirectly by the list the edge appears on. An example of a graph with eight vertices and nine edges is shown in Fig. 12.3.

We model a graph as a whole using a dynamic array of vertices. Each vertex in the graph maintains data and a list of the edges that point away from that vertex. Each of the edges has a field that refers to the head end of that edge. The representation of the graph of Fig. 12.3 is shown in Fig. 12.4. The left portion shows the vertex array. The arrow at the bottom indicates that it is a dynamic array and will grow as the size of the graph grows. The edges are at the right. Each edge is on a list corresponding to the tail of the edge, and each edge holds a reference to the vertex at its head. In

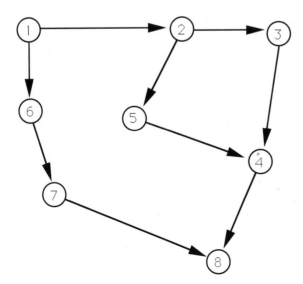

FIGURE 12.3

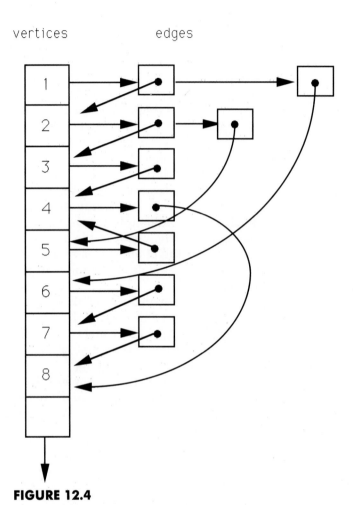

FIGURE 12.4

the vertices are shown some data which in this case are just the integers corresponding to the order in which the vertices were created. Just as in Fig. 12.3, Fig. 12.4 indicates that vertex 1 has an edge to vertex 2 and an edge to vertex 6, etc.

Graphs are collections, since the vertices, and perhaps the edges, hold data. They have positions and rather complex iterators. A graph position refers to some vertex. Iterators may iterate in several orders. One obvious order is that of vertex creation. In another, called depth-first order, chains of edges are followed, yielding vertices as we go until a vertex is found that lacks outward-pointing edges or whose outward-pointing edges point to vertices already yielded. This is very much like pre-order processing in a tree. The opposite order, called breadth-first order, involves processing the near neighbors of a vertex before processing the farther neighbors. It is similar to level-order processing in a tree.

Many operations on graphs are complicated by the possibility of loops in paths through the graph. We don't want our algorithms to follow paths forever, obviously. We must therefore know which vertices have been processed as an algorithm progresses. One way of doing this is to give unique names to the vertices and save the names of the vertices processed. Another way is to mark the nodes when we process them so that we know not to repeat a process. The latter method is easier, but requires that only one process be active at a time, unless we provide a multiplicity of possible marks. We provide a single Boolean field, fMarked, to indicate that a vertex has been marked, and methods for setting, clearing, and checking this mark. Inserting an edge into a vertex involves nothing more than inserting it into the fEdges list and incrementing fOrder, which keeps track of the number of edges pointing out from the vertex. The other methods of SVertex should be obvious.

```
class SGraph;
typedef SGraph *PGraph;
class SVertex;
typedef SVertex *PVertex;
class SEdge;
typedef SEdge *PEdge;

PGraph newGraph ();

class SGraph: public SCollection {
    public:
        SGraph();
    virtual                 ~SGraph ();
    virtual void            edgeFromTo (PVertex,
                            PVertex);
    virtual PVertex         newVertex (PObject);
    virtual void            unmark (void);
    virtual PQueue          depthFirstOrder (void);
        // Produces a new list (queue) of the
        // vertices in depth first order.
        // Does not modify the graph itself
        // (except possibly the marks).
    virtual PQueue breadthFirstOrder(void);
        // Produces a new list (queue) of the
        // vertices in breadth first order.
        // Does not modify the graph itself
        // (except possibly the marks).
```

```
            virtual PStack depthFirstSort(char &detect);
                // Produces a new list (stack) of the
                // vertices in topological order.
                // Set detect = TRUE to obtain cycle
                // detection. Then it will be set TRUE
                // if the graph has one or more cycles.
                // Does not modify the graph itself
                // (except possibly the marks).
                        // Must disable insert and remove.
            virtual void            insert (PObject);
            virtual void            remove (PObject);
            virtual char            empty (void);
            virtual PIterator       newIterator (void);
            virtual PPosition       newPosition (void);
            virtual char            member (classtype c);
            virtual PObject         Clone (void);
            virtual void            writeIt (void);

        protected:
            PDynamicArray       fVertices;
            int                 fNumberOfVertices;
            virtual       int sizeOf (void);
        friend SGraphPosition;
        friend SGraphIterator;
    };


    class SVertex: public SObject {
        public:
                SVertex (PObject);
            virtual             ~SVertex ();
            virtual void        insertEdge (PEdge);
            virtual char        member (classtype c);
            virtual PObject     Clone (void);
            virtual void        writeIt (void);

        protected:
            PObject         fValue;
            PList           fEdges;
            int             fOrder;
            char            fMarked;
            virtual int     sizeOf (void);
            virtual void    mark (void);
            virtual void    unmark (void);
            virtual char    marked (void);
```

```
        friend SGraph;
        friend SGraphPosition;
        friend void nbrsOf (PVertex v, PQueue Q);
        friend void topSort (PVertex v, char &detect,
                              PStack P, char oldDetect);
    };

class SEdge: public SObject {
    public:
            SEdge (PVertex head);
        virtual PVertex     head (void);
        virtual char        member (classtype c);
        virtual void        writeIt (void);

        protected:
        PVertex         fHeadVertex;
        virtual int    sizeOf (void);
        friend void nbrsOf (PVertex v, PQueue Q);
    };

class SGraphPosition;
typedef SGraphPosition *PGraphPosition;

class SGraphPosition: public SPosition {
    public:
            SGraphPosition (PGraph g);
        virtual             ~SGraphPosition (void);
        virtual void        toHead (void);
        virtual void        useNextEdge (void);
        virtual PObject     at (void);
        virtual void        toVertex (int n);
        virtual PVertex     vertexAt (void);
        virtual PEdge       direction (void);
        virtual PVertex     nextHead (void);
        virtual char        member (classtype c);
        virtual PObject     Clone (void);
        virtual void        writeIt (void);

        protected:
        PGraph          fGraph;
        PVertex         fPosition;
        PListPosition   fDirection;
        virtual     int sizeOf (void);

    };
```

```
class SGraphIterator;
typedef SGraphIterator *PGraphIterator;

PGraphIterator newGraphIterator ();

class SGraphIterator: public SIterator {
   public:
         SGraphIterator (PGraph g);
         // Initialize and reset to iterate
         // in vertex definition order.
      virtual            ~SGraphIterator (void);
      virtual char       nextItem (PObject&);
         // Yield the vertices in definition order.
      virtual char       nextDepthFirst (PObject&);
         // Yield the vertices in depth-first
         // order. Must initialize
         // with resetDepthFirst.
      virtual char       nextBreadthFirst (PObject&)
         // Yield the vertices in breadth-first
         // order. Must initialize
         // with resetBreadthFirst.
      virtual char       nextTopological (PObject&);
      virtual void       resetDepthFirst (void);
         // Reset the iterator so that it will
         // iterate in depth-first order using
         // nextDepthFirst.
      virtual void       resetBreadthFirst (void);
         // Reset the iterator so that it will
         // iterate in breadth-first order
         // using nextBreadthFirst.
      virtual void       resetTopological (void);
      virtual void       reset (void);
         // Reset to yield vertices in definition
         // order using nextItem.
      virtual char       member (classtype c);
      virtual PObject    Clone (void);

   protected:
      int                fPosition;
      PQueue             fList;
      virtual int        sizeOf (void);

};
// REQUIREMENTS For Use
//    initLists ();
```

Similarly, an edge has a simple protocol with obvious meanings. Initialization involves only setting its fHeadVertex field. The method head retrieves a reference to the head of an edge, and writeIt writes the edge by sending writeIt to its head vertex. A simple extension of initialization would permit the edge to contain data. We would need a new instance variable to hold the data, of course.

The graph itself is a collection that has a PDynamicArray object to hold references to the vertices and an integer field to remember the number of vertices. The vertices are stored in an initial section of the large array, and a new one is entered by extending the array by one cell. Therefore we maintain the vertices in the array in the order of their creation. We make no provision for the removal of vertices or edges in a graph. If removal methods are needed, they could be supplied in subclasses of SGraph. Graph initialization involves creation of the fVertices array and setting fNumberOfVertices to zero. To write a graph, we could just give the data in the vertices, but it is more informative to give for each vertex the data in it and in the vertices at the other ends of edges pointing away from it. This is redundant, but it shows the structure of the graph more clearly. We make no attempt to draw the graph in two or more dimensions.

```
void SGraph :: writeIt (void) {
    PVertex v;

    for (int i = 1; i <= fNumberOfVertices; ++i) {
        v = PVertex (fVertices -> at (i));
        v -> writeIt ();
        cout << " : ";
        v -> fEdges -> writeIt ();
        cout << "\n";
    };
};
```

A new vertex is created and inserted into the fVertex array by a generator method of SGraph. It returns a reference to the vertex, in case the user desires to operate on the vertex in some way. The parameter becomes the data stored in the vertex. At creation the vertex has no edges, so the graph is not a connected graph. In fact, our graphs are not required to be connected. The internal array of vertices always remembers which vertices belong to which graph, so following the edges is not necessary for finding other vertices in the graph.

```
PVertex SGraph :: newVertex (PObject o) {
    PVertex result;
```

```
      result = new SVertex (o);
      failnull (result);
      ++fNumberOfVertices;
      fVertices -> atPut (fNumberOfVertices, result);
      return result;
};
```

We create a new edge by passing two vertices to the edgeFromTo method. It is a generator also. It creates an edge whose head is the "to" vertex and inserts it in the edge list of the "from" vertex. The method does not return a reference to the edge. An edge should be in the edge list of only one vertex. This protects us from disaster. (Why?)

```
void SGraph :: edgeFromTo (PVertex f, PVertex t) {
   PEdge edge;

   edge = new SEdge (t);
   failnull (edge);
   f -> insertEdge (edge);
};
```

The method unmark sends unmark to all of the vertices in the vertex array, setting in turn all of the fMarked fields to FALSE.

```
void SGraph :: unmark (void) {
   for (int i = 1; i <= fNumberOfVertices; ++i)
      PVertex (fVertices -> at (i)) -> unmark ();
};
```

The next two methods, depthFirstOrder and breadthFirst-Order, are intended to help us construct iterators. They can be used by clients directly, however. Each of them constructs a list of the vertices in the graph and returns it. They do not modify the graph in any way. The list they return is a new list with references to the vertices in the graph. This list is actually a queue and can be used with dequeue to retrieve the vertices in the specified order or be deleted if no longer needed, without danger to the graph from which it was constructed. They both begin by creating a new queue and unmarking the graph. They both proceed by enqueueing vertices so that when they finish, all of the vertices appear in the queue. They both finish by returning the completed queue. They both process the entire vertex list of the graph, generally working in order of vertex creation.

The depthFirstOrder method recursively processes the vertices reachable from the current vertex. When it processes a vertex, it marks it, inserts it into the queue that it is constructing, and then processes all of the unmarked vertices reachable along edges from that vertex. Since it processes a vertex before the neighbors, it is like pre-order tree processing. If we list the vertices of the graph of Fig. 12.3 in depth-first order, we obtain 1, 6, 7, 8, 2, 5, 4, 3. We could give several other lists. This one is determined partially by the order in which we followed the edges. Another possible depth-first order is 1, 2, 3, 4, 8, 5, 6, 7. Note that the order is also determined partly by the order in which the vertices are defined. If we had defined the same graph but created the vertices in order 5, 6, 7, 8, 1, 2, 3, 4 instead, a depth-first ordering could be 5, 4, 8, 6, 7, 1, 2, 3.

```
void nbrsOf (PVertex v, PQueue Q) {
    PVertex x;
    PObject e;
    PIterator IT;

    v -> mark ();
    Q -> enqueue (v);
    IT = v -> fEdges -> newIterator ();
    while (IT -> nextItem (e)) {
        x = PEdge (e) -> head ();
        if (! x -> marked ()) nbrsOf (x, Q);
    };
    delete IT;
};

PQueue SGraph :: depthFirstOrder (void) {
    PQueue result;
    PVertex v;
    int i;

    result = newQueue ();
    unmark ();
    for (i = 1; i <= fNumberOfVertices; ++i) {
        v = PVertex (fVertices -> at (i));
        if (! v -> marked ()) nbrsOf (v, result);
    };
    return result;
};
```

The same process is performed by breadthFirstOrder as by depthFirstOrder with one important difference. Since depth-first processing is done recursively, it is equivalent to using a stack to process the data. We saw this in our investigations of recursion removal. If we replace that stack with a queue but otherwise use the same algorithm, we get a process that also processes all of the nodes. This is breadth-first order. Instead of processing the neighbors of a node as soon as possible (recursion or stack processing), we process them as late as possible. The following procedure could be arrived at by removing the recursion from the above process and replacing the stack so introduced with another queue. The details are left to the truly committed. Note that only unmarked vertices are put into the new queue. When we remove them, we must still check whether they are marked, because they may have become marked when we followed another path back to them. If we list the vertices of Fig. 12.3 in breadth-first order, we could get 1, 6, 2, 7, 5, 3, 8, 4.

```
PQueue SGraph :: breadthFirstOrder (void) {
    PQueue Q, result;
    PVertex v, w;
    PObject e;
    int i;
    PIterator IT;

    unmark ();
    Q = newQueue ();
    result = newQueue ();
    for (i = 1; i <= fNumberOfVertices; ++i) {
        v = PVertex (fVertices -> at (i));
        if (! v -> marked ()) {
            Q -> insert (v);
            do {
                v = PVertex (Q -> Dequeue ());
                if (! v -> marked ()) {
                    v -> mark ();
                    result -> enqueue (v);
                    IT = v -> fEdges -> newIterator ();
                    while (IT -> nextItem (e)) {
                        w = PEdge (e) -> head ();
                        if (! w -> marked ())
                            Q -> insert (w);
                    };
                    delete IT;
                };
            } while (! Q -> empty ());
        };
    };
    delete Q;
    return result;
};
```

The final method in this group, depthFirstSort, yields a stack in which the vertices of the graph are listed in an order called topological order. If this ordering is applied to a directed graph with no cycles, each node is listed before any of the nodes that can be reached from it. If the graph has cycles, then this won't (can't) be true, but the process still produces the vertices on each cycle in order of the cycle. Our original graph in Fig. 12.3

has no cycles. One topological ordering is 1, 2, 3, 6, 7, 5, 4, 8. If we reverse the directions of the edges from 2 to 3 and from 3 to 4, we form a cycle from 5 to 4 to 3 to 2 to 5. Then one topological ordering of the graph is 1, 6, 7, 5, 4, 3, 2, 8. Note that a topological sort is similar to a post-order tree walk *in reverse*. The process is developed in a similar way to such a post-order walk. We process the vertices recursively, stacking a vertex in the output stack only when all nodes reachable from it have already been stacked. We also permit depthFirstSort to return an indication of whether the graph has cycles. Since such extra processing is expensive in time, we signal the method if we want it done. If we set the parameter detect of this method to TRUE, the routine will indicate whether the graph has cycles. It uses the same parameter, detect, to return the value. The method depthFirstSort is a function that returns a stack of the vertices listed in topological order.

The method proceeds by creating a stack, unmarking the graph (this), remembering if the user wants cycle detection, and calling the recursive procedure topSort on the first vertex. When that procedure returns, the other unmarked vertices are sent to topSort until all vertices are marked. The function topSort marks the vertex sent it and then works through the edges that start at that vertex. If an edge has an unmarked head, topSort is called recursively on that vertex. When the recursion returns, the vertex is stacked. Since recursions involve vertices that can be reached, and since each vertex is stacked after the recursions, each vertex is pushed after the vertices reachable from it. Cycles are detected through the examination of the vertices that appear in the edge lists. If a vertex is already marked, it has been seen somewhere. If it is not in the stack, it was marked in the current recursive chain and thus is part of a cycle.

```
void topSort (PVertex v, char &detect, PStack P,
              char oldDetect) {
    PIterator IT;
    PVertex w;
    PObject e;

    v -> mark ();
    IT = v -> fEdges -> newIterator ();
    while (IT -> nextItem (e)) {
        w = PEdge (e) -> head ();
        if (! w -> marked ()) topSort (w, detect, P,
                                       oldDetect);
        else
            if (oldDetect && !detect && ! P ->
                element (w)) detect = TRUE;
    };
    P -> push (v);
    delete IT;
};
```

```
PStack SGraph :: depthFirstSort (char &detect) {
    PStack result;
    PVertex v;
    char doDetect;
    int i;

    unmark ();
    result = newStack ();
    doDetect = detect;
    detect = FALSE;
    for (i = 1; i <= fNumberOfVertices; ++i) {
        v = PVertex (fVertices -> at (i));
        if (! v -> marked ()) topSort (v, detect,
                                        result, doDetect);
        else if (doDetect && !detect &&
                ! result -> element (v)) detect = TRUE;
    };
    P -> push (v);
    return result;
};
```

12.4.1 Graph Positions

Graph positions are used when it is necessary to navigate a graph manually rather than by using iterators or the results of the graph-ordering methods. Position is implemented as a vertex in a specific graph and a list position in the edge list of that vertex. Thus a position refers to both a vertex and an edge pointing out from that vertex. We have methods that go to a vertex by index number in the array, move to the head along which the current position points, or set the direction to the next edge in the edge list. We can also retrieve the vertex at the current position and its data, the edge of the current direction, and the vertex at the head along that edge. The position movement methods all require that the instance variable fDirection be updated so that it is always a list position for the current vertex.

```
SGraphPosition :: SGraphPosition (PGraph g):
                SPosition (g) {
    fGraph = g;
    fPosition = PVertex (g -> fVertices -> at (1));
    fDirection = PListPosition (fPosition -> fEdges
                            -> newPosition ());
};
```

```
void SGraphPosition :: toHead (void) {
   if (fDirection != NULL) {
      fPosition = PEdge (fDirection -> at ()) ->
                              head ();
      delete fDirection;
      fDirection = PListPosition
         (fPosition -> fEdges -> newPosition ());
   };
};
```

12.4.2 Graph Iterators

Our graph iterators iterate only over the *vertices* of a graph. This is adequate for many problems, but in others the edges are more important. An edge iterator class could easily be built if this were needed. Graph iterators are complicated in two ways. First, a large number of sensible orderings of the vertices are possible. We could use depth-first, breadth-first, or topological orderings or iterate in the order of creation or in an arbitrary order. The second complication is that graphs can contain loops or cycles. They complicate only the implementation and not the concept, but they require us to keep more information if the iteration order involves tracing the edges. Graph iterators have four different next methods, corresponding to creation, depth-first, breadth-first, and topological order. Creation prepares an iterator only for creation-order iteration using the standard method nextItem. If we want one of the other iteration orders, we also need to call the associated reset method and use a corresponding next method.

Creation-order iterators are easy to implement and fall into a pattern seen several times previously. The fPosition variable of an iterator is used for creation-order iteration and holds a reference to a cell number in the array of vertices of the graph which is the index of the next vertex to be returned by nextItem. We initialize it to one. The variable fList is initialized to the value of a newly created queue. The method reset sets the position back to that of the first vertex.

```
SGraphIterator :: SGraphIterator (PGraph g):
                     SIterator (g) {
   fPosition = 1;
   fList = newQueue ();
};
```

The method nextItem returns items until this -> fPosition exceeds the size of the graph.

```
char SGraphIterator :: nextItem (PObject &o) {
   char result;
```

```
    result = !fDone;
    if (result) {
        o = PGraph (fCollection) -> fVertices
            -> at (fPosition);
        if (fPosition < PGraph (fCollection) ->
            fNumberOfVertices)
            ++fPosition;
        else
            fDone = TRUE;
    };
    return result;
};
```

All of the other iteration methods rely on having more information available. In fact, each captures the state of the graph at the time of reset and uses this state information to perform an iteration. Each keeps a list of the vertices of the graph in the desired iteration order in a queue named fList. They obtain this list by calling one of the methods of SGraph. For example, resetDepthFirst calls depthFirstOrder to obtain a queue, which it saves in fList. resetTopological obtains a stack by calling depthFirstSort and transfers the contents to a new queue. Once the iterator is properly reset, a next method merely dequeues and returns an item from this queue. This proceeds until the queue is empty. Note that because the state of the graph is captured at time of reset, an iterator must not be used to remove vertices from a graph. Doing so would make the queue of vertices invalid, making the iterator invalid.

```
void SGraphIterator :: resetDepthFirst (void) {
    reset ();
    delete fList;
    fList = PGraph (fCollection) ->
        depthFirstOrder ();
};

char SGraphIterator :: nextDepthFirst (PObject &o) {
    char result;

    result = !(fDone !! fList -> empty ());
    if (result) {
        o = fList -> Dequeue ();
        fDone = fList -> empty ();
    };
    return result;
};
```

Because the order of iteration is completely determined by the ordering of `fList`, the other `next` methods are identical to this one. In fact, they can call this one, or, alternatively, we could get along with only this one method for ordered iteration.

12.5 Intervals

An interval is an increasing arithmetic sequence of integers, whose successive elements always differ by the same value. For example, 1, 5, 9, 13, 17, is an interval that proceeds from 1 to 17 by 4. Each element except the first is four more than the previous. An interval is characterized by the three values, `from`, `to`, and `by`, that describe, respectively, its starting point, its end point, and the difference between successive members. The size of an interval is the number of values it contains. The size of our example is five. This size is fixed for a given interval and cannot be changed. Nor can the contents of an interval be changed. Therefore, the `insert` and `remove` methods of our `SInterval` class must be rebuilt so as to result in errors if called. This is the case for all fixed-size collections, in fact. The method `at` gives the contents of some indexed location in the sequence. For the sequence above, `at(4)` is the fourth item, which is 13.

```
class SInterval;
typedef SInterval *PInterval;

PInterval newInterval (int from, int to, int by);

class SInterval: public SCollection {
    public:
            SInterval (int from, int to, int by);
        virtual int           at (int);
        virtual int           size (void);
        virtual void          insert (PObject) {
                                  Error ("SInterval ::
                                      insert: Fixed-size
                                      collection.");};
        virtual void          remove (PObject) {
                                  Error ("SInterval ::
                                      remove: Fixed-size
                                      collection.");};

        virtual char          empty () {
                              return (FALSE);};
        virtual PIterator     newIterator (void);
        virtual char          member (classtype c);
        virtual void          writeIt (void);
```

```
    protected:
        int                 fFrom;
        int                 fTo;
        int                 fBy;
        virtual int         sizeOf (void);
    friend SIntervalIterator;
};


class SIntervalIterator;
typedef SIntervalIterator *PIntervalIterator;


class SIntervalIterator: public SIterator {
    public:
            SIntervalIterator (PInterval);
        virtual char      nextItem (PObject&);
        virtual void      reset (void);
        virtual char      member (classtype c);


protected:
    int                 fNext;
    virtual int     sizeOf (void);


};


// REQUIREMENTS For Use
//      initLists ();
//      initIntegers ();
```

The initialization ensures that the sequence is an increasing one. It maps an attempted nonincreasing sequence into an increasing one.

```
SInterval :: SInterval (int from, int to, int by) {
    fFrom = from;
    fTo = to;
    fBy = abs (by);
    if (fBy == 0) fBy = 1;
    if (fTo < fFrom) {
        fTo = from;
        fFrom = to;
    };
};


int SInterval :: at (int i) {
    int result;

    result = fFrom + (i - 1) * fBy;
    if (i > 0 && result <= fTo) return result;
```

```
        else Error ("SInterval :: at: Out of range.");
};
```

The most common use of intervals is to create one and then create an iterator over it, permitting operations similar to that of for loops in standard C or Pascal. For example, if we wanted to process every other element in the list EvalList, we would do something such as the following.

```
anInterval = newInterval (1, EvalList ->
                               length (), 2);
IT = anInterval -> newIterator ();
while (IT -> nextItem (v))
    process (EvalList -> atLoc (PInteger (v)
                                    -> value ()));
delete IT;
delete anInterval;
```

The operation of the iterator in this class is standard.

```
char SIntervalIterator :: nextItem (PObject &o) {
    char result;

    result = !fDone;
    if (result) {
        o = asInteger (fNext);
        fNext += PInterval (fCollection) -> fBy;
        fDone = fNext > PInterval (fCollection) -> fTo;
    };
    return result;
};
```

12.6   MULTILISTS AND BAGS

A bag is like a set except that containment can be multiple. In sets containment is a binary (Boolean) concept. Either an object is in the set or not. An object can appear in a bag several times, so removal of an object from a bag may leave it in the bag as well. As an implementation strategy we build the bag class, SBag, as a subclass of SCollection and use an instance variable, fElements, from a new class, SMultiList, which is a specialization of an SList. An SMultiList is built from nodes that maintain a cardinality associated with the object that they refer to. Therefore, when an object is stored three times in a multilist, it is present only once in a single node, and the cardinality of that node is 3.

```
class SMultiList;
typedef SMultiList *PMultiList;
class SMultiListIterator;
```

```
typedef SMultiListIterator *PMultiListIterator;
class SMultiListPosition;
typedef SMultiListPosition *PMultiListPosition;

PMultiList newMultiList (void);

class SMultiList: public SList {
   public:
         SMultiList (void);
      virtual void               insert (PObject);
      virtual void               remove (PObject);
      virtual void               removeFirst (void);
      virtual PListNode          newNode (PObject o,
                                 PListNode n =
                                        SList :: zed)
      virtual PIterator          newIterator (void);
      virtual PListPosition      newPosition (void);

   protected:
      class SMultiListNode;
   public:
      typedef SMultiListNode *PMultiListNode;
   protected:
   class SMultiListNode: public SListNode {
      public:
            SMultiListNode (PObject,
                           SList :: PListNode);
         virtual char   member (classtype c);
         virtual void   writeIt (void);
         int            fCount;
         virtual int    sizeOf (void);

      friend SMultiListIterator;
   };
};

class SMultiListPosition: public SListPosition {
   public:
         SMultiListPosition (PMultiList);
      virtual void   next (void);
      virtual void   insertFirst (PObject);
      virtual void   insertAfter (PObject);
      virtual char   last (void);
      virtual void   toFirst (void);
      virtual void   deleteNext (void);
      virtual int    cardinalityOf (void);
```

```
             virtual char      member (classtype c);
             virtual void      writeIt (void);
        protected:
           int fWhich;
           virtual SList :: PListNode nodeAt ();
           virtual int sizeOf (void);
        friend SMultiList;
        friend SMultiListIterator;
   };

   class SMultiListIterator: public SIterator{
      public:
             SMultiListIterator (PMultiList);
             virtual char      nextItem (PObject&);
             virtual void      reset (void);
                  // {fDone = fCollection -> empty ();};
             virtual char      member (classtype c);
             virtual void      writeIt (void);
             virtual PObject   Clone (void);
        protected:
           PMultiListPosition fPosition;
           virtual int sizeOf (void);
   };
```

A multilist is a linked list of nodes of a new kind. A multilist node maintains a count of the number of times the object referred to is contained in the multilist. We need to override the insertion and deletion methods to maintain this new field, fCount. In particular, insertFirst is disabled. If possible, insert increments the cardinality of an existing node containing the object.

Most of the maintenance of a bag is handled by the more primitive class, SMultiList. A bag is obtained primarily by a reshaping of the protocols.

```
class SBag;
typedef SBag *PBag;
class SBagIterator;
typedef SBagIterator *PBagIterator;

PBag newBag (void);

class SBag: public SCollection {
   public:
          SBag (void);
        virtual               ~SBag (void);
        virtual char          element (PObject);
        virtual void          insert (PObject o);
```

```
        virtual void         remove (PObject);
        virtual PBag         intersection (PBag);
        virtual PBag         bagUnion (PBag);
        virtual PBag         allBut (PObject);
        virtual char         subset (PBag);
        virtual char         empty (void);
        virtual PObject      Clone (void);
        virtual int          cardinality (void);
        virtual int          cardinalityOf (PObject);
        virtual PIterator    newIterator (void);
        virtual char         member (classtype c);
        virtual void         writeIt (void);
    protected:
        PMultiList fElements;
        virtual SList :: PListNode newNode
                        (PObject, SList :: PListNode);
        virtual int sizeOf (void);
    friend
        SBagIterator;
};

class SBagIterator: public SIterator {
    public:
            SBagIterator (PBag);
        virtual char     nextItem (PObject&);
        virtual void     reset (void);
                // {fDone = fCollection -> empty ();};
        virtual char     member (classtype c);
        virtual void     writeIt (void);

    protected:
        PMultiListPosition fPosition;
        virtual int sizeOf (void);
};
```

When a multilist node is created and initialized, its fCount is set to one. Thereafter it is increased or decreased as we insert or remove items having the same value from the list. When the count goes to zero, we can remove and dispose of the node.

```
SMultiList :: SMultiListNode
            :: SMultiListNode (PObject o, SList ::
                                PListNode n):SListNode (
    if (n != NULL) fNext = n;
    fCount = 1;
};
```

```
void SMultiList :: insert (PObject o) {
   PMultiListNode aNode;
   PMultiListPosition aPosition;
   WhereFound how;

   if (! element(o)) {
      aNode = PMultiListNode (newNode
                                 (o, fFirstNode));
      fFirstNode = aNode;
   }
   else {
      aPosition = PMultiListPosition (newPosition ());
      how = aPosition -> search (o);
      if (how == IsHere) {
         ++(PMultiListNode ((aPosition -> fHere)) ->
                                 fCount);
      }
      else {
         ++(PMultiListNode ((aPosition -> fHere ->
                                 fNext)) -> fCount);
      };
   };
};

void SMultiList :: remove (PObject o) {
   PMultiListPosition P
   PMultiListPosition Q;
   PMultiListNode N;
   WhereFound where;

   P = PMultiListPosition (newPosition ());
   Q = PMultiListPosition (newPosition ());
   where = P -> search (o);
   switch (where) {
      case IsNext: {
         N = PMultiListNode (P -> nodeAt ());
         Q -> moveTo (&P);
         Q -> next ();
         if (Q -> cardinalityOf () == 1) {
            P -> SListPosition :: deleteNext ();
         };
         else {
            N = PMultiListNode (N -> fNext);
            --(N -> fCount);
         }
      }; break;
```

```
            case IsHere: {
                removeFirst ();
            }; break;
            case NotFound:;
        };
        delete P;
        delete Q;
    };
```

The corresponding methods of SBag just pass the message along to the fElements instance variable. It is extremely important in the insert method to create an SMultiListNode and not one of its ancestors. This is why we override the newNode method in SMultiList.

The logic of union and intersection were seen before when we studied ordinary sets.

```
PBag SBag :: intersection (PBag s) {
    PBag result;
    PIterator IT;
    PObject aValue;
    PBag copy;

    result = newBag ();
    copy = PBag (s -> Clone ());
    IT = newIterator ();
    while (IT -> nextItem (aValue)) {
        if(copy -> element (aValue)) {
            result -> insert (aValue);
            copy -> remove (aValue);
        };
    };
    delete copy;
    delete IT;
    return result;
};
```

We get the number of times a given element is contained in a bag with the cardinalityOf method.

```
int SBag :: cardinalityOf (PObject o) {
    PMultiListPosition p;
    WhereFound where;
    int result;

    result = 0;
    p = fElements -> (SMultiListPosition)
                     newPosition ();
```

```
      where = p -> search (o);
      if (where != NotFound) {
         switch (where) {
            case IsNext:{
                p -> next ();
            }; // Continue.
            case IsHere: {
                result = p -> cardinalityOf ();
            };
         };
      };
      delete p;
      return result;
};
```

The iterator for bags has to maintain a reference to a position in the implementing list. It may seem strange, but a bag iterator yields only the distinct elements in the bag. The idea of a bag is not that there are several similar items in a bag but that a given item is in the bag several times. The containment is repeated, not the element. Of course, if an iterator operating according to the other interpretation is needed, it can be simulated by this one combined with a for loop running cardinalityOf times.

```
SBagIterator :: SBagIterator (PBag s): SIterator (s) {
   fPosition = (PMultiListPosition) s ->
      fElements ->
      newPosition ();
};

char SBagIterator :: nextItem (PObject&o) {
   char result;

   result = ! fDone;
   if (result) {
      o = fPosition -> at ();
      if (fPosition -> last ()) {
         fDone = TRUE;
      };
      else {
         fPosition -> next ();
      };
   };
   return result;
};
```

12.7   SUMMARY

Intervals, heaps, multilists, bags, and dictionaries are advanced storage structures. Dictionaries implement mathematical functions. Heaps are useful in sorting and in situations in which a full sort is not required but a partial sort is. In a heap, a path from root to leaf is sorted. Multilists and bags generalize lists and sets, respectively.

A graph can be thought of as a collection structure, but it is much more than that. There is a very rich literature of graphs in mathematics, where the main interest is in the relationships between things and not in any storage capability. Graphs model these relationships well in some situations, and in our implementation of them as a storage class, auxiliary information can be held at the vertices.

We also saw, in this chapter, an application of recursion removal. Depth-first processing of a graph can be easily accomplished recursively. Replacing the recursion stack with a queue gives us similar breadth-first algorithms that are useful in their own right.

EXERCISES

12.1 (12.2) Correct the errors in `SHashDictionaryIterator :: nextItem`.

12.2 (12.3) How must `SHeap` be changed if we want it to be a subclass of our dynamic array class instead of just a collection? What are the consequences of this for space and time efficiency?

12.3 (12.3) Prove what was said concerning the behavior of `filterUp` and `trickleDown` that if the heap property holds except for one cell, `filterUp` and `trickleDown` restore it to the whole heap.

12.4 (12.3) Build the required heap iterator class.

12.5 (12.4) The `depthFirstOrder` and `breadthFirstOrder` methods can be generalized in the following way. We ensured that all vertices would appear by processing the entire vertex list of the graph. We also processed this list in order of vertex creation. Sometimes it is desired to obtain only the nodes reachable from a given vertex and to obtain them in some particular order. Implement this idea.

12.6 (12.3) Give a verification for the loop in the body of `heapSort`. Its invariant is Fig. 12.2.

12.7 (12.3) A method of heaps that destroys the heap property is a bit strange. It is out of place, actually. Rebuild `heapSort` so that, rather than sorting itself, it returns a `PArray` with the elements of `this` in sorted order. One way of doing this is to create the array variable at the beginning, copy the elements of `this` into it, and then use `SArray :: at` and `atPut` to rearrange it. The array is returned as the function result of `heapSort`, which leaves its own elements unaffected.

12.8 (12.4) Build an edge iterator class for our graphs.

## PART THREE

THE
APPLICATIONS

PROGRAM TRANSLATION

Yes, madam, and, moreover,
Some thousand verses of a faithful lover,
A huge translation of hypocrisy,
Vilely compiled, profound simplicity.

    Shakespeare, *Love's Labours Lost*

In this chapter we shall examine some of the principles of language translation and some of the things that compilers and interpreters must do to translate programs from the source form in which they are written by programmers into the form in which they are used by computers. We shall see that for modern languages the tree structure is fundamental to the translation process, primarily because today's languages have a nested structure, which leads naturally to a tree representation.

13.1   SYNTAX OF LLLBI'T AND BABY PASCAL

In this section a simple language is described that is adequate for writing simple programs. It has a semantics, or meaning, much like that of C or Pascal, but its syntax, or structure, has a form that makes writing a translator easy. This form is called prefix form, because each structure in the language starts with a keyword that describes the structure completely. Pascal also has such a structure for nearly every construct. However, we shall require more from our programmers in this simple language. We shall also require that each structure in a program be enclosed in parentheses so that the nested nature of the program be made explicit. Thus, a simple program in this language might be the following single statement.

```
(if, (<=, X, (*, -22, M)), (else, (:=, y, 1),
                           (:=, X, (+, X, 33)))))
```

Translated into a Pascal-like syntax, it says

```
IF X <= -22 * M THEN
    y := 1
ELSE
    X := X + 33;
```

The overall structure is that of an `if` statement, which requires two additional parts. The first of these is always an assertion, or logical statement. In this case the assertion is a `<=` assertion, which itself requires two additional parts, each of which are expressions. The first expression of the `<=` assertion is the identifier X. The second is a `*` expression, or multiplication, with its own two parts. The second part of an `if` structure is either a statement or, as we have here, an `else` structure. An `else` structure begins with that keyword and consists of two statements. In this case, both of the statements in the `else` structure are `:=`, or assignment, statements, which require an identifier and an expression. Note that the parts of each structure are separated by commas.

The syntax of the complete language is given below in the Backus-Naur form (BNF), which was introduced in Section 7.9. BNF is a collective, recursive definition of a set of names, called nonterminals. The definition is given in terms of the same nonterminals and another set of symbols, called terminals, that are assumed to be defined elsewhere or to stand for themselves. In our usage here a nonterminal is always enclosed in angle brackets. Therefore, <program> is a nonterminal. A BNF is written as a list of statements, called productions, each of which is a definition of the nonterminal on its left-hand side. The symbols on the right side give one or more possible definition forms of the nonterminal on the left. Our terminal symbols are such symbols as (, :=, and the word `identifier`, which is seen to be a terminal because of the lack of angle brackets. Generally, if two symbols appear juxtaposed on the right side of a production, the corresponding terminals or nonterminals are to appear concatenated in some string whose form is a legal form of the nonterminal being defined by the right-hand side. The only exception to this rule is the vertical stroke, !, which indicates alternate forms of the definition. Therefore, the second production in the grammar below can be read as the following: A statement can be an `if` statement, an assignment, a concatenation, or a `while` statement. Each of the forms is defined in other productions. For example, an `if` statement can be a left parenthesis followed by, in order, the word *if*, a comma, an assertion, a comma, and either an `else` structure or another statement.

```
<program>           ::= <statement>
<statement>         ::= <if> | <assign> | <concat> |
                        <while>
<if>                ::= (if, <assertion>, <statement>)
                        | (if, <assertion>, <else>)
<assign>            ::= (:=, identifier, <expression>)
<concat>            ::= (;, <statement>, <statement>)
<while>             ::= (while, <assertion>, <invar>)
<invar>             ::= (invar, <assertion>,
                          <statement>)
<else>              ::= (else, <statement>,
                          <statement>)
<expression>        ::= <sum> | <difference> |
                        <multiplication> | <quotient> |
                        identifier | integer
<sum>               ::= (+, <expression>, <expression>)
<difference>        ::= (-, <expression>, <expression>)
<multiplication>    ::= (*, <expression>, <expression>)
<quotient>          ::= (/, <expression>, <expression>)
<assertion>         ::= <less> | <equal> | <greater> |
                        <greaterEqual> | <notEqual> |
                        <lessEqual> | <and> | <or> |
                        <exist> | <all> | <not>
<less>              ::= (<, <expression>, <expression>)
<equal>             ::= (=, <expression>, <expression>)
<greater>           ::= (>, <expression>, <expression>)
<greaterEqual>      ::= (>=, <expression>, <expression>)
<notEqual>          ::= (#, <expression>, <expression>)
<lessEqual>         ::= (<=, <expression>,
                          <expression>)
<and>               ::= (and, <assertion>, <assertion>)
<or>                ::= (or, <assertion>, <assertion>)
<exist>             ::= (exist, identifier, <assertion>)
<all>               ::= (all, identifier, <assertion>)
<not>               ::= (not, <assertion>, -)
```

The terminal identifier is defined as a string of characters of which the first is alphabetic and the rest are alphabetic or numeric. Similarly, an integer is a string of digits, perhaps preceded by a minus sign.

Although in the BNF the nonterminals are all defined, we generally specify one of them as being primary. Often this is the nonterminal on the left side of the first production. Thus, we take the above BNF as a whole to define its first nonterminal symbol, <program>. The BNF then describes a collection of strings in the following way. A string is legal for a BNF if it can be produced by the following rules. First, write down the primary nonterminal symbol. As long as a nonterminal remains in the string under consideration (called a sentential form), choose the production whose left-hand side is that nonterminal and replace the nonterminal in the string with any of the alternatives on the right-hand side of that production. Stop when only terminal symbols are left. The result is called a sentence in the language defined by the BNF. The BNF is also called a grammar, because it defines the structure of a language.

A language that can be defined in terms of a BNF such as above is called a context-free language. There is a very rich theory of languages of this type. Generally speaking, a push-down automaton as discussed briefly in Chapter 5 is adequate to process such languages. The interested student is encouraged to explore the topics further in any good book on language theory or on the theory of automata. A good introduction is found in [Rayward-Smith, 1983].

The sequence of steps from the primary nonterminal to the final string is called a derivation. For the above example of the if statement, a derivation might be the following.

```
<program> ->
<statement> ->
<if> ->
(if, <assertion>, <else>) ->
(if, <lessEqual>, <else>) ->
(if, (<=, <expression>, <expression>), <else>) ->
(if, (<=, identifier, <expression>), <else>) ->
(if, (<=, identifier, <multiplication>), <else>) ->
(if, (<=, identifier, (*, <expression>, <expression>
      <else>) ->
(if, (<=, identifier, (*, integer, <expression>))
      <else>) ->
(if, (<=, identifier, (*, integer, identifier)),
      <else>) ->
(if, (<=, identifier, (*, integer, identifier)),
      (else, <statement>, <statement>)) ->
(if, (<=, identifier, (*, integer, identifier)),
      (else, <assign>, <statement>)) ->
(if, (<=, identifier, (*, integer, identifier)),
    (else, (:=, identifier, <expression>),
      <statement>)) ->

(if, (<=, identifier, (*, integer, identifier)),
  (else, (:=, identifier, integer), <statement>)) ->
(if, (<=, identifier, (*,integer, identifier)),
  (else, (:=, identifier, integer), <assign>)) ->
(if, (<=, identifier, (*, integer, identifier)),
    (else, (:=, identifier, integer),
      (:=, identifier, <expression>))) ->
```

```
(if, (<=, identifier, (*, integer, identifier)),
    (else, (:=, identifier, integer), (:=, identifier,
    <sum>))) ->
(if, (<=, identifier, (*, integer, identifier)),
    (else, (:=, identifier, integer), (:=, identifier,
    (+, <expression>, <expression>)))) ->
(if, (<=, identifier, (*, integer, identifier)),
    (else, (:=, identifier, integer), (:=, identifier,
    (+, identifier, <expression>)))) ->
(if, (<=, identifier, (*, integer, identifier)),
    (else, (:=, identifier, integer), (:=, identifier,
    (+, identifier, integer))))
```

The final form of our example was derived from this by replacing the terminals identifier and integer with some of their possible values.

   The relationship between such derivations and the translation problem is that a compiler must discover this derivation, or an equivalent one, to determine if the program it is trying to translate is a legal program. If a form cannot be found that matches some symbol in a supposed program, the translation must fail. There is a relationship between what we have done here and trees, because the above derivation is the successive construction of subtrees of a tree. When this tree is completed its leaves are only terminals and are the symbols in our program, in the correct order. We start to build the tree by writing down the primary nonterminal, but this time it is a node in a tree. Then, instead of replacing nonterminals, if a node represents a nonterminal, we give it child nodes, one for each symbol in the right-hand side of some production. Therefore, after the first few replacements in the derivation above, we have the tree shown in Fig. 13.1. We next replace the assertion at the left leaf with a lessEqual form. After a few more replacements we get the tree shown in Fig. 13.2.

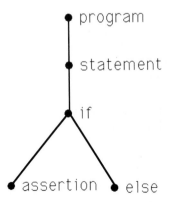

FIGURE 13.1

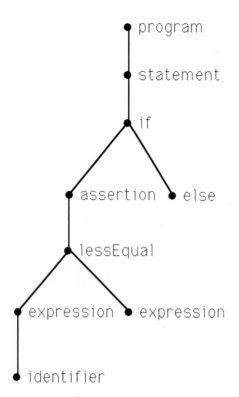

FIGURE 13.2

> ## Parse Tree
>
> A tree in which the interior nodes represent the nonterminals of a BNF and the leaves represent its terminal symbols. Subtrees of a node represent the right hand side of some production for the nonterminal represented by the node.

Both terminals and nonterminals appear at the leaves. We are finished when there are no more nonterminal leaves. The result is called a parse tree. We haven't exactly conformed to our rule for building this tree. We haven't written down the parentheses or the commas at all, nor have we written down the terminals for the initial keywords, such as `if`, in the forms, because the node from which the children derive leaves us enough information to know what they must be. Thus our form is sometimes described as an abstract syntax tree. A more compact form of the abstract syntax tree is sometimes obtained by replacing each node having only one child with the child node itself. The above tree might be represented by Fig. 13.3. A complete parse tree is much more easily shown in this more compact form. Fig. 13.4 shows an abstract parse tree for the original example. A pre-order walk of this tree gives the original program structure.

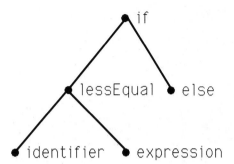

FIGURE 13.3

If from any `expression` node we walk according to in-order protocol until we return to the node for the last time, we obtain the infix form of the expression. If we were to write out a representation for each leaf on such a walk, we would be translating from the original prefix form into infix form. There is one small difficulty with this, however. Because our original language was fully parenthesized, we did not need to discuss the precedence of the operators. With the infix form we must either use parentheses or find a way to write down partially parenthesized expressions taking operator

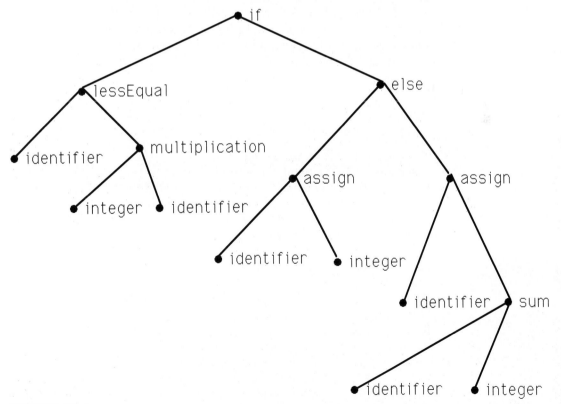

FIGURE 13.4

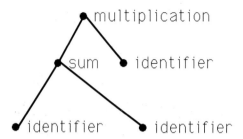

FIGURE 13.5

precedence into account. The former method is much easier. The rule is simply this: Write down a left parenthesis when moving down a branch on an in-order walk of an `expression`. Write a right parenthesis when moving up. If we do this for the tree of Fig. 13.5, we arrive at `((identifier) + (identifier)) * (identifier)`.

If we also choose which structures to walk according to pre-order protocol and which to walk according to in-order protocol, we can easily translate the fully parenthesized prefix program into one more familiar and similar to Pascal.

Our purpose in this chapter is to create abstract parse trees for our little language, which we call LLLBI'T (Looks Like Lisp, But Isn't) because of its superficial resemblance to Lisp, which also uses a fully parenthesized form. The pronunciation, of course, is lilbit. We shall then produce an output in Baby Pascal, which is an equivalent, but more familiar, form. For example, Baby Pascal for our example is

```
IF {X <= [-22 * 55]} THEN
    y := 1
ELSE
    X := [X + 33] END IF
```

The form that we use here is a little richer than Pascal, since we enclose assertions in braces and expressions in square brackets. Note that the `if` form is still a prefix form, though we have added the additional words THEN and ELSE to replace what were originally commas, and an ending pair of keywords for readability. Assertions, expressions, and assignments have been translated into an infix form.

Our first task in carrying out this translation is to decide what our classes are to be and how we shall represent them. The most natural way to describe the things needed in a translation is to look at the grammar that defines the language. If we are to handle the grammar then we must handle its nonterminals. Therefore it makes sense to build structures for statements, assignments, `if` statements, etc. We could construct a class for each nonterminal in the grammar. Then we could give each class methods by which it would handle all of the right-hand sides possible for the nonterminal that it represents. Thus the class `SIf` will need to know about the two possible forms of an `if` structure, and the class `SStatement` class will need to be able to distinguish the four possible forms of a statement. This would give us 23 or 24 classes (depending on whether we wanted a class for programs, which are the same as statements according to the grammar). The behavior of many of these classes is the same as that of others, because sums and differences have the same behavior in a translation. It is only in an execution that they behave differently.

The main class in this ADT is `SStatement`, which is a subclass of `SBinaryTree`. We use a binary tree, because we want to represent a program as a tree. We have carefully constructed the language so that binary trees would be sufficient. Our purpose was not to define a real language for programming but to illustrate the principles and how the principles relate to our data abstraction techniques. The other structures are represented by classes that derive from a binary tree node through a new class, `SNonTerminal`. We want this new node class because we don't want to build a class for each nonterminal and so must remember somewhere what kind of node we are dealing with. Therefore `SNonTerminal` needs an instance variable, `fKind`, in which we save the node type when the node is generated. We then have separate classes for each statement type, assignments, concatenations, `if` statements and `while` statements. We have an assertion class but no subclasses for the various kinds of assertions. On the other hand, we have an expression class, though we build seven subclasses of this for all of the specialized expressions. Our purpose in treating assertions differently from expressions is purely pedagogical. We want to demonstrate the difference between the form of object-oriented programs (`SExpression`) with subclasses versus the form of ordinary programs (`SAssertion`) that must take account of a variety of situations using ordinary constructs, such as `switch` statements. The difference is quite dramatic. Finally, we need a class to represent the `else` structure. This gives us eight subclasses of `SNonTerminal`: `SAssign`, `SIf`, `SConcatenation`, `SWhile`, `SExpression`, `SAssertion`, `SElse`, and `SInvariant`. `SExpression` has seven additional subclasses: `SIdentExpression`, `SParamExpression`, `SIntLitExpression`, `SSum`, `SDifference`, `SProduct`, and `SQuotient`. The complete header interface is shown below, though some of the methods will be discussed in the next chapter. In this chapter we are primarily interested in the `parse` and `writeIt` methods of each class. Later in the chapter the `simplify` methods will be discussed as well.

```
#ifndef __Verification__
#define __Verification__

#include "pBinaryT.h"
#include "pString.h"
#include "pSet.h"
#include "Scan.h"
#include "PInteger.h"
```

```
class SStatement;
typedef SStatement *PStatement;

PStatement newStatement ();

class SStatement: public SBinaryTree {
   public:
         SStatement ();
```

Required Classes

```
SObject
    SBinaryTreeNode
        SNonTerminal
            SExpression
                SIdentExpression
                SParamExpression
                SIntLitExpression
                SSum
                SDifference
                SProduct
                SQuotient
            SAssertion
            SIf
            SConcatenation
            SAssignment
            SElse
            SInvariant
            SWhile
    SCollection
        SBinaryTree
            SStatement
        SList
        SSet
        SStack
        SString
    SMagnitude
        SCharacter
        SInteger
        SIterator
        SBinaryTreeIterator
        SListIterator
        SSetIterator
    SListNode
```

```
            virtual void        computePrecondition
                                (char *Assrt);
            virtual void        parseString (char * inp);
            virtual void        parseProgram
                                (char *filename);
            virtual void        listProof (void);
            virtual void        simplify (void);
            virtual char        member (classtype c);
            virtual PObject     Clone (void);
            virtual void        writeIt (void);

    protected:
        virtual int     sizeOf (void);
    friend SIf;
    friend SWhile;
};

class SNonTerminal;
typedef SNonTerminal *PNonTerminal;

PNonTerminal newNonTerminal (PObject o, token k);

class SNonTerminal: public SBinaryTree::
        SBinaryTreeNode {
    public:
            SNonTerminal(PObject o, token k);
        virtual PNonTerminal    computePrecondition
                                (PNonTerminal);
        virtual PNonTerminal    makeProofFragment
                                (PNonTerminal);
        virtual void            parse (void);
        virtual void            findFree (PSet F,
                                          PSet B);
        virtual PNonTerminal    simplified (void);
        virtual token           kind ();
        virtual char            member (classtype c);
        virtual void            writeIt (void);

    protected:
        token           fKind;
        virtual void    attachPrecondition
                        (PNonTerminal);
        virtual int     sizeOf (void);
    friend SIf;
    friend SAssignment;
    friend SConcatenation;
    friend SElse;
```

```
      friend SWhile;
      friend SInvariant;
};

class SExpression;
typedef SExpression *PExpression;

PExpression newExpression (token k);

class SExpression: public SNonTerminal {
   public:
         SExpression (token k);
      virtual void             parse (void);
      virtual void             findFree (PSet F,
                                         PSet B);

      virtual void             replaceFree
                               (PString, PExpression)
      virtual PNonTerminal     simplified (void);
      virtual char             member (classtype c);
      virtual void             writeIt (void);

   protected:
      virtual int    sizeOf (void);

};

class SIdentExpression;
typedef SIdentExpression *PIdentExpression;

PIdentExpression newIdentExpression (void);

class SIdentExpression: public SExpression {
   public:
         SIdentExpression (void);
      virtual void    parse (void);
      virtual void    findFree (PSet F, PSet B);
      virtual void    replaceFree (PString,
                                   PExpression);
      virtual char    member (classtype c);
      virtual void    writeIt (void);

   protected:
      virtual int sizeOf(void);

};
```

```
class SParamExpression;
typedef SParamExpression *PParamExpression;

PParamExpression newParamExpression (void);

class SParamExpression: public SExpression {
   public:
         SParamExpression(void);
      virtual void     findFree (PSet F, PSet B);
      virtual void     replaceFree (PString,
                                      PExpression);
      virtual char     member (classtype c);
      virtual void     writeIt (void);

   protected:
      virtual int      sizeOf (void);

};

class SIntLitExpression;
typedef SIntLitExpression *PIntLitExpression;

PIntLitExpression newIntLitExpression (void);

class SIntLitExpression: public SExpression {
   public:
         SIntLitExpression(void);
      virtual void     parse (void);
      virtual void     findFree (PSet F, PSet B);
      virtual void     replaceFree (PString,
                                      PExpression);
      virtual char     member (classtype c);
      virtual void     writeIt (void);

   protected:
      virtual int      sizeOf (void);

};

class SSum;
typedef SSum *PSum;

PSum newSum (void);

class SSum: public SExpression {
   public:
         SSum(void);
```

```
        virtual PNonTerminal    simplified (void);
        virtual char            member (classtype c);
        virtual void            writeIt (void);

    protected:
        virtual int sizeOf     (void);

};

class SDifference;
typedef SDifference *PDifference;

PDifference newDifference (void);

class SDifference: public SExpression {
    public:
            SDifference (void);
        virtual PNonTerminal    simplified (void);
        virtual char            member (classtype c);
        virtual void            writeIt (void);

    protected:
        virtual int    sizeOf (void);

};

class SProduct;
typedef SProduct *PProduct;

PProduct newProduct (void);

class SProduct: public SExpression {
    public:
            SProduct(void);
        virtual PNonTerminal    simplified (void);
        virtual char            member (classtype c);
        virtual void            writeIt (void);

    protected:
        virtual int sizeOf (void);

};

class SQuotient;
typedef SQuotient *PQuotient;
PQuotient newQuotient (void);
class SQuotient: public SExpression {
    public:
```

```
            SQuotient(void);
        virtual PNonTerminal       simplified (void);
        virtual char              member (classtype c);
        virtual void              writeIt (void);


    protected:
        virtual int    sizeOf (void);



};

class SAssertion;
typedef SAssertion *PAssertion;

PAssertion newAssertion (token k);

class SAssertion: public SNonTerminal {
    public:
            SAssertion (token k);
        virtual void              parse (void);
        virtual void              findFree (PSet F,
                                            PSet B);

        virtual void              replaceFree
                                  (PString, PExpression);
        virtual PNonTerminal     simplified (void);
        virtual char             member (classtype c);
        virtual void             writeIt (void);


    protected:
        virtual int    sizeOf (void);
      friend PAssertion buildAlls (PAssertion N,
                                   PSet F);
};

class SIf;
typedef SIf *PIf;

PIf newIf (void);

class SIf: public SNonTerminal {
    public:
            SIf(void);
        virtual void              parse (void);
        virtual PNonTerminal     computePrecondition
                                  (PNonTerminal);
```

```
        virtual void            findFree (PSet F,
                                          PSet B);
        virtual char            member (classtype c);
        virtual void            writeIt (void);

    protected:
        virtual int     sizeOf(void);

};

class SConcatenation;
typedef SConcatenation *PConcatenation;

PConcatenation newConcat (void);

class SConcatenation: public SNonTerminal {
    public:
            SConcatenation (void);
        virtual void            parse (void);
        virtual PNonTerminal    computePrecondition
                                (PNonTerminal A);
        virtual void            findFree (PSet F,
                                          PSet B);
        virtual char            member (classtype c);
        virtual void            writeIt (void);

    protected:
        virtual int     sizeOf (void);

};

class SAssignment;
typedef SAssignment *PAssignment;

PAssignment newAssignment (void);

class SAssignment: public SNonTerminal {
    public:
            SAssignment (void);
        virtual void            parse (void);
        virtual PNonTerminal    computePrecondition
                                (PNonTerminal A);
        virtual void            findFree (PSet,
                                          PSet);
        virtual PNonTerminal    simplified (void);
        virtual char            member (classtype c);
        virtual void            writeIt (void);
```

```
protected:
    virtual int    sizeOf (void);

};

class SElse;
typedef SElse *PElse;

PElse newElse (void);

class SElse: public SNonTerminal {
   public:
        SElse (void);
        virtual void              parse (void);
        virtual PNonTerminal      computePrecondition
                                  (PNonTerminal A);
        virtual void              findFree (PSet,
                                           PSet);
        virtual char              member (classtype c);
        virtual void              writeIt (void);

    protected:
        virtual int    sizeOf(void);

};

class SWhile;
typedef SWhile *PWhile;

PWhile newWhile (void);

class SWhile: public SNonTerminal {
   public:
        SWhile (void);
        virtual void              parse (void);
        virtual PNonTerminal      computePrecondition
                                  (PNonTerminal A);
        virtual void              findFree (PSet F,
                                           PSet B);
        virtual char              member (classtype c);
        virtual void              writeIt (void);

    protected:
        virtual int    sizeOf (void);

};
```

```
class SInvariant;
typedef SInvariant *PInvariant;

PInvariant newInvariant (void);

class SInvariant: public SNonTerminal {
   public:
         SInvariant (void);
      virtual void              parse (void);
      virtual PNonTerminal      computePrecondition
                                (PNonTerminal A);
      virtual void              findFree (PSet F,
                                          PSet B);
      virtual char              member (classtype c);
      virtual void              writeIt (void);

   protected:
      virtual int     sizeOf (void);

};
#endif
```

The nonterminal class doesn't do anything useful for our purposes here so its details will be discussed later, except for the following point. When we create a node either directly or by creating an object in one of its subclasses, we give fKind a value of the enumerated type token so as to describe the node. This type is defined in another file, scan.h, described below. The token enumeration from that file is the following:

```
typedef enum {endSym, ifOp, elseOp, whileOp,
              invarOp, andOp, orOp, notOp,
              ImpliesOp, existOp, allOp,
              assignOp, concatOp, Comma,
              LParen, RParen, LBrace, RBrace,
              LAngle, RAngle, ID, INTLIT, plusOp,
              minusOp, mulOp, divOp, EQOp, NEOp,
              LOp, GOp, LEOp, GEOp, ParamOp, eofSym,
              kpb, kpl, kpr} token;
```

These tokens are used internally in the translation program to represent the tokens that a LLLBI'T programmer would use to write a program. Some of the values in this type, such as kpb, are used for special purposes, as will be discussed in Chapter 14.

13.2   **SCANNING LLLBI'T**

As in our operator precedence translation of expressions, we use a scanner to break up the input string of characters representing an input LLLBI'T program into tokens or symbols in the language. The purpose of the scanner is to read enough of the input so that it can determine a symbol, such as : =, a keyword, such as if, or an identifier or integer, and return a code indicating the class of the token and, if necessary, its spelling.

The general form of the new scanner is identical to that of the previous one, because it, too, simulates the operation of a deterministic finite automaton. The difference is that it is a bit more sophisticated, because we require it to deal with multiple-character identifiers and integers. We also require that it distinguish between keywords, such as if and identifiers, such as ifDone. The scanner used here is more sophisticated than is needed for LLLBI'T. It recognizes a few symbols that are not in the language. Generally speaking, it is adequate for our use, though occasionally it does the wrong thing if we use an identifier that it believes should be a keyword, such as end. It also recognizes a few symbols that we shall not need until the next chapter. The codes that it recognizes have symbolic names that are encoded in our type token described above.

When the scanner recognizes the word if, it signals the fact by returning a value ifOp from the above list. Since we want the spellings of identifiers and the numeric values of integers, the scanner must return these as well. Therefore, we create a variable for the information to be returned. The type of this variable is a struct of which one field is a type union.

```
typedef struct {
    token currentToken;
        union {
            struct {
                char itsSpelling[256];
            } butIntLit;
            struct {
                int itsValue;
            } justIntLit;
        } tok;
} _tokenBuffer;
```

We also need a Boolean variable, tokenAvailable, to tell us whether the contents of tokenBuffer are currently valid. The variable tokenBuffer has a field called currentToken, of type token. If the value of this field is INTLIT, tokenBuffer has an additional field, itsValue. Alternatively, if the value of currentToken is one of the values in the range from elseOp to allOp, tokenBuffer has a field called itsSpelling, which is a string. It is the programmer's responsibility to fill in the currentToken field correctly and then to use either the field itsSpelling or the field itsValue. They are not both defined for a given legal value of tokenBuffer. The variable tokenBuffer is defined in the header part of the scanner and is therefore a visible global variable. Each call to the scanner routine nextToken ensures that the tokenBuffer is filled with a legal value. The field currentToken tells what kind of token was seen in the input, and the other field (either itsSpelling or itsValue) gives the additional information. The rest of our public interface and the global data of the implementation section for the scanner follows.

```
token nextToken (void);
void match (token);
void toss (void);
void initScanner (char *);
void initScannerString (char *);
void closeScan (void);
```

The globals defined in the implementation part are the following:

```
_tokenBuffer tokenBuffer;
FILE *scanFile;
char tokenAvailable;
char LineBuffer[MaxLineLength];
int LineLength;
int LinePtr;
char EofFlag;
char haveFile;
```

The variable scanFile holds the file variable for the source file if we use one. We don't need to read a file, however. We can either parse a file or include an entire program in a single string and simply scan and parse it. This is why two initialization routines exist for the scanner unit. If we want to scan a file, we call initScanner with the name of the file. If we want to scan only a single string, we call initScannerString instead, sending it the string to be scanned.

```
void initScanner (char *fileName) {
   EofFlag = FALSE;
   haveFile = TRUE;
   LineLength = 0;
   LinePtr = MaxLineLength+1;
   if ((strcmp(fileName, "") != 0) ) {
      scanFile = fopen (fileName, "rt");
   }
```

```
else {
   haveFile = FALSE; EofFlag = TRUE;
};
toss ();
};
```

When the user calls `nextToken`, the scanner performs the following.
If `tokenAvailable` is TRUE, the token buffer is valid, so `nextToken`
only returns. If it is FALSE, the input is read until it is clear which
is the next token in the input, `currentToken` is set appropriately,
`tokenAvailable` is set to TRUE, and `nextToken` returns. The function `toss` sets `tokenAvailable` to FALSE so that the next call to
`nextToken` advances the input and returns a new token. In this way we
reuse `currentToken` as often as needed, calling `toss` only when we
know `currentToken` is no longer needed.

The procedure `match` is used when the user knows what the next token is supposed to be and wants to discard it. For example, in LLLBI'T
commas are required in several places. If we call `match (Comma)` and
the next token is a comma, then the comma is discarded, and the next call
to `nextToken` returns the symbol after the comma. However, if the token
is not a comma, the program is halted.

`LineBuffer` holds the string being scanned, or if we are using a file, a
line of the file being scanned. `LineLength` is the logical length of this line,
and `LinePtr` is the index of the current character being scanned. The variables `haveFile` and `EofFlag` indicate whether a valid file is to be scanned
and whether the current file being scanned is exhausted, respectively.

A number of auxiliary routines aid the scanner in returning the next
token. One of these is the built-in function `atoi`, which is called when we
have seen a digit in the input and therefore expect more. We want to know
the value of the integer that the string of digit characters represents. We
send `atoi` a string of digits and get back an integer.

Another important auxiliary function is `CheckReserved`. When we
see a string of characters that begins with an alphabetic character, we save
characters in `tokenBuffer` until we see a character that is neither alphabetic nor numeric. We then call `CheckReserved`, which looks at the
spelling in `tokenBuffer`. If the spelling matches one of the keywords,
it returns the token value of that reserved word. If it matches none of the
keywords, it returns the token value of an identifier.

```
token CheckReserved () {
    token result;
    str255 theWord;

    strcpy (theWord,
            tokenBuffer.tok.butIntLit.itsSpelling);
    if (((strcmp (theWord, "END") == 0)) ||
        ((strcmp (theWord, "end") == 0))) {
```

```
            result = endSym;
         }
      else if (((strcmp (theWord, "ALL") == 0)) !!
          ((strcmp (theWord, "all") == 0))) {
         result = allOp;
         }
      else if (((strcmp (theWord, "EXIST") == 0)) !!
          ((strcmp (theWord, "exist") == 0))) {
         result = existOp;
         }
      else if (((strcmp (theWord, "AND") == 0)) !!
          ((strcmp (theWord, "and") == 0))) {
         result = andOp;
         }
      else if (((strcmp (theWord, "OR") == 0)) !!
          ((strcmp (theWord, "or") == 0))) {
         result = orOp;
         }
      else if (((strcmp (theWord, "IF") == 0)) !!
          ((strcmp (theWord, "if") == 0))) {
         result = ifOp;
         }
      else if (((strcmp (theWord, "NOT") == 0)) !!
          ((strcmp (theWord, "not") == 0))) {
         result = notOp;
         }
      else if (((strcmp (theWord, "ELSE") == 0)) !!
          ((strcmp(theWord, "else") == 0))) {
         result = elseOp;
         }
      else if (((strcmp (theWord, "WHILE") == 0)) !!
          ((strcmp(theWord, "while") == 0))) {
         result = whileOp;
         }
      else if (((strcmp (theWord, "INVAR") == 0)) !!
          ((strcmp(theWord, "invar") == 0))) {
         result = invarOp;
         }
      else if (((strcmp (theWord, "PARAM") == 0)) !!
          ((strcmp(theWord, "param") == 0))) {
         result = ParamOp;
         }
      else {
         result = ID;
         };
      return(result);
   };
```

The scanner also has three procedures for dealing with `LineBuffer`. The first of these, `GetNewLine`, fills it up from the input file when necessary. `Advance` increments `LinePtr` by one so that we advance a character in the `LineBuffer`. `Inspect` checks whether more characters are available and if so returns the current character, the one referenced by `LinePtr`. If `LinePtr` is greater than `LineLength`, `Inspect` calls `GetNewLine` before returning a character. It also forces a halt if it is called when `haveFile` is FALSE.

```
void GetNewLine () {
    int I;
    char ch;

    LineLength = 0;
    if feof (scanFile) EofFlag = TRUE;
    else
    if (!EofFlag) {
        while (fscanf (scanFile, "%c", &ch) != 0
            && !feof (scanFile)
            && ch != EOLN
            && LineLength < MaxLineLength) {
            LineBuffer[LineLength] = ch;
            ++LineLength;
        };
        fscanf (scanFile, ""); ch = " ";
        for (I = LineLength; I < MaxLineLength; ++I)
            LineBuffer[LineLength] = " ";
        cout << "\n";
        for (I = 0; I < LineLength; ++I ) {
            cout << LineBuffer[I];
        };
        cout<< "\n" ;
        LinePtr = 0;
    };
};

char Inspect () {
    char result;

    if (LinePtr >= LineLength) {
        if (haveFile) {
            GetNewLine ();
        }
        else {
            EofFlag = TRUE;
        };
    };
```

```
      result = LineBuffer[LinePtr];
      return (result);
};

void Advance () {
    ++LinePtr;
};
```

The following two procedures help manage TokenBuffer. Clear-Buffer, used when we need a new token, sets itsSpelling to the empty string. BufferChar appends its parameter (usually the current input character) to the spelling in TokenBuffer so that the spelling can eventually be made available to the user.

```
void ClearBuffer () {
    strcpy (tokenBuffer.tok.butIntLit.itsSpelling, "")
};

void BufferChar (char C) {
    strncat (tokenBuffer.tok.butIntLit.itsSpelling,
           &C, 1);
};
```

The main routine of the scanner, nextToken, is only a short control function that calls the private function getNextToken, which does all of the work.

```
token nextToken () {
   token result;

   if(EofFlag) return eofSym;
   if (!tokenAvailable) {
      tokenBuffer.currentToken = GetNextToken ();
   };
   result = tokenBuffer.currentToken;
   return (result);
};
```

Much of getNextToken is very repetitive, so only parts of it are shown, mainly the parts that are different from the scanner that we saw in Chapter 5. The structure is a long case statement, which has one case for each of the possible token types. Because some tokens, such as < and <=, have the same initial spelling, we may need to look at more than one character before deciding on the token.

```
token GetNextToken () {
   token result;
```

```
char CurrentChar;
char Finished;

ClearBuffer ();
Finished = FALSE;
while (!Finished) {
   GetNextChar (CurrentChar);
   if (CurrentChar == '\0'){ Finished = TRUE;
                              result = eofSym; }
   else
      if ((CurrentChar == tab) ||
                        (CurrentChar == " ")) {
      // Nothing.
      };
      else if (isalpha (CurrentChar)) {
         BufferChar (CurrentChar);
         while (!Finished) {
            if (isalpha (Inspect ()) ||
                        isdigit (Inspect ()) ||
                        Inspect () == '_') {
               BufferChar (Inspect ());
               Advance ();
            }
            else {
               result = CheckReserved ();
               Finished = TRUE;
            };
         };
      }
      else if (isdigit (CurrentChar)) {
         BufferChar (CurrentChar);
         while (!Finished) {
            if (isdigit (Inspect ())) {
               BufferChar (Inspect ());
               Advance ();
            }
            else {
               result = INTLIT;
               Finished = TRUE;
            }
         }
         tokenBuffer.tok.justIntLit.itsValue =
            atoi (tokenBuffer.tok.butIntLit.
                  itsSpelling);
      }
      else {
         switch (CurrentChar) {
```

```
case '(': {
   result = LParen;
   BufferChar (CurrentChar);
   Finished = TRUE;
}; break;
case ')': {
   result = RParen;
   BufferChar (CurrentChar);
   Finished = TRUE;
}; break;
   ⋮
case '<':
   if (Inspect () == '=') {
      BufferChar (CurrentChar);
      Advance ();
      result = LEOp;
      BufferChar (CurrentChar);
      Finished = TRUE;
   }
   else {
      result = LOp;
      BufferChar (CurrentChar);
      Finished = TRUE;
   }; break;
case ':':
   if (Inspect () == '=') {
      BufferChar (CurrentChar);
      Advance ();
      result = assignOp;
      BufferChar (CurrentChar);
      Finished = TRUE;
   }
   else {
      LexicalError (Inspect ());
   }; break;
case '-': {
   while ( Inspect() == ' ' )
      Advance ();
   if (!isdigit ((Inspect ()))) {
      if (Inspect () == '>') {
         Advance ();
         result = ImpliesOp;
      }
      else {
         result = minusOp;
      };
```

```
                            BufferChar (CurrentChar);
                            Finished = TRUE;
                        }
                        else {
                            result = GetNextToken ();
                            tokenBuffer.tok.justIntLit.
                            itsValue = 0 - tokenBuffer.tok.
                                justIntLit.itsValue;
                            Finished = TRUE;
                        };
                    }; break;
                    default:
                        if (!EofFlag) {
                            LexicalError (CurrentChar); }
                        break;
                };
            };
        };
        if (!Finished) {
            result = eofSym;
        };
        tokenAvailable = TRUE;
        return (result);
    };
```

13.3   RECURSIVE DESCENT PARSING

The technique by which we translate from LLLBI'T to Baby Pascal is
called recursive descent parsing. It is recursive because all of the `parse`
methods of our various classes potentially call each other, making them
mutually recursive. It is called descent parsing because we construct
the parse tree from the top down, from root to leaves. The technique is
a special kind of parsing, known as predictive parsing because at each
stage we are able to predict the form of the subtree below a node simply by looking at one or a few symbols from the input program. For example, when we see `if` in the input, we know that we need subtrees
(nodes) to represent one assertion and either a `<statement>` or an
`<else>`.

The main control process for the translation is either `SStatement`
`:: parseProgram` or `SStatement :: parseString`. The structure of these is the same. They initialize the scanner, telling it what is
to be scanned. They then discard the opening left parenthesis and look at
the next token. If it is the first token in a statement, they create a node
appropriate for that statement type and send the new node the `parse`

message. This call makes the newly created node parse the input, causing other `parse` methods to be called. Each `parse` method called reads some of the input, constructs a tree node (and its children) equivalent to the input read, and returns that tree as the function result. Thus, the initial call of `parse` returns a tree node. `SStatement :: parseProgram` then attaches this node as the root of its own tree. At this point, because the original call has returned, the entire program has been read by the various `parse` methods that were called as a side effect of calling the first one.

```
void SStatement :: parseProgram (char *filename) {
   token aToken;

   initScanner (filename);
   match (LParen);
   aToken = nextToken ();
   toss ();
   if(aToken == assignOp !! aToken == concatOp
      !! aToken == ifOp !! aToken == whileOp)
      fRoot = doParseNode (aToken);
   else
      syntaxError
         ("TStatement :: parse: Bad initial token.");
   match (RParen);
};
```

The only difficulty in this is the very first step in which we must create a tree node of the appropriate kind and send it the `parse` message. Because aToken can be any of `assignOp`, `concatOp`, `ifOp`, or `whileOp`, corresponding to the four statement types, we have a four-way switch statement, with each case looking something like the following:

```
assignOp: {
   anAssign = newAssign ();
   aNode = anAssign -> parse ();
};
```

Because we can use this pattern in other places, we gather all of these cases into the single procedure `doParseNode`, which constructs a new node appropriate for the token just read and passes this node the `parse` message. The `doParseNode` procedure then returns the result of the parse, which is an object in `SNonTerminal`.

```
PNonTerminal doParseNode (token which) {
   PNonTerminal result;
```

```
    switch (which) {
       case assignOp: result = newAssignment ();
          break;
       case concatOp: result = newConcat (); break;
       case ifOp: result = newIf (); break;
       case whileOp: result = newWhile (); break;
       case elseOp: result = newElse (); break;
       case invarOp: result = newInvariant ();
          break;
       default: syntaxError (" in DoParseNode");
          exit (1);
       };
  result -> parse ();
  return result;
};
```

This switch statement could be distributed among the various class methods, but it can't be avoided because we must test a token and then, based on the value, create an appropriate node. This node then continues the parse for us. Because the node has a specific class type and because the parse method for a class knows how to read input and construct a tree node (nonterminal, actually) appropriate for that type of construct, we are able to distribute the complexity of the parse among several classes, making each one responsible for only a bit of the detail.

Let us emphasize the general plan of parsing by recursive descent. We first look at a significant token in the input. For example, the token *if* following the opening parenthesis tells us that the program statement is an if statement. We therefore create an object in class SIf and pass this new object the parse message. This object is responsible for scanning an assertion and either an else structure or a statement. It performs these steps by creating further nodes and passing them the parse message. When these parse routines finish, the if object attaches the created nodes to itself as its left and right children. The left child is an assertion node, and the right child is either an else node or a nonterminal of some kind. The if object then matches the final parenthesis in the construct that caused its own creation and returns. The if object, in fact, has created itself. But the beauty of the technique is that the assertion node that the if generated also created itself.

```
void SIf :: parse (void) {
   token aToken;

   match (Comma);
   if (nextToken () == LParen) toss ();
   fLeft = doParseAssertion (nextToken ());
   match (Comma);
```

```
    match (LParen);
    aToken = nextToken ();
    toss ();
    if (aToken == assignOp !! aToken == concatOp !!
        aToken == whileOp !!
        aToken == ifOp !! aToken == elseOp)
        fRight = doParseNode (aToken);
    else
        syntaxError ("SIf :: parse");
    match (RParen);
};
```

Note something very important. This procedure reads some of the input but not the open parenthesis or the `if` token. This was done by the creator of the node executing this code. This procedure does handle the commas and the closing parenthesis directly. It also handles the components of the `if` structure but it does so indirectly, by creating other nodes. The two calls to `doParseAssertion` and `doParseNode` create these other nodes and parse them. The important thing to note is that each of these calls does the same thing as this procedure. Namely, they read a bit of the input and create and attach further nodes. They read enough of the input, directly or indirectly, to ensure that when we return to this procedure the input has advanced to the next token that is part of this structure but not a part of a substructure. In particular, an assertion nested within an `if` structure must end with a right parenthesis. `SAssertion :: parse` is responsible for consuming this final parenthesis.

The structure of `SWhile :: parse` is nearly identical. The only difference is that the second subpart is always an invariant, so we need only call `doParseNode (invarOp)` for the second call.

```
void SWhile :: parse (void) {
    token aToken;

    match (Comma);
    if (nextToken () == LParen) toss ();
    fLeft = doParseAssertion (nextToken ());
    match (Comma);
    match (LParen);
    aToken = nextToken ();
    toss ();
    if (aToken == invarOp)
        fRight = doParseNode (aToken);
    else
        syntaxError ("SWhile :: parse");
    match (RParen);
};
```

The parse method of SConcatenation is also similar, the difference being that both parts are statements, requiring us to create a node for the correct statement type.

```
void SConcatenation :: parse (void) {
    token aToken;

    match (Comma);
    match (LParen);
    aToken = nextToken ();
    toss ();
    if (aToken == assignOp !! aToken == concatOp !!
        aToken == ifOp !! aToken == whileOp)
        fLeft = doParseNode (aToken);
    else
        syntaxError ("SConcatenation :: parse");
    match (RParen);
    match (Comma);
    match (LParen);
    aToken = nextToken ();
    toss ();
    if (aToken == assignOp !! aToken == concatOp !!
        aToken == ifOp !! aToken == whileOp)
        fRight = doParseNode (aToken);
    else
        syntaxError ("SConcatenation :: parse");
    match (RParen);
};
```

The first part of an assignment is always an identifier, so we just fill this into the assignment node itself as its data. We don't use the left child of such a node. The right node is always an expression.

```
void SAssignment :: parse (void) {
    match (Comma);
    if (nextToken () == ID)
        fValue = newString
            (tokenBuffer.tok.butIntLit.itsSpelling);
    else
        syntaxError ("SAssignment :: parse");
    toss ();
    match (Comma);
    if (nextToken () == LParen) toss ();
    fRight = doParseExpression (nextToken ());
};
```

The parts of an else node are always two statements.

```
void SElse :: parse (void) {
   token aToken;

   match (Comma);
   match (LParen);
   aToken = nextToken ();
   toss ();
   if (aToken == assignOp !! aToken == concatOp !!
      aToken == ifOp)
     fLeft = doParseNode (aToken);
   else
     syntaxError ("SElse :: parse");
   match (RParen);
   match (Comma);
   match (LParen);
   aToken = nextToken ();
   toss ();
   if(aToken == assignOp !! aToken == concatOp !!
      aToken == ifOp)
     fRight = doParseNode (aToken);
   else
     syntaxError ("SElse :: parse");
   match (RParen);
};
```

An invariant node has an assertion for its first part and a statement for its second.

```
void SInvariant :: parse (void) {
   token aToken;

   match (Comma);
   if (nextToken () == LParen) toss ();
   fLeft = doParseAssertion (nextToken ());
   match (Comma);
   match (LParen);
   aToken = nextToken ();
   toss ();
   if (aToken == assignOp !! aToken == concatOp !!
      aToken == ifOp !! aToken == whileOp)
       fRight = doParseNode (aToken);
   else
     syntaxError ("SInvariant :: parse");
   match (RParen);
};
```

The methods that parse expressions are similar. An expression parser looks at the next token to determine what sort of expression it is to parse. If it is a left parenthesis, it must look at the next token to see what sort of an expression is to be parsed. As usual, the commas and ending right parenthesis must be matched.

Most of the expression types consist of two subexpressions. For example, a sum consists of the two expressions to be added. The default `parse` method is defined in `SExpression` itself. It needs to be overridden only in `SIdentExpression` and `SIntLitExpression`, where the expression consists of a single term.

```
void SExpression :: parse (void) {
    // The default case, with two subexpressions.

    toss ();
    match (Comma);
    if (nextToken () == LParen) toss ();
    fLeft = doParseExpression (nextToken ());
    match (Comma);
    if (nextToken () == LParen) toss ();
    fRight = doParseExpression (nextToken ());
    match (RParen);
};
```

If the token is an identifier or an integer, we must save the spelling in the node itself and not attach a subnode.

```
void SIdentExpression :: parse (void) {
    fValue = newString
        (tokenBuffer.tok.butIntLit.itsSpelling);
    toss ();
};

void SIntLitExpression :: parse (void) {
    fValue = asInteger
        (tokenBuffer.tok.justIntLit.itsValue);
    toss ();
};
```

In contrast, all parsing of assertions is done within a single procedure. Note the `switch` statement in the `parse` method of `SAssertion`. It would not be present if we had built subclasses for all of the assertion types. The `parse` method is a bit longer, because we have to save the type of assertion in the node itself, since we don't have a full complement of subtypes for it. The token tells us what the type is, but the token is not what we want to store, so we need something like a switch statement to sort it out. Other than this, the `parse` method has the same structure as before.

```
void SAssertion :: parse (void) {
   token aToken;
   if (nextToken () == ID){
       fValue = newString
           (tokenBuffer.tok.butIntLit.itsSpelling);
       toss ();
   }
   else {
       aToken = nextToken ();
       toss ();
       match (Comma);
       switch (aToken) {
           case ParamOp: {
               if (nextToken () == LParen) toss ();
               fLeft = doParseAssertion (nextToken ());
               match (Comma);
               if (nextToken () == LParen) toss ();
               fRight = doParseExpression (nextToken ()
           }; break;
           case orOp:
           case andOp: {
               if (nextToken () == LParen) toss ();
               fLeft = doParseAssertion (nextToken());
               match (Comma);
               if (nextToken () == LParen) toss ();
               fRight = doParseAssertion (nextToken ())
           }; break;
           case notOp: {
               if (nextToken () == LParen) toss ();
               fLeft = doParseAssertion (nextToken ());
               match (Comma);
               match (minusOp);
           }; break;
           case existOp:
           case allOp: {
               fValue = newString
                   (tokenBuffer.tok.butIntLit.itsSpelling
               toss ();
               match (Comma);
               if (nextToken () == LParen) toss ();
               fRight = doParseAssertion (nextToken ())
           }; break;
           case EQOp:  case NEOp:  case LOp:
           case LEOp:  case GOp:
           case GEOp: {
               if (nextToken () == LParen) toss ();
               fLeft = doParseExpression (nextToken ())
```

```
                    match (Comma);
                    if (nextToken () == LParen) toss ();
                    fRight = doParseExpression (nextToken ());
                }; break;
            };
        match (RParen);
        };
};
```

The result of creating a statement and sending it a `parse` message is that the statement, which is a tree, empty at first, becomes filled as the parse continues. The order in which it is filled is that of a pre-order walk of the parse tree. For the example in this chapter, this tree is shown in Fig. 13.4. We create first the `if` node and then an assertion node, and then we complete the assertion node with a `lessEqual` relation. The first argument of the `lessEqual` relation is an expression with an identifier value, and the second is an expression whose value is a multiplication. As the parse continues, each node creates and parses any subnodes that it requires and attaches them to itself. Each is in turn attached by its caller to some other node, until the entire tree is built.

Note the large difference between the handling of expressions and assertions, even though the two are very similar. To add another expression type, we would create a new subclass of `SExpression` and give it about four methods. To create a new kind of assertion, we must find the four or so methods of `SAssertion` that might apply to the new form and modify them by adding new cases. We might even have to reformulate some of the code if we optimized it at all. This leaves us open to the introduction of errors, not just for the newly added features, but for the older code as well. Object-oriented programming has a clear advantage in this area. This difference will appear again in the next section.

13.4   THE OUTPUT OF THE TRANSLATOR

After the parsing of an `SStatement` object, the object itself represents its own parse tree. We can use iterators or whatever to walk this tree, and as we walk it, we can perform various transformations or output the information seen. Our current purpose is to produce an output of an equivalent program written in Baby Pascal, which was discussed earlier. The method we employ is to implement the `writeIt` methods of each of our classes and vary the protocol (in-order, pre-order, etc.) in each class to get the desired effect. For example, in the expression class we want to output a parenthesized in-order expression, so we use an in-order protocol at such nodes.

The `writeIt` method of `SStatement` sends `writeIt` to its root node, `fRoot`. An `if` node writes the word *IF*, sends `writeIt` to its left child, writes the word *THEN*, sends `writeIt` to its right child, and finally writes the words *END IF*. This is a pre-order node, because the word *IF* is written first. While nodes are nearly the same.

```
void SIf :: writeIt (void) {
    cout << "\nIF ";
    fLeft -> writeIt ();
    cout << " THEN ";
    fRight -> writeIt ();
    cout << " END IF";
};

void SWhile :: writeIt (void) {
    cout << "\nWHILE ";
    fLeft -> writeIt ();
    cout << " DO ";
    fRight -> writeIt ();
    cout << "\nEND DO ";
};
```

A concatenation node writes a semicolon between the output of its left and right children. It is an in-order node. Assignment nodes and else nodes are similar.

```
void SConcatenation :: writeIt (void) {
    fLeft -> writeIt ();
    cout << " ; ";
    fRight -> writeIt ();
    cout << "\n";
};

void SAssignment :: writeIt (void) {
    cout << "\n";
    fValue -> writeIt ();
    cout << ":= ";
    fRight -> writeIt ();
};

void SElse :: writeIt (void) {
    fLeft -> writeIt ();
    cout << "\n";
    cout << " ELSE ";
    fRight -> writeIt ();
};
```

An invariant node formats its output quite differently. The right child, a statement, is written first, then the word *Invar*, and then the left node.

Therefore an invariant condition is written just before the *END DO* of the loop it is contained in.

```
void SInvariant :: writeIt (void) {
   fRight -> writeIt ();
   cout << "\n { Invar: ";
   fLeft -> writeIt ();
   cout << " }";
};
```

If its expression is an identifier or an integer, an expression node writes out the data in the node, which is a string or an element of SInteger. Otherwise, it writes the left and right children separated by the appropriate operator symbol. Brackets are put to the left and right of multipart expressions, as well.

```
void SExpression :: writeIt (void) {
   cout << "[" << "an expression" << "]";
};

void SIdentExpression :: writeIt (void) {
   fValue -> writeIt ();
};

void SParamExpression :: writeIt (void) {
   cout << " [ ";
   fLeft -> writeIt ();
   cout << "^";
   fRight -> writeIt ();
   cout << " ] ";
};

void SIntLitExpression :: writeIt (void) {
   fValue -> writeIt ();
};

void SSum :: writeIt (void) {
   cout << " [ ";
   fLeft -> writeIt ();
   cout << " + ";
   fRight -> writeIt ();
   cout << " ] ";
};
```

The other arithmetic expressions are similar to SSum.

Assertion nodes are more complex, because of the variety of forms of assertion. We also try to format the assertions in a generally mathematical way, especially `all` and `exist` assertions, which use the data in the assertion node and the right child but have no left child. Also, a `not` node has a left child but no right child. Since all of these except the `not` node must write a right child, we factor the writing out of all of the cases and write it at the end of `SAssertion :: writeIt`.

```
void SAssertion :: writeIt (void) {
    cout << " { ";
    switch (fKind) {
        case ID: fValue -> writeIt (); break;
        case ParamOp: {
            fLeft -> writeIt ();
            cout << "^";
        }; break;
        case allOp: {
            cout << "ForAll ";
            fValue -> writeIt ();
            cout << " ! ";
        } ;break;
        case existOp: {
            cout << "ThereExists ";
            fValue -> writeIt ();
            cout << " ! ";
        }; break;
        case andOp: {
            fLeft -> writeIt ();
            cout << " and \n ";
        }; break;
        case orOp: {
            fLeft -> writeIt ();
            cout << " or \n ";
        }; break;
        case notOp: {
            cout << " not ";
            fLeft -> writeIt ();
        }; break;
        case EQOp: {
            fLeft -> writeIt ();
            cout << "=";
        }; break;
        case NEOp: {
            fLeft -> writeIt ();
            cout << "#";
        }; break;
```

```
        case GOp: {
            fLeft -> writeIt ();
            cout << ">";
        }; break;
        case LOp: {
            fLeft -> writeIt ();
            cout << "<";
        }; break;
        case GEOp: {
            fLeft -> writeIt ();
            cout << ">=";
        }; break;
        case LEOp: {
            fLeft -> writeIt ();
            cout << "<=";
        }; break;

    };
    if (! (fKind == notOp !! fKind == ID))
        fRight -> writeIt ();
    cout << "}";
};
```

13.5   SIMPLIFICATION OF A PARSE TREE

This section discusses how a tree representing a program might be simplified before it is output. It just touches the surface of a very complex subject. An optimizing compiler for a language such as Pascal does something similar to what we do here but is much more sophisticated. The main idea is to replace the parse tree, which represents the structure of a program, with a different tree of equivalent structure that has more convenient or more efficient substructures. For a compiler, a tree is equivalent if the program it translates to produces the same result as the original program, though perhaps in a different way, perhaps one that is much faster or requires less space in memory.

At the SStatement level (tree level) the method simplify applies the node method simplified to its root and attaches the return value as the new root. Nonterminals have a functional method simplified that returns a tree representing a simplified version of themselves. The default simplified method for a nonterminal is to pass simplified to the left and right children and attach the results as its own fLeft and fRight.

```
PNonTerminal SNonTerminal :: simplified (void) {
    fLeft = PNonTerminal (fLeft) -> simplified ();
    fRight = PNonTerminal (fRight) -> simplified ();
    return this;
};
```

An assignment node has only a right child, so we pass `simplified` to that node, which is an expression. The other statement types, as well as else nodes and invariant nodes, use the default method.

```
PNonTerminal SAssignment :: simplified (void) {
    fRight = PExpression (fRight) -> simplified ();
    return this;
};
```

It is at the level of expressions and assertions that simplification becomes interesting. As an example of some of the things that can be done, suppose an expression is a sum, and suppose that both of the children are just expressions of type `IntLit`, meaning that they have an integer stored in the node itself. We could perform this addition in the simplifier and then transform the sum node into an `IntLit` node, in which we store the result. The original child nodes of the sum are no longer needed.

Before attempting this, however, we should simplify both of the children of that sum node, because even if they aren't originally integer literals, the simplification step might leave them so. In general, the parts are better simplified before the whole. Simplification is sometimes called a bottom-up process, since we simplify the lower parts of the tree before the upper parts, even though we start the simplification step at the root. This is similar to a bottom-up or post-order tree walk, in which we visit the children before we visit the node itself.

```
PNonTerminal SExpression :: simplified (void) {
    return this; // Subclasses will do more.
};

PNonTerminal SSum :: simplified (void) {
    PNonTerminal result, newLeft, newRight;

    result = this;
    newLeft = PExpression (fLeft) -> simplified ();
    newRight = PExpression (fRight) -> simplified ();
    if (newLeft -> kind () == INTLIT
        && newRight -> kind () == INTLIT) {
        result = newIntLitExpression ();
```

```
      result -> fValue = PInteger (newLeft -> fValue)
          -> add (PInteger (newRight -> fValue));
   };
   return result;
};
```

Again, the other arithmetic expressions are similar.

Other expression simplifications are possible. Some of them are dangerous in general, especially with real data because of possible round-off problems. It is theoretically possible to build the laws of mathematics into our simplifier so that we could look for such things as a sum node below a product node, in which case we could apply a distributive law. It is not generally attempted in a real compiler for a variety of reasons. One simple reason is that such simplifications take a lot of testing, taking time. A more fundamental reason is that the number abstractions built into computers only approximately model the concepts on which they are based. A mathematician has no notion of overflow in integer computations. Round-off error is indeed a mathematical concept, but it is in general a rather deep one. Real numbers in a computer don't generally obey the commutative and associative laws of ordinary real numbers. On the other hand, if a symbolic rather than numeric computation is desired, all of these simplifications (and more) may be appropriate.

Assertions provide more simplification possibilities. A comparison node, such as `lessEqual`, below a `not` node can be simplified to a single `greater` node if we reverse the left and right children. Double `not` nodes can be eliminated altogether.

```
PNonTerminal SAssertion :: simplified (void) {
   PAssertion result, anAssertion;
   PNonTerminal newLeft;

   result = this; // Default return value.
   switch (fKind) {
      case ID: {
         // Nothing.
      }; break;
      case ParamOp: {
         fRight = PAssertion (fRight)
            -> simplified ();
      }; break;
      case allOp:
      case existOp: {
         fRight = PAssertion (fRight)
            -> simplified ();
      }; break;
      case andOp:
      case orOp: {
```

```
            fLeft = PAssertion (fLeft)
               -> simplified ();
            fRight = PAssertion (fRight)
               -> simplified ();
      }; break;
      case notOp: {
         newLeft = PAssertion (fLeft)
                  -> simplified ();
         switch (newLeft -> kind ()) {
            case allOp:
            case existOp:{
               anAssertion = newAssertion (notOp);
               anAssertion -> fLeft = newLeft
                  -> fRight;
               if (PAssertion (fLeft)
                  -> fKind == existOp)
                  result = newAssertion (allOp);
               else
                  result = newAssertion
                     (existOp);
               result -> fValue = newLeft
                     -> fValue;
               result -> fRight = anAssertion
                     -> simplified ();
            }; break;
            case notOp: {
               result = PAssertion
                     (newLeft -> fLeft);
            }; break;
            case ID:  case ParamOp:   case andOp:
            case orOp: {
               fLeft = newLeft;
            }; break;
            case EQOp:  case NEOp:   case LOp:
            case LEOp:  case GOp:
            caseGEOp: {
               switch (PAssertion (newLeft)
                     -> fKind) {
                  case EQOp: result
                     = newAssertion (NEOp); break;
                  case NEOp: result
                     = newAssertion (EQOp); break;
                  case LOp: result
                     = newAssertion (GEOp); break;
                  case LEOp: result
                     = newAssertion (GOp); break;
                  case GOp: result
```

```
                                       = newAssertion (LEOp); break;
                            case GEOp: result
                                       = newAssertion (LOp); break;
                    };
                    result -> fLeft = newLeft
                               -> fLeft;
                    result -> fRight = newLeft
                               -> fRight;
              }; break;
              default:
                    result = this;
          };
      }; break;
      case EQOp:  case NEOp:  case LOp:
      case LEOp:  case GOp:
      case GEOp: {
          fLeft = PExpression (fLeft)
              -> simplified ();
          fRight = PExpression (fRight)
              -> simplified ();
      }; break;
    };
    return result;
};
```

13.6   DESIGN REVISITED

A few elements of the design of the program translator may be questioned.
In this section we explore a few alternatives.

The first major issue is that the scanner presented above is not object-
oriented at all. It is composed of a set of ordinary procedures that work
together to produce the global variable tokenBuffer. These procedures
use some static memory, defined in the implementation section of the scanner, to keep track of the scan. As a result of this design decision, two files
cannot be scanned at once. Once our main program sends one of the parse
messages to a statement object, the parsing must finish before we can parse
any other program. It might be useful in languages such as Modula-2, where
a program is spread over several files, to suspend the parse of one file so
that we can parse another. This is not possible with the current design,
because the state of the current parse will be destroyed if we reinitialize
the scanner.

A solution to this problem is to create a class, SScanner, whose
instance variables are the static variables of the current scanner and
whose methods are the procedures and functions of the current scanner. In
this way, whenever we need to scan a new program, we just create a new

scanner object to do the scan. This object internally maintains its own state. This flexibility comes at a small cost, however. We have to communicate to a `parse` routine which scanner it is to use. We do this either by including a new scanner instance variable in each class that has a parse method or by passing the scanner to a parse routine as a parameter.

If the scanner is rebuilt as a class, we should probably build a class with subclasses to replace the type of the variable `tokenBuffer`. The class could have only one instance variable, `fToken`, to hold the type of the current token, and subclasses corresponding to each variant of type `union` of the current declaration of `tokenBuffer`.

Another design issue that affects the code greatly is the degree of refinement of our class hierarchy. On the one hand, we could build only a statement class and a nonterminal class without the additional subclasses of the latter. We would need additional instance variables within the node class to distinguish the various sorts of nodes that we have in our tree. We would then need a `case` statement in the `parse` routine for the nonterminal class. Each case would carry out the parsing of one kind of construct in the program, perhaps by calling a specialized method for the purpose.

On the other hand, we could build a class for every nonterminal in our original grammar for LLLBI'T. We would then have eleven additional subclasses of `SAssertion`. They would require many more constructors, but not much more code, because most of the methods can be inherited. The one difference would be that where we have determined the class of a node by looking at an instance variable in the node, we would, instead, use the `member` function to tell us the class of the node.

A third possibility would be to rewrite the `parse` methods so that a given `parse` method in a class is designed to parse direct subclass structures of that class rather than structures of the class itself. Then the `parse` method of `SIf`, for example, would have knowledge of the structure of an assertion, a statement, and an `else` structure from the original language. This is a bad design for two reasons. First, it saves us nothing in complexity. We still need to look at a token and use a `case` structure to handle it correctly. Second, it causes us to repeat things, since `while` nodes also need to know about statements and assertions. We can do this with procedures, of course, but it is much cleaner to associate the assertion parsing code with the assertion class.

13.7   SUMMARY

The syntactic structure of a modern programming language is defined in terms of trees. These trees are in turn described by means of a BNF or equivalent formalism. For an appropriate grammar the recursive descent method described in this chapter is adequate for analyzing the language and forming the basis of a translation to another language. This is the general idea on which compilers, such as the C++ compiler, are built. C++ uses a more powerful but similar method. Not all compilers build the parse tree as we have done here. Some content themselves with a single pre-order (or post-order) walk of the tree where only a very small part of the tree exists at any one moment.

The object-oriented technique aids in such tree building, because the decisions about how to handle a particular kind of node in the tree are localized within the class defining that node type rather than being distributed over many procedures that have responsibility for many node types. This distinction should be clear from the difference between the implementations of SAssertion and SExpression. A new kind of expression is easily added because we need only build a new class describing it. To add a new assertion, we need to modify several procedures that have responsibility for all assertion types. This localization of the changes required when extending software is one of the chief benefits of object-oriented programming.

In the next chapter we shall extend these ideas, building on our tree notion and doing more tree rewriting as we did when simplifying programs in Section 13.5.

EXERCISES

13.1 (13.1) Consider the concatenation operator `;`. In Pascal this separates and hence concatenates two statements: `X := 1 ; Y := X + 1`. If S, T, and U are statements, what is the meaning of `S ; T ; U`? Is it equivalent to `(S ; T) ; U`, or is it `S ; (T ; U)`? Or are these two statements the same? Stated another way, the question is "Is the concatenation operator associative?" Note that when we parenthesize statements, we are not suggesting that this is legal Pascal. We do so merely to indicate what pieces of a program are to be considered to be a unit. Therefore, `(S ; T) ; U` means to do S `; T` first and follow the result of that with U. On the other hand, `S ; (T ; U)` means to do S first and follow that with `T ; U`.

13.2 (13.2) At the end of the chapter, we suggested that LLLBIT could have an object-oriented scanner. Build a class for this scanner. Its methods should be the scanning functions discussed in Section 13.2. Its instance variables should be any globals that we depend upon to remember things between calls of nextToken. Except nextToken, most of the methods should be protected.

13.3 (13.4) Write down a grammar for Baby Pascal. Note that only the productions from LLLBIT that mention some terminal symbol need to be rewritten. For example, `<statement>` has the same definition, but the new definition of `<if>` is

```
<if> ::= IF <assertion> THEN <statement> END IF ¦
     IF <assertion> THEN <else> END IF
```

13.4 (13.4) The procedure CheckReserved actually searches for keys in a dictionary. The keys are the keywords of LLLBIT, and the values are the token symbols. Reimplement `CheckReserved` taking advantage of this. Hold this information in an element of `SDictionary`. This dictionary will have to be initialized (once only). You will need an `initScanner` procedure for this and will have to ensure that it is called.

13.5 (13.4) Rebuild `SAssertion` so that its methods distribute functionality over a set of specialized subclasses rather than use `case` statements.

## CHAPTER 14

PROGRAM VERIFICATION

For I have ever verified my friends,
Of whom he's chief, with all the size that verity
Would without lapsing suffer.

  Shakespeare, *Tragedy of Coriolanus*

The Sentence of the Judge ... is a sufficient Verification of the Law of Nature in that individual case.

  Hobbes, *Leviathan*

L LLBI'T, like ordinary Pascal, is an imperative language. We execute a program for some effect on the memory and the input and output devices of the computer. Programs in such languages can be defined in terms of what they do. Imperative programming languages can be contrasted with functional languages, which evaluate expressions. Such programs are defined in terms of what functions they compute. Lisp is a functional language. Another family of languages is the logic languages, such as Prolog. These are defined in terms of the relationships they represent, which are more general than functions. Imperative languages carry out some process, and their programs are expressions of some algorithm. Said another way, a program in an imperative programming language describes the steps by which we carry out a computation rather than just the results desired.

In this chapter we shall develop a method of defining imperative languages called algebraic semantics. As with many of the topics in the book, this is only an introduction to a much deeper subject. An understanding of it will make you a better programmer, however, because it will give you a way to think about the correctness of your programs that is very powerful. We shall also develop methods of our language translator class to aid us in determining the correctness of our programs.

14.1   SOME BACKGROUND FROM LOGIC

In the following, the behavior of program statements in LLLBI'T will be discussed. Imagine a computer memory. Imagine that some variable names are mapped to that memory and that those variables have values. We say that the memory is in a certain state. Another way to describe a memory state is to say what is true about it. We might say "$x = 4$" or "$y < 27$", for example. Statements such as these are called predicates. They can be TRUE or FALSE, depending on the current state of the machine. They involve variables, some that are program variables and, occasionally, some that are auxiliary, used only in our reasoning process. We say that a predicate describes a set of states. It describes a set of states rather than a single state because a statement such as "$y < 27$" can be TRUE for many states of the memory. Unless the memory consists of a single cell, even the statement "$x = 4$" can be TRUE in many ways, for example, y could be 5 or 44.

When we want to represent abstract, rather than concrete, statements, we use roman capitals, P or Q, for predicates. If we want to emphasize that a predicate is defined in terms of variables, we list them using a functional notation such as P (x, y). In fact, a predicate is a function from some set to the truth values. The following is an example of the use of predicates

```
{x < 28 and x > 5}   (:=, x (+, x, 2))
    {x < 30 and x > 7}
```

Here we have written two predicates, one on either side of a LLLBI'T statement. We put the predicates in braces, so they look like Pascal comments. (LLLBI'T doesn't have comments.) The meaning of what we have written is this. If the machine is started up in a state in which the first predicate is TRUE and we then execute the program fragment in the middle, the machine will then be in a state in which the right predicate is TRUE.

Note that the last statement in the previous paragraph, which gives the meaning of our little example, is itself a predicate. Therefore it can be either TRUE or FALSE. If it is always TRUE, we call it a specification of the program statement it contains. The first predicate is called a precondition, and the second is called a postcondition. In general, a specification has the form

```
{P} S {Q}
```

where P and Q are predicates, which may involve variables, and S is a program fragment. Note that it isn't the form that makes it a specification. It is the truth of the associated predicate: If P is TRUE and then we execute S, then Q will be TRUE.

Specification

If whenever the program S starts in state P it necessarily terminates in state Q, then {P} S {Q} is a specification of S.

Specifications are used in defining programs, developing programs, and proving that programs do what they are supposed to do. The standard way to describe to a programmer what is wanted from a program is to describe the input and output conditions of the machine that the program will need to deal with. The input conditions are just an elaborate precondition. The output conditions form a postcondition. The specification for the, as yet unwritten, program is "If the inputs to the program have form... and the program is executed, then the outputs will have the form...." This is the same as our specification predicate. The programmer in effect is given {P} {Q} and is asked to fill in the middle to create what we have called a specification.

Precondition and Postcondition

If {P} S {Q} is a specification, P is called a precondition and Q is called a postcondition.

Suppose we have two predicates, Q and R, and the implication Q -> R is TRUE. This means that either R is TRUE or Q is FALSE (or both). That is, to say that Q -> R is TRUE is to say that whenever Q is TRUE, R is also TRUE. In this situation we say that R is a logically *weaker* statement than Q. We also call Q *stronger*.

Now suppose we have a specification {P} S {Q}. If R is weaker than Q, it follows that {P} S {R} is also a specification. Likewise, if B is stronger than P, it follows that {B} S {Q} is a specification. The rules are that you can strengthen a precondition or weaken a postcondition without breaking a specification. We would really like to move the other way. We would like our preconditions to be as weak as possible and our postconditions to be as strong as possible. In other words, we would like programs to work in as many initial states as possible and to do as much as possible. For a given program statement, if {A} S {Q} and {P} S {Q} are specifications and A -> P is TRUE, we prefer the second specification, because it has the weaker precondition.

Notice that the predicate P -> TRUE is always TRUE. For this reason we call the logical constant TRUE, which is a predicate, but a constant one, the weakest predicate of all. Similarly FALSE -> P is always TRUE, for any P. Therefore we call the logical constant FALSE the strongest predicate of all. If we give as precondition TRUE, we are saying that it doesn't matter what state we start the program in. By giving FALSE as precondition, however, we say that the specification cannot be met. A program that has an infinite loop can be said to have the precondition of {FALSE}. A natural example of a program with the precondition {TRUE} is the following.

```
{TRUE} (:=, x, 1) { x = 1 }
```

If we start the program in any state, we will wind up in the state {x = 1}.

Weaker and Stronger Predicates

If P -> Q, then P is called stronger and Q is called weaker. TRUE is the weakest predicate of all. FALSE is the strongest predicate of all. Strong predicates are more specific. Weak predicates are more general.

In the following sections we shall use some additional terminology and results from logic. The statement A **or** B formed from the two statements A and B is called a disjunction. Similarly, A **and** B is called a conjunction. De Morgan's formulas are

1. **not** (A **and** B) = (**not** A) **or** (**not** B)
2. **not** (A **or** B) = (**not** A) **and** (**not** B)

The statement A -> B is equivalent to (**not** A) **or** B. However, if A and B involve any free variables, such as x, what we generally mean when we write A -> B is (for all x | A(x) -> B(x)), so this is equivalent to (for all x | (**not** A(x)) **or** B(x)). This will be important in what follows.

We have defined a rather general form for assertions in LLLBI'T. In particular, we permit assertions to contain universal and existential quantifiers. The assertion (all, x, (<, x, x + 1)) claims that for all values of the variable x, x is less than x + 1. The word all is called a universal quantifier, and the statement is a universal quantification. Similarly, (exist, x, (<, x, y)) is an existential quantification. It claims that there is some value of x less than y. The occurrence of a variable name immediately after a quantifier, such as x here, is called a binding occurrence of the variable. If the variable appears in the following expression and the occurrence there is not bound again at some inner level, we say that that particular occurrence of the variable is a bound occurrence and that it is bound to this quantifier. A variable that is not bound is free. The only occurrence of *y* in (exist, x, (<, x, y)) is a free occurrence. A bound variable is like a local variable in a C++ or Pascal procedure. The change to the global variable having the same name does not affect the local variable. A free variable is similar to a global (nonlocal) variable.

14.2   THE SEMANTICS OF LLLBI'T AND BABY PASCAL

Algebraic semantics is a way of defining the meaning of programming languages by using specifications. We shall give specifications of the elementary statements of LLLBI'T and of the ways that statements may be combined into programs. If we give weak preconditions and strong postconditions, we sufficiently restrict what can occur in between, so the specifications define the statements. In particular, we proceed in the following way. Suppose we start with a program fragment S and a postcondition Q. Suppose we then find some precondition P so that {P} S {Q} is a specification. Suppose also that P is the weakest such precondition that can be used. This means any weaker statement P' would not give us a specification. If Q is sufficiently general, we can say that {P} and {Q} define the meaning of S.

For example, consider the assignment statement (:= , x, e) where e is any expression that can be legally formed in LLLBI'T. Suppose we want to establish some postcondition, Q (x), that involves the variable x. In other words, we want Q to be TRUE of x after executing the program fragment (:=, x, e). Then before the statement is executed, Q should be TRUE of e. Therefore we say that

{Q(e)} (:=, x, e) {Q(x)}

is a defining specification of the assignment statement. If we start the assignment in a state in which Q is TRUE of e and then assign e to x, we end in a state in which Q is TRUE of x.

To give an example of this we examine the statement (:=, x (+, x, 2)), shown earlier in the chapter. If we want to establish the postcondition Q (x) = (x < 30 and x > 7) after executing the statement, Q (e) must be true before. But e is the expression (+, x, 2), or x + 2 in infix form. Therefore, by substituting x + 2 into Q (x) for all occurrences of x we get Q (e) = Q (x + 2) = (x + 2) < 30 and (x + 2) > 7, which is x < 28 and x > 5. Therefore, our precondition is (x < 28 and x > 5).

This sounds easy enough, but there is something very subtle here. We are using this as the *definition* of the assignment. We can see that it gives the following meaning to the assignment statement: In a state in which Q (e) is TRUE, and the value of x is not inconsistent with the truth of Q (e), the assignment (:=, x, e) gives x a value so that Q (x) is then TRUE *and nothing else has changed*. Said another way, the assignment changes the state only of x, and not of other entities. Execution of the assignment (:=, x, e) makes a very local change in the state. Finally the *evaluation* of e doesn't change anything at all. It is a pure evaluation without side effects.

Therefore, when we give {Q(e)} (:=, x, e) {Q(x)} as a defining specification for the assignment, we declare that the language does not permit side effects to occur when we evaluate expressions used in assignments. Pascal is not precisely like this. We can say X := foo; in Pascal where foo is a function being called. If foo changes some global variables, the state has changed beyond the change in X. It is precisely this about global variables in our programs that causes them to be frowned upon. They make the effects of statements, and hence of programs, much harder to determine, and therefore they make programs much harder to understand.

We summarize what we have done above with the assignment by saying that {Q(e)} (:=, x, e) {Q(x)} is the algebraic semantics of the assignment statement. An alternate form of this will be helpful in what follows. If {P} S {Q} defines the algebraic semantics of S, we write P = Wp (S, Q), which is read "P is the weakest precondition for which {P} S {Q} is a specification." For the assignment statement this becomes Q(e) = Wp ((:=, x, e), Q (x)).

Weak Precondition Wp (S, Q)

If {P} S {Q} is any specification, then P -> Wp (S, Q). Wp (S, Q) is thus defined to be the weakest precondition, R, such that {R} S {Q}.

A precondition or a postcondition is nothing more than an **assertion** that something is true. LLLBI'T has a way to represent assertions. They are a fundamental part of conditionals and loops and can also represent preconditions and postconditions. If we want to represent a specification as a tree, we need three branches for the parts: precondition, statement, and postcondition. If we restrict our implementation to binary trees, we can use the scheme of Fig. 14.1 to represent a specification using two binary tree nodes as cement to hold the structure together. For the example shown previously the specification would look like Fig. 14.2.

We want to establish algebraic semantics (specifications) for each of the parts of LLLBI'T. The next case is even simpler than the assignment statement. When assertions and expressions are evaluated in LLLBI'T, no change whatever occurs to the program state. Thus, if we evaluate an assertion, such as (<, a, (+, b, 2)), and want {Q} to be TRUE

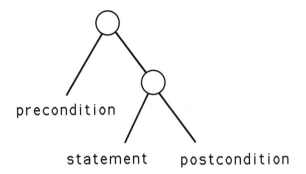

FIGURE 14.1

precondition

statement   postcondition

afterwards, {Q} must be TRUE before as well. Therefore we can summarize the algebraic semantics of expressions and assertions as

```
{Q} <assertion> {Q}
{Q} <expression> {Q}
```

In Pascal the semicolon acts as an infix form of a concatenation operator: S1 ; S2. Concatenation simply indicates that the statement on the left is to be executed before the statement on the right. In LLLBIT, using our prefix form for all statements, we write this as (;, S1, S2). In order to express the meaning of this exactly, we seek to write down what

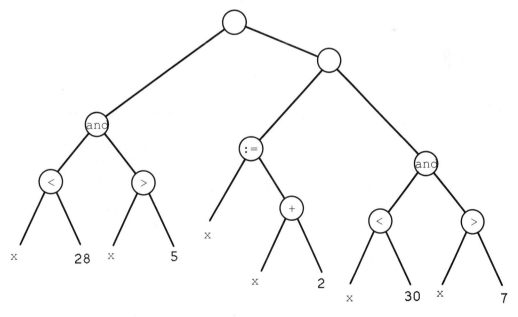

{x<28 and x > 5}   (:=, x (+, x , 2)) {x < 30 and x > 7}
FIGURE 14.2

we mean by `Wp ((;, S1, S2), Q)` where `Q` is an arbitrary predicate. The question is "What state must we start in so that first executing `S1` and then executing `S2` will leave us in state `Q`?" If this state is called P, after executing `S1` we must be in a state in which executing `S2` will leave us in state Q. This means that the state `P'` that we are in after executing `S1` must be stronger than `Wp (S2, Q)`. If we are seeking the weakest P that does this, we can take `P'` to be the same as `Wp (S2, Q)`. Thus, Pmust be `Wp (S1, Wp (S2, Q))`. Therefore we conclude that defining the concatenation operator by

```
Wp ((;, S1, S2), Q) = Wp (S1, Wp (S2, Q))
```

exactly expresses "First execute `S1` and then execute `S2`."

As an example of this, consider the program fragment `y := 1; y := y + 2`, which we have expressed in the normal infix form rather than the LLLBI'T prefix form. Suppose we want to establish `{y = 5}` at the end of this. We must first compute `Wp (y := y + 2, y = 5)` using the assignment rule. This precondition is `y + 2 = 5`, which simplifies to `y = 3`. Then we must compute `Wp (y := 1, y = 3)` using the assignment rule again. This gives `1 = 3`, which simplifies to FALSE. Therefore our precondition in the specification of this fragment is FALSE, indicating the impossibility of achieving the desired postcondition. If we try again with the postcondition `{y <= 5}`, we arrive in two steps at the precondition `1 <= 5`, which simplifies to TRUE, indicating that in *any* starting state we can achieve `y <= 5` through the execution of `y := 1; y := y + 2`.

The `if` statement in LLLBI'T, like the `if` statement of Pascal, has two forms. One form has a statement as the second operand, and the other form has an `else` construction as the second operand. We shall consider these two cases separately. Since `else` fragments appear only in `if` statements, we shall in effect be giving the semantics of `else` parts as well as those of `if` statements.

To define what we mean by `(if, A, S)` where A is an assertion and S is a statement, we consider that A may be TRUE or FALSE. If it is FALSE, the statement is not executed at all. If it is TRUE, S is executed. Therefore, if we want Q to be TRUE when we finish, in those cases in which A is false, Q must be true initially. This is because the evaluation of A will not change the state, and S will not be executed at all, so it can't change the state. Therefore, the state does not change, and we must be in the final state originally. However, in those cases in which A is TRUE, S is executed and represents the only means of changing the state. Therefore we must begin in state `Wp (S, Q)` in those situations in which A is TRUE. We can say all of this compactly as

```
Wp ((if, A, S), Q) = (A and Wp (S, Q))
    or ((not A) and Q)
```

This says we must start with both A and Wp (S,Q) TRUE or with A FALSE and Q TRUE. Note that we can express the right-hand side of the above definition in LLLBI'T. It would become

```
(or, (and, A, Wp (S, Q)) , (and, (not, A, -), Q))
```

In defining concatenations and if statements we have been defining Wp in terms of itself. We are, in effect, recursively defining a function, Wp, associated with the language. The recursive definition is valid because we are defining a structure in terms of the parts of that structure. Since all structures have a finite number of parts, and since we give separate definitions for the elementary parts (assignment statements) this recursive definition is valid.

When an if statement has an else part, the analysis is only slightly more complicated. We seek Wp ((if, A, (else, S1, S2)), Q) for arbitrary A, S1, S2, and Q. An if statement is executed through the calculation of A, which does not change the state. If A evaluates to TRUE, we execute S1, leaving us in state Q. If A is FALSE, we execute S2, also leaving Q TRUE. This says that in those situations in which A is TRUE before executing this if statement, WP (S1, Q) must also be TRUE. Likewise, if A is FALSE, we must begin in state Wp (S2, Q). This is summarized as

```
Wp ((if, A, (else, S1, S2)), Q) = (A and Wp (S1,Q))
    or ((not A) and Wp (S2, Q))
```

For example, examine the following if statement in Pascal.

```
IF a  <  b THEN
    x := a
ELSE
    x := b;
```

We want to verify that the statement always leaves us in the state {x is the smaller of a and b}. Saying that something always leaves you in a given state means that the precondition is the constant TRUE for that given postcondition. If we apply the assignment rule separately to the two statements in the if construction, we see that the precondition for x := a would be (a is the smaller of a and b). Likewise, the precondition for x := b would be (b is the smaller of a and b.) Translating into the form given in the definition of the semantics of if, we see that the precondition may be stated as ((a < b) **and** (a is the smaller of a and b)) **or** ((a >= b) **and** (b is the smaller of a and b). If we give the usual interpretation to the word *smaller* in case a and b are the same, this evaluates to TRUE **or** TRUE, which is TRUE. Therefore the fragment *always* leaves x in the required state.

14.2.1 Proving Loops

The situation with while statements is much more complicated. The meaning of the while statement (while, A, (invar, B, S)) is as follows. If A is FALSE, do nothing. On the other hand, if A is TRUE, execute S and reexecute the entire while statement. (The invariant, B, is not used in the execution at all. It will be discussed shortly.) This definition is a recursive one: while is defined in terms of while. The actual definition is

```
(while, A, (invar, B, S)) =
   (if, A, (;, S, (while, A, (invar, B, S)))))
```

Note well that this is a potentially infinite recursion, because loops are potentially infinite. This expresses the difficulty with loops. A loop represents a potentially infinite computation. Therefore the logical statement defining a loop has an infinite number of clauses. Wp ((while, A, (invar, B, S)), Q) means approximately the following. To execute (while, A, (invar, B, S)) and leave Q TRUE: If A is initially FALSE, we must begin in state Q. If A is initially TRUE, we execute S, and if the loop exits at this point, it must leave Q TRUE. However, if A is still TRUE, we execute S for the second time, and if A is then FALSE, Q must be TRUE. However, if A is *still* TRUE, we execute S a third time. *Then* if A is FALSE, Q must be TRUE, and so on for an infinite number of clauses. Although we can't write down such a statement, understanding it is not a particularly hard logical problem. One can express the meanings of such statements in terms of something like the limit processes of calculus.

If the loop never exits, and it might not, we cannot say that we leave Q TRUE at the end, because there is no end. Therefore to write a loop construct, we must see to two things to be sure that some postcondition is met. First, we must guarantee that the loop does exit. Next, we must guarantee that when the loop exits, it leaves the postcondition TRUE. If we can start a loop in which a precondition guarantees both of these parts, we can be sure that we terminate with the postcondition TRUE. We may not have the weakest such precondition, but if we do our work well, we will be able to establish a sufficiently weak precondition that we can use. Precisely speaking, however, it won't express the meaning of the while statement.

Before we begin the formal discussion of the while statement, we need a bit of mathematical background. Suppose the function $b(s)$ has only integer values and is strictly decreasing. Then for sufficiently large values of s $b(s)$ must be negative. There are only a finite number of possible values that b can have between any positive value and zero, since it is strictly decreasing and therefore takes strictly smaller integer values for larger values of s. The type of s doesn't matter as long as it has magnitude. Such functions help us ensure that loops exit. Suppose we have a Pascal WHILE statement such as

```
WHILE E DO
    S;
```

Suppose we have a function b whose domain is expressed in terms of program variables, such as x and y, and whose range is the integers. Suppose that when we start to execute the WHILE statement, these variables are all initialized so that b is some integer. Suppose, in addition, that we can establish two conditions. The first is that if b <= 0, E is FALSE. The second is that each time we execute S, changing the state of the machine and hence the variables defining b, b strictly decreases. If it has the value B before the execution of S, it necessarily has a value less than B afterward. These two conditions ensure that the loop is eventually exited. We can't execute S more than a finite number of times before b takes on a nonpositive value, at which point E is FALSE and the loop terminates.

We can express this property of the function b by saying {b = B} S {b < B}. Another way to say this is to say that (b = B) -> Wp (S, b < B). As an example of the use of this, suppose we are looking at the linear search algorithm.

```
WHILE (x > 0) AND NOT found DO
    IF M[x] = target THEN
        found := TRUE
    ELSE
        x := x - 1;
```

If the target does not appear in the array M, the bound function b (x) = x is adequate for our purposes. Each time we execute the body, we decrease this function, since we decrease x. Therefore, b must eventually be nonpositive, but in this case the loop test becomes FALSE. On the other hand, if the target does appear in M, the same bound function will serve, because the only time that execution of the body fails to reduce the bound is when we reach the target, in which case we provide for an alternate exit.

Now we turn to the other part of the problem of proving a loop correct: that if a loop exits, it leaves its postcondition TRUE. Since a loop can execute an arbitrarily large number of times before it exits, the state of the program can change an arbitrarily large number of times before then. Therefore we need additional help in knowing what to expect to be TRUE when we exit. This help comes from the idea of an invariant. An invariant is a predicate whose truth value does not change from TRUE to FALSE under certain conditions. Loosely speaking, its truth doesn't vary, and hence the name. We have already seen class invariants. These are statements that the class methods maintain in the TRUE state. For example, in the fraction class we maintained all values in lowest terms. This was a class invariant. Here we look at loop invariants. A loop invariant doesn't change from TRUE to FALSE as the loop executes.

Technically speaking, a loop invariant, I, for the loop

```
WHILE E DO
    S;
```

obeys the rule that if E and I are TRUE and we execute S, I remains TRUE. Another way to say this is that `(E and I) -> Wp (S, I)`. We don't consider or care about the situation in which we start with E FALSE, since then we won't be executing S anyway. We also don't care about the case in which we begin with I FALSE, since we handle that in a special way, as discussed next.

Suppose that we are trying to execute the above loop and that we want to establish some postcondition Q after the execution. Suppose we can prove three things. First, we can prove that some assertion, I, is indeed a loop invariant. Second, we can prove that `((not E) and I) -> Q`. Finally, we can prove that I is TRUE before we begin the execution of the loop. Then if the loop exits, it leaves the postcondition TRUE. The reasoning is as follows. I is initially TRUE. We check E, without changing the state. If E is FALSE, both `not E` and I are TRUE, so Q is TRUE and we are not executing anything that would change the state. Alternatively, if E is TRUE, both E and I are TRUE, and so when we execute the body S, we leave I TRUE. We are now in the same state in which we started all of this: I is TRUE and we are about to evaluate E. As long as we stay in the loop, the invariant condition keeps I TRUE. As soon as we exit the loop, `(not E)  and I` ensures that Q is TRUE.

The following five requirements summarize the proof that a loop exits and establishes its postcondition. We must find an integer function b and an assertion I that satisfy the following.

1. I is TRUE before the loop begins.
2. `(E and I) -> Wp (S, I)`
3. `((not E) and I) -> Q`
4. `(b <= 0) -> not E`
5. `(b = B) -> Wp (S, b < B)`

If we find such b and I, we can conclude that the loop exits with its postcondition Q TRUE. Therefore, we can use as a precondition for the loop the statement formed from the conjunction (and) of I and assertions 2 through 5. (The statements 2 through 5 certainly contain free variables, the variables of the program. They must be interpreted as being true for all values of their free variables. See the discussion of free variables at the end of Section 14.1.)

The conjunction of assertions 1 through 5 is not the weak precondition for the loop, but it does imply it. In what follows we shall be concerned only with the first three points in the above list, not because the others are less important, but because the first three are easier to deal with. The understanding is that proof that the loop is exited must be established separately.

Coming up with a loop invariant is not a trivial task. If it were, the complete automation of the creation of programs would be possible. Creating loop invariants takes creativity, just as writing loops that do what we want takes creativity. In LLLBI'T the programmer must state a loop invariant with every loop. The form of a `while` statement in LLLBI'T is (while, E, (invar, A, S)), where the `invar` clause contains an assertion, the loop invariant, and a statement. It has this form partly to emphasize that the programmer is responsible for the behavior of a loop.

Returning to our example of sequential search: Suppose the array M has indices from 1 to 100.

```
WHILE (x > 0) AND NOT found DO
    IF M[x] = target THEN
        found := TRUE
    ELSE
        x := x - 1;
```

The postcondition desired is (`target` is not in `M[1]` through `M[100]` or else `M[x]` = `target`). A valid loop invariant is I, where

I = (`target` is not in `M[x + 1]` through `M[100]`)

To prove that the statement I is a loop invariant for this loop, we first compute the weak precondition Wp (S, I) where S is the IF statement forming the body of the loop. To do this, we must also compute the weak preconditions for each of the conditionally executed statements in the body. The resulting weak precondition Wp (S, I) is

((M[x] = target) **and** (target is not in M[x + 1] through M[100]))
or
   ((M[x] <> target) **and** (target is not in M[(x - 1) + 1] through M[100]))

This simplifies to

((M[x] = target) **and** (target is not in M[x + 1] through M[100])) **or**
   ((M[x] <> target) **and** (target is not in M[x] through M[100]))

Now note that if the WHILE condition, (x > 0) AND NOT found, is TRUE and the invariant I is also true, the above weak precondition must also be TRUE (with the caveat that x must also be no greater than 100). This is because M[x] either is or is not the target. If it is, the first disjunct is TRUE. If it is not, the second is TRUE. In either case one of the clauses in the **or** construction is TRUE. This establishes point two of the loop plan: I *is* an invariant.

Now let us look at the third point in our five–point loop plan. If E is FALSE but I is TRUE, either x `<= 0` or found is TRUE. If I is also TRUE, the case x `<= 0` yields that target is not in M[1] through M[100]. The case found = TRUE gives us that M[x] = target. However, it is not correct to say that the truth of both I and found implies that M[x] = target. We need to look back at the code to see this. However there is a better way. Suppose that instead of the above invariant, we take as our loop invariant the slightly more complex statement

I = ((found **and** M[x] = target) **or** target is not in M[x + 1] through M[100])

An argument similar to the one above shows that this is indeed an invariant. Furthermore, when the loop test is FALSE and this is TRUE, we get the desired postcondition in both cases. If x `<= 0`, the second clause gives the desired conclusion. If found = TRUE, the second clause must be FALSE, but the first one gives the desired result.

The final step in executing this search loop for the desired effect is to initialize it properly. We must ensure that the loop invariant is TRUE before we begin execution. Without initialization this can seldom be realized. In this case we could initialize the loop by setting x and found:

```
x := 100;
found := M[x] = target;
```

With this initialization the second invariant is TRUE. Therefore a correct program for sequential search is the following:

```
x := 100;
found := M[x] = target;
WHILE (x > 0) AND NOT found DO
    IF M[x] = target THEN
        found := TRUE
    ELSE
        x := x - 1;
```

If the postcondition is "target is not in M[1] through M[100] or else M[x] = target," the precondition is TRUE.

14.3   COMPUTING PRECONDITIONS

In this section will be discussed the remaining methods of the classes SStatement, and SNonTerminal and the descendants of the latter. The purpose of all of these methods is to take a tree developed using the parse methods of Chapter 13 and a postcondition supplied by the user, and compute the precondition according to the rules presented in Section 14.2. What we shall do is create an *annotated tree*, or *proof tree*, which contains the precondition, statement, and postcondition for the program as well as for each of its components. The details are somewhat intricate, but the object-oriented method permits us to separate the details into a number of relatively simple cases, which we can handle separately. It also gives us the means of exploring the effect of making changes in the specifications. The methods that we need to develop are shown in the partial specification below.

```
class SNonTerminal: public SBinaryTree
   :: SBinaryTreeNode {
   public:
       virtual PNonTerminal     computePrecondition
                                    (PNonTerminal A);
          // This is a proof fragment,
          // including a parsed statement.  A is a
          // parsed postcondition. Compute and
          // return the proof tree.
       virtual PNonTerminal     makeProofFragment
                                    (PNonTerminal A);
          // Construct a two-node fragment with
          // three children.
          // Attach this as the middle child
          // and A as the right child.
       virtual void             findFree (PSet F,
                                          PSet B);

       virtual token            kind ();
       virtual void             writeIt (void);


   protected:
       token           fKind;
       virtual void    attachPrecondition
                          (PNonTerminal A);
          // This is a partial proof fragment
          // with precondition A.  Attach A at the left.
          ⋮
};
class SStatement: public SBinaryTree {
   public:
       virtual void    computePrecondition
                          (char *Assrt);
       virtual void    listProof (void);
          ⋮
};
```

```
class SExpression: public SNonTerminal {
   public:
      virtual void     findFree (PSet F, PSet B);
      virtual void     replaceFree (PString v,
                                         PExpression e);
         // This is a parsed expression.
         // v represents a variable name. e is a
         // parsed expression.  Replace all free
         // occurrences of v in the expression
         // this with a reference to e.
      ⋮
};

class SIdentExpression: public SExpression {
   public:
      virtual void     findFree (PSet F, PSet B);
      virtual void     replaceFree (PString,
                                         PExpression);
      ⋮
};

class SParamExpression: public SExpression {
   public:
      virtual void     findFree (PSet F, PSet B);
      virtual void     replaceFree (PString,
                                         PExpression);
      ⋮
};

class SIntLitExpression: public SExpression {
   public:
      virtual void     findFree (PSet F, PSet B);
      virtual void     replaceFree (PString,
                                         PExpression);
      ⋮
};

class SAssertion: public SNonTerminal {
   public:
      virtual void     findFree (PSet F, PSet B);
      virtual void     replaceFree (PString v,
                                         PExpression e);
         // This is a parsed assertion.
         // v represents a variable name. e is a
```

```
                        // parsed expression.  Replace all free
                        // occurrences of v in the assertion this
                        // with a reference to e.
            friend PAssertion buildAlls (PAssertion N,
                                         PSet F);

                ⋮

};

class SIf: public SNonTerminal {
    public:
        virtual PNonTerminal        computePrecondition
                                    (PNonTerminal);
        virtual void                findFree (PSet F,
                                             PSet B);

                ⋮

};

class SConcatenation: public SNonTerminal {
    public:
        virtual PNonTerminal        computePrecondition
                                    (PNonTerminal A);
        virtual void                findFree (PSet F,
                                             PSet B);

                ⋮

};

class SAssignment: public SNonTerminal {
    public:
        virtual PNonTerminal        computePrecondition
                                    (PNonTerminal A);
        virtual void                findFree (PSet,
                                             PSet);

                ⋮

};

class SElse: public SNonTerminal {
    public:
        virtual PNonTerminal        computePrecondition
                                    (PNonTerminal A);
        virtual void                findFree (PSet,
                                             PSet);

                ⋮

};
```

```
class SWhile: public SNonTerminal {
   public:
      virtual PNonTerminal    computePrecondition
                              (PNonTerminal A);
      virtual void            findFree (PSet F,
                                        PSet B);

         ⋮
};

class SInvariant: public SNonTerminal {
   public:
      virtual PNonTerminal    computePrecondition
                              (PNonTerminal A);
      virtual void            findFree (PSet F,
                                        PSet B);

         ⋮
};
```

As an example of the use of these methods, suppose that we first parse the assignment statement (:=, x, (+, x, 2)), which produces a parse tree. Then we compute Wp ((:=, x, (+, x, 2)), (and, (< , x, 30), (> , x, 7))). This was the example used in Section 4.2

```
ST = newStatement ();
ST -> parseString ("(:=, x, (+, x, 2))");
ST -> writeIt ();
cout << "\nproof\n";
ST -> ComputePrecondition
   ("(and, (<, x, 30), (>, x, 7))");
ST -> writeIt ();
```

The output produced is the following. The first line is produced by the first ST -> writeIt (). The last five lines come from the second writeIt.

```
x :=  [ x + 2 ]
proof

{ { [ x + 2 ] < 30 } and
   { [ x + 2 ] > 7 } }
x := [ x + 2 ]
{ { x < 30 } and
   { x > 7 } }
```

Figure 14.2 shows the tree that is equivalent to the output. The only difference is that this proof fragment is not as highly simplified as the tree shown in the figure.

The methods of SNonTerminal don't do very much. The method computePrecondition generates an error, because we should always be sending this message to a subclass object. The protected method attachPrecondition just attaches the parameter on the left. Only makeProofFragment does anything useful, which is to create a two–node subtree such as the one shown in Fig. 14.1. It attaches a reference to this as the middle child and attaches its parameter A at the right. Since this proof fragment is three nodes constructed from two nodes, we can refer to the right child as first -> fRight -> fRight. The middle child is first -> fRight -> fLeft. At this point first -> fLeft is not filled in. It will eventually be filled in with the precondition. At this point the postcondition, A, is the right child, and the statement, this, is the middle child. The two statement nodes used to construct the proof fragment are tagged with the constant kpb (proof block) so that we can test for them. They are mostly used for debugging. The companion values kpl and kpr are used to control printing. The tag of a kpb node can be changed to kpl or kpr to prevent printing.

```
PNonTerminal SNonTerminal :: computePrecondition
                            (PNonTerminal) {
    Error ("SNonTerminal :: computePrecondition:
                            Handle in subclass.");
    return NULL;
};


PNonTerminal SNonTerminal :: makeProofFragment
                            (PNonTerminal A) {
    PNonTerminal first, second;

    first = newNonTerminal (NULL, kpb);
    second  = newNonTerminal (NULL, kpb);
    first -> fRight = second;
    second -> fRight = A;
    second -> fLeft = this;
    return first;
};

void SNonTerminal :: attachPrecondition
                    (PNonTerminal A) {
    fLeft = A;
};
```

A proof tree completely filled in will have a proof fragment for the root, the precondition at the left, a dummy node at the right, the statement (annotated with subproofs) as the left child of the dummy, and the postcondition at the right of the dummy. This is shown symbolically in Fig. 14.1. Most of our computePrecondition methods will call MakeProofFragment, especially in those classes that represent statements such as `if` and `while`.

The `writeIt` method of `SNonTerminal` is intended only for the dummy nodes of a proof fragment. All other nodes are in a subclass and have their own `writeIt` methods. We need this method because a proof fragment corresponding to an assertion or an invariant has a special form that the other nodes do not have. When we construct such a fragment, we encode its first and second nodes. We write neither the left child of a `kpr` node nor the right child of a `kpl` node. This will be discussed again when the `computePrecondition` methods of `SElse` and `SInvariant` are shown.

```
void SNonTerminal :: writeIt (void) {
    if (fLeft -> member (assertion)) cout << '\n';
    if (fKind != kpr) fLeft -> writeIt ();
    if (fRight -> member (assertion)) cout << '\n';
    if (fKind != kpl) fRight -> writeIt ();
    if (fRight -> member (assertion)) cout << '\n';
};
```

The `computePrecondition` method of `SStatement` is the main control procedure for the computation of preconditions. Before we can call this method, we need to call `parse` so that the statement `this` is a parse tree. Then we can call `computePrecondition`, sending a string as parameter. This string is the postcondition for which we want to compute the precondition. The first thing we need to do is to transform this string, `Assertion`, into a tree. We can do this easily if we embed it into an artificial `if` statement, parse the `if` statement, and then extract the left subtree of the result, which is the assertion of the `if` statement. This result is named A. We then send `computePrecondition` (A) to the root of the tree `this`. This root node performs the calculation by sending `computePrecondition` to its children recursively as necessary, for constructing the proof tree. When this call returns its value, aTree, we attach it as the root node of the tree `this`. This use of the `parse` method and an artificially constructed statement is typical of how the `computePrecondition` methods work. The `parse` method is our primary means of constructing trees. We can use it as a helper to construct trees with specified structures.

```
void SStatement :: computePrecondition
                    (char *Assertion) {
    PAssertion A;
    PStatement aux;
    PBinaryTreeNode aTree;
    char auxStr[200];
```

```
    aux = newStatement ();
    strcpy (auxStr, "(if,");
    strcat (auxStr, Assertion);
    strcat (auxStr, ",(:=, z, 0))");
    aux -> parseString (auxStr);
    if (aux -> fRoot -> fLeft -> member (assertion)) {
        A = PAssertion (aux -> fRoot -> fLeft);
    }
    else {
        syntaxError
            ("SStatement :: computePrecondition:");
    };
    failnull (fRoot);
    aTree = PNonTerminal (fRoot)
        -> computePrecondition (A);
    failnull (aTree);
    fRoot = aTree;
};
```

It remains to discuss the computePrecondition methods of the SNonTerminal subclasses and the replaceFree methods of assertions and invariants. The computePrecondition methods are all sent an assertion tree, A, that represents some postcondition. They don't need to deal with parsing a string representing the postcondition, because others, such as SStatement :: computePrecondition, take care of that step. The computePrecondition message is sent to some node that represents a part of a program. The method computes the corresponding precondition of this portion using the postcondition supplied as a parameter. The simplest of these methods is SAssignment ::

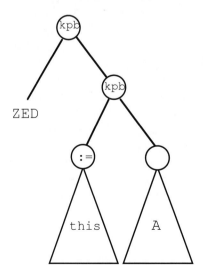

FIGURE 14.3

ComputePrecondition. We begin by sending makeProofFragment (A) to this. This constructs a tree such as that shown in Fig. 14.3.

Recall that an assignment tree has no left child. If the assignment is (:=, v, e) for a variable v and an expression e, the variable v is the data field of the assignment node itself and the expression e is parsed and attached as the right child of the assignment. The execution of the rest of the computePrecondition method calculates the precondition that is to replace the zed node. This calculation is accomplished by cloning A and replacing all references to the assignment variable in the clone, pre, by the expression on the right-hand side of the assignment. The method replaceFree in class SAssertion does this. The method replaceFree replaces all free occurances of its first parameter with its second parameter in whatever assertion object receives the message replaceFree. We send replaceFree the variable, which is encoded in the root of the assignment as the data field. We also send it the right-hand expression, which is just the right subtree of this. What we get back is a clone of the original postcondition with all free occurrences of the variable name replaced by the expression of the assignment. This is just the required precondition for the assignment, so we attach it using the attachPrecondition method.

```
PNonTerminal SAssignment :: computePrecondition
                          (PNonTerminal A) {

    PNonTerminal result;
    PAssertion pre;
    PString aString;

    result = makeProofFragment (A);
    pre = PAssertion (A -> Clone ());
    aString = PString (fValue);
    pre -> replaceFree (aString, PExpression (fRight))
    result -> attachPrecondition (pre);
    failnull (result);
    return result;
};
```

The computePrecondition method of concatenation statements is of similar complexity. We again begin by constructing a proof fragment from this and the parameter A. Since this is a concatenation statement, the first substatement is attached as the left child and the second is the right child of this. Therefore we compute the precondition of the right subtree of this, using the postcondition A. The result is saved in temp. This result is a proof tree, so we extract its left child, which is the precondition. We call this inter. If the concatenation is (;, S1, S2) and we call the postcondition A, inter represents Wp (S2, A). Therefore we compute the proof tree of the left subtree of this using inter as the postcondition this time. The result is again called temp. Again we extract the left child of temp, which is the precondition, Wp (S1, Wp (S2, A)). This we attach to the left child of the originally constructed proof fragment and return this completed proof tree. Note that twice we computed new trees and called them temp. We don't free these trees. Instead, we attach them as they are constructed as the right and then the left children of this. In fact, these trees, computed by a computePrecondition method, represent proof trees, and as such have the children of this within them as children. This embedding occurs when each computePrecondition calls makeProofFragment. What we are doing is modifying this so that whereas originally it represents only a statement, at the end it represents a proof of the statement. It still contains the statement part. The nodes representing the statement are encoded starting at the middle child of the proof fragment. This modification of the tree itself enables us later to print out the program with each part annotated with preconditions and postconditions.

```
PNonTerminal SConcatenation :: computePrecondition
                                     (PNonTerminal A) {
    PNonTerminal result, temp;
    PAssertion inter;

    result = makeProofFragment (A);
    temp = PNonTerminal (fRight) ->
        computePrecondition (A);
    fRight = temp;
    inter = PAssertion (temp -> fLeft);
    temp = PNonTerminal (fLeft) ->
        computePrecondition (inter);
    fLeft = temp;
    result -> attachPrecondition (PAssertion
                                     (temp -> fLeft));
    failnull (result);
    return result;
};
```

Figure 14.4 shows a concatenation tree for two assignment statements. Figure 14.5 shows the resulting proof fragment if the postcondition is

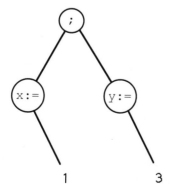

FIGURE 14.4   1   3

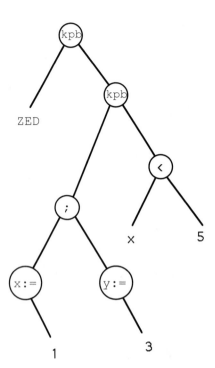

FIGURE 14.5

just the simple assertion x < 5. It is shown as it is immediately after the proof fragment is created but before any preconditions are computed. In the next step the precondition of the second statement is computed from the precondition at the right. The result is shown in Fig. 14.6. Note that the precondition is the same as the postcondition, since the assignment involves the variable y and the postcondition does not contain any reference to y. The arrow indicates the position of this intermediate precondition, `inter`.

Next we must compute a precondition for the left tree of `this`, still the tree rooted at the concatenation node. We use `inter` as the postcondition this time, but it is the same as the original postcondition. The result is shown in Fig. 14.7. Fig. 14.7 indicates the location of the node `temp`. Its left subtree has the precondition of the left statement of the original. It is equivalent to (<, 1, 5), which is the same as TRUE. This might or might not be inferred by our simplification routines, however, depending on what we have done in them. In any case, this is the precondition of the entire concatenation statement, and it is next attached in place of the `zed` node in the originally constructed proof fragment. When `SConcatenation :: computePrecondition` returns, this tree will become the root of the `SStatement` object that started this computation.

The method `SIF :: computePrecondition` has two parts, corresponding to the cases of a statement or an `else` construction as the second argument. Both cases proceed similarly, first constructing an auxiliary parse tree, `aux`, that gives the general structure that the desired precondition is known to have. We discover this form by looking at the semantics

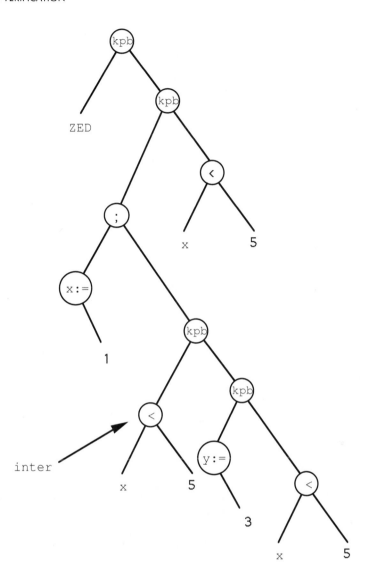

FIGURE 14.6

of the if statement. We previously discovered that Wp ((if, e, S), A) = (e **and** Wp (S, A)) **or** ((not e) **and** A), or, in LLLBI'T, Wp ((if, e, S), A) = (or, (and, e, Wp (S, A)), (and, (not, e, -), A)). A parse tree equivalent to this expression has an or node as its root and and nodes for both of its children. It is depicted in Fig. 14.8. The parser can construct this tree for us if we give it an artificially constructed if statement to parse that has an assertion of this general form. We then extract the assertion from the resulting tree and call it pre. Then we must simply replace the four leaves of this assertion with the proper subtrees. We replace the e with the assertion of this, the if statement being computed. The replacement is represented by the left subtree of this. We replace A with the postcondition. To get the

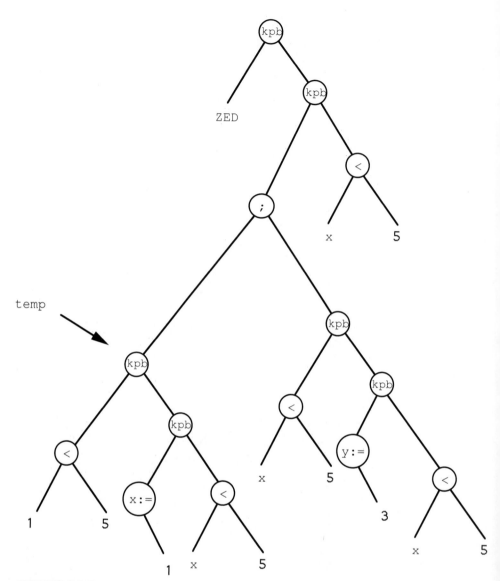

FIGURE 14.7

replacement for the leaf, Wp (S, A), we must recursively call compute Precondition on the right child of this and extract the left child of the resulting proof tree when computePrecondition returns.

```
PNonTerminal SIf :: computePrecondition
                    (PNonTerminal A) {
    char Asrt[200];
    PAssertion pre, inter, inter2;
    PNonTerminal result, temp;
    PStatement aux;
```

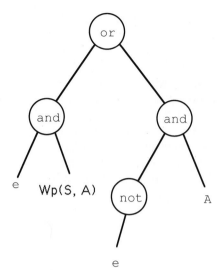

FIGURE 14.8

```
aux = newStatement ();
result = makeProofFragment (A);
temp = PNonTerminal (fRight)
  -> computePrecondition (A);
inter = PAssertion (fLeft);
fRight = temp;
if (PNonTerminal (fRight) -> kind() != elseOp) {
  strcpy (Asrt, "(if, (or, (and, fLeft, inter),
     (and, (not, fLeft, -), Aa)), (:=, z, 0)) ");
  aux -> parseString (Asrt);
  pre = PAssertion (aux -> fRoot -> fLeft);
  pre -> fLeft -> fLeft = fLeft;
  pre -> fLeft -> fRight = inter;
  pre -> fRight -> fLeft -> fLeft = fLeft;
  pre -> fRight -> fRight = A;
}
else {
  strcpy (Asrt, "(if, (or, (and, fLeft, inter),
     (and,(not, fLeft, -), inter2)), (:=, z, 0)) ");
  aux -> parseString (Asrt);
  pre = PAssertion (aux -> fRoot -> fLeft);
  inter2 = PAssertion (temp -> fRight -> fRight);
  pre -> fLeft -> fLeft = fLeft;
  pre -> fLeft -> fRight = inter;
  pre -> fRight -> fLeft -> fLeft = fLeft;
  pre -> fRight -> fRight = inter2;
};
```

```
    result -> attachPrecondition (pre);
    return result;
};
```

   We proceed in the same way if we have an `else`, except that the form of the eventual precondition is slightly different, as determined by the semantics of the `IF e THEN S1 ELSE S2` form. This tree is shown in Fig. 14.9. Again, we let the parser construct this tree for us and then compute the two Wp nodes recursively and fill in all of the leaves to get the result. We get the two Wp nodes by sending `computePrecondition` to the `else` clause. When it returns its result to the variable `temp` , we extract the two required nodes from it. Since an `else` structure is not a statement, and since it needs to provide us with two preconditions, one for each of its statements, this returned proof tree is specially encoded so that we can find the desired information easily. The precondition of the left (first) statement is in the usual location at the left of the first node of the proof fragment, that is, at `temp -> fLeft`. The precondition of the second statement, however, is at the right of the second node of the proof fragment, that is, at `temp -> fRight -> fRight`. This is where we normally store postconditions for statement nodes.

   The behavior of `SElse :: computePrecondition` must conform to the description in the previous paragraph. We compute the preconditions of the two statements of the `else` construction with separate recursions and then attach them at the left and at the far right in the proof fragment. We also encode the nodes of the proof fragment (the nodes labeled kpb in Fig. 14.3), labeling the top node kpr and the one to the lower right as kpl. These codes are used by SNonTerminal :: writeIt so that these pre- and postconditions to the left of the kpr node and to the right

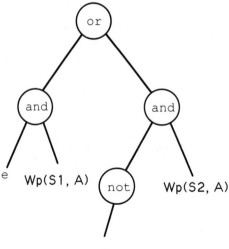

FIGURE 14.9

of the kpl node won't be printed. After all, else nodes don't really
have preconditions and postconditions of their own. It is their parts that
do. This encoding is rather unusual in object-oriented programming and
could be avoided through the use of additional classes. However, it is a
special situation, requiring a special solution of some sort. The solution
here is rather minimal. Since it represents exceptional behavior it represents a potential problem for the maintenance and extension of these
classes.

```
PNonTerminal SElse :: computePrecondition
                         (PNonTerminal A) {
    PNonTerminal result, temp;
    PAssertion pre, other;

    result = makeProofFragment (A);
    failnull (result);
    result -> fKind = kpr;
    PNonTerminal (result -> fRight) -> fKind = kpl;
    temp = PNonTerminal (fRight) ->
        computePrecondition (A);
    other = PAssertion (temp -> fLeft);
    fRight = temp;
    temp = PNonTerminal (fLeft) ->
        computePrecondition (A);
    pre = PAssertion (temp -> fLeft);
    fLeft = temp;
    result -> attachPrecondition (pre);
    result -> fRight -> fRight = other;
    return result;
};
```

The computePrecondition method of SInvariant is similar to
that of SElse. An invariant node represents the statement part of a while
construction and its associated invariant. computePrecondition attaches the precondition in the expected location, but it also leaves a copy
of the invariant to the right of the kpl node so that it can be easily found.
It also encodes the nodes of the fragment so that the printing of the precondition and the invariant are suppressed when the SInvariant proof
fragment is written.

```
PNonTerminal SInvariant :: computePrecondition
                            (PNonTerminal A) {
    PAssertion pre;
    PNonTerminal result, temp;
```

```
result = makeProofFragment (A);
result -> fKind = kpr;
PNonTerminal (result -> fRight) -> fKind = kpl;
temp = PNonTerminal (fRight) ->
    computePrecondition (PAssertion (fLeft));
pre = PAssertion (temp -> fLeft);
fRight = temp;
result -> attachPrecondition (pre);
result -> fRight -> fRight = fLeft;
failnull (result);
return result;
};
```

We saw in Section 14.2 that we are unable to compute the weakest precondition for a while statement. What we shall do is take the postcondition expressed by the user and the loop invariant encoded in the while statement itself and compute a precondition using the first three rules of our proof method for loops. We shall not take the bound function into account; we are leaving verification of loop exit to be examined separately.

We are computing the *sufficiently weak precondition* SWp ((while,B, (invar,I,S)), Q) = I **and** ((B **and** I)->Wp (S, I)) **and** (((**not** B) **and** I)->Q). To do this, we apply the rule that

$$X{-}{>}\,Y = (\mathbf{not}\,X)\,\mathbf{or}\,Y$$

as well as the De Morgan Rule

$$\mathbf{not}(X\,\mathbf{and}\,Y) = (\mathbf{not}\,X)\,\mathbf{or}\,(\mathbf{not}\,Y)$$

We obtain

```
I and ((((not B) or (not I)) or Wp (S, I))
    and ((B or (not I)) or Q)),
```

which is written in LLLBI'T as

```
(and, I, (and, (or, (or, (not, B, -), (not, I, -)),
    Wp (S, I)), (or, (or, B, (not, I, -)), Q))),
```

and in this form it can be parsed by our methods. The equivalent tree is shown in Fig. 14.10.

However, the components of this expression all depend on free variables. The program itself and the assertions we make are expressed in terms of variables. Only the left child of the root, which represents the initial state, is to be established independently of free variables. The others must be interpreted as being universally quantified by each such free variable. For example, if the loop uses the variables x and y and the invariant is expressed in terms of these but no other variables, some occurrences

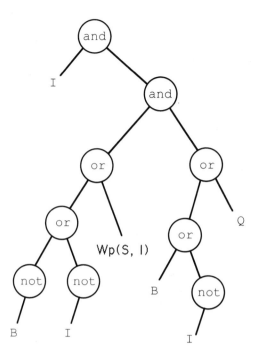

FIGURE 14.10

of x and y will be free. Therefore, if we want to assert the truth of
I and expr for some expression, expr, that depends on these two
variables, we must actually establish the truth of the assertion shown in
Fig. 14.11. In order to construct this tree, we must be able to determine the
free variables in any assertion. This is the purpose of the findFree methods of the nonterminal classes. Each of these is recursive. The parameters
F and B are two sets, initially empty. They represent the free and bound
variables, respectively. Whenever the message findFree is received by
a nonterminal object, it determines if any variables in the node should be
added to F. If a node is not a quantification node (an assertion of type kAll
or kExists) and contains a variable name, it inserts that variable name
into F if is not in B. If the variable is not bound, it should be free. The
node then recursively sends findFree to its children because they might
contain assertions or expressions. If the node is a quantification node, the
variable stored in the node is inserted into B because this is a newly bound
variable. It then recursively sends findFree to its own expression, the
right child. Then, before it returns, it removes the same variable from B,
because in the containing node that variable is not bound.

Most of the versions of findFree just pass on the message to one or
both of the child nodes. Only SExpression and SAssertion need to
do any work. For example, SExpression :: findFree looks like the
following:

```
void SExpression :: findFree (PSet F, PSet B) {
    PExpression (fLeft) -> findFree (F, B);
```

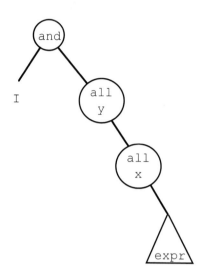

FIGURE 14.11

```
    PExpression (fRight) -> findFree (F, B);
};
```

Three of its subclasses need different versions of findFree. The others use the default version defined above.

```
void SIdentExpression :: findFree (PSet F, PSet B) {
    if (!B -> element (fValue)) F -> insert (fValue);
}; // If an identifier expression is not bound,
   // it is free.

void SParamExpression :: findFree (PSet F, PSet B) {

    PExpression (fRight) -> findFree (F, B);
};

void SIntLitExpression :: findFree (PSet, PSet) {
    // Nothing. These don't have identifiers at all.
};
```

SAssertion -> findFree handles the special logic of quantifiers.

```
void SAssertion :: findFree (PSet F, PSet B) {
    switch (fKind) {
        case ID: if (! B -> element (fValue))
            F -> insert(fValue); break;
        case ParamOp: PAssertion (fRight)
            -> findFree (F, B); break;
        case allOp:
```

```
            case existOp: {
               B -> insert (fValue);
               PAssertion (fRight) -> findFree (F, B);
               B -> remove (fValue);
            }; break;
            case notOp: PAssertion (fLeft)
               -> findFree (F, B); break;
            default: {
               PAssertion (fLeft) -> findFree (F, B);
               PAssertion (fRight) -> findFree (F, B);
            };
      };
};
```

Given these methods, we can build SWhile -> ComputePrecondition by constructing a tree such as the one in Fig. 14.11. We first construct the general form, using Fig. 14.10 as a template, assuming that there are no free variables. We then find the free variables and adjust this tree for each such variable. The procedure buildAlls constructs the chain of quantification nodes from the set of free variable names.

```
PAssertion buildAlls (PAssertion N, PSet F) {
    PAssertion result, aNode;
    PIterator IT;
    PObject v;

    result = N;
    IT = F -> newIterator ();
    while (IT -> nextItem (v)) {
        aNode = newAssertion (allOp);
        aNode -> fRight = result;
        aNode -> fValue = v;
        result = aNode;
    };
    delete IT;
    return result;
};

PNonTerminal SWhile :: computePrecondition
                         (PNonTerminal A) {
    PAssertion invar, cond, inter, pre, looper, final;
    PNonTerminal result, temp;
    PStatement aux;
    char Asrt[200];
    PSet invarFree, looperFree, finalFree, bound;
        // invarFree is the free variable set
        // for the loop invariant.
```

```
strcpy (Asrt, "(if, (and, theInvar,
    (and, theLooper, theFinal)), (:=, z, 0))");
aux = newStatement ();
aux -> parseString (Asrt);
pre = PAssertion (aux -> fRoot -> fLeft);
aux -> fRoot -> fLeft = aux -> newNode (NULL);
delete aux;
aux = newStatement ();
strcpy (Asrt, "(if, (or, (not, Invar, -),
      (or, theCond, thePost)),
      (:=, z, 0))");
aux -> parseString (Asrt);
final = PAssertion (aux -> fRoot -> fLeft);
aux -> fRoot -> fLeft = aux -> newNode (NULL);
delete aux;
aux = newStatement ();
strcpy (Asrt, "(if, (or, (not, Invar, -),
      (or, (not, theCond, -), thePre)),
          (:=, z, 0))");
aux -> parseString (Asrt);
looper = PAssertion (aux -> fRoot -> fLeft);
aux -> fRoot -> fLeft = aux -> newNode (NULL);
delete aux;

result = makeProofFragment (A);
temp = PNonTerminal (fRight) ->
    computePrecondition (A);
    // Proof of the statement part for
    // postcondition A.
inter = PAssertion (temp -> fLeft);
fRight = temp;

invar = PAssertion (fRight -> fRight -> fRight);
cond = PAssertion (fLeft);
final -> fLeft -> fLeft = invar;
final -> fRight -> fLeft = cond;
final -> fRight -> fRight = A;

looper -> fLeft -> fLeft = invar;
looper -> fRight -> fLeft -> fLeft = cond;
looper -> fRight -> fRight = inter;

    // Find the free variables in each part.
invarFree = newSet ();
looperFree = newSet ();
finalFree = newSet ();
bound = newSet ();
```

```
      invar -> findFree (invarFree, bound);
      cond -> findFree (invarFree, bound);
          // InvarFree contains free variables
          // of the loop invariant and
          // loop condition.
      looper -> findFree (looperFree, bound);
          // looperFree contains free variables of the
          // computed precondition of the loop statement.
      final -> findFree (finalFree, bound);
          // finalFree contains free variables of the
          // postcondition.
      delete bound;

      pre -> fLeft = invar;
      pre -> fRight -> fLeft = buildAlls
          (looper, invarFree -> setUnion (looperFree));
          // Rule 3 of plan involves only invariant,
          // loop test, and statement precondition vars.
      pre -> fRight -> fRight = buildAlls
          (final, invarFree -> setUnion (finalFree));
          // Rule 2 of plan involves only invariant,
          // loop test, and postcondition vars.

      delete invarFree;
      delete looperFree;
      delete finalFree;

      result -> attachPrecondition (pre);
      failnull (result);
      return result;
   };
```

Now we must examine the replaceFree methods of SExpression
and SAssertion. The purpose of these is to replace free occurrences of
the variable v with copies of the expression e. In SExpression we replace all occurrences. Most expressions have two parts, and this method
is a pair of switch statements, one for each subexpression. When we find
an identifier in the expression, we check whether it is equal to the parameter v. If it is, we attach the expression e in its place. Since the parse
trees of expressions are defined recursively, we perform this recursively on
subexpressions.

```
void SExpression :: replaceFree
                    (PString v, PExpression e) {
    // Result depends on what is attached to this.
```

```
          switch (PExpression (fLeft) -> fKind) {
             case ID: if ((v) ->
                equal (fLeft -> fValue)) fLeft = e;
                break;
             case INTLIT: break;
             case plusOp: case minusOp: case mulOp:
                case divOp:
                PExpression (fLeft) -> replaceFree (v, e);
          };
          switch (PExpression (fRight) -> fKind) {
             case ID: if ((v) ->
                equal (fRight -> fValue)) fRight = e;
                break;
             case INTLIT: break;
             case plusOp: case minusOp: case mulOp:
                case divOp:
                PExpression (fRight) -> replaceFree (v, e);
          };

};
```

The specialized expressions define their own versions.

```
void SIdentExpression :: replaceFree
   (PString, PExpression) {
   // Nothing.
};
```

Parameterized expressions have only the right child.

```
void SParamExpression :: replaceFree
                           (PString v, PExpression e) {
   if (PExpression (fRight) -> kind () == ID) {
      if ((v) -> equal (fRight -> fValue)) fRight = e
   }
   else
      PExpression (fRight) -> replaceFree (v, e);
};
```

```
void SIntLitExpression :: replaceFree
                           (PString, PExpression) {
   // Nothing.
};
```

Conceptually, SAssertion :: replaceFree is similar to SExpression :: replaceFree except that in assertions of type kAll and kExists it calls itself on the expression only if the variable of name v is different from the variable being bound. If a variable is used in a wider context but bound in a smaller one, replacements of the free occurrences of the variable by SAssertion :: replaceFree do not affect bound occurrences. Note that the difference in structure between this single method and the methods of SExpression and its subclasses is due to the lack of subclasses of SAssertion.

```
void SAssertion :: replaceFree
                     (PString v, PExpression e) {
    switch (fKind) {
        case ID: {
            // Nothing.
        }; break;
        case ParamOp: {
            if (PExpression (fRight) -> kind () == ID) {
                if (v -> equal (fRight -> fValue))
                    fRight = e;
            }
            else
                PExpression (fRight) -> replaceFree (v, e);
        }; break;
        case allOp:
        case existOp: {
            if (!v -> equal (fValue))
                PAssertion (fRight) -> replaceFree (v, e);
        };break;
        case notOp:{
            PAssertion (fLeft) -> replaceFree (v, e);
        }; break;
        case andOp:
        case orOp: {
            PAssertion (fLeft) -> replaceFree (v, e);
            PAssertion (fRight) -> replaceFree (v, e);
        }; break;
        case EQOp:
        case NEOp:
        case LOp:
        case LEOp:
        case GOp:
        case GEOp: {
            switch (PExpression (fLeft) -> kind ()) {
                case ID:
                    if (v -> equal (fLeft -> fValue))
                        fLeft = e; break;
```

```
        case INTLIT: break; // Nothing.
        case ParamOp:
        case plusOp:
        case minusOp:
        case mulOp:
        case divOp: PExpression (fLeft)
            -> replaceFree (v, e);
    };
    switch (PExpression (fRight) -> kind ()) {
        case ID:
            if (v -> equal (fRight -> fValue))
                fRight = e; break;
        case INTLIT:break; // Nothing.
        case ParamOp:
        case plusOp:
        case minusOp:
        case mulOp:
        case divOp: PExpression (fRight)
            -> replaceFree (v, e);
    };
  }; break;
    };
};
```

14.4   PROVING PROGRAMS CORRECT

In this section we shall look at a simple loop program. We shall prove it correct by hand and then consider the output of the above program.

The program, written in ordinary Pascal, is a simple counter that begins at 1.

```
x := 1;
WHILE  x <  99  DO
x :=  x + 1
    {Invar:  {x <  100}}
END;
```

We would like to establish that the program always ends with $x = 99$. The specification has precondition TRUE and postcondition $x = 99$. We proceed by working through the five–point plan. We are given a proposed loop invariant. We need to discover a bound function limiting the number of times the loop executes before exits. It must be a decreasing function. How about $b(x) = 99 - x$? Each time we execute the body of the loop we increase x and therefore decrease b. Both x and b are integers. Finally, if b yields 0, x must be 99, so the loop will exit. We have established parts 4 and 5 of the loop plan.

Certainly the initialization of the loop, x := 1, leaves the invariant, x < 100, TRUE, so we need only prove points 2 and 3. If the loop condition is FALSE, x >= 99. If I is TRUE, then x < 100. Therefore x is 99, fulfilling the postcondition, so part 3 is valid.

To establish part 2, we must first compute the weak precondition of the loop statement x := x + 1, using the invariant, x < 100, as a postcondition. This gives x + 1 < 100, by the rule for assignments, which is equivalent to x < 99. Now if the loop condition is TRUE, we have x < 99. If the invariant is TRUE we have x < 100. Therefore if both of these are TRUE, we must have x < 99, so that this precondition is TRUE. This finishes the proof of the program.

This program can be expressed in LLLBIT as

```
(;, (:=, x, 1), (while, (<, x, 99), (invar,
    (<, x, 100), (:=, x, (+, x, 1))))))
```

Suppose that this program is stored in a file, aLoop.txt, and that we want to establish the postcondition x=99. We could run it with the following commands.

```
initLists ();
initBinaryTrees ();
initIntegers ();

ST = newStatement ();
ST -> parseProgram ("aLoop.txt");
ST -> writeIt ();
cout << "\nproof\n";

ST -> computePrecondition ("(=, x, 99)");

ST -> Simplify ();
ST -> writeIt ();
```

The output produced would be

```
    (;, (:=, x, 1), (while, (<, x, 99),
        (invar, (<, x, 100), (:=, x, (+, x, 1))))))

x := 1 ;

WHILE  { x <  99 } DO

x :=  [ x + 1 ]
    {  Invar: { x <  100 }   }
```

```
END DO

proof

   {   { 1 <   100 }   and
       {   { ForAll  x :   {   { x >=   100 }   or
       {   { x >=   99 }   or
       {   [ x + 1 ]   <   100 }   }   }   }   and
       { ForAll   x :   {   { x >=   100 }   or
       {   { x <   99 }   or
       { x =   99 }   }   }   }   }   }
     {   { 1 <   100 }   and
       {   { ForAll   x :   {   { x >=   100 }   or
       {   { x >=   99 }   or
       {   [ x + 1 ]   <   100 }   }   }   }   and
       { ForAll   x :   {   { x >=   100 }   or
       {   { x <   99 }   or
       { x =   99 }   }   }   }   }   }
 x := 1
   {   { x <   100 }   and
       {   { ForAll   x :   {   { x >=   100 }   or
       {   { x >=   99 }   or
       {   [ x + 1 ]   <   100 }   }   }   }   and
       { ForAll   x :   {   { x >=   100 }   or
       {   { x <   99 }   or
       { x =   99 }   }   }   }   }   }
   ;

   {   { x <   100 }   and
       {   { ForAll   x :   {   { x >=   100 }   or
       {   { x >=   99 }   or
       {   [ x + 1 ]   <   100 }   }   }   }   and
       { ForAll   x :   {   { x >=   100 }   or
       {   { x <   99 }   or
       { x =   99 }   }   }   }   }   }
 WHILE   { x <   99 } DO

   {   [ x + 1 ]   <   100 }
 x :=   [ x + 1 ]
   { x <   100 }

   {   Invar:   { x <   100 }   }

END DO

   { x =   99 }
   { x =   99 }
```

Some of the assertions about the program are printed several times, because the program proves each of its parts recursively and writing out the tree writes all of the parts.

We must verify that the program works. In particular, we must examine the computed precondition

```
{{1 <    100 } and
  {{ForAll x !{{x >= 100} or
  {{x >=   99} or
  {[ x + 1 ] < 100}}}} and
  {ForAll x !{{x >= 100} or
  {{x < 99} or
  {x = 99}}}}}}
```

to see exactly what it means. We expect that the program *always* leaves us with x = 99, so this precondition should be equivalent to TRUE. Simplifying its form gives

```
    {{1 < 100}
and
    {{ForAll x !{
        {x >= 100} or {{x >= 99} or
            {[ x + 1 ] < 100}}}
    }
and
    {ForAll x !{
        {x >= 100} or {{x < 99} or
            {x = 99}}}}}
    }
```

The first conjunct, 1 < 100, is certainly TRUE. The second can be simplified to

```
{{ForAll x !{
    {x >= 100} or {{x >= 99} or
    {x < 99}}}
}
```

This simplifies further to

```
{{ForAll x !{
    {{x >= 99} or {x < 99}}}
}
```

This is TRUE also. The third conjunct is TRUE by examination. Therefore the precondition is TRUE, so the program is valid always, provided, of course, that we can also establish that the loop exits.

If we try to establish the postcondition x = 100, which is an error, the verification program produces the following computed precondition.

```
{{1 < 100} and
   {{ForAll x !{{x >= 100} or
   {{x >= 99} or
   {[ x + 1 ] < 100}}}} and
   {ForAll x !{{x >= 100} or
   {{ x < 99 } or
   {x = 100}}}}}}}
```

Analyzing this we see that it is equivalent to TRUE and TRUE and FALSE since

```
{ForAll x !{{x >= 100} or
{{x < 99} or
{x = 100}}}}.
```

is FALSE. The assertion is not TRUE for all x; x = 99 is an exception.

14.5   SUMMARY

Program verification is important because it is impossible to determine that a program meets its specification by testing. Testing only shows you that you still have errors in the code. It cannot tell you that you have no errors, unless the program is trivial. In order to show that a program is correct, we must apply logic to its analysis, much as a mathematician does.

We saw verification previously when we examined the sorting algorithms in Chapters 6 and 8. Here we have used a tree–rewriting methodology to automate the process. The language LLLBI'T was designed to make this possible, since it requires that a user supply an invariant with every loop. Creativity is needed in coming up with these invariants, however; you should not be misled into thinking that it is a simple job. Some methods by which this can be done in many cases are found in [Gries, 1981].

EXERCISES

14.1 (14.3) Develop a method for writing out only the overall proof of a program without writing all of the intermediate proof fragments.

14.2 (14.3) Design a means of incorporating the bound function into our proof methods.

14.3 (14.3) Implement your design of Exercise 14.1.

DATABASE NORMALIZATION

Such a dependency of thing on thing
As e'er I heard in madness.

   Shakespeare, *Measure for Measure*

For the table, sir, it shall be served in; for the meat, sir, it shall be covered;

   Shakespeare, *Merchant of Venice*

In this chapter we shall examine an important problem in database theory that has important consequences in practice. Creating a good relational database design requires skill and the application of this theory. We shall also see important applications of our set and binary search tree abstractions.

15.1   RELATIONAL DATABASES

A database is a repository for information. A relational database stores information in the form of tables, called relations, and permits a set of operations, the relational operators, to be applied to these tables. Relations and relational operators conform to a simple mathematical theory, which makes possible certain reasoning about the consequences of the operations. The theory also provides a way of controlling redundancy in a database. Redundancy causes problems in all databases, because of the added time and space for dealing with copies of information. More importantly, redundancy

571

in a database can lead to information loss if the copies of pieces of information are not kept consistent. For example, I currently receive two copies of some notices from the Association for Computing Machinery because they have my name in their database in two different forms. Therefore they think I am two people. I receive *many* copies of some mail-order catalogs for a similar reason.

To a mathematician, a *relation* is any subset of a Cartesian product. Given a finite collection of sets, $A, B, \ldots$, of which some are perhaps repeated, the Cartesian product, $A \times B \times \cdots$, is the set of all ordered tuples $(a, b, \ldots)$ where a is in A, b is in B, etc. If we give distinct names to the sets, we can view a Cartesian product as a table whose columns are labeled by the set names and whose rows are the tuples. We can view each column as being *labeled* with its set name and hence consider the order of the columns of the table as being unimportant. Said another way, a Cartesian product whose sets are listed in a certain order is *isomorphic* to any Cartesian product with the same sets listed in another order. The *isomorphism* is established by providing a matching between the elements (tuples) of the two sets, that preserves all relevant operations. For example, we might provide three sets: *Names, Addresses,* and *Phone Numbers*. We might repeat the phone numbers twice, using the names *Home Phone* and *Business Phone*. We abbreviate these names as *N, A, H, B* for *Name, Address, Home Phone,* and *Business Phone*. The Cartesian product $U = N \times A \times H \times B$ is the set of all tuples (name, address, phone number, phone number). If we rearrange the order, we have an equivalent structure.

A relation is any subset of such a Cartesian product. For example, we might take the subset, *Employee,* of the Cartesian product U that consists of all the names, addresses, and home and business phone numbers of the employees of a certain business. The names used to build the relation are called *attribute* names. At a certain time the employee relation might look like the following:

Name	Address	Home Phone	Business Phone
Fein, Jacob	10 Oak	555-1234	555-2234
Hai, Sari	3 First	555-4312	555-3312
Low, Judith	22 Elm	555-2314	555-3314
Ng, Lai	92 Third	555-2134	555-1134
Ng, Mary	92 Third	555-2134	555-4434
Smith, John	52 Maple	555-3214	555-2214

Since relations are sets, we can form their unions and intersections. Since they are subsets of Cartesian products, we can project them onto any subset of their attributes. For example, projection onto *Name* and *Address* yields the first two columns in the table. However, projection onto *Address* and *Home Phone* yields only the five elements shown below.

Address	Home Phone
10 Oak	555-1234
3 First	555-4312
22 Elm	555-2314
92 Third	555-2134
52 Maple	555-3214

Suppose we have another relation, *Dependent,* that also has employee names for one attribute, and another which represents the name of a child of the employee. Note that in each row/column position in a relation we store only a single value. *Dependent* might look like the following.

Name	Child
Fein, Jacob	Tony
Fein, Jacob	Marcy
Hai, Sari	Abi
Hai, Sari	Mara
Hai, Sari	Lora
Smith, John	Tim

One operation that can be performed on the *Employee* and *Dependent* relations is the *natural join*. To form the natural join, we first form a Cartesian product of the two relations, treating them as sets of rows. In this product the *Name* attribute labels two different columns. We then remove all rows in which the *Name* attributes do not match. Thus, in the Cartesian product, two of the rows will be

Name	Address	Home Phone	Business Phone	Name	Child
Ng, Mary	92 Third	555-2134	555-4434	Hai, Sari	Abi
Smith, John	52 Maple	555-3214	555-2214	Smith, John	Tim

We remove the first of these, because the *Name* attributes are different, and retain the second. Finally, we project this onto a relation having only one copy of the common attributes. The resulting table is as follows.

Name	Address	Home Phone	Business Phone	Child
Fein, Jacob	10 Oak	555-1234	555-2234	Tony
Fein, Jacob	10 Oak	555-1234	555-2234	Marcy
Hai, Sari	3 First	555-4312	555-3312	Abi
Hai, Sari	3 First	555-4312	555-3312	Mara
Hai, Sari	3 First	555-4312	555-3312	Lora
Smith, John	52 Maple	555-3214	555-2214	Tim

If we wish to provide this information in a database, it is preferable to store the two tables, *Employee* and *Dependent,* rather than this last one. There are two reasons for this. The first is that some employees are missing from it, since they don't have dependents. The second is that some of the information is redundant. Fein's address and phone numbers appear twice in the table. If Fein moves, we need to update all such information. If we don't do it faithfully, we lose the ability to determine Fein's address.

Note that if we know a person's name in the *Employee* relation, we know all there is to know about her or him, because the name determines a unique row in this relation. Such an attribute, or collection of attributes, is a *weak key.* A *key* (strong key) is a minimal set of attributes that forms a weak key. It is minimal if no attribute can be removed from it and still maintain the weak key property. In general, a relation can have several keys. *Business Phone* is another key of *Employee*. The combination of *Name* and *Child* is a key in the join of *Employee* and *Dependent*. A combination of attributes that forms a key is a *composite key.* Note that the projection of a relation onto a set of attributes that contains a key is a relation of the same cardinality as the original.

More generally, we say that an attribute, X, depends functionally on a collection of attributes (perhaps a single attribute), S, provided that the collection would form a weak key in a relation that had only the attributes $\{X\} \cup S$. In other words, having values for all of the attributes in the collection would imply that only a certain unique, determined value was possible for the other. If D depends functionally on attributes A, B, and C, we write

$$A, B, C \rightarrow D$$

and call this a functional dependency, also saying that A, B, and C functionally determine D. Functional dependencies carry the meaning, or semantics, of the data. To say that *Name* functionally determines *Address* is to say that a person has only one residence. Sometimes the restrictions implied by functional dependencies are physical. In a biological database, *Number of Legs* depends on *Species*. Sometimes the dependencies are social or merely conventional. The dependency between *Name* and *Address* is only an approximation of reality, since some people do have several addresses. We may just decide on a principle address for the purposes of the database.

In any case, an understanding of the underlying dependencies is fundamental to building a correct database, since they can prevent us from entering data that makes no sense. They can also be the basis of building efficiency into the database, as we shall see.

It is also important to remember that a key or functional dependency is not to be interpreted as a mere artifact, a consequence of the data that we happen to be storing in the table at a given moment. A key or functional dependency is a relationship between the sets from which the tables in the relation are built. In fact, then, *Name* is not a good candidate for a key in a realistic system, since you will likely need to represent two different employees who happen to have the same name. This is why social security numbers are so important as a means of identification in the United States. They can be relied on (approximately) to determine an individual uniquely.

15.2   REDUNDANCY AND DECOMPOSITIONS

A relational database is a collection of relations. What the appropiate relations should be is not always clear to the designer of a database. The attributes that must be stored are usually more easily determined because an attribute is the smallest unit of information. One method of database design is to start with all of the attributes needed in the database and to think of them as labeling columns in a single relation, the *Universal* relation. Of course, some sets are represented several times, with different names. We then consider projections of this relation onto various subsets of the attributes. Generally speaking, the sets of attributes that form the projections are not disjoint.

For example, in designing the database that contains *Employee* and *Dependent,* at some point there was a list of attributes that contained *Name, Address, Business Phone, Home Phone,* and *Child.* Two projections were made to get *Employee* and *Dependent,* but both contain the *Name* attribute. These projections (or some equivalent ones) were made to avoid the redundancy implied by the relation that contained all of these attributes. For example, we saw above that the address of an employee with several children would be listed several times in such a universal relation. That redundancy was a consequence of functional dependencies. If *Name* functionally determines *Address,* storing *Name* twice in a table requires that we store the *Address* the same way in both tuples. If *Name* does not functionally determine *Child,* we don't want *Name, Address,* and *Child* in the same table.

The following is a small part of a database for an airline scheduling system. It is presented here as a universal relation so that we can examine some of the inherent problems.

When a flight number is assigned, a plane will fly between a fixed source and destination on a regular basis. The flight number and the date determine the unit of service. In this database are the following functional dependencies.

Pilot	Flight	Date	Departs	Plane
Cushing	83	9 Aug	10:00 A.M.	B747
Cushing	116	10 Aug	1:00 P.M.	B747
Clark	281	8 Aug	6:00 A.M.	Airbus
Clark	301	12 Aug	6:00 P.M.	Airbus
Clark	83	11 Aug	10:00 A.M.	Airbus
Chin	83	13 Aug	10:00 A.M.	B747
Chin	116	12 Aug	1:00 P.M.	B747
Copley	281	9 Aug	6:00 A.M.	DC9
Copley	281	13 Aug	6:00 A.M.	DC9
Copley	412	15 Aug	1:00 P.M.	DC9

Flight, Date → Pilot (A pilot can only fly one plane at a time.)

Flight, Date → Plane (It only involves one plane.)

Flight → Departs (Flight number is just an encoding of departure time.)

Pilot → Plane (This airline's policy enforces this as a safety measure.)

These dependencies can be shown in a dependency diagram as in Fig. 15.1. A box is drawn around each attribute and around each group of attributes on which some other depends. It is easy to see from this diagram that *(Flight, Date)* forms a composite key to the relation. To an experienced designer the pattern of arrows also indicates problems.

One of the problems with using the universal relation to store this database is the amount of redundancy in it. For example, the fact that flight 281 leaves at 6:00 A.M. is encoded more than once. If this time should change, we must update every tuple in which this information is saved. Another problem is that some information is here that might be lost inadvertently. For example, if flight 412 is canceled on 15 August for some reason and we remove that tuple from the database, we lose all information about flight 412, including the time that it is supposed to leave.

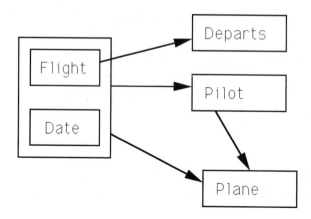

FIGURE 15.1

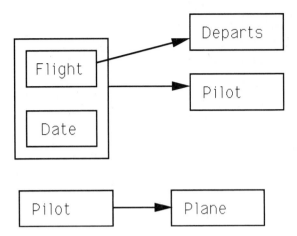

FIGURE 15.2

A solution to both of the above problems is to save projections of this data rather than a single table. We might save *Pilot* and *Plane* in a separate table and remove *Plane* from this one. The new table would have one row for each pilot, and *Pilot* would be its key. This would leave us in the situation of Fig. 15.2.

Another table could be for *Flight* and *Departs* and have the key *Flight*. We could then remove *Departs* from this table. The design would then be as in Fig. 15.3.

We don't have a single table from which to answer such questions as "What time does Copley fly on 9 August?" If we need this information, we must join tables having the appropriate information. In this case we join (*Flight, Date, Pilot*) with (*Flight, Departs*) to get the required information. Of course, this implies that starting with a table, then forming projections, and then joining projections brings us back to the original table. This is, in fact, not always true. The join can yield more tuples than we started with. These extra tuples are not extra information. In fact they represent loss of information, since they have valid attribute values in them, but invalid combinations of values. They might tell us that Chin is to fly both a Boeing 747 and an Airbus, violating company policy. When such invalid combinations occur, we say that the decomposition (set of projections) has a lossy join. The opposite of this is the lossless join property and is an important design goal. One theorem of relational theory is that if some relation in a decomposition contains all of the attributes of some key, the decomposition is lossless. There are algorithms to check other situations.

> **Lossless Join**
>
> A decomposition is lossless if the natural join of the relations in the decomposition yields the original relation that was decomposed.

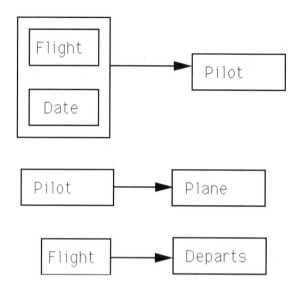

FIGURE 15.3

Another important factor in a decomposition is easy verification that the functional dependencies hold. In the original table this verification is relatively easy because the table is short and all of the information is in one place. We can verify that no pilot appears on two rows with different planes. When we decompose the table, we must be able to verify the same thing, or else we shall need separate processes to guarantee the constraints. If our decompositions are done so that each functional dependency has all of its attributes, on both the left and right sides of the arrow, within a single projection, we can be assured that they all hold. This was the basis for the decomposition above. However, if none of our projections contained, for example, both *Pilot* and *Plane,* it would be difficult to verify that the restriction *Pilot → Plane* was being observed. Preservation of dependencies under decomposition is another important goal of design.

The final goal we are concerned with is the minimization of redundancy. For a variety of reasons, that is a difficult task. There are degrees of redundancy, and the goal is to achieve a high degree of redundancy removal. This is discussed in the next section.

15.3   THE NORMAL FORMS

Generally speaking, the normal forms represent degree of removal of redundancy in a database. The normal forms are either numbered or named, and they form a scale of quality of database design. In order of increasing strength, the common normal forms are first, second, third, Boyce-Codd, fourth, and domain-key. Strictly speaking, first normal form is not a redundancy form. It simply states that in a relational database each attribute is single-valued, meaning that only a single value appears in a row/column position. We have been assuming this all along.

In any database it is possible to achieve the third normal form and ensure that all functional dependencies are met and that the decomposition has a lossless join. In this chapter we shall present an algorithm that achieves this and develop a program to carry it out. To move higher than third normal form, you might need to give up either dependency preservation or lossless joins. This is sometimes done, though reluctantly. For a further discussion of this deep topic, consult a good book on database design. Here a great deal will be left unsaid about the topic, including definitions of other kinds of dependencies.

Before we continue with the definitions of the second and third normal forms, we need a few additional definitions. An attribute is *prime* if it is contained in some key; otherwise, it is *nonprime*. Since relations may have several keys, one must be singled out and called the *primary key*. A key that is not the primary key is sometimes a *candidate key*. A *superkey* is a set of attributes that contains a key. A functional dependency $A \rightarrow B$, with A and B sets of attributes, is *trivial* if B is a subset of A. Finally, an attribute B is *partially dependent* on a set of attributes A if there is a proper subset C of A such that $C \rightarrow B$.

> ## Second Normal Form
>
> A relation R with attributes $A, B, \ldots$ and a set of functional dependencies is said to be in second normal form (2NF) if it is in first normal form and each attribute of R is either prime or not partially dependent on a candidate key.

Our flight data relation is not in 2NF because the attribute *Departs* is not prime, because although it appears in no candidate key, it is partially dependent on the key (*Flight, Date*), since it depends on *Flight* alone. The functional dependency that offends 2NF, or makes it break, is *Flight* $\rightarrow$ *Departs*. We can achieve 2NF easily in such a situation by taking the attributes of the offending dependency as a separate relation and removing the right-hand side of the offender from the original. The result may not be 2NF, but if the rule is applied often enough, all of the resulting relations will be. Since 2NF is not enough for most purposes, we will not generally execute this algorithm. More powerful methods give us higher levels.

A functional dependency $M \rightarrow N$ offends 3NF if N is not a part of any candidate key, M is not a superkey, and N is not a subset of M. In this case N can be said to depend on the primary key through M, since M depends on that key. That is to say, if K is a key, then $K \rightarrow M \rightarrow N$. For this reason such offending dependencies are called transitive, and a relation is sometimes defined to be in 3NF if it is in 2NF and no nonprime attributes depend transitively on the primary key. Sometimes the wording is that all attributes have full functional dependence on the primary key. Even with *Departs* removed, our flight-data relation is not 3NF, because *Plane* is transitively

---

Third Normal Form

A relation R with attributes $A, B, \ldots$ and a set of functional dependencies is said to be in third normal form (3NF) provided that it is in second normal form and that each functional dependency $X \to Y$ of R satisfies one of the following: (a) $X \to Y$ is trivial, (b) X is a superkey for R, or (c) Y is prime.

---

dependent on the primary key. The offending functional dependency is *Pilot → Plane*. Again, we can achieve 3NF by repeatedly factoring out the attributes of offending dependencies. In this case we let (*Pilot, Plane*) be a separate relation and remove only the right-hand side, *Plane,* of the offender. Also in this case there are better methods.

15.4

THIRD–NORMAL–FORM, DEPENDENCY–PRESERVING, LOSSLESS–JOIN DECOMPOSITION

The theorem on which we shall depend for the rest of this chapter was published in 1979 by Biskup, Dayal, and Bernstein [p. 143 ff.]. It requires that we are able to form a simplification called a *minimal cover* of an arbitrary set of functional dependencies. How to do this is discussed in Section 15.5. Given that this simplification is possible, by the following rule we can achieve a decomposition of the database into 3NF with preservation of all dependencies and also with the lossless join property.

Biskup, Dayal, Bernstein Theorem

Let R be a relation and F a set of functional dependencies that is a minimal cover.

1. Construct a single relation from all the attributes of R that do not appear in any functional dependency in F, and continue to step 2.

2a. If all of the remaining attributes of R appear in a single functional dependency in F, output all of these attributes as a single relation.

2b. Otherwise, for all functional dependencies $X \to Y$ in F (X and Y are sets of attributes) output the relations (X, Y).

3. If the result of the above steps is not lossless, also output any key of R.

4. If any of the relations output above are entirely contained in any other, omit the smaller one.

15.5   **MINIMAL COVERS**

All of this is simple enough. All the work is in constructing the minimal cover. Once again, we need a few definitions before we can proceed. We assume that we have a relation R and a set F of functional dependencies on the attributes of R. If A is a set of attributes, A^+ is the set of all attributes that depend functionally on A. If $A^+ = R$, then A is a superkey of R. A^+ is called the *closure* of A.

Given A, we compute A^+ in the following way. We set $A^0 = A$. We get A^{k+1} by starting with A^k and inserting all attributes of Y, such that $X \to Y$ is a functional dependency and X is a subset of A^k. Eventually, for some k, $A^k = A^{k+1}$, since we start with a finite set. This A^k is A^+.

Given a set, F, of functional dependencies, its closure, F^+, is the set of all functional dependencies that can be derived from F by the simple set of rules called Armstrong's axioms.

Armstrong's Axioms

1. If Y is a subset of X, then $X \to Y$.
2. If $X \to Y$ is in F^+, so is $WX \to WY$ for any attribute set W.
3. If $X \to Y$ and $Y \to Z$, then $X \to Z$.

The problem with F^+ is that effectively it is not computable. It potentially contains exponentially many elements. This has a double meaning. First, if we start with some set of functional dependencies that we wish to maintain in a database, there may be an extremely large number of other dependencies that can be derived from them and therefore must also be maintained. Second, it may take an extremely long time to compute all of the dependencies, even if we wanted only to list them, much less check whether they hold individually.

Be careful to distinguish between A^+ where A is a set of attributes and F^+ where F is a set of functional dependencies. The first is a set of attributes that are fixed once we fix values for A. The latter is a set of functional dependencies that can be derived from F. A^+ is easily computed; F^+ is not.

A set, F, of functional dependencies is said to *cover* another set G, if $F^+ = G^+$. We can check whether F covers G without computing F^+ or G^+ by checking whether any dependency in G can be derived from dependencies in F and whether any dependency in F can be derived from dependencies in G. To make the first check, it is enough to take the left-hand side X of a functional dependency $X \to Y$ in G and show that Y is a subset of X^+, computing X^+ using only the functional dependencies of F. Note that the cover relationship is an equivalence relation. It is reflexive, since every set of dependencies covers itself. It is symmetric, because if F covers G, G covers

F. Similarly, it is transitive: if *F* covers *G* and *G* covers *H*, *F* covers *H*. There is a rich mathematical theory of such relations.

Minimal Cover

A cover F is *minimal* if the following conditions are satisfied.

1. The right-hand side of every functional dependency in *F* consists of a single attribute.
2. If $X \rightarrow Y$ is in *F*, the set with this functional dependency removed is not a cover of *F*. (No redundant dependencies occur.)
3. If $X \rightarrow Y$ is in *F* and *Z* is a proper subset of *X*, *F* with $X \rightarrow Y$ replaced by $Z \rightarrow Y$ is not a cover of *F*. (No redundant left attributes occur.)

Let us compute a minimal cover of our flight-data database.

Flight, Date → Pilot
Flight, Date → Plane
Flight → Departs
Pilot → Plane

The first rule is already met, though it might not have been if we had combined the first two dependencies into the single one with both *Pilot* and *Plane* on the right. We seek to establish the second point by throwing out some redundant dependencies. We can check whether a dependency is redundant by tentatively removing it and then seeing whether it can be derived from the remaining ones. The last cannot be removed, since no other dependency involves *Pilot* on the left. Similarly, the third cannot be removed, since none of the others has *Departs* on the right. The first must be retained for a similar reason. We seek to determine whether (*Flight, Date*) → *Plane* must be retained. We compute (*Flight, Date*)$^+$ using the algorithm above. The first rule says that *Plane* is in (*Flight, Date*)$^+$. Therefore, the last one says that *Plane* is in (*Flight, Date*)$^+$. Therefore the right-hand side of (*Flight, Date*) → *Plane* is in the closure of its left-hand side, and so (*Flight, Date*) → *Plane* holds. Since it was derived from the others, it is redundant, and can be dropped.

Flight, Date → Pilot
Flight → Departs
Pilot → Plane

To check the third point, we see whether any left-hand attributes can be dropped without affecting the coverage. We obviously cannot drop attributes from those relations having only a single attribute on the left, so we focus on the first. We proceed by determining whether the given set implies one with an attribute missing. Suppose we attempt to determine whether *Date* → *Pilot*. Since none of the above functional dependencies has *Date* alone on the left, the answer must be no. Similarly we ask about *Flight* → *Pilot*. In this case there is more hope, as *Flight* → *Departs* appears. The actual method employed is to compute the closure (*Flight*)⁺ using the current set of functional dependencies. We see quickly that this is (*Flight, Departs*), and since it does not contain the desired right-hand side, we fail. Thus we have a minimal cover. Therefore, a decomposition of our flight database into three relations is (*Flight, Date, Pilot*), (*Flight, Departs*), (*Pilot, Plane*). This is 3NF, dependency-preserving, and lossless. It is lossless because (*Flight, Data*) is a key to the entire database. If we form the projections onto these relations, our database becomes as follows.

Pilot	Flight	Date
Cushing	83	9 Aug
Cushing	116	10 Aug
Clark	281	8 Aug
Clark	301	12 Aug
Clark	83	11 Aug
Chin	83	13 Aug
Chin	116	12 Aug
Copley	281	9 Aug
Copley	281	13 Aug
Copley	412	15 Aug

Pilot	Plane
Cushing	B747
Clark	Airbus
Chin	B747
Copley	DC9

Flight	Departs
83	10:00 A.M.
116	1:00 P.M.
281	6:00 A.M.
301	6:00 P.M.
412	1:00 P.M.

15.6 A PROGRAM FOR DOING DECOMPOSITIONS

Our database ADT defines two classes. The first implements sets of functional dependencies, and the other implements individual functional dependencies. A relation is considered to be composed of all attributes used in any functional dependency. The classes provide facilities to read a file of dependencies, compute a minimal cover, and output a list of relations constituting a decomposition. We only consider point 2b of the Biskup, Dayal, Berstein theorem, so a user will need to determine whether the decomposition is lossless, normally by determining whether any output relation contains a key. Most of the work is in computing a minimal cover, and that is where we focus our work. When applied to the flight–data dependency list, the program produces the decomposition shown above. Another more complex, if abstract, example is the following. Let the input file contain the following list:

```
a,b          -> c;
c            -> a;
b,c          -> d;
a,c,d        -> b;
d            -> f,e;
b,e          -> c;
c,f          -> d,b;
c,e          -> f,a;
END
```

Then the output is the following:

```
c,  e,  f
c,  f,  d
b,  e,  c
d,  e
c,  d,  b
a,  b,  c
```

Note that the input file lists several functional dependencies, separated by semicolons and terminated by the word END. The program depends on this format. The attribute names can be formed like identifier names in C or Pascal.

```
Required Classes

SObject
    SFunctionalDependency
    SBinaryTreeNode
    SCollection
        SList
        SSet
            SFDSet
        SStack
        SBinaryTree
            SBinarySearchTree
        SBSTSet
        SString
    SListNode
    SMagnitude
        SChar
```

```
class SFDSet;
typedef SFDSet *PFDSet;
class SFunctionalDependency;
typedef SFunctionalDependency *PFunctionalDependency;

PFDSet newFDSet ();

class SFDSet: public SSet {
    public:
            SFDSet ();
        virtual void           parse (char *aFileName);
        virtual void           produce ThirdNF (void);
        virtual PSet           allBut (PObject);
        virtual char           member (classtype c);
        virtual PObject        Clone (void);
        virtual void           writeIt (void);

    protected:
        virtual int       sizeOf (void);
        virtual char      checkImplication
                          (PBSTSet aLHS, PString target);
        virtual void      minimize (void);
        virtual void      redundantFD (void);
        virtual void      redundantLHS (void);
        virtual void      redundantRelations (void);

};


PFunctionalDependency newFunctionalDependency
    (PBSTSet l, PString r);

class SFunctionalDependency: public SObject {
    public:
            SFunctionalDependency (PBSTSet l,PString r);
        virtual                ~SFunctionalDependency ();
        virtual void           parse (void);
        virtual void           trivialImplication (void);
        virtual char           member (classtype c);
        virtual PObject        Clone (void);
        virtual void           writeIt (void);

    protected:
        PBSTSet          fLHS;
        PBSTSet          fRHSSet;
```

```
    PString          fRHS;
    virtual int      sizeOf (void);
  friend SFDSet;
};
```

To decompose a database, create a new FDSet and tell it to parse a file. This reads the input file and creates a set of functional dependencies that already conform to part 1 of the theorem. Then tell the set to produceThirdNF. The result will be the list of relations shown above.

```
initLists ();
initBinaryTrees ();
initCharacters ();

aFDSet = newFDSet ();
aFDSet -> parse ("flight.dep");
cout << ("\nThird--Normal--Form,
        Lossless-Join, Dependency-Preserving
        Decomposition.");
aFDSet -> produceThirdNF ();
```

The parse method of SFDSet uses the scanner that we discussed in Chapter 13. Scanning is a fairly standard practice. It differs in the particular symbols and keywords needed in a particular application, but it is easy to construct one that works in a lot of situations.

The parse method creates new objects of SFunctionalDependency and lets them parse themselves. Essentially the parse of a functional dependency works by reading the input and collecting the strings to the left and right of the arrow token into two separate sets representing the left and right sides, respectively. When the functional dependency returns from the parse step, we replace it with a set of functional dependencies whose right sides have only single attributes. We do this by iterating over the set on the right, constructing a new functional dependency for each item returned, and inserting it into this, since an SFDSet is a specialization of an SSet.

```
void SFDSet :: parse (char *aFileName) {
  PFunctionalDependency aFD, aNewFD;
  PObject v;
  PIterator IT;

  initScanner (aFileName);
  while (nextToken () != endSym) {
    aFD = newFunctionalDependency
        (newBSTSet (), NULL);
    aFD -> parse ();
    IT = aFD -> fRHSSet -> newIterator ();
```

```
               while (IT -> nextItem (v)) {
                   aNewFD = newFunctionalDependency
                       (PBSTSet (aFD -> fLHS -> Clone ()),
                       PString (v));
                   aNewFD -> trivialImplication ();
                   aNewFD -> fRHSSet -> insert (v);
                   insert (aNewFD);
               };
           delete IT;
           delete aFD;
           };
       };
```

In order for a functional dependency to be parsed it needs to be initialized. Its left-hand side, fLHS is always a set of attributes (objects of SString), its right-hand side is either a binary search tree set, fRHSSet, or a single SString, fRHS. SFunctionalDependency :: parse only constructs left-side and right-side sets. These sets are objects of SBSTSet because of the efficiency of binary search trees. The later algorithms will be very complex, and we need the set processing to be as quick as possible. See Section 10.4 for a complete discussion of sets implemented as binary search trees.

```
SFunctionalDependency :: SFunctionalDependency
                              (PBSTSet l, PString r) {
    fRHSSet = NULL;
    fLHS = l;
    fRHS = r;
};
```

SFunctionalDependency :: parse uses two auxiliary procedures. The method ident just gets the next string from the scanner. The method idList repeatedly calls ident to insert the results into the left-side and right-side sets.

```
PObject ident(void) {
    match (ID);
    return newString
        (tokenBuffer.tok.butIntLit.itsSpelling);
};

void idList (PBSTSet s) {
    s -> insert (ident ());
    while (nextToken () == Comma) {
        toss ();
        s -> insert (ident ());
```

```
    };
};

void SFunctionalDependency :: parse (void) {
    fRHSSet = newBSTSet ();
    idList (fLHS);
    match (ImpliesOp);
    idList (fRHSSet);
    match (concatOp);
};
```

The `produceThirdNF` method is nothing more than a formatter. It first calls the `minimize` method to organize the work. When that returns, it writes out the left and right sides of the functional dependencies that were produced. This is essentially rule 2b of the theorem.

```
void SFDSet :: produceThirdNF (void) {
    PObject g, s;
    PFunctionalDependency f;
    PIterator IT, JT;

    minimize ();
    IT = newIterator ();
    while (IT -> nextItem (g)) {
        f = PFunctionalDependency (g);
        JT = f -> fLHS -> newIterator ();
        while (JT -> nextItem (s)) {
            s -> writeIt ();
            cout << " ";
        };
        f -> fRHS -> writeIt ();
        cout << "n";
    delete JT;
    };
delete IT;
};
```

The method `minimize` outputs some messages and calls the three work routines. The method `redundantFD` searches for and removes redundant functional dependencies from the set `this`. The method `redundantLHS` removes redundant attributes from the left sides of the dependencies remaining after the first step. The method `redundantRelations` finds and removes every functional dependency whose attributes are all contained in the attributes of another relation after the second step. After the second part the cover is minimal. The third is provided merely to produce a good relational design with little redundancy. Note that although the only thing printed is a list of relations, we have actually done more than that. After the execution of `minimize`, the `PFDSet` `this` represents the minimal cover. Further processing can be done on this representation if desired.

```
void SFDSet :: minimize (void) {
    cout << "Removing redundant dependencies.\n";
    redundantFD ();
    cout << "Removing redundant left-side
            attributes.\n";
    redundantLHS ();
    cout << "Removing redundant relations.\n";
    redundantRelations ();
    cout << "Done.\n";
};
```

The method `redundantFD` checks for redundant functional dependencies and removes them from `this`. A functional dependency is redundant if it is implied by the others. It is implied by the others if we get the attribute on the right-hand side when we compute the closure of the left-hand side of it using only the other functional dependencies. `SFDSet :: parse` has ensured that only a single attribute appears on the right-hand side. We iterate over `this` to access the functional dependencies in sequence. For each functional dependency we execute a loop to compute the closure. It begins by creating a set containing all other functional dependencies. It then sends this new set the message `checkImplication`, which computes the closure of its first parameter and determines if that contains its second parameter. If so, the item is removed. This entire process may need to be repeated several times, since a functional dependency listed late may depend on others listed earlier. We must either repeat the outer iteration or let `checkImplication` repeat its scan several times. We build a repeat loop here that loops until a scan of all functional dependencies does not remove any.

```
void SFDSet :: redundantFD (void) {
    PFunctionalDependency removeThis, f;
    char changes;
    PObject x;
    PIterator IT;
    PFDSet a;

    IT = newIterator ();
    do {
        changes = FALSE;
        removeThis = NULL;
        while (IT -> nextItem (x)) {
```

```
        f = PFunctionalDependency (x);
        if (cardinality () > 1) {
            a = PFDSet (allBut (f));
            if (a -> checkImplication
                (f -> fLHS, f -> fRHS)) {
                removeThis = f;
                changes = TRUE;
            };
            delete a;
        };
    };
    if (removeThis != NULL)
        remove (removeThis);
    IT -> reset ();
  } while (changes);
  delete IT;
};
```

SFDSet :: redundantLHS determines whether any of the functional dependencies remaining after performing redundantFD have redundant attributes in their left-hand sides. An attribute is redundant if the
current set of functional dependencies, including the one under consideration, implies one built from the current one by removing the attribute from
the left side. Thus A is redundant in A, B, C -> D provided that we can
derive B, C -> D using all of the current functional dependencies including A, B, C -> D. At the outermost level redundantLHS iterates over
the functional dependencies and uses a loop to attempt to remove attributes.
This loop iterates repeatedly over the left-hand attributes of the functional
dependency it is sent, checking whether that attribute can be removed. It
does this by using another loop, which checks whether a functional dependency with that attribute removed is implied by all of the functional dependencies in this. Of course, it only needs to check if the
functional dependency, f, that it is checking has more than one left-hand
attribute. The inner loop calls checkImplication to determine the
closure of the left-hand side and check whether that contains the right
side.

```
void SFDSet :: redundantLHS (void) {
    PString removeThis, a, target;
    char changes;
    PObject x, y;
    PIterator IT, JT;
    PBSTSet s;
    PFunctionalDependency f;
    JT = newIterator ();
```

```
    while (JT -> nextItem (x)) {
        f = PFunctionalDependency (x);
        if (f -> fLHS -> cardinality () > 1) {
            IT = f -> fLHS -> newIterator ();
            do {
                changes = FALSE;
                removeThis = NULL;
                while (IT -> nextItem (y)) {
                    a = PString (y);
                    s = f -> fLHS -> allBut (a);
                    failnull (s);
                    target = f -> fRHS;
                    failnull (target);
                    if (checkImplication (s, target)) {
                        removeThis = a;
                        changes = TRUE;
                        IT -> Short ();
                    };
                };
                if (removeThis != NULL) {
                    f -> fLHS -> remove (removeThis);
                    f -> fRHSSet -> remove (removeThis);
                };
                IT -> reset ();
            } while (changes);
            delete IT;
        };
    };
    delete JT;
};
```

The method `redundantRelations` treats the functional dependencies in the set `this` as if they were just relations. At the time it is executed, the `fRHSSet` of each of its functional dependencies contains all of the attributes that appear in the functional dependency. We use two iterators over `this` to extract pairs of functional dependencies. If one is a subset of the other, we don't need the smaller one. However, using iterators over `this` to remove elements of `this` is a dangerous game. Its success depends critically on the specific implementation of our set iterator. Normally it is not done. It is done here only for efficiency. Two nested iterators mean two nested loops. Checking subset relationships between sets inside such a structure implies four nested loops. It is important that we speed this up however possible. Since a set iterator's internal state is always ahead of the item just returned, that item can be safely removed. However, if the other iterator refers to the item just removed, we will have an error. One (terrible) solution is to reset both iterators whenever we remove an item. This would require redoing a lot of work. A better solution is to look at exactly what is going on within the nested loops. Think of the process as representing a two-dimensional matrix, with IT determining the row and JT determining the column. Assuming that JT is nested inside IT and that IT returns item i and JT returns j, we see that if we remove i, then JT need not continue within that row, since we have just removed all the items in the row. Therefore, if we short-circuit JT, we exit that loop and advance the outer loop. If we also reset JT, then this process amounts to continuing at the beginning of the next row, so no work is wasted.

```
void SFDSet :: redundantRelations (void) {
    PBSTSet copy;
    PIterator IT, JT;
    PObject i, j;

    IT = newIterator ();
    JT = newIterator ();
    while (IT -> nextItem (i)) {
        copy = PFunctionalDependency (i) -> fRHSSet;
        while (JT -> nextItem (j))
        if (!i -> equal (j))
            if (copy -> subset
                (PFunctionalDependency (j) -> fRHSSet))
                remove (i);
                JT -> Short();
            };
        JT -> reset();
    };
    delete IT;
    delete JT;
};
```

The method checkImplication is used by redundantFD and redundantLHS. It checks whether the closure of its first parameter contains its second and, if so, returns TRUE to its caller. It begins with a copy of the first parameter, since the first parameter is trivially implied by itself. It then repeatedly iterates over the functional dependencies in this, seeing if any attributes should be inserted into the copy. The right-hand side of a functional dependency should be inserted if all of its left-side attributes are in the copy, which is, of course, more than a copy if changes are made to it. The procedure exits when it determines that the second parameter should be included, or when further changes cannot be made to the copy.

```
char SFDSet :: checkImplication
                (PBSTSet aLHS, PString target) {
    char result, changes, searching;
```

```
PBSTSet copy;
PObject k;
PFunctionalDependency f;
PIterator IT;

result = FALSE;
copy = PBSTSet (aLHS -> Clone ());
IT = newIterator ();
do {
    changes = FALSE;
    searching = TRUE;
    while (IT -> nextItem (k) && searching) {
        f = PFunctionalDependency (k);
        if (f -> fLHS -> subset (copy)) {
            if (! copy -> element (f -> fRHS)) {
                changes = TRUE;
                copy -> insert (f -> fRHS);
                if (f -> fRHS -> equal (target)) {
                    result = TRUE;
                    searching = FALSE;
                };
            };
        };
    };
    IT -> reset();
} while (changes && searching);
delete IT;
delete copy;
return result;
};
```

The method `allBut` is essentially the same as the set version. The
only difference is the type of value returned. We need an `SFDSet` so that
we can use the additional operations. The code is the same except for the
type of the local variable result, which is what will eventually be returned.

```
PSet SFDSet :: allBut (PObject o) {
    PFDSet result;
    PIterator IT;
    PObject v;

    result = newFDSet ();
    IT = newIterator ();
    while (IT -> nextItem (v))
        if (!v -> equal (o))
            result -> insert (v);
```

```
        else
            IT -> Short ();
        return result;
};
```

15.7   SUMMARY

Relational databases form the foundation of much current database design
and implementation. Most computer programmers in business and industry
come across them frequently. Designing a good relational database (not a
database processing system, just the database itself) requires both art and
science.

The basis of the science part is normalization. Database normalization
minimizes the redundancy in a given database. Redundancy causes a number of difficulties and can result in the loss of information. Normalization
involves a number of competing requirements, which sometimes conflict
with each other. The first requirement is that of a high degree of normalization, which implies a low degree of redundancy. We have discussed part
of the range of normal forms that are commonly used in industry. Since, in
practice, the normalization level is increased by the decomposition of the
database into relations, we must be sure not to lose information when we
do the decomposition. For this reason we require that our decompositions
have the lossless join property. Finally, since the meaning of our data is carried by the key-value relationships as expressed in functional dependencies,
we must ensure that every functional dependency imposed on the database
also holds in its decomposition.

As we have seen in this chapter, algorithms exist that achieve all these
things. These algorithms can be carried out in reasonable time and so are
feasible for implementation in computer programs.

EXERCISES

15.1 (15.2) We gave a very inadequate presentation of lossless join decompositions.
Investigate the topic in a good book on database theory, such as [Korth and Silberschatz, 1986], and develop an algorithm to check whether a decomposition
is lossless.

15.2 (15.6) We needed to redefine `allBut` in class `SFDSet` for no other reason
than to ensure that it returned a `PFDSet` rather than an ordinary `PSet`.
Suppose that in `SSet` our definition were the following:

```
PSet SSet :: allBut (PObject o) {
    PSet result;

    result = PSet (Clone ());
```

```
        result -> remove (o);
        return result;
};
```

Would we need to redefine it in SFDSet? What is the trade-off? Is there any reason at all not to have done it that way originally? Choose between the two implementation strategies and justify your choice. Find an even better implementation in SSet if possible.

MEMORY USAGE

The prince will in the perfectness of time
Cast off his followers; and their memory
Shall as a pattern or a measure live,
By which his grace must mete the lives of others,
Turning past evils to advantages.

 Shakespeare, *Henry IV* Part 2

Sleeping neglection doth betray to loss
The conquest of our scarce cold conqueror,
That ever living man of memory,
Henry the Fifth

 Shakespeare, *Henry VI*

Fig. A.1 is a diagram of the inside of a hypothetical computer that is very similar to the conception of computers that is utilized in C++ or Pascal programs. The CPU (central processing unit) provides basic functionality, such as arithmetic and comparative operators, that C++ uses in its expression evaluation. It also provides linkages between memory and various I/O (input/output) units, such as disk drives, keyboards, and printers. We shall examine the various ways in which many languages use the memory of the computer.

Memory is shown in this schematic as being divided or partitioned into four parts, program, globals, stack, and heap. In fact, in most computers the memory is best viewed as a long array of small cells, each with an address, which can be thought of as its proper name and consists of an integer in some range starting at zero (Fig. A.2). A computer with one megabyte of

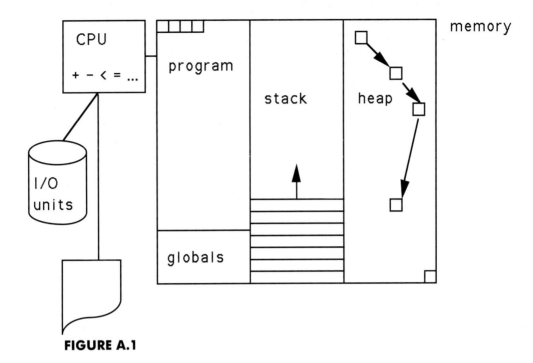

FIGURE A.1

RAM (random access memory), for example, has addresses or memory-cell names in the range from 0 to 1,048,576, which is the square of 1024, which itself is one kilobyte ("one k"). One kilobyte is not 1000 but 1024, because computers typically do arithmetic in base 2, and $1024 = 2^{10}$, the closest power of 2 to 1000. Each cell is a small electronic component that may be set to any of $256 = 2^8$ different states. Such a component is called a byte. A byte can also be thought of as being composed of eight binary digits, or bits, since this many binary digits are capable of 256 different values.

C++ treats these memory cells in different ways depending on what data types we use in our programs. First, though, we must realize that both the program itself, after being translated into machine code, and the data it manipulates are stored in the memory of the computer. The program and portions of the operating system occupy some of the cells, and we have called the section of memory that they occupy the program section. If the CPU is told to interpret some section of memory as a program, it treats the data encoded there as instructions. The function of the C++ compiler and other

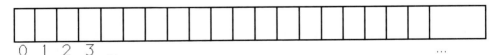

FIGURE A.2

system programs is to translate our C++ programs into a code acceptable to whatever computer we are using, to load these translated instructions into some program area of the memory, and finally to tell the CPU where to find these instructions so that they can be executed.

The data the program uses is stored in various places, depending on how it arises in the program. As is shown above, there are (conceptually, at least) three main areas for data, globals, the stack, and the heap. A given computer may use a slightly different scheme, but thinking of it in this way is helpful in any case. These three data areas will be discussed later, after discussion of the ways in which data can be encoded into the bytes of the memory.

A.1   SIMPLE TYPES

If a type of data can be encoded with 256 or fewer possible different values, a single byte can hold a constant or variable of that type. For example, the Booleans of Pascal have only two values, so the compiler in Pascal commonly uses a byte to hold a Boolean and to encode TRUE as binary 1, which in eight bits is 00000001, and to encode FALSE as 0, or 00000000. Another common coding is to use -1 for TRUE, because in the typical two's complement encoding this is 11111111. (Two's complement encoding is explained below, when integers are discussed). This latter encoding has the side effect of making TRUE less than FALSE, because comparisons use the arithmetic interpretation of the encoding. Note, however, that many computers use a minimum of two bytes to hold any datum. This will likely be the case if it is faster to access a two-byte item than a one-byte item. On such computers Pascal uses the keyword `packed` to tell the compiler that space is more important than time and that it should use the minimum possible amount of space to hold an item.

Likewise, the characters can be encoded with fewer than 256 patterns. The most common character encoding method has 128 standard characters, though many computer manufacturers use the other 128 patterns for a special graphics character set, simplifying the creation of some simple screen graphics. Thus a byte and a character are often thought of as being the same thing.

If you create an enumeration type with less than 256 different values, such as

```
typedef enum {red, green, blue, yellow} colors;
```

the compiler will probably use a byte to store a value of this type. The encoding will most likely be red = 00000000, green = 00000001, blue = 00000010, and yellow = 00000011, which are 0, 1, 2, 3, respectively. This makes red less than green and makes green the successor of red as well as the predecessor of blue.

If a data type requires more than 256 values, the compiler clumps some contiguous range of bytes together and treats it as a group. For example, an int (integer) in many microcomputer versions of C++ has a value from −32768 to +32767. This range has 65536 different values, which are the possible different encodings of 16 bits: $2^{16} = 65536$. On these computers, the C++ compiler is using two consecutive bytes to make up an integer. For example, some integer variable might use bytes 345678 and 345679 as in Fig. A.3. The individual bits of these two bytes can also be thought of as being numbered, and here they are numbered from 0 through 15. The leftmost bit, or bit 15, also called the most significant bit (MSB), is the sign bit, meaning that the value stored here (a zero or a one) tells whether the integer is positive or negative.

The nonnegative integers use standard base-two encoding in these 16 bits, so that 5 is 0000000000000101. Negative numbers are usually encoded with the method called two's complement. To get a negative 16-bit two's complement number, you take the equivalent positive number written out to 16 bits, change all the bits, and then add 1, doing the arithmetic in base 2. (A carry to the seventeenth bit is ignored.) Therefore, to get -5, we start with 5, shown above, and change all of the bits, getting 1111111111111010. Then we add 1, getting the result of 1111111111111011. Notice that the MSB is a 1, indicating that this number is negative. This encoding has a number of nice properties that make it the method of choice. For example, −1 is 1111111111111111. If we add 1 to this and ignore the final carry, we get 0000000000000000, which is zero, of course. If we take a negative number and apply the process described above (change all of the bits and add 1), we get the equivalent positive number. Therefore, the process is its own inverse. Finally, the process is easy to build into a computer, so a computer can easily be made to subtract. All we need to do is negate the subtrahend with the two's complement process and then add the result to the other number.

Mainframe computers and some micros use 32 bits instead of 16 bits for integers and internally do something similar to what we have described. On such computers the range of integer values would be -2^{31} to $+2^{31} - 1$, or from −2,147,483,648 to +2,147,483,647. Most microcomputer versions of C++ that use only 16 bits for an integer use 32 bits for a long, another of the built-in numeric data types. It is useful for larger values, but it takes up twice as much space in the memory.

Real numbers are often stored using four bytes. The thirty-two available bits are divided up into three sections, but the details vary widely between

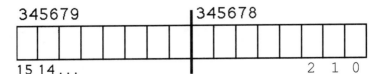

FIGURE A.3

manufacturers. One scheme is to have the MSB (bit 31) for the sign bit, then 8 bits for the exponent, interpreted as a binary power of 2, and the remaining 23 bits used to hold the significant digits of the number. This gives the equivalent of seven to eight decimal digits of accuracy. Many compilers also provide one or more 64-bit versions of real numbers, with the extra 32 bits used to extend the exponent, the mantissa, or both. Ten-byte (80 bit) real number versions are also available.

A.2   STRUCTURED TYPES

Arrays are made up of a fixed number of items of a given data type. They are called homogeneous because every element in an array has the same type. If an array had three elements, and each of those elements required four bytes, we would need twelve bytes to hold the entire array (Fig. A.4). The system would assign twelve contiguous bytes to the array and would make the address of one of these the address of the entire array. Most likely it would be the smallest numeric address. The address of the entire array would be saved by the compiler in its internal tables in one of several ways, depending on how the array was declared. (Globals are slightly different from procedure parameters and locals, as will be explained below under memory usage.) The address of a static, globally declared array can be used directly and is saved in the compiler's tables so that references to the array can be handled by the compiler by consulting these tables.

To access the components of the array, the compiler makes a computation based on the size of the components and the address of the entire array, called the base address. For example, the first element has an address that is the same as the array address. The second has an address that is numerically the sum of the array address and the size of a single element. In general, item n is found at address

```
baseAddress + (n - 1) * elementSize
```

For a more detailed example, consider an array, A, whose type is

```
float [15]
```

This array has fifteen components of size 4 bytes each. They are numbered 0 through 14. If we suppose that the base address of A is 612348, the first

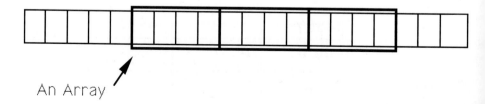

FIGURE A.4   An Array

component, A[0], is at this address, and the third, A[2], is at 612348 + 2 × 4 = 612356. In general, component A[k] is at location 612348 + k * 4. That is to say, the item with subscript k has address

```
baseAddress + (k - lowBound) * elementSize;
```

where lowBound is the value of the smallest legal subscript: zero in C and C++. Of course, the subscript k must be less than or equal to the high bound as well. The high bound is always one less than the size in C++.

This address can be computed very quickly, making arrays very efficient for a homogeneous storage structure. Arrays in Pascal are of fixed size in order that the system can easily assign addresses to arrays in memory and know where they end as well as begin, so that space is efficiently used. C++ uses a more flexible scheme, in which the length of the array need not be known until run time. Every cell is still required to have the same size. Note that it is the fact that the cells used have consecutive addresses that makes the above computation possible and fast. If the address of each element were unrelated to the addresses of the others, the computation would be more complex and hence take longer.

Variables of the struct type hold heterogeneous data. A struct or record is made up of several fields, but each field may have its own type and hence its own size. The size of a struct is the sum of the sizes of its components plus some overhead. Again, the computer stores a record in contiguous bytes, but a computation like that used for arrays is not possible. Instead, the compiler stores a table of field names and sizes for each record type declared in a program. When a variable of that type is used, the compiler translates field references for the variable by consulting this table. For example, the following struct type

```
typedef struct {
    char truth;
    float size;
    char code[3];
} sample;
```

might require twelve bytes for storage: two for a character variable, four for a real number, and six for an array of three characters. The form of its storage is shown in Fig. A.5. During the compilation the compiler could store these sizes or, more likely, store the offsets from the beginning of the

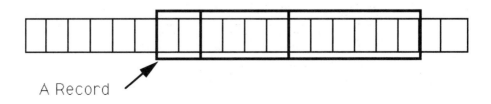

FIGURE A.5   A Record

record for each field. Therefore, truth would be given offset 0, size offset 2, and code offset 6. Each offset is the offset of the previous field plus the size of that previous field. If the record B is of this type and has address 54664, the reference B.size is a reference to the four bytes starting at $45464 + 2 = 45466$. Note that a reference to B.code[2] needs to use both record addressing to find the array B.code and array addressing to find component 2.

A.3   POINTERS AND REFERENCE VARIABLES

Pointer variables in Pascal, C, and C++ and reference variables of C++ hold addresses of other memory locations and hence addresses of other data. Many computers today use a scheme in which an address is represented in four bytes, or 32 bits. Thus we can address up to $2^{32} = 4,294,967,296$ different memory locations (four gigabytes). Very few computers have this much actual memory, but the potential is there, and some operating systems (virtual memory operating systems) use the system disk as a supplement to RAM so that programs can be written that assume this much memory is available, with the operating system shuffling data back and forth between RAM and the disk to permit the program to run. In any case, if an address requires four bytes, a pointer variable or a reference variable requires four bytes also. The encoding of these bytes is whatever the hardware requires for an address. In some computers this is just a positive integer; in others it is more complex. This difference between computers is just one more reason why a C++ program must be compiled separately on each computer model on which it is to be run.

The important thing to remember about pointer and reference variables is that they don't contain data themselves. They just tell us where the data is to be found. Most often the data is in the memory section called the heap, so pointers and reference variables are said to point into or refer to locations or data in the heap. See Fig. A.6. In the following declaration of two types,

```
typedef struct {
   char truth;
   float size;
   char code[3] ;
   } sample;
typedef sample *samplePtr;
```

we declare that a variable of type samplePtr will require four bytes (it is a pointer) and that it is intended to always point to an item of type sample, which requires 12 bytes, as we have seen before.

In fact, if we declare a variable SP of type samplePtr, it doesn't necessarily point to any location in particular, because C++ does not generally

`mainList` is four bytes in size, and its value is the address of the heap cell containing the integer 5. That cell can be referred to only via the variable `mainList`. The cell itself is said to be anonymous, as it does not have a name of its own. We refer to it by constructing a name from `mainList` and the dereferencing operator `*`. Thus, `*mainList` is a constructed name for this cell, which is a variable of type `listNode` and therefore has fields `data` and `next`. Therefore `(*mainList).data`, which may be rewritten as `mainList -> data`, is 5, and `mainList -> next` is a pointer to somewhere, in this case to the node that contains 3. Continuing in the same way, we find that `mainList -> next -> data` is 3 and that `mainList -> next -> next` is NULL.

To simplify such names, we commonly use auxiliary variables. Therefore, after the assignment

```
auxList = mainList -> next;
```

which is legal because both sides of the assignment are of type `integer-List`, we find that `auxList -> data` is 3 and `auxList -> next` is NULL. The effect of the assignment is shown in Fig. A.8. However, if `mainlist -> next` were never properly initialized, the above assignment statement could cause a crash. Even if it doesn't, most subsequent uses of `auxList` will cause a crash or produce incorrect program results. Note that `mainList` and `auxList` themselves are not in the heap (they are probably globals) but point to elements in the heap. This distinction will be ignored in the rest of our pictures, and the heap boundary will not be drawn explicitly.

Suppose we make the assignment `auxList = NULL` in the context of Fig. A.8. Then `auxList -> data` is no longer 3 and, in fact, is an illegal construction and will cause an error in our C++ program. The error is not caught by the compiler, however. Dereferencing NULL is illegal, because NULL is not a cell. Note, however, that the cell containing 3, is still available, because we still have the indirect reference to it via the name `mainList`. However, if we should next make the assignment `mainList -> next = NULL`, which is legal, we would be left in the state of

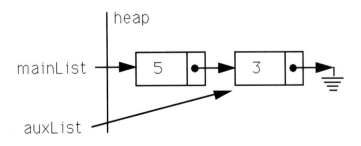

FIGURE A.8

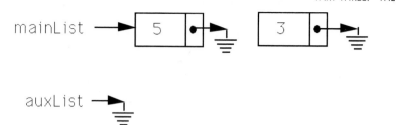

FIGURE A.9

Fig. A.9. In this state we would not have any reference to the node containing a 3 at all. It would be a lost node, and the space it occupies would be lost to our C++ program. If such losses occur too often or with large nodes, our program could fail when we try to execute new, because no room would be found in the heap for the allocation. It is very important to be aware that if the node containing 3 were not the last node in the list, nodes that followed it in the list would also be lost. However, if we execute mainList ->
next = NULL while auxList still points to the node containing 3, the node (and any following nodes) are not lost, but they are no longer attached to the list. We would be in the state shown in Fig. A.10. It is very important to always keep a pointer, directly or indirectly, to every node in the system. Otherwise, as when letting go of a tow rope or cutting a fishing line, you lose something.

The correct way to shorten a list is as follows. Suppose we are back at the state of Fig. A.8, in which mainList refers to the node that holds 5 and auxList refers to the node that holds 3. Then executing the statement

```
delete auxList;
```

permits the heap management system to recapture the space occupied by the node holding 3 so that this space can be reused later. The correct sequence of operations to remove this node and also leave us in a valid testable state is shown in Fig. A.11. The effect of the statements is shown after the statements. We have left the list with NULL at the end and have left auxList in a valid, known state. Prior to the last two statements, both auxListand mainList -> next were undefined.

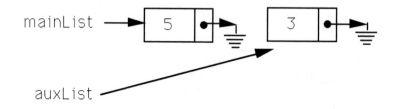

FIGURE A.10

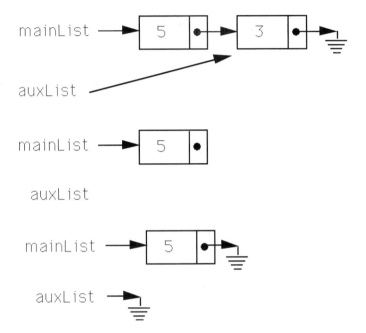

FIGURE A.11

POINTER OPERATIONS FOR LISTS

In this section we shall see some code fragments for standard list operations that assume that pointer variables are used. Normally these fragments are best implemented as procedures, since it is easy to make small but important errors. In most cases the order of the statements is critical. You are encouraged to develop list pictures for each fragment showing the step by step changes to the list and its associated variables. We assume that the above type declarations have been made and that mainList, auxList, and thisNode are all of type IntegerList. We also assume that mainList is a pointer to the first node on the list.

The code for the initialization of a list is very simple:

```
mainList = NULL;
```

The purpose of this code is to establish a testable condition for the end of a list. In fact, after this is established, we have as invariant that every list is terminated by NULL.

To insert a new node at the head of a list, as its new first node, we execute the following:

```
auxList = new (ListNode);
auxList -> data = . . .
auxList -> next = mainList;
mainList = auxList;
```

The auxiliary variable `auxList` is very important. If we start with `mainList = new (ListNode)`, we have lost the list.

Assume that a list has been properly initialized and perhaps has had some nodes inserted. Often we need to position an auxiliary variable, such as `auxList`, to point to some node in the list other than the first. The way to do this is to set `auxList` to point to the head of the list and then move it by stages to successive nodes. This process is called walking the list. Walking a list also involves some stopping condition that depends on our purposes. If we want to position our auxiliary to the last node, we look for a node whose `next` field contains NULL.

```
auxList = mainList;
if (auxList != NULL)
    while (auxList -> next != NULL)
        auxList = auxList -> next;
```

Note the initial test. It is required in order to take care of an empty list. If this test were not done, the test in the following `while` statement could cause an error, because NULL cannot be dereferenced.

Other stopping conditions are slightly more complicated. Suppose we want to stop with `auxList` pointing to a node whose data field is `val`. If we can be sure without testing that such a node is in the list, it is enough to have the following:

```
auxList = mainList;
while (auxList -> data != val)
    auxList = auxList -> next;
```

We don't even need the initial test we saw previously, because the guarantee of a node containing `val` ensures that the list itself isn't empty. Suppose, however, that we want to position `auxList` to a node containing `val` if it exists, but we aren't sure that it does exist. We also want to know whether the search for the node was successful. The above code is not adequate, because it implies an infinite loop in the case in which no such node exists, although the infinite loop is terminated by a system error when we walk past the last node.

Often we need to walk a list until we find a node whose data is `val` but actually need a pointer to the node previous to this node. Since backing up along a pointer variable is not possible, we must be careful to avoid both error and extremely complicated nesting of control structures. An easy way to accomplish this is with an auxiliary pointer variable, such as prevNode.

```
auxList = mainList;
prevNode = auxList;
done = FALSE;
while (! done ) {
   if   (auxList == NULL)
      done = TRUE;
   else if   (auxList -> data == val )
      done = TRUE;
   else {
      prevNode = auxList;
      auxList = auxList -> next;
        };
   };
```

Testing at the end to determine exactly where we are is somewhat complex, because we need to consider that we may have found the val node at the beginning, in the middle, or not at all. However, if it was found in the middle, prevNode is such that prevNode -> next == auxNode.

Having learned to walk a list, we can now consider how to insert nodes at positions other than the head. First we walk the list to some point in the list using the auxiliary variable auxList. We then insert a node after auxList but before any current successor of auxList.

```
thisNode = new (ListNode);
thisNode -> data = . . .
thisNode -> next = auxList -> next;
auxList -> next = thisNode ;
```

Next we examine processes to remove nodes from lists. Removal from the head of a list is the easiest, as we have a well-determined pointer to the head.

```
if (mainList != NULL) {
   auxNode = mainList;
   mainList = mainList -> next;
   delete (auxNode);
   };
```

If auxNode might be used for other purposes after this, especially if it is to be tested in later code, then setting auxNode to NULL at the conclusion is important.

Finally, we examine removal from the middle of a list. First we need to assume that we have walked the list and have managed to set `prevNode` to point to the node whose successor is the node to be removed. We admit the possibility that the successor to `prevNode` is NULL, but we are assuming that `prevNode` itself is not NULL.

```
if (prevNode -> next != NULL) {
    thisNode = prevNode -> next;
    prevNode -> next = thisNode -> next;
    delete (thisNode);
    };
```

After the execution of the above, `thisNode` might have to be set to NULL, depending on its later use.

A.6   ALIASES

When we execute a simple assignment between pointer variables,

```
auxList = mainList;
```

we do not get two different lists. In fact, `auxList` and `mainList` refer to the same list after this operation. Sometimes `mainList` is best thought of as being the name of the list itself (instead of a pointer to a list). Thus after the above assignment we have two different names for the same list. Two names that refer to the same thing are aliases. Aliases must be dealt with carefully. Some operations apply to all aliases of an item, and some apply to only the name used in the operation. For example, if `auxList` and `mainList` are aliases for some list and we execute

```
delete (auxList);
```

then we have made both `mainList` and `auxList` invalid. This operation applies to all aliases. However, if we execute

```
auxList = auxList -> next;
```

then `auxList` is no longer an alias for `mainList`. The reference `main List` has not been changed, but the reference `auxList` now refers to a new list (a sublist of the list `mainList`).

Disposing of an item in the heap that has aliases is an especially difficult problem. After such a disposal, any use of an alias that expects the item to have a value will be an error. Thus, if `auxList` and `mainList` are aliases and we execute `delete (auxList)`, `mainList -> data` is not a proper reference. Nor is `if (mainList == NULL) . . .` valid because `mainList` has no valid value. Therefore, considerable thought needs to be given to disposal of heap entities in the presence of aliases.

Because of this potential difficulty, it is important to remember when aliases are created and to keep track of operations that affect all aliases. Generally speaking, an operation affects all aliases if it changes the datum itself as disposal does. An operation affects only the name used in the operation if it doesn't change the datum but changes how we refer to or view the datum, as stepping down to the next node does.

Aliases are formed in assignment of pointer variables as shown above, but they are also formed when we pass a pointer variable to a procedure or function by value. Consider the following simple procedure, which changes the value of a node of a list.

```
void SetIt (IntegerList  node, int val ) {
    node -> data = val;
};
```

When we call this procedure, as in `SetIt (auxNode, 77)`, the value parameter `node` of the procedure is an alias for the argument `auxNode` of the call. The change made to `node` in the procedure is effective for the argument `auxNode`. This is a very useful behavior, but it must be used wisely.

This problem has a reverse side. If you create a heap entity inside a procedure, you must remember that local variables always disappear when the procedure exits. If `otherList` is of type `IntegerList` and is local to some procedure and we call `otherList = new (listNode)`, a `listNode` will be created in the heap and `otherList` will be made to point to it. When the procedure returns, `otherList` no longer exists, but the `listNode` in the heap is not deallocated (unless the programmer does it). It will be lost space if we are not careful. The programmer must remember to pass some reference to the node outside the procedure or else dispose of the node inside the procedure. One way to pass the reference out is to use a function return value. Other ways are reference parameters and global variables. A value parameter is not enough, however. There is a very subtle effect here, especially in light of what was said about value parameters and aliases above. The call to `new` using a value parameter of the current procedure or assigning the result of a call to `new` to a value parameter would not affect the value of the argument used with that value parameter. The value of the address of the new node must be passed out.

A.7   REFERENCE VARIABLES AND OBJECTS

C++ also permits the creation of the special class of variables called reference variables. These are like pointers, since they are indirect references to things, often things created in the heap with `new` and destroyed with delete. With a pointer variable X, the name X itself is only an address, and we use *X as a name of the thing pointed to, usually a record. With reference variables, however, the indirection notation (* or ->) is not used at all. If Y is a reference variable, the name Y could refer either to the reference or to the object referred to, depending on the context. We do not use the notation *Y at all. Therefore, if Y and Z were declared to be references to type SList (a class type), the assignment

```
Y = Z
```

makes Y a reference to the same list that Z references. The names Y and Z are aliases for the same list. The assignment does not create a new list with the same values, so Y and Z are references to the same object, which is a list. However, if we wish to refer to the insert method of this object, we just say Y.insert, and the name Y here means the object itself. Because reference variables have some special rules, we have not used them in this book.

A.8   HOW THE HEAP WORKS

The heap is a large area of memory that is directly managed by the C++ programmer through calls to the built-in functions new and delete. These functions are often developed in assembly language for efficiency. One simple scheme to implement them is as follows. Suppose we divide the entire heap up into four-byte chunks. Each chunk is, therefore, big enough to hold an address but nothing else. Suppose we store in each chunk the address of the next chunk, but in the last we store some other value, such as 0. In effect, what we have done is make the entire heap a long linked list of nodes that just store references to other nodes and nothing else. Now the heap manager is given the address of the beginning of this list. This list is called the *free list*.

When the running C++ program executes a statement such as

```
mainList = new (listNode);
```

which requires, say, that eight bytes be allocated, the execution of new takes two consecutive nodes off of the free list and sets mainList to be the address of this eight-byte block. The new value of the major pointer to the free list is then the old value of the next node in the free list, i.e., the first location following the block just returned. If a block is required whose size is not a multiple of four, the call to new returns a slightly larger block whose size is a multiple of four.

A call to delete (mainList), which returns eight consecutive bytes to the system, is handled by giving the first four bytes the value that is the address of the second four bytes, giving the second four bytes the current value of the header of the free list, and giving the free list a value that is the address of this entire eight-byte block. Thus the block is put on the head of the free list for later use.

Now a subsequent call to new will reuse this block if it requires eight bytes. However, if it needs more than eight bytes, it must search the free list for a consecutive set of blocks whose total size is as large as required, because the heap (through new) must always return a contiguous block of memory.

Real C++ systems use a more sophisticated scheme than the one described above. In particular, it would be very difficult with this method to find those blocks on the free list that were adjacent to one another and could be combined into larger blocks.

MEMORY USAGE

Data declared in the outermost lexical scope (the main program level) of our program are global data and can be used by any function in the program. They are collected in the global area of memory. They are distinguished from local data by having fixed addresses, which the compiler can compute and which can be included directly into the machine-language version of our programs.

Data that are local to functions in our program, both function parameters and local variables, are handled differently. Such data are managed in the area of memory called the system stack. It is called a stack because the operations that modify it are insertion and removal at the top, or beginning. Insertion is called push, and removal is called pop. In the system diagram at the beginning of this appendix, this area has an arrow indicating that it can grow (because of push).

We examine stack structures as one of our abstract data types in the main text (Chapter 7, on linear structures), but the operation here is slightly different. The system stack behaves like a stack, since we change it only with push and pop, but it is treated as if we can examine any item in it at any time. Normally, we think of a stack as being opaque and allowing access only to its top. Here, however, we think of it as being transparent. In some ways we consider it to be an array and examine its contents by position or index, and in some ways we consider it to be a linked list of nodes referenced by pointers.

The things pushed onto the system stack are called stack frames, or activation records. Each function has an activation record, which is pushed onto the stack each time it is called and removed from the stack when it terminates. The activation record of a function is of fixed size and fixed internal structure, but different functions have activation records that are different and even of different sizes. The activation record associated with a given function is determined by the number and types of its parameters, its local parameters, and perhaps the amount of temporary storage that is required to evaluate complex expressions in its code. The activation record contains the values of the parameters and local variables of a procedure while it is executing. The compiler determines a size and internal structure for the activation record of each function.

Note that in C++ we assume that only one function is active at any one time and that when one function calls another, the caller is suspended until the function called finishes. Thus the active lifetimes of functions are strictly nested, the called function starting after and finishing before its caller. This strict nesting is equivalent to a hierarchical structure (every nested structure is equivalent to a tree, with the outermost item equivalent to the root). The main program is the root of this tree. This activation tree is a static view of the program in action. At any given instant during the operation of the program, the system stack can be thought of as a path in this tree from some node back to the root. The leaves of the tree correspond to functions that do not themselves call any functions. Each execution of the program can result in a different activation tree, because the functions called might depend on the data in the program. If a program has a function call within a loop, the activation tree may be infinite. The activation trees of programs that have recursive functions are also potentially infinite in extent, since once a recursion begins, it is often not possible to guarantee when it will end, even when we are certain that it will eventually terminate. In some badly designed programs the repetition or recursion will, in fact, be infinite.

In Section A.6 we examined the function SetIt, whose declaration was

```
void SetIt (IntegerList node, int val);
```

This function has a pointer parameter (4 bytes), and an integer parameter (say 2 bytes). It has no local variables and has a very simple code. Its activation record might look like Fig. A.12. When the function is run, the values of the actual parameters at the time of call are copied to the val and node areas of the activation record. The other fields are for use by the system and are discussed later. Whenever a function wants to access its own parameters or locals, they can be found in the activation record at the top of the stack. A given parameter is always at the same fixed offset from the top of the stack at the time it is needed. Thus addressing may consider

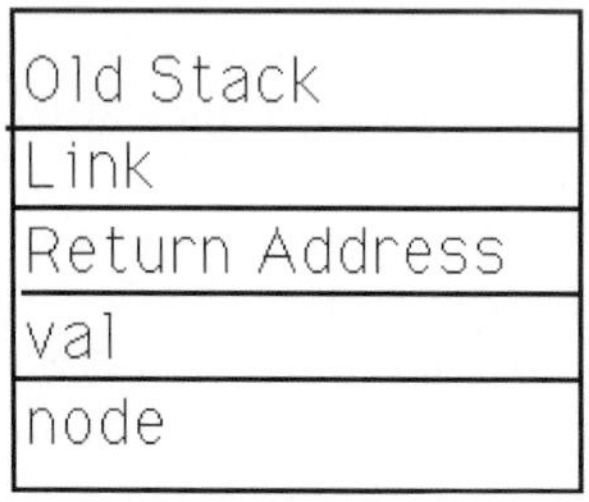

| Old Stack |
| Link |
| Return Address |
| val |
| node |

FIGURE A.12

the stack to be an array whose zero entry is at the very top of the stack, and whose size is the size of an activation record. The top of the stack itself is maintained by the system, often in one of the hardware registers. The stack might look like Fig. A.13 if the main routine had called the function `adjustList`, which in turn called `SetIt`. The value shown for `val` is 235, and the value of `node` (actually an address in the heap since node is a pointer) is 12987. The values of `OldStack` etc., are not shown yet.

If `SetIt` were to call another function, a new activation record for that function would be pushed onto the stack. When `SetIt` finishes, the top activation record is removed by the system, and `TopOfStack` is adjusted to the top of the activation record that was present when `SetIt` began. This is the purpose of `OldStack` within the activation record. It always holds the address of the top of the stack before the current activation record was pushed. It is like a pointer. We can restore the master stack pointer from this position when any function returns. In our supposed layout `val` can be found at an offset of twelve bytes from the top of the stack if we assume that each of the auxiliary fields is four bytes long, which is typical.

Each stack frame has a few special fields. Here we have shown a scheme in which three such fields are used. The `ReturnAddress` field holds the memory location of the code to be executed after this routine ends. It is the address of the machine-language instructions immediately after the point of this function call in its caller. It is placed into this slot of the activation record as part of the call process. The `OldStack` field holds the address of the stack top that was current when the caller of this routine was executing. It is placed there as part of the call process and is restored to the stack-top pointer as part of function return.

The `Link` field shown above is not actually present in C or C++ but is used by Pascal compilers and those implementations of C or C++ that provide interlanguage call facilities. It is sometimes called the static link, and its purpose is to enable the running program to find data that were

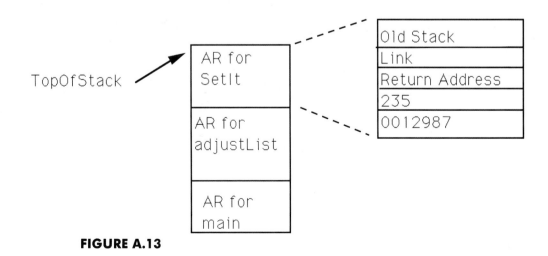

FIGURE A.13

declared in some function that contains the current function. Such data are called nonlocal data. In Pascal, nonheap data can be of three kinds. Global data are declared in the outermost program or unit. Local data are the parameters and locals of a given routine. Nonlocal data are the other data visible to a function. In a block-structured language such as Pascal, data are nonlocal to one function if they are defined within another function that contains the first. For example, consider the following situation, which is artificially contrived. Suppose we have a sort function, which works by exchanging values in an array. One of its activities is a swap, or exchange, of values. We might have the following declarations:

```
PROCEDURE sort (...);
VAR temp: integer;
   PROCEDURE SWAP (VAR A, B: integer);
   BEGIN
      temp := A;
      A := B;
      B := temp;
   END;
BEGIN {sort}
   :
   SWAP (...);
   :
END;
```

The variable temp is neither local to SWAP nor global. It is nonlocal within SWAP but local in sort. The activation record for SWAP will have two parameter fields in addition to its other fields. The activation record for sort will have a field for the local temp among its other fields. At run time, the Link field of the activation record for SWAP will refer to the activation record for sort. This is easily seen, because the sort routine is the function in the program text that contains the definition of SWAP (Fig. A.14). The rule for the link pointer is that it points to the activation

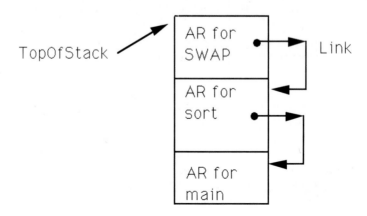

FIGURE A.14

record of the function in which it was defined (the block structure ensures that one must be on the stack), and if there are several such activation records (which might occur in case of recursion), it points to the one on the top.

Note that the `OldStack` field refers to the run-time caller of the routine whose activation record is on top, but its `Link` field refers to its textual container in the program itself. These need not be the same. For example, a function can call itself or call an ancestor other than its immediate container.

Since C and C++ don't allow functions to be nested, there is no possibility for such nonlocal data. Thus the link pointer is not necessary, and procedure call is slightly more efficient than in Pascal.

A.10   WHY THE STACK? ANSWER: RECURSION

The stack-based function activation and parameter-passing mechanism is rather complex. Earlier languages, such as FORTRAN and COBOL, used a simpler mechanism. The benefit of this complication is that it makes recursion easy to implement. Recursion is the name for the act of a function's calling itself. Such a function is called recursive. The technique is important because an important class of problems exists for which a solution is easily stated in terms of a solution to a simpler case of the same problem. For a trivial example, suppose you have a large pile of sand, `BigPile`, to move from point A to point B, and your only tool is a teaspoon. The task can be accomplished with repetition, as in the following. We create the procedure `MoveAPileOfSandWithATeaspoon` and give it as parameter a pile of sand of arbitrary size.

```
To MoveAPileOfSandWithATeaspoon (BigPile):
   WHILE BigPile is not empty DO
      move a teaspoon of sand from A to B.
```

However, another way to say this is

```
To MoveAPileOfSandWithATeaspoon (BigPile):
   IF BigPile is not empty THEN BEGIN
      move a teaspoon of sand from A to B;
      MoveAPileOfSandWithATeaspoon (rest of BigPile);
   END
```

There are only a few differences between these pieces of code. They are both fundamentally repetitive, though only the first uses a `while` construct. The second simply applies the same process to a smaller pile of sand. Of course the first does also, but it isn't stated that way. In a certain sense, this is the power of abstraction. We create a name to stand for a process: moving a pile of sand. We also *define* the process thoroughly. We may give such a definition without using computer programming language or methodology.

The important thing is that our definition of the process be complete and correct. Then we want to *describe* our process. Note that we may consider that the process already exists and that we just want to describe it. Since the process exists, we can use it by using its name and parameters. We can even use it to describe itself. Thus there is nothing wrong with a self-referential description such as we gave in the second example above.

An example of a recursive C++ program is one to generate the *n*th term of the Fibonacci sequence, 1, 1, 2, 3, 5, 8, 13, 21, 34.... This is an infinite sequence of integers with a number of interesting physical and mathematical properties. It can be thought of as a simple way to describe the growth of a population. Except for the first two values, both ones, each term is the sum of the two previous terms. Thus, a mathematician would define the Fibonacci sequence as $Fib(x) = 1$ if $x < 3$, and $Fib(x) = Fib(x-1) + Fib(x-2)$ otherwise. This definition is recursive, because it is self-referential. A C++ function for computing any given term in the sequence closely models the definition itself.

```
int Fib (int x) {
   if (x < 3)
      return 1;
   else
      return Fib (x - 1) + Fib(x - 2);
};
```

The self-referential uses of the name of the function within its definition/description are called recursive calls. This function has two recursive calls, the two separate calls of Fib within the definition of the function itself.

Part of the beauty of C++ is that such a self-referential, or recursive, description can be the code of the procedure. However, a few things must be kept in mind when using recursion, though these are mostly in the realm of common sense. First, it doesn't make sense to describe the solution of a particular problem in terms of exactly that same problem, or a more complex problem. We can't define or describe "move a pile of sand" by "move a pile of sand." Therefore, a recursive procedure must not execute itself with exactly the same data. Usually this means that the parameter of the recursive call must be simpler than the parameter with which the procedure itself is called. In Fib this is achieved because the arguments of both recursive calls are less than x, the formal parameter of Fib. Also, we must see to it that the simplest cases are handled without recursion. In the above code we declare that Fib should be 1 for values of the argument less than 3.

Therefore, to implement recursion properly, we need to provide an if or switch statement so that not every execution of the procedure will call itself. This must provide for some simple, or base, cases solved without recursion. Also, all recursive calls must be expressed in such a way that repeated recursion will eventually result in one of the base cases being executed. This is the case with Fib, as the recursions use smaller parameters and we have provided separate solutions for all small values, i.e., those less than 3.

Recursive functions work like any other functions in C++. When a function calls itself, the parameters are placed into a new activation record on top of the current one, and the code begins anew. Since the local variables of a function are also in the activation record, each execution of a recursive function has separate copies of all locals so that they do not interfere with each other. Note, however, that a function such as Fib does a lot of recursion, meaning that there are a lot of activation records. Therefore, the program takes a lot of space and time: space for the activation records and time to push them on and pop them from the stack.

EXERCISES

A.1 (A.5) Develop the list operations into functions. Give special thought to the proper parameters of these functions.

A.2 (A.5) Develop step-by-step diagrams showing the changes made by the list operations.

A.3 (A.5) An alternate way to terminate lists is to have the last node refer to itself rather than to NULL. With this scheme a list might look like Fig. A.15. The test for end of list is someNode -> next == someNode, rather than someNode -> next == NULL. Discuss this method. What is easier, and what is harder? What happens to the list operations when this is used?

A.4 (A.8) Consider a memory management scheme in which the free list of the heap is organized as a list of variably sized nodes, each of which contains a size field (first four bytes) as well as a next field (next four bytes). The node is treated as if it were size bytes long. Initially only one node is on the list, its size is the size of the heap, and its next is zero. A call to new searches the free list for the first node equal to or larger than the required size, and either this node is returned (if it is exactly the right size) or a node is carved out of it, with sizes adjusted. A call to dispose searches the entire free list for one adjacent to the memory being freed. If one is found, the memory is coalesced into it. If none is found, the memory is added to the end of the free list (either end will do). Compare this method with the one described in the text. Which scheme is simpler, and which is faster? How would you write a program to simulate the operation of each scheme?

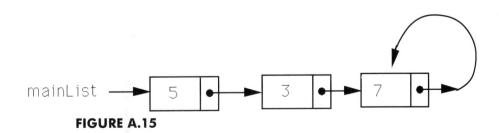

FIGURE A.15

A.5 (A.9) Explain how the collection of `Link` pointers for a running program represents a tree. What is the root of this tree? What are the leaves? What does a path from leaf to root represent? Consider the hypothetical program below. Note that only a few of the statements in each function are shown. Nor are any of the data shown that the program requires. What do the `Link` fields of the activation records in the stack look like both before and after `dryer` calls `baker` for the first time? What do they look like before and after `dryer` calls `apple` for the first time? (Run the program by hand starting with `main`.)

```
Program test;

PROCEDURE apple;
    PROCEDURE baker; {nested inside apple}
    BEGIN {baker}
        IF...THEN
            baker;
        apple;
    END;

    PROCEDURE cooker; {nested inside apple}
        PROCEDURE dryer; {nested inside cooker}
        BEGIN {dryer}
            baker;
            apple;
        IF...THEN
            cooker;
        END;

        BEGIN {cooker}
            dryer;
            baker;
        END;

BEGIN {apple}
    cooker;
    baker;
END;

BEGIN {main}
    apple;
END.
```

MORE ON C++

B.1   OPERATORS AND THEIR PRECEDENCE AND ASSOCIATIVITY

The following is a list of the operators of C++ in order of precedence. All operators associate left to right except the groups marked (RTL).

Highest precedence

1. `::` scope resolution operator
2. `()`, `[]`, `->`,`.` parentheses and member access
3. prefix-postfix `++`, `--`, unary `+`, unary `-`, `new`, `delete`, `delete[]`, `!`, ones complement `~`, `&`, pointer `*`, `(type)`, `sizeof` (RTL)
4. `.*`, `->*` pointer to member access
5. `*` multiplication, `/` division, `%` modulo (remainder)
6. `+` addition, `-` subtraction
7. `<<`, `>>` shift operators and output to and input from streams
8. `<`, `<=`, `>`, `>=` size comparison
9. `==`, `!=` equality testing
10. `&` address-of
11. `^` bitwise exclusive **or**
12. `|` bitwise inclusive **or**
13. `&&` logical **and**
14. `||` logical **or**
15. `?:` conditional expression (RTL)
16. `=`, `+=`, `-=`, `*=`, `/=`, `%=`, `&=`, `^=`, `|=`, `<<=`, `>>=` assignment operators (RTL)
17. `,` comma operator

Lowest precedence

B.2   SYNTAX OF C++

Keywords

asm	auto	break	case	catch
char	class	const	continue	default
delete	do	double	else	enum
extern	float	for	friend	goto
if	inline	int	long	new
operator	private	protected	public	register
return	short	signed	sizeof	static
struct	switch	template	this	typedef
union	unsigned	virtual	void	volatile
while				

The full syntax of C++ is extremely rich. Consult your system documentation for details. The best currently available definition of the language is [Ellis & Stroustrup, 1990]. That book is written for professionals, not for novices. A more readable description of the language may be found in [Lippman, 1989].

B.3   LINKING C++ AND BUILDING EXECUTABLE PROGRAMS

Different C++ systems have different requirements for creating an executable program. There are at least two main approaches to this problem. The first is exemplified by the UNIX operating system and by the Macintosh Programmer Workshop (MPW). Here you create a file (the makefile) that describes the dependencies between files and the requirements for rebuilding the executable file when one or more of the components is updated. These systems provide an automated tool, called make or build, that processes a makefile, examining the dependencies and executing the compiler or linker as necessary depending on the dates of the files that are described in the makefile.

The second approach to building is used in Borland C++ as well as a number of other systems. Here, the user creates a *project window* within the programming environment and adds all of the .cp files to the project using menu commands. The system itself is responsible for determining dependencies, using the #include directives that appear in the files themselves. An executable is built using another menu command that processes the files in the project.

Exerpts from a sample MPW makefile appear below. They are contained in a file called driver.make; the suffix .make is recognized by the build tool provided with the MPW. To create an MPW tool, the user selects `Build . . .` from the menu. In the following, # introduces comment lines, and ∂ permits the continuation of an instruction onto the following line. Braces, { }, yield the value of a symbol. The name and the braces surrounding it are replaced by the definition of the symbol. My comments are enclosed between ‹‹ and ›› and usually imply that some of the lines of the file have been excluded for brevity. These comments are not legal in such a file. We assume that the `main` function of the project is contained in a file called `driver.cp`.

```
# File:        driver.make
# Target:      driver
# Created:     Sunday, May 26, 1992 6:02:28 PM

OBJECTS = ∂
    DRIVER.CP.O   ∂
    POBJECT.Cp.o   ∂
    PCOLLECT.Cp.o   ∂
    PMAGNITU.Cp.o   ∂
    PCHARACT.Cp.o   ∂

‹‹More here. One line for each file.››
‹‹This defines a symbol called OBJECTS.››


    PBag.Cp.o ∂
    PTree.Cp.o

# Define dependencies for each file.
MagDep = PObject.H PMagnitu.H
CollDep = PObject.H PCollect.H
IntDep = {MagDep} {CollDep} PInteger.H
ListDep = {CollDep} {MagDep} PList.H ListWrit.cp
‹‹More here.  One line for each file.››
‹‹In the above line {CollDep} will be replaced››
‹‹by its definition: PObject.H PCollect.H.››
BagDep = {MultiListDep} PBag.h
TreeDep = {BTreeDep} PTree.h

HEADERS = ∂
    PCHARACT.H   ∂
    PCOLLECT.H   ∂
    PINTEGER.H   ∂
    PLIST.H   ∂
‹‹More here. One line for each file.››
‹‹This defines a symbol called HEADERS.››
    PBag.H ∂
    PTree.H
```

```
# Following is the link command that produces the
# tool called driver.
# ƒ is option-f on the Macintosh keyboard.
driver ƒƒ driver.make {OBJECTS}
    Link -d -c 'MPS ' -t MPST ∂
       {OBJECTS} ∂
       "{CLibraries}"CplusLib.o ∂
       "{CLibraries}"StdCLib.o ∂
       "{Libraries}"Stubs.o ∂
       "{Libraries}"Runtime.o ∂
       "{Libraries}"Interface.o ∂
       -o driver

# Following are the dependencies needed to drive
# the compiler.
DRIVER.Cp.o f  DRIVER.Cp INITCLAS.H {HEADERS}
    CPlus   DRIVER.Cp
PCOLLECT.Cp.o f  PCOLLECT.Cp {CollDep}
    CPlus   PCOLLECT.Cp
PINTEGER.Cp.o f  PINTEGER.Cp {IntDep}
    CPlus   -s Mags PINTEGER.Cp
PLIST.Cp.o f  PLIST.Cp {ListDep}
    CPlus   -s Lists PLIST.Cp
<<More here.  Two lines for each .cp file.>>
<<The first line defines dependencies on>>
<<source files and the second gives the>>
<<compile command necessary to build the>>
<<object file.  The -s name options give the>>
<<Macintosh memory segments in which the code>>
<<should be placed permitting functions likely>>
<<to be used together to be loaded together.>>
PBag.Cp.o f  PBag.Cp {BagDep}
    CPlus   -s Lists PBag.Cp
PTree.Cp.o f  PTree.Cp {TreeDep}
    CPlus   -s Trees PTree.Cp
```

B.4   MORE C++: USE OF DIRECT OBJECTS

In the main part of this book we relied entirely on indirect objects: objects referred to by pointers. For completeness we shall discuss what must be added to our classes to enable us to safely use direct objects, that is, objects used directly, without pointers. Such use of objects is not, strictly speaking, object-oriented, though it does have valuable uses. In particular, ADT's can be built using direct objects and work very well. We give up the advantages of virtual functions, however, and therefore give up the benefits of the dynamic binding principle.

Direct objects are those data items whose type is a class type, such as SList or SListIterator. They are implemented in C++ in much the same way that a struct of C or record of Pascal is implemented: as a block of data stored in the run-time stack. A difference is that direct objects also have access to their methods and respect the privacy constraints on members of the class. Since they form blocks of data, assignments of objects of different types and the meanings of such assignments are restricted. In particular, if SB is a subclass of SA, and if b is a variable of type SB and a is a variable of type SA, b can be assigned to a, but not conversely (see an exception to this below). Also, when the assignment is made, the members of b that are not part of the definition of SA are simply truncated and lost. The mathematical term for this is projection. Assignment projects the subclass onto the superclass. The reason why we can't assign variable a to variable b is that b would be partly empty, since a has no fields or methods to supply to the parts of b that are not described in SA.

If we want to use classes in our structure to instantiate direct objects, we need to understand a few things about how they fit into C++ and therefore what we must do to provide for safe use.

First, and most importantly, C++ was designed to make direct objects completely safe for clients. Said another way, the designer and the builder of a class should be able to provide services that never need to be circumvented and that can be used without error. The language and its compiler work together to help ensure this. For example, if we want to use a list iterator as a direct object, we need to declare a variable of type SListIterator. It is not enough to just say

```
SListIterator IT;
```

however, since the constructor of a list iterator requires a parameter; namely, the list over which the iterator works. It is not enough to apply this iterator after the declaration, since that might be forgotten, leaving us with an uninitialized variable, which C++ wants to avoid. Therefore, the compiler makes us name an existing list in the declaration, as in

```
SListIterator IT (aList);
```

If this is not done, the compiler will complain. If the constructor had no parameters, the first form would have been acceptable. Note that the compiler sees to it that the constructor is called before any use of the object, so we may be assured that the iterator is safe to use just by giving its declaration.

If a direct object is declared as a global variable, its lifetime is the life of the program run of which it is a part. However, if a direct object is declared local to a function or a method, then the life of that object is just that of the block in which its definition appears. Thus the object disappears at the end of each invocation of the function (at the end of the block in which the definition appears). At this time the variable goes out of scope. The compiler calls the destructor when this occurs, so the programmer doesn't need to call it. If the programmer does not write a destructor, the compiler applies a default destructor and that is leaving too much to the compiler. Note, however, that we can have an inherited constructor, even if we don't write one for a new class.

Therefore, the first lesson for those who want to use direct objects is that each class should have a constructor and a destructor. We have provided these in our library already.

The next thing to be concerned with is whether the designer of a class anticipates that users will want to assign direct objects from one variable of the class to another within the same class. If the class has no member variables that are pointers or indirect objects, the compiler will handle the assignment correctly, but if the class has such member variables (as most of our classes have), the actions provided when we say

```
SListPosition P(L),Q(L);
 ⋮
P = Q;
```

are not necessarily sufficient. The compiler provides a copy of the individual fields of Q into those of P. For pointers this means that aliases are created. Later, when P and Q come to the end of the scope in which they were created and the destructor is applied, such a pointer member can be destroyed twice, causing a program crash. That won't happen in our list-position class, since the destructor of a position doesn't destroy the list or node member that it contains references to. If we were to provide such assignments in our list class, however, at the end of the scope the destructor would try to destroy the first node (and hence subsequent nodes) more than once. After the first destruction the second attempt would cause the program to fail. The solution to this is to provide a special operator for the compiler to use when it carries out assignments so that we can avoid the default behavior provided by the compiler.

To make assignments safe, we need to overload (not override) the assignment operator and provide a special version for the class to use. C++ provides ways to overload the assignment operator both as an ordinary function (for use by ordinary variables) and as a class method (for use by objects). We need the latter form, of course. In our list class, where such a method would be vital, we need to provide a method with the prototype

```
SList& SList :: operator = (SList &L);
```

which says that within class SList we overload the assignment operator (operator =) to provide a version that is passed a reference to a list and returns a reference to a list. This returned value is the one assigned. Technically, the prototype could be

```
void SList :: operator = (SList &L);
```

so that the method returns nothing, but it is more consistent with C and C++ that an assignment is an expression whose value is the value assigned. If either of these is provided, a message is sent to the object on the left of the assignment whenever the user writes something like the following:

```
SList A, B;   // Which require no parameters
              // since we have a parameterless
              // constructor.
A = B;
```

For SList the full method would be something like our clone method for lists, except that it is copying in the opposite direction and must free the existing nodes if any exist. There is one special problem with the assignment operator, however. An object should never be permitted to assign itself to itself.

```
SList& SList :: operator = (SList &L) {
    PListPosition P;
    PIterator IT;
    PObject anItem;

    if (*this == L) return *this;
        // Don't do anything.
    while (fFirstNode != zed) removeFirst ();
        // Empty this.
    IT = L.newIterator ();
    P = PListPosition (newPosition ());
    while (IT -> nextItem (anItem)) {
        if (P -> afterLast ()) {
            P -> insertFirst (anItem);
        }
        else {
            P -> insertAfter (anItem);
            P -> next ();
        };
    };
    delete P;
    delete IT;
    return *this;
};
```

The next issue concerns whether it is anticipated that the user will need to pass a direct object to a method or function as an ordinary (value) parameter or return a direct object as the return type of a function. Since it is hard, in most cases, to guess what all of the needs of a client might be in the future, it is usually safest to assume that it might happen. Therefore we need what is called a copy constructor, which, again, supplants the default behavior of the compiler in these cases. The issues are very similar to those of the overloaded assignment operator. If we pass a value parameter that is a direct object, a copy of it is made. The default behavior will be a field-by-field copy of the original. Later both objects will be destroyed. If the object has a pointer or indirect object that is destroyed by a destructor, we shall have a disaster, as the destructor will be applied twice. The solution is to provide a special constructor. Again, for SList, it should have the following prototype:

```
SList :: SList (SList&);
```

This constructs one SList from another. It is also used when we declare a new SList and initialize it with a value that is another SList. The full method is very similar to our assignment operator except that nothing is returned and the object hasn't been initialized when this starts, since it is a constructor.

```
SList :: SList (SList &L) {
    PListPosition P;
    PIterator IT;
    PObject anItem;

    fFirstNode = zed;
        // Initialize object properly.
    IT = L.newIterator ();
    P = (PListPosition) newPosition ();
    while (IT -> nextItem (anItem)) {
        if (P -> afterLast ()) {
            P -> insertFirst (anItem);
        }
        else {
            P -> insertAfter (anItem);
            P -> next ();
        };
    };
    delete P;
    delete IT;
};
```

The next issue matters only when the user might need to create arrays of direct objects, as in

```
SList arrayList [10];
```

The difficulty here is that the SList objects in the array must be passed a constructor and a parameter list cannot be given in this case. Therefore, the class should provide a parameterless constructor or else provide another mechanism for creating such lists. SList already has such a constructor, so nothing more must be done here. For us an array of SListIterator objects would be especially problematical, since an iterator makes no sense unless we know what its list is, and knowing this is its initialization and hence its construction. Here, we could provide a parameterless constructor, make it private so that no code could call it outside the class, and provide a method that returns an array of iterators on some list. This array will need to be pointed to by a pointer, but the iterators that make it up can be direct.

The next capability is less likely to be needed. If direct objects are to be compared == or !=, the default behavior provided by the compiler is likely to be wrong, and these should be provided by the class designer. The contents of these are similar to what we have seen in our magnitude classes. Note, however, that it is very disconcerting to a user if A == B is TRUE but B == A is FALSE. It is also disturbing if A == B and A != B are both TRUE or both FALSE. Special care needs to be taken in these cases to assure that the usual sense of these is maintained. The prototypes for these in class SListNode should be

```
int SListNode :: operator == (SListNode&);
int SListNode :: operator != (SListNode&);
```

The operator != can be easily implemented in terms of ==, making some of the rules hold automatically:

```
int SListNode :: operator != (SListNode &N) {
   return ! (*this == N)
};
```

Finally, if a class needs to provide assignments between its own objects and objects of other classes or even ordinary data, it must provide either additional operators or constructors to achieve the translations needed by the assignments. For example, if the proper scaffolding is put into place in our classes, SStrings objects can be assigned to ordinary (char*) strings, and SList objects can be assigned to SArray objects.

For our first example of translating across the assignment operator, consider the problem, just mentioned, of assigning an SArray to an SList. The most sensible idea for this is to put items into the list in the order in which they are located in the array. What we wind up with is a list with the same elements as the array and in the same order. To achieve this, we need a constructor in the SList class that will do a translation. It might require in some circumstances that the target class (SList here) be a friend of the source class (SArray), but that won't be needed here. The prototype of the transforming constructor is

```
SList :: SList (SArray&);
```

which indicates that it creates an SList out of an SArray (but it doesn't modify the array.) The body of the constructor, using the public interface of SArray, just extracts the elements from the array in reverse order and inserts them into itself.

```
SList :: SList (SArray &a) {
    fFirstNode = zed;
    for (int i = a.physicalSize (); i > 0;) {
        insert (a.at (--i));
    };
};
```

This constructor is called automatically whenever an assignment is done from an SArray to an SList or when an SArray is type-cast to an SList.

Our last example of a translation shows how to make possible the assignment of an SString to an ordinary string. The techique of the above example would work for the converse operation but not here, since the target is not a class. For this we need to use a special feature of C++, which treats the name of a type as an operator. A translation function (it isn't a method) can be declared as a member operator within class SString with header

```
SString :: operator char* (void);
```

Note that the assignment operator does not appear in this declaration. The assignment is not the operator; the type char* itself is, and in fact this operator will be useful outside assignments. In fact, in any context in which the compiler expects a char* the programmer can use an SString instead, and the compiler will ensure that this operator is used. The body provides a translation from the current class, SString, to a char*. Since the user may want to modify the returned char* and not modify the SString that was the original source, we shall do some copying in the body of the operator. This gives us the following:

```
SString :: operator char* (void){
    char *result;

    result = new char[fLength + 1];
    :: strcpy (result, fValue);
    return result;
};
```

Summary of the Rules

To use direct objects in the class `Class`, you must provide the following:

1. A constructor, preferably one with no parameters.

    ```
    Class :: Class(void);
    ```

2. A destructor. If you are also using pointer-based objects, it should be virtual.

    ```
    Class :: ~Class (void);
    ```

3. An overloaded assignment operator.

    ```
    Class & Class :: operator = (static Class&);
    ```

4. A copy constructor.

    ```
    Class :: Class (static Class&);
    ```

5. (Optional) Overrides of the operators == and != if these comparisons need to be made within a class.

    ```
    int Class :: operator == (Class&);
    int Class :: operator != (Class&);
    ```

6. (Optional) Other translating operators and constructors, if assignments must be made between classes or between a class and ordinary data.

B.5   SAFER POINTERS: SOLVING THE DELETION PROBLEM

Throughout this book objects have been referred to through pointers, but the pointers weren't themselves objects. Here we shall see how to create a class whose objects behave just like pointers. In addition, we shall use the technique to automate the `delete` operation for objects so that the programmer doesn't need to consider when and where each object in some class should be deleted. The example will be our `SAssociation` class, since when we use associations to build dictionaries, a given association could be inserted in several different dictionaries and therefore have several aliases. It might be difficult, under these circumstances, to determine when an association was no longer needed, because it has just been removed from the last dictionary of which it was a member.

Our general technique is to keep track, in any association, of exactly how many references there are to that association, thus counting aliases. When this number drops to zero, we can delete the association, but not before. Since aliases can be created in many ways, we want to control the generation process so that we can manipulate the count of references for each potential creation.

The first change we need to make is to give SAssociation the new protected field fRefCount, which can be an int. In this field we shall keep track of the number of references (aliases) of the object. When we create a new association, it will be set to 1. The initialization of fRefCount can be done in constructors of SAssociation. Next we declare the new class RAssociation (reference to an association) and make it a friend of SAssociation. This new class will behave as a pointer-to-associations class and will manage the reference counts other than the initialization. Objects in this class will be used as direct objects rather than dynamic objects, so it doesn't need virtual functions, though it does need the refinements that were discussed in the previous section of this appendix. Its only member (instance) variable is a PAssociation, fRepresentation, and this variable (together with the copy constructor, the assignment operator, and another operator to be discussed shortly) manages its behavior as a pointer. The declaration of this new class is as follows:

```
class RAssociation: public SObject {
   public:
      RAssociation (PObject k, PObject v);
      ~RAssociation (void);
      RAssociation (RAssociation&);
      RAssociation &operator = (RAssociation&);
      PAssociation operator -> ()
         {return fRepresentation;};
   protected:
      PAssociation fRepresentation;
};
```

This declaration consists almost entirely of constructors and overridden operators. The operator of most interest is ->, the pointer dereference operator. The operator is declared to return a PAssociation: a pointer to an SAssociation. The implementation is just to return the fRepresentation member. When we use an RAssociation, RA, which is a direct object, in a context such as

```
RA -> writeIt ();
```

the system applies this operator, which normally couldn't be applied to a direct object, and the operator returns a PAssociation, which is a pointer. The ordinary (or possibly, in another class, overridden) operator -> is then applied to this returned pointer, so that in this case, fRepresentation will get the writeIt message.

In order for this scheme to work, however, we need the other constructors and the overridden assignment operator, for these catch the creation of aliases.

The main constructor is simple and merely creates a new SAssocia-tion to use as the representation. Recall that the construction of fRepresentation also initializes the fRefCount member of the newly created SAssociation.

```
RAssociation :: RAssociation (PObject k, PObject v) {
   fRepresentation = new SAssociation (k, v);
};
```

Next we need the destructor, which for a direct object, such as an RAssociation, will be called automatically by the system whenever such an object goes out of scope.

```
RAssociation
   :: ~RAssociation (void) {
   if (--fRepresentation -> fRefCount <= 0) {
      delete fRepresentation;
   };
};
```

This destructor decrements the count in its fRepresentation in-stance variable and checks whether it has just become zero. If so, fRep-resentation itself, which is a pointer, is also deleted. Note that if several RAssociations have references to the same SAssociation, the RAssociations are aliases. Therefore, we can't delete fRepresentation each time we remove an RAssociation but only when the last alias disappears.

The next two members are the key to all of this working correctly, since it is in assignment expressions and in other copying of RAssociations that aliases are created. Therefore, we need to provide a copy constructor and an overload of the operator =. The copy constructor illustrates what we need to do:

```
RAssociation :: RAssociation (RAssociation&a) {
   fRepresentation = a.fRepresentation;
   fRepresentation -> fRefCount++;
};
```

When we copy an RAssociation, either by passing it as a value parame-ter to some function or returning it by value from a function, we simply copy the representation of the source into the destination (which is the object be-ing constructed) and increment the reference count in the representation.

The assignment operator is somewhat similar but a bit more subtle. First, we have the problem that the object named on the left side of the assignment is already a reference to some association. We therefore need to decrement a reference count for that object and delete it if the count has become zero. Then we must perform the assignment and updating of the new reference count. Finally, we return the object copied as the result of the operation. This should be returned by reference however, and not by value, or the copy constructor will also be called to make a copy, and therefore the reference count will be incremented twice rather than once. As usual, we guard against the assignment of one object to itself.

```
RAssociation & RAssociation :: operator =
                                (RAssociation &a) {
    if (fRepresentation != a.fRepresentation) {
        if (--fRepresentation -> fRefCount <= 0) {
            delete fRepresentation;
            };
        fRepresentation = a.fRepresentation;
        fRepresentation -> fRefCount++;
    };
    return *this;
};
```

This completes the items necessary for creating a smart pointer, which is the name given to this sort of a class. There is, however, one additional thing we might want to do. When we treated associations previously, we noted that, as magnitudes, they have the usual magnitude operations equal and less (and those derived from these two). Previously we could not easily overload the == and < operators because we were working through pointers. Now, however, with a class simulating pointers, we can overload these operators and the other comparison operators; thus <=, for example, can be used between RAssociations.

These last two sections have described advanced uses of C++. More material of this sort and an introduction to how C++ is used by professionals in practice can be found in [Coplien, 1992].

B.6   PROCEDURES AS PARAMETERS TO OTHER PROCEDURES

Often it is useful to pass one function as a parameter to another. One very useful example is a sorting function designed to sort into either increasing or decreasing order. We can devise the procedure so that it calls the function compare () when it needs to test two elements to see what order they belong in. We can then pass the compare function in to the sort function. A user of the sort function will write a compare function appropriate to the situation and then pass it to sort.

In C and C++, we pass functions as parameters by passing a pointer to a function. Suppose, for example, we have two comparison functions, such as

```
char less (int a, int b) {return a < b};
char greater (int a, int b) {return a > b};
```

We can then devise the sort routine to take either of these as a parameter, as follows:

```
void sort (int *vector, int length,
           char (*compare) (int, int)) {
   ⋮
   if (compare (x,y))
   ⋮
};
```

According to this definition, sort receives an array named vector as input (represented by a pointer to an int) and rearranges its contents. It also requires a parameter that is pointer to function. The parentheses around *compare are needed so that the compiler can correctly determine that we want a pointer to a function of two integers returning a character and not a function returning a pointer to a character.

Inside the body of sort, the compare function is used in the ordinary way, by supplying it parameters of the required types and getting back a value of its return type. We can call sort itself with

```
sort (anArray, 20, less);
```

The function less will be used in place of the argument compare.

Sometimes the caller of such a function must be able to pass additional information along with the function parameter, less, and the information must be known only to the caller and to less, but not to the function sort. If this is anticipated when we design sort, we can devise both less and sort to make it possible, though doing so is a bit complicated. The trick involves creating a pointer to a struct that is to contain the required information. Then we write both less and sort so that they can take such a pointer as an additional argument. For complete flexibility we designate the pointer as (void*), which is a generic pointer: a pointer to anything, which prevents any sort of type checking by the compiler and so puts additional responsibility on the programmer to avoid errors. Our new declarations of less and greater would be

```
char less (int a, int b, void *more)...
   return a < b};
char greater (int a, int b, void *more)...
   return a > b};
```

The declaration of sort would then be

```
void sort (int *vector, int length,
           char (*compare) (int, int, void*),
           void *link) {
    ⋮
    if (compare (x, y, link)) . . .
    ⋮
};
```

Note that both sort and compare have an additional parameter, link, of type void* and that compare is called with this additional parameter.

Of course, if this is to make any sense, less and greater need to make use of the additional information. We could, at the place from which the call is made, create a struct type info as in

```
typedef struct {
    int x;
    ⋮
} info;
```

At the place from which we want to call sort, we package our required extra information inside such a record:

```
info myRecord;
myRecord.x  =  . . .
```

We can also declare less and greater so that they access such a record, as in

```
char less (int a, int b, void *extra) {
    if (((info*) extra) -> x ==  . . .) . . .
    return a < b
};
char greater (int a, int b, void *extra) {
    if (((info*) extra) -> x ==  . . .) . . .
    return a > b
};
```

Note that the new parameters of less and greater must have type void* so that the functions will be compatible with the first parameter of sort. We would then call sort using something like

```
sort (anArray, 20, less, &myRecord);
```

passing a pointer to the struct myRecord. This record would then be passed by sort to the routine less as its third parameter.

| B.7 | **INTERNAL ITERATORS** |

Both C and C++ have a way to pass a function as a parameter to another function (actually, it is a pointer to a function that is passed). We can use this facility to add a method, EachDo, of the following form to each collection class, starting with SCollection:

```
virtual void    EachDo (void (*DoToItem)
                    (PObject item, void *StaticLink),
                    void *StaticLink);
// Execute DoToItem (o) once for each
// object in the collection in an order
// appropriate to the collection.
```

We can't implement it in this class, because we don't have any collection implementation in the abstract class. We can define it to be a pure virtual function, a call to Error, or by giving it an empty function body, just a no-op. The protocol is established, however, and every subclass of SCollection will be required to implement EachDo. EachDo has two parameters: the first is a function pointer to a function of two parameters, and the other is an untyped pointer. The second parameter provides a means for the caller of EachDo to send additional information to the first parameter if it is needed. The method EachDo executes DoToItem (obj . . .) once for each object in the collection. EachDo is itself *a lot* like a for loop in C, which executes a statement once for each integer in a range. Here we execute a procedure once for each object in a collection. If we wanted to implement EachDo for our SFiniteStack class, the following would do.

```
void SFiniteStack :: EachDo (void (*DoToItem)
                    (PObject item,
                    void *StaticLink),
                    void *StaticLink) {
    for (int i = fTop; i >= 0, i--)
        DoToItem (fElements[i], StaticLink);
};
```

If SFiniteStack were a subclass of SCollection, this would be an override method. We could use it by creating some procedure that was consistent with the procedure type of DoToItem, such as the following:

```
void CountIt (PObject o, void *StaticLink) {
    count++;   {Increment a global variable.}
};
```

We could then send the message

```
ExpressionStack.EachDo (CountIt, NULL);
```

and count would be incremented by the number of elements currently in the stack. CountIt ignores its input parameters and just increments count. The overall effect on count comes from the fact that CountIt is executed once for each object in the stack. Although the example here is so simple as to be useless, it does illustrate a very powerful technique that can be used in all of our collection classes. The extra parameters of type void* are used so that the caller of EachDo supplies additional information to the procedure used in place of DoToItem. We can create any struct with any information whatever and pass a pointer to it when we call EachDo, which should pass the same pointer (or possibly another) to DoToItem.

Now that we have built EachDo in our collection classes, four additional methods, Collect, Reject, FirstThat, and Select, can all be implemented within SCollection by using EachDo. Then subclasses such as SList will redefine EachDo but not the other methods.

For example, when some SList object, SomeList, is sent the Collect message and executes Collect, it sends the EachDo message in the body of Collect. The message EachDo represents the method of that subclass, even though Collect, which sends the message, is defined in the superclass. In effect, the object sends the EachDo message to itself, as illustrated in Fig. B.1. This is the dynamic binding principle again.

These additional iterator functions are shown below. They are included in SCollection and are generally not overridden in subclasses.

```
virtual PObject    FirstThat (char (*select)
                       (PObject item, void *StaticLink),
                   void *StaticLink);
    // Return a reference to the first object in
    // the collection for which select is TRUE.
    // Return NULL if there is no such object.
virtual void    Select (PCollection c, char
                       (*select) (PObject item,
                       void *StaticLink),
                       void *StaticLink);
    // Send c->insert(o) for all objects o in
    // this for which select (o) returns TRUE.
```

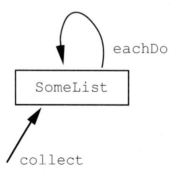

FIGURE B.1

```
virtual void    Reject (PCollection c, char
                    (*select) (PObject item,
        void *StaticLink), void *StaticLink);
    // Send c -> insert (o) for all objects o in
    // this for which select (o) returns FALSE.
virtual void    Collect (PCollection c, PObject
                    (*transform) (PObject item,
                    void *StaticLink),
                    void *StaticLink);
    // Send c -> insert (x) for the result x returned
    // by transform (o) for each object o in this.
```

FirstThat executes select once for each object in the collection until some call returns TRUE. Then FirstThat quits and returns the object that caused select to return TRUE. It is relatively easily implemented using EachDo, which will exist in every subclass of SCollection. In order to use EachDo, we first need to construct a function to pass to it as parameter DoToItem. This can't be the same function that the user of FirstThat passes as the parameter *select, because they have different parameters and a different purpose. We call this new ordinary function selectFirst. It needs a function prototype such as:

```
selectFirst (PObject item,void *StaticLink);
```

which is consistent with the first parameter of EachDo.

When we call EachDo, passing selectFirst, EachDo has select-First called once for each object in the collection. Then selectFirst must ensure that select (passed to FirstThat) is called on the same object, communicate back whether select returns TRUE and, if so, which object returned TRUE. The question then arises as to how we can write selectFirst in a generic way so that it can be passed any select function and can communicate back the information as it learns it. The solution involves the extra StaticLink pointers to EachDo and to the function that EachDo is passed.

We first define (in PCollection.cp; it needs to be done only once) a struct named firster:

```
struct firster {
    char found;
    void *link;
    PObject result;
    char (*select) (PObject item, void *StaticLink);
};
```

This struct has fields for a Boolean (char) variable, found, and for a generic pointer so that any object or other data can be passed in, an object reference for the return value, and a function pointer whose signature (parameters and return type) is the same as that of the parameter to be passed to FirstThat. A pointer to a record such as this is passed to selectFirst as its StaticLink parameter. Before we call selectFirst, we create such a record f in FirstThat and fill in its fields with initialization data:

```
f.found = FALSE;
f.result = NULL;
f.select = select;
f.link = StaticLink;
```

When we call EachDo, passing a pointer to this record, it makes this data available to selectFirst, including the function select, which we really want executed.

Inside selectFirst we then simply execute select, which we get from the record passed in, and remember when we first see TRUE.

```
void selectFirst (PObject item, void *L) {
   if (((firster*) L) -> select (item,
   ((firster*) L) -> link) &&
   ! ((firster*) L) -> found) {
      ((firster*) L) -> found = TRUE;
      ((firster*) L) -> result = item;
      };
};
```

Finally, here is the complete FirstThat code.

```
PObject SCollection :: FirstThat (char (*select)
                                   (PObject item,
                                    void *StaticLink),
                                   void *StaticLink) {
   firster f;

   f.found = FALSE;
   f.result = NULL;
   f.select = select;
   f.link = StaticLink;
   EachDo (selectFirst, &f);
   return f.result;
};
```

Note that EachDo does indeed process every element of the class. We play a trick by changing result only the first time select(o) returns TRUE. Without the extra guard in the if statement within selectFirst, we would return the last item for which select returned TRUE, not the first.

FirstThat is used by creating a testing procedure to be passed as the value of the parameter select. For example, a procedure might test an object that stores a number, returning TRUE if the value is positive. Such a procedure would be used as the actual parameter in place of select. FirstThat would then return the first object in the collection that stored a positive value.

Select and Reject are quite similar except that they build up collections of the objects for which select returns TRUE or FALSE, respectively. The collection is not created by Select or Reject, so it must be created and initialized before a call to these methods. Select is shown below, and Reject is similar. Select needs a new struct type to pass the required information. Reject can use the same record.

```
struct selecter {
    PCollection c;
    void *link;
    char (*select) (PObject item, void *StaticLink);
};

void selectAll (PObject item, void *L) {
    if (((selecter*) L) -> select (item,
            ((selecter*) L) -> link))
        (((selecter*) L) -> c) -> insert(item);
};

void SCollection :: Select (PCollection c,
    char (*select) (PObject item,
                    void *StaticLink),
                    void *StaticLink) {
    selecter f;

    f.select = select;
    f.link = StaticLink;
    f.c = c;
    EachDo (selectAll, &f);
};
```

Collect also inserts into a collection but does so by performing a transformation on each object in the collection and returning some object. This transformation procedure, transform, operates on an object and produces another object in some way. Collect then inserts all of the generated objects into the collection c. For example, a procedure could change the signs of numeric objects. Another example is that of a procedure that picks the largest object out of a set. We could use collect to form a set of the largest elements in all the sets in a collection of sets. Again, we need a new struct type to hold the information that needs to be passed to the function that is itself passed to EachDo.

```
struct transformer {
   PCollection c;
   void *link;
   PObject (*transform) (PObject item,
                           void *StaticLink);
};

void collectAll (PObject item, void *L) {
   (((transformer*) L) -> c) ->
   insert ((((transformer*) L) ->
   transform (item, ((transformer*) L) -> link)));
};

void SCollection :: Collect (PCollection c,
                     PObject (*transform)
                     (PObject item,
                     void *StaticLink),
                     void *StaticLink) {
   transformer f;

   f.transform = transform;
   f.link = StaticLink;
   f.c = c;
   EachDo (collectAll, &f);
};
```

Note that `Collect` calls `EachDo` and indirectly calls `insert` as well, neither of which is implemented in this class. However, if we redefine `SFiniteStack` to be a subclass of `SCollection`, override `insert` so that it just calls `push`, and implement (reimplement) `EachDo` as shown above, `Collect` will operate correctly in `SFiniteStack` as inherited, because of the dynamic binding principle. It doesn't need to be reimplemented. For example, if an expression negation procedure had the declaration

```
PObject negateIt (PExpression  o, void *StaticLink);
```

then we could say, in the language of an earlier example,

```
expressionStack
   -> Collect (auxiliaryStack, negateIt, NULL);
```

The effect would be to push the negative of each element in the expression stack (from the top down) onto the auxiliary stack without disturbing the expression stack, assuming that `auxiliaryStack` was properly created and initialized.

Note how important it is that objects in a subclass interpret all messages in their own context. If an `SFiniteStack` gets the `Collect` message, it executes an inherited method. That inherited method is still executed by our stack, however, so the calls to EachDo and insert that appear in it are message names that our stack associates with its own methods, not the dummy methods of SCollection. Again we see autonomy of objects in action.

The methods EachDo, Collect, Select, Reject, and FirstThat are all examples of internal iterators. They repeat, or iterate, an operation over the elements of some collection.

> **External Iterator**
>
> A class that implements iteration over another class.

> **Internal Iterator**
>
> A method of a class that implements iteration over that class.

We also see that writeIt can be implemented with the internal iterator EachDo. The reader is encouraged to try it before reading further. It is enough to pass NULL for all StaticLink fields, since we don't need to pass information just to write the object, which is passed separately in any case.

```
void doWrite (PObject o, void *L) {
    o -> writeIt ();
};

void SCollection :: writeIt (void) {
    EachDo (doWrite, NULL);
};
```

Internal iterators in a few concrete classes will be discussed next.

Internal Iterators for Lists

The internal iterator EachDo is easy to implement for lists. It walks the list nodes and passes to DoToItem the contents of the node and the pointer, StaticLink, that was passed to it. Since the node class is nested inside the list class and has a public interface, we can operate directly on the nodes.

```
void SList :: EachDo (void (*DoToItem)
                             (PObject item,
                              void *StaticLink),
                              void *StaticLink) {
    PListNode aNode;

    aNode =     fFirstNode;
    while (aNode != zed) {
       DoToItem (aNode -> value (), StaticLink);
       aNode = aNode -> fNext;
    };
};
```

Internal Iterators for Trees

EachDo can be built using a tree iterator. It uses in–order logic to apply its
parameter DoToItem to each value stored in the tree.

```
void SBinaryTree :: EachDo (void (*DoToItem)
                                   (PObject item,
                                    void *StaticLink),
                                    void *StaticLink) {
    SBinaryTreeIterator IT (this);
    PObject anItem;

    while (IT.nextItem (anItem))
       DoToItem (anItem, StaticLink);
};
```

An alternative way to build the internal iterator that doesn't depend on
an external iterator (which seems like cheating) is to write it recursively.
It should recursively iterate over the left subtree, perform DoToItem on
the value in the node itself, and then iterate over the right subtree. The
problem is that the subtrees are in a different class, SBinaryTreeNode.
Therefore this needs to be done in two parts. The following code must
be used in SBinaryTree, and the recursive method must be added to
SBinaryTreeNode. The latter does the work.

```
void SBinaryTree :: EachDo (void (*DoToItem)
                                   (PObject item,
                                    void *StaticLink),
                                    void *StaticLink) {

    fRoot -> EachNodeDo (DoToItem, StaticLink);
};
```

The procedural parameter supplied for DoToItem must, of course, be known at the point that the EachDo message is sent. However, it need not be known at the point of definition of EachDo. For example, suppose countIt, which increments a static (global) variable each time it is called, is defined as follows:

```
void countIt (PObject v, void *S) {
   ++count;
};
```

If we then execute the code

```
count = 0;
tree -> EachDo (countIt, NULL);
cout << count;
```

we learn the number of (internal) nodes in the tree named tree.

Internal Iterators for SRTrees

EachDo can be easily built here using the same idea that was used in SRTree :: writeIt.

```
void SRTree ::
   EachDo (void (*DoToItem)
              (PObject item,
               void *StaticLink),
              void *StaticLink) {
   DoToItem (fValue, StaticLink);
   if (fLeft != nil) fLeft -> EachDo (DoToItem,
                                      StaticLink);
   if (fRight != nil) fRight -> EachDo (DoToItem,
                                        StaticLink);
};
```

This internal iterator walks the tree using a pre-order protocol and applies the procedure DoToItem once to each value stored in the tree. A similar method, EachSubTreeDo, applies a procedure to each subtree in the tree, rather than each value.

```
void SRTree ::
   EachSubTreeDo (void (*DoToItem)
                    (PRTree item,
                     void *StaticLink),
                    void *StaticLink) {
   DoToItem (this, StaticLink);
```

```
% 646
if (fLeft != nil) fLeft ->
   EachSubTreeDo (DoToItem, StaticLink);
if (fRight != nil) fRight ->
   EachSubTreeDo (DoToItem, StaticLink);
};
```

The method subTree can utilize EachSubTreeDo to check if the parameter is a subtree. Implementations using external iterators are also possible. We need the auxiliary procedure checkSubTree, which subTree will pass to EachSubTreeDo. The method subTree also needs to share information with the procedure that it sends to EachSubTreeDo. Therefore, we need a struct to hold this information. We need to pass in the tree we are searching for and get back a Boolean to inform us if it was found.

```
struct cst {
   char found;
   PRTree t;
};

void checkSubTree (PRTree o, void *result) {
   if (o == ((cst*) result) -> t)
      ((cst*) result) -> found = TRUE;
};

char SRTree :: subTree (PRTree t) {
   cst *info;
   char result;

   info = new cst;
   info -> found = FALSE;
   info -> t = t;
   EachSubTreeDo (&checkSubTree, info);
   result =  info -> found;
   delete info;
   return result;
};
```

We can pass information local to subTree to the procedure EachDo and have it passed in turn to checkSubTree, even though EachDo was written previously without knowledge of this particular use or the kind of data that would be passed.

EXERCISES

B.1 (B.5) Implement the comparison operators, ==, <, <=, etc., in class RAssociation so that they behave like equal, less, lessEqual, etc. of class SAssociation. Do this by overloading the operators.

B.2 (B.6) To see the generality of passing procedures, create, compile, link, and run the following. File exe.h has only four lines.

```
#ifndef exe
#define exe

void doSomething (void what (void*), void *link);
#endif
```

File exe.cp contains

```
#include "exe.h"
void doSomething (void what (void *), void *link){
    what(link);
};
```

File main.cp contains

```
#include <iostream.h>
#include "exe.h"

typedef struct {
    int input;
    int ans;
} dr; // Data record.

void countIt (void *data) {
    // Compute and return 1+2+...+n = n * (n + 1) / 2.
    dr *local;

    local = (dr*) data;
    local -> ans = (local -> input *
                    (local -> input + 1)) / 2;
};

void main (void) {
    dr package;

    package.input = 5;
    doSomething (countIt, &package);
    cout << package.ans << '\n';
};
```

B.3 (B.6) Change the first executable line of main in Exercise B.2 from

```
package.input = 5;
```

to

```
cin >> package.input
```

and execute the program again. You are expected to provide input integers when it runs. Note that the input has no prompt. You may provide one.

B.4 (B.6) Continuing the above exercises, file `test.cp` has eleven lines (two of them are blank).

```
# include <iostream.h>
# include "exe.h"

void printIt (void *msg) {
   cout << (char*) msg << '\n';
};

void main (void) {
   char *hello = "Hello world.";
   doSomething (printIt, hello);
};
```

Compile, link, and test this program.

B.5 (B.7) Implement the recursive internal iterator method:

```
void SBinaryTreeNode ::
   EachNodeDo (void (*DoToItem) (PObject item,
                                 void *StaticLink),
                                 void *StaticLink) {

```

in `SBinaryTreeNode` as was described in Section B.7. Implement both an in–order and a pre–order version. It is intended to be called only by `SBinaryTree :: EachDo`, so it should probably be a private method of `SBinaryTreeNode`.

B.6 (B.7) Implement a method, `propagate`, in `SBinaryTreePosition` similar to `EachDo`. `propagate` is an internal iterator used to apply a procedure to each position at and below the current tree position. Note that it is an operation on positions, not on trees. Otherwise, it is similar to `EachDo`.

GLOSSARY

Abstract class A class included for organizational purposes only. Objects are not directly created within an abstract class. They lack initialization methods (unless inherited). Classes with pure virtual functions are always abstract. Classes with no public constructor are often abstract, though they may be under the control of another class.

Abstract data type (ADT) A collection of related data abstractions and a set of rules governing their interactions. An example is the collection list, list node, list position, and list iterator. *See also data abstraction.*

Alias If more than one name are used to refer to some quantity, the names are called aliases. When a name can be used to destroy the object to which it refers, as is the case with dynamic objects, special care must be taken when programming with aliases.

Allocation The process of creating a data object. Global data are allocated at program initialization. Local variables are allocated when the function is called. Heap data, including indirect objects, are allocated when the program executes an allocation function or operator such as new.

Assertion A Boolean statement that is supposed to be TRUE at a certain point in the execution of a program. Examples are preconditions and postconditions of functions and methods. A FALSE assertion indicates a program error.

Base class A class used as the basis for inheritance. If *B* inherits from *A*, then *A* is a base class of B. *See derived class.*

Block   A grouping of declarations and expressions. For example, the body of a function is a block.

Cast   Occasionally it is necessary to treat a variable declared to have a certain type as if it had a different type. For example, in many situations in object-oriented programming, a variable of a base class must be cast to a derived class. A type cast accomplishes this. The programmer must ensure that the cast is valid, since the compiler does not help.

Class   The fundamental abstraction mechanism of object-oriented programming. It is typically used to implement a data abstraction, though it is not restricted to this. It represents a binding between a set of data values (instance variables) and a set of procedures and functions (methods) used to manipulate the values. A class is a factory for objects of a certain kind.

Class feature   Those items declared within the scope of a class definition. They include instance variables, methods (including constructors and destructors), nested types (including classes), variables, and procedures. Friends of a class are not class features. *See member.*

Class hierarchy   The structure of the relationships between classes. When classes are derived from other classes, they extend the hierarchy downward. Since C++ has multiple inheritance, the class "hierarchy" is somewhat misnamed, since it actually a graph and not strictly a tree (hierarchy).

Client   A unit that uses another. The user is the client; the unit used is a service module or a provider.

Clone   A process for creating and initializing a faithful copy of an object.

Compilation unit   A subset of a program that can be submitted to the compiler. It is sufficiently complete that the compiler will accept it. In C++ a compilation unit is a single file, containing declarations and definitions, together with the files that it includes (and that the included files include).

Complexity   The complexity of a problem can be characterized by the efficiency of the most efficient program that can solve that problem. Complexity is thus the inherent difficulty of solving the problem.

Concrete class   A class that we use to create and initialize objects. We call this process of creation and initialization "instantiation." It is characterized by having a special generator function or a public constructor method for its instances.

Constructor method   A method written by the programmer but called by the system as part of the construction and initialization of any object, whether static or dynamic. A class can have several constructors, as long as they have different parameter lists. A constructor's name is the name of the class.

Data abstraction   A set of data values, a set of operations on those values, and a set of rules governing the behavior of the operations. An example is the type `int` with operations +, -, etc. and rules such as the commutative and associative rules.

Data decomposition A methodology of program development in which the overall problem to be solved is decomposed into its data elements. This is in contrast to procedural decomposition, in which the problem is decomposed into processes.

Data encapsulation Packaging elements of data (and perhaps the processes that operate on the data) into a syntactic unit, such as a record, class, or compilation unit. The purpose is to create higher-level logical units, abstracting from the details of the implementation.

Declaration The introduction of the name and characteristics of a program entity.

Dereference Obtaining access to a data entity that is referenced by a pointer or reference variable. The dereference operator for pointers in C++ is -›.

Derived class A class that has one or more parent classes. If *B* inherits from *A*, then *B* is a class derived from *A*. *B* is a derived class. *See base class.*

Destructor A method written by the programmer but called by the system as part of the destruction and deallocation of an object, whether static or dynamic. A destructor can be virtual, but it does not have parameters. There can be only one per class. Its name is the class name preceded by a tilde (~).

Downstream A file (or program) that includes another is said to be downstream from the other and uses what flows downstream from the other.

Dynamic binding In object-oriented programming, this is delaying until run time the choice of a (virtual) method to be executed in response to a message. It may be impossible to know at compile time (hence while doing static analysis of the program) which method will actually be executed.

Dynamic object An object referenced by a pointer, reference variable, or reference parameter. It virtually executes all messages sent to it (if they were declared virtual.) *See static object.*

Encapsulation Any means of indicating that some construct in a program is a semantic unit. Procedures encapsulate operations. Functions encapsulate expressions. Classes encapsulate data types.

Extendible software Software is extendible if adding to the functionality of a component is relatively easy without extensive rewriting, especially the rewriting of other components.

`extern` The `extern` directive introduces the name of a data variable into a C++ header file (usually), and indicates that its declaration appears elsewhere.

External iterator A separate class that manages iteration. It permits a method to be called repeatedly. `SListIterator` is an example of an external iterator.

Floating-type data   C++ has a variety of types that can hold real values. Among them are `float`, `double`, and `long double`, in order of increasing size and precision.

Forward class declaration   The introduction of the name of a class without introducing the names or characteristics of its features. This is needed so that mutually recursive definitions can be made.

Friend class   When two classes, by the nature of their abstractions, need to be designed together, it is helpful to implement them together. In such a case one class can declare that the details of its own implementation should be visible to that other class. It does so by indicating that the other class is a friend class. Friends can be overused. The key concept is that if the abstractions are linked, the implementations can be linked. See `SList` and `SListPosition` for an important example.

Friend function   An ordinary function can be declared to be a friend of a class. The protected and private details of the class are open to the function. It is still not a method, as it cannot be virtual and has no reference to `this`.

Generator function   An ordinary function, provided as a convenience to clients, that returns a properly initialized dynamic object that has been checked for success of the allocation.

has-a   A relationship between two classes that indicates that one class has a class member that is of the type of the other. For example, in our hierarchy we can say that a list *has-a* list node.

Header   A file in C++ that contains declarations needed by a variety of compilation units. Headers give the public, or exported, part of a compilation unit.

`# include`   The directive that allows one text file to be included into another. Standard practice is to isolate the public parts of compilation units into headers and then include them as needed.

Indirect object   *See dynamic object.*

Information hiding   Any means of making some information invisible in some parts of a program. Its purpose is to prevent client code from taking advantage of implementation details, especially details used to maintain invariants and details that can change. If these details were seen and used, the invariants could not be guaranteed and the changes would be more costly. In C++ the primary means of hiding information is with protected and private class features. Other means include using local variables in functions and including some details in files that other files do not `include`.

Inheritance   Mechanism by which we can declare a class to have all features of another class except those that we specifically change. In C++ the only modifications possible are replacing function bodies and changing the visibility level (public, private, protected) of a feature. A class (the derived class) that inherits from another (the base class) is a subtype of that other. The new class can, of course, add new features to those it inherits.

Instance variable   A variable that is internal to an object. An instance variable is usually private or protected. The instance variables are said to partition the state of an object-oriented program. The internal state of each object is determined by the values of its instance variables. Work is done in an object-oriented program by sending messages to objects, which then execute methods, some of which change the state of the instance variables and hence of the computation.

Integer-type data   C++ has a variety of integer types. In order of increasing size and range, these include `char`, `short`, `int`, and `long`.

Interface   The collection of available features of a compilation unit or of a class is called its interface. For ordinary clients the interface of a class is the set of public features of the class. For an heir of a class, the interface consists of the public and protected features. For a compilation unit the interface is the items declared in the header.

Internal iterator   A method of a class that provides iteration or repetition over objects of that class.

Invariant   An assertion that is supposed to be true (or at least its truth is a constant) over a range of statements in a program. One common example is a class invariant that is supposed to be true always. In actuality, it is necessary to make it false briefly while methods of that class are in operation, but its truth is restored before the method finishes so that to a client it always appears true.

is-a   A relationship between classes that indicates that an object of one class is also in the other class. In our hierarchy we say that a list *is-a* collection. This relationship is created through inheritance.

is-like   A relationship between classes that indicates similarity between their objects. This can be implemented in a variety of ways, among which is the reuse of code through inheritance. If we implement the set class as a subclass of the list class, we could say that a set *is-like* a list.

Iterator   A mechanism for managing repetition or iteration. A simple example is the `for` loop. *See external iterator and internal iterator.*

Loop invariant   A predicate that does not change from TRUE to FALSE while the loop executes. More precisely, if a loop invariant is TRUE at the top of the loop and the loop conditional test is also TRUE, the loop invariant is also TRUE at the bottom of the loop.

`make`   A program supplied with the UNIX operating system and elsewhere that assists in the construction of software by managing the compilation and linking processes.

`makefile`   A file that describes the requirements of building a program from its components that is read by the program `make` to guide the construction process. Some systems require that this file be created by the programmer. Others automate its creation from an examination of the source files.

Member   Features of a class are called its members. These consist of data members, member functions, static members, and static member functions.

Message   The means by which one object requests a service from another object. A message consists of the name of an object and the name of one of its methods. If the object is direct, the object and the method name are separated by a period. If the object is referred to by a pointer, then -> separates the object name from the method name.

Method   A function or procedure that an object uses to provide a service to other objects. Each object has a fixed collection of methods that it uses to provide services.

Mixin class   A class whose purpose is to provide some property to another class. Mixin classes are used only in multiple-inheritance schemes, in which the class mixed in provides additional functionality. Examples of mixin classes are SMagnitude, in the hierarchy discussed in this book, as well as Printable, which enables objects to be printed on external printers, Storable, which enables objects to be stored in a database, and so on.

Multiple inheritance   A feature of C++ and some other languages that enables a class to have many parent (base) classes. When used wisely (and sparingly), this can simplify the creation of complex objects.

Object   The basic building block of a running system. The objects are the data of an object-oriented system. They provide a partitioning of the state of the running program. Objects are service providers (and requesters). They act by executing methods in response to messages that request service. They are autonomous, in that the methods they execute are personal to themselves. Other, similar, objects can respond to the same messages by executing different methods.

Override   The reimplementation of an inherited virtual method.

Parent class   When one class inherits from another, the latter is called the parent class, or base class.

Polymorphism   "Many forms." In object-oriented systems this refers to the fact that objects can have several types. They have the type of all classes in their inheritance chain. It also implies that the same message-sending text can be interpreted in different ways at different times in the running program, because the object receiving the message may not be the same each time the message statement is executed and the interpretation of the message is done by the object.

Postcondition   An assertion that the programmer of a method (or ordinary function) ensures on exit provided that the preconditions were true on entry.

Precondition   An assertion that a method or function requires to be true before the method is called. The caller must ensure the truth of any precondition.

Predicate A function that returns a Boolean result.

Private member A feature of a class that is intended to be used only within methods of that class (and its declared friends), and not by its clients or heirs.

Procedural decomposition A methodology in which the problem at hand is considered to be a process and the program for solving the problem is created by breaking the process down into its components, which are solved individually. This is in contrast to data decomposition.

Protected member A feature of a class that is intended to be used only within methods of that class (and its declared friends) and by its heirs, but not by its clients.

Protocol The header of a function or method, which gives the requirements for using it, or the declaration of the public (or protected) parts of a class, which gives the requirements for using them. Protocol is the rules that an ADT must obey.

Provider A unit that is used by another. All units are providers to the programs that use them.

Pseudo class A class declared for documentation purposes only, and not implemented. An example in our hierarchy is the numeric class, of which SFraction, SComplex, and SInteger are logical descendants.

Public member A feature of a class that is intended to be used anywhere the class name is visible, including methods, heirs, and clients of that class.

Pure virtual function A method of a class that is declared to have no body in that class. The prototype of the method is followed by =0 to indicate this. No object of a class that has a pure virtual function can be created. It is, in effect, a command to heirs to provide a body for this function. It is intended to introduce a protocol for a method into a hierarchy, without actually defining a method. SMagnitude :: less is an example.

Qualified name In some contexts the name of a member of a class must be preceded by the name of the class. This is needed, for example, to gain access to a static member of a class. C++ uses the : : operator for this purpose, as in SList :: zed.

Reference parameter A parameter of a function that has the semantics of a const pointer parameter but uses the syntax of a direct variable. Direct syntax is used both within the function and in calls of the function. The system sees to the construction of the pointer and its dereferencing.

Reference variable In standard C++ terminology this is a variable that is implemented as a const pointer variable and has most of the semantics of a pointer variable, but uses the syntax of direct variables. In a more general context it is any mechanism, including pointers and more abstract means, that is used to refer to an item indirectly. In this book we generally use the latter meaning. Pointers for us are references to objects.

Reusability of software   The ability to reuse components of one program in other programs and on other machines.

Scope   When a name is declared, its scope is that part of the text of a program in which the name can be seen and the declaration applies. For example, if we declare a name in a C++ method, its scope is the remainder of that method. If we declare a protected class method, its scope is that class declaration, all methods of that class, and all heirs and friends.

Server   *See provider.*

Static class members   Class features that are not instance variables or methods are called static class members. These may be types, including classes, variables, and ordinary functions. They are referred to by prefixing (qualifying) the name of the thing with the name of the class. `SList :: zed` is an example.

Static member function   An ordinary function declared within the scope of a class.

Static object   An object whose type is a class type (not a pointer or reference to a class type). It executes all messages sent to it statically even if they were declared virtual. "What you see is what you get."

Stronger assertion   If assertion *A* logically implies assertion *B*, then *A* is called the stronger assertion. The strongest assertion of all is the constant FALSE, since it implies all other assertions.

Strongly typed language   A language is called strongly typed if each data item has a single well-determined type and if the language provides rules that minimize the combinations of data items of different types within the same expression.

Subclass   A class that inherits directly or indirectly from another is said to be a subclass of that other. A subclass extends the other class, known as a superclass.

Superclass   If a class inherits directly or indirectly from another then the latter is a superclass of the former. *See subclass.*

Token   The smallest meaningful unit of a programming language is a token. Tokens are built from ordinary characters, including alphabetical characters. For example, in C++ the tokens include `void`, `while`, `+=`, etc.

Type cast   A means by which one item (including objects) can be viewed as if it had a different type, including various means of actually converting it to that type. A type cast is the name of a type or an expression defining a type enclosed in parentheses preceding the name of the item that is being cast. It is an error to type-cast an object to a type unless it is of that type or a conversion to that type has been provided.

Type conversion A mechanism by which an item of one type can be converted to another type. C++ provides many automatic conversions, such as between the various built-in numeric types. C++ also provides a means by which the creator of a class can provide conversions from other classes using special methods. We have not used this facility, because it is used only with static objects, which we have avoided.

`typedef` A C++ keyword that is used to introduce a name for a type.

Upstream A header file that is included by another unit or program is said to be upstream from that other file. The items used flow downstream to the user.

Verification A logical process that is used to prove the correctness of a program.

Virtual method A method intended to be overridden. Most methods are virtual. The exceptions include `Error` and the special constructor methods of each class.

Weaker assertion If assertion A logically implies assertion B, then B is called the weaker assertion. The weakest of all assertions is the constant TRUE, since all assertions imply it.

BIBLIOGRAPHY

[Beck & Cunningham, 1989] "A Laboratory for Teaching Object-Oriented Thinking." Kent Beck and Ward Cunningham. *OOPSLA '89 Conference Proceedings, ACM SIGPLAN Notices* 24 (October), no. 10.

[Bentley, 1986] *Programming Pearls*. Jon Bentley. Reading, MA: Addison-Wesley.

[Biskup, Dayal, and Bernstein, 1979] "Synthesizing Independent Database Schemas." J. Biskup, U. Dayal and P. A. Bernstein. *Proceedings of the ACM Sigmod International Conference on Management of Data:* 143–152.

[Coplien, 1992] *Advanced C++: Programming Styles and Idioms*. James Coplien. Reading, MA: Addison-Wesley.

[Dijkstra, 1972] "Structured Programming." Edsger Dijkstra. *In Software Engineering, Concepts and Techniques*. ed. Buxton et al. New York: Van Nostrand Reinhold.

[Ellis & Stroustrup, 1990] *The Annotated C++ Reference Manual*. Margaret A. Ellis and Bjarne Stroustrup. Reading, MA: Addison-Wesley.

[Floyd, 1963] "Syntactic Analysis and Operator Precedence." R. W. Floyd. *Journal of the ACM*, 10, no. 3: 316–333.

[Graham, 1991] *Learning C++*. Neill Graham. New York: McGraw-Hill.

[Gries, 1981] *The Science of Programming*. David Gries. New York: Springer-Verlag.

[Horowitz & Sahni, 1987] *Fundamentals of Data Structures in Pascal*. 2nd ed. Ellis Horowitz and Sartaj Sahni. Rockville, MD: Computer Science Press.

[Korth & Silberschatz] *Database System Concepts*. Henry Korth and Abraham Silberschatz. New York: McGraw-Hill.

[Lippman, 1989] *C++ Primer*. Stanley Lippman. Reading, MA: Addison-Wesley.

[Manber, 1989] *Introduction to Algorithms: A Creative Approach*. Udi Manber. Reading, MA: Addison-Wesley.

[Meyer, 1988] *Object-oriented Software Construction*. Bertrand Meyer. Englewood Cliffs, NJ: Prentice Hall.

[Miller, 1956] "The Magical Number Seven, Plus or Minus Two: Some Limits on Our Capacity for Processing Information." G. A. Miller, *Psychological Review*, 63: 81–96.

[Papadimitriou & Steiglitz, 1982] *Combinatorial Optimization*. Christos Papadimitriou and Kenneth Steiglitz. Englewood Cliffs, NJ: Prentice Hall.

[Pohl, 1991a] *C++ for C Programmers*. Ira Pohl. Redwood City, CA: Benjamin-Cummings.

[Pohl, 1991b] *C++ for Pascal Programmers*. Ira Pohl. Redwood City, CA: Benjamin-Cummings.

[Rayward-Smith, 1983] *A First Course in Formal Language Theory*. V. J. Rayward-Smith. Cambridge, MA: Blackwell Scientific Publications.

[Roberts, 1986] *Thinking Recursively*. Eric Roberts. New York: John Wiley & Sons.

[Sedgewick, 1988] *Algorithms*. 2nd ed. Robert Sedgewick. Reading, MA: Addison-Wesley.

[Teague, 1972] *Computing Problems for Fortran Solution*. Robert Teague. New York: Canfield Press.

INDEX

DATE DUE

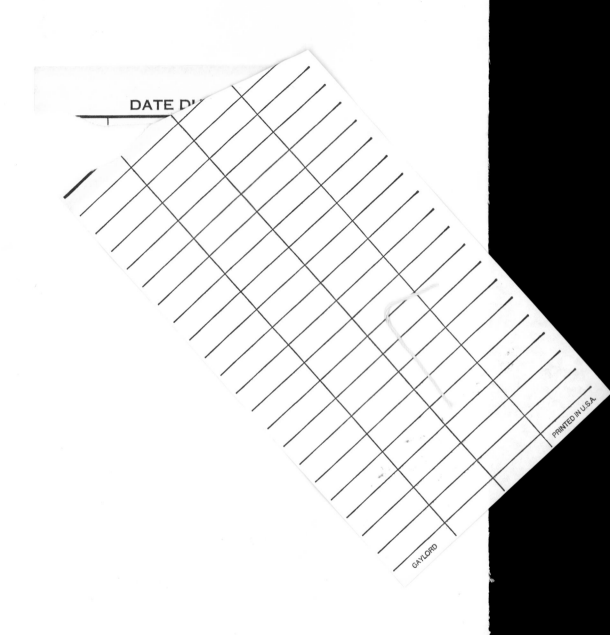

GAYLORD   PRINTED IN U.S.A.